Ba...
Song:
A Bayou History

By
Rebecca DeArmond-Huskey

Rebecca De Armond - Huskey

to Charlie Mac,
I know you will enjoy reading the history
of the old bayou that is so important to many of
your constituency.

HERITAGE BOOKS, INC. *best wishes,*

Rebecca

This project was supported in part by a grant from the
Arkansas Humanities Council and the National
Endowment for the Humanities

Published 2001 by

HERITAGE BOOKS, INC.
1540E Pointer Ridge Place
Bowie, Maryland 20716

1-800-398-7709
www.heritagebooks.com

ISBN 0-7884-1937-4

A Complete Catalog Listing Hundreds of Titles
On History, Genealogy, and Americana
Available Free Upon Request

Table of Contents

Preface

*"I hope that there will be others to
tell other things about bayous."*
Harnett T. Kane, 1943

The Bayous of Louisiana

Bayou Bartholomew and its environs have long been overlooked in the annals of history. While the importance of the Mississippi, Arkansas, and Ouachita Rivers has been noted, the historical role of the bayou has been neglected. When I was conducting research for *Beyond Bartholomew: The Portland Area History*, I began to realize the considerable contribution the bayou had made to the opening up and development of the interior Delta. I also learned from interviews that the bayou was the center of culture and recreation until recent years and that people associated with it have an enduring affection for it. I could not rid myself of the idea that the history of the entire stream should be written.

When the Bayou Bartholomew Alliance was formed in 1995, one of its stated goals was to "educate the people...about the esthetic and ecological value of [the bayou] and its historical significance to the region." I resolved that a book on the history of the bayou would be my contribution to this objective. A book on this subject would also fill a void in published history

In the summer of 1997 I conducted a preliminary research survey of archives in Arkansas, Louisiana, and Mississippi to determine if there was enough available material to serve as the foundation for a book. The references were meager and dispersed, but this only reiterated the need for such a publication. After considerable deliberation, I decided to undertake the project and in the spring of 1998 began interviewing people who had a lifetime association with the bayou or who could otherwise contribute information. After seventy-three interviews, I had gained an immense amount of information as well as an even deeper insight into the prominence of the bayou in the lives of those who lived along it. Documents found during the archival research phase, conducted from November 1998 until March 1999, confirmed my theory. The bayou had always played a major role in the area's history beginning with the Native Americans and continuing through the progression of colonialism, territorial settlement, steamboating, the timber industry, and agriculture.

There were endless decisions to make during the writing, which took place from March 1999 until May 2000. With thousands of details at hand, which should I include and which should I eliminate? Knowing that this would presumably be the only work to ever be published on this area, I opted for the liberal approach. This homage to Bayou Bartholomew meanders like the stream itself, and at each turn there is a story. It was written first and foremost for the people who I call bayouphiles. Students of history, archeology, cultural anthropology, economic geography, sociology, and folklore will also benefit from the diverse material presented. Genealogists will find that although the family histories begin with bayou families, they go back in time to many other states and countries.

It is my hope that this book will inspire and encourage all who read it to help the Bayou Bartholomew Alliance in its effort to restore and preserve the natural beauty of this historic and once pristine stream.

Acknowledgments

The adage, ask and you shall receive, worked exceedingly well for obtaining information for this book. There were even times I did not have to ask; it simply came to me. Although the material from archives and publications supplied needed documentation for relevant historical events, the response from an interested public enriched many pages with firsthand experiences as well as additional documented material. Research and writing are rather lonely tasks, and the personal involvement with people who love the bayou was rewarding and encouraging.

I am especially indebted to the seventy-three people who allowed me to interview them. Their information and stories enliven the text and make history more enjoyable to read. Many of them also provided originals or copies of germane documents and photographs. Those who generously shared research compiled through the years were Eloise Robertson Means, Marion Robertson Doles, Ruth Mayo Boone, Fay Bowe, and Bobby Abraugh. John B. Currie Sr. gave access to his collection of the *Delta News*. Duke Shackelford loaned his old copies of *Eastern Louisiana: A History*. Mark and Sheila Hawkins served as hosts for the Parkdale investigations. Many, too numerous to mention, shared genealogical research that was the result of years of research.

Some friends joined in on the research trail. Robert B. Owens helped immensely with the steamboat research and accompanied me on several research trips; Lon Martin was always willing to find obscure data, and Jann Woodard supplied numerous abstracts from old newspapers. A. J. Stewart guided me for two days on the preliminary research trip to Bastrop and Monroe and arranged a meeting with Dr. Russ Williams. George Sims, a bayouphile *cum laude*, always stood by, eager to help.

The most enjoyable part of research is field trips to sites. Sheila Hawkins guided me to every building in Parkdale and related its history. John B., Mary, and Johnny Currie showed me the outlying area at Wilmot. Ralph Kinnaird and Billy Bobby Abraugh introduced me to the entire length of the bayou in Morehouse Parish. Ralph also arranged exciting visits to two sunken steamboats. Susan Holley led me to the Leonidas Spyker home site, the Abraham Scribner monument, and the ruins of a steam gin and sawmill. Steve Atkins took me to Mason Cave and Cora's Bluff. Through Nell Hestand I found Worley Jones who conducted me and others to the source of the bayou on his property time after time. Benton and Mike Hunt guided me to a cypress Choctaw log in Overflow Creek. Joe Cope, Sammy Wells, Buck Burton, and Roy Wayne Huskey escorted me to the Arkansas River where we retrieved a Choctaw log. Lewis and Carmen Redden accompanied me on several trips to film segments on bayou history for their "Louisiana Back Roads" program on KNOE-TV, Monroe.

Colleagues and friends in specialized fields of study donated their time and information. Judge Morris S. Arnold offered material for the chapter on the colonial period and after reading it offered suggestions to clarify some issues. John House gave me a crash course in elementary geology and contributed greatly to the old Arkansas River channel explanation and the segment on archeology. He also read the chapter and suggested improvements. Marvin Jeter supplied additional information on archeological sites in Drew and Ashley Counties. Serving as humanities scholars for the Arkansas Humanities Council grants were Willard Gatewood, Alumni Distinguished Professor of History (Emeritus) of the University of Arkansas, Fayetteville; John L. Ferguson, Director, Arkansas History Commission; David Moyers, Publisher and Editor of the *Ashley County Ledger*; Linda Webster, Associate Professor of Speech at the University of Arkansas, Monticello; Lavelle Cole, Professor of History at Ouachita Baptist University; and Curtis Merrell, Director of the Arkansas River Education Service Cooperative and Chairman of the Board of the Bayou Bartholomew Alliance. Special appreciation goes to Drs. Gatewood, Ferguson, Moyers, and Merrell for reading and correcting the completed manuscript. Jann Woodard, Linda Webster, and Robert Mitchell served as grant evaluators. Barbara Clayton Mitchell read and corrected the manuscript before it was sent to the official readers. Once again my family and friends patiently stood by as I fervently pursued the work of research and writing.

I am especially grateful to Charles Sidney Gibson, who encouraged me to undertake the project when I was hesitant to make a decision. Gratitude goes to the Arkansas Humanities Council for grants to help with the expense of the preliminary research survey, oral history project, and writing phase and to the institutions and people who donated funds to the Bayou Bartholomew Alliance on behalf of the project.

Partial funding for this work was provided by:

The Arkansas Humanities Council
Gus Pugh Sons, Portland
JW Pugh Interests, Portland
Dermott Drainage District
Duke Shackelford, Bonita
SouthEast Arkansas Bank (Delta Trust), Portland
First National Bank, McGehee
Hibernia Bank, Bastrop
Lephiew Gin Company, Dermott
Union Bank, Monticello
Bonita Motor Supply & Hardware
Commercial Bank, Monticello
Mer Rouge State Bank
John C. Yeldell, Bastrop
Dorothy Mack, West Monroe
Kenneth Dashiell, Bastrop

Photographs

One of the Taylor Mounds previous to cultivation at Hollywood Plantation

The Haunted Hawkins House, built 1912, at Parkdale

Part One

The History of the Bayou

To Bartholomew come with me,
Where the cypress grows and the holly tree;
Where the sweet magnolia scents the air,
And one sees beauty everywhere.

The cotton, like great flakes of snow
Whitens the fields where'er you go;
While all around, dense forests stand,
The wall in nature's fairy land.

The southern moon gleams on the trees,
The moss festoons sway in the breeze;
Weird shadows move o'er water fair,
And heaven's stars are mirrored there.

The tinkling banjo and the song,
The merry laugh of tenant throng,
And mocking birds delight the ear,
Unused to such sylvan sounds to hear.

From *Memories of Hollywood*
By Oliver W. Jennings, 1893

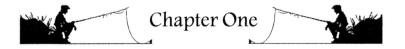

Chapter One

Ancient Springs, Rivers, and Peoples

The Source

These springs never quit running.
Worley Jones

Clear, cold water perpetually seeps from springs about halfway up the western hillside. Five immense springs line the slope for several hundred yards. The largest seep area covers an acre or more, and the smallest is about fifty yards in diameter. Bright green ferns, arum, arrowhead, gentian, boneset, and nettle squeeze their roots into the sodden bogs and define the boundaries. These splashes of green sprawl beneath a hardwood canopy composed of beech, red oak, post oak, shagbark hickory, gum, ash, and elm. Underneath these woodland giants are maple, mulberry, cherry, persimmon, pawpaw, and dogwood. The shaded ground below is clear of undergrowth, and a natural park-like atmosphere prevails. Several inches of clear water remain on the surface of the springs as the excess spills out into a labyrinth of small channels. These trenches merge into larger, deeper ones, and the water trickles downward to a waiting bayou bed composed of rocks and sand. During the absence of recent rain, the first half-mile of Bayou Bartholomew looks like a clear mountain creek. After the last spring flows into it, however, the embryonic stream immediately assumes bayou characteristics – a slow moving, meandering waterway in a well-defined channel. At this point, the bayou is only fifteen to twenty feet wide during normal flow.

North and west of the spring area, which is one and a half miles due south of Hardin in Jefferson County (in Section 24, T5S-R11W), are five runoff channels extending for several miles. These ephemeral tributaries contribute only rainwater to the bayou. They eventually merge into two channels that meet and form one bed approximately a hundred yards above the first spring. Some water, from the alluvial aquifer, remains in this bed at all times, but does not maintain a flow during dry periods. The clear pools in rocky beds need rain to create a flowing stream, but once the last spring runs into the channel, the bayou becomes a perpetual waterway. At this point Bayou Bartholomew begins its long journey through the southeast Arkansas and northeast Louisiana Delta to its juncture with the Ouachita River north of Sterlington, Louisiana. The 359-mile tortuously winding course has the distinction of being the longest bayou in the world.

A report issued by U. S. Congress in 1878 stated that the source of the bayou issued from Birds Spring sixteen miles west of Pine Bluff.[1] There is an indication that German Springs, several miles north of Hardin, once flowed into the bayou, perhaps before the east-west embankments of roads and railroads as well as intensive timber harvesting blocked the course. An undated, unsigned, hand-drawn map shows the bayou heading at this spring.[2] Goodspeed made note of German Springs as a mineral spring, along with White Sulphur, Cantrells, and Lees Springs in Jefferson County in 1889.[3] From Jefferson to Ashley County there is a series of springs located along the same general north-south line that possibly has the same underground aquifer as their source. From north to south these are German, Jefferson, the unnamed bayou springs, and Sulphur Springs in Jefferson County followed by Parnell Springs in Cleveland County. On each side of the Saline River in Drew and Bradley Counties there is a Sulphur Springs, and in Ashley County southwest of Crossett is another Sulphur Springs.

Benton Hunt of Morehouse Parish told this story about the bayou's source: "When my folks came down here from Missouri in the 1890s, they came upon a spring coming out of a rock. It was a rocky hill and then flatland and a little stream. They followed the stream and it was Bayou Bartholomew. An old trail went along the side of it. When they came to Overflow Creek in Ashley County, they left the bayou and followed it to Zachary. We went back up there in the late thirties or early forties and found it. An old road went by it."

Mary Roane Tomlinson, writing in 1938, told a different version. "Like all true bayous, Bartholomew has no natural spring for a source...."[4] However, it does have a spring source, and furthermore it is acclaimed for its abundant springs. Anyone familiar with the bayou will mention its springs. "Byrd Lake, a bayou oxbow, is fed by springs." (Helen Byrd, Jefferson County) "They were everywhere. We kept them cleaned out and put our milk and butter in them and drank from them." (Bessie Fuller Green, Lincoln County) "The springs threw up sand and that made a good sandy bottom." (John Edd Curry, Lincoln County) "We put a pipe in them to force out the water to use for drinking." (Earl Kitchens, Ashley County) "The bayou was full of them – they kept it full. When we were wading or swimming we could feel the cold water." (Oren Robertson, Morehouse Parish) "It is spring fed all up and down. There was a spring in a cypress stump four by four by two feet deep. All travelers knew where it was and would stop and drink from it." (Frank Day, Morehouse Parish) "It would not be a bayou if not for the springs. It purifies itself every twenty-five to

forty feet because of them.   We lived off the springs of Bayou
Bartholomew." (Benton Hunt, Morehouse Parish.)

From River to Bayou

*A river is never quite silent; it can never
of its nature be quite still; it is never
quite the same from one day to the next.*

Roderick Haig-Brown, *A River Never Sleeps*

Although Tomlinson's 1938 comment about the bayou having no spring for a source was misleading, she was correct in her next statement. "It has been conjectured that in some remote period Bayou Bartholomew was an old channel of the Arkansas River, or the trace of the still mightier current of the Mississippi."[5] Free-flowing streams are constantly changing – that is one of their main characteristics. Riparian dwellers easily notice banks caving in, sandbars switching from one side to the other, and occasional changes of courses caused by new channels cutting through. Running water always takes the less obstructed course. Or as Henry Thoreau put it, "Thus in the course of ages the rivers wriggle in their beds, till it feels comfortable with them. Time is rather cheap and insignificant."

Mark Twain noted such alterations in the Mississippi during his days as a river pilot. In *Life on the Mississippi* he wrote, "The Mississippi is remarkable in still another way – its disposition to make prodigious jumps by cutting through narrow necks of land, and thus straightening and shortening itself. More than once it has shortened itself thirty miles at a single jump! These cut-offs have had curious effects: they have thrown several river towns out into the rural districts, and built up sand-bars and forests in front of them...[It] is always changing itself bodily – it is always moving sideways...Nearly the whole of that one thousand three hundred miles which La Salle floated down in his canoes, two hundred years ago, is *good solid dry ground* now." What Twain did not mention is that the river is also lengthening itself by eroding new bends in other places. One of the most lamentable losses in Arkansas history is the river's carving away of its bank until the old town of Napoleon completely slid into its waters in 1874.

Timothy Flint, writing in 1835, said in reference to Bayou Barthelimi and other similar streams, " . . .long, deep, and winding water-courses in these alluvial swamps, which seem to have been dug out by the hand of nature, as navigable canals...."[6] They *were* "dug out by the hand of nature." A million years ago, during the Pleistocene epoch, glacial ice sheets covered much of the northern hemisphere. As the earth warmed again, melting glaciers fed streams carrying glacial outwash. The current Mississippi Alluvial Plain began forming at this time. Ancestral rivers carved channels preceding the present channels of the Mississippi and Arkansas Rivers.[7]

Dr. John H. House wrote, "Within the [Arkansas River] Lowland, most land surfaces are thought to date to the Holocene, the last 10,000 years since the end of the Pleistocene or Ice Age. The major exceptions are scattered terrace remnants representing extensive former floodplain surfaces laid down during the melting of Pleistocene glaciers between 12,000 and 120,000 years ago. These remnants include the terrace between Ladd and Tarry along the Jefferson-Lincoln County line and Macon Ridge to the east between Lake Village, Arkansas, and Sicily Island, Louisiana."[8] Seven older meander belts for the Arkansas River identified by geologists are west of the Mississippi River and east of Little Rock and Bayou Bartholomew. The Arkansas created Macon Ridge, west of Bayou Macon, approximately 30,000 years ago as the river flowed east of it in its third path. The river eventually switched west of the ridge and carved out a new (fifth) path in the area of the Beouf River.[9] The next course appears to be represented by segments east of the modern river between Little Rock and Pine Bluff, portions of Bayou Bartholomew between Pine Bluff and Dermott, and channels along Lighterwood and Bonne Idee Bayous in Louisiana.[10]

A new cutoff south of Little Rock formed the seventh and last pre-modern meander belt. This path followed a course corresponding to present-day Plum Bayou north of the present river, passed just east of Pine Bluff, and then followed a southern route along a course corresponding to present-day Bayou Bartholomew to its confluence with the Ouachita River.[11] The scalloped outline of the edge of the pine timbered terrace west of the modern-day bayou reflects the meandering of the Arkansas River. The many oxbows flanking the bayou are likewise vestiges of the ancient river. Approximately 2,500 years ago the Arkansas began to divert to its present channel, and between 1,800 and 2,200 years ago, it left the present bayou channel entirely. The present-day course of Bayou Bartholomew reflects the Arkansas River when it was in a partial-flow regime. Part of the flow of the river was then diverting through a crevasse into the swamps to the east where it eventually formed the present-day Arkansas course to the Mississippi.[12] In 1994 the eminent geologist, Roger Saucier, revised his 1974 estimate of the bayou channel being the active bed between 4000 and 1800 B.P. to at least a few hundred years earlier after House identified Late Archaic artifacts from the Plum Bayou Meander Belt. Artifacts from sites on the banks of the Arkansas were also used to determine the 2500 B.P. date for its present channel.[13]

Recently uncovered evidence may eventually establish a collaborative date and more precise location of the last connection of the Arkansas with the bayou. In 1996 when new sewer lines were being installed in the

Grider Field area south of Pine Bluff, the crew encountered stumps at a depth of twelve feet. John House investigated the site. He believes the stumps are cypress and estimates their age to be around 2,000 years. Radiocarbon dating of the stumps would help date the shift. Also noticing the character of the lower sediments, he wrote, "It was clear that this was an old oxbow of the Arkansas River that had been filled in with alluvium. On aerial photographs, you can see traces of the old channel."[14]

House uses a metaphor, palimpsest, to figuratively describe the changes in the river channel. A palimpsest is a manuscript (stone, papyrus, parchment, for example) used over and over again with the original writing having been erased. Since the erasure is incomplete, what was written before is still slightly visible. And so it is with the geological tableau. "Think of the landscape as actually a patchwork or collage – or palimpsest. Some time around 2,000 years ago, the Arkansas River picked up a giant pencil, turned it end-for-end, and erased the portion of its old meander belt lying athwart its new course in the bottoms east of Pine Bluff. Much of the old landscape was scooped away and fell into the swift water of the migrating channel. Other parts of the old landscape were buried under fresh flood sediments. Then the river turned the pencil end-for-end again and drew a new landscape with channels and oxbows oriented toward the modern river and having nothing to do with the alluvial features that were there before. But portions of the old meander belt to the north and south were not erased. We see them along Plum Bayou north of the present-day Arkansas and along Bayou Bartholomew to the south."[15]

The Arkansas River begins in central Colorado in the Rocky Mountains as a small, clear mountain stream. One can easily jump across it as it begins its long journey to the Mississippi. It then passes through Kansas before entering Oklahoma northwest of Tulsa. At this point it begins to carry the distinctive red soil associated with this area, and this buried red sediment maps the course of the old riverbed in Arkansas and Louisiana. In contrast, sediments carried by the Mississippi are characteristically gray. A soil sample taken at Pine Bluff in the late 1800s found sixteen feet of red clay and twenty-six feet of orange colored sand under seventeen feet of other soil types. The modern river continued to deposit red sediment on farmland, and farmers sought these places for cotton production. Goodspeed wrote, "The well-known red sediment of the river, which has so much to do with cotton growth, was supposed by Dr. Owen [a geologist] to percolate into the lower soils, reaching the cotton rootlets, for good cotton will grow on sand-bars where corn would not thrive."[16] The red deposits are evident all the way to the mouth of the bayou and on into the Ouachita River. The French traveler, C. C. Robin, visited Ouachita Post (Monroe) between 1803-1805 and noted, "The soil on the left [east] bank, however, being flat and covered with a thick layer of humus overlying the reddish subsoil is fertile, and will be inexhaustible for a long time."[17]

Another indication of the "well-known red sediment of the river" is Red Fork Bayou, a fork of Cypress Creek in Desha County. It was called the Red Fork "because when the Arkansas was on the overflow, [it] carried surplus Arkansas River red water into the Mississippi."[18] During the 1991 excavation of the Taylor Mounds near Winchester, the trenching revealed "alternating bands of…yellowish sands and reddish clayey sands, deposited during major floods of the [Arkansas] River at intervals on the order of a few decades apart."[19] Actually any trenching conducted along the bayou meander belt reveals this red sediment. USDA county soil surveys assign soil types along Bayou Bartholomew and Beouf River to soil types elsewhere associated with the Arkansas. These lower red deposits indicate the locations of the old Arkansas meander belts.[20]

The naming of streams after their sediment-colored water was not uncommon. The Mississippi has long been known as the Muddy Mississippi. The water of Bayou Bartholomew is characteristically drab green to green except during rainy periods when it assumes a brown color from runoff. When running over hard bottom shallows in Morehouse Parish during low water intervals, the water is clear, and the rapids resemble those of a mountain stream. It even retains its individual color once it empties into the Ouachita. Tomlinson wrote, "Rivermen and others testify that the reddish green waters of [the bayou] remain discernible beside the limpid stream of its host…until both join the powerful churning current of the Mississippi."[21]

In the early 1800s the Ouachita emptied into the Mississippi via the Black and Red Rivers through what is presently known as Upper Old River. With the final removal of the logjam near the head of the Atchafalaya in 1855, this river increased dramatically in size and flow with water from the Mississippi and Red Rivers through the Lower Old River arm of the Old River Loop. Silting in both Upper and Lower Old River arms eventually created impediments to navigation through the channels. After several efforts by the Corps of Engineers failed to correct the problem, Upper Old River filled in completely by 1896. The lower arm then received water from the Mississippi and Red (and therefore the Ouachita) and diverted the flow into the Atchafalaya. In 1959 a navigation lock installed at the head of the Atchafalaya once again allowed passage of boats from the inland rivers to the Mississippi.[22] Although some Red River water is diverted into this lock, the Red essentially empties into the Atchafalaya, which in turn empties into the Gulf of Mexico southwest of New Orleans. Here ends the long voyage of the bayou that first arose from springs in southeast Arkansas.

From springs to bayou to river to sea – but what is a bayou? The word almost defies precise definition, and lexicographers differ in their attempts, with some saying it is an inlet from rivers and lakes and others saying it is an outlet. The inlet-outlet confusion comes from the fact that during floods, bayous serve as a relief with larger streams flowing back into them. When this happens the bayous flow backward for they are flatland steams with barely a discernible drop in bed level in most places. Bayou land is mostly flat and wet with outlying swamps and marshes situated below the water table. The flatland bayous are therefore sluggish and languid. Most bayous were created, as Bartholomew was, by the shifting of old river channels.

The bayou appellation exists only in the southernmost states from Georgia and Florida to Texas. The word originates from the Choctaw *bayuk* for small river or creek. The Choctaws of southern Louisiana used a similar word, *bogu*, for river, and called a bayou *kwahonoshe'*. The town of Bogalusa derives its name from the Choctaw *bogu* and *losa* (black) probably in reference to the dark water of the Mississippi. The Atchafalaya River (named a bayou on old maps) is likely from the Choctaw *chafa* (one) and *falaya* (long).[23]   The French explorers interpolated the Choctaw words into their own language, and *bayuk* became *bayouc* or *bayouque.* Anglo-Saxon settlers dropped the hard consonant, and the word became bayou. Among the variety of old spellings are bayoue, bayoe, bayeau, and bayau. Pronunciation still varies slightly according to region from *bi-oo* to *bi-o* to *bi-a* with the latter two being favored by bayou dwellers. An astute linguistic ear can determine where a person is from by how he pronounces the word.

Early cartographers variously named the same streams river or bayou, denoting their own confusion about the term. J. H. Colton's map of Louisiana has River Bartholomew, and his later railroad and township map of Arkansas names it a bayou. Some early maps show the Saline River as Bayou Saline. Hon. H. Bry wrote in 1847, "On the eastern side of the Ouachita the first considerable stream met with is the Bayou Salines...The next important river is the Bartholomew . . .." In a footnote he said that the bayou, Bartholomew, "ought to be [called a] river."[24] Clarence B. Moore echoed Bry's thoughts in 1909. "We are unable to say why Bartholomew is called a bayou, and residents along its banks are equally in ignorance as to the explanation. The Saline, rising in Arkansas and joining the Ouachita, as does Bayou Bartholomew, and of no greater size than Bartholomew, is called a river."[25]   The Saline is considerably wider than the bayou, although the bayou does become much broader in Louisiana. The Beouf was also variously named as river or bayou. Local people living near the head of Bartholomew often referred to it as a creek. "We called it Hyde Creek after the previous owners when we were growing up here in the fifties," said Worley Jones, owner of the property at the source. "We didn't know it was Bayou Bartholomew until we were grown."

Moore observed, "Bayou Bartholomew, comparatively deep in the winter season, and narrow so that the traveler on it has the cosy [*sic*] sensation of journeying on a canal...." The "cozy sensation" is created by the colossal cypress trees that line its banks with their branches extending over the water. Cascading from the branches are long, swaying tendrils of Spanish moss that the Louisiana Indians called *Itla-okla* for "tree hair." The first Frenchmen referred to it as *Barbe Espagnol* (Spanish beard) because of its similarity to the long, black beards of the Spanish explorers before them. The later Spaniards, resenting this term, changed the name once more to *Cabello Frances* for "French Hair." The Indians still preferred Spanish beard and this eventually translated into Spanish moss.[26] William Dunbar noted in 1804 "no long moss here" at a point on the Ouachita about midway between "Great Saline Bayou" (the Saline River) and Bayou Bartelemi.[27] This bromeliad air plant, mostly associated with coastal regions, begins as far north as Lake Wallace in southern Drew County. By the time the bayou reaches Lake Enterprise at Wilmot, the festoons of moss become a salient feature of the bayou panorama.

Cypress knees of infinite gnarled shapes line the banks giving further definition to the stream. The bayou ambience changes constantly from season to season. Spring brings the lacey first green of dainty cypress leaves which transform to lush green in summer. The leaves of cypress are among the first to turn golden brown in autumn, and they soon fall to the water where they float like frail little boats. In winter the stark, bare trees stand as towering, distinct monuments. The bayou milieu is further denoted by the unceasing transformation created by the play of sunlight, moonlight, and clouds as changing light trickles through the overhead canopy and reflects from the water.

The French mistakenly assigned such descriptions as "sleeping water" or "dead stream" to these bayous. Although a current is hardly perceptible in normal flow, a bayou may appear to be sleeping, but it is far from dead. Geographically, Bayou Bartholomew serves as a primary drainage outlet for over 997,000 acres. Historically, it was the favored site for the first American Indians and settlers who also used it for transportation. Its virgin hardwood forests beckoned the lumbermen who rafted logs down it and set up steam-powered sawmills on its banks. The farmers quickly claimed the extremely fertile soil within its bends and used its water for their steam gins. Steamboats brought supplies and exported the white bales of cotton. This bayou was a fundamental component of the infrastructure of the southeast Delta until the coming of the railroads in the 1890s. It was also the center of culture and recreation until recent times. Today the bayou still provides the farmers its productive soil as well as water for irrigation.   Hunters and fishermen still enjoy its woods and waters. The bayou lives on in the memories of those who called it home – their unique and singular special place.

The First Bayou People

There's arrowheads all over that bayou.

Shorty Lyle

Changing nature left buried sediment and old channel scars for the geologists to ponder, but early man also left viable evidence to use in piecing together the story of the unwritten past. The first American Indians appeared in the southeastern United States sometime before 12,000 years ago. They were probably descendants of nomadic Asians who perhaps 23,000 years ago crossed a land bridge from Siberia to Alaska and then drifted southward following the grazing herds of animals they hunted. Little is known about these prehistoric people except what can be gleaned from their stone tools. Prehistoric Indians in Arkansas were Paleo Indian (before to 8000 B.C.), Archaic (8000 B.C. to 1000 B.C.), Woodland (1000 B.C. to A.D. 900), and Mississippian (A.D. 900 to A.D. 1541).

These periods are based upon changes in material culture such as projectile points, pottery, and in the evident lifestyles of the inhabitants. The Paleo Indians were roving hunters with no permanent villages. Beyond the borders of Arkansas, archeologists have found the Paleo Indian's distinctive fluted spear points with the bones of extinct Ice Age animals such as mastadon, mammoth, and long-horned bison. In Arkansas archeologists have found many distinctive Dalton style spear points and accompanying flint hide scrapers and woodworking tools. These date to about 10,000 years ago and indicate the growing human populations and changing lifeways after the end of the Ice Age. During the Archaic period, they still roamed, but began to return to certain areas to hunt and fish. They also began to grind their stone as well as flake it.

Major changes in lifestyle occurred during the Woodland period. Continuing to hunt, they also began to make pottery, grow crops, settle in villages, and build mounds for burial purposes. Recently archeologists working in the region of the mouth of Bayou Bartholomew made a startling discovery about the roots of Woodland lifeways. They learned that the building of mound cermonial centers extends to to some 6,000 years ago into the middle of the Archaic time span. (See Frenchman's Bend below.) This trend continued in the Mississippian period when they became more settled, having larger villages and cultivating more food crops. They built temple mounds for religious ceremonies and buried their dead in cemeteries. De Soto encountered and described the Late Mississippian period Indians when he was in Arkansas and Louisiana from 1541 to 1542 - the beginning of recorded history. The Protohistoric period (1541–1700) generally covers the time from De Soto to the first white settlers. During this time Spanish and French explorers encountered the Quapaw, Koroa, Tunica, Mentou, and Taensa in southeast Arkansas and the Caddo, Koroa, Chickasaw, Tunica, Taensa, and Choctaw in Morehouse Parish. The Historic period (1700-1835) includes the first settlement to the last migration across the state during the Indian removal.[28]

Bayou Bartholomew and its environs offered these early inhabitants the most fertile land for their crops, good hunting and fishing, and a transportation route. Along the bayou banks are numerous village and camping sites, which will be revealed in the following tour down the bayou. The alluvial land forms (the outer terraces and oxbows) associated with the bayou were created by the Arkansas River in comparatively recent geological times. The archeological sites on the older river oxbows near the bayou are about 3,000 years old, and the oldest sites on the bayou itself are somewhat more recent.[29] The Bartholomew-Macon archeological region includes most of the southeast Delta south of Star City and Dumas. These two bayous are the region's "two archeologically best-known streams."[30]

The archeological tour, which is numbered for clarity, begins at the headwaters and follows the bayou downward to its mouth. **(1)** Locals at the spring area source found numerous artifacts consisting mainly of points. The location has not been investigated by archeologists, and the occupation is unknown. **(2)** Only a few miles downstream from the source, archeologists John Miller and David Williamson found twenty-six sites by shovel testing only in woods and pastures during a survey for the nearly twelve mile long Bartholomew Bypass Route west of Pine Bluff. Occupation at these sites ranged from Middle to Late Archaic (5000-1000 B.C.) to Woodland with a possible Plum Bayou culture (A.D. 700-900). Additionally they found a number of components relating to nineteenth and early twentieth century. After dirt removal began for construction of the bypass in 1990, John House resurveyed the area and found three small sites apparently representing Archaic occupation. A nearby barrow pit yielded a Scottsbluff point that is estimated to date to around 7000 B.C.[31]

(3) At the Highway 15 (Olive Street) Bridge on the south edge of Pine Bluff, Bayou Bartholomew leaves the pine-forested uplands and enters the alluvial Delta. A short distance downstream, however, in the vicinity of Ladd in Jefferson County and Tarry in Lincoln County, the bayou flows against the flank of a line of low hills. These slight elevations are remnants of a floodplain created from glacial outwash during the waning Ice Age tens of thousands of years ago. Much of the city of Pine Bluff rests on another terrace remnant of this floodplain surface. This land is veneered with a layer of wind-deposited silt or loess, dust picked up by the wind from the outwash of melting glaciers in the Midwest. This is reflected in the characteristic pale soils. Archeological collections from the Ladd-

Tarry terrace include Dalton type projectile points dating back 10,000 years, left by some of the state's first inhabitants.

(4) South of Tarry and about two miles north of Yorktown, a field on the east bank of the bayou shows (under certain conditions) a dark stain in the soil a hundred or more feet in diameter. This stain marks the location of a former small mound that was leveled for farming in the 1950s. When the mound was being leveled, a local collector found a "conch shell necklace fragment." Recent explorations of the site by archeologists produced "battered clear quartz crystal and fragments of clay tempered pottery decorated with cord-impressed paddles or ziz-zag stamping suggesting that the occupation dates between 1500 and 2000 years ago." A very large mound (approximately two hundred feet in length and around fifteen feet high) at Bethlehem Church on the east bank of the bayou about a mile north of Yorktown remains to be investigated. Partial excavation units could determine if it is an outlying part of the Ladd-Terry terrace or if prehistoric American Indians built it. Another mound on the east bank of the bayou about a mile below Yorktown is about 120 feet in diameter and 10 feet high. Modified now by cultivation, erosion, and casual digging, this mound once probably had a rectangular flat-topped pyramid configuration. Plain clay-tempered pottery fragments and tiny corner-notched chert arrow points found around the base of the mound suggest occupation contemporary with the Toltec Mounds east of Little Rock, which places these people at this site around A.D. 700 to 1000.[32]

(5) In 1882 Edward Palmer, representing the Smithsonian, excavated more than four large mounds on the bayou at the Taylor plantation near Winchester. In three of them he found pottery, mussel shell, bone and stone implements, and turtle shells. Prior to his visit, farmers had plowed up skeletons, and locals uncovered others. Palmer also excavated the Tillar Mound 450 feet away from the bed of the bayou on the J. T. W. Tillar farm two miles from the Taylor place. One foot below the surface of the nine-foot high mound, he found pottery and human skeletons.[33] Artifacts from recent excavations at the Tillar Mound and other Tillar phase sites suggest they were in use in the A.D. 1500 and 1600s. Archeologists returned to the Taylor Mounds in 1991-1992. Marvin Jeter of the Arkansas Archeological survey identified Plum Bayou components dating around A.D. 850 at the Taylor Mounds and confirmed evidence of occupation from around A.D. 100-200 to possibly around A.D. 1300.[34]

"Members of a priestly hierarchy" probably occupied Plum Bayou culture mounds with the majority of the people living on farms in the local area. Larger mound sites (Toltec Mounds near Little Rock, for example) were aligned "for observations of solstices, equinoxes, and other celestial phenomena." The people hunted (mainly deer), fished, gathered mussels and wild plants, and farmed. They cultivated native plants such as goosefoot, maygrass, little barley, knotweed, sumpweed, and sunflower. They also grew some maize. Pottery was predominantly plainware but was infrequently incised with designs. The people commonly used quartz crystals from the Little Rock and Hot Springs vicinity as stone tools and "perhaps for magic [religious ceremonies] and fortune-telling." The Boydell Mound contained these crystals.[35]

(6) In 1969 and 1970 archeologist Martha A. Rolingson, with the help of local amateur archeologists, conducted an intensive survey along the bayou in Ashley County from Boydell to Wilmot. They recorded more than a hundred sites and tested five that were named Wilson Brake, Henderson, McArthur, Currie, and Ellis Pugh. Data collected revealed the following cultural occupations: Botsford phase (Poverty Point period, 1500-600 B.C.), Grampus phase (Tchula period, 600-100 B.C.), Alligator Point phase (Marksville period, 100 B.C.–A.D. 400), Dry Bayou phase (Baytown period, A.D. 400-700), deYampert phase (Coles Creek period, A.D. 700-1100), Bartholomew phase (A.D. 100-1400), and Wilmot Phase (late Mississippi period, A.D. 1400-1600).[36]

The Wilson Brake site is by Wilson Brake, an oxbow of the bayou south of Portland and a natural levee of an old river channel. The team found red clay at a depth of thirty centimeters. Artifacts collected indicated two periods of occupation, the Alligator Point phase of Marksville period and Bartholomew phase of early Mississippi period. The survey examined, but did not excavate three other mounds in the vicinity, Wilson #2, Bell, and Robert Lee. Rolingson concluded that this group was the location of a small village or hamlet.[37]

The Henderson site is on the west bank of the bayou directly across from Lake Enterprise at Wilmot. Five gravestones on one end of the mound indicate Christian burials between 1849 and 1877, a not uncommon use of these mounds. The two mounds proved to be a major occupation site (village) for the Bartholomew phase with an Alligator Point phase also indicated. A clay human effigy head and a stone table or palette suggested that ceremonial activities were held on these mounds.[38]

Shelby McArthur dug into dark brown soil on his farm on Big Bayou a few miles east of Portland in 1970. His pocketknife uncovered portions of a human skull. By the time an Archeological Survey representative visited the site, two burials were fully exposed. Twenty-six postmolds in two different lines suggested the presence of two circular buildings. Seven shallow burials, underneath these former houses, contained the skeletons of five infants and three adults and some gravegoods. This Bartholomew phase hamlet contained bones of fish, turtle, turkey, opossum, rabbit, squirrel, gopher, mouse, raccoon, fox, mink, and deer.[39]

The Currie site is located on a small rise two miles west of the bayou and two miles east of the edge of the hills in the middle of Overflow

Swamp. Not a suitable farming area, this place was likely used as a hunting camp. The survey found an unusually high number of deer bone and antler tools in two concentrations as well as scattered about the area. These included awls, handles, scrapers, and tips from deer and raccoon. Other bone fragments were from opossum, squirrel, rabbit, skunk, fox, turkey, fish, horse, and pig. Some post molds indicated the presence of a shelter. Human bone fragments implied the shallow burial (disturbed) of two to four individuals. Various pottery types suggest four different occupation periods: late Marksville or Baytown (A.D. 100-300), Coles Creek, Bartholomew phase, and Wilmot phase.[40]

Located on the backslope of the bayou levee on Dry or Deadman's Bayou is the Ellis Pugh site. Local collectors and deep plowing had previously destroyed a burial ground. Badly disturbed by farming at the time of the survey, sufficient artifacts, including ceramics, fired clay, stone, and worked bone, told the story of five separate occupations. Phases represented are Alligator Point, Dry Bayou, deYampert, Bartholomew, and Wilmot with the latter two representing the longer or larger.[41]

Rolingson concluded her research in the area by identifying the Bartholomew phase as a Plaquemine adaptation in the lower Mississippi Valley, specifically into the upper Beouf Basin from approximately A.D. 1200-1400. Based on evidence available in 1976, she suggested that these people came either out of the Tensas Basin in Louisiana or from the Ouachita River Valley. From the distribution of settlements she noted "the preference for site locations on relative high points of land, in proximity to Bayou Bartholomew and oxbow lakes or to the backslope streams, with easy access to all microenvironments with the bottom lands."[42]

(7) Archeologists returned to the Bayou Bartholomew survey area in 1977 and 1978 to conduct salvage excavations at Boydell Mound A which was to be leveled to clear a house construction site. This mound is located on the bayou which is a relict levee of an old Arkansas River channel. Associated with this site is Mound B, located approximately 150 meters to the southeast on Highway 165. This mound contains the Christian burials of members of the Waddell family who died from 1879 to 1958. Harriet Waddell's second husband, a Mr. Womack, was probably buried in Mound A in the 1860s.[43] Before the 1977-1978 excavation of this mound, locals found half of a child's coffin during soil removal.[44] Seven different prehistoric burials within the mound contained fragmentary skeletal remains of at least fifteen individuals who lived there from around A.D. 1100-1400 (Plaquemine culture). The estimated time span of occupation is A.D. 900-1200. Pottery collected represented periods from early Coles Creek (A.D. 900) to a phase of Plum Bayou culture.[45]

Defining the Boydell Catchment as "a catchment circle with the Boydell Mound A in the center and a 2KM radius," the survey recorded sixty sites. Of these, eighteen were prehistoric, twenty-six historic, and sixteen a combination of both. Periods represented ranged from Late Archaic to Bartholomew Phase with the latter being predominant. Forty-two sites contained historic material dating from 1850 or earlier to recent years. Most of these were located along the banks of the bayou, indicating that early settlers as well as American Indians favored this location.[46]

John House wrote, "Results from the 1977-78 work at Boydell, together with subsequent discoveries at Taylor Mounds, have prompted archeologists to rethink the origins of the post-A.D. 1200 Bartholomew phase. We now know that Coles Creek period (A.D. 700-1200) habitation middens and mound construction stages underlies Bartholomew Phase levels at these sites. These early residents of the bayou appear to have had strongest cultural ties not to the Tensas Basin on the south but rather to the north to the Arkansas River and Plum Bayou Culture."[47]

(8) What may prove to be the oldest mound in Arkansas is on the bank of Lake Enterprise, an old Arkansas River oxbow, at Wilmot. Two limited investigations took place in 1991 and 1992. Two small test pit excavations produced 7 whole, 16 partial, and 416 fragments of Poverty Point Objects.[48] Archeologists returned in 1997 and "dug deeper." Under the direction of Marvin Jeter, workers excavated a trench, which reached four meters in depth, and found numerous baked "clay balls" (actually they are made of silt, not clay). These Poverty Point Objects date from about 1500 B.C. (an example of an older oxbow date). Jeter theorized that this site may have been a "last stop" for Indians traveling to Poverty Point near Epps, Louisiana, a site famous for widespread trade. Other components found in the mound were plant remains, non-local stone fragments, a deer mandible with teeth, other deer bones, and mussel shells. The absence of pottery indicated the mound predated pottery making, and the presence of charcoal implied that it was used as feasting site.[49] Identification and radiocarbon dating of the plant remains will determine if the mound is indeed the oldest known mound in Arkansas.

Having no local supply of stone to use for hot rock cooking, the Poverty Point culture improvised a method for cooking by inventing the earth oven and clay balls. "A hole was dug in the ground, and hot 'clay balls' were packed around the food, and the pit was covered...Some archeologists have cooked in earth ovens, made like those at Poverty Point. They found, if they always put the same number of Poverty Point objects in the oven every time they cooked, that the shapes (cylindrical, biconical, spheriodial, etc.) controlled how hot the pit got and how long it stayed hot. Using different shaped objects was apparently the cook's means of regulating cooking temperature...."[50] Archeologists also found Poverty Point objects at another site near Wilmot and at the Grampus Sand Pit site on Lloyd's Bayou (Perkins Slough west of Montrose).[51] Clifton L. "Curly"

Birch said he found clay balls in holes in three places along the bayou bank near Tillar.[52] The Neimeyer-Dare (Darragh) site near Bonita, Louisiana, contained a large amount of the objects.[53]

(9) An earlier archeologist, Clarence B. Moore of the Academy of Natural Sciences of Philadelphia, visited the lower reaches of the bayou in early 1909 during his exploration along the bayou. Traveling in his steamboat, *The Gopher*, from the mouth of the bayou to Portland, Moore and his crew investigated fourteen mounds and cemeteries in a four-month period. (Here the tour will begin at the mouth and go up the bayou.) Stopping first at a mound near Sycamore Landing, where investigation was refused, he then explored a nearby cemetery on a slight rise in a cultivated field. He found thirty-eight traces of human remains from two to four feet deep and surmised from the large number of artifacts that many burials had disappeared. Graveware included arrow points, shell beads, pottery, and ceremonial pipes made of earthenware, limestone, and sandstone. Pottery represented the Coles Creek and later Mississippi periods. Eleven elaborately made ceramic pipes are similar to ones found later on up the bayou to Tillar and beyond. The pipes reminded Moore of the smoking ceremony described by Charlevoix, "in which the smoke was blown first to the sky, then to the earth ('above' and 'below'), and then around the horizon, or to the four quarters."[54]

A few miles up the bayou from Sycamore Landing, Moore stopped at Keno Plantation where he hit the "jackpot." In a cultivated field one-quarter of a mile from the bayou, the survey encountered 255 traces of human remains from the surface to a depth of three feet. Many burials by this time had disappeared. Graveware consisted of a circular wooden staff, masses of iron oxide, clay pipes, glass beads, a sandstone ceremonial axe, sheet-brass and copper, a small bell of thin sheet-brass (possibly a hawk bell), a brass disk with human hair (believed to be) preserved by copper salts, a pendant of hematite, and 485 exquisite pottery vessels, which Moore, in naivete, labeled as "inferior" much to the dismay of contemporary archeologists. This is a late Protohistoric site dating from the 1600s and perhaps into the 1700s. The pottery is mostly representative of a Tunican archeological culture (perhaps Koroa) with a large number probably being trade vessels from the Caddos. The hematite pendant is likely from the Poverty Point period.[55]

Stopping at the Ward place on a farm owned by T. L. Day, Moore found another cemetery containing thirty-one burials on a slight rise within sight of the bayou. Lying from near the surface to a depth of slightly more than two feet, all but one were practically intact. He wrote, "It was evident that the skeletons...had been placed in the ground when denuded of flesh, as bones were often out of place and small bones, in some instances were missing." Grave objects consisted of earthernware vessels, deer antler tines, mussel shells and hoes, tortoise carapaces, deer and raccoon bone implements, and chert pebbles. In a nearby field to the north, they found more than eighty chert arrowpoints, lanceheads, and knives in a short time, but no cemetery.[56]

At Seven Pines or Miller Landing the crew unearthed thirty-four burials from just under the surface to a depth of three feet on a slight rise one-quarter of a mile from the bayou. Graveware consisted of thirty-nine ceramic vessels and four clay pipes. The party searched a nearby field "celebrated for years for its yield of plummet-shaped pendants of hematite," but none were found. S. J. Harrell presented them with one of these specimens, which were from the Poverty Point period.[57]

Visiting S. J. Harrell's plantation near Mounds Landing, the party excavated a cemetery on a small elevation one-half mile from Bray Landing. Some of the skeletons were extended and intact and others were bunched in bone heaps. With the burials were twenty-six pottery vessels and eleven clay pipes. A nearby mound 22 feet high by 140 feet square with a summit-plateau of 50 square feet yielded neither bones nor artifacts. Moore noted that the alignment of the mound did not face celestial cardinal points. A small pool of water not far away probably marked where soil was removed to build the mound. The workers discovered artifacts about a hundred yards away from the mound, and excavation there uncovered thirteen skeletons in a back-extended position plus a bunched burial of one individual. Near surface burials indicated that others had been plowed away. Fourteen ceramic vessels were with the burials, but only a few were intact.[58] The large mound, now called the Matheny Mound, is still intact.

From Lind Grove Landing to Portland the survey turned up less evidence of aboriginal occupation. At Lind Grove they found signs of occupancy but only one skeleton and scattered bones. N. H. Huff informed them that previous plowing had unearthed many human bones. Two medium size mounds at Wilmot, one said to contain modern burials, were "much dug away previous to our visit" and were not investigated. They trenched a large mound at Noble Landing south of Parkdale, but did not find any bones or artifacts. The team did not disturb a mound on the bayou bank at the Carlock place (west of Sunshine) as it had recently been used as a cemetery. They did find "an extensive dwelling-site thickly strewn with bits of musselshell, fragments of pottery, and other debris" on level ground nearby. A low mound long cultivated on the Sherrer place south of Portland produced five or six skulls and bones but no artifacts. The last site visited was a small mound a half mile from Alligator Point on the bayou west of Portland. Previously disturbed considerably by "a seeker after treasure," the team did not excavate the site.[59]

(10) In the region centering on the confluence of the bayou with the Ouachita, archeologists recently made discoveries that are changing prevailing views of American Indian prehistory. Here, over the decade of the 1990s, an interdisciplinary research team headed by archeologist Joe Sanders of Northeastern Louisiana University, soil scientist Thurman Allan of the USDA Soil Conservation Service Monroe office, and geologist Roger T. Saucier of the U.S. Army Corps of Engineers identified evidence for a mound-building American Indian culture dating between 5,000 and 7,000 years ago.

The five mounds at Frenchman's Bend, located about three miles south of the juncture of Bayous Bartholomew and DeSiard, are among the newly-identified Middle Archaic mounds of northeast Louisiana, along with Watson Brake, Hedgepeth Mounds, and Hillman's Mound. Excavating at Frenchman's Bend in 1992 and 1993, the investigators recovered distinctive double-notched Evans projectile points, fired clay blocks of unidentified function, and samples of charcoal subsequently dated to between six and seven thousand years ago. Coring revealed that the occupation strata at Frenchman's Bend are overlain by the distinctive red alluvium deposited by the Arkansas River and therefore must date much earlier than the presence of the river in the Bartholomew meander belt between 1,800 and 2,200 years ago.

These recently discovered mounds pre-date the Poverty Point mounds and earthworks by as much as four thousand years. This discovery is prompting archeologists to re-think their most basic assumptions about the development of American Indian cultures. It is becoming apparent that the outlines of prehistoric cultural development were quite complex and that early Native Americans did not everywhere remain simple, nomadic hunter-foragers over several millennia following the end of the Ice Age.[60] [End of tour]

Unfortunately, many American Indian occupation, burial, or ceremonial sites have been destroyed by land leveling and plowing. However, people still find signs of their presence along the bayou. "On most any ridge around the bayou you can pick up arrowheads, and we find them in spring plowing." (Harvey Chambliss, Jefferson County) "There were mounds on the Jeff Davis tract. They were definitely manmade." (Sam Williamson, Jefferson County) "We found artifacts on every mound around here." (Lloyd Smith, Lincoln County) "There were artifacts on the old bayou bed near Oak Grove Chapel." (Robert Mitchell, Lincoln County) "There's arrowheads all over that bayou." (Shorty Lyle, Lincoln County.) "There were mounds around Persons Bridge, Tarry, and Yorktown." (Alvie Pugh, Lincoln County) "When our house burned we plowed the ground and unearthed relics. It was on a high ridge that never floods." (Edgar Norris, Lincoln County) "They are scattered everywhere – especially around Syrene Church and on the bayou banks." (Andrew Pickens, Desha County) "We picked up arrowheads on the Lambert place north of Baxter. On the old Bilgeischer place there was a high place claimed to be an Indian camp." (Amos Sledge, Drew County) "There were lots of artifacts on land not prone to flood. We found pottery, clay pipes, and flint rock." (Robert Crawley, referring to Crawleys [Tatum] Bend, Ashley County)

The stories continue in Morehouse Parish, Louisiana. "On that large mound [Matheny] between the bayou and Venoy Kinnaird's farm we found clay pots, sherds, and points." (Ralph Kinnaird) "We leveled a mound behind the house. It was full of artifacts, but there was no sign of a burial." (Benton Hunt) "We found arrowheads all around the Vester field." (Gaston Harrison) "I found Poverty Point objects and plummets at Niemeyer-Darrah Brake." (Bobby Abraugh) "My dad talked about his mother grinding corn on rock artifices." (Thelbert Bunch)

The last American Indians to live in Arkansas, other than the Cherokees, were the Quapaws, their name having come from "U-gakh-pa" which meant Downstream People. The Quapaws were known to the French as "Arkansea" from their tribal name which meant "South Wind" in the Illinois (Algonkian) language. Warfare and the ravages of European introduced disease greatly reduced their number by the early nineteenth century. By 1805 only 575 remained at villages near Arkansas Post. Continual westward expansion and greed for good land created a series of treaties whereby the government gradually dispossessed them of their land claims. By 1818 they only had about two million acres on a tract defined by a line running from Arkansas Post to the Ouachita River and from Little Rock to the Saline River. Bayou Bartholomew ran through this area in Jefferson, Lincoln and Drew Counties. More so-called treaties followed that eventually pushed the few remaining Quapaws out of the territory by 1834.[61]

During the great removal of the Cherokees from southeastern states in the 1830s, they followed the "Trail of Tears" and its various branches through northern Arkansas. Choctaws and Chickasaws from east of the Mississippi also crossed the territory on their own "trails of tears." One of these crossed Bayou Bartholomew in northern Ashley County on a route from present Lake Village through Camden and Foreman to Texas.[62] The story of Native Americans on the bayou and elsewhere had a sad ending. These once free and proud people, who lived off the land and respected it, were dislocated and reduced to a life of poverty and slackened pride by white man's rapacity. The early French and Spanish explorers and settlers did, however, share something in common with the American Indians. They likewise used the bayou as a transportation route and hunting ground.

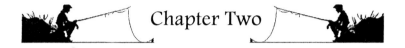

Chapter Two

The Colonial Wilderness

French and Spanish Foundations

> ···*he begs also the grant along the Bayou*
> *Barthelemi, from its source to its mouth*···.
> **Baron de Bastrop, 1797**

Perhaps the first white man to meet American Indians on Bayou Bartholomew was Hernando De Soto. Charles Hudson places part of the path of the conquistador in southeast Arkansas from Jefferson to Desha County. According to his interpretation, the exploration party spent the winter of 1541-42 at Autiamque (possibly the Hardin site east of present Redfield) on the River of Cayas (the Arkansas). In March they set out in search of Anilco and spent the night at Ayays (probably in present southeastern Jefferson or northeastern Lincoln County). After reaching Anilco (probably located at the Menard site in Arkansas County), the party traveled a short distance to Guachoya ("on the bank of the Mississippi River somewhere east of present McArthur in Desha County." (Coincidentally, De Soto Landing is on the Mississippi due east of McArthur.) After De Soto died there, his men "traveled toward the northwest, probably following a trail which ran through the chiefdom of Catalte, which probably comprised Tillar phase sites along Bayou Bartholomew." The De Soto Expedition Commission places the route from northeast Arkansas to the Camden area and down the Ouachita Valley with De Soto's death occurring in northeast Louisiana.[1]

Many years passed before another white man came in contact with Bayou Bartholomew. The French explorer, Robert Cavalier, Sieur de La Salle, claimed the region for France in 1682. La Salle's men eventually mutinied and murdered him in 1687 on the Trinity River in Texas. Duhaut, the perpetrator of the revolt, assumed command. Meanwhile La Salle's former lieutenant, Henri de Tonty, while searching for him in 1686, stopped at an Indian village near the mouth of the Arkansas River where six of his men wanted to remain. These Frenchmen established the first permanent settlement, Arkansas Post, in what would become the state of Arkansas.

Henri Joutel, a member of the La Salle expedition, decided to continue marching in hopes of finding the great river that would take them to Canada. Six men chose to go with him. They were Father Anastase Douay, Father Cavelier, Cavelier (La Salle's nephew), De Marle, Tessler, and a young French lad, Bartholomew.[2] The party crossed southern Arkansas not far north of Texarkana and Camden, dropped slightly south, crossed the Saline River, and veered slightly northeast to cross Bayou Bartholomew and on to the post.[3] They arrived July 24, 1687, and Joutel recorded the names of two of the founders, Couture and de Launay. He also entered in his journal that "Little Bartholomew, the Parisian," wanted to remain at the post when the Joutel band left for Canada. Thus the name, Bartholomew, first appeared in Arkansas history and represents one of the first few European names recorded in seventeenth century Arkansas.[4]

Joutel wrote that he crossed the River of the Koroa, a stream that eventually became known as Bayou Bartholomew. In the late spring of 1690, Tonty visited a village of the Coroa (spellings differ) on the bayou near present Wilmot "twenty-three leagues from his trading station on the Arkansas River." He also noted a Mentou village along the bayou east of present McGehee. Assuming French traders to be at a Coroa village on the bayou, Tonty sent two of his men up it to summon them down. On a return trip from Texas later the same year, he crossed the River of the Coroa once more, perhaps in the Bastrop area. The Courrois (a variation of Coroa) are shown on an unnamed tributary of the Ouachita, which appears to be the bayou, on a 1716 map. The bayou was then left undisturbed for nearly a century except as a hunting ground. Trappers began roaming in the 1730s from Pointe Coupee Post in Louisiana through Arkansas and into Missouri. Although the Ouachita and Saline Rivers were used as water routes, they found these streams dead-end passages as both headed in higher terrain with a long and difficult portage to the Arkansas. Filhiol observed that seventy leagues from the mouth of the Ouachita the water became low and rapid.[5] Surely the trappers discovered that by entering the River of the Coroa off the Ouachita, they could canoe to within a day's portage over level land to the Arkansas which would connect them to the White and Mississippi.

Although the small band of Frenchmen at Arkansas Post made no effort to colonize inland, some French-Canadian hunters and Indian traders went westward from the Arkansas and Mississippi Rivers in search of bear oil, hides, and beaver and otter pelts.[6] They undoubtedly found the bayou an obliging route to the Ouachita River and from there an access to markets in New Orleans. These folk were a roving breed and did not concern themselves with stationary dwellings, but some possibly built crude shelters on the bayou bank.

France ceded the Province of Louisiana (which included Arkansas) to Spain by a secret treaty in 1762, but Spanish sovereignty did not exist until 1766 with the arrival in New Orleans of Antonio de Ulloa, the first governor. A census by districts taken in 1769 revealed only 110 inhabitants of the Washita District, which included nearly all of northeast Louisiana, and southern Arkansas. Settlement began on Bayou Bartholomew on the lower end from the mouth upward. Francois Bonnaventure, an Indian trader, established a trading post at Point Pleasant in 1775. This bayou trade center attests to a substantial number of hunters on the bayou at that time with their goods predictably being brought downstream from their camps. Bonnaventure claimed approximately 2,000 acres and named his place "Old Cabbins."[7] However, colonization did not begin until 1795.

Governor Miro appointed Don Juan Filhiol, already in the Ouachita Valley by 1780 or 1782, commandant of the District of Ouachita in 1783. Miro ostensibly wanted to gain some control over French hunters who had been operating in the region since the late 1760s. Filhiol made his first post on the Ouachita River at Ecore a' Fabri (Camden), but moved his headquarters to Ouachita Post in 1784. He did not succeed in taming the intransigent hunters and left "perhaps upwards of a hundred" along the Ouachita and Saline Rivers.[8] A small settlement of families - Fogle, Buleet, Acan, and LeBoeuf - was on the Saline at present Longview in Ashley County in the early 1770s.

The significance of Bayou Bartholomew did not escape Filhiol's notice. He observed that it, along with the Tensas, Boeuf, Saline and Little Missouri, were navigable in high water. He was also impressed with the land adjoining the bayou. "The lands that border it from one end to the other are fine and high, very suitable for agriculture." The commandant was aware of this alluvial soil and its great, yet unused, potential for agriculture. He attempted to motivate the hunters to move to the fine bayou land and begin farming.[9] They simply had no interest. Why work to clear land and stay on it to cultivate it when the forest abounded in game? These people were hunters - first and foremost. They lived off the land and their diet was primarily meat. Filhiol described them in a 1784 letter to Governor Miro: "These men make a business of the hunt, and they are riveted to it worse than savages...Their lodgings are made with six forks and some bark or with some pliant poles and some bear skins. Their beds are skins of beasts. A loin cloth of a third of an ell of limbourg forms the men's summer garb, rags suffice for the women. Their winter wardrobe consists of deer skins...The flesh of beasts that they kill is their only food, boiled, grilled and steeped in bear grease when they have it...." Some did make small clearings and planted maize, pumpkins, and melons; but once planted, they did not attend to the crop.[10] In other words, they went hungry rather than work the land.

When the hunters left to live in the woods for months, their families survived the best they could. Henry Bry described their wretched condition: "Of these early colonists, the women created a matriarchy which formed a bulwark against constant destructive forces. Left alone for six or more months a year, they had to be the protectors and providers for their families. Hunger of the young was their constant worry. Often in an effort to assuage hunger pains, they would put belts or leather straps around the children's stomachs and gradually tighten them to stifle the starving sensations. And when a woman had to be away from her child, she would use an ingenious substitute for a commercial pacifier to entertain him or her. A piece of bear or pork fat would be given to the child to suck - but only when the precaution had been taken to tie a leather string to the fat and the infant's big toe. If the child tried to swallow the tasty morsel and thereby choke himself, the first impulse was to kick, and off goes the pork from its dangerous position."[11]

Governor-General Miro's successor was Francois Louis Hector, the Baron de Carondelet, who was more interested in colonizing the area. The area around the mouth of the bayou and upstream from it attracted some of the first settlers as revealed in Carondelet's 1795 letter to Filhiol. "You have not yet informed me of the distance from the Fort [Miro] to Bayou Barthelemy . . .[The fort] appears to me rather distant from Bayou Barthelemy, where the inhabitants at the new settlement would therefore suffer much from the Indians."[12]

James Morrison was one of the earliest settlers. He received a grant for 2,000 arpents (an arpent is .85 of an acre) from Miro at and near the mouth of the bayou in 1790. In return for the grant Morrison was to bring in sixteen families and locate a saline or salt deposit. He selected a home site two leagues from the mouth. George Hook, Morrison's son-in-law, settled on Morrison's land at Point Bartholomew (at the mouth) in 1795. It was later revealed during a long dispute with Maison Rouge, who wanted to build his fort at Morrison's place, that Morrison's grant was actually for land near either Rapides or Natchitoches Post. He simply chose 4,000 arpents along Bartholomew instead - reasoning that it would be of equal value to the 2,000 arpents in a more established place. James McLauchlin arrived in 1793 and received a grant from Governor Carondelet for four hundred arpents six and one-half miles from the mouth. He married Sarah Morrison, daughter of James Morrison. McLauchlin, a steamboat captain before coming to Louisiana, received an appointment as surveyor for the Spanish government in 1799. He later held positions as justice of the peace, captain of the militia, parish treasurer, and judge.[13]

Carondelet discussed the importance of the bayou as a navigable waterway in a 1797 letter to Filhiol: "I wish to have a direct communication from Washita to Arkansas, as well in low as in high waters, considering that if we fall out with the Americans, it would be convenient to have a land communication with Upper Louisiana [Arkansas]. Some think that the Bayou Barthelemy is navigable for canoes as far as near the river Arkansas. You might ascertain that by inviting some bold hunter, to whom a reward would be given, to go through that way to Arkansas, from whence he should bring a hunter of Arkansas, who would likewise be paid by the government. They should observe during the journey, in the principal points, the quantity of water. I wrote on the same subject to the Commandant of Arkansas." Carondelet wanted to establish a northern route west of the Mississippi River to Upper Louisiana as part of his defense plan for the province. The route, planned with short portages, would go up Bartholomew to the Arkansas River and thence into the White and St. Francis Rivers. This would allow direct communication between New Orleans and the settlements to the far north without using the Mississippi.[14]

The bayou did serve as a water route from Arkansas Post to Ouachita Post and points below on the Ouachita River. Before the establishment of Ouachita Post, the Mississippi River was used as the waterway of choice to go to the lower Louisiana settlements, but when the Mississippi was high, the bayou was an alternate route.[15] The trail connecting the two posts, the Arkansas Post-Louisiana Trace, also ran parallel to the bayou on its western side. The Chemin a Haut (high route or high road) was in the area of the Ashley County creek of that name. Chemin a Haut Creek runs into the bayou just below the Louisiana line.

Carondelet encouraged colonization by ordering two extensive land grants to the Marquis de Maison Rouge and the Baron de Bastrop. Their commission in return for these grants was to bring in settlers. The Maison Rouge Grant lay generally south of Bayou DeSiard, which joins Bayou Bartholomew near Sterlington, and the Bastrop Grant lay north on both sides of Bartholomew. The Bastrop Grant extended east of Bayou Macon, took in most of the present day parishes of Ouachita, Morehouse, and West Carroll, and extended well into southern Arkansas.[16]

Both colonizers wanted land along Bayou Bartholomew. Maison Rouge wanted a fort near the mouth, and Bastrop especially asked for the prerogative of selecting his acreage on it. Maison Rouge established his home on the bayou and selected a site for his fort on land already claimed by Morrison. In a letter to the governor, Maison Rouge observed that the soil on the bayou was "a thousand times superior to the hole" at Canot Prairie (near the post). The Marquis eventually relocated to Ronde Prairie south of the bayou and north of Fort Miro. Struggling to keep his small colony operative, he ventured to Arkansas Post in 1797 to purchase wheat seed. He returned late in the planting season with insect infested grain and sold it to some willing to risk the odds. The harvest proved adequate, but the flour mill was not yet built, so their efforts were in vain.[17]

Bastrop's plan, for his own profit, was to raise wheat for flour production. For this, he asked for the water power rights on Bayou Bartholomew and De Siard as well as for six *toises* (38.4 English feet) of land along the banks of each. He wrote to Governor Carondelet on June 12, 1797, for permission to dam De Siard for the establishment of flour mills, which needed dikes to provide water power. To prevent possible disputes he also asked for "the grant along Bayou Barthelemi, from its source to its mouth, of six *toises* on each bank, to construct upon them the mills and works which he may find necessary; and prohibiting every person from making upon the said bayou any bridge, in order that its navigation may never be interrupted, as it ought to at all times remain free and unobstructed...." Carondelet issued a decree using almost the exact wording the same day granting him this right. Construction for the DeSiard mill began in 1798, but it was not operating by the next year's harvest. C. C. Robin noted in 1804 that grain was rotting in storehouses for lack of a mill.[18]

Bastrop entered into a contract in 1798 with a New York state land speculator, Colonel Abraham Morhouse, to issue grants to settlers in a continued effort to colonize the area. The baron convinced Morhouse to purchase "a one-twelfth interest in his twelve square league land tract." Morhouse arrived in 1799 and settled on Bastrop's property. Meanwhile Bastrop was involved "in one of the most intricate commercial deals ever executed by a small entrepreneur of his status." The final result of the Bastrop schemes and deals was that Morhouse wound up with less than he bought, but did manage to sell approximately a hundred tracts between 1804 and 1813. Three settlements were established: Mer Rouge, Prairie Jefferson (Oak Ridge), and Point Pleasant. [19] Morhouse settled near Mer Rouge, and when the parish was formed in 1844, it was named after him with the addition of the *e* in the spelling.

Dunbar and Hunter, on their exploration of the Ouachita River in 1804, stopped at Bastrop's plantation, reported as being three miles above Fort Miro. Dunbar described it as "...a small settlement containing only 500 persons of all ages and sexes...There are three merchants settled at the post, who supply the inhabitants at very exorbitant prices with their necessaries; those with the garrison and two small planters and a tradesman or two constitute the present village." As his party moved upriver, he noted settlements on the "rich land" of the Bayous Siard and Barthelmi.[20]

After Robin visited Ouachita Post in 1804, he wrote of Bastrop: "His blind stupidity prevented him from noticing that he was the principal victim of this policy [trade monopoly]. If he had generously provided for the provisioning of the district, he would have enticed great numbers of settlers to come there. He could have made an immense fortune overnight, and by the most honorable of means, but far from getting people to come as settlers into these wildernesses, becoming for them a father or at least a protector, he repelled from his concession those who were nearby." Robin noted that most settlements were on the east bank of the river because of the fertile soil. "These settlements are spread out for twenty miles above the post. On the same side of the Ouachita are found the Bayou's communication with the river, circling across the prairie. One called *Bayou de Siard* and the other *Bayou Bartholomew.* The banks of both are thickly settled."[21]

Spain ceded Louisiana Territory to France by secret treaty in 1800, and in 1803, the United States bought the land for fifteen million dollars - about four cents an acre. Grant challenges, court suits, and debts finally caused Bastrop's vision of building an empire in his Great Wilderness to fade. Undaunted, in 1805 he went to Texas, still a Spanish territory, and talked Governor Cordero into giving him another land grant! Still the *poblador*, he attempted to bring his former Ouachita colonists to Bexar, but they did not want to leave. By 1806 he was in the freighting business in San Antonio and was elected the second *alcalde* (mayor) of the town in 1810. His finest claim to fame came in 1820 when Moses Austin attempted to establish a colony of Americans in Texas. Refused an audience with Spanish officials, Bastrop used his influence and interceded on Austin's behalf. Austin obtained permission for the colony, but died before it succeeded. His son, Stephen F., assumed the venture and between 1821 and 1824 brought in three hundred families, "The Old Three Hundred," to found a small colony named San Felipe de Austin. Baron de Bastrop, whose real (Dutch) name was Felipe Enrique Neri, died in Saltillo, Mexico, on January 3, 1827. In 1837 in recognition of his friendship with Moses Austin, the town and county of Mina changed the name to Bastrop.[22]

The name of Bastrop lived on in Louisiana as well. The Morehouse Parish seat was named after the colonizer. The name also continued in less flattering ways. Many of the Bastrop - Morhouse claims were never proven; the ones that were eventually wound up in an embroilment questioning legal title that lasted for years beginning in 1851 when Congress passed an act for the settlement of the land claims in the Bastrop Grant. Of the 117 sales made by Morhouse that show up in this settlement, 35 were on Bayou Bartholomew. One of the most notorious disputed claims centered on Aaron Burr, former vice-president of the United States. A Kentuckian, General Charles Lynch, bought into the Bastrop claim and in 1806 sold 350,000 acres to Burr. During Burr's trial the government accused Burr of using this settlement scheme as a facade for ulterior motives that amounted to treason. Attorneys maintained that he only plotted to settle Spanish sympathizers there so they could march quickly to Texas in case war erupted between the U.S. and Spain. After the trial, which acquitted Burr, the land reverted to Lynch who sold it to Edward Livingston, whose brother, Robert, was involved in the Louisiana Purchase.[23] The Livingston tract surrounded Bayou Bartholomew in north Louisiana and extended into Arkansas.

Bastrop left a similar situation in Texas. The *Telegraph and Texas Register* ran the following notice in 1838: "Adm. Notice. County of Bexar, Republic of Texas. All persons are hereby notified that lands advertised to be sold in May by John W. Smith, clerk of said county, as adm. of est. of the late Baron de Bastrop do not belong to the said estate...Said lands belong to the est. of the late Juan Martin de Veramendi." Veramendi was the former governor of Coahuila and Texas, and the father of Maria Ursulita Veramendi, who married Jim Bowie.[24]

In 1805 Congress created a commission to investigate Spanish grants held by Arkansans. Only 160 were acknowledged. The commission legitimized grant claims in the following counties: Arkansas (68), Phillips (18), Crittenden (16), Jefferson (15), Monroe (11), Cross (10), St. Francis (9), Pulaski (8), Independence (3), White (2), Lee (2), Prairie (1), and Lawrence (1). One of the Pulaski County grants was called the "Bartholomew Spanish grant." Located east of North Little Rock, it was bought by Peter Le Fevre Sr., who arrived in Arkansas around 1789. Part of this parcel was eventually passed on to Le Fevre's great-grandson, A. Howard Stebbins.[25]

Filhiol himself laid claim to one of Arkansas's wonders. Hearing from buffalo hunters about some hot springs with "wondrous virtues of the water," he sent two men to bring a sample to him. Three Osage Indians met them and made signs that threatened scalping and burial. The men "got their jug of water and fled." Filhiol wrote to Miro in 1787 and asked for a square league of land containing the *Aquas Calientas*, which was granted. The following year he journeyed to see the fabled springs and wrote that they were surrounded for miles by crystal rock. The United States eventually did not honor this claim although Filhiol's heirs fought to retain ownership.[26]

France gave way to Spain, and Spain to the United States, and the colonizers left behind a legacy of letters and documents which are invaluable in the interpretation of the region in the 17th and 18th centuries. For example, Filhiol's 1786 detailed account of the Ouachita Valley, which includes the lower bayou, names the "Ferocious and Wild Beasts." These included panther, bobcat, lynx, wolf, fox, opossum, raccoon, polecat, rabbit, squirrel, otter, beaver, bear (abundant), deer, and "wild oxen" (buffalo). He also mentioned turkey (common), swans, cranes, geese, "bustards," ducks (six months of the year), and "clouds of wood-pigeons." The most common fish listed were gar, catfish, buffalo and fresh-water drum. Others were spoonbill catfish or sturgeons, pikes, bass, perch, trout, sunfish, crappie, big mouths, Opelousas catfish, sardines, and eel. Turtles were common, and alligators were thinned out in the region.[27]

The dominant trees, he wrote, were oak, sweetgum, walnut, pine, sassafras, ash, elm, mulberry, locust, sycamore, willow, bitter pecan, olive, poplar, linden, birch, holly, arrow-wood or service tree, elder, wild cherry, sorb apple, pawpaw, persimmon, plum, and sumac. Some plants mentioned were agrimony, angelica, elecampane, crane bill, maiden-hair, chervil, centuary, eye-bright, larkspur, targon, ginger, mallows, gentian, ginseng, wild indigo, St. John's wort, cat's paw, plantain, cinquefoil, dragon's blood, Solomon's seal, wild valerium, and golden rod.[28]

The inhabitants, he said, "consist of scum of all kinds of nations...who have become stuck here through their fondness for idleness and independence...They excel in all the vices and their kind of life is a real scandal. The savages, though uncivilized, who have opportunity to see them, hold them in contempt...The women are as vicious as the men, and are worthy companions of their husbands...Lazy to the uttermost, what can their industry be! If they hunt a little it is only to satisfy their primary needs of life."[29]

The small amount of trade disappointed the commandant. "All the district's annual trade does not exceed 6[000] to 7000 pots of bear oil, 2000 deer skins, 2000 pounds of suet, 500 beaver pelts and 100 otter pelts. What a difference this would make if the same number of men were real farmers! The hogs alone that they would raise, considering how easy it is, would guarantee more than that by their lard alone...." By comparison, to suggest what was available to an ambitious hunter at this time, the average annual shipment from Arkansas Post in the early 1800s "contained over forty thousand French pounds of deerskins, along with the pelts of twelve thousand raccoons, five hundred bears, twenty-five hundred to three thousand beavers, and three hundred otters." This enormous amount of goods was not brought in by the vagabond white hunters, but by the Osage Indians.[30]

Bear provided more than hides for shelter or sale; their fat and tallow were valuable commodities. The fat was rendered into oil that was used for cooking and in lamps, and tallow (the harder fat) was used for candle making. Dunbar addressed this subject: "The hunters count much of their profits from the oil drawn from the Bear's fat, which at New Orleans is always of ready sale, and is much esteemed for its wholesomeness in cooking, being preferred to butter or hog's lard: it is found to keep longer than any other oil of the same nature, without turning rancid; they have a method of boiling it from time to time upon sweetbay leaves which restores it or facilitates it conservation." A French hunter, Arclon, who lived on the upper Ouachita made log troughs that were used to transport the oil down the river.[31]   The community of Oil Trough, in Independence County, is named for this device.

Life was not easy for these earliest settlers.   Laurence Cavet, who settled at Prairie Rondo in 1790 and later moved to 240 arpents on Bayou Bartholomew, died intestate in 1812.   An inventory of his estate gives some indication of the sparseness of worldly goods.   His most valuable possession was the land that was appraised at $1,500 and sold to Hugh Stephenson for $1,100.   Next in worth was his livestock that consisted of two head of (illegible, probably oxen), three horses and one old mare ($60), fifteen head of cattle in the woods ($150), and twenty hogs ($60). One old wagon was appraised at $25 and two old plows and guys were worth $15.   Rounding out his equipment were four hoes, two axes, three augers, one saw, a large froe, a spade, a small cotton hand gin, and a Spanish bridle and saddle.   The household furnishings included a table, six chairs, two old blankets, a bedstead, two pots and one Dutch oven, a dozen bottles, six plates, cups and saucers, knives and forks, a tureen, a cypress chest, two flatirons, a candlestick, a box of razors, two new hats, and a looking glass.   The mirror, appraised at $10, was the most valuable household item.[32]

The Bartholomew Name

An Arkansas Indian named Chalmet was hunting in
the Ouachita region on Bayou Barthelemy⋯.
Balthazar de Villiers, 1781

Bartholomew is a Hebrew name which may have been a patronymic version of "Son of Tholmai." Saint Bartholomew, one of the twelve apostles, is mentioned in the Bible in Matthew (10:3), Mark (3:18), Luke (6:14), and Acts (1:13). Tradition holds that after a long evangelistic crusade, he was martyred by being flayed alive and crucified. He is represented as carrying his skin in his hand in Michelangelo's *Last Judgement* in the Sistine Chapel. The Feast of Bartholomew, held in his memory on August 24, was celebrated in London at the opening of Bartholomew Fair from 1113 to 1855. The surname became widespread in Europe and was also used as a boy's given name.[33]

The fate of the young Parisian, Bartholomew, who elected to remain at Arkansas Post in 1687, is not known. He possibly chose to become a hunter or fur trader, embraced an Indian lifestyle, and took an Indian woman for a wife, which was common practice. If he did, his descendants may be among the next recorded named Bartholomews in Arkansas history. Jacques Michel and Renaul Barthelemy were living in a household with one woman at Sotehouy below the former Law's colony in 1723, and a Bartelemias was living on the bank of the Arkansas River in 1726. The 1726 Louisiana census noted, "All the inhabitants are poor and live only through Indians' hunting." Joseph Barthelemy was in the Fort Carlos III (Arkansas Post) militia in 1780.[34]

The *Catholic Register of Arkansas* contains many Bartholomew names with various spellings. Some came from Canada as evidenced by the nickname, *dit* (called) Quebec. Angelique Berthelemy Quebec was the godmother to Simon, son of Genevieve Berthelemi Quebec and Francois Coussot. (Joseph) Barthelemi Quebec married "an Indian of the Kances [or Cances] Nation," whose name became Margarita upon her baptism on August 19, 1793. The same day they were married, and their four children were legitimized. Three of their children, Louis (about age nine), Francois (age twelve), and Joseph (age three), were baptized the previous week. The day after their marriage, their eighteen-year-old daughter, Therese, received baptism. Other Bartholomew names in the register are Joseph Barthelemi and wife, Felicete DuChassin, whose sons, Pierre, Martin, and Francois, were baptized June 20, 1820. Marianna Fayasse and Louis Barthelemi's children, Joseph, Helene, Pierre, and Martin, received baptism the same day. In 1848 Martin Barthelemy was a sponsor for some young children at their baptism.[35]

The names appear with slightly different spellings in *Baptisms Of Whites Of The Parishes Of Rivera De Las Arcas*. Francis or Francisco, son of Francisco Coussot and Genovesa Bartelmey, was born in 1779 and baptized in 1796. His grandmother, Maria Bartelmey, was deceased. When the priest officiated at the baptism of their son, Pedro (who was born in 1790), in 1797, he wrote that the maternal grandparents were "unknown Salvages [savages]," which was a term for Indians. The notation was the same for the baptism of their next two children. Angelica Bartelemy was godmother to Maria Souligny in 1798, and Juana Bartolemeo was godfather to Rosalia Bonne in 1802. The same year Bartholome Quebedo and Margarita were named maternal grandparents of Joseph Kebed, son of Joseph Souligny and Francisca Quebedo (Kebed). Teresa (Therese) Bartelemi married Francisco Hembeau (Imbeau), and baptismal records for two of their children give Joseph Quebec and Margarita Bertelemi and Jose Quebu and Margarita Bartelemi as maternal grandparents.[36]

President James Monroe signed a land grant to Louis Barthelemy on August 9, 1824. The 640-acre tract was along the Arkansas River in the vicinity of Arkansas Post and adjoined the southeast corner of a section belonging to Joseph Bartholomew.[37] To qualify for a grant, a person must have occupied the land for ten years. It is not determined if this Louis Bartelemy is the same man Thomas Nuttall saw at Pine Bluff in 1819. The bayou was probably not named after these Bartholomews; it was more than likely named after the first at Arkansas Post, the young Parisian. Filhiol's 1786-1788 map of the Ouachita River environs and Trudeau's 1797 map of the Bastrop Grant shows Bayou Bartelemy. The name changed from the River of the Coroa to Bayou Barthelemy by 1781, the earliest known date the name appeared in written history.[38]

The French and Spanish explorers and colonizers acknowledged the worth of Bayou Bartholomew as a transportation route and noted the remarkable fertility of the adjoining land. Although a significant amount of settlement took place on the lower bayou in Morehouse Parish during the colonial period, the settlers paid scant attention to developing the agricultural potential. Only after the United States bought the Louisiana Purchase in 1803 did a new breed of settlers begin to arrive. The resolute pioneers also used the bayou for transportation and hunted in its forests, but they turned their attention to clearing land for agriculture. Many, recognizing the advantages offered by the bayou, chose its banks for their homeplace.

⚓

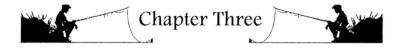

Chapter Three

Early Bayou Settlements in Southeast Arkansas

Jefferson County

Pine Bluff

The early settlers at Pine Bluff, located on the banks of the Arkansas River, probably paid no attention to the trickle of a small bayou to the south even though it bore a common local name. In 1819 Ambrose Bartholomew was living on the north side of the river, and Louis Bartholome was on the south side. These men were hunters. The first permanent settler was a French trapper and hunter, Joseph Bonne, who came in 1819 and built a wigwam on the riverbank in 1825. This house and a log house owned by a Mr. Prewett constituted the settlement. John Derreiusseaux came in 1825 and settled nearby. Others south of the river at this time were Bailey, Morrison, and Arrington. Bonne opened the first tavern, and afterwards, James Buck and Drew White also kept taverns. Mr. Fugate opened the first store. Some of the first businessmen there were Dorris, Maulding, Hewes, James, Scull, Tucker, Bird, Greenfield, and Kay. [1]

The county court met either in Joseph Bonne's log house or at other homes until Jacob Brump erected a courthouse in 1839. This building was replaced in 1856 by a two-story painted brick structure with one-story wings. The town gradually emerged as a river trading point. Trade increased when the Little Rock & Napoleon Railroad was laid between Pine Bluff and Chicot (on the Mississippi River) in 1869. The St. Louis, Arkansas & Texas Railroad, known as the Cotton Belt, came through around 1880. [2] From Bonne's lone log house on the bank of the river, Pine Bluff grew to be the fourth largest city in the state and the largest in the Delta.

Byrd Lake

Peter Paul Byrd Sr. moved from El Dorado to Pine Bluff between 1890-93 and engaged in the cotton brokerage trade. He was the son of John Henry Byrd, a well-known portrait painter. Byrd and his sons, George Conlin and Henry Boyd, later bought a large tract of land along the bayou south of the town. George Conlin Byrd returned to Pine Bluff in 1919 and, with his brother, began to develop a farm at Byrd Lake. "It was way out in the county then," explained Helen Byrd, daughter of George. Fifty-second Street was only a dirt lane that ended after Ohio Street. They built three houses, a commissary, barns, and a sorghum mill. Cotton was the primary crop, but the farm also consisted of a large truck patch and a dairy.

The brothers decided to develop the lake, an oxbow of Bayou Bartholomew. Fed by springs and surrounded by large cypress trees, it was a naturally beautiful setting. They built a colossal dance pavilion that was screened and raised high off the ground. A grand piano had its place within. In 1913 the area was dedicated and named Doris Park, after the brother's half-sister, Ellen Doris (who married James Crow Thompson Jr.). "At that time," said Helen, "Doris Park and Sulphur Springs were the only place to go for entertainment." During the Depression, the pavilion had a different use. George Byrd Jr., in an attempt to raise money for college, began raising game fowl and illegal cockfights were held in a pit in the dance hall for about two years. In 1978 the Natural Heritage Commission purchased 144 acres of the Byrd land, and the area is protected as part of the Arkansas System of Natural Areas.[3]

❧❧❧❧

The Jefferson Davis Tract

The bayou, still an embryonic stream, leaves Pine Bluff to wend past Grider Field and Ladd to the east. Jeff Davis once owned a large tract of land on the bayou west of there. The ex-president of the Confederate States acquired this land in a roundabout way. In 1836 Samuel W. Dorsey of Louisiana purchased a 2,100-acre tract that was never developed. He left his land to his wife, Sarah Ann, and she, being childless, willed it in 1878 to Davis, "my most honored and esteemed friend," with subsequent title to go to Varina, his youngest daughter. Varina Davis willed it to her mother, who willed it to her only surviving child, Margaret, wife of Joel Addison Hayes.

A few years before 1908, Charles H. Triplett of Pine Bluff was visiting in Colorado and became acquainted with a Mr. Hayes, who was president of the First National Bank of Colorado Springs. The sale of this property was discussed and Triplett investigated the plot upon his return. He found it "covered with squatters, in tracts ranging from a few acres to clearings of considerable size." Some of them had been in possession long enough to acquire ownership by virtue of the statute of limitations. Triplett secured quitclaim deeds from them and from the others he took rent notes acknowledging ownership to Mrs. Hayes. He bought the tract from Hayes the same year and began to develop it for farmland.[4]

❦

Bayou Settlers

Carland Hardwick settled in the vicinity of Grider Field by 1844. He wrote that year to J. Hines Trulock, "I am told a very fine settlement of land was discovered in the time of the overflowing by persons looking out for higher land. About 12 or 15 miles Southeast of my place between the Arkansas River and the Bouyo Bartholomew, some 5 or 6 miles back from Fish's Store. I am told this settlement of land which I allude to is several feet above the highest water and several families has and is settling there." Names mentioned in the letter were Bachen [?], Barksdale, Tarver, Wilson, Dardeene, and Datch. William Alexander Noel, M.D. bought a plantation south of Pine Bluff on Bayou Bartholomew in 1853. The family moved to Pine Bluff in 1865 so that the children could receive a better education. Dr. Noel practiced medicine in Pine Bluff for fifty years until his death in 1903.[5]

Derreiusseaux Cemetery, on a high ridge east of the bayou, bears the names of early area settlers. Sarah Derreiusseaux Bean, born in 1858, was buried there in 1883. Wm. W. Cogbill died in 1893. Other names on markers are Bean, Rodgers (died 1889), Abernathy (died 1918), Fleetwood, and Haynes. A Pointer family burial lies in a thicket near the Gibb Anderson place.

H. B. Chambliss worked for the C. H. Clowers Co. at Tarry as a young man and then began farming for himself on a rented bayou farm. In 1932 he bought a large tract east of Ladd and south of Grider Field and moved to that location. Hill Acres School was located at the present site of Grider Field. The two-room school went through the ninth grade. The Grider family sold this land to the U.S. government during World War II. Pine Bluff School of Aviation was established by the U.S. Army Air Force and trained over 9,000 pilots for the war.

Before the land was cleared for farming, sawmills cut timber from the cypress brakes. Canals were built to float timber from the brakes to the mills and perhaps during high water were rafted down the bayou. Traces of these canals can still be seen in this area. John and Jimmy MacIntyre, operating as MacIntyre Bros., ran a sawmill at Ladd. They also had a gin and store on their farm.[6] ❦

Lincoln County

Tarry

Bayou Bartholomew enters Lincoln County west of Tarry, an old farming settlement. Settling near there in the 1870s were the families of Tom and Lizzie Vining and their daughter, Mandy Mae, who was married to James Bradshaw. The Bradshaws had four children: George, Grafton, John, and Ida.[7] Tarry Post Office was established in 1892 and continued in operation until 1965. Henry Wallace Thomas and his wife, who succeeded him, were the last two postmasters, and consequently the post office was located in their store.

The McGehee brothers, J. D. "Jim," Bob, Will, and Clayton, owned a plantation and McGehee Bros. Store. They also operated a steam-powered sawmill on Thirteen Acre Lake, a gristmill, gin, and blacksmith shop. The McGehee home, a large two-story that burned, was located at the present site of the late Mrs. H. W. Thomas home. The Taliferro family owned a plantation and mercantile. C. H. Clowers Co. owned a plantation, gin, and mercantile. R. L. "Bob" Thomas was at one time part owner of the Clowers store. He and his brother, Henry Wallace Thomas, bought out the McGehee store and ran it under the name of Thomas Bros. The building burned and was rebuilt in 1933. The concern eventually became H. W. Thomas General Merchandise. When H. W. Thomas died in 1948, his wife continued its operation until she retired in 1986 at age ninety. The town also had a black masonic lodge. "On Saturdays there would be two to three hundred people in town," said Mrs. Thomas.

Lois Baldwin arrived in Tarry in 1916 to teach and married H. W. Thomas the following year. The local school went to the twelfth grade and had a two-month summer term and a three-month winter term. Mrs. Joe Henry Hardin followed Mrs. Thomas as teacher. The schools consolidated with Star City around 1931. Dr. Joe Henry Hardin was an early doctor at Tarry followed by Dr. Billingsly around 1921. Dr. Patton came from Ladd to see patients in the old post office building during the 1920s. The town never had a church, but all denominations met at the school for services. Baptizings were held in Thirteen Acre Lake. The town began to decline during the 1930s, and all that remains presently of this once bustling farming center is the old Thomas store. The post office corner remains exactly as it was left in 1965. Canned goods, patent medicines, and a good supply of shoes still line the wooden shelves. A wood burning heater and lonely bench stand alone in the center of the building.[8]

Yorktown

From Tarry the bayou continues its southeasterly course to Yorktown where it is bridged on Highway 425. The community is named after a York family who settled there before 1859. E. York was living in Bartholomew Township (now in Lincoln County) in Jefferson County in 1860. Sue Gipson's grandmother, Sally York who married Alex Smith, was born near there as a York slave. Joseph Lane Hunter graduated from a Harvard College in Alabama in 1855 and settled on the bayou south of Yorktown in 1858. Two years later he wrote to his father that he was planning to build a gin. He married Lucy Hudson, daughter of James A. Hudson, in 1861. The following year he enlisted in the Confederate army and served for the duration of the war. The bayou farm was successful, and in 1884 Hunter moved to the top of the ridge above the bayou and built a new home. Part of his orchard still stands near Hunter Hill Road. One of Hunter's daughters married a Turchee whose family were early settlers. A Mr. Burns had a store in this area from around 1890 to around 1960.[9]

Other area settlers were Alexander, Calloway, Cawthorne, Copeland, Coblert, Cotton, Goulsby, Horace, Miller, Morrison, Ollar, Pitts, Saint, Spellman, Smith, and Sonedraker. The Waters family settled at Yorktown in 1882. Other early names connected with the settlement are Baugh, Bones, Bradshaw, Brickley, Dabney, DeBruce, Edwards, Fuller, Goins, Green, Hughes, McLemore, McWhorter, McBride, Pendleton, Richmond, Ryall, Sneed, Taylor, Thompson, and Tracy. Alabama Nelson came to the area as a slave and after the war eventually acquired land where George Couch presently lives. Dock Gipson, an ex-slave, arrived with Bill Britley in 1865.

Oak Grove Baptist Church was organized in July 1861, and in 1872 Joseph L. Hunter donated thirty acres on Bayou Bartholomew for the church and cemetery. Church records dated April 8, 1885, state that by that time most members had died or moved away. Yorktown First Baptist Church had its conception in 1924 when an evangelist, J. D. Sayers, conducted a tent revival on the school grounds. Fifty people converted and thirty-two were baptized in the bayou. A Sunday School and weekly prayer meeting were organized. John Grumbles Sr. from the Star City Baptist Church conducted these meetings in the school until a church was built in 1934. Lumber from the old Oak Grove building was used in the construction. Corldon Patton was the first pastor. A new church was erected in 1978 with the old building becoming the fellowship hall. In 1933 W. M. Guinn and R. M. Moore organized Yorktown Freewill Baptist Church in the Waters' schoolhouse. The following year a building was completed on land donated by Bob Atkinson.[10]

The African-American community established Mt. Nebo Baptist Church in 1879. Some preachers who served later were Joseph P. Williams, A. L. Brantley, S. J. Nash, Dabney, Booker, and Singleton. Baptizings were held in the bayou at a site about two miles away. Bethel Church #2 was built between Yorktown and Tarry by the early 1900s. Rev. Daniel Bush was an early preacher there. Sneed Chapel served the black community at nearby Phenix.[11]

A. V. Verdue built a one-room schoolhouse in the late 1890s near the Ferd Simms home north of Copeland Creek. Mrs. Partridge from Tennessee was the first teacher. Minnie Sawyers and Ruby Gray Hunter (Nobles) taught there later. Teachers and students often had to wade the creek after heavy rains. Waters School, built by Mr. Verdue in 1911, was near the home of Mrs. Peter Bell Waters. Teachers there were Myrtle Clowers, Julia Rogers, Donna Brockman, Eula Crow, Mellie Crow, Lizzie Norton (Dixon), Bertie Nichols, Lela Trussell (Newton), Lill Stephenson (Thomas), Mary Lee Spears, Professor Jeff Reynolds, and Fred Grumbles. This school was used until around 1937 when it was replaced by another building north of it. During World War II the school consolidated with the Grady School District

Black children attended school in a building near Mt. Nebo Church where Laura Smith was an early teacher. Some other teachers were Mrs. Demery, Mrs. Cruthfield, and Mr. Cooper. Sweethome was a rural school for blacks in the early 1900s. Ethel Allen and Eliza Spicer taught there. Morgan School replaced this school on Tracy Road around 1919. Located on the west side of the bayou south of Tarry, this one-room school went through the eighth grade and had twenty to thirty students. Ethel Allen was a teacher.[12]

By 1881 the settlement was large enough to call for a post office, which was established that year and continued until 1921 when mail was rerouted to Tarry. Yorktown Post Office was reestablished in 1943 when the Phenix office closed. Nestled on the bank of the bayou, the town consisted of several stores, a cotton gin, gristmill, blacksmith shops, and two sawmills. Bob Atkinson owned one of the earliest stores and was succeeded by Lee Thomas. Walter White owned a store, which contained the post office, and a gin on the bayou. Neb Ryall owned a sawmill. Dr. J. M. Short and Dr. Rickett were early physicians. Before a bridge was built across the bayou in 1878, Atkinson Ford served as a low water crossing.[13]

⚜

Crigler, Meroney, Fresno

From Yorktown the bayou continues its curving route through open farmland and passes south of Crigler, Meroney and Fresno. Furth Post Office opened at Crigler in 1902, and the name changed to Crigler in 1937.

The post office was discontinued in 1957. A government resettlement program developed at Furth during the 1930s on land sold by E. P. Ladd.

Meroney was a railroad shipping point for cotton and crossties. E. P. Ladd owned a sawmill and V. L. Hill owned one south of the bayou. Horace Socia's father owned tie mills in the area. Brockman and Joyce owned stores, and there was a gin in the town. Meroney Post Office existed from 1910 to 1931. The community swimming hole was half a mile down from the bridge.

Fresno was another rail stop to the east. "It was a thriving community once," said John Edd Curry. "It was first called Cold Spur which was just to the east of Fresno. They had a store and a gin." Deep Bayou Post Office was located there from 1917 to 1921.[14]

✖✖

Persons Bridge, Todd, Star City

The bayou flows past the old Sorrells Ferry site near the mouth of Deep Bayou. Theodoric Finley Sorrells moved his family from Pine Bluff in 1861 or 1862 to his bayou plantation that he had been running for several years. This family later moved to Tyro. Downstream from Sorrells Ferry is Persons Bridge seven miles east of Star City. The bridge was named for the Person family who lived on the west bank. William Davis Person moved to the county in 1852 and developed a plantation. He was also a surveyor and blacksmith.[15] During the first half of the 1900s, the bayou swimming hole was located in front of Bill Person's house. The baptizing site for the black community was up from the bridge and down from the Herman Gassaway place. Persons School, in a one-room building with eight grades, was located west of the bayou during the 1920s. Persons Chapel, an African-American church, was built west of the school in the 1930s. Some Slavonians came to the area in the late 1800s and cut stave bolts, which they rafted down the bayou in the spring. Joe Stennis, who stayed in the area, was one of this group. A Mr. Trantham owned a gin on the bayou in this area in the early 1900s.

The little town of Todd on the bank of Cane Creek was two miles west of the bridge. Todd Post Office existed from 1908 to 1927 with mail going to Meroney at its closure. The town had three stores (owned by James Martin Lyle, Mansfield Scott, and Andrew Woodard) and a gristmill (owned by Lyle). Bud Leal (or Lelg) owned a sawmill and blacksmith shop. John K. Lyle, Woodard, Tiner, and Littlejohn owned bayou farms nearby.[16]

Cane Creek emptied into the bayou near there before it was dammed to make a lake for Cane Creek State Park in the 1980s. Cane Creek Church, a log building, was the site of the first county court held in Lincoln County on April 24, 1871. Judge George H. Joslyn presided and the following justices of peace attended: J. M. McKittrick, E. H. Smith, Henry Palmer, William Lewis, D. M. Neal, Burnett Washington, Thomas Ashcraft, and George Hilliard. J. Chris Chestnutt Jr. was appointed to consult with the owners of the building to obtain permission to make alterations and repairs. Two small log additions were added as wings for jury rooms. The court met again in July and established road and school districts. Commissioners appointed by the governor to locate a permanent county seat reported that they had selected a site on the Little Rock, Pine Bluff & New Orleans Railroad near Varner. At the September term, a petition was presented to change the selected site to a more central location. An election was held in October 1871, and citizens voted in favor of removal. In December the court accepted a new location suggested by the commissioners. The new county seat was to be called Star City. The two log additions to the church were moved to the new site and placed end to end for a clerk's office. By February 1872, the court moved to Star City. A log calaboose was soon built. A new jail replaced the old calaboose in 1887 but burned soon after its construction. The courthouse and another jail were constructed in 1880.[17] This courthouse is on the National Register of Historic Places.

R. R. Rice Sr. of Varner continued to use his political influence (he was sheriff and later a representative) to move the county seat to his town. An election was held in 1880 that defeated a proposal to move court to Varner or Tyro. Captain Bob, as Rice was called, finally got his way, however, and the Varner District was created in 1885. Included in this second judicial district were the townships of Kimbrough, Choctaw, Wells, Auburn, and part of Bartholomew. A courthouse and jail were constructed there on land donated by Rice. Later Deputy Sheriff Edward T. Smith tired of the "shenanigans" going on at Varner and had a friend in the legislature to introduce a bill to do away with the second county seat. Representative R. R. Rice suggested they ask Smith to tell them his reasons for wanting the removal. Smith replied, "I can't tell you what a dirty hole has been created at this second court house or county seat – whiskey, crooked men and dirty women, and I could tell you more in private conversation. Do as you think best, but I am asking you to get rid of a dirty hole." The legislature immediately did away with Rice's private courthouse.[18]

⚜

Rose Hill

The bayou continues southward from Persons Bridge for around three miles and then makes a turn northward to Batchelor Bridge. Within the bend, which contains nearly two sections of choice farmland, is the old community of Rose Hill. This area is also referred to as the old Moore place. Other early names associated with the area are King, Collins, and

Calhoun. The Summerford family arrived in the area in 1866. Summerford Ford was on the bayou about a mile due south of Persons Bridge. There was also a ford at Rose Hill. An old site on the Moore place is called Sam Pete Field.

Rose Hill Baptist Church, built of logs before or soon after the Civil War for the black community, was on the old Moore plantation. It also served as the first school. Andrew Pugh told his son, Alvie, that the church was "a little log house by the cemetery" and across the road from it. He also said that services were held in a brush arbor before the church was built. George Pugh and his wife, Alice Jasper, both freed slaves, married around 1869 and moved from near Avery to Rose Hill where they raised their family. Alice Jasper was the daughter of Annie (Burks) and Peter Jasper, who left Virginia in 1858 and lived on what is now the Avery place, according to Alvie Pugh, grandson of George Pugh. A slightly different account by Luther M. Jasper of this family is that Peter and Annie (Burk) Jasper moved from Virginia to Tyro in 1858 and settled on 280 acres. They attended church at Rose Hill. In the early 1900s, George Pugh bought 160 acres on the bayou and began farming. He also installed a steam-powered sawmill around 1905 and was in the lumber business.

Early preachers at Rose Hill were Major Hull, Johnson Mayfield, Jim Williams, Pete Jasper, and James Henderson. Wess Hubbard taught school there in the 1890s. Alvie Pugh, born in 1912, went to school under the tutelage of Spencer Gondor, Mr. Castleberry, and Mr. Chandler. The school went through the eighth grade and continued in operation until consolidation with Star City. The old log church was replaced by another building around the turn of the century. This building was torn down recently and part of it moved across the bayou to its present location with new additions being made.[19] Rose Hill Cemetery, marking the location of the old church, reposes on the bayou bank.

⚜

Batchelor Bridge, Avery, Wells Bayou

Downstream (yet about three miles northeast) from Rose Hill, the bayou passes by the abandoned Batchelor Bridge. Joseph and Sarah Batchelor and William Batchelor were living in Smith Township (then in Drew County, now Lincoln) in 1850. On the east bank, tombstones bear the names of Sarah Attella (1856-1924) and Thomas Eldridge (1851-1913) Batchelor.[20] Batchelor Bridge served as the bayou crossing on the Varner-to-Monticello road which went through Avery, Rose Hill, Tyro, and Coleman. Jess Leatherman and Richard Jasper operated sawmills near the bridge.

About six miles to the north, where Cross Bayou runs into Wells Bayou, is the site of Avery Plantation, which Captain John Bates Avery

began to establish in 1877 when he bought 160 acres. Tucker, Triplett, and
McCloy previously owned parts of this land. Avery's holdings eventually
amounted to 1,300 acres. Captain Avery, who had served in the Union
army, arrived in Pine Bluff driving a herd of mules around 1867. He
established a mule barn, which he later named J. B. Avery & Son, on
Barraque Street. While managing Rob Roy Plantation near Altheimer for
John M. Gracie, he met Josephine Dyer at a social gathering at Arkansas
Post and married her in 1877. The couple had no children, but after the
death of her sister, Octavia (Mrs. Hans Siegfried J. Johnson), in 1887, they
took her six month old son, John Bates Avery Johnson Sr., to raise as a
foster son. The other Johnson children, Joe W. and Charles H., were raised
by Octavia's brother, Charlie Dyer.

Captain Avery built a two-story house that contained six bedrooms and
a dogtrot. Around thirty tenants worked eight hundred acres with a hundred
mules. The prison at nearby Varner supplied additional hands. The
plantation settlement consisted of a commissary, gristmill, sorghum mill,
gin, blacksmith shop, and sawmill. Avery Post Office, established in 1891
with Captain Avery as postmaster, was in the commissary. The post office
closed in 1916 with mail going to Meroney. Upon Captain Avery's death
in 1931, the plantation became the J. B. A. Johnson Estate and continues to
operate on a rent basis.[21]

Avery School existed in the 1920s and consisted of one room with six
grades. Donna Brockman taught there in the 1920s and boarded with the
Averys. Children later went to Wells Bayou School. Church services were
held in the school until the congregation split and built their own churches.
The group from Mills built at Dark Corner on land acquired from Jim
Smith, and Smyrna Missionary Baptist Church was established June 15,
1890.

There was a school at Dark Corner before the Wells Bayou School was
built. Marion A. Hudson, an early resident, was a founder of the Wells
Bayou School. Mills Post Office, four miles east of Avery, opened in 1895
and closed in 1914 with mail going to Dumas. St. Harmony Church served
the black community and another black church was on the bayou above the
Finn place. A black family, Liza (Livingston) and Will Jasper, moved
there in 1906 and rented the Dr. Duckworth (of Monticello) place for
around fifty years. Their children attended Bailey Chapel School, which is
now Thomas Chapel Church.[22]

The John Henry Bradley family moved in wagons from Warren
(Bradley County) to Wells Bayou in 1872. Arriving in the area in 1887
was a widow, Lina Terry Norris, with her six young children ranging in
ages from eighteen to four. Her husband, Marshall Norris, died in
Mississippi in 1884. The woman arrived by train to Reedville and walked
to the Marion Hudson place where they made a crop the following year.

The family then worked on the Godfrey place at Avery (1889-90), Batchelor place (1891-92), Avery Plantation (1893), Tom Johnson place at Wells Bayou (1894), Ed Hagood place at Tyro (1895), Morgan place near Tyro (1896), and the Price place at Wells Bayou (1896-1905). Her sons, Enoch Edgar and Billy Bob Norris, bought land near southeast of Avery in 1905 and began farming as Norris Brothers. Their descendants continue to farm this land.[23]

Garrett Bridge

Garrett Bridge, down the bayou from Batchelor Bridge, is an old farming community on the bayou northeast of old Greenmount and Tyro. Dr. E. C. G. Anderson owned a large farm there before the Civil War, but the family lived at Tyro. His son, E. C. G. Anderson Jr., eventually moved to the bayou farm. Les Curry of Tyro married the daughter of E. C. G. Anderson Jr. and joined the farming operation. Edward Tucker Smith, who lived and farmed at Tyro before the Civil War, bought a four hundred acre farm on the bayou from Mrs. Amanda Youngblood in 1900, and his sons worked this land. Smith continued to add to his land holdings and his son, Clay King Smith, eventually took over the bayou farm. Other early settlers in the area were Guy Mooney, Arch French, Blagg, Jones, and Farmer. Buck Finn owned a large farm, which he rented out, north of the bridge.

Anderson Chapel, a Baptist church, was built on the Anderson place and named for E. C. G. Anderson Jr. "It looked more like an old barn than a church," said Anderson's grandson, John Edd Curry. After the school was built, the church used that building until the present church was erected in 1948. Rev. Ralph Douglas was an early pastor. An Assembly of God church was on top of the hill west of the bayou by the 1940s. A church for the black community was on the west side of the bayou where the Alvie Lay home is located. Percy Dancer was an early preacher. In the woods near the church site is a slave cemetery.

Garrett Bridge School, located at the present site of Harold Farmer's house by the bridge went through the eighth grade. In the early 1940s, Brother E. D. Allison was principal of the three-room school. Teachers were Dorothy Wright (Mrs. Rob Gardner), Miss Lock, and Mary Farmer. The school closed upon consolidation with Dumas around 1948. Across the road from the school was Lozeir's Grocery. Jim Jones owned a cotton gin near the bridge by the 1920s. Cotton was hauled to Monticello.[24]

Greenmount, Tyro

Greenmount was an early hill settlement in Lincoln County (then Drew). Green Mount Post Office was established in 1855 with John Smith Sr. as postmaster. Following Smith were James S. Evans (1857), Rowena J. Stiles (1868), Amanda Weaver (1870), and Thomas Hagood. Ables Creek and its tributaries lay between Greenmount and Tyro, and during high water transportation across the bottoms was nearly impossible. For this reason, the post office moved to Tyro (with a name change) in 1879 where it remained until 1953 with mail going to Pickens. Early postmasters at Tyro were Thomas Hagood, Joseph W. Barnett (1883 and 1888), William D. Barnett (1886), Robert C. Collins (1893), Eddie T. Hagood (1896), Moses Collins (1898), and John Collins (1901).[25]

During the late 1800s, Tyro was the second largest town in Lincoln County and was considered for the site of the county seat in 1880. Greenmount School, a pay school, existed during the Civil War. George W. Rowell (later Dr. Rowell) was the teacher. Greenmount Church served the community, but is no longer extant.

Among the earliest settlers at Greenmount were John Smith and his son, Thomas Sidney Smith, who arrived there after a short stay at Collins. Smith's slaves, who went by the surname of Thomas, accompanied him. John Smith installed a horse-powered gin, and his son, John King Smith, had a sawmill. Thomas Sidney Smith received two land grants, one in 1856. His son, Edward Tucker Smith, farmed at Tyro, but later moved his family to Monticello so his twelve children could receive a good education. One of Edward Tucker Smith's sons, Henry Waterson Smith, became a prominent southeast Arkansas circuit court judge, and another, Clay King Smith, continued in the family farm at Garrett Bridge.

One of the earliest settlers at Tyro was Bob Curry's father, who came in the 1850s. The William Cammel Richardson and the Paschall families were there before the Civil War. Robert Lee Collins, whose family migrated from Mississippi to Coleman (Drew County) in 1855, settled at Tyro and owned a general store and was postmaster. Richard Tiner was a local farmer and served as justice of the peace. His brother, Ben, operated a gristmill in the town. Tyro grew as a stave mill and small farm town. The first school was in an 18x24' building, but was replaced with a larger structure by 1912. Several small general stores served the public. A round dancehall called the Roundhouse provided a place for social gatherings.

Dr. E. C. G. Anderson practiced medicine there before the Civil War and owned a farm on the bayou at Garrett Bridge. Dr. George W. Rowell, son of William Rowell who settled there about 1868, began medical practice at Tyro in 1871, and in 1884, opened a mercantile business. Dr. William C. Kimbro came in 1886 and practiced medicine and established a farm. Dr. Watts was serving in the early 1900s. Dr. Ray W. Smith was acting postmaster in 1925. The hill land soil gradually depleted and the farmers relocated to the Delta. During the Depression, many moved to Dumas. The little town vanished, but the community remained.[26]

Tyro Union Church and Tyro Missionary Baptist Church were early churches. The cemetery contains the names of many early residents who died before 1900: Bowles, Barnett, Brown, Buford, Clowers, Collins, Davidson, Eastham, Elliott, Fain, Gibson, Hagood, Irwin, Johnson, Jones, Kimbro, King, Lay, Lockhart, Morgan, Nuckols, Paschall, Payne, Petty, Phillips, Phelps, Price, Puryear, Rowell, Taylor, Thompson, White, and Youngblood. Also buried there is a slave, Burl Lay. Burl and his brother, Moses, were sent from Dancyville, Tennessee, to Elizabeth Dancy Lay by her brother.[27]

⋘⊙⋙

Gourd

Downstream from Garrett Bridge, Bayou Bartholomew continues a southeasterly course and then turns northward where it gyrates through nearly an entire section of land and almost meets itself on the return loop. "You can throw a rock from one part of the bayou to the other here," said Andrew Pickens. Named after the shape of the bayou, Gourd became a black settlement after the Civil War. Around six hundred people populated the area during the late 1800s and early 1900s. Brooks and Mariah Livingston moved from Louisiana in 1890 in a wagon pulled by oxen and bought a farm.[28]

Wesley Williams was an early settler and owned around six hundred acres on the bayou. His son, York Williams Sr., in addition to farming, owned a grocery store and served as postmaster, teacher, and minister. Jerusalem Baptist Church was located at the entrance into the "gourd" and the congregation held annual baptizings in the bayou. Gourd School served the students through the eighth grade. Prof. E. E. McBeth was a teacher and principal and his wife also taught.[29] Gourd Post Office existed from 1902 to 1917, when mail went to Walnut Lake. The small farmers began leaving during the Depression, and the area was eventually taken over by large-scale farming operations.

⋘⊙⋙

Desha County

Dumas

Dumas, located several miles east of the bayou in Desha County, grew as a trading point when the railroad came through in the late 1870s. Finley Holmes bought 12,000 acres of land in this area in 1851. He divided the land among his children with the Dumas tract going to Marcia Holmes Tredwell and Francis and Abercrombi Holmes. A son, A. C. Holmes, came in 1854 with seventy-five slaves to clear land in the area near Dumas. Two years later he brought his bride from Memphis down the river and then by horseback to his plantation between Dumas and Walnut Lake. William B. Dumas (of French descent) came in 1870 and bought 940 acres from Abercrombi Holmes. By 1890, three hundred acres were in cultivation and a steam-powered gin was operating. He also had a stave manufacturing business. The town was named for this man, the first permanent resident. The first mercantile store was owned by him and in 1879 carried a stock of goods valued from $3,000 to $5,000. Gus Waterman, born in Germany, established a mercantile business at Pendleton on the Arkansas River in 1875 and in 1879 relocated to Dumas. His stock was valued at $10,000 to $12,000 that year. W. B. Meador came to Dumas in 1887 and established a store. He was instrumental in organizing the Methodist Church 1897.[30]

Charles Dante, who emigrated from Poland to the U. S. in 1893, arrived in 1897. When he stepped off the Iron Mountain train at the budding town, he saw "two stores, a gin, a union church and a few houses." He established a small mercantile, which he enlarged in 1902. Two years later he built an even larger store, the Globe. Dante married Toney Steil in 1900, and at that time there were only eight families living in the town, which was clustered around the depot. The Dante family donated land for the school, several churches, and the museum.

The town continued to grow during the first three decades of the 1900s. W. F. Puryear established a general store before 1911. His son, Oscar, continued this business as O. I. Puryear & Sons. Lee Bros. General Merchandise and Cox Bros. General Store were in existence by 1916. R. A. Adcock joined his brother-in-law, James Adams, in his grocery store in 1922. This concern purchased a wholesale business around 1925 and operated it until 1935 when Adams retired. The firm became R. A. Adcock & Sons Co. in 1954 with Ralph Clayton as manager and partner. Bowles and C. W. Meador opened Meador Pharmacy in 1917. Ernest Smith had a garage and blacksmith shop that was the forerunner of Smith

Steel, Inc. Porter & Eastman General Merchandise originated during this time. David Oscar Porter Sr. was an early Dumas merchant and planter. D. O. Porter Store, a mercantile, was in business by the early 1940s. Sam Wolff opened Wolff Brothers Department Store in 1925. John Puryear Hardware Store began business in 1931. Hagood's Goodyear Store was in operation by the early 1940s. W. E. Bud Adams owned a mercantile for fifty-four years and ran Bud's Big Dip, an ice cream stand.[31]

Dumas incorporated in 1904 and for a time was the site of a second district county seat. The first county seat at Napoleon was abandoned in 1874 as the Mississippi River continued to wash away the town. Watson became the new seat and a courthouse was built there on land donated by L. W. Watson. The new rail line bypassed Watson in 1878, and Arkansas City became the county seat the following year. Court continued to meet at the Watson District until the second courthouse located at Dumas. The Dumas District was abandoned in the early 1900s and the courthouse was used for the school. I. N. Moore Sr. arrived in 1906 and opened a law practice. He eventually served as city attorney and mayor. He also served three terms each as state representative and senator. His son, Robert S. Moore Sr., served as county sheriff for twenty-five years before his death in 1973.

Dumas Post Office was created in 1879. Fred Lucas founded a newspaper, the *Dumas Clarion*, in 1899. M. A. Birdwell was publishing this paper by the 1920s and Ralph Moore was publisher in the 1940s. Melvin and Charlotte Schexnayder purchased the paper from Moore in 1954. Merchants and Farmers Bank served the community and were in a new brick building in 1909. The first medical doctor was Thomas H. Bowles, and Dr. Joseph A. White followed him. Dumas continues to prosper as an agricultural and small industrial center. The Sam Terry house, built in the 1850s from hand-hewn cypress logs and moved from its original location on Oakwood Bayou, houses the Desha County Museum.[32]

⁂

Walnut Lake, Pickens

Bayou Bartholomew bends eastward into Desha County at Fletcher Brake and approaches the farming community of Pickens. Walnut Lake Post Office originated there in 1879 after the coming of the railroad. Three of Finley Holmes' sons settled in the area. Nathaniel Holmes came immediately after the war and established a plantation at Walnut Lake. He married Flora Tillar, daughter of Maj. J. T. W. Tillar. By the late 1880s, his holdings were 880 acres with 450 in cultivation. Abercrombie Holmes, brother to Nathaniel, settled nearby in 1867 on a section of land that had 320 acres in cultivation by late 1880. His second marriage was to Lundie Tillar, sister to Major Tillar. A daughter by his first marriage, Claudia, married L. W. Proctor, deputy sheriff of the county. The couple resided at Walnut Lake. Another Holmes brother, A. C., lived on a plantation in the Dumas-Walnut Lake area. Other early area landowners were LaGrone, McKennon, Bankston, and Berry. Dennie P. Terry and his wife, Cora Charlotte Bancroft, were residents of Walnut Lake from 1890 to 1900. Terry was the son of Sam Terry who settled in the Oakwood Bayou area, between Dumas and Backgate, in the 1850s.[33]

William Alexander Pickens moved his family to Selma (Drew County) in 1868-69 and established a sawmill. His son, Reuben A. Pickens, began farming on his own in 1875 at age twenty-three and soon after went to work in a mercantile. He first opened a mercantile in Tillar and in 1881 moved to Walnut Lake where he established a large sawmill operation and began farming with his brother, Will. At this time, his Delta landholdings were mostly timbered, and part of the sawmill effort was to clear land for cultivation.[34]

Walnut Lake boomed as a lumber town and trade point. Ladd Canal, parts of which are still visible, was dug at this time to raft timber from the Gibson Brake area in Lincoln County to Walnut Lake.[35] Reuben Pickens set up R. A. Pickens & Son Company as a mercantile and farming enterprise. A plantation commissary was in place by 1883. This building was replaced in 1948 and is still in use. "Walnut Lake was a metropolis in the 1880s," said Andrew Pickens, great-grandson of Reuben. "There were stores, a depot, a water tower for the trains, and probably a gin."

Reuben A. Pickens began his farming operation on four hundred acres of bayou land with sixty in cultivation.[36] As the company grew with partnerships, the holdings eventually reached 14,494 acres with 10,250 in cultivation at its peak in the early 1950s. Reuben's son, B. C. Pickens, joined the enterprise and managed it until his death at age fifty-three in 1932. At this time, in honor of this man, the citizens petitioned to change the name of the town to Pickens. Managership then fell to his son, R. A. Pickens.

The company eventually restructured as a partnership. Early partners were F. G. Godfrey (manager of the Stock Farm), B. F. Keahey (manager of the Wilburn Place), Clyde LaGrone (manager of the Bayou Place), M. Buck Westbrook (manger of the Berry Place), W. I. Adams (manager of Holmes Farm), Doyle Rowland (manager of Lake Farm), and Lamar Grisham (manager of the commissary). When the operation began the transition from mule to tractor in the 1950s, it owned 475 head of work stock. "Back in the sharecropping days, they probably had 2,000 head of mules," said Andrew Pickens. Before mechanization, the farm had over seven hundred tenants and sharecroppers.

Walnut Lake School, a one or two room building, and several outlying schools served the white community until the 1920s. Four small schools for blacks existed until the 1950s when they consolidated with Dumas. The blacks attended Syrene Church (and school), Bethel, and St. Paul. Walnut Lake Cemetery is located on land donated by the Pickens family. R. A. Pickens, grandson of Reuben, donated land for Walnut Lake Country Club and was instrumental in its organization in the 1930s.[37]

Unlike so many other Delta farming towns, Pickens did not languish in the past. The village, nourished entirely by a well-managed farming operation, continues to thrive. Reuben Andrew Pickens, who plowed his first row there in 1881, would be proud.

꩜

McGehee

A railroad town, McGehee is located a few miles east of the bayou's last sweep into Desha County. Benjamin McGehee, a surveyor and farmer, bought an unimproved farm near there and settled in 1858. His son, Abner, bought 160 wooded acres west of his father in 1872, cleared the land, and built a house. Continuing to add to his holdings, he eventually owned 2,640 acres, 300 of which were in cultivation by 1889. He also had a gin. After the railroad came through McGehee's farm in 1878, he opened the first store, a plantation commissary, in the new town. With railroad construction booming in the area, McGehee sold ties cut from his land, engaged in contracting, and was the station agent.

McGehee Station or Holly Glade, as the stop was called, became McGehee when the post office was created in 1879. Abner McGehee was the first postmaster. Typical for a railroad town, the next business to open was a saloon and gambling hall owned by Jim Fitzhugh. His monopoly was quickly broken as Walter McKennon, Dilworth Bros., Ben Thompson, Jacob Poye, and W. J. Brannon soon opened more saloons. "Gambling and drinking were just about the only forms of entertainment then," said Leland Lockhart, who came as a railway laborer in 1903. At that time the town was "surrounded by woodland with water standing in it most of the year. Black Pond Slough was practically a lake that extended almost to the banks of Bayou Bartholomew." The only farms in the area then were those of McGehee and the Hyde place about four miles north of McGehee's.[38]

The town grew slowly from this humble beginning, and after the rail yards and roundhouse were built in 1905, it was large enough to incorporate, which occurred the following year. Erwin and Bell opened the second store. Rosenzweig opened a clothing store, the Grand Leader, in 1908. Isadore Friedman and his father opened the next store. Other early known merchants were Sam Wolchansky, J. E. Erwin (hardware), Selman (grocery), and Joe Lang (bakery). The first bank opened in 1906 under the leadership of Mr. Thane.[39]

Dr. J. M. Stuart was the first physician. Dr. James C. Chennault entered Dr. Stuart's practice in 1904. Dr. Chennault later established his own practice and was joined in it by the town's first nurse, Fannie Hyde (Mrs. John Liggin). Next to his office was the law office of a young attorney, James Merritt, who eventually served as judge of the Second Chancery District from 1955 until his retirement in 1972. Dr. Paine was the first dentist.[40]

The business district was nearly destroyed by fire in 1908. Some whiskey barrels caught fire and the men rolled them into Crooked Bayou, which runs through the town, in an effort to save the contents. McGehee went into a decline after the railroad abandoned its roundhouse and depot, but it continues to sustain an economic base supported largely by agricultural interests.[41]

Drew County

Hollywood Plantation

In 1818 a young surveyor, Peter Gilam Rives (pronounced Reeves), left his home in Virginia and headed west in search of new land. Arriving in Arkansas (then Missouri Territory) the same year, he laid claim to government land in present Crittenden, Drew, Desha, and Lincoln Counties. The Drew County land was recorded as "the Rives Tract."

While surveying this acreage in 1819, he built a large one-room log cabin on a high bluff overlooking the bayou at the point where the old Choctaw Indian Trail crossed the bayou at a low water ford. Around this wilderness headquarters, he cleared some land and planted cotton, corn, maize, melons, vegetables, and fruit trees. He also constructed a crude yet functional sawmill.[42]

An 1833 government survey made note of "P. G. Rivers' farm" in Section 6-11S-R4W. The report also mentioned Widow Williams' farmhouse, Widow Gray's farmhouse, and A. I. Cook's farm near the bayou in sections 28 and 27. By 1836 Rives was on his land in present Crittenden County with improvements made and a comfortable home built. The same year he married a young, wealthy, twice-widowed lady, Martha Goodloe Robertson Arnold, and brought her to his wilderness home where they lived for the remainder of their lives. Martha's two daughters from her previous marriages, Mary E. Robertson and Martha Arnold, remained in a convent in Kentucky. In 1843 Mary E. Robertson, age eighteen, left the convent to visit relatives in Union County, Kentucky. There the beautiful and wealthy heiress met Dr. John Martin Taylor, a practicing physician and also well-to-do. They immediately fell in love and were married a few months later.

The couple invested in land in Kentucky and also bought the Rives land in southeast Arkansas that consisted of "thousands" of acres. Assuming ownership of the bayou land in 1844, they left half of their many slaves in Kentucky to raise tobacco and sent the others on flatboats to the Rives location to work the cotton fields there. Between 1844 and 1846 huge virgin cypress logs were felled to fashion their bayou home. The old Rives cabin was used as a separate kitchen for the big house. The two-story house was built from slightly squared log beams roughly six inches thick and twelve to sixteen inches wide and notched for joints. Cracks between the beams were filled with hand-rived cypress shakes, and other chinks were filled with a white plaster made from lime and sand.[43]

The house, still extant, has two large (24'x24') rooms separated by a dogtrot on the first floor and three rooms on the second story. A stairway leads from the dogtrot to the upper floor, and brick chimneys stand at each side of the house. The house was moved back away from the bayou once or twice as the bayou banks caved in. Such a move took place around 1880 and at this time the chimneys were replaced, an attached kitchen ell was built, and weatherboarding was added. The original Rives cabin was then used as a smokehouse.[44] This pioneer cabin was moved to the Drew County Historical Museum where it stands in excellent condition.

On the grounds of this self-sustaining plantation were quarters for house servants, a smokehouse, a cypress log stable, barns, gardens, and orchards. A large underground cistern provided the water supply, and laundry was done in the bayou. A floating bridge of cypress logs chained together and anchored to trees on the bank allowed passage across the bayou to the fields and cotton gin. The slave quarters were located about a fourth of a mile from the house on the west side of the bayou. There also was a slave church and burying ground, now known as Cypress Grove Cemetery. The cemetery consists of about two acres with many unmarked graves. Of the marked graves, the earliest birth date is 1865 and the earliest death date is 1907. A commissary was built in later years, probably after the Civil War when tenants replaced slaves.

The Taylors named their place Hollywood Plantation after the impressive stands of holly trees on the property. Their embossed stationary read: "Hollywood Plantation on Bayou Bartholomew." The family commuted between their plantations in Arkansas and Kentucky. They built a magnificent home, Mauvilla, on the Ohio River near West Port. This house was built in 1855 according to a Louisville newspaper. "It had nineteen rooms, an observatory on top, a spiral stair leading from the great entrance hall to the observatory, hardwood floors, a stone porch, a roof supported by Corinthian columns, a balcony with an iron balustrade opening from the second story." Mrs. Taylor died at Mauvilla in 1868, and in 1876 Dr. Taylor sold that plantation and returned to his bayou home for the last time. He rented the Wells home in Monticello and hired a housekeeper and servant for his children. Continuing to live at the plantation, he visited the children once a week. Dr. Taylor died in 1884 at age sixty-five and "at his own request was laid to rest under the holly trees on Bayou Bartholomew land which he had owned and loved for more than 40 years."[45]

After Dr. Taylor's death, his sons managed to buy back much of the family land that was lost after the Civil War. With the bayou winding 12 miles through 11,000 acres of Taylor farmland in Drew, Lincoln, and Desha County, 17 bridges were built across the bayou to get to farmland. The eldest son, Henry, managed the plantation until the youngest son,

Rives, reached his majority, and they then divided the land. A son, Benjamin, managed the interests for a few years until Jim Fitzhugh became manager. Around 1895, sons Jonathan Gibson and John Martin Taylor organized the Valley Planting Company with A. W. Nunn of Pine Bluff as third major stockholder and manager. John D. Currie of Pine Bluff became manager in 1901 and moved the Valley headquarters to Winchester where the company bought a brick store, a gin, and 200 acres of land. Dillard H. Saunders, who married Dr. Taylor's granddaughter, Mildred Taylor Bradford, managed the concern from 1921 to 1925. The original homeplace with 6,000 acres was eventually sold out of the family, but heirs still own much of the Taylor land.[46] A post office, Rives, established in 1888 at Hollywood, discontinued in 1910 with mail going to Winchester.

❧❀❦❀☙

Winchester

Bayou Bartholomew bends eastward through the old Hollywood Plantation and nears Winchester before it changes to a southerly course. Probably named for the birthplace (Winchester, Kentucky) of Dr. Taylor, this town grew up around the railroad that came through in the late 1870s. Robert H. Wolfe and J. T. W. Tillar established R. H. Wolfe & Company, a mercantile store, in 1893. J. T. Cheairs & Son were also early merchants. The town incorporated in 1912 with C. A. Myers, mayor; Hardy Peacock, recorder; J. T. Peacock, treasurer; and S. G. McHan, marshal.

Winchester's population peaked to around 2,500 between 1912-1919 and during this time the town had a bank, two cotton gins, Winchester Broom Works, and several general merchandise stores. C. W. Oswald established a drug store that remained in business for many years. A newspaper, the *Winchester Independent*, ran for a few years with C. A. Myers as editor. Cotton, logs, crossties, and other wood products were shipped from this location.[47]

A skating rink built by a Mr. Sessions in the early 1900s provided entertainment. Soon after the end of World War II, Calvin Moss began showing movies in Winchester as well as at Backgate and Rohwer. "None of the Moss theaters were what you usually think of as a theater. They were just wooden buildings with a small porch and ticket booth and wooden benches to sit on. Burlap bags, filled with ice, were hung in front of the huge wall fans to cool the building, and coal stoves were used in the winter. His wife and daughters sold tickets, sold popcorn and soft drinks, made cold in a wash tub with ice and covered with an old quilt," explained Calvin's daughter, Virginia Flesher.[48]

A one-room school, built around 1900, also served as a meeting place for the first church groups. The Methodist Episcopal Church South was organized in 1902 with eleven members: John T. Cheairs Sr., Mrs. Ana L.

Cheairs, John T. Cheairs Jr., Mrs. May K. Cheairs, Mrs. Ida O. Knox, Hardy Peacock, Mrs. E. Courtney, Mrs. Elizabeth Taylor, Hettie H. Gibson, William McCarver, and Mrs. Emma D. McCarver. Presiding Elder was Cadesman Pope and the pastor was J. J. Mellard. The Methodist Episcopal Church was built in 1912, and Hopedale Baptist Church was built around 1947.

A school for white students was built in 1913, and Roy L. Bryn of Kentucky was hired as the first teacher. A school for blacks was built soon afterwards. Complete consolidation to Dumas took place in 1956. Virginia Moss Flesher described the Winchester school during the late 1940s: "The school had one room for first through third and another for fourth though sixth grade. We had an auditorium with a stage and a kitchen, where I recall Mrs. Merritt (Twila Ann's mother) cooking our meals, which we ate at our desks. Large stoves in the center heated the rooms. There were no bathrooms - just two outhouses out back. There was a bridge near [Aaron] Zeno's home, and friends lived across the bayou [Coon Bayou] from them. Also I crossed the footbridge near the trestle to get to school and sometimes even walked on the trestle. Many times, friends would ride bikes on the old Tillar Highway and play by the bayou, walking across footbridges along the way or just sitting on the bridges, watching the bayou move along...."[49]

Like many other small Delta towns, Winchester went into a decline after the stock market crash in 1929 and the ensuing Depression. With the advent of mechanized farming after World War II, tenants and small farmers moved away leaving the area in the hands of corporate farmers. Winchester Gin Company survived and remains in business along with two small stores.

⁂

Tillar

Located two miles to the east of the bayou in northeast Drew County (with part of the town being in Desha County), Tillar emerged as a railroad town when the Little Rock, Mississippi River & Texas Railroad was re-routed from Varner to Halley (through McGehee) between 1875 and 1879.[50] Major J. T. W. Tillar of Selma donated land for the right-of-way and built a depot. The man for whom the town was named never lived there although it did become headquarters for his son, Frank, who managed the plantation and business interests. The large planters who lived at Selma, but farmed in the Delta, gradually begin to move down from the hills to the new settlement. By 1879 when the post office formed, the population was around two hundred. The town incorporated in 1906 with D. P. Terry as mayor.

Ed Grisham opened a blacksmith shop, possibly the first business in the area, around 1880. The Grisham house was situated on the county line, and it is said that they ate in Desha and slept in Drew County. Ben Tillar, son of Major Tillar, sent Grisham and his sons, Frelan, Arthur and Rasco, to Mexico to use their equipment in the Tillar gold field. Arthur died there, and soon after they returned to Tillar. Frelan continued blacksmithing, and Rasco became an engineer with the Missouri Pacific Railroad.[51]

Planters entered the mercantile trade developing in the new settlement. Chesley Clayton and Zachary Taylor Prewitt, both from Selma, opened the first stores in 1875. Frame and Hugh Henry owned a general store from 1882 to 1894. Attached to their two-story frame building was a lean-to shed that housed a saloon. The Henrys sold their store to Frank Tillar and Billy Paschall around 1894. D. P. Terry bought the business in 1900 and operated it as D. P. Terry Co. until it burned in 1915. During the association of William A. Birch with the Henry concern, the business operated as Henry Bros. & Birch. R. W. Harrell, son-in-law of Robert H. Wolfe, entered the mercantile business in 1884 and was later joined by his son, Willie, and his son-in-law, Howard Slemmons. Upon Harrell's death in 1900, his other sons, Jeff and Virgil, bought the interest of Slemmons, and the firm became R. W. Harrell & Sons. Jeff Dishong and Judge Wood opened a mercantile under their names in 1897. Dishong later sold out to Wood and the business became Wood & Sons. Jesse R. and T. A. Prewitt succeeded Wood in 1912 with the firm becoming Prewitt Bros. This store closed in 1941 after the death of T. A. Prewitt.[52]

Robert H. Wolfe, in the mercantile business with Major Tillar at Winchester, consolidated his farm and mercantile interests with Tillar in 1895, and at this time the business became Tillar & Company with the headquarters moving to Tillar. In 1909 the enterprise incorporated, and the name changed to Tillar Mercantile Company with Wolfe as manager. Two other stockholders, Thomas Franklin "Frank" Tillar and A. C. Stanley, were equal partners. The combined lands owned by the company members amounted to between nine and ten thousand acres at this time. Around 1913 Wolfe bought Stanley's mercantile stock and sold it to W. S. Wood, E. S. Terral, B. C. Prewitt, Lawrence Wolfe, and M. R. Davidson, members of the Tillar Mercantile Company. The company dissolved in 1948 and reorganized as three separate concerns with the Frank Tillar interests becoming Tillar & Company with Vernon W. Scott as general manager.[53]

Also coming to Tillar from Winchester was J. T. Cheairs & Son General Mercantile in 1905. Fred Whiting joined this business and the name changed to Drew Mercantile Co. E. S. Terral served as manager until 1912 when he entered the Tillar Mercantile Co. Pete Sain managed the store until it burned in 1917. Sain then built a brick mercantile store which he ran until 1948 when he sold it to Ben and Dorothy Salter. Arriving from Mississippi in 1906 were J. H. Ballard, R. H. Ballard and V. A. Peacock who established Ballard Peacock Co. Peacock left the firm in 1912 to join J. B. Hogue Mercantile. A fire a few years later destroyed the Hogue building as well as Hawley Bros. Building Company. B. Cleve Prewitt built a livery stable and sale barn around 1906. When Prewitt joined Tillar Mercantile, he sold the business to a Mr. Appleton. Subsequent owners were Lige Rogers, Roman and Bill Mullis, Bob Durham, and Russell. The building burned in 1920 while under the ownership of J. B. Hogue. Other business concerns between the late 1880s and 1920 were Isaac Penticost's watch and clock repair shop, J. W. Conner's store, John Palmer's restaurant, Gillespie Bros. Dry Goods, L. A. Clayton's store, Dennie Moore's Place, C. A. King's store, T. A. King's store, and Ben Marks' pressing shop.[54]

S. O. Tillar, a grandson of Major Tillar, moved there in 1883 to become one of the town's first physicians. Other early doctors were A. C. Stanley, Tom Stanley, Jeff Meade, Dan Carroll, J. T. Cheairs, Troy Cheairs, and C. H. Kimbro. Dr. G. W. Fletcher moved from Snyder in 1905 and opened a drug store and medical practice. He sold the drug store in 1914 to F. P. Watson who continued in business until 1955. Dr. Sims provided dental care.

Valley Hotel, built around 1891, was a two-story frame structure with eight rooms. Pete Sain bought the establishment in 1911 and turned over management to Mrs. Mary Bryant in 1913. Mrs. Will McCarver was the last to operate it in 1919. The Breedlove Hotel, built in 1895 and operated by Mollie Breedlove, was also a two-story frame building. It was razed in 1914. The Hartsfield House, owned and operated by Mr. and Mrs. J. W. Hartsfield, was in operation by 1894. These hotels contained neither plumbing nor running water. J. W. Barnett built a modern two-story brick hotel around 1918. Four saloons thrived until a dry vote in 1906 moved the liquor trade to McGehee.[55]

The editors of the *Drew County Advance* visited the town in 1894 and spoke to a crowd of over 250. They gave the following account: "Knowing that there were but few stopping places en route...and not wishing to impose too many burdens upon them, we went through to Tillar, reaching the comfortable hostelry of J. W. Hartsfield just at sunset. Messrs. Jas. Cotham, R. L. Herd, and J. H. Hammock had preceded us...The roads [were] so dry and dusty that on our arrival it was hard to distinguish the coloring or complexion of garment or skin. Free ablutions, however, and the whisk brush renewed our youth and we started to take in the town. We noted signs of substantial improvements since our last visit. Several new and handsome dwellings have gone up – a new mill and gin and a handsome school building. The spirit of enterprise seems to be present and Tillar, we think, is destined to be the most important station on the road...."[56]

Primarily an agricultural center, Tillar and Company, D. P. Terry, Prewitt Bros., and Mrs. Caldwell owned gins. Hampton Pugh later bought the Caldwell gin. Drew Oil Mill operated there from around 1900 to 1919 when it moved to Monticello. A Mr. Ketcherison built a sawmill in 1901 and operated it until he moved it to Cominto (Drew County) in 1910. The Bank of Tillar opened in 1904 followed by the establishment of Citizens Bank in 1913.[57]

In August 1881 a small congregation met under an oak tree in Frank Tillar's yard to organize a Methodist Episcopal Church, South. They continued to hold services under the tree until cold weather, when they met in the homes of members. E. N. Evans was the first preacher. J. T. W. Tillar, Anna E. Whiting, and A. E. Hughes donated land for a church, which opened the following year. The simple frame building was replaced by a brick structure in 1913. Built by Monk and Ritchie of Pine Bluff, the church was named Frank Tillar Memorial Methodist Church. Mrs. Frank Tillar donated $8,000 of the $8,500 construction cost. An outstanding example of a masonry Classical Revival-style church, this building was placed on the National Register of Historic Places in 1996. Baptist and Presbyterian congregations held services there until they were able to build. Successive pastors were J. W. House, Milburn Raiford, W. R. Harrison, J. C. Coulson, and W. C. Hilliard.[58]

The First Baptist Church of Tillar organized December 28, 1908, with Rev. J. Tomme of Monticello at the helm. A new church was built in 1912. Rev. C. D. Wood was an early pastor. Tillar Presbyterian Church was also built in 1912 on land donated by R. H. Wolfe. Ministers there were Ben Ingram (1885), Rev. Dilham, J. W. Wilson, E. A. Hollingsworth, and S. D. Shell. The church was later replaced by a second building that burned in 1962, and the small congregation moved to McGehee.

The first school opened in 1880 in a renovated smokehouse called "freeze-out" in derision of the air inlets between the planks. The hardy students and teachers entered a two-story frame building in 1894. Three fraternal organizations – the Masons, Knights of Pythias, and Woodmen of the World – shared the cost of the structure with the school board. This building was razed in 1949 after the construction of a two-story brick edifice. Early teachers were Dave Gates (1880-83), Mrs. Hill (1884), Sam Benson (1895), Carrie Embree (1887-87), A. B. Banks (1888-89), Maurice Chestnut (1890), Maude Montague (1891), Carrie Embree (1892-93), Hattie Stanley (1894), Lizzie Deaner (1895), Octavia Wilson (1896), Cainby Brice (1897), H. D. Avery (1899), and Professor Wynn (1901-02).[59]

Tillar Cemetery lies five miles west of the town on a five-acre plot donated by Mrs. J. T. W. Tillar in 1910. R. H. Wolfe and Mrs. D. P. Terry were instrumental in the formation of this cemetery. The first internment was Will Watt Stitt, who died April 13, 1910. [60] Gravestones bear the names of many of the early settlers and their descendants in this peaceful setting on the bank of Bayou Bartholomew.

Selma

Situated "in the hills" two miles west of Bayou Bartholomew and six miles west of Tillar, Selma was an early Drew County settlement. John R. Dentz filed a land patent for eighty acres in 1852. Samuel Dickson was operating a sawmill by the following year. The Lovitt Spivey family arrived in 1853. Joshua Thomas Westbrook Tillar arrived from Hernando, Mississippi, in 1855 and soon married Antoinette Prewitt, daughter of Jacob M. Prewitt. He returned to Mississippi where he managed a mercantile store but returned to Selma in 1857 and established a store there. He entered the Confederate service at the outbreak of the war and upon his return was known as Major Tillar. [61]

Other settlers were the families of Robert S. Taylor, John Haisty, William H. Isom, J. S. Harvey, M. A. Harvey, Weatherall, and Richard Stanley and his sons, James P. and A. C. Stanley. Chelsey C. Clayton, born in Arkansas County in 1831, owned a mercantile store from 1874 to 1879. William A. Pickens, with sons, Reuben A. and William S., arrived in 1869 and established a sawmilling operation. Charles L. Pickens, who came to Monticello in 1860 and engaged in the mercantile trade, moved to Selma in 1885. [62]

In 1871 Tillar deeded land (previously owned by Dentz and then Prewitt) for the town. Incorporation took place in 1876 and about the same time, John Haisty deeded cemetery land for Selma Cemetery. Dr. A. C. Stanley, T. P. Howell and Company, and J. R. Shelton and son owned mercantile stores by 1881. Mrs. Smith operated a boarding house. [63] Selma Post Office was established in 1857.

A Methodist Episcopal Church, South building was begun in 1873 on landed deeded the previous year by Major and Mrs. Tillar to trustees James E. Spivey, John B. Shelton, and Alpheus D. Breedlove, but the structure collapsed under a snowstorm before it was completed. The congregation met in an old school building and in the Baptist church until 1885 when the Baptists sold the church to the Methodists. M. Blalock, deacon of the Baptist church, deeded the property to James P. Stanley, J. T. W. Tillar, and Wm. H. Isom, trustees of the Methodist church, for the sum of $790.43. A Mr. Rector constructed this building in 1874. [64] The white frame building, built of hand-hewn lumber and containing a hand-carved pulpit and alter, is on the National Register of Historic Places.

With the coming of the railroad to Tillar, planters and merchants gradually began an exodus to that point of trade. Planters were already using the Delta farmland but did not live there because of the threat of malaria in the swampy terrain. At first the men lived in the back of their stores when weather did not permit the horseback ride back to Selma. Eventually they built homes in Tillar but returned to their Selma homes during the summer months. This custom continued until around 1900. By 1904, Selma, also called "Shanghai," consisted of "the post office, a general mercantile store, the one-room school, church, a saloon, a one-room log calaboose, and a grist mill."[65]

Major J. T. W. Tillar, instrumental in the founding of Selma, Winchester, Pickens, and Tillar, became a leading citizen of the state. His interests were not limited to farming and merchandising. In addition to his vast plantations in the southeast Delta (at one time he had as much as 2,500 acres in cotton), he also owned a large estate in Texas, which his son, Ben, managed. He was also involved in banking and founded and was first president of the Citizens' Bank of Pine Bluff in 1887. Moving to Little Rock in 1888, he helped form the Arkansas Building and Loan Association, where he served as president for six years. He was also a director of the German National Bank of Little Rock and of the National Livestock Bank of Fort Worth, Texas. Other positions he held were as vice-president of the Arkansas Fire Insurance Company and the Goodbar Shoe Company of St. Louis. Involved in politics, he served as a delegate to the Democratic National Convention and was elected to the Arkansas legislature in 1873. When Major Tillar died in 1908, he was considered the wealthiest man in Arkansas.[66]

⚜

Old Catholic Monastery

A Discalced Carmelite Monastery once stood less than a mile west of the bayou west of McGehee. In 1918 Friar Cyril Corbato, priest of St. Winand's Catholic Church in McGehee, purchased 220 acres of land from Charles T. Duke. He then proceeded to oversee the construction of "a modest monastery…for the Missionary Fathers of their order to rest and recuperate from their labors and journeys." The structure was sixty-five by fifty-eight feet with an eight by nine foot offset on the north wall for a bell tower. It contained "many small rooms with doors opening outward into a hallway which completely surrounded the inside of the building" and an open courtyard in the center. The outside walls were unpainted wood. The Carmelites used the retreat until 1927 when diocesan priests replaced the order. By 1934 the building was abandoned and it was razed in 1956. At some point after the retreat house was in place, Father Corbato realized that he had mistakenly built it just above his property line on land belonging to Adam Walker, a black man who lived nearby. In 1934 Walker and Corbato exchanged deeds for 3.10 acres each to correct the mistake. Corbato deeded the property to the Discalced Carmelite Fathers of Oklahoma in 1938. All that remains of the structure are the honeysuckle covered concrete foundations.[67]

⚜

Baxter

The bayou next passes by Baxter where its fertile land drew some of the earliest settlers to Drew County. John Smith and his wife, Sarah Bowden, settled below Baxter (near present Dermott) around 1810. Goodspeed wrote, "Soon after his settlement, some of his relatives and friends followed and settled near him, which made one of the first white settlements in this part of the State." By 1830 Smith's neighbors in Bartholomew Township were Jesse Condren, Cyrus Hathaway, Jonathan Blythe, John Stewart, Thomas Wyatt, and Samuel Wyatt. The Smith family was on the bayou in present Lincoln County by 1836 and was living on the bayou about thirty miles south of Pine Bluff when he died in 1862. Edward Wiley claimed land between Baxter and Dermott in 1810, and he and Stephen Gaster were living there by 1830. Wiley owned twenty-one slaves and Gaster had three. Their neighbor was John Smith, owning fifteen slaves. Reese Bowden, brother-in-law to Gaster, arrived in 1831. Stephen Gaster was married to Mollie Bowden, and their child, Elizabeth, born in 1833, is the first recorded child born in present Drew County. Gaster's first wife died and he married her sister, Martha. Samuel Townsend joined these bayou settlers by 1835. Ezekiel Owens settled on the bayou in Drew County in 1834.[68]

Stephen Gaster settled on the south side of the bayou about a mile west of Dermott and south of Baxter. In 1848 he obtained a license to establish a ferry at his place.[69]   Gaster's smokehouse, blacksmith shop, and potato house remained intact on the homesite until around 1950. The smokehouse was moved to the grounds of the Drew County Historical Museum.

Everett Skipper arrived before 1854 and settled on the bayou near Gasters Landing. He eventually bought the Gaster home and owned 1,000 acres of land. He was listed in the 1860 census as a farmer and merchant. His son, William Franklin "Willie" Skipper, was born there in 1856 and as a young man learned the mercantile trade as a clerk for Baker & Taggart at Collins. He then returned to Baxter and went into the mercantile business with W. R. Taggart and W. H. Lephiew.

Skipper and Lephiew later bought out Taggart, and the firm became Skipper & Lephiew. They conducted a large furnishing business and owned several cypress shingle mills, one located upstream from Baxter. W. H. Lephiew was the son of Henry H. Lephiew who moved to Monticello from Alabama in 1849 and opened a grocery store. In 1870 he moved to his various farms in the Baxter-Collins area, eventually settling one mile south of Baxter. As a teenager W. H. Lephiew clerked at Duke's store. After Willie Skipper's death in 1896, the business continued as W. H. Lephiew. Lephiew moved to Dermott in 1902.[70]

Bartholomew Post Office was established near Gaster's Landing on November 29, 1832, with John O. Dabney as first postmaster. Succeeding postmasters were Edward Wiley (1834), John Smith (1837), Edward Wiley (1838), Reese Bowden (1838), William Moore (1849), Charles McDermott (1850), and S. A. Duke (1867). The actual location of this post office moved up and down the bayou to the homes of the various postmasters and by 1892 it was at Wilmot. Maps dated 1838 and 1862 show Bartholomew at the present site of Baxter.[71] Maps dated 1860 and 1864 show "Bowdens" at the site. On June 13, 1832, the *Gazette* reported, "It gives us much pleasure to announce to our readers that the mail route from this place [Little Rock] via Pine Bluff in Jefferson County, Cabeen's in Union County, Bayou Bertelemi, and Old River to the Mississippi River at Villemont in Chicot County may now be considered as permanently established and the public may hereafter expect a regular weekly mail on this route. This is an important route affording as it does our only direct channel of communication with Chicot and intermediate communities."[72]

Baxter owes its founding to Salathiel Allen Duke, a Republican Radical Reconstructionist originally from Ohio and later of Keokuk, Iowa. During the Civil War Duke worked for the government in placing freedmen ("freed" by the Emancipation Proclamation in 1862) on abandoned southern plantations. After the war he set out to find a place to settle and found what he wanted on Bayou Bartholomew. Arriving in 1866, he purchased 478 acres near Gaster's Landing and lived there until 1872 when he laid out a new town where the Little Rock, Mississippi River and Texas Railroad crossed the bayou. He named his town Baxter after Governor Elisha Baxter, who was embroiled in a battle with Joseph Brooks, a Reform Republican, over who had won the governor's race in 1872. Duke sided with Baxter during the Brooks-Baxter War because Baxter favored restoring the right to vote to southern Democrats. Baxter Post Office was created March 17, 1873, with Duke as postmaster.[73]

Duke continued to buy more land, built a plantation store, S. A. Duke and Company, on the west bank of the bayou, and erected a large house hewn from virgin timber to the west of the store. By the 1880s the community's population was around six hundred with the majority being black. Duke's only child, Charles T. Duke, entered in partnership with his father in 1881 and bought him out in 1907. At that time they owned 9,000 acres along the bayou with 3,000 in cultivation. Charles T. Duke married Willie Slemons, daughter of William F. Slemons, a resolute disciple of the Confederacy who lived in Monticello. Their children were Elizabeth "Betty" (Mrs. W. R. McCloy), Marguarite (Mrs. Robert F. Hyatt), and Katharine (Mrs. Henry H. Tucker).[74]

Baxter was also an important steamboat landing and the head of navigation on the bayou. As a little girl, Betty Duke had the job of checking and recording the water stage each day. With an outlying Negro population of around 2,000, it boasted one of the few black newspapers published in the state. The *Baxter Vidette* was "moderate in viewpoint and well written." Schools were established for both races, the white school being a one-room building. Early teachers there were James Wilson, Marie Bell, and Mrs. Erwin. In addition, the town at one time had four saloons, one of them being owned by J. F. Patton.[75]

With the onslaught of automobile traffic and the ensuing dust, Charles Duke attempted to move the family home back from the road around 1914. When the move began, the house, put together with wooden pegs, pulled apart and had to be reconstructed. Elizabeth and Will McCloy later occupied the house and remodeled it in the late 1920s. Will McCloy operated a gin and a general store. "The old store was gone by 1940," said Garvin Adcock, who lived at Lambert Bend up the bayou at that time.[76]

The Dub Kimbrell family moved to Panther Brake Plantation (the Henry Tucker Estate) south of Baxter in 1936. Estelle Kimbrell Works remembered the McCloy gin and riding to the Baxter school in Thomas Woolridge's pickup truck, which served as the school bus. "It had a cattle frame above the bed with a tarp over it and three benches for us to sit on," she said. At this time, the two-room school went through the sixth grade, and Mrs. Bulloch was a teacher. Behind the old church building was a black church. "Those were the days," said Estelle. "When we weren't in school or working in the field, we were on that bayou. It was the center of our lives."[77]

❧❦❧

Collins

Collins, situated four miles west of Baxter and just above the Delta divide of Cut-Off Creek, was first settled by Benjamin Franklin Collins in 1856. He bought a section of land from Samuel Swartwont who had purchased it in 1836 from some homestead claimholders, Charles F. Moulton and Daniel Lowe. Cut-Off Post Office, near present Collins, was established in 1850 with Peter Farquhar as postmaster. William R. Smith became postmaster in February 1857, and Benjamin Collins succeeded him in November of the same year. The post office became Collins in 1873.[78]

A stage stop on the Gaines Landing Road, the location attracted planters who preferred to live in the hill country while farming land in the bottoms. Benjamin Collins built a two- story home and began farming with slave labor. He also operated a sawmill, gristmill, and gin. An 1865 map shows "Collins Mill" at the location and another mill just south of it.[79] Other early families in the area were R. M. L. Baker (by 1856), Stephen Bulloch (1856), Sam Gibson (1849), J. F. Donaldson, Trice, Talley, and Roper. John Wesley McShan was there by 1858. He hand-planed the lumber for Collins' house, which was later used as a hotel. C. M. Boyd moved from Hamburg to Collins and clerked in a store from 1872 to 1877. He went into a partnership with J. T. W. Tillar in 1877 and bought him out in 1888. He moved to Monticello in 1880 but continued to manage his bayou farms. Considered the largest planter in the county in 1893, he owned 5,000 acres of bayou land with over 1,000 in cultivation.[80]

A letter from Collins published in a local paper in 1883 stated: "We have six stores in our little town, one family grocery and one bar-room." Harris & Brown carried the largest stock and was managed by B. F. Benson and assisted by A. A. Everett. E. A. Harris, the senior partner, lived in Monticello. The next largest house was Tillar & Boyd with Charles F. Wells managing and Hartsfield and Thomas Boyd as salesmen. Following were S. M. Courtney & Company and Baker & Taggart. Jonathan Weatherall owned the grocery and was assisted by his brother James Weatherall. S. R. Bulloch kept the bar and his clerk was R. F. Christmas."[81]

Methodists and Baptists used the same building for church until 1883 when they constructed their own buildings. The Baptist church was called Gill Gall Church. A Christian Church was built in 1884 and was used for the schoolhouse until a school was erected in 1918. This was a twelve-year school until 1930 when it became a seven-year school. Dr. R. N. Smith, who came around 1900, and Dr. A. M. Lisenbee, who came around 1913, were the town doctors. The Mississippi, Ouachita & Red River Railroad reached the town, which was the end of the line, in 1875. At this point, it became a booming trade center. Cotton, crossties, and hogs were the principal exports. When the Iron Mountain line took over the MO&RR and the rail was completed to Monticello, a depot was built at Collins. Rev. F.R. Somervell, the Baptist minister, was agent.

Collins incorporated on August 15, 1892. The thirty residents signing the petition to found the town were: F. M. Campster, H. L. Biggs, J. S. Courtney, S. R. Bulloch, J. F. Donaldson, M. F. Christmas, N. H. Evans, Thomas Ross, Robert Duncan, J. H. Wallace, J. E. Bowden, M. S. Collins, D. S. Lovett, W. A. Graham, J. P. Weatherall, J. R. Spivey, W. B.

Crenshan [sic? Crenshaw], R. H. Russell, W. A. Courtney, C. E. Bulloch,
F. H. Biggs, C. E. Gannaway, J. F. Norman, J. A. Trice, J. A. Weatherall,
James Gaster, J. C. Morris, W. J. Bailey, F. R. Trotter, and J. T. Blanks.[82]

Another saloon was built and keepers were R. L. Baker, Tom Cole, and
Victor Moss. A livery stable was remodeled into a store owned by J. A.
Trice. J. D. Hunt later bought out Trice and in 1920 sold to P. G. Hoffman.
Near the end of World War I, a Mr. Fowler built a theater, but it was closed
by 1920. Other businessmen in the early 1900s were: P. G. Hoffman
(hardware), Dr. R. N. Smith (drug store), Walter Gaster, W. H. McShan,
Henry Bulloch, W. C. Roper, M. S. Collins, W. E. Lang, Emanuel
Courtney, W. B. Barksdale (later owned by W. C. Bulloch), John Ogles
(later owned by J. B. Hunt), and Oren Ogles (second hand store). W. C.
Roper owned a gin that was operated by W. E. Fowler and Walter Morgan.
J. J. Couey established Collins Lumber Company in the 1920s. Leavitt
Land and Lumber Company had a two-story office building with Joseph
Mack in charge.[83]

The railroad contributed to the rapid growth of Collins and it eventually
contributed to the demise of the town. When Monticello and Warren
became primary railroad trade centers, Collins went into a decline. The
Great Depression delivered the final blow, and the town slowly ebbed
away.

❦

Blissville, Jerome

The bayou continues its southern course through its namesake township
in Drew County where it passes Townsend Lake to the west and nears
Jerome to the east. Old Townsend Road once led from Jerome to Old Troy
through the Cut-Off Creek bottoms passing south of Dr. Bulloch's place.
Blissville Post Office, named after Bliss-Cook Oak Company, opened
there in 1900. Based in Saginaw, Michigan, the local mill was managed by
M. A. Bates, who also built a cotton gin. The concern became Jerome
Hardwood Company in 1908 with "a very stern German named Moehler"
as manager. Locals began to refer to the town as Jerome, the name of
Moehler's son, at this time, but the name did not become official until
Jerome incorporated on March 16, 1920. The post office name changed to
Jerome the same year.

The lumber town flourished. Bliss-Cook built a general store and two
hotels to house its hands, one for each race. The hotel for whites on
Mississippi Avenue contained forty-five rooms. It burned in late 1928 or
1929. The black hotel was "down in the quarters." John D. Currie of
Montrose managed the general store until 1937 when he hired Mrs. Hazel
Byrd to operate it. Mr. Cone owned a drugstore. Dr. Baker was the first
doctor, and Drs. Parmalee and Burge followed him. The school went

through the ninth grade and had a gymnasium, auditorium, cafeteria, home economics building, and two elementary buildings. After consolidation with Dermott in 1950, the main building was moved to the black school in Dermott. Jerome Baptist Church purchased the home economics building and the red brick elementary building became the community center.

The sawmill burned in 1927 but the planing mill continued to operate until around 1930. Alice-Sidney Dryer presently occupies the site of the planing mill. In 1937 the company sold the town and surrounding land (located in Drew and Chicot County), to Sam Wilson of Montrose.[84] In March 1939, Wilson sold this property to the U.S. Government for $100,000. Included in the sale was the entire town of Jerome (houses, store, cotton gin), 3,508 acres of land, sixty-five head of mules, and three tractors. Thirty-six families were moved from the Sunnyside Plantation resettlement near Lake Village. Jointly administered by the Farm Security Administration and the National Youth Administration, this project was the first of its kind in the United States.

Plans called for 737 acres to be farmed by a cooperative association composed of members of the colony. The NYA unit was to bring in fifty young men and women each between the ages of eighteen and twenty-five to farm 325 acres as a co-op. They proposed to set up a sawmill, work shop, meat-curing plant, potato curing house, chicken hatcheries, and blacksmith shop. Teaching self-sufficiency was the goal. The NYA clients would be paid to work a hundred hours a month the first year with other time devoted to the co-op labor. The FSA families borrowed approximately $250 from the Chicot County FSA as spring "furnish." They were expected to pay back all expended on feed, food, seed, and subsistence within a year. They were given five years to pay back capital expenditures such as mules and tools. Adjoining this project was another tract of 11,114 acres in the Beouf River bottoms. Although it was inaccessible throughout the rainy season, twenty-nine houses were completed by 1937. Each unit contained a four-room house, complete with running water and electric lights.[85] The project made some headway for a few years, but by 1942 was defunct. After the bombing of Pearl Harbor, the government transferred the land to the war department for use as a relocation center for Japanese-Americans.

Wartime hysteria swept the country after Japan bombed Pearl Harbor, and as a result of this, the government interned Japanese citizens in ten camps situated throughout the U.S. Another Arkansas based camp was at Rohwer in Desha County. Berte Knox Carr was a building foreman for the Jerome camp and took his family on a tour before it was occupied. His daughter, Joan Carr Willis, wrote: "I can remember driving miles and miles through plowed fields with no vegetation...with occasional sharecropper houses so remote...I know it must have been devastating to have to give up everything – because of the wartime hysteria that was so rampant in the country at that time."[86]

Known as the Denson Relocation Camp, the 10,054-acre site received its first resident on October 6, 1942. Organization of communal life was swift. The *Denson Communique*, a newspaper, had its first issue on October 22, 1942. This was a semi-weekly mimeographed paper written in both English and Japanese. The last issue was published June 6, 1944. On January 4, 1943, Denson High School opened. A G. Thompson, a former superintendent of schools at Lake Village, was in charge of the school.[87] Mrs. Willis remembered attending a home economics conference in Lake Village during this time. "The area girls came with mothers driving them and chaperoning. The Japanese girls came in Army vehicles with armed army guards. That's when it hit you – this is not right. As far as the handiwork and sewing – we should have stayed home. Their work was like something professionally done. It was exquisite."[88]

T. H. Greenway worked as a laborer on the camp construction, making a dollar an hour. His son, Herbert Von Greenway, recalled the attitude of the community toward the Japanese. "We hauled garbage from the camp to our hogs. Sometime they would hitch a ride on wagons to go to the bayou to fish. They didn't speak much English, but they were friendly people. We already had Chinese in Dermott and we didn't think much about it. It was just like black people – we didn't think anything about it. We were only prejudiced against people who wouldn't work."[89]

A Protestant non-denominational church, Denson Church, held meetings in the dining room of Block 33. Buddhist services and funerals were also conducted there. In March 1943, the camp population peaked at 8,497. Jerome was the first camp in the country to be completely evacuated with the last resident leaving on June 30, 1944.[90] The camp was later used for German prisoners of war.

The government began selling parcels of this land after the war, and John Baxter bought the town (store, gin, water system) and land surrounding it. Baxter then sold to Charles Clifford Gibson Sr. who with his son, C. C. Gibson Jr., made this the site of their farm headquarters and ran the store and gin.[91] Jerome is nearly vacant now except for the Alice-Sidney Dryer and Cokely's Store. A tall, lone smokestack stands behind a commemorative marker at the relocation center site on Highway 165 – a silent reminder of an unfortunate past episode.

Chicot County

Dermott

Bayou Bartholomew makes a slight curve into northwest Chicot County at Dermott, where Dr. Charles M. McDermott and his brother, Edward, bought land in 1834. Dr. McDermott, a resident of East Feliciana Parish, Louisiana, married Hettie Smith of Natchez in 1833 and during a visit to her Mississippi relatives in 1834, he was told about "the rich land of Barth, which never did overflow; where there were plenty of bears and deer."[92] He left soon after to investigate and after crossing the Mississippi River, borrowed a horse from Sandy Faulkner (the "Arkansas Traveler"), who lived south of Gaines Landing, to make the trek through the wilderness country. Arriving at Edward Wiley's place on the bayou, he found "Steven Gaston [sic Gaster], Rease [sic Reese] Bowden, Easly Hurd, Hilly Hones [probably Billy Jones], and old John Smith and Parson Gross, all settled with good log cabins and a few negroes, making crops of corn and killing plenty of bears."[93]

He wrote, "I bought the preemptives of Gross and his son Sterely Gross, which fronted the bayou in Section 6, T 14, R 3 W [along the bayou at Dermott], expecting to buy the backlands on Gum Ridge when they came on the market. I got some other small tracts from the Government and then went home...." His brother, Edward, attended to the plantation "after his return from the Florida war."[94]

In 1844 McDermott moved his family to the bank of the bayou and began permanent settlement.[95] They lived in cabins on the bayou for seven years before he built a large house "across the road" (at the later location of the hospital). A granddaughter, Emma Shaw Smylie, described the house, called Bois D'Arc. "It was a two-story structure built by free negroes from the North Few nails were used in its construction. The plaster on the walls was mixed with hair. It had a front (broad) porch of one hundred feet and side porches of fifty feet both up and down stairs. The upper porch had side banisters and the top was plastered. The floor slanted outward. The wide front steps extended from the second story to the ground. There were four rooms opening on front, each 20x20x20, and all plastered and with wide fireplaces. Behind there were four more rooms opening on side galleries."[96] This design was typical of Louisiana houses of the period. The reference to the home being built by "free negroes from the North" is dubious. McDermott owned slaves, and it is unlikely that he hired northern labor for the construction. If he did, it was very unusual if not unique.

Located on the old Gaines Landing Road from the landing on the Mississippi to Monticello and a day's journey from the river, this house became a regular stopping place for pioneers heading west. One visitor described the "abounding hospitality" which included having their dusty feet washed in cedar tubs brought out by servants.[97] Family lore alludes to some ulterior motive on the part of the host for his display of hospitality. He had sons and daughters and his brother's orphaned children who would need acceptable spouses, and there was not much to choose from in the area. When the William Allen Daniels family stopped over in 1858, McDermott swapped land to Daniels in exchange for their wagons, "thus ensuring that he would stay in Dermott as he would not have means to move further."[98]

Charles McDermott graduated from Yale in 1828 and returned to Louisiana where he received instruction in medicine from his brother-in-law, Dr. Henry Baines, a distinguished physician from London. A prominent correspondent to the *Scientific American*, McDermott was among the first to discourse upon and advocate the germ theory of disease origin. He was also an inventor and received patents on the common iron wedge (1875), an iron hoe, and a cotton-picking machine (1874).[99] He is most recognized, however, for his innovative efforts to build a flying machine. His design received a patent in 1872 and was exhibited at the Southeast Arkansas Fair in 1874, the state fair in Little Rock in 1882, and the Centennial Exposition at Philadelphia in 1876. Once he hauled one of his machines by wagon to Washington, D.C. for patent application. When the Wright brothers gave a public demonstration in 1908, two of McDermott's contemporaries who were there commented, "Why, that's Charlie McDermott's machine! ."[100]

McDermott built a fine home named Finisterrae near Monticello and moved his family there in 1858. After the Civil War, he returned to the bayou plantation to grow cotton but soon took his family to Honduras where he attempted to found a secessionist colony. That failing, he returned to his bayou home where he died in 1884 and was buried on the grounds of his home. A large grove of pecan trees planted by the family forms a backdrop for his tombstone and stands as a living memorial to this pioneer [101]

By 1890 Hattie (Crenshaw) and C. E. Peddicord occupied the house, where they raised a cousin, Mabel Winston, who became the First Lady of Arkansas in 1928 as wife of Governor Harvey Parnell. The eighty-five-acre home site eventually passed out of the family, but was bought back by Emma Shaw Smylie who sold the land, reserving the cemetery plot, in 1904 to Dr. W. K. Baker. Mrs. Smylie also sold three acres nearby for the town cemetery. The McDermott house was taken down in 1918, and on the white plaster walls of the veranda were the still legible names of travelers who stayed at the hospitable bayou home.[102]

Dermott was named for this man, and its township (first named Franklin) was named for John Jones Bowie, brother to James "Jim" Bowie of Alamo fame. An early news article asserts, "Colonel [Jim] Bowie paid several visits to his relatives on Bayou Bartholomew on the site of Dermott, John J. Bowie's place...."[103] Records do not specify John Bowie owning this land, but he was in the county as early as 1828. The family moved in 1800 to Louisiana, where by 1819, John, James, and another brother, Rezin, were smuggling slaves for the pirate, Jean LaFitte. An 1825 bill of sale for three slaves from John Jones Bowie to James Bowie "for a consideration of two thousand arpens of land" was notarized in Catahoula Parish and later recorded in Chicot County. Unfortunately, no location or description of the land was given. In 1828 John J. Bowie was buying and selling land in the county with nine transactions being recorded at Villemont. A mortgage recorded on March 28, 1828, reveals Bowie still a resident of Catahoula Parish. He moved to the Lakeport area prior to 1830 as that year he sold property there identifying it as "the place where I now reside."[104] He was still in the county in 1833 as he signed a petition that year.[105] By 1836 he was in Helena and in 1857 he purchased a plantation at Halley, five miles east of Dermott.[106] There John Jones Bowie was buried in 1859 in an unmarked grave at his request. In the Halley Cemetery there is a small plot enclosed by an iron fence with the name "Old Bowie" on it. Bowie Township in Desha County (Halley area) was also named after this pioneer.

John Bowie's son, James Bowie, born in 1835, was elected sheriff of Chicot County in 1856 and in 1861 entered the Confederate Army. He was killed in action and his body was sent to Arkansas to be buried by his father.[107] John Bowie's brother, Rezin, designed a knife that was fashioned by his blacksmith, Jesse Cliffe. The knife was eventually given to his brother, Jim, in whose hands it gained its lasting name, the Bowie knife.[108]

A story passed down through time alleges that General Zachary Taylor passed through the present town of Dermott while surveying a route for the Indian removal, which took place in the 1830s. Following the Gaines Landing Road, which led from Gaines Landing on the Mississippi, he paused to rest under a large oak and blazed it with an axe. Located on the north side of West Gaines Street between the old Golden lot and the Racquet Club, the tree was known as the "Zachary Taylor tree" for many years. The giant tree, a swamp chestnut oak with a nineteen foot, seven inch circumference, reportedly the second largest in the state, still stands although the mark is no longer evident.

Another antebellum settler on the bayou nearby was Dr. William Crenshaw, who owned a small plantation and practiced medicine. Dr.

Crenshaw had "visions that this part of Arkansas would some day be the garden spot of the world." After the Civil War, he asked his nephew, Rueben Crenshaw, to come for a visit. Rueben stayed and became the first postmaster of Bend Post Office which was formed in 1875. This office was probably named after the prominent bend in the bayou there. Bartholomew Post Office, created in 1832 and located at Gaster's Landing several miles upstream from the settlement, served the area until this time. The name changed from Bend to Dermott on May 25, 1877 with John B. Daniels postmaster. He was the son of William A. Daniels who bought land on the bayou in 1858. The Daniels land included the present South Trotter Street area of the town.[109]

The first public institution in Dermott was a small church built by McDermott, who converted from Catholicism and became an ordained Presbyterian minister. On the first Sabbath the family was in their bayou log house, he held services for his family and Negroes. His brother, Edward, was at the other end of the house with his "wicked friends." The following day, Edward offered one hundred dollars to build a place of worship. Dr. McDermott had a small church built in the yard for his white neighbors and his   slaves as well.   A storm blew away the original building, and the congregation built another one after the Civil War. Rev. J. A. Dickson of Monticello officially organized this church as the New Bethany Presbyterian, later to be named the Dermott Presbyterian Church, in 1868 while McDermott was in Honduras. The bayou settlement, centered along Gaines Landing Road (now Gaines Street), also had a general store that was kept by M. B. Shaw and Matthew Allison.[110]

It took a railroad to expand the community. The Mississippi, Ouachita & Red River Line was planned to run through the area in 1852, with Charles McDermott subcontracting for four miles east of the west border of Chicot County. The roadbed was roughly constructed, but only eighteen miles of track were ever laid from the eastern terminus at Gaines Landing and this was after the Civil War. The rail reached Dermott in 1872, and in 1875 the Little Rock, Mississippi River & Texas Railroad bought the assets of the then defunct MO&RR.[111]   John Crenshaw, brother to Rueben, arrived in Dermott in 1881 as depot agent. According to his daughter, Martha Crenshaw Burleigh, the first depot was located "about a mile west on what is now [1961] Mrs. Walter Bowden's place. It was a part of the Crenshaw place." When the north-south line of the Houston, Central Arkansas & Northern Railroad intersected with the east-west Iron Mountain at Dermott in 1887, the village experienced new growth. The station house was a small frame building where Main Street crosses the railroad. A second was built later at the intersection of the two railways. James Alfred Morris Sr. came in the early 1900s as railroad master.

The budding town contained the rail station, and a gin, store, and saloon. Several years later, two additional stores and a barbershop were in operation. John Crenshaw and his brother, Jim, built a general merchandise store, which was attached to the railroad station. By this time, the post office was located in the station, where John Crenshaw also kept a small drug store. In 1883 Morris & Kimpel were "doing a tremendous furnishing business," and Harrison of Monticello bought the J. C. Crenshaw mercantile. Jack Winston managed this firm.[112]

Dermott was described in 1892 as "a thriving, hustling little city...the largest between [Little Rock and Monroe]." Agriculture constituted the major economic base with 2,500 bales of cotton being shipped the previous year. The hardwood timber industry was second in importance. In 1891, eight hundred cars of staves, two hundred cars of pilings, and smaller loads of crossties were shipped out of the town. The French Oak Stave Company began operation in 1891 under the management of E. Ehrman and employed over 150 men. Charles T. Duke & Co., managed by P. K. Savage, carried a large inventory of general merchandise. The Dermott Compress and Storage Company, with a capability of five hundred bales a day, was near completion. The only thing lacking was a "good hotel." William D. Trotter, who married Mabel McDermott, established a general merchandise store in 1886.[113]

By 1888 Duke and Company built a new store, which was managed by Pat Savage and Buckner. They were selling "an immense quantity of goods and buying most of the cotton," giving strong competition to the Kimpel and Trotter firms. In retaliation, perhaps, Morris & Kimpel opened a branch store at Baxter, Duke's stronghold. J. P. Holland & Bro. sold out to J. W. White. W. D. Trotter & Co. moved into a new store on Main Street. J. B. Mercer purchased the drugstore of Philander McDermott (which had been established in 1885). C. L. Adams & Co. opened a store on Main Street "with a nice stock of fancy groceries." W. S. Adams was manager. The Hotel Crenshaw was in operation by this time.[114]

Dermott incorporated on July 11, 1890, with J. Tom Crenshaw as mayor, W. K. Splawn as marshal, and David Kimpel as treasurer. Serving the board of aldermen were Charles T. Wells, John T. Crenshaw, S. M. Owens, L. C. Crute, and W. S. Smiley. Dermott owes its most attractive feature to Mayor Crenshaw and his recorder, C. H. VanPatten, who were responsible for planting the grand oak trees which still line the streets.[115]

An "unknown pioneer citizen" wrote in 1935 of his recollection of the town in the 1890s: Front Street (now Iowa) faced the east-west railroad and during the 1890s was the entire business district. From east to west, and north of the street Elvin Gaster and V. E. Moss owned a saloon. To attract customers they had a small zoo on the side of the building. "The animals confined were a very large and ill-tempered bobcat, a number of squirrels, a rattlesnake, and other fauna...." Next to the zoo, Captain Miller ran a rooming house. The Exchange Bank & Trust Company later occupied this site. Across the street was a large mercantile owned by S. A. Duke & Co. being managed by P. K. Savage. Mr. Bissell later had a mercantile business there. Morris, Kimpel & Wells (Charles F.) owned a large mercantile. J. T. Crenshaw Jr. owned a drugstore at the corner of present Iowa and Freeman Streets. Across the street from there a black man by the name of Bailey ran a small fancy grocery store. Ben Kimpel, S. E. Greenburg, Sam Silbernagel, and B. A. Kimpel owned other businesses on Front Street. Theodore F. Martin was a "popular hotel man at Dermott" in 1895. Hugh N. Brooks owned a butcher shop by 1889.[116]

Main Street was the principal residential section. Homes recalled there by the "unknown pioneer" were those of J. T. Crenshaw Sr. (corner of now Peddicord), J. T. Crenshaw Jr., J. A. Anderson, Seaman (later occupied by Dr. Blanks), Dr. Phil McDermott, Elvin Gaster, Judge Charles F. Wells, Dr. H. C. Stinson, V. E. Moss, and J. B. Mercer. The Baker home stood at the junction of present Pecan Street and Gaines Landing Road. The Seaman home was the last on Main Street, and the Moss home was at the corner of Main and present Speedway. Beyond these homes was cultivated farmland. Also mentioned were Colonel R. A. Buckner, Johnny and W. P. Ottman, Woolfolk, Dr. Luther Buckner, Smylie Owens, Captain Tom Owens, E. A. Fowler, and Mr. Crawford ("the village blacksmith and his two motherless children"). Others there during this time were the families of Tom Crenshaw, Peddicord, and Winston. Mmes. Peddicord and Winston were daughters of Dr. Crenshaw. On the outskirts were the farm families of McDermott, Mercer, Hurd, and Daniels. Mrs. Mercer was the daughter of Charles McDermott, and Mrs. Hurd was his adopted niece.[117]

W. H. Lephiew moved in 1902 from Baxter to Dermott where he opened a large mercantile business and bought a gin. He eventually established the first power plant and operated it for several years before selling it to the town. The mercantile store was sold to the Valley Mercantile Company in 1913. Lephiew moved his office to the Crenshaw Building in 1917, and the family business is still located there. Around 1920 David Kimpel entered partnership with the Lephiew gin, and the concern became Kimpel & Lephiew Gin Company.[118] Lephiew later bought out Kimpel. In addition to managing his large farming operation, he also owned shingle mills in the area. Management of the gin and farm operation passed to his son-in-law, R. H. "Butch" Dennington and continues to be directed by his son, Lephiew Dennington.

Henry Bordeaux opened a drug store in 1903, and it was still in operation twenty years later. J. C. Hoffman established Dermott Grocery & Commission Company in 1904 and remained in business until 1929 when it moved to Eudora. H. E. Courtney opened a grocery store on Iowa

Street around 1906 and was still in business twenty-four years later. L. M. Singleton entered the grocery trade on Main Street between 1905-1910. Orr Hardware Company, owned by S. E. Orr, opened on Arkansas Street in 1909. He carried a line of hardware, harnesses, furniture, and groceries. Part of the business included an undertaking department and offered an auto hearse, caskets, robes, and funeral supplies.[119]

The hardwood lumber industry, which began there in 1891 with the location of the French Oak Stave Company, continued to grow. Leavitt Land & Lumber Company constructed a large mill a few miles west of Dermott in 1908 and cut over 28,000 acres of timber. In 1913 the name was changed to Dermott Land & Lumber Company with headquarters in Dermott by that time. M. E. Bird owned and managed the commissary connected with the company. In 1919 he sold out and returned to his home at Wilmar in Drew County. C. R. Bates was manager and secretary in 1930. Schneider Stave Company, managed by O. A. Lowe, built a slack barrel stave mill around 1907. One of the largest industries in the town, it could produce 45,000 staves per day. Slack barrel staves were made into barrels for shipping dry products such as flour. Bimel-Ashcroft Manufacturing Company located there around 1910 under the management of C. Helmstetter and produced oak and hickory tool handles, single trees, neck yokes, and automobile and wagon spokes. Frank Herbert Dennington joined this firm in 1913 as a machinist. W. P. Bynum came in 1912 and built a mill that turned out tight barrel staves and circled heading. These products were used in the manufacture of whiskey barrels. The buildings and grounds of Bynum Cooperage covered fifteen acres. Sherer Burleigh came to Dermott when he was twenty-two to manage a handle mill established earlier by his grandfather who lived in Scotland. Other hardwood mills were Mark's Veneer and Frecraton, which produced flooring.[120]

By 1910 the town had two hotels, the Moss and the Wilkinson. Joe Wiseman came to the town in 1910 and opened a small clothing store that flourished at the corner of Iowa and Freeman Streets. This store eventually moved to the corner of Iowa and Main where it remained as a family business until the 1990s. Adolphus Prothro launched Prothro's Jewelry on Iowa Street around 1910, and that store also continued in business until recent times when it relocated to Dumas. Two saloons were in competition in 1911 with H. L. Van selling Old Charter whiskey for $1.50 per quart against Bowden & Bowden's $1.65 price. Two new theaters opened in 1912 - the Alex, owned by W. T. Alexander, and the Dixie. Pope Blythe purchased the Dixie the following year. Mrs. Ella Neal owned and operated the City Hotel, with rooms available for a dollar a day. Ellen Grubb also ran one of the Dermott hotels.[121]

A fire in February 1913 started in the Post Office Cafe and destroyed the nearly completed brick Iron Mountain depot, the Wilkinson Hotel (a frame building on the corner of Iowa and Arkansas Streets), and Van and Bowden's saloons. Endangered were the buildings of the Annex Hotel, Exchange Bank, Moss Hotel, Porter Brothers and Kirkpatrick General Merchandise Store, Dermott Bank, and Alex Theater. Charles Duke organized the Dermott Hotel Company in April 1913. Located on Arkansas Street, Hotel Dermott opened in February the following year with a "brilliant social function" celebrating the $65,000 structure. Oliver Higgins opened a barbershop in the hotel where he offered "Baths for Sale" at six for one dollar. David Kimpel organized the Chicot Hotel Company in 1913, and the following year it was under the management of T. A. Wilkinson, who also managed the Hotel Dermott. Harvey Parnell purchased the Lephiew Livery Stable in 1913.[122]

Another fire occurred in May 1914 that originated in the Kennedy Hotel and destroyed it. Also consumed was the building occupied by the Dermott Realty Company, Blount and Moss, Ander's Law Office, and Davis Tailor Shop. The Exchange Bank burned as well as Mrs. Skipper's millinery shop, E. G. Hammock's Law Office, Dante's Dry Goods Store, and Gregg's Grocery & Meat Market. In August fire originated in the Kimpel house occupied by Dr. H. C. Stinson and burned the Dermott News office, Clarke & Clark Store, and the new Kimpel home. Glass was broken in Hanchey's Drug Store and the post office. Kimpel immediately made plans to erect a large building on the corner of Main and Front Streets to house six stores and office rooms. Planning to occupy this building were Clarke & Clark, Blanks Brothers, A. Prothro Jewelry, the Dermott News, E. G. Hammock Law Office, and Kimpel's office.[123]

Central Drug Store was established around 1914 under the proprietorship of H. D. Elliot, a registered pharmacist. It was located at the corner of Main and Iowa Streets. C. F. Dowden was selling Studebaker wagons, buggies and harness by 1914. In 1915 C. H. McCroskey purchased a confectioners and billiard parlor from A. T. Bowden and was to be assisted by George Newman. In January 1916 V. E. Moss assumed proprietorship of the Chicot Hotel where fifty rooms were available for seven to ten dollars per month. Mrs. W. S. Daniel became resident manager of the Chicot Hotel that was to be run as a "high class rooming house." This hotel and the Hotel Dermott were now under the ownership of J. C. Douglas.[124]

By 1916 Dermott was a boomtown with seven hardwood mills in operation employing 1,100 men and a payroll of $83,000 a month. The Dermott Bank and Trust Co. and the older Exchange Bank held deposits of around $500,000. Dermott Wholesale Grocery's accounts were more than a million dollars a year. Electric lights and a sewage system were in place.

There was also an ice cream factory and a bottling plant. Sixteen passenger trains passed through each day, and the population was 3,500.[125]

Hanging on beneath one of these trains was a young hobo from Polluck, Louisiana, riding the rails in search of work. Ed Wagner got off and wandered into Louie Belser's mercantile store on the west corner of Main and Iowa Streets (later the location of Pinkus Liquor Store). Belser offered to put him up for the night if he would clean up the store. "He did such a good job that Mr. Belser let him stay on," said Jim Wagner. When he saved enough money, he sent for his wife and baby son, James. In 1923 Ed became manager of Belser's Texaco Station located across from the Methodist Church. Oliver Higgins later ran this station.[126]

In 1918 Henry Gaster sold his interest in the Valley Mercantile Company to his partner, P. O. Bynum, and bought the interest of C. M. Measel in the Dermott Hardware and Furniture Company. C. H. McCroskey built a new theater, the Allied. H. H. Dyer was the funeral director and embalmer with the Orr Hardware Company. John Baxter arrived from Hampton to begin a law practice. R. W. Baxter purchased Walker Lumber Company, owned by A. R. Walker and J. F. Delaney, and formed Baxter Lumber Company in 1919. H. D. Elliot and C. M. Measel bought the former Hanchey Drug Store from R. W. Baxter. Drs. J. A. Thompson, M. R. Hanchey, and A. C. Blanks bought People's Drug Store and the name became Dermott Drug Company. Mr. and Mrs. C. T. Kennedy leased the Chicot Hotel.[127]

The Bank of Dermott, organized in 1922, experienced rapid growth under the leadership of its directors, A. B. Banks, S. B. Meek, R. M. Scott, John Baxter, C. B. Bowman, D. Kimpel, M. C. Magness, Joe Niven, and Vann M. Howell. Its first location was near the depot.[128]

In 1924 N. F. Bynum purchased the Dermott Drug Company from L. E. Hoke, A. C. Blanks, and J. A. Thompson. W. R. Drummond opened a photographic studio. (Drummond was still in business during the 1927 flood, and many of his photographs remain in private and institutional collections.) C. M. Measel and H. D. Elliot dissolved the Central Drug partnership. M. R. Hanchey bought the Dermott Drug Store in 1925 and renamed it Hanchey's Pharmacy. The Dermott Furniture and Undertaking Company opened with Henry Gaster as general manager and T. M. Downey in charge of the undertaking department.[129]

L. W. Wilson resigned as manager of the Peoples Lumber Company and was succeeded by C. B. Owens in 1927. Silbernagel & Co. established a wholesale grocery in a building on Arkansas Street, which was also occupied by the Coca-Cola Company. H. E. Courtney moved into his new building on Front Street. Morgan & Lindsey, a variety store under the management of F. D. Massey, opened in 1927 and stayed in business until the 1970s. Coca-Cola Bottling Company, a distributing center for the Pine

Bluff Company managed by Herman Watts, moved to a new location by the railroad on Highway 35. Dermott Machine & Boiler Works was established in 1928 on North Main under the management of N. L. Vaughn. Howard and Wisner, owned by W. H. Howard and J. C. Wisner, offered "general blacksmithing, body building and wood working" at their shop on North Main.[130]

In 1929 Will "Frog" Parker opened Frog's Feed Store. The new Municipal Building on Arkansas Street opened in February. Work began on paving streets; "White Way" lighting was installed, and natural gas was available. Lamar Stinson arrived to join his father in the Southern Motor Company. Dermott had nearly 4,000 residents around 1930. The many business concerns were for the most part owned by local capital. The timber industry was still contributing to economic growth. Dermott Land & Lumber Company was no longer cutting timber, but formed the Industrial Machinery Company which engaged in buying liquidated industrial equipment, particularly sawmill machinery. Schneider Stave Company, Bynum Cooperage, Bimel-Ashcroft, Burleigh, Mark's Veneer, Frecraton, and Peoples Lumber Company remained in business.[131]

The Dermott and Chicot Hotels were still in operation. Trade continued for Orr Hardware, Louie Courtney's grocery, Dishongh Grocery, Hoover Dry Cleaners, Bulloch Brothers, Valley Mercantile, Blanks Brothers Grocery (owned by Charlie and Andrew Blanks), C. E. Singleton Grocery, Delta Drug (owned by Mabel Ford and Abbott Kinney Sr.), and Prothro Jewelry. In October 1935 fire destroyed the Dermott Hotel, Orr Hardware, and the post office. This occurring in the midst of the Depression, "people shook their heads and said that Dermott was destined to become a ghost town."[132] The Legion Hut was built on Freeman Street by WPA labor. This building became a legend in its time as people from surrounding counties flocked to the all-night dances on Saturday. "It was cooled by air blowing over ice on the outside," remembered Clifton Trigg.

Jewish families owning clothing stores were Joe Wiseman, Joseph Cohen, Hi Pinkus, and Abe Abrams. Sam Nusbaum was associated with his father-in-law, Joseph Cohen. Abe Abrams employed Joe Goldstein, who later ran the business. "Mr. Abrams arrived in town with only a pack on his back," said Butch Dennington. Ely and Jack Dante owned a mercantile, and Tinnerbar and Wachanskey owned clothing stores. Although the town accepted the Hebrew populace, some merchants were concerned about the new competition. "Charlie Skipper fell out," remarked Clifton Trigg. "They will tear us to pieces, he said."

Chinese families immigrated to Dermott as peddlers and eventually established the grocery stores of Y. L. Tow Company (owned by Suen), S. Yee Poy, Y. H. Wahl, (owned by Lee Jaim "Jimmy" Wahl), Herbert Leung, King, Lee, and Couy. A Chinese man also owned Sam's Cafe (the

Iron Mountain Cafe). The King store was located near the present Belser Lee's Royal Liquor Store on Iowa Street.[133]

The Chinese children attended the public school, but were soon disallowed this privilege. "They were so studious, so far ahead of the other students, that the school board decided they could not attend," recalled Clifton Trigg. After this, Mrs. Belser took in the children and taught them. Belser Lee was named after this woman. They were eventually permitted to return to the public school. "The Chinese children helped to ease the tension," said Butch Dennington. Most of the descendants of these Chinese families became university graduates and entered professions.

Four motor companies were thriving in the early thirties. Southern Motor Company, managed by R. P. Stinson and in business for about ten years, was located by the depot and offered Buick cars and accessories. J. N. Pearson sold Chevrolets at his three year old Dermott Motor Company on North Main. This business began as the O.K. Service Station. Kimpel Motor Company, managed by E. P. Kimpel, opened in 1925 near the depot and sold Ford cars as well as Lincoln and Fordson tractors. George and Jack Kelley sold the "famed Nash automobile" at their West Garage and "drive-in filling station." J. J. Sumner operated Dermott Service Station on Main Street. Magnolia Service Station was about ten years old and under the management of O. E. Owens, who was also a wholesale dealer for Magnolia Petroleum Company.[134]

Dermott was also a dairy town. A dairy was operating by 1916 with another needed "to supply local demand." R. L. Woolfolk resumed operation of Homewood Dairy in 1927. A Mr. Fanning and a Mr. Baker owned other dairies. Tom Trigg (who came to Dermott in 1919) bought a dairy from a Mr. Thomas north of town in 1929. Tom and his son, Clifton, rose at four to milk nine cows each. The mother had the milk bottled by the time they finished, and Clifton made the delivery route to the Dermott Hotel and three Chinese groceries. Henry Trigg ran a dairy south of Speedway. A Mr. Kirby later owned a dairy, and a Mr. Daniels had a dairy with a herd of about thirty cows south of town. Charles Bishop, Jack Ellis, and James Dottery were milkers there. Charles recalled those days, "Every morning and every evening we three boys would walk down there to milk the cows. For every four cows those boys could milk, I could milk seven. He paid us five dollars a week.[135]

Ed Wagner established Wagner Oil Company, a Lion bulk plant, and Wagner Service Station, which was located at Main and Speedway in 1936. Wagner Motor Company opened in 1947 with three Dodge vehicles in stock. Wagner's son, James, later joined in business. Chester Courtney and Clifton Trigg formed Courtney-Trigg Company, a dry goods, drug, and grocery store, in 1944. The grocery business was eventually sold to Y. L. Tow. The partnership was dissolved in 1950 with Trigg taking the dry goods store and Courtney taking the drug store. Trigg's Department Store opened in 1952.

The first newspaper, the *Dermott Incubator*, was established in 1892 by John H. Page, but was out of business two years later. The *Dermott News*, founded by J. A. Watkins of Warren, began publication in 1910 and was leased the same year to D. L. Newman. The following year G. E. Kinney bought the paper and published it until 1916 when he sold it to Joe Sitlington of Little Rock. By 1924 the Kinney family was publishing the paper.[136]

The first church established was the New Bethany Presbyterian, later to be named the Dermott Presbyterian Church. Having its unofficial beginning in the small building in Dr. McDermott's yard, the church was organized in 1868 under the direction of Rev. J. A. Dickson of Monticello while McDermott was in Honduras. The original McDermott church building was blown away by a storm and another one was erected after the Civil War. This building was used until the church moved to the "union church" on Freeman Street. Baptist and Methodist congregations used this building as well. The Presbyterians eventually built a church on Peddicord Street. Founding elders were J. F. Lowery and Pineo Hurd with M. B. Shaw as deacon. When McDermott returned from Honduras, he was elected an elder. Rev. Dickson served as pastor until 1870 and was followed by Alex P. Henderson.[137]

A Methodist church was in existence by 1883 with services being conducted by Rev. Wright. The Dermott Methodist Church was founded in 1886 under the initiative of John T. Crenshaw and his cousin, Mrs. Hattie Peddicord. J. Tom Crenshaw organized a Sunday School in 1891. Some early members were Mabel Winston (later Mrs. Harvey Parnell), Mrs. Susan Elizabeth Crenshaw, and Mrs. Reubye Crenshaw Edwards. The Methodists bought the union church building and used it until January 1914, when they moved to the corner of Main and Peddicord Streets. The Dermott Methodist Church burned in March 1924, and a new structure was built with first services in it being held in August the following year.[138]

The Baptist congregation organized on May 12, 1904, under the direction of Rev. N. C. Denson. The first Sunday School superintendent was W. J. Raborn. Some of the early members were Mrs. Mae Courtney, Mrs. Ouida Johnson, Mrs. Evelyn Baker, Mrs. W. H. Lephiew, and Mrs. W. S. Daniels. Rev. Denson's wife at this time was the former Ellen Grubb, a staunch Methodist, and she gave the church a lot next to her home in the 200 block of South Main. The first church was built there with W. H. Lephiew contributing generously to the construction. When a new church was built in 1926, it was located at South Main and Speedway.[139] This building was replaced in the 1950s.

In 1912 the Benedictine diocese, headquartered at St. Winands's (now St. Mary's) in McGehee, erected St. Leo's, a small mission church in Dermott. Father Matthew was priest, and Father Galoni followed him the next year. A local lodge of B'nai B'rith was organized in 1913. Having no temple, Eli Dante began holding services in his home in the early 1920s. The congregation, invited from the entire area, soon outgrew Dante's house, and they began to meet on the second floor of a theater. Dante moved in 1927, and members traveled to Pine Bluff and Little Rock to synagogues until Isadore Pinkus opened his home for services in 1940. The group later met at various places in McGehee until Temple Meir Chayim was built there in 1947. Featuring Gothic architecture with Mission decorative influences, the building is on the National Register of Historic Places. The Church of Christ congregation built a church in 1939, and the following year the Assembly of God had a building. In 1952 there were fourteen black churches in the town.[140]

Dermott's earliest settler was a Yale graduate and attentive to the education of his children and nieces. French masters and governesses he brought up from New Orleans conducted this antebellum schooling. A local governess (from Ashley County) was Marguerite Nunn, mother of the late Janie Withers Pugh of Portland. Families continued in-home tutoring until the first white school was organized in 1885. Martha Burleigh wrote, "The Negro children already had a school [by this time] and they had a very nice building. There were something over 50 Negro children. This building was located where the Tom Spurlock home now is [West Gaines and South Trotter Street]."[141] The presence of an organized black school and the lack of a white school at this time reflect the influence of the Reconstruction government as well as perhaps the white opposition to tax supported schools.

Tom Crenshaw was president of the school board and was the only literate and only white member. Twelve enrollments were required, and Crenshaw could only register ten, so he "fudged" the ages on his daughter, Reubye, and his nephew, Will, both age four, to bring the number to twelve. The state would provide a teacher, but there was no building. An abandoned cabin in a cotton field "about a quarter of a mile south of the Negro school" became the schoolhouse. It had a large front room and a shed room on the back with wooden shutters and a dirt chimney. After one six-month summer term there, they were allowed to use the black school on alternate terms. Miss Anna Morgan (later Mrs. J. J. Baugh of Searcy) was the first teacher at this school. The twelve students attending the first year school were Martha Crenshaw (Mrs. Sherer Burleigh), two cousins named Will Crenshaw, Reubye Crenshaw (Mrs. R. C. Edwards), Eula Mercer, Kate Mercer (Mrs. Vance Bordeaux), Arthur and Ada McDermott, and Frank, Mary, Gordon, and Maggie Hurd. By the time the enrollment increased to around thirty white children, a new school was built.[142]

The new school was "practically a duplicate of the Negro building - no better, no worse." It was built "about two years later...on the present [1941] location of the Dermott Gin Company's gin on Speedway Street." Professor H. G. Boyle, formerly of Little Rock was principal of the white school in 1892. The first unit of a two-story brick school was completed on School Street in 1908, and that year it became a graded school. Alma Daniels (Mrs. U. C. Barnett) was the first graduate.[143] This impressive building served until 1976 when a modern complex was built at another location.

By 1915 Dermott High School was "one of only nine Arkansas schools on the accredited list of schools in the South and Southwest." The following year it was proclaimed as a "designated State High School, the only one in the southeast part of the State." Always excelling in football, the Dermott team beat A&M College with a score of 24-0 in 1919 and later won the state championship.[144] U. C. Barnett, superintendent in 1908, suggested that annual contests in literary and athletic events be organized. He met in Montrose on November 28, 1908, with superintendents John H. Belford of Lake Village, Victor L. Webb of Hamburg, David C. Hastings of Crossett, and J. R. Anders of Portland. Out of that meeting, the Southeast Arkansas Literary and Athletic Association was formed, the first of its kind in the state. Six other schools joined, and the first contest was held in Dermott in April the following year. From 1911 to 1924 Dermott hosted at least seven of these events. In 1916 the local paper announced, "Five special trains will bring visitors" to the contest. The association spread to statewide districts and ultimately came under the control of the Arkansas Athletic Association.[145]

A private school for black students, the Southeast Baptist Academy, opened November 20, 1899, under the administration of the Baptist Southeast District Association. The group chose Dermott for the location, as it was known "for the prominent Blacks who lived there...Many of the businesses in the downtown section are owned and operated by Negroes." A boarding school requiring tuition, the curriculum offered Greek, Latin, and Hebrew in addition to regular courses.[146]

The Arkansas Baptist State Convention divided in 1934, and the Regular ABSC assumed responsibility for the Dermott school with the Consolidated ABSC sponsoring Arkansas Baptist College in Little Rock. The academy was called Morris Booker Memorial High School and College at this time. A twelve-year old boy, born on Bayou Bartholomew at Gourd in Lincoln County, entered in 1941, earning extra money by cutting firewood. York Williams Jr. graduated in 1946 as valedictorian and returned in 1957 as president. By this time the financially insecure institution was near collapse. Buildings were in disrepair and students were entering integrated institutions with the idea that "their institutions were inferior and incapable of delivering quality education" as a result of the 1954 *Brown vs. Board of Education* Supreme Court decision.

Williams quickly began a statewide fund-raising effort, formed a reputable faculty, and solicited students, which he attracted by implementing a student work program for tuition and fees. By 1960, the academic and extracurricular programs were the best in the history of the school, and enrollment exceeded a hundred. The effects of integration continued to threaten enrollment, and by 1970 the institution was wavering. Dr. Williams adjusted the program to a senior high and two-year college and obtained a federal grant to establish a day care center. The buildings were dilapidated, and in 1974 the school bought and moved into the old Chicot County High School (the former black school) facility nearby.

Many students who received their early education at Morris Booker became distinguished leaders in their professions. The father of Samuel L. Kountz from Lexa paid his son's tuition with a wagonload of sweet potatoes and sorghum syrup each year. Kountz was the first black to enter the University of Arkansas Medical Sciences School and became a pioneer in organ transplant surgery. Peaches Davis, daughter of school trustee and treasurer, Matthew Davis, graduated from Fisk University and returned to Dermott to manage her father's funeral home. One local boy under Williams' tutorage had a terrible case of stuttering. Dr. Williams, perhaps remembering Demosthenes, advised, "Go down to the bayou and find you some rocks. Fill your mouth with rocks and talk with them in your mouth." The youth followed the advice, and Don Glover graduated from Howard University with a degree in jurisprudence and became mayor of Dermott and Circuit Court Judge.[147]

Dermott, named in honor of a medical doctor, has a history of many qualified physicians. Dr. Charles McDermott and Dr. William Crenshaw attended to patients before the Civil War. By 1887, "a number of Negro medical doctors held their practices in Dermott. A Dr. Banks was one among many in the town." The name of Dr. Duke, one of the early black doctors, remains inscribed on an Iowa Street building facade. Drs. Philander McDermott, Edward O. McDermott, Harry C. Stinson, A. C. Blanks, and Luther Buckner were practicing by 1890. Dr. W. K. Baker, who died in 1911, was another early doctor. Dr. Elwood Baker began a practice in 1902. In 1913, Dermott had five physicians known as the "Busy Bees" - E. E. Barlow, Elwood Baker, Boal, R. L. Barr, and Blanks. Dr. J. A. Thompson was there by 1919 and served a long term as Health Officer. Dr. J. T. Blanks was practicing in the 1920s.[148]

The town enjoyed good health. After the cemetery was established, it was said that it was ten years before anyone was buried in it. However, a hospital was ultimately established, largely through the efforts of Dr. E. E. Barlow. St. Mary's Hospital, under the direction of the Benedictine Sisters, opened July 1, 1940. Mother Columba was president of the board, and the staff was composed of Drs. H. W. Thomas, Major Smith, and T. C. Wilson. The same year, Dr. E. E. Barlow and his son, Dr. Brian E. Barlow, opened Barlow & Barlow Clinic. The Dermott Clinic, owned by Dr. H. W. Thomas and Dr. Brian E. Barlow, followed. By 1952 Dr. C. V. Reeves ran "one of the most modern clinics for Negroes in the state," and Dr. N. R. Parker was another "well-known Negro physician." A new hospital, Dermott-Chicot Memorial, opened in June 1971 at which time St. Mary's closed. This hospital served the outlying area until it closed on March 31, 1990. In 1920 the local paper ran the following notice: "The Doctors of Dermott announce that, beginning January 1st, 1920, owing to the high cost of living, they will charge $3 for an ordinary day visit, and that charges for night visits, country visits and other medical services will be increased in proportion." A veterinarian, Dr. J. C. Beyea, established there by 1912. Serving the general area, he advertised that he would "answer telephone calls on the first train day or night."[149]

Dermott has always been well represented in the legal and political arenas. Among the earliest known barristers were J. H. Hammock and his son, E. G. Hammock, who opened a practice in 1911. J. H. Hammock was elected mayor the following year and was also appointed as delegate to the Democratic State Convention. E. G. Hammock was elected Chancery Judge in 1919. Col. R. A. Buckner, described as "of Chesterfelian deportment and legal ability," opposed Judge Z. T. Wood for Chancellor in 1912 and accepted J. M. Golden in his law practice in 1920. Anders Law Office was open by 1914. Dudley Crenshaw, a graduate of Harvard Law School, joined the law firm of E. G. Hammock in 1916. John Baxter arrived in 1918 to practice law.[150] Harvey Parnell was elected representative from the county in 1918 and later served as senator and lieutenant governor. He became governor in March 1928 upon the resignation of Gov. Martineau, was elected to the office in November, and re-elected in 1930.

John Frank "Mutt" Gibson Sr. graduated from Dermott High School and was admitted to the bar in 1939. Elected City Attorney the same year, he held that office for almost forty years. He served in the state senate from 1967 until his death in 1980. Appointed to fill his term was his cousin, Jack Gibson, who won re-election and held the office until 1993. The Gibson Law Office continues to operate with Gibson's son, Charles Sidney, and his grandson, C. S. "Chuck" Gibson II, at the helm. John Frank Gibson Jr. maintains a law practice in Monticello. Other Gibsons who became attorneys were Robert and his son, Bynum, and Charles Clifford Gibson III.

Betsy Morris Rodgers, great-granddaughter of Willie F. Skipper, remembered slipping off to the Skipper Bridge over the bayou at the east edge of town. "That's where everyone went to smoke," she laughed. "It was also a courting place. The old bridge was in such bad shape, people would tear planks off it for firewood." Garvin Adcock, whose family rented the R. T. Smith farm near Skipper Bridge around 1940, said Dermott was "pretty boomie" at the time. "There were three drug stores, three Chinese grocery stores, three liquor stores, three gins, and the staves mills. You couldn't walk down the street on a Saturday night - it was filled with people, and a lot of them in a state of drunkenness."

Butch Dennington and Clifton Trigg grew up together in Dermott. They recalled the rough and tumble days of the saloon era and the Dermott Hotel, which stayed open all night and where the men would congregate after their dates. Big bands such as Herbie Kaye, Blue Steel, and Les Brown performed at the hotel and the Legion Hut. "They danced from midnight to dawn and then went for breakfast." Butch remembered the early leadership of men like W. E. Lephiew, John Baxter, and a Mr. Johnson.

Charles Bishop was born in 1912 at 915 South Trotter Street. "My memories of my time there are good ones. We had a good school, good churches, and good doctors. But the best thing was the swimming hole past old man Buckner's place, which was right on the bank of the bayou. We would go over there every day. When we came back through, he would give us watermelon - all we could eat." This group of boys was composed of Coil and Indman Moore, Howard Turner, Durwood Gregg, Billy Curley, James Wagner, Robert Thompson, Lee Naron, and Butch Dennington. Charles related the story of Col. Buckner's burial. "Back then, when someone died, you got fixed up and put in a coffin and were kept in the house overnight. And so folks went out there to sit up, and a little after it got dark, everyone was told that they may as well go home since Col. Buckner wouldn't be buried until the next day. The Colonel was buried right out back behind the house. And a fence was put up and so was a tombstone." Buckner Lane, near the cemetery, was another preferred courting area in later days.

Not far downstream from Skipper Bridge on the edge of the town are the Dermott Cemetery and McDermott family burial. Inscribed on the tombstones are the names and dates of the early settlers, founders, and citizens. The pecan trees planted by the McDermotts and the oak trees planted by the early leaders continue to adorn the streets, and the town is still surrounded by farmland. Trains continue to roll through but no longer stop at a bustling depot. The grand hotels and the lumber mills are only a distant memory. But this bayou town, still quite remarkably populated by descendants from its early inhabitants, continues to thrive. A long ago description remains appropriate: "Where the Old Southland and the New South come together: the Old South of hospitality, flower gardens and southern cooking, and the New South of industry, trade and diversified farming. It is a good place to live."[151]

≈≈§≈≈

Lake Wallace, Hudspeth

The bayou leaves Dermott and soon passes by Lake Wallace, an oxbow from its old channel. This lake, located in both Drew and Chicot Counties, was variously called Five Mile Brake, Smylie Brake, and Wallace Brake. Samuel Wallace and Wallace Dickson are early names associated with the area. The Dickson family owned nearby Enterprise Plantation. Part of the Duke Estate farm managed by Henry Tucker extended down from Baxter to Panther Brake and Lake Wallace. Tucker owned a large cypress lodge near the spillway. Before the Game & Fish Commission dammed the lake in the early 1930s, several fields were cultivated within the present lake area. The original dam was partially destroyed after heavy rain in the spring of 1939, and plans were drawn in August for a permanent dam and spillway. In September, local sportsmen organized the Lake Wallace Association to solicit $15,000 "to preserve the popular fishing resort…it must be completed before fall rains or the lake will go out and be irrevocably lost." Construction began in October.[152]

Deadman's Camp was a sawmill camp in the area. "A fellow came through there and worked at that camp. He died and since they didn't know who he was or where he came from, they just buried him there. Then they started calling it that," related Amos Sledge, who lived at the lake in the 1940s. The bayou swimming hole was near the bridge that crossed to the spillway. Lake Wallace, covering 350 acres, continues to be a favored fishing place. Giant cypress trees, emerging out of clean, reflecting water, their limbs adorned with Spanish moss, form a picturesque setting. The growth of Spanish moss begins in this area and continues down the bayou.

Below Lake Wallace the bayou at one time made a long eastward bend to the Chicot County line at Hudspeth. The narrow neck of land separating the channel was dug out in the 1920s to cut off the long loop. Hudspeth was a train stop and had a post office from 1890 to 1931. A grocery store owned by Mr. Hall was still operating in the 1930s. A school for black children was also there.[153]

≈≈§≈≈

Ashley County

Slemons, Morrell, Boydell

Bayou Bartholomew enters Ashley County shortly after leaving Jerome and passes an old steamboat landing variously called Nellie, Slemons, Morrell, and finally Boydell. Nellie Post Office was established in 1869 and continued until 1871. Mrs. Harriet Womack was first postmaster. Slemons Post Office opened in 1878 a few miles down the bayou at Green Pugh Bend north of Lake Grampus. Postmasters at Slemons were Jerome R. Rogers (1878), L. Hancock (1878), Jerome R. Rogers (1879), A. E. Jackson (1880), Green Pugh (1881), and Thomas H. Baldy. At some point during this time, the post office moved near the present site of Boydell. Angeline Stubblefield Waddell wrote, "On Bayou Bartholomew just above Boydell there was a boat landing named Slemons. Steamboats from New Orleans made their way up the bayou, bringing supplies from New Orleans and returning with bales of cotton. This was in the late 1800s." The name changed to Morrell in 1890 and to Boydell in 1914. The earliest known person in the area was Jesse McGary, who owned a plantation there as early as 1827. Thomas Baldy moved from Fountain Hill (Ashley County) to Slemons in 1877 and bought six hundred acres of bayou farmland. In 1888 he established a mercantile at Slemons.[154]

Harriet May Waddell came by carriage and covered wagon from Wakesboro, North Carolina, in 1859 and homesteaded a large tract of land. With her was her nine-year-old son, James Madison Waddell, who, at her death in 1904, became her only heir. After her arrival the widowed Mrs. Waddell married a Mr. Womack. He died shortly thereafter and was buried in an Indian mound on the bank of the bayou. Mrs. Waddell, her son, and his wife, Olivia Spencer Waddell, and three other family members are buried on an Indian mound east of Highway 165 at Boydell. T. L. Cagle bought the 1,900-acre Waddell plantation in 1918. Another prominent early family was Boyd, and the name of the town is derived from a combination of these two names.

Micajah Stinson moved from Troy in Drew County after 1800 and settled on the bayou north of Boydell. Claude Simpson, who was married to a Boyd woman was another early settler. The Bulloch family is also associated with this area. Arriving later were the families of Aubrey and Allen Harrison, John Sedberry, Clyde Rufus Russell, Maglothlin, Peder, and Standard. W. A. Roddy established one of the first stores. Eighteen year old John A. Gibson came in 1874. He began working as a farm hand for Boyd and learned the mercantile trade by clerking in Roddy's store. He eventually bought the store, which then became J. A. Gibson & Son, the son being Charles Clifford Gibson Sr. This store was known as the "Big Store," which distinguished it from the "Little Store" which was owned by John A., June, William Edward, and Charles Clifford Gibson, Sr. The "Little Store" was used only for furnishing their tenant farmers. S. C. Bulloch, Claude Simpson, William Gammel, and Clyde Russell owned other stores. Robertson bought the Simpson store and later sold it to G. H. Richardson. Jim Riley eventually took over the Richardson store.

A two-story hotel, the Red Onion, was built because the Blissville Lumber Company first planned to establish there. A Mr. Bussell owned a blacksmith shop, and Charles C. Gibson Sr. installed a gin. An earlier gin was located on the bank of the bayou near the steamboat landing.

At one time the town had two liquor stores, and a Mr. Hollis owned a black honky-tonk which was patronized by the whites as well. Nearby stood a conveniently located calaboose. Sam Gibson served as a town marshal. At one time, the town had two liquor stores. A large stock pen was situated near the railroad. June Gibson traded in cattle, and mule and horse traders frequented the town. Early doctors were J. P. Barker, Elwood Baker, George W. Fletcher, and D. C. Lee.[155]

Boydell School went through the twelfth grade. Early teachers were Mrs. Roger Mills, Edna Bond Gibson, Mabel Thompson, Nettie Wilson, Jimmie Thurman, Mrs. Praul, and Carouse. The school eventually consolidated with Portland. James Madison and Olivia Waddell donated land for Morrell Methodist Episcopal Church, South in 1905. A nondenominational community church known as Union Church was between Jerome and Boydell at the present site of Union Cemetery. Serving the black community was Evergreen Baptist Church. Located on the bayou northwest of town, this church is still in existence.[156]

⚜⚜⚜

Thebes

Located about two miles west of the bayou and west of Montrose was the village of Thebes with the outlying community stretching to the bayou. An unknown pioneer built a log house on the west bank of the bayou conceivably by the mid-1830s. Clark or Patton could have been the builder as they had a cotton gin near the site by 1837.[157] Robert W. Noble bought the property in 1856 and sold it three years later to Samuel B. Wiggins. Wiggins' daughter, Laura, married W. F. McCombs Sr., and the land passed to McCombs after Wiggins' death. After Laura died, McCombs married Fannie, daughter of Green Wood Pugh.

The McCombs plantation, which included land other than the Wiggins tract, reached from the foot of Overflow Hill to the bayou, and came under the management of a son, Ashton, when the father moved to Hamburg in 1866. A plantation commissary was in place by this time. McCombs installed a horse-drawn gin at the intersection of the east-west railroad and the Upper Portland Road in 1898. He also built a ferry for people hauling cotton from the east side of the bayou. McCombs Landing was a steamboat stop and became the head of navigation in the late 1800s.

Thebes Post Office was established March 7, 1900, with Wright A. Haley as postmaster, and closed in 1918. St. Peter's AME Church and Cemetery served the large African-American community, and whites attended it as well. The church also served as the schoolhouse for black students. The building burned around 1925, and children were then bussed to Portland. The town had a café for blacks that was run by Melvin Brown and later by Henry Burke. The McCombs store closed by 1933, and Eunice and Emmit Pamplin opened a store in 1935, which continued in business until 1957. They sold to Jim and Bessie Corder the following year, and the Corders ran it until it burned in 1973 [158] Thebes is deserted now, but the old Wiggins Cabin, moved to Crossett and restored, can still be seen.

❧❦❧

Montrose

Three miles east of the bayou lies the town of Montrose, which was built as a result of the Mississippi River, Hamburg & Western Railroad coming through in 1898. William T. Cone donated four acres the previous year for the town site to be called Cone City. The east-west line made connection with steamboats on the Mississippi River and ran to Hamburg. Montrose Post Office was established August 12, 1898, with John A. Roop as postmaster.

Cone installed a steam-operated cotton gin in 1897 and built Cone Hotel. The town incorporated July 6, 1904. First town officers were G. H. Richardson, mayor; G. A. Franklin, recorder; and G. W. Moody, W. T. Cone, W. H. Shipman, William James, and Scott Burns, aldermen. Being a railroad town and therefore filled with male employees, one of the issues addressed by town ordinances was that of prostitution. Houses of ill fame or bawdyhouses and "lewd women" were subject to fines and imprisonment. In 1917 the council addressed the problem of gambling machines in the town. Saloons for both races were numerous and the calaboose received frequent occupation.

Owning mercantile stores were H. P. Riley (by 1919), A. E. Alsobrook, T. R. Pugh Sons Company, Young, J. B. Wooten (1914), W. L. Gammel (1914), John Currie, John H. Alexander, Sam Wilson (1919), and Kerr. Robert Lee and Aubrey Bawcom had grocery stores, and E. J. Austin owned a meat market. Dermott Grocery Company was a wholesale house.

Victor Edwards arrived in the early 1920s to work in Malone's Drug Store. After graduating from pharmacy school, he returned and went into partnership with John Fletcher and eventually bought Fletcher's interest in the store. In 1926 Sam Wilson bought the W. T. Cone plantation, home, and gin. He established a mercantile store and was later joined in this venture by his brother-in-law, John D. Currie.

The Bank of Montrose opened in 1910 with W. T. Cone owning a major portion of the stock. After being embezzled by an employee, the bank closed in the early 1920s. The small brick building is the only business structure remaining in the town and is used as an office by the Shackelford family business. Frances Shackelford, an adopted daughter of Sam Wilson, occupies the original W. T. Cone house. A modern school building replaced the original frame school in 1927. Originally going through the twelfth grade, by 1948 eight grades were left and the school closed around 1965. The black public school went through the twelfth grade and consolidated to Lake Village in 1948. An industrial school for blacks, established under the efforts of Rev. Ralph Amos, opened in 1902. The Montrose Industrial School existed for only a few years and was lost by foreclosure.

The Methodist Episcopal Church South was built in 1910, and the town also had a Southern Baptist Church. African-American churches were First Baptist, Evening Star Baptist, Zion Methodist, Mt. Pisbey Methodist, Mt. Pilgrim, Sanctified, and New Providence. W. T. and Leona Cone deeded land for the Missionary Baptist (1906), AME (1912), and First Baptist (1914). The Baptist Church # 2 was built on land north of town that was donated by Sam and Frances Wilson in 1916. The town may have had its bawdyhouses and saloons, but it also was well supplied with churches and preachers. Rev. George Wine said that at one time, eleven preachers lived in Montrose. W. T. Cone deeded land for "a white and colored cemetery" in 1912.

With trains rolling through from both east-west and north-south, the depot at the intersection swarmed with activity. The original depot burned and was replaced by 1914 by the Iron Mountain Rail Company. Early rail agents and operators were a Mr. Brislair, Mr. and Mrs. U. E. Barker, William Guise, Marvin Watson, and Murray Streeter. In 1932 the eastern line to Luna Landing was abandoned, but the train continued to run from Montrose to Crossett until around 1948.[159] The north-south line, now MoPac, continues to run through the town, but no longer stops. Surrounded by farmland, Montrose thrived as an agricultural center until the Great Depression. Population, and therefore business, continued to decline as hundreds of tenant farmers gradually left and were replaced by mechanized farming in the 1940s and 1950s.

Holly Point (Old Portland)

The bayou continues its southern sweep through Ashley County to pass by the site of Holly Point and old Portland. John P. Fisher and his wife, Rebecca Journigan, arrived from Louisiana by 1834 and bought a homestead claim. Fisher erected a two-story home on the west bank. Built of sawn cypress lumber and resting on hand-hewn sills of heart cypress, the house contained two bedrooms upstairs and two large and three smaller rooms downstairs. The family lived in the kitchen, a separate building, until their home was completed. Steamboats from New Orleans delivered the windowpanes, furniture, and household provisions. Barns and outbuildings, still in use in 1939, were built of hewed and notched cypress logs measuring twenty inches wide, four inches thick, and eighteen feet long.

Col. Sam Bell acquired the Fisher property by 1869 and lived there with his family. During the Bell occupancy, the house became "a show place and a center of community and social activity." In 1874 Noah E. Moats bought the plantation and home, which eventually passed to his stepdaughter, Bertha Hollaway, who married first Allen Lindsey and second James Oliver Bain. The property consisted of more than 1,300 acres when it was eventually divided between the Lindsey and Bain heirs. Continuously occupied throughout its history, the Greek Revival style home, presently owned by William Holland, is on the National Register of Historic Places.

The Fisher family was not alone in the bayou wilderness. Their neighbors to the north were the family of James Lee Hollaway, who settled there in 1844. William Brady and several other families were there when Hollaway arrived. Daniel J. Cammack came by 1856 and married one of Fisher's daughters, Nancy, the same year. After Cammack's death, his widow married Jack McBride, who lived there. Cammack's father, Lewis J., came around 1857 and settled a few miles to the east Other antebellum settlers in the nearby area were Dr. F. L. Sherrer, John Albert Barringer Sr., Harrell Wells, William Benjamin deYampert, and Joel Wilson. Joe Miller, who died in 1894 at the age of eighty-six, was an early resident. His home on the bayou was "always the favorite resort for friends and travelers...."[160] Mrs. E. J. Camak (a daughter of Wylie J. Cammack) said in 1937 that Joe Miller was the first settler there and he operated a ferry.[161]

After the Civil War more settlers came to the area. Wylie J. Cammack, son of Lewis Cammack, came immediately after the war and bought land a few miles east of the bayou. The father of Marshall Whitesides arrived in 1867 and moved away in 1891. Edward Woolard came in 1868 and in 1876 bought 160 acres on Gum Ridge three miles southeast of the settlement. He married Georgiana Barringer. Willis A. Cain arrived in

1872 and bought land on the bayou. He married James Hollaway's daughter, Alice. Cain served as deputy sheriff for many years, was director of the school, and operated a ferry. Daniel G. Owen established a lumber mill on the bayou north of Holly Point in 1880.[162]

The vicinity had enough population by 1851 to demand a post office. Holly Point Post Office was established that year on the west bank of the bayou near the Fisher home. Postmasters were Henry C. Deal (1851), John Bullock (1853), and John M. Sherrer (1858). This post office was discontinued September 20, 1858, and was most likely located a short distance down the bayou at the Sherrer home at this time. The post office reopened in 1872 with Lamaruex Bloomer postmaster and was then located on the bayou west of Sunshine.

Holly Point was a steamboat landing that the boat hands called simply "the port." When a new post office was established there on August 10, 1857, it was given the name Portland and was on the east bank of the bayou. Robert S. Hazzard was first postmaster. The post office was discontinued in 1867 and reestablished in 1872 with James P. Reeves as postmaster. Subsequent postmasters were John C. Hollaway (1873), John C. Ryan (1876), Deberry F. Dunn (1878), William J. Price (1879), and John C. Bain (1879). The office closed in 1880 and then reopened with Fred L. Sherrer postmaster. After closing once more, it opened again in 1883 with Edward F. Woolard as postmaster. John D. Hollaway followed him in that position in 1886.[163]

A town emerged around the port. Robert F. Hazzard, Frank Hazzard, and Enoch Gardnier were listed as merchants in the 1860 census. Frank Hazzard owned a general store and John Cicero Bain owned a mercantile. At the end of the Civil War two stores remained in business.[164] John David Hollaway bought out the firm of Cammack & Jackson in 1886. Carrying a "general line of plantation supplies," he was grossing $8,000 to $10,000 by the late 1880s. James O. Bain began farming on the bayou in 1882 and a year or two later opened a plantation store that grew into a general mercantile. His annual sales in the late 1880s amounted up to $15,000. In 1889 Dolphus Leroy Bain joined his half- brother in this concern, which included a steam gin and a cotton and cottonseed brokerage.[165]

A one-room school was established south of the town at Alligator Bluff. Tom Gardner was an early teacher. Cola Cammack began attending this school around 1866. "When Cola was a little girl the three-months school of the section was located at Alligator Bluff church – the site of the present cemetery. She and neighboring children walked the two miles in a pig trail, which the constant pattering of little feet soon made a ditch. When it rained…they took off their shoes and waded merrily to school." H. R. Withers, a Methodist circuit rider, first preached at this church in 1851. A Missionary Baptist Church was organized in 1857. The two congregations used the same building on alternate meeting days. The local masons chartered Crescent Lodge in 1860, and it continued until 1881. Dr. F. L. Sherrer set up a medical practice in 1860. When the railroad came in 1890, the town began to move to a new location on the line two miles to the east.[166] The site of old Portland is on a farm road that turns north on the east side of the bridge off Highway 278. Three-fourths of a mile up this road, a silver maple tree marks the location of this once flourishing steamboat port town.

※◎◎※

Portland

The Houston, Central Arkansas & Northern Railroad from McGehee to the Louisiana line was completed June 25, 1890, and the merchants at old Portland gravitated to the new trade center. The mercantile firm of J. O. and D. L. Bain opened that summer. Pugh Bros. & Co., Dean & Cone, Camak & McQuiston, and A. P. Hollaway & Co. owned general merchandise stores by 1892. E. J. Christian & Co. owned a drugstore, and Dr. Christian was practicing medicine. Pugh Bros. & Co. opened in 1892 with R. A., T. R., and D. B. Pugh, and W. F. McCombs as members. The firm incorporated the following year with the name changing to Pugh Brothers Company. Dean & Cone became Dean & Co. with J. D. Dean at the helm. In 1893 Richard J. McBride opened a mercantile, and T. C. Lloyd opened a hotel.

A square mile was laid out for the town with the depot being in the center. Charles T. Scott, John M. Crawford, Lamereux Bloomer, Lewis Cammack, Hosea George, James L. Hollaway, and Ruben Russ previously owned this land. A notice for application to incorporate signed by R. A. Pugh, J. C. Bain, and E. J. Camak was filed July 20, 1893, and incorporation took place in October. The post office moved to the new location. Postmasters following John D. Hollaway were Ella F. Bethune (1895), Mamie A. Savage (1898), William E. Edmiston (1902), Joseph E. Herren (1911), Sidney A. Herren (acting, 1913), A. W. Cammack (1913), William E. Edmiston (1922), Lola B. Gregory (1934), and Floyd L. Kelley (1963).

Fire was a constant threat. Bain Brothers steam gin and mill burned in the first fire in November 1893. Shortly after that, on November 14, a fire broke out in a storage building owned by R. A. Pugh & Bros. and spread rapidly though the business section. Lost in this fire were Christian's drug store, "the Chinaman's store," and the stores of Bain Bros., Mrs. Hollaway (a millinery) R. J. McBride, E. F. Woodard, J. S. Hall (a meat market), and "a small store owned by some Negroes" were also lost. Ed Sedberry perished in the Pugh building. Only the stores belonging to Dean & Co. and E. J. Camak remained on the west side of the railroad.

In spite of this catastrophe, the town continued to grow. Portland had a newspaper, the *Portland Enterprise*, published by M. R. White, by 1895. T. A. Corson began publishing the *Portland Index* in 1908, but the paper was short-lived. By 1895 three Blind Tigers (unlicensed saloons) were doing business. A calaboose was constructed on land deeded to the town by D. L. and Lottie Dean Bain. The city fathers saw to it that it would serve its purpose. The brick walls were over two feet thick and the roof was also brick. The ten feet by twenty feet structure was divided into two cells and each had a small window opening and a steel door. The calaboose was a busy place - especially on weekends. Used until around 1960, this building still stands behind the Portland Bank and is the oldest structure in the town.

The timber industry invaded the town and stimulated more growth. W. H. Wells, who lived south of town, produced over a half million barrel staves in 1896. American Forest Lumber Company was a large mill located at the site of the present Wilson-Pugh Gin. Stell & Boothby Stave Mill was operating by February 1897. Wiley Cammack's hotel was doing a "rushing business" that year.

The town suffered its second fire in August 1902. Frank Hazzard's grocery, the Matthews Hotel, and several smaller buildings burned. A third fire broke out in July 1904 and destroyed G. R. Berry's store, Dean & Co., and the Portland Hotel, which was owned by Mrs. Gaines. Dr. A. E. Cone's office and J. R. Duerson suffered some loss. Dean & Co. rebuilt using brick. In October the same year, fire consumed Wheeler Cypress Lumber Company at Dean Brake about a mile north of town. This mill was also replaced.

The first bank in Ashley County opened there in 1900. Portland Bank began business with a capital stock of $20,000. J. D. Dean was president, and J. C. Bain was vice-president. Directors were D. B. Pugh, C. M. Matthews, T. R. Pugh, D. L. Bain, and J. A. Dean. Seven years later, the bank's assets were $114,857. People's Bank opened in January 1908 with J. C. Bain as president and E. J. Camak as vice-president. Other directors were D. L. Bain, J. A. Dean, Thomas P. M. Compere, W. T. Cone, and W. E. Dean. By March the total resources were $40,212. Both of these institutions persevered during the Great Depression and never closed their doors. "They closed the front door, but left the back door open," said Tom Pugh.

Three cotton gins dotted the town. Bain Gin Company, Jess Dean, and T. R. and J. W. Pugh owned them. The Bain Gin ceased operation around 1925, and the Dean Gin closed around 1930. The Pugh Mercantile Gin came under the ownership of J. W. Pugh after the death of T. R. Pugh in 1922. J. W. Pugh's grandsons, Benton and Joel Newcome and Robert D. Pugh, replaced this gin with Portland Gin Company in 1965. Henry Naff and T. R. Pugh's sons, Felix, Gus, and Joe, built Naff-Pugh Gin in 1926. The partnership was dissolved in 1954, and Hamp Pugh, Naff's son-in-law, operated this gin until around 1963. In 1954 Felix and Gus Pugh established Gus Pugh Gin Company. This company became Wilson-Pugh Gin in 1970 when Mrs. Sam Wilson, Frances Shackelford, and the daughters of Felix Pugh entered the partnership. Gus Pugh and his sons, Tom, George, and Augustus "Bubba", built GPS Gin Co. in 1977.

Portland Oil Mill, a cottonseed oil firm, began production in 1902. J. C. Bain was president and directors were D. B. Pugh, J. D. Dean, Justin Matthews, R. A. Pugh, A. C. Stanley, and J. A. Dean. It was called "the largest and finest between Pine Bluff and Monroe." [167] The oil mill warehouse, located behind J. W. Pugh Company, burned in August 1939, destroying 400 pounds of raw wood stored in it.[168] J. D. Dean established Dean & Co.'s Tannery in 1907. Managed by Fritz Lempke, a German harness maker, the tannery turned out harnesses, skirting, bridles, lace, and buckskins.

On August 7, 1907, fourteen structures burned during the most destructive fire the town ever witnessed. Destroyed were the buildings of J. W. Cammack, W. R. Roddy, D. L. Land, A. W. Cammack, Austin Estate, Portland Bank, Pugh Bros., J. D. Dean store, Mrs. H. A. Harris (hotel), G. A. Lindsey Drug Store, and the E. J. Christian Estate store. Two residences burned, one belonging to E. J. Camak. Pugh Bros. rebuilt with brick and opened under the new name of Pugh Mercantile Co. Bain & Co. also built a brick store that year.

Undaunted, the town continued to grow as more business ventures were established. Lining the west side of Main Street during the 1910s were Ed Wahl's grocery, Hawkins Dress Store, George Brown's City Drug, Cochran & Rogers Mercantile, Leroy Bain's drugstore, T. H. Hamm's grocery, Bain Mercantile, Boysen Grocery & Meat Market, Pugh Mercantile Co. (owned by T. R. & J. W. Pugh), Berry's hotel (above the Pugh store), Liggit's Drug Store, Cammack Mercantile, a warehouse, and The Leader (a discount outlet store owned by J. W. Pugh). The J. D. Dean store and Willie Dean's hardware store were on the east side of Main Street. Dr. Cone owned a boarding house and bakery. The yellow depot stood by the tracks in the center of town. Wright-Bachman Mill was in place just north of the present home of Bob Pugh. [169] J. J. Lowrey had a plumbing, roofing, and metal and tin working business by 1912.[170]

Even though the town's population averaged around 500, Portland had a swimming pool. An artesian well flowed generously, and many carried water from it to use for their laundry. Country folks hauled it home for drinking water. Mayor Leroy Bain had a 1,000-foot pipe driven into it in 1911. The Portland Bathing and Amusement Club was formed as a corporation in 1912 to finance a swimming pool that would use the well for its water supply. The pool, complete with dressing rooms, opened July 4 the same year. It was a well-frequented spot until the water level began to drop as more wells were driven. It eventually filled with sand and was abandoned. In March 1939 the water was tested and found to contain good medical qualities, but was unsuitable for domestic use. The pipe was pulled and sold to an oil company in El Dorado. Henry Naff then supervised repairs on the old pool, filled it with filtered city water and a chemical, and the pool opened again in June of the same year. It was abandoned again after a few years.[171]

Although Portland suffered a decline when the hardwood mills depleted their supply of timber and begin to move out after World War I, as well as during the early 1920 economic depression, more expansion continued until the Great Depression. Hugo H. and A. J. Gregory opened a mercantile. Herren & Cochran changed hands to become Cochran & Rogers, and a later division created W. W. Rogers Store and Cochran and Company. Dr. Cockerham established Portland Drug. Lem Hong took over Ed Wahl's grocery. Lester Peebles established a Chrysler-Plymouth dealership. Percy Trim and Petit Giles had cafes. Wells Hardware & Lumber Co., owned by Carl Wells, was still open in 1929.

The depression of the 1930s caused many concerns to flounder. As mechanized farming began to replace the dwindling tenant population after World War II and into the 1950s, the town's size began to decrease. T. R. Pugh Sons Company, owned by Felix, Joel Withers "Joe," and Gus Pugh stayed in business until 1963. Pugh & Company, owned by J. W. Pugh, closed in 1960. Cochran & Co., the last remaining large mercantile store, closed in 1966. The large farming interests continued, however, and the economy of the town remains stable.

Although Portland never had a hospital, qualified physicians continually served the populace. Dr. F. L. Sherrer, who began a practice at old Portland at the age of nineteen, graduated from the University of Alabama. His son, Fred Morrell Sherrer, followed in his footsteps and practiced there until his death in 1927. Dr. E. J. Christian moved to Portland in 1881 and practiced for two years before returning to Mobile to complete his training. He returned in 1884 and continued serving until his death. Arriving from Tulane Medical School around 1898 was Dr. Henry Enoch Cockerham. He married Mary Frances Pugh in 1899 and remained there until his death in 1952. Dr. Andrew E. Cone, born at nearby Snyder in 1876, was the last of the old-fashioned country doctors to serve the community. He died in 1958. Medical service is presently provided by Mainline Health Clinic.

The little one room school at Alligator Bluff was abandoned when the town moved, and children were soon attending school in a two-story, four-room frame building on Bain Avenue. Teachers at the new school were

Mrs. Margarite Withers, Tom Compere, Alle Pugh Roddy, and Irene Hope. This building became the masonic lodge after a fine new schoolhouse was completed in 1902. The large brick two-story building containing four classrooms had to be enlarged with an annex in 1907. A gymnasium was completed in 1930, and in 1947 an additional classroom building and a home economics and industrial arts building were added. A new school was built in 1966, and the old school, once labeled "the finest public building in Ashley County," was condemned and demolished. Serving as superintendents were Tom Compere, John Anders, Mr. McGuire, G. R. Wilson, Mrs. G. R. Wilson (taking her husband's position when he entered WWI), Mr. Montgomery, Mr. Marble, J. H. Hudson, B. F. Albright, H. O. Splawn, Frank Purifoy, B. F. Walker, Fred Greeson, H. S. Hopkins, and Lloyd Crossley.

Early teachers were Gertrude Bain, Jayne Rogers, Irene Hope (Mrs. Tom Compere), Miss Peak, Cleo Reeves, Jessie Ladd, Mae Boysen Lindsey, Mrs. Tracy, Mrs. Hayden, Freda Nutt, Mr. Camp, Hattie Bell Stewart, Zura Jones, Mrs. Adams, Mary Jane Higgs Wren, Hudson Wren, Clare Davis, Ike Laws, George Evelyn Cone, Mrs. Gerald Gay, Frances Devaney (Mrs. Sam Wilson), Clyde Ellis, Mabel Amburn, Agnes Ellis, Minnie Reah Ha Ha Jackson, Bessie Sherrer Thornton, Wanda Gary, Maxine Gary Cochran, Mildred Pamplin, Mrs. B. F. Albright, Dell Atkins Grantham, Robbie Nobel Hoggard, J. E. Hoggard, Mrs. Starr, Virginia Lee Cleveland, Dickie Bain Adams, Maude Hill, Mrs. Patterson, Mrs. Ellington, and Emma Mazanti.

Three elementary schools and a high school for blacks were built around 1907. The high school burned in the mid-1920s, and elementary grades went to classes in the Number Two Church until a new building was erected before 1930. Early teachers were Charles King (principal), A. J. Smith, Maude Green, Margaret Reed, Georgia Potte, Loula Potte, Mrs. Hubbard, Maggie Reed, Coretta Johnson, and Mrs. Fudge.

Pugh Bros. Co. deeded land on March 15, 1895, for a Methodist Episcopal Church, South. Trustees for the new church were E. J. Camak, A. L. Hollaway, and J. O. Bain. A one-room building was soon constructed when Rev. McClintock replaced Rev. Walsh as pastor in 1896. The frame building with a belfry faced south on Bain Street. The interior was furnished with a pulpit, choir stand, and oak benches. A hand pumped organ supplied the music and a pot-bellied stove or palmetto fans provided air-conditioning. Rev. J. R. Dickerson arrived in 1922 or 1923 and after preaching three sermons in the now leaking, dilapidated building, tore it down. The congregation met in the school during construction of a new building. Upon completion of the basement in 1924, services were held there. The first service was held in the new sanctuary in April 1926.

J. O. and Battie Bain and E. J. and Emma Christian gave land in 1892 for a Baptist church on Second Avenue. It is not known if a church was ever built there, but by 1910 the Baptist church owned land at its present location. Before the church was built, the congregation met in the lodge hall. A new church was dedicated on December 4, 1921. This church became a full-time church around 1940. When a new building was constructed in 1966, the original bell from the old church was hung in front of it.

The black community had a church at Free Negro Bend by around 1850 when the Carlock family donated land for Number Two Baptist Church. This church relocated to Portland in 1891 on land sold by Emit and Celia King. Trustees were Joe Louis, William Moore, Rev. George, Green Bridkly, Frank Brown, and Emit King. Located on the southern border of the town, the church moved in later years to a site donated by Gus Wilson for a church and cemetery. A log building was constructed across the road from Number Two Cemetery. A frame building, began in 1899 by Rev. Jeffery, was completed in 1901 when Rev. W. W. Booker was pastor. This building was replaced in 1965. The bell from the old church at Free Negro Bend hangs in the bell tower, which was erected in 1978 by the Robert Dean (Bob) Pugh family as a memorial to BeEssie Donaldson.

Green Grove AME Church was established in 1894 on land deeded by Emit and Celia King. Sam Simpson, Moses Bush, and Wesley Thonitue [? illegible] paid fifty dollars for the land located west of the compress. Travelers Rest Baptist Church was organized in 1898 on land also deeded by King in King's Addition. Providence Baptist Church was established about the same time on land deeded by Virginia Martin Wilson. Bain's Chapel AME Zion was located north of GPS Gin.[172]

Three properties in Portland are on the National Register of Historic Places. These are houses built by Jesse Dean, J. W. Pugh, and Henry Naff. Charles Thompson designed the Dean and Pugh homes. One mile west of the town, Portland Cemetery occupies the original cemetery site at Alligator Point. Below the cemetery is the location of the old swimming hole. Situated on a high bluff overlooking the bayou, aged markers stand in mute testimony to those who carved a settlement out of the wilderness.

∼✺✦✺∼

Free Negro Bend

Three miles below Portland, the bayou forms a large westward bend around Anthony Lake. First known as Horseshoe Lake, Mr. Raycroft was farming south of it by 1841 and had two neighbors, Brooks and Simms. Carlock Plantation was there by 1850 and was still in operation in 1879. Andrew Elijah Jackson Jr. bought 238 acres between 1856 and 1871.[173] T. A. Jackson of Hamburg owned land there in 1909.[174] Lamareaux Bloomer bought 318 acres at the north point of the bend in 1858. His land lay within the area of the Holly Point Post Office after it moved south from Portland. Henry Morschheimer owned a plantation there before the Civil War. His descendants, Henry, Louis, Charles, and Mrs. Edwin Gregory continued to manage the holdings. Dr. H. L. Anthony arrived in 1874 and established a plantation. In 1889 he owned 620 acres with 170 in cultivation.[175]

Lucius Webb deYampert established Sunshine Plantation around 1850. After the Civil War he gave forty acres each to his freed slaves.[176] John Lucius deYampert also began selling parcels to freed slaves, probably in connection with the Freedmen's Bureau. The area then became known as Free Negro Bend, a Reconstruction settlement. Early black families who lived there were those of Plato D. Ransom Sr., J. P. Ransom, George W. Gee, Peter Sims, Homer L. Johnson, Ned Moffatt, Joseph Dunn, and Birdner. Steve and John T. Wilson lived on the west side of the bayou. Although the descendants of some of these families still live there, most of the land ultimately reverted to white ownership.

Number 2 Baptist Church was established around 1850 on the Carlock Plantation and later relocated to Portland. St. Marion Missionary Baptist Church and Cemetery were located at the brake of the same name. The church was eventually moved to its present location on Highway 156. The cemetery contains many sunken, unmarked graves and was probably in use before the Civil War. Of the remaining marked stones, three bear prewar birth dates. Children attended school at this church as well as at Sunshine to the east and at Holly Grove, a black settlement west of the bayou.

Point Pleasant Post Office was established on the bayou in 1860 with Thomas B. Savage postmaster. It closed in 1868 with Martha C. Tebbs postmaster. Holly Point Post Office reestablished from its old Portland site in 1872 on the bayou about two miles northwest of Sunshine. Lamareaux Bloomer was postmaster, and the office was serving 300 families. Bloomer and Riley Currington owned ferries in "the Bend," as it is now called. A steamboat landing was located there. Plato Ransom Sr. owned a gin and store and provided overnight accommodations for farmers hauling cotton overland to Eudora.[177]

In the early 1930s people began to call Anthony Lake a different name. Bob Pugh explained, "There was a lot of interest then in the opening of King Tut's tomb in Egypt. Someone caught a big alligator or gar out of the lake and someone made the remark that it was so big it must have come from King Tut's tomb. Then they began calling the lake King Tut Lake. In the 1930s and 1940s fifty percent of the people called it that." Earl Bishop wrote that he did not know it was ever called anything but King Tut.

Sunshine

Sunshine, east of Free Negro Bend, was once a busy village with stores, cotton gin, lodge hall, and school. Daniel G. Owen, a lumberman from Michigan, opened up a sawmill there in 1880. By 1889 he was milling 5,000 to 6,000 feet of cypress daily.[178] George Beltz located American Spur Sawmill there in the early 1900s and built a camp for the hands. Dr. H. L. Anthony settled there in 1874. W. L. Blanks, J. C. Bain, Henry Naff, William deYampert II, and Dr. H. E. Cockerham owned later farms in the area. Sunshine was a rail stop for lumber and cotton.

Sunshine Post Office opened in 1887 and closed in 1916. Primarily inhabited by blacks, Glasco King was the first postmaster and the office was in his store.[179] King was afforded an education by a deYampert as a result of an accident on his plantation. When he was nine years old, his shirt got caught in the gin equipment, and his arm was injured. Blood poisoning ensued, and the arm had to be amputated at the shoulder. After keeping the boy in his house for a year, deYampert sent him to Corbin School in Pine Bluff. Glasco King became a schoolteacher and preacher and was the first black to be appointed justice of the peace in Ashley County. He was influential in bettering the lives of his contemporaries. He stated before he died that he wanted everyone he had taught to put a shovel of dirt on his grave. "When he died in 1942, there was a line of people two hundred yards long at St. Marion's," said Herman King.[180]

Mr. Barrow owned a store and blacksmith shop. Later James Williams and James Hall owned stores. Hall's store closed around 1953. Two churches, Freewill Baptist and Baptist Missionary, served the black community. A two-story lodge hall for the Knights of Pythias also served as a church and school building. Teachers at Sunshine Chapter School were Glasco King, R. Porter King, Monroe Harris, and Homer L. Johnson. Black landowners in the area were Barrow, Isaac Armstrong, Brisco Wilson, John Nelson, and Bruin Jackson. Sam and Gus Wilson established Sunshine Plantation in 1936 on land bought from Bruin Jackson. Pecan groves indicating the Cockerham farm site and a lone railroad sign are the only visible remaining signs of this village.[181]

⁂

Poplar Bluff, Parkdale

The bayou continues on its southward path and makes a long eastward bend to go through Parkdale. The original settlement there was Poplar Bluff on the east bank of the bayou. In 1857 John Tillman Hughes erected a mercantile store at the steamboat landing, and this was the beginning of the new town. Hughes was born around 1826 in Georgia, the son of George D. Hughes who migrated to Union County, Arkansas, before 1857.

John Tillman Hughes married Mariah Louisa Cole in Ashley County in 1856. She was the daughter of William G. Cole who came to Ashley County from Alabama around 1842 and moved to Union County by 1850.

John William Morris, born in 1841 in North Carolina, came with his father, William Morris, to Beech Creek Township west of Poplar Bluff in 1848. At age sixteen, John William Morris began clerking in the Hughes store and lived with the Hughes family. After service in the Confederate Army, he returned to the family farm before the war was over and in 1866 moved to a farm on the bayou at Poplar Bluff. The same year he engaged in a business with a Mr. White.[182] Morris evidently bought land there by 1862 as he paid taxes in Poplar Bluff that year. In 1868 he established his own mercantile store at Poplar Bluff. By 1878 he was in partnership with Isaac Cohen doing business as Morris & Cohen. They advertised "dry goods, boots, shoes, hats, bagging, ties, and general plantation supplies."[183]

The area became moderately populated before the Civil War. John W. Harris arrived before 1850 and managed bayou farms that belonged to his uncle. He went to California seeking gold in 1850 and returned two years later. He married Mrs. Martha Gregory and became a wealthy farmer, owning 1,200 acres of land on Bayou Bartholomew. William L. Butler came in 1856 and bought land that he farmed until returning to Alabama in 1860. After serving in the Confederate Army, where he achieved the rank of colonel, he returned to his Poplar Bluff land in 1866. His plantation grew to contain five hundred acres in cultivation. Major Lavelle Butler was mayor of Parkdale during Reconstruction.[184]

Archibald Crawford Nobles moved to Beech Creek around 1858 and in 1862 settled on the bayou one mile south of the town. John Sims Barnes arrived in 1857. His daughter, Susan Rebecca, married Nobles' son, James Samuel "Jim." The Barnes farm lay south of the town and included over 2,000 acres. Barnes built a horse-powered gin and later installed a steam gin. The boiler from the steam gin could still be seen in 1940. Hosea George moved from Union County, Arkansas, to Bayou Bartholomew in 1857 and engaged in farming. His son, Gaston P. George, carried on the family farm and added to it, eventually owning around 1,000 acres with 375 in cultivation. Gaston George entered the mercantile business in 1887 or 1888 with William T. Harris, his brother-in-law. In 1889 Harris & George carried a stock of $2,000 and grossed $12,000 annually. William T. Harris moved to the area with his siblings and mother, Mrs. S. L. Harris, in 1862. After serving in the Confederate Army for a few years, he returned to Poplar Bluff and became a farmer. In 1889 he owned 240 acres with 150 in cultivation. John M. Sherrer came to Poplar Bluff in 1859 and lived there until his death in 1868. His son, F. L. Sherrer, was a physician at Portland.[185]

Settlement continued after the Civil War. Captain James P. Clark, who came to the county in 1854, established a plantation on Gum Ridge near Parkdale soon after the war. He served as sheriff of the county from 1886 to 1894. Ten-year old Thomas L. Atkin arrived in 1867 with his mother (formerly Mrs. David Atkin) and stepfather. When he was twenty-three years old he purchased 120 acres and began a successful farming undertaking. He owned a steam gin and a small merchandising business. Robert D. Radford settled there in 1872. After farming in Extra and DeBastrop Townships for six years, he entered an equal partnership with W. L. Blanks to form Radford & Blanks, a mercantile. He also owned 260 acres on nearby Gum Ridge with 150 acres in cultivation in 1889.

Jason C. Hill came from Louisiana in 1874 and rented the Moore place. After farming it for five years, he bought 80 acres to which he later added another 160. He also owned a gin and gristmill. The family lived at Poplar Bluff. His brother, Reuben, also settled in Ashley County.[186] William Sanford Fuller, who married Mary Elizabeth "Johnnie" Stanley, owned a farm in DeBastrop Township by 1880. His wife was born at Wilmot in 1867. Their first two children were born at Wilmot in 1887 and 1888 and both were buried at Parkdale in 1888. Their other three children were born at Parkdale from 1890 to 1896. Moving there in 1887 was Columbus C. Wolfe, whose father, Philip S. Wolfe, settled in Drew County in the 1840s. The Wolfe family lived at Poplar Bluff and had around sixty-five acres in cultivation. Wolfe's daughter, Ella, married Frank Barnes. Jesse Thomas Files farmed a section of land in the bend of the bayou north of Poplar Bluff by the 1880s. His son, William Thomas Files Sr., continued to oversee the farm in later years. Both men engaged in the mercantile trade at Parkdale. William Thomas Files Jr. eventually farmed this land and was also a Parkdale merchant.[187]

Lake Enterprise Post Office was created in 1856 in the Wilmot area. On July 18, 1860, the name was changed to Poplar Bluffs (the *s* spelling was never used) with John Tillman Hughes as postmaster. A grove of poplar trees stood on the bayou bluff near where Leroy Gardner later lived. The last poplar tree from this grove fell around 1995. When the railroad came in 1890, the post office name changed to Parkdale because freight shipments were being confused with Poplar Bluff, Missouri.[188]

Poplar Bluff incorporated in January 1889 becoming the second incorporated town in the county. R. M. Roberts was mayor; Frank Barnes was marshal; and the population was around two hundred. Mercantile firms at this time were J. W. Morris, Radford & Blanks, and Harris & George. H. C. Dade owned a grocery store. A gin and gristmill were in operation with from 3,000 to 4,000 bales of cotton being produced annually. Fraternal orders at this time were the masons, Knights of Pythias, and Order of Eastern Star.

J. W. Morris owned the largest mercantile, which carried a $10,000 stock and was grossing $60,000 in 1889. The steamboat landing was in front of his store, which was where Edwin Gregory later lived. Steamboats also stopped at Nobles' Landing south of the town. Also in the trade on the banks were saloons. "Blind Tigers were on the bayou at Poplar Bluff," said Ernestine Nobles Sprinkle. Cross & Banny were running a large sawmill on the bayou two miles upstream by 1889.[189]

Robinson Ferry provided transit across the bayou where the old road between Grand Lake and Hamburg intersected the road running north and south on the east side of the bayou. This site is just west of Childress Chapel. The location became known as Old Ferry when a new ferry was installed in town at present Highway 8. The first bridge was constructed in 1910 and could be turned to allow passage for the boats. Cecil Kelly found wooden piers, planks, and nails in a gully just north of the present bridge, indicating the probable site of the first bridge.[190]

A Missionary Baptist Church organized in 1857. A two-story building erected at the cemetery in the 1850s most likely served this congregation as well as the Methodists. In the 1870s the Baptists built a two-story frame structure at the cemetery. The second story was used for the lodge hall, and the first story was used for the church and school. The congregation made an unsuccessful effort to revive the church around 1907 and decided to sell it. Dr. B. F. Holiday bought the building for a hundred dollars. The following year Parkdale Methodist Church was organized in the old Methodist church. Founding members were Mr. and Mrs. J. S. Barnes, Mr. and Mrs. J. H. Bell, Mr. and Mrs. J. A. Cockrell, Mrs. L. B. Cockrell, N. T. Foster, Mr. and Mrs. T. L. Nichols, R. H. Nichols, Mrs. W. S. Nichols, Inez Nichols, Mr. and Mrs. W. A. Pierce, Noble Daniel, and Mrs. F. A. Barnes. Sunday School was held in the school building until a church was erected in 1910 on property donated by Norwood George. The first ministers were Rev. M. N. Deloach from Crossett and Dr. A. J. Fawcett of Hamburg. Rev. T. M. McGehee came in 1912. Other early pastors were Otto Mathis (1914), N. C. Denson (1918), F. N. Carter (1920), L. T. Gutheric (1921), A. A. Weeks, (1922), W. O. Taylor (1925), J. A. McKinney (1929), A. D. Langston (1929), Gearing, New, Wade Hopkins, (1937), Keith Babb (1939), Clanton ((1941), Claud Hughes ((1947), and Heartsall Atwood (1951.) The building was remodeled in 1925 with the upstairs balcony being turned into a second story.[191] The charming structure still stands as one of the town's historic buildings.

The Methodist Episcopal Church, South moved from the cemetery in the late 1800s into a new log church north of where N. P. Atkins later lived. A third church was built in 1904 under the leadership of Rev. J. R. Dickerson on land and with lumber donated by Mr. and Mrs. John W. Morris. Dickerson oversaw the building of the present church in 1926 on land donated by Mr. and Mrs. C. C. Morschheimer. The concrete blocks were molded and cured on site. The lumber from the dismantled church was used to build Green Grove Church for the black community on Morschheimer's farm.[192]

Parkdale Cemetery, located on the bayou at the south edge of town, is on land given by a freed slave, according to Mary Morris Foster. Her grandmother told her that anyone could be buried there and that no lots were ever sold. A cemetery and church for African-Americans was located to the south of the white cemetery. It is now abandoned and overgrown, and no markers are present. Thomas Compere Sr. gave land on the bayou west of town for Childress Chapel and Cemetery.[193]

The first public school was built around 1884 on the north side of town at the edge of a cypress brake. This was a one-room frame building where around thirty students attended three months a year. Classes were held there for about eight years. After the railroad came, this building was torn down and rebuilt across the track at the northeast corner of town. A private school was held in the living room of the W. E. Barnes house. A school was later built outside of the town limits near the home of S. O. Savage. Children then attended Savage School for three months and went to the school in town for an additional three months. School was held in the Methodist Church until a two-story frame school was built in 1908. This school became the first nine-month school. It was torn down in 1917 and a brick structure built in its place. The first "school hack" (hired driver and vehicle) in the state was instituted when Dry Bayou School consolidated with Parkdale. Ernestine Nobles Sprinkle said that the first school was on land owned by H. S. Hill. "It was called the Grove. Political meetings and barbecues were held there," she said. This site was apparently near the old baptizing site off Grove Street. The first school for black children was Savage Grammar School.[194]

When the railroad came, merchants abandoned their bayou location and moved a few blocks east to the railroad, and new buildings soon lined the west side of the track. Other entrepreneurs soon joined them. Parkdale Bank was open by 1905. L. W. Perdue and M. C. Hawkins, M. D. were dealers in drugs and druggist's sundries by the first decade of the 1900s. T. L. Nichols and J. J. Daniel were doing business as Nichols & Daniel by 1907. They advertised as a cash dealership in general merchandise. Finch Bros. Pharmacy was in operation by 1909. A. C. Blanks and W. E. Barnes had a general merchandise store by 1911. Nichols Brothers owned a mercantile by 1912. Caldwell & Bell opened an auction house for general merchandise in 1912. M. R. White published a newspaper, the *Parkdale News*, for a few years beginning in 1900. The Parkdale Telephone Exchange was in place by 1912, and phone service for one month cost $3.50. Bob Acres managed the company. Arkansas Power and Light supplied the town with electricity around 1927, and a water system was installed in 1930.[195]

Some of the many stores during the 1920s-1930s were W. L. Dew, W. T. Files General Merchandise, Slocum Furniture, John Howard Nobles Sr. Merchandise, J. H. Caldwell (stayed in business until around 1978), Franklin Smith (later Ozelle and Walter Morris), Sam Wiseman (a women's clothing store later owned by H. S. Hill), T. W. Echols, Gregory & Jackson (later E. D. Gregory Co. and until recently owned and operated by Carl Dean Miller), Radford & Guice, Percy Morris, C. C. Morschheimer, McCraken Grocery & Market, John Ralph, and John W. Morris. South of the stores was a two-story Negro Masonic and Eastern Star building. In the same area was the calaboose. "It was a little square wooden building with four little windows with bars," remembered Mary Morris Foster. East of the tracks were Saline Grocery Wholesale and Hayes Store (later owned by Buatt). Herman Morris was dealing in general merchandise in the 1940s. J. D. Guice's father had a blacksmith shop, and Ed Murphy owned a service station. A two-story hotel was located behind the station. The old depot was moved to the Parkdale Gin lot where it was used as a warehouse until it burned around 1993.[196]

J. K. Barnes, J. T. Ralph and E. D. Gregory owned gins. The Gregory Gin is now a cooperative operating as Parkdale Gin and is the only remaining gin in the town. In September 1939 Parkdale was ginning more cotton than other area towns. Parkdale gins had turned out 2,600 bales and was followed by Portland (2,350), Wilmot (1,850), and Montrose (950). Kellough Lumber Company moved to Monroe during the 1930s. Rainer sawmill was located north of town. It was later bought by Bowden and continued to operate until the early 1950s. Herman Morris and William T. Files had the Amuse-U Theater for a few years. William T. Files Jr. opened a John Deere dealership in 1937 and continued this business until 1950. From 1952 to 1959 he owned a Massey-Harris dealership.[197]

Several colored "joints" were east of the track. C-Berg, managed by Tom Rowen and later by Rabbit Parker, was one of the most frequented. Richard Robinson operated one of these honkytonks by the Caldwell store. "You could hear the music all over town," said Ernestine Sprinkle. Mark Hawkins, born in 1938, could "barely remember" the many saloons in the town. The white men also simply gathered in the stores for their recreation. "The older folks said that all the old stores had a back room where the men met to drink and gamble," he said. The town also had a liquor store until the early 1960s.

The first known physician at Poplar Bluff was Dr. Reece, who organized a company for the Confederate Army there in 1861. Dr. Benjamin F. Holiday was practicing by the early 1900s. He was married to Mary Frances Morris, daughter of John William Morris. Dr. Holiday was killed while driving a team of horses across the bayou bridge. "My father told me that they went wild and jumped off the bridge," related Mark Hawkins. Dr. Charles Parkel opened a practice before 1898. Dr. Robert G. Williams also had a practice. Dr. Martin Cassetty Hawkins was the next physician to serve the town. After graduating from the University of Louisville School of Medicine in 1893 he went to Texas. In 1895 he began a practice in Parkdale that continued until his death in 1953. Although he bought his first automobile in 1912, he continued to call on patients in the remote countryside by horseback or buggy for several years.[198]

Fire destroyed part of the town in early April 1940. Two buildings and a barn owned by Dr. R. G. Williams burned. H. P. Buatt Grocery & Market occupied one building, and the other contained Williams' fertilizer, cotton, and cottonseed business. Buatt quickly rented the C. C. Morschheimer store building at the north end of Main Street. By June, Williams rebuilt these stores using brick, and Buatt moved back to his original location.[199] Several smaller fires later consumed other Main Street buildings and still others were destroyed by a tornado in 1990.

Parkdale Chemical Co., until recently owned by Mark Hawkins, had its warehouse on the old Hawkins drugstore site and its office in the old theater building. Properties on the National Register are the Dr. M. C. Hawkins house, built in 1911 and owned by Mark Hawkins, and the Dr. Robert George Williams house, presently owned by C. A. Bawcom. The oldest structure in the town is probably the old Frank Barnes house, which was built in the 1870s by Archibald Nobles.

Parkdale was still a lively town in the middle 1950s. "We still had five or six grocery stores then and still had tenant farmers. It was so crowded on Saturday nights, you could not get up and down the streets," said Mark Hawkins. "It was lively until the seventies, and then everybody just left," declared Ernie Sprinkle. Although the business district is deserted now, the residential section reaching to Bayou Street along the bayou retains a tranquil, appealing atmosphere reflective of the past.

❦

Hawkins Landing, Lake Enterprise (Old Wilmot)

The bayou leaves Parkdale to curve through open farmland for three miles before reaching Lake Enterprise at Wilmot. Hawkins Landing is shown on early maps south of Lake Enterprise in 1854 and near present Wilmot in 1863. John L. Hawkins became the first postmaster on December 16, 1845. He also farmed and owned a gristmill, gin, and store. Thomas Kimbrough succeeded Hawkins as postmaster in 1851. The office moved to Line, Louisiana, in 1854 with Thomas M. Jones as postmaster. Hawkins Landing Post Office moved to its former location in 1866 and closed the next year. James W. Hawkins, son of John L.

Hawkins, was born at Hawkins Landing in 1846 and joined the firm of Files & Morris in 1866 "at the rejuvenated office of Hawkins Landing."[200]

Lake Enterprise Post Office opened in 1856 with Thomas Clower as postmaster. Archibald Calhoun became the next postmaster in 1858. This post office relocated to Poplar Bluff in 1860 with a name change. The next post office to serve the area was Bartholomew, located two miles to the north in 1880. This post office relocated to Wilmot in 1892, and the name became Wilmot. Rachel L. Allen was postmaster and her sister, Mattie M. Allen, succeeded her in October. Lightfoot Post Office was two miles west of bayou from 1906 to 1911 with Mollie Stokes, a black, as postmaster. Another area post office was Savage, which existed from 1899 to 1904 in Section 21 to the southwest. The name of Hawkins Landing Post Office in Morehouse Parish changed back to Line and changed again to Cypress in 1890. At this time the office moved back into Ashley County, near the state line, in 27-19S-5W. This office was discontinued in 1907.[201]

Joseph H. Williamson, a justice of the peace for Chicot County, which then stretched west to the bayou, was living on Lake Enterprise in 1841. An 1844 map of the area shows "Williamson's Farm and Cotton Gin" on the bayou at the south end of Lake Enterprise. John T. Carnahan, born in Chicot County in 1849, the son of J. T. and Elizabeth (Bird) Carnahan, was living at Bartholomew in 1889. He owned a gin at Ohio Landing and a sawmill "in the swamp." His wife was Mattie Summer. Dr. Ben F. Moore came to Bartholomew immediately after the Civil War and practiced medicine. He also had a 125-acre farm that was worked on shares. When Grant Township formed in 1889 on the west side of the bayou, the voting place was set at "Moore's Store at Bartholomew." Dr. James Dean settled on a plantation west of Wilmot before 1850 and died there in 1858. His neighbor across the bayou to the east was J. D. Bragg, who also owned a plantation. Bragg served as state legislator and is buried in an unmarked grave at Parkdale.[202]

David Milton Grant and his wife, Nancy C. Waitts, moved from Georgia in 1851 and settled across and down the bayou from Wilmot at what would become known as Grants Ferry. Grant Township was named after this man. He owned a large farm and was the largest taxpayer in the township. The Grant name did not continue as his son, John Milton, was killed in the Civil War, and his other son, Joseph Pinckey, died soon after his marriage to Alice Dean. One daughter, Elizabeth married Samuel Watkins, and his other daughter, Mary Frances, married Thomas Stanley. After returning from service in the Confederate Army, Thomas Stanley farmed and owned a gin on the bayou. Buried in the Grant Cemetery (on the present Fred Montgomery place) are David and Nancy Grant, Elizabeth (Grant) and Samuel Watkins, and Althena Beard (daughter of Thomas and Frances Stanley and wife of W. B. Beard).[203]

The African Methodist Society organized Shady Grove African Methodist Church in 1886 with Rev. Sherman Green as pastor. The congregation met in a one-room school building on the east bank of the bayou. Membership increased, and in 1898 the members built a church. The black community organized the First Baptist Church in 1888. White residents attended church at nearby Gaines.[204]

❧❦❧

Wilmot

When the railroad reached the settlement in 1890, John T. Allen, father of the aforementioned postmasters, already had a store on the bayou northwest of the depot and near the present bridge. One or two other stores were also at this location. The steamboat landing was north of the present bridge at the old Owensteen place, which is now owned by Jim Johnson. More merchants followed the railroad. William B. deYampert II and J. W. McGarry established deYampert & McGarry, a mercantile, in a frame building on the south edge of town. W. T. and A. B. Cone built Cone & Company on the bank of Lake Enterprise west of the depot. Dr. E. O. McDermott came with the railroad as its physician and tie contractor. He opened a mercantile store in 1893 and operated it until his death when it was taken over by his son, Harry McDermott. Dave and Oscar Brown were later merchants.[205] Addie Claire Neely Holt moved to the town around 1894 to teach music. Her husband, John Thomas Holt, worked at the railroad yard.[206]

David Rankin Perkins, a black, came to Wilmot at its beginning from Jones, Louisiana, where he was teaching school in the summer and attending Alcorn College in Mississippi during fall and winter. With a partner, he established Perkins & Douglas, one of the first mercantile stores in the town. He and his wife, Mattie Martin, both taught school. He also established a farm and served as rural mail carrier for many years. All five of their children graduated from college and entered professions. Three became teachers and one was a physician. A son, John, returned and taught in Wilmot and Parkdale. He later began operating the family farm.[207]

Although the town was named for or by the railroad surveyor, the actual founder was J. W. Harris. He bought land before the railroad came and then sold it in parcels. He also had a large farm and was a moneylender. Signing the petition for incorporation in 1896 were: Dr. E. O. McDermott, W. L. Bell, L. T. Murphy, W. A. Brame, J. D. Kinnabrew, H. W. Walker, Mary Allen, Robert Cofton, P. B. Burnside, William Harris, Dr. J. M. Chambers, Mrs. E. Brown, J. W. Price, B. B. Statton, Tom Allen, D. Braswell, R. C. Norris, A. F. Brame and Co., J. B. Allen, A. E. Jackson, D. E. Watson, H. Smith, deYampert & McGarry, Cone & Co., George F.

Barnett, Douglas & Perkins, J. W. Harris, James Jones, and W. P. Mosely.[208]

Arriving in 1899 were the Brame brothers: Jefferson Davis "Jeff," Augustus Foster, Walter Acker, William Milan, Henry Davis, and Thomas Quitman. Jeff and A. F. Brame built a large mercantile store. They constructed a large brick vault in the back of the building and operated a private bank until it failed around 1909. This building still stands and is known as Janes Store. After the bank failed, four of the brothers, Jeff, A. F., Walter, and Henry, moved to Seminole, Oklahoma, and established businesses. Jeff Brame moved back to Wilmot in 1911 and opened a new mercantile. J. D. Brame Jr. continued to manage the store for many years. Jeff Brame and his son, J. D. Jr., served as mayor. J. D. Brame's daughter, LaDell, married J. D. Brown, a Wilmot native who owned a store.[209]

Beautiful Lake Enterprise provided a scenic backdrop for the new town that built east of the railroad. A roundhouse stood at the present location of the John B. Currie home. An oil mill was built by 1902, and Arthur Wooten's father arrived that year to work in the mill. A saloon opened the same year. Ed Franklin arrived in 1902 with his sister and nephew. His brother, Tillon, had come before him. Ed Franklin's grandsons, Les and James Franklin, became area farmers. Earl Newton joined the mercantile firm of deYampert & McGarry. A shingle mill owned by deYampert & NcGarry was located by the lake. Cypress was logged from the lake, and during periods of low water, the stumps as well as piles of shingles are still visible.[210]

Wilmot Bank opened in 1906 with W. B. deYampert II as president and A. M. Keller as cashier. Major stockholders were deYampert, Keller, J. W. Harris (Keller's father-in-law), Mrs. Molenkoff (Harris' daughter), and Walter Davies. Keller eventually bought out the deYampert interest. This bank failed during the Depression in 1933, and Keller went to work for the deYampert mercantile. "The corresponding bank was A. B. Banks in Foydyce. When it went broke, forty banks in Arkansas went with it," explained John B. Currie. Citizens Bank was in business for a few years with Jack Burns, president; A. E. Jackson, principal stockholder; and L. W. Perdue, cashier. It liquidated around 1925. Jack Burns was successor to McDermott's tie contracting business. Wilmot State Bank was organized in 1937. Major stockholders were Willie Wilhite, Sam Wilson, J. B. Shackelford, G. B. Stovall, Dr. M. C. Crandall, Edward Dunning, Mary Virginia deYampert, and William B. deYampert III. This bank continued until recent times when it was acquired by SouthEast Arkansas Bank (now Delta Trust).[211]

By 1911 J. C. Kistler built a theater. Growth continued and by 1912 the population was around a thousand. Advertising itself as "The Queen City of the Bartholomew Valley," the town had a newspaper, a deep well was nearing completion, a large drainage effort was underway, and a new school was in place. Plans were being made for a water works, electric lights, and "a woodworking plant and large new gin are practically assured." City officials were J. R. Byrd, mayor; B. B. Statton, recorder; R. R. Lashlee, marshal; and J. B. Burns, A. F. Wooten, and C. L. Hill, aldermen.[212]

Prominent in business and professions at this time were W. B. deYampert II, E. J. Newton, Dr. E. O. McDermott, A. M. Keller, Dr. A. D. Knott, Ben C. Tiller, Dr. H. N. Princehouse, Edward J. Doyle, J. C. Kistler, Dave Brown, Harold A. Keith, and DeWitt Talmadge Henderson. A. M. Keller, W. B. deYampert, and Dr. McDermott dealt in real estate. Average deposits in the Wilmot Bank were $150,000. McGarry and Byrd owned a mercantile. Fong Ginn and Fritz Schwendimann owned grocery stores. Other businesses were Wilmot Motor Company (owned by the Smith brothers), Wilmot Ice & Fuel, William Smith's Fixit Shop, Bell Gasoline and Oil Company, Clifford and Bragg deYampert's store, and W. L. Perdue Drug Store. Mrs. Anna Jones operated a restaurant and meat market, and Albert Taylor had a butcher shop. Fred Haberyan was a local contractor for staves, stave bolts, hickory billets, wagon axles, and other wood stock. Dr. E. O. McDermott opened a new furniture store that also carried coffins and burial supplies. William L. Fuller, grandson of David M. Grant, owned a Sinclair service station.[213]

The train stopped to unload and load stock. W. N. Wilhite owned a livery stable and dealt in the horse, mule, and cattle trade. Wilhite and William deYampert were still shipping cattle from there in the late 1940s. John June Gibson came in 1917 and was in the horse and cattle business. One of the first stock dealers in Wilmot was Ben Miller, who lived at nearby Dry Bayou. John Henry Walker Jr. recalled the excitement created when mule shipments were unloaded for Wilhite in the late 1930s and early 1940s. "When the mules were being moved to his barn, everyone in town would rush to get to see John Metcalf as he herded the mules. He would lead 35 or 40 mules on horseback. The mules would follow him while he rode his horse in the lead. When she [his horse] came off the railroad tracks, the horse would rear up and walk on her hind feet. From right off the tracks, all across the highway – on her hind feet! It was amazing to see. John would be holding the reins and that big horse would be reared up and prancing across the highway, surrounded by [the] mules."[214]

The Commercial Hotel, a large brick structure owned and managed by Dr. and Mrs. E. O. McDermott stood on the bank of Lake Enterprise. After Mrs. McDermott retired, the A. B. Cone family ran this hotel. A hotel located two doors east of the Methodist church reopened in 1912. The advertisement stated, "Arrivals on the night train will know the house by the red light." A Mr. Hughes was managing a hotel there in the late 1940s.[215]

Lawrence & Hudson had the City Barber Shop and Pool Hall in 1922. By 1924 the town was still progressing. Carl Wells established Wells Hardware & Lumber Company and also owned a furniture store, gin, and grain elevator. The oil mill owned Hammett Grocery, a wholesale business. Officers of the company were S. C. Alexander, president; A. W. Nunn, vice-president; and C. D. Rutledge, manager. Managing Wilmot Mercantile were Dave Brown, president; W. C. Carter, vice-president; and Oscar Brown, secretary-treasurer. Wilmot Drug Co. was in business and featured a soda fountain. H. J. Harker managed the Corner Café. William B. deYampert's mercantile was in a brick building. His plantation included 4,000 acres of cotton and 1,000 acres of corn. Mayor was A. M. Keller. C. E. Larrison built an icehouse in 1925 that stayed in operation until 1960.[216]

A golf course was in place by 1930. "I think it was built around 1922," said John B. Currie. "The greens were sand with oil on them and they were fenced to keep the cows and their droppings off. The ways were unfenced and the cows kept them grazed down." Currie told the story of a mysterious man, Lee Edwards, who frequented the golf course during the 1930s. "People thought he may have been a gangster hiding out. He had a lot of money, drove a big car, and built a big log house out on the lake. He played golf all the time and called himself a golf pro. He stayed around for a long time and then just disappeared."[217]

Frank and Brigita Janes migrated from Yugoslavia and settled in East Carroll Parish, Louisiana, where they owned a plantation, timberland, and a sawmill. With the onslaught of the Great Depression, Janes gave his land away and sold his company. He came to Wilmot and bought a grocery store with money he obtained by pawning his wife's three-carat diamond ring. Janes Store continued in business until the early 1990s. It was later managed by Buddy and Catherine Janes and finally by Tommy Janes.[218]

After suffering through the years of the Great Depression, Wilmot continued to make progress during the following decade. Owning large mercantile stores in the 1940s were Benton and Jim Cone, W. B. deYampert II, Leslie M. Tullos, and Herman S. Brown. J. D. Brame, Harry McDermott, and G. B. Stovall owned dry good stores. Bernice Smith, Fritz Schwendimann, Fong Ginn, and Anna Steed, a black, owned groceries. The oil mill and Hammet Wholesale continued in business. William B. deYampert II opened a John Deere dealership and had a groundhog sawmill. John Kidwell installed a sawmill on the bayou bank in the 1930s, and his son, J. T. Kidwell, continued running it during the 1940s. Gins were owned by W. B. deYampert, Gus Pugh (Wilmot Gin), and R. C. Wells. Wells Hardware was still in business. Lee Foster managed the Strand Theater, which was owned by the Kistler family. Tanner "Cowboy" Hayden operated Cowboy's Barber Shop, and Bonnie Denham ran a boarding house. Bell's Pool Hall and Domino Parlor provided a gathering place for the men. Bell also managed a hotel.[219]

Wilmot's first newspaper, the *Wilmot Weekly,* published its first issue on April 11, 1912. J. P. Doyle, who was from Wisconsin, owned it. Doyle soon sold the paper to a group of local businessmen. A. M. Keller became manager with Edward H. Dunning as editor and D. T. Henderson as associate editor. The paper was discontinued for an interval during World War I. John P. Hosmer revived it in 1920 and continued publishing until he sold it to the *Ashley County Ledger* in 1933. The *Weekly East Ashley Enterprise* was established in 1938 by Nathan Bolton, publisher of the *Morehouse Enterprise,* a Bastrop newspaper. D. D. Tilbury was editor during the early 1940s. This paper merged with the *Crossett Observer* in 1946.[220] Ida Margaret Newton established the *Delta News,* which ran from March 9, 1939 to December 19, 1940.

A $12,800 contract for a new school building was given in 1908 to W. J. Doyle. The two-story brick structure was completed in 1911 for a cost of $17,500. At a school board meeting in May 1912, J. A. Burns was reelected president; A. F. Brame resigned from his position as secretary, and B. B. Staton was elected as secretary. Dr. M. C. Crandall served on the school board from 1927 to 1967. A public school for blacks was built in 1909 at a cost of $400, which included the tearing down of an old school building on the bayou. The new structure was 30x50 feet. Before this time school was held in houses or churches. The earliest known school was on the Leach Plantation in 1884 with A. J. Smith as teacher. The following year Rev. E. D. Washington became the teacher, and the school moved to the John Wesley AME Zion Church.[221]

Wilmot Colored School burned in 1941, and classes were held in churches and the Masonic Hall until a new school was built in 1948. This was the first nine-month school and the first high school. William C. Slack was the first principal of Wilmot Colored High School and Mrs. Margaret LeGrande was second. Seven students graduated in 1948. The name changed in 1960 to Slack-LeGrande High School, and in 1970 the school closed. William C. Slack was born in Parkdale in 1893, the son of Betty Elizabeth (Jones) and William Beauregard Slack. William Beauregard Slack was born in 1870 in Parkdale, the son of Mary Robinson, a Negro, and John Slack, who was a white physician. William B. Slack's mother died when he was very young, and his father moved to Monroe, Louisiana. A white family in Hamburg adopted him, and he received some schooling. William C. Slack graduated from Branch Normal College (later AM&N and UAPB) at Pine Bluff in 1926 with high honors. His first teaching job was at Dry Bayou in 1922. Professor Slack, as he was known, used his education to freely help members of the black community. The W. C. Slack Memorial Park in Wilmot was dedicated in his honor in 1992.[222]

The first church in the area was west of Wilmot near the Gaines Community. A Methodist circuit rider with the Bartholomew Circuit, Dr. Winfield, was serving in 1851. Mt. Gilead Methodist Church was eventually established at Gaines. The congregation later joined the Wilmot Methodists, who met first in Old Union Church. Among the early families associated with this church were Lural S. Eatmon (Eatman), Walter Brame, Ben Staton, Ed Jones, A. E. Jackson, W. B. deYampert II, and A. M. Keller. By 1900 the church was a halftime church with Parkdale and at later times was associated with Portland and Lake Village. The church acquired fulltime status in 1919.[223]

Rev. N. C. Denson organized Wilmot Baptist Church in 1908, and in the following year the church became part of the Bartholomew Baptist Association. The congregation also met in the Union Church until they completed a building soon after the 1927 flood. The black community organized the First Baptist Church in 1888 with Rev. Charlie Hicks as pastor. The first deacons were B. Bozeman, Spencer Hicks, and Emmett King. Following Rev. Hicks as pastor were: T. B. Hillard, Rev. Sims, Jessie Carter, T. C. Greggs, W. W. Booker, D. Hoston, C. W. Russell, Rev. Suggs, A. D. Ford, and James Crockett.[224]

The African Methodist Society organized Shady Grove African Methodist Church in 1886 with Rev. Sherman Green as pastor. The congregation met in a one-room school building on the east bank of the bayou. Membership increased, and in 1898 the members built a church. J. B. Gabe was a member at this time. This building was replaced in 1933, and a new church was built in 1954. Trustees in 1933 were Andrew J. Lee, P. H. Holmes, D. R. Perkins, P. B. Clayborne, Lonnie Wilder, Pearl Bowden, Emmon Harrison, and W. M. Bowden. Rev. J. W. Nelson was pastor.[225] Other African-American churches are John Wesley AME Zion, Second Baptist, and Sweethome Baptist.

Miller's Chapel, a Methodist institution, served the community of Dry Bayou, a few miles east of Wilmot. Buried in nearby Dry Bayou Cemetery are William Anderson Miller, who died in 1883, and his wife, Eleanora, who died in 1902. Other pre-1900 burials there are Addie Boyette (wife of James L. Boyette, 1897), James Radford (1885), and Martha Radford (1876). Three children of Ace Morgan were buried in the late 1890s. The church existed for approximately seventy years.[226]

A long line of physicians cared for the citizens of Wilmot. The first was Dr. E. O. McDermott who arrived in 1892 as a railroad doctor. By 1912 five more doctors were practicing: H. N. Princehouse, Charles H. Watkins, L. T. Cobb, L. C. Barnhart, and A. D. Knott. Dr. Watkins may have been an African-American as he was writing the "Colored Column" in the

Wilmot Weekly. Dr. R. E. Lindsey opened a dental office in Princehouse Drug Store. Dr. M. C. Crandall arrived by 1917 and practiced into the 1960s.[227] A Dr. Thompson was there by the 1940s.

During the 1950s, with the loss of the large tenant population and the advent of mechanized farming, the business district went into decline. All the large mercantile stores closed with the exception of deYampert's, which is still in business. Large agricultural interests support the town. Lake Enterprise provides a picturesque setting for recreation. It is as appealing now as it must have been to the settler, Joseph Williamson, in 1841. Elizabeth Brown, a seventh or eighth grader, described this lake in 1940 in an essay entitled "Moonlight on Lake Enterprise." Her account follows.

"The rising moon threw golden rays across the water forming a path of gold. Here and there this path was broken by the weird shadows of the ghostly cypress trees which wore their gray witch's cloak of Spanish moss. The moon reflected all of the colors of the rainbow upon the dark waters and shone through the haunted trees leaving them aglow with cool grandeur. The evening stars were beginning to appear in the blue sky and the gentle breeze formed ripples on the water, making the shadows dance and sway. The sleeping birds and frogs seemed to be part of this lordly enchantment. The lonely hollow stumps recalled early memories of goblin dens and the bright moon and twinkling stars overhead proceeded to keep watch over this magnificent masterpiece."[228]

⁂

Gaines, Crawley's Landing

The bayou leaves Wilmot to complete its final journey through southeast Arkansas. It approaches the old community of Gaines, which had a church and cemetery. School was held in the church. Early families in this area were Grant, Wilhite, Eatman, White, and Gaines. Griffin Plantation was owned by the parents of Rebecca Genevia Griffin who was born in 1865 and married Robert Page Crawley Sr. One of her sisters married Will Gaines, who owned a gin there before he relocated to Little Rock to enter the cotton brokerage trade. Gaines Street in Little Rock is named after this man.[229]

The remains of an old ferry are exposed during low water directly south of the Eatman place. This ferry is noted on an 1844 map and may be the Phillips Ferry (later Grants), which was in operation by 1841. L. S. and Battle (or Bartle) Eatman were paying taxes on this land in 1865.[230] Lural S. Eatman was a leader at the old Mt. Gilead Church in the Gaines area.

The large westward bend of the bayou below Gaines is known as Tatum Bend. Edward Tatum settled in this area by 1860 with his wife, Martha, and three children, Camillus, Annie, and Briscoe. A Methodist preacher, Samuel Hawes, with his wife, Sarah, and two children, William and Lizzie, were in the Tatum household.[231] On the returning eastward stretch of Tatum Bend was Crawley's Landing, an antebellum steamboat landing. J. Fred Crawley Sr. and his brother, William G. Crawley, moved to Jefferson County in 1853 and began buying land. J. Fred Crawley Sr. married Amanda (Phillips) Tiller in Pine Bluff in 1855, and from 1855 to 1857 bought six hundred acres along the bayou in Ashley County. N. P. Jones previously owned one of these parcels. Crawley built a large two-story home on the west bank and established Crawley's Bend Plantation. The owner of 156 slaves, he built a slave hospital near his house. Crawley took his slaves to Texas during the Civil War and afterwards returned to the plantation only to abandon it and move to Tennessee.

Crawley's son, Robert Page Sr., eventually traded real estate in Tennessee for part of the plantation and returned to it. He married Rebecca Griffin at Gaines in 1887. His half-brother, John Fred Crawley Jr., came with him but ultimately settled in Texas. Mattie Crawley Lee and Julia Ida Jolly Crawley, daughters of J. Fred Crawley Sr., inherited the remainder of the plantation. The plantation home burned between 1902-1905. The land was eventually sold out of the family, but twenty-eight acres of the Ida J. Crawley Plantation is still owned by Robert A. Crawley, grandson of Robert Page Crawley Sr.[232]

The Oscar Haynes family moved to this area in 1911 and bought 227 acres of the original Crawley Plantation. Vesper Haynes, a son, continued to farm there for many years. Alex Crawley, son of Robert Page Crawley, Sr. continued to farm part of the Crawley land. The Haynes and Crawley children attended school at the Gaines church and later at Wilmot. Oscar Haynes took over operation of the old Crawley ferry and ran it until around 1922. The people of the neighborhood then built a floating bridge to replace the ferry.[233] David Doles Sr. bought more than a section within Tatum Bend around 1940 and the land continues to be farmed by his descendants.

 Chapter Four

Early Bayou Settlements in Northeast Louisiana

Morehouse Parish

McGinty

Bayou Bartholomew crosses into Morehouse Parish, Louisiana, and immediately passes by the communities of McGinty and Zachary where it forms a boundary, with McGinty lying to the east and Zachary to the west. McGinty is on low land with most drainage going east to Boeuf River through what was swampland before major drainage efforts took place beginning in the early 1950s. Camp and Cypress Bayous were dredged to make canals to the Beouf, which also lost its natural bed to a dredged channel. Holly Ridge rises west of the Boeuf providing good sandy farmland in an area otherwise plagued by buckshot. After this swampland was cleared, some farmers began to experiment with growing rice on the poor buckshot land, and their efforts were successful.

George Washington McGinty, born in 1827 in Georgia, is one of the first known settlers. His first wife, Mary Adeline Davis (a cousin to Jefferson Davis), was buried in Sawyer (McGinty) Cemetery in 1877. Their daughter, Mary Elizabeth, married Ray Marshall McDowell of Bonita, and the couple moved to McGinty after several years. George Washington McGinty's second wife was Mrs. Julia Lawrence Sawyer, a widow. Her sons, Narvin and Verner Sawyer, eventually inherited the McGinty land. Another early settler was G. W. Kimbrough who was born in 1840. His young children were buried in Jones Cemetery between 1882 and 1891, and his wife, J. W. Kimbrough, was buried in 1887.[1] A single stone in the Wolfe family burial indicates that Nettie, wife of D. D. Wolfe, died in 1902. Dudley Daniel Wolfe was the son of Columbus Wolfe of Parkdale. The Wolfe Estate contains a "lost forty," a timbered area surrounded by the Naff farm. Walter Fredrick Chiles was also one of the earliest settlers. He was born in 1849 in Alabama and married Octavia Burnham of Mississippi. Two of their daughters were born in Arkansas.

Bartholomew's Song

Chiles was a notary public, and his name appears on numerous legal documents filed from the area. The Ramshur family now owns the Chiles place.[2]

William Adrian Doles, born in Virginia in 1807, was elected justice of the peace in Morehouse Parish in 1844 and as sheriff in 1848. His son, Francis King "Frank" Doles, born in 1851, carried mail from Girad, Louisiana, to Bastrop and on to Hamburg, Elan, and Poplar Bluff in Arkansas as a young man. Frank's son, Ellis Adrian, married Ina Honeycutt at McGinty in 1906. They owned a farm on Lighterknot Creek, near Crane Lake, where they were neighbors to George Howell. After moves to Parkdale and Mist, they returned to McGinty and lived on the Nunn place. They later moved to Jones and in 1919 settled in Bonita. Pat Doles, brother to Frank, bought 360 acres when McGinty was first being settled, and this land was eventually divided among his children. Jim Doles, son of Pat, became a large farmer and was killed in 1931 at one of his tenant houses, the present location of the Bobby Abraugh home. His widow, Kate Madison, then married James Taylor and moved off the Doles homeplace, which went into legal succession to Jim Doles' relatives. Howard and Bill Doles, sons of Ellis, formed a farming partnership with their brother-in-law, Willis Bert McCready who married Ina Katherine Doles.[3]

George Washington Naff, sheriff and tax collector of Morehouse Parish, began buying tracts of land there in the late 1890s and early 1900s. He eventually accumulated around 2,500 acres with at least half of it being wooded. Naff offered this land to tenant farmers who moved in, cleared thirty acres or less, and then began to farm. "Naff had the largest plantation in the Jones-Bonita area. At its peak there were thirty-five to forty families working it. All the tenants were white. It was one of the few working plantations that had all white tenants," Bobby Abraugh said. Crawford Arnold Mayo II became overseer for Naff around 1934.[4]

Sherrod Armstrong and William Jackson McCarty were other early settlers. William Alonzo Boone came to McGinty from Extra community in Ashley County around 1900. Thomas Yeldell, who married Mary Lillie McCain, owned a farm and sawmill there until 1919. Henry Jackson McCarty also operated a sawmill. Wesley Bunch, son of Louis Bunch who moved there in the early 1900s, began working for Naff around 1930 and became his overseer in 1946. He then rented the farm and was joined in a partnership by his son, Thelbert, in 1956. Thelbert's son, Perry, took over management in 1991.[5]

James B. "Jim" Shackelford came to McGinty in 1918 and bought eight hundred acres, a steam gin, and a commissary from Arthur Wooten. He also leased land from Wolf & Silbernagle and continued to buy additional land to add to his Hollyhurst Plantation which eventually grew to around

2,200 acres. The family lived in an old house on Bayou Bartholomew until it burned in 1934, and they moved to Jones. He continued to operate the old gin, which he converted to electricity around 1930, until 1938. He later built a gin at Bonita. Jim Shackelford's son, Duke, entered the farm operation in 1949 and continues to manage it.[6]

The Great Depression brought waves of tenant farmers, who had been released from smaller farms, to this plantation area. Most were hired as day laborers with the landlord furnishing them a house. Among these were the families of Yeager Abraugh, Joe T. Chandler, Will Wooden, Davidson Rogers, Abe Johnson, Tom, Albert and Monroe Tubbs. Others were Bray, Hopkins, Hardgraves, Blackard, Doke, West, Moore, Chappel, Chesney, and Stallings. Some of them bought forty-acre plots in a Farm Security Administration development and some managed to fulfill the requirements to keep the land. Most who did not enter the FSA program worked on the Ober plantation west of Jones as renters.[7]

McGinty was a segregated community with about an equal population of black and white families. Poca Hunter, an illiterate but well respected black, acquired six to seven hundred acres there at some point after the Civil War. His family does not know if this land was homesteaded or "perhaps some white man 'heired' it to him."[8] Buster Ford said Hunter told him that he worked for wages of $2.50 a week and paid fifty cents an acre for most of his land, which he had to clear. Hunter owned a nice house that had a large room reserved for white travelers. The guests were frequent and enjoyed the hospitality of their host. This uneducated man donated land for the first known school, Hunter's Institute, for his race. Hunter's daughter, "Pokie," became a schoolteacher.[9]

One of Hunter's daughters, Mahala, married Seymour Richmond, who homesteaded 136 acres. Richmond, who worked as a railroad porter for forty-eight years, had a house constructed in 1897 by William Carter and Son. The two-story structure of red cypress with beaded ceilings is still extant, although in poor condition. Seymour Richmond went to school only through the third grade, but he and his wife saw to it that their nine children received a good education. All of the sons attended college and one, Will, became a schoolteacher. The oldest son, Thomas Cleveland, graduated as valedictorian from Alcorn College. After graduating from Meharry Medical College in Nashville, Tennessee, in 1917, he returned to McGinty and set up a medical office in the family home where he practiced until his death in 1968. As his reputation as an outstanding physician grew, white people began to seek his services. At first he turned them down but eventually began to treat them. When he took the Louisiana state medical exam, he finished first out of the sixty-two applicants. Some of the furniture from the Richmond house, as well as his ledgers, are in the Snyder Museum at Bastrop.[10]

Bob Jackson and his wife, Sally Mays, both descendants of slaves, moved to McGinty in the 1890s and homesteaded 160 acres. Their grandson, James "Buster" Ford, was born there in 1915. Nick Webb and his wife, Liza Jackson, bought a sixty-nine acre farm around 1929. Liza was born into slavery on the Pipes plantation near Collinston, Louisiana, and Nick's parents were former slaves at Collinston. Page Webb, son of Liza and Nick, was born at McGinty in 1913. Other known early African-Americans there were Cy and Tishia Robinson and the Kelleys.[11]

McGinty Grade School began through the efforts of George Washington McGinty who made the application to the school board. He died in 1907, so the first school was built before this time by Walter Fredrick Chiles, a carpenter. A second school built of brick replaced the first building by 1926. The third school contained an auditorium and a cafeteria. After graduating from the sixth grade, students attended Bonita School. Early teachers were Alcenia Ogden, Lonnie Doles (1913-14), Owen Todd, Eva Harrington (1914-15), O. B. Todd, Bernice Patton, Eva Harrington (1916-17), and E. L. Hart, Helen M. Beard, and Addie Mae Eubanks (1925-27). H. G. Hammons was principal from 1927-30. Teachers for the 1927-28 term were Mrs. Irma Braddock and Mrs. Will McKoin. Nannette Ogden and Irene McDougal began teaching in 1929. Jack Bostwick was principal from 1931-33. J. Conner Speir (1933-1935), Mrs. Grover C. Harp (1935-1942), and Fred H. Beavers (1943-44) followed him. Mrs. Nannette Ogden Sawyer became principal in 1944 and served until the school consolidated with Bonita in August 1958. Other teachers were R. R. Jemison, Mollie Farmer, Dora Bostwick, Louise Eckles, Mollie Blackman, Virginia Gibson, Virginia Jernigan, Dorothy Ann Wathen Myers, Riva Allison, Dessie Gammill, Sara Grigg, Minnie R. Harris, Marion Doles, Gracie Cockrell, Iris Jo Reynolds, Edith Crossley, Tessie Ellis, Esta Henderson Freeland, Katherine McCready, Mrs. A. E. Calhoun, Cornelia Calhoun, Ethel Fluitt, Mrs. Thelma Doles, Opal Adair, Alice Granberry, Jane D. Pippin, and Oren Robertson.[12]

First church services were held in a tent until a union church was built. In 1919 Mrs. William Jackson (Annie) McCarty bought the land the church was on from a Mr. Peterson and donated it to the churches. Methodist and Baptist congregations held services in a large old house on the land until they erected their separate buildings only ninety feet apart. New Hope Baptist Church was organized in 1903 with Rev. T. G. Morgan as pastor. Charter members were Mr. and Mrs. John G. Watkins, Mr. and Mrs. Sherrod Armstrong, and Mrs. A. E. McCarty. Rev. P. J. Deason was serving as pastor when John Winfrey and Lon Boone were ordained as deacons in 1915. Subsequent early pastors were H. B. Mercer, C. N. Walker, J. C. Higginbotham, Riggins, and Roger M. Baxter (1942). The first building was rebuilt in 1942 with two wings added, and the Naff

Estate donated a parsonage. A new brick church was built in 1965. The Methodist church moved to Jones in 1938 and eventually merged with the Bonita congregation. The old church at McGinty was torn down and the present New Hope Baptist Church occupies the site. The cemetery marks the location of the old schoolhouse.[13]

Jane (Doles) and Ralph Pippins owned a small store at the crossroads in the late 1940s. The preferred place to be in the community was the swimming hole in the bayou near the Shackelford gin and store.

⁂

Zachary

Bayou Bartholomew borders the community of Zachary on the east, and Overflow Creek and the hills define its western boundary. Robert Zachary was living in Ward Four in 1850, and a Robert Zachary filed on 110 acres in 1874. Eugene Page Zachary and wife, Jesse Peterkin, were listed in the 1900 Morehouse Parish census in the Zachary area. A Zachary family lived on Hopkins Hill above the bayou and owned the first known ferry at this crossing. In later years, F. M. "Fay" Hopkins, who also lived on the hill, ran a ferry there that remained in operation until a bridge was built around 1930. The ferry remains in the bayou below the bridge and is visible about a foot under water during low water periods. Robert Crawley said he remembered seeing graves near the ferry site.[14] Oren Robertson also recalled graves there and said he saw "bones sticking out of a vault."[15] Hopkins owned farmland below the hill and had a gin on the bayou.

Most of the land at Zachary was in possession of large landowners and the community was one of tenants until they gradually began to acquire their own farms. Zachary and Hopkins are names most associated with land west of the bayou. William Penn McCain bought land around 1895 and settled near present Merganser Road. His daughter, Bell, married Edward Korjan in 1914 and after farming at Tatum Bend for a number of years, they moved to a farm on the bayou at present Ed Korjan Road. McCain sold sixty-eight acres to Korjan in the 1920s and in 1934 sold the remaining land to Bealie Parker. McBraugh, Luther Hamilton, Robertson Woods, and Cay Walker were other early landowners. Joe Franklin, W. F. Doles, Mrs. E. P. Zachary, Mrs. Mabel Adams, Mrs. S. E. Day, F. M. Hopkins, and T. Lovett owned large tracts east of the bayou by 1920.[16]

The Bunyan Bell family moved to Zachary in 1921 and sharecropped for Tom Banister. The following year they rented land from Jesse Zachary. Their daughter, Katie, married Roosevelt Parker, son of Willie Parker who moved to Zachary around 1912. Charles Edward Sikes moved to the Willis Doles farm in 1929. Some other tenants there at that time were Barney Mixon and Monroe Fincher. Howard Huffty, Roosevelt

Parker, Ben Hunt, Wiley Willis, Virgil Boney, and Ed Korjan were area commercial fishermen.[17]

Bruce Blanks owned a plantation on the east side of the bayou and during the 1920s ran a grocery. Mike Doles owns the old Blanks homeplace. Ben Hunt arrived in the 1890s and sharecropped for Blanks until 1932 when he moved onto a forty-acre plot on the plantation and began clearing land. By 1936 they had cleared seven acres and began farming. They eventually cleared twenty acres. Ben Hunt's son, Benton, bought land from Mrs. Marion Day in 1951 and in 1964 bought three hundred acres at the Blanks homeplace. This sharecropper's son increased his farming acreage to 1,200 with an additional 4,000 rented. Chester Arrington brought his family to the Blanks farm in 1921 and later moved across the bridge where they farmed. The John Bevils family lived on the bayou north of the Blanks place in the first decade of 1900. Bevils was remembered for his patent medicines, Bevil's Lotion and Corn Remedy, which he peddled around the country.[18]

Katie Bell Parker described Zachary Elementary School, located on the bayou by the church, as having two rooms with a wood-burning heater. Her teachers were Mrs. Brice, Mrs. Williams, and Levi Smith. The building burned in 1934. Dorothy Korjan Mack wrote, "I will always remember the date because on the morning of February 14, 1934, many of the children and their parents, as well as the teachers, met around the ashes and remains of what had been [the school] for one last time. My first grade teacher, Miss Green, gave us all a valentine, possibly the first 'bought' valentine that many of us had ever received. In a few days we walked to Zachary Bridge to catch the school bus which took us to Bonita School." Luther Travis, Sherrod Armstrong, and George Armstrong drove the "school wagon." The community built Calvary Baptist Church in 1931. Among those helping in the construction were George Armstrong, Fulton Chambers, T. D. Armstrong, and Oscar Franklin. Rev. Higgenbotham and Billy Bell were early preachers. This church is still in existence.[19]

Zachary was a strictly segregated community. "No blacks were allowed to live across [west] the bridge here", said Benton Hunt. "They could only come as day laborers. They finally let the first one live here in 1946." The local swimming hole was below the ferry and the later bridge. Another swimming hole was on the Brixey place. The bayou leaves Zachary on a general southwest course to swing past Horseshoe Lake (also called Jones Lake), one of its old oxbows.

⚜

Jones

The small town of Jones is situated east of Jones Lake and the bayou. Dr. Ambrose Wyatt Jones I, born in 1810 in North Carolina, settled there by 1853 as his two-year-old son, Ambrose, was buried in the Jones-Hadley Cemetery that year. This is the earliest marked burial in the cemetery. In 1860 he owned 65 slaves, 12 slave dwellings, 580 acres of improved land, and 362 acres of unimproved land. His stock consisted of 13 horses, 25 mules and asses, 30 milk cows, 12 oxen, 16 sheep, 150 swine, and 83 other cattle. He had 3,000 bushels of corn, 327 bales of ginned cotton, 30 pounds of wool, 100 bushels of peas and beans, 50 bushels of Irish potatoes, and 400 bushels of sweet potatoes.[20] These statistics indicate a well-established plantation at that time.

Born there in 1856 to Dr. Jones and his wife, Elizabeth Giles Godfrey, was Ambrose Wyatt Jones II, who also became a medical doctor. He married Mala Leavell and they had one son, also named Ambrose Wyatt Jones, who married Emily Mason. This couple had no children. All the other children of Dr. A. W. Jones and Elizabeth died before they married except for Amelia (married J. A. Peterkin) and Eliza L. (married W. H. Hadley). Amelia died in 1881 at age twenty-three leaving two children: Jessie D. (married E. P. Zachary) and Mabel A. (married Weston Adams). Minors at the death of their mother, Jessie and Mabel received one-fourth interest in Amelia's share of the A. W. Jones Estate. The estate consisted of 500 acres known as the Robinson Tract on the west side of Bayou Bartholomew, 3,000 acres known as the A. W. Jones Plantation on the east side of the bayou, and 600 acres of woodland "in or near or east of the line of Peterkin Plantation." Thus the original Jones land passed to the Hadley, Zachary, and Adams heirs.[21]

Also buried at Jones-Hadley Cemetery are Amelia Jones (born 1850; died 1856), Amelia A. E. Jones Peterkin (died 1878, age 23; wife of J. A. Peterkin) Dr. Ambrose W. Jones (1810-1860), and Dr. Ambrose Wyatt Jones (1856-1906). Hadleys buried there are Ellie Belle (1884-1885; daughter of W. H. and E. L. Hadley), Robert J. (1859-1890; son of James and H. H. Hadley), and William Holmes (1854-1913; son of James and Hanna Holmes Hadley). Octavia (Burnham) and Walter Frederick Chiles were buried in 1902 and 1927 respectively. The only other marked burial is Lee Shelton (1890-1902), daughter of J. T. and Anna Shelton. This cemetery is in a field east of Jones Cutoff Road slightly north of the Jones Lake Road intersection. It is located on the old Hadley plantation where there once stood a large two-story house. William Hadley was born in Arkansas in 1852 and was listed in the 1900 Morehouse Parish census as a merchant and landowner with his wife, Liza.[22]

A church, Jones Chapel, existed by 1858, and a school was planned to open early the following year. Seven-year-old Johnnie Crawley wrote from Crawley's Bend to a newspaper in January 1859. "I go to Sunday-school at Jones chapel in Morehouse Parish, Louisiana. Last November the new library was received, and our kind superintendent, Dr. W. A. Jones, gave each of the scholars a Testament and Hymn-book. He also presented beautiful Bibles to Corinna Wilson and Camilas Tatum as rewards...I have to drive gin-horses for about two weeks, and then I am going to start school to Mr. Brewer – a dear, good Methodist preacher, whom we all love. So you may soon look for a letter from me in my own writing."[23]

Jones did not become a town until after the arrival of the Houston, Central Arkansas and Northern Railroad in 1890 from Monroe to the Louisiana line.[24] When the Arkansas segment of this line from McGehee reached its Louisiana counterpart in June the following year, Jones became a busy thoroughfare. A small village grew around the depot, the center of activity. When the post office opened on August 27, 1890, with William H. Hadley as postmaster, there were "about 150 in the village" with a total patronage of 500. John B. McKoin established a mercantile in 1890 and continued in business for ten years. He then became a cottonseed buyer and was still in that venture in 1914. McKoin is listed in the 1900 census as a hotelkeeper. Others in business by that time were William Hadley (merchant and landowner), William L. Pugh (merchant), Jasper Jones (saloonkeeper), Robert Gannaway (photographer), Jasper Sawyers (saloonkeeper), and David Glass (saloonkeeper). Eugene Zachary was listed as a farmer and landowner. As more tenants moved to the neighboring plantations, the outlying population grew and augmented the town's development. Thomas Jefferson "Jeff" Haynes, John Knox Nunn, William Lester "Snig" Pugh, George Washington Naff, and Jim Shackelford owned large farms. The Shackelford farm at one time had around seventy families on it.[25]

The Haynes plantation was on the bayou at Haynes Landing. Jeff Haynes, who married Althea Blanks, operated a private bank in the early days of the town. The Haynes holdings passed to their daughters, Mary (Mrs. William Augustus "Bill" Ober) and Allyne (Mrs. Fred Petty).[26] The Pettys named their farm Modoc Plantation after the prominent Modoc Bend in the bayou. Ober's Bluff on the bayou was within the Ober farm.

Bill Ober moved to Jones in 1920 and established a mercantile store. He later enlarged this business to include Ober Wholesale Grocery, and the red brick building that housed this concern still exists. Knox Nunn owned a large general merchandise store by the railroad tracks. In this store, pool tables offered entertainment for his customers. Not so pleasurable there was the availability of coffins.[27] William L. Pugh and E. P. Zachary also owned mercantiles. Leland Pierce, Vernon Slocum and Earl Watts owned grocery stores by the early 1940s. There was also a drugstore and blacksmith shop.

William L. Pugh, Bill Ober, and Vernon Slocum owned gins. The Pugh Gin later became Jones Co-op Gin. In 1964 Wesley and Thelbert Bunch bought the old Slocum Gin from Union Oil Mill of West Monroe and operated it until they built Bunch's Gin in 1980. The name changed to Jones Producers Gin in 1980 as more stockholders joined the company. Upon consolidation with the Shackelford Gin at Bonita in 1997, the company became Jones Producers Gin, Inc.[28]

Several sawmills operated in the area. Jacob Niemyer and Thomas J. Darragh of Little Rock began buying tracts of land north of Jones in January 1891. Doing business as Niemyer & Darragh, they purchased ninety-four acres of cypress brake land from Frank Haynes in sections 11 and 14, T23N-R8E, and ninety-five acres from R. B. Sadler in sections 10 and 15, T23N-R8E. In September 1899 they bought a parcel of land in section 15, T23N-R8E from Farm Land Company, based in Minnesota, and established a shingle mill on that land, a location that became known as Niemyer-Darragh Brake.[29] Smaller mills were owned by Earl Watts in Jones and Jesse Harris at Graveyard Brake. Singer Sewing Machine Company owned a large tract where they cut lumber for the machine cabinets. Phin Kimball ran large sawmills at nearby Kimball and Laark above the state line.[30]

The Doodlebug Express stopped daily for roundtrip service between Collinston, McGehee, Little Rock, and Memphis. "You could get on in the morning and go to Little Rock and be back by five in the afternoon," Jack Gibson recalled. The freight trains hauled stock in addition to lumber products. John Anderson Gibson, in the cattle and horse trade, moved there in 1930.[31]

Physicians who served the area were Ambrose Wyatt Jones Sr. (1858), Jordan Harrison (1860), L. M. Cheek (1860), R. M. Ryan (1860), Ambrose Wyatt Jones Jr. (1880), and Thomas Madison Jones (1880). Dr. William Joel McWilliams was practicing by the early 1890s. His daughter, Iris, who married John Knox Nunn, was born there in 1893. Dr. Bunnie M. McKoin, son of John B. McKoin, opened an office in 1912 and moved to Mer Rouge two years later. Dr. M. W. Owens conducted a long practice before moving to Bonita in 1927. He was the last physician in the town.[32]

Jones Elementary School, built in 1920 by Gray Barham, was a large two-story brick structure. When the school consolidated with Bonita in 1939, Bill Ober bought the building with plans to convert it into a hotel and cafe for tourists and visiting baseball players. Ober had built a ballpark where the town's "first class" baseball team played against other teams in the Cotton State League. He died before the remodeling was done, and Duke Shackelford bought the structure and had it taken down. When he built a new house, he used the bricks as well as the fan lights from the old school.[33] Teachers at Jones were Mrs. Lucy Nunn Pugh, Mrs. Hugh D. Harkness Boone, Elizabeth Rogers, and Annie B. McAdams. Lucy Pugh was principal.

The history of Jones Pentecostal Church is directly connected to the old Black Cat Saloon, a black honky-tonk. Jesse Harris, a well-known and successful moonshiner, built the church on the site of his saloon after his conversion in the early 1950s. First located on Harris's land at Graveyard Brake about a mile north of town, a modern building was later constructed in town. "The church has been very successful with a large following and competent ministers," Bobby Abraugh said. The Black Cat Saloon had its heyday during the 1930s. Ed Bell opened Bell's Saloon in Jones during the 1920s and had a flourishing business until the mid-1930s.   The building, later used as the post office, still stands east of the highway.

Gladys Parks Shackelford, who moved to Jones in 1934, described the area in an interview with a local paper when she was ninety years old. "We had no roads we could travel on except in the dry summer time. The roads had too many mudholes in the winter.... A brand new Oldsmobile set up and rusted because we couldn't go anywhere in it," she said.[34]

When a WPA Writer's Program author passed through in the late 1930s, he described Jones as "a small village with a cotton gin" with a population of one hundred. The only other thing he noted was the Knox Nunn house. "The Log House, opposite the depot, is of unusual size for its type of construction. It was built in 1936 of logs cut in near-by brakes. The gabled roof is covered with crude shingles hewn with adz and drawknife from cypress blocks."[35]   This exceptional house, presently owned by J. C. Doke, still stands in excellent condition.

The oldest house in the town is the Edgar Bell home, a simple box-frame structure that stands next to the old saloon building. The Jim Shackelford home (built in 1939), the Mrs. Bill Ober home, and the Duke Shackelford home (built in 1978) are large plantation type houses. The vine-covered red brick building that housed Ober's Wholesale Grocery is the oldest extant commercial building. Most childhood recollections are not centered on the town. Those good memories go back to the bayou swimming holes at Ober's Bluff, McGinty, and Zachary.

⚜

Lind Grove

The bayou leaves Jones Lake and heads west to the foothills where it meets the confluence of Overflow Creek. From this point to below the mouth of Chemin-a-Haut Creek, the bayou is generally "against the hills," the west bank being called the "high bank." From Overflow Creek it goes by Haynes Landing, Oak Landing (an old steamboat landing and turnaround near Hopkins Hill), Modoc Bend, and Cora's Bluff. Gaston Harrison, born in 1900, told how Cora's Bluff was named: "Uncle Bascon Harrison said a little girl lived on top of the high, steep bluff. She was playing and fell off of it and died. They buried her in Cora's Bluff Cemetery." The earliest marked grave in this cemetery is Mildred E. Crawford who was born in 1873 and died in 1875. She was the daughter of J. R. and Martha Crawford. Also buried there are George R. Crawford and wife Emma (Allen) Crawford. Bascon Harrison and wife, Ida Crawford, and James G. Harrison and wife, Martha (Westbrook), are among others. Across the bayou from Cora's Bluff Bridge was the John Knox plantation.[36]

About two miles downstream from Cora's Bluff, the bayou makes a sharp westward bend at the site of old Lind Grove, one of the first settled areas in the parish along with Prairie Mer Rouge, Prairie Jefferson (Oak Ridge) and Point Pleasant. One of the first roads, the Lind Grove Road (now the Old Bonita Road), ran from there to Monroe.[37] When steamboats began coming up the bayou, Lind Grove became a landing and turnaround. The village, situated on the bayou bank among a grove of linden trees, first consisted only of a store and warehouse. Lind Grove Post Office was established February 19, 1857, with Aaron H. Brewer as postmaster. Sequential postmasters were James E. Warnock or Womack (1857), George M. Harrison (1868), and William R. Watt (1875-1890).[38]

Twenty-one year old Aleck K. Watt settled near there in 1848. He spent the first winter in a crudely built log cabin and slept with his firearms nearby to protect himself from wild animals. In 1853 he married Mary Jane Haynes of Berlin Community in Ashley County. After serving in the Confederate Army throughout the Civil War, he returned to his plantation on the bayou and opened a dry goods store at Lind Grove. Having no children of their own, Julia Haynes, Mary Watt's niece, came to live with the couple as a young girl. Julia was the daughter of John D. and Mary Haynes, whose other children were Martha, Emma, and Jeff. Julia Haynes married Newton H. Huff in 1875. Their children were Anna, Alexander Kincade (1884-1918), Emma Williamson, John, Robert, and Ellis. Newton Huff was clerking in a store at Lind Grove when he met his wife, and it was there that they made their home.[39]

Also owning stores were Wolff & Montgomery and Bond & Williams. Major Ellis owned a saloon and his nephew, George, clerked in it. A gin and large warehouse were also there. By February 1875, W. R. Bunckley was dealing in "Dry Goods, Boots, Shoes and Plantation Supplies." John W. Bowe, a timber buyer, was a customer at Bunckley's store, which T. W. Ellis bought by 1877. Bunckley & Williams General Merchandise was in business by December 1886, and by January 1880, W. F. Watt was selling "Dry Goods, Groceries, Notions, Hardware, Hats, and Plantation Supplies." George Ellis was a clerk or manager and J. E. Phelps was a customer. J. W. Bowe settled his account with Watt in December 1881 with his receipt being signed by R. M. Hardy. Wolfe & Silbernagle were buying cotton by 1882. Simon Parker and deHart owned stores. The deHart business later became Thomas Mercantile.[40] Physicians were L. E. Renwick (1860), L. D. Williams (1860), and Lee Dreisbach ((1891).[41]

Other early known people associated with this area were Mrs. M. E. Gibson (nee Duckworth), Dr. L. N. Renwick, Julius Williams, M. F. Williams, Winfield Scott, Ed Spikes, Joe Warnock, Dr. Tom Jones, Dr. Wyatt Jones, and Ghearing.[42] In later years two Lovett brothers, J. D. and Will, lived on the west side of the bayou at nearby Lovett Bend where J. D. Lovett was murdered and buried in 1921. Robert Cain presently owns this property.[43] Demarquis Ellis Harp moved his family three miles southeast of Lind Grove (just north of the Highway 165 overpass) in 1880 on land purchased from a Mr. Hersey. Lumber for their second house, built in 1882, arrived at Lind Grove on a steamboat. His sister, America Missouri Harp, married Warren Alexander Montgomery in 1860, and the couple settled in this area. It was their child, Charles Warren Montgomery, who owned the store at Lind Grove and later at Bonita.[44]

Lind Grove School was in existence by 1873 with Mrs. Lizzie Beauchamp as the teacher. James A. Williams was teaching in Ward Ten in 1874. Representing the ward on the parish school board in 1875 was W. F. Watt. Following Watt in the position were Jubal A. "Jobe" Williams (by 1887), Charles Weiss (1887), and John A. Williams.[45]

Steamboat trade began a moderate decline with the coming of the railroad, and as business at the landing decreased, merchants began to move their firms to Bonita or Bastrop. A. K. Watt and H. N. Huff were living near there in 1909.[46] Green Grove Methodist Church is on part of the site of old Lind Grove.

≈≈◎≈≈

Bonita

Settlement was taking place along Bayou Bonne Idee, east of Lind Grove, long before the railroad came. The first known settlers in the area were James and Robert McDowell who came there in 1844. They were married to sisters, Ellen and Elizabeth Barnard. Robert and Elizabeth settled less than a mile from the present Bonita Post Office on what is still known as the McDowell place. Their son, Ray Marshall, married Mary Elizabeth McGinty and their first child, George Robert "Bob", was born there in 1885. Bob McDowell married Vinnie Mae McLeod and they lived in Bonita throughout their lives. Their children were Alton, Fred Keith,

James Robert, George, Thomas Todd, Mary Elizabeth (Lyne), and Pauline (Hale).[47]

Ransom Bunckley and his third wife, Minerva Richmond, married in Franklin County, Mississippi, in 1854 and moved to Morehouse Parish the same year. He bought a large plantation near present Bonita and named it Bonne Idee. Bunckley's first wife was Catherine Pickett and all of his children were from this marriage. Their firstborn, Nathan, stayed in Franklin County on the large plantation that was established by Ransom's father, John, around 1806. Nathan was a physician and successful planter. His son, William, inherited the Bonne Idee plantation upon the death of his grandfather, Ransom, in 1870. Family history indicates that William was raised there "since he was a child." He married first Mahala (?) and second Ella Watson of Hamburg, Arkansas. William continued the operation of the plantation until around 1902 when he moved to Hamburg. Ransom Bunckley was a member of the old Bartholomew Methodist Church and Masonic Temple. He was buried on the plantation, and a daughter, Emma R., born in 1852, died in 1886 and was buried in Mound Cemetery.[48] The grand two-story home was still in use in 1943 but was taken down in the 1960s by Duke Shackelford, present owner of the Bunckley land.

The area was a well-populated settlement before the coming of the railroad. A Mr. Dawson was within the present town limits by 1857. That year he built an exquisite, two-story, thirteen-room house embellished with gingerbread trim and scrollwork.[49] A public school was in existence before 1885. Thomas Young Harp II, son of Demarquis Ellis Harp, remembered the schoolteacher, Harrison George, who boarded with them that year. Harp began the first grade in 1887 in a school that was located "up on the Weiss farm about half way between the old steam boat landing, Lind Grove...and the present ball playing town of Bonita." Students attending school before 1890 were Marion Ashley, "Punch" Causey, Lillian Causey, John Whittaker, Tom Bullock, and Cammie Mayo. Julia Wright (Mrs. Ben Rowlinson) was teacher from 1887-1889, and Mrs. Lizzy Beauchamp taught from 1889 to 1891.[50]

Harp described the school when he was sixty-four years old: "The building was of rough sawn clapboards and rough flooring, unceiled with one uncertain window...It was equipped with a box wood brass hooped cedar water bucket and a tin dipper. Some time later the old dipper became holey from rust, then some thoughtful person sacrificed their personal chew of sweet gum and plugged the holes. A set valuation of seventy-five dollars for the building and equipment would have delighted a profiteer. The 'privacies' were a large red oak tree for the girls while the boys patronized a big post oak. A boy was never excused while a girl was on vacation – vice versa."[51]

Although a settlement existed there, it was the coming of the railroad that formed the town. A construction locomotive first puffed through in the summer of 1890. By the beginning of the school term, the HCA&N freight and passenger depot was in place. The railroad conductor, given the task of naming the stops, was impressed by the luxuriant green emanating from the dense forest, marshes, and fields and named the town Bonita, Spanish for beautiful. Most farmland at this time was out along the bayou or on the sandy ridges. The area of the town was mostly forested. T. Y. Harp wrote, "The right of way cleared down through the virgin forest seemed to be the coldest spot on earth. It seemed to funnel the cold north wind in winter. In summer it incubated heat almost unbearable."[52] Local legend says that Jay Gould rode in his private car when the first train arrived. The HCA&N met with Gould's St. Louis, Iron Mountain & Southern at McGehee, and Gould purchased the HCA&N in 1893.[53]

The new town materialized swiftly. A. S. Washburn's 1890 survey laid out the town in blocks and lots. Bonita Post Office was established August 6, 1890, with William W. Denhem as postmaster. Wolff & Montgomery was the first store to relocate from Lind Grove. They advertised as "Dealers in Dry Goods, Notions, Boots, Shoes, Hardware and Groceries" and "Highest Price Paid for Cotton."[54] Other general merchandise stores opening in 1890 were Bunckley & Williams, Harry Buatt, Bond & Williams, Scott Brothers, and the Rocket, which a Mr. Bush owned. Stamper and Calloway opened a drugstore, and Warren Montgomery had a livery stable. Montgomery also bought the Dawson house and remodeled it into a hotel for rail passengers, drummers, and visitors. Dances and parties were also held in the hotel. Scott Brothers Saloon rounded out the brand new town.[55]

The school also moved to the town. Mrs. Beauchamp conducted classes during the 1890-1891 term "in an old abandoned jerry built saloon, even cruder than the one on the Weiss farm." (The abandoned saloon is indicative of a settlement there before the arrival of the railroad.) T. Y. Harp once again described the amenities available at the school: "The cabinet d'aisance as we French so aptly call it, was the bank of the old cypress brake. If one went far enough down the slope the bank acted as a screen against the view of any passer-by on the old road leading to Lind Grove. On the whole it was something of an improvement to the oak trees on the old grounds. At least, gravity and a freshet added something to sanitary conditions."[56]

A new building erected in the summer of 1891 was about a hundred feet away from the old saloon. The location was within the present cemetery. Harp began the third grade in this wonderful, modern structure, which he described: "About 25x50 feet in dimension, ceiled and walled with matched dressed lumber, it was perfection and luxury rampart...."

The windows even raised and a steeple housed a bell that had "the nastiest tone ever possessed by metal." Manufactured desks replaced the torturous homemade benches. And – finally – "just under the dip of the hill there stood Two Chic Sales Mansions. Both, I presume, were two holers...."[57]

A. W. Meadows conducted the next two terms (1891-1893). Some students during this time were Burgess "But Baby" Young, A. K. Huff, Grover Harp, John Stamper, Stuart "Bummer" Causey, John Huff, Bob Huff, Ed Jones, Filmore Williams, and Talbot Williams. During extremely hot weather, Mr. Meadows sprinkled the floor with water from the cypress brake, which also provided drinking water. "[It] was dipped from the cypress brake after the scum had been knocked off." Boys also went to Captain Bunckley's backyard well where hound dog hair and chicken droppings clung to the well rope. Once the boys found "numerous white grubs floating around" in it. After much debate, they scooped the larger ones off and took it on to the school. Thereafter they drew from the well in Bunckley's horse lot. If one drank quickly, "the livery stable taste wasn't so pronounced."[58]

Miss Mary Cross was principal from 1893 to 1895 with Mrs. R. W. Hope as assistant. Students mentioned by Harp during these years were Jap Jones, Sidney Williams, and Buatt Jones. Miss Irma McCord taught from 1895 to 1897, and the children adored her. Harp wrote, "Miss Irma was an outstanding woman in all phases of life – a great teacher with unusual character. She was possessed with a gentle disposition that was limitless and had the faculty of teaching the why of things." Some students under her were Emma Huff, Zelpha Searcey, Jimmy Faust, and John Stamper. Justice Fred M. Odom arrived in the fall of 1897 to "ride herd over the old school," and a Mr. Wallace replaced him the following year. The school building was also used for church services, a lodge hall for the Woodmen of the World, a skating rink, and a dance pavilion.[59]

Arriving around 1893 with a pack on his back and a suitcase in hand was Jacob "Jake" Seligman. He peddled goods from the case for a few years until he was able to build a general merchandise store. His wife, Rose, helped in its management. They sold dry goods, material, clothing, shoes, hardware, feed and seed, groceries, wagons, buggies, surreys, and coffins. Kerosene lamps provided light and these were eventually replaced by Coleman lanterns. He installed a dynamo in the 1920s, and the store became the first business to have electric lights. Heat came from a wood or coal-burning heater. Seligman later built a brick building to house his business.

Jacob died in 1910, and his seventeen-year-old son, Hymann, assumed management. By 1918 Sam Hanna was a partner. Some managers were Alvin Allen, Jeff Posey, Ralph McCready, Omer Bryan, and Clifton Reeves. Marion Robertson (Doles) began clerking on Saturdays around

1927. She began at 7:30, had thirty minutes for lunch, and worked until midnight, for which she was paid two dollars. "The Seligmans were civic minded and helped many people," she said. Hymann I. Seligman opened a second store in Bastrop in 1923, and this business is still in operation under different ownership.[60]

John Williams installed the first cotton gin, near the cemetery, in 1895. A shingle mill began operation on the cypress brake by the town in 1899 but was only in business for about two years. Houses were also filling up the town lots. Robert Hope began construction on his two-story colonial manor in 1893 and finished two years later. This house stayed in the Hope family until 1981 when Elroy and Martha Glossup purchased it. Robert Hope was born on the bayou in Ward Two in 1870. He married Lula Belle Harp, daughter of J. N. Harp in 1893. After she died, he married her sister, Hattie Harp. Winfield Scott built a house in 1892, and around 1898 the Harry Buatt family moved into their new home.[61]

In 1903 Jacob Seligman made a trip to Baton Rouge to file for incorporation, and the governor proclaimed Bonita a bona fide town on December 19 of that year. Dr. Robert L. Credelle was first mayor with Jake Seligman, Charles Calhoun, D. E. "Mark" Harp, and Harry W. Buatt as aldermen. Edgar Jones was elected as first marshal. Charles Weiss succeeded Denham as postmaster in 1893. Following Weiss were William Denham (1897), Jennie L. Slandfer (1898), Hunter P. Buatt (1899), Mattie Harp (1900), Belle B. Sawyer (1902), Robert B. Daniel (1906), Myra M. Jones (1908), Lillian Causey (1919-1931) and James F. Harp (1931).[62]

In 1910 the population was 273 and the town continued to grow. Ray Robertson arrived in 1918 as the rural mail carrier, a position he held for forty years. Bonita Motor Company, under the ownership of Dr. A. B. Anthony and Scott Buatt, was in operation by 1925. J. N. Jones, R. C. White, and Francis Brown later owned this company. John Anderson built a large two-story mercantile. Mr. Wing and Mrs. Wong Shee Gee arrived in 1927 and opened a grocery store that is still run by their descendants. During the 1920s Mr. and Mrs. T. P. Miller built a dry goods store that continued in business by their daughters, Opal and Jewel, until 1988. Scott Buatt owned a large grocery store. Jones Mercantile, owned by Jasper N. "Jap" Jones, was the largest in town. Jim Denham and Arthur Baggett had drugstores. A bank owned by Bastrop National served the town until it closed at the beginning of the Depression. Jasper Jones had purchased the old Williams gin, and Ellis Doles owned a mule barn.

Bonita became a lumber town. The first mill to locate there was a shingle mill on the cypress brake north of the cemetery. It was there by 1899 and operated for about two years. In 1919 Eckord & Leonard built a stave mill on Henry Street between Fifth and Sixth Streets. The company also built shotgun houses for their workers. This mill also only stayed in business for about two years. Organization of the Bonita Lumber Company began in May 1919 when Nelson H. Walcott and Charles Palmer of Providence, Rhode Island, appointed F. E. Stonebreaker of Memphis to represent them as agent and attorney to organize the charter. Stonebreaker was general manager of the Crittenden Lumber Company, which also had its headquarters in Rhode Island with a large mill at Earle in Crittenden County Arkansas. The first board of directors, all of whom were stockholders, were Nelson H. Walcott (one share), Charles P. Palmer (one share), F. E. Stonebreaker (500 shares and president), Chester L. Walcott (vice-president) and T. A. Ware (one share and secretary). Leland Thornton was treasurer and owned one share. Crittenden Lumber Company also bought 1,495 shares. Locating in the northern part of the town, the company built the mill, an office, a large two-story boarding house, and ten mill houses. F. E. Stonebreaker managed the mill until Chester Walcott moved to Bonita and assumed that position around 1923. The company bought a section of land in Beouf Swamp and installed a dummy line railroad to haul out the logs. According to a 1920 article published by the Southern Alluvial Land Association, the company owned "many thousands of acres of both timbered and cut-over lands in the Bonita vicinity." The company shipped the hardwood lumber to a furniture company in Canada. When all the select timber was cut by around 1928-29, the mill closed.[63]

Louisville Cooperage Company established a heading mill across the railroad on the Bonne Idee in 1921. They also built a green shed, drying shed with a kiln, an office, commissary, and several tenant houses. This company also ran a dummy line into the swamp to cut white oak. R. C. White was manager, and Harry Tucker managed the commissary. The company moved to Monroe in 1927, and Pat McCleary and Claude Watt purchased the mill. McCleary's daughter, Agnes, was bookkeeper and office manager. Pat McCleary and his son were killed in an accident in 1935, and Agnes and James Wyatt continued operating it until Wyatt's death in 1941. R. C. White purchased Wyatt's interest, and he and Agnes managed the mill until they sold it to Calvert Distilling Company in 1946. Eloise Means wrote, "The mill whistle was blown at 7, 12, 15 minutes to 1, 1, and 4 each day. Nearly everyone set their clocks to this time. There were two fires at the mill. The signal for a fire in those days was three pistol shots. The citizens of the town always responded quickly to the fire alarm. At one of these fires they formed a bucket line from the Bonne Idee to the fire and put it out. The other time the green shed caught fire but it burned before it could be extinguished. Robin Jordan and his brother-in-law, Ben Lowe, owned the last mill in the town. They installed a planing mill at the old location of the Bonita Lumber Company in the late 1930s and operated it for about five years.[64] The mills provided work for many and contributed to the growth of the town. However, they left the surrounding countryside in ugly devastation.

Huge tracts of hardwood timber were cut. The Humble or Little Missouri tract contained over 40,000 acres. Another large tract near Bonita was known as the Schenley tract, presently owned by Mer Rouge Farms. This cutover land sold only by the section for fifteen dollars an acre. After it was drained in the early 1950s, the timber was cut again, and the owners began to think about a new use for the land. Gerrard H. Mountjoy, who had married the daughter of lumberman Phin Kimball, decided clear the land for rice production. News of his success spread, and others began to emulate his lead. The price then rose to three hundred an acre and increased again to seven hundred.[65]

Ellis Doles was marshal in 1924, and Bob McDowell served as marshal during the 1930s. There was a calaboose and later a jail to serve their clients.[66] Four trains stopped daily, one of them was a fast passenger train, the "Hotshot." "It went sixty miles an hour instead of forty," said Oren Robertson. "On Saturday nights you could not walk down the street. The town was filled with black tenants. They came in cotton wagons," Cecil Harp said.

Saloons were prevalent. Some saloon owners were Lee Buatt, Pete Ginn, and Claude Copeland and Noel Towles, partners. "At one time Front Street had four of them," Bobby Abraugh said. Cecil Harp also remembered four at an earlier time. "There were three churches and four saloons. A tornado came around 1950 [1951] and destroyed every church and never touched a saloon!" he said.[67]

The population of Ward Ten in 1929 was 1,500, and Bonita was still progressing. Jasper N. Jones was mayor, and town council members were Walter Baggett, J. W. Montgomery, and H. A. Sisson. W. H. Tucker was marshal. A municipal waterworks and Bonita Telephone Company were in place, and electricity and natural gas were available. Three gins, owned by Jasper Jones, Ellis Doles, and Jim Shackelford, were running. The latter two were in their first year of operation, and the Jones gin would soon close. The Doles gin burned around 1951. Three lumber mills were the leading industries. A new high school was in place, and Baptist and Methodist churches "had admirable houses of worship."[68]

The Great Depression ended the town's progress. The lumber mills moved out and small businesses folded. When the WPA writer passed through in the late 1930s, the population was 507. Evidently, nothing about the town impressed him or her. The only mention was: "South of Bonita, US 165 runs through forests of oak, gum, and hickory. Water-filled ditches and swamplands border the road."[69]

Ellis Doles built some cabins in 1930 to rent to travelers. His brother, Will, came from Texas to manage the business which "flourished" until the roads were improved around 1933. Mr. and Mrs. Boyd Smith bought the old Dawson-Montgomery house in 1940 and rented out apartments. In 1940 the Ellis Doles house burned and he then built a store with living quarters in the back. "Mrs. Doles started her business with one barrel of flour and a few small articles. When these were sold, she took the money she had made and bought another barrel of flour and a few other things." Her son, Howard, entered the business and was a partner until his death in 1966. The business grew to include a meat market, and she worked in the store until 1972. Doles Grocery & Meat Market stayed in business until around 1983 under the management of Mrs. Doles' daughter, Ina Katherine McCready, who took it over upon her retirement from teaching in 1972. The vacant building is still extant.[70]

Edwin Robertson, son of Ray Robertson, opened Robertson's Grocery in 1940 and stayed in business until 1960. His brother, Oren Robertson, began showing movies in his father's mule barn in 1946, and two years later built the Village Theater. "There had to be a balcony for the blacks. We charged ten cents for children and twenty-five cents for adults," Oren said. Arthur Baggett bought the theater in 1951 and then sold it to Mrs. Gene Gee. It closed in the late 1950s. Oren's next venture was a skating rink. In 1951 he bought a tent, wooden floor, and skates and opened for business. Two years later, he closed the rink and put in a variety store. Louis Means, who first came to Bonita in 1941, returned in 1947 and the following year established a blacksmith and automobile mechanic shop. Hollis McCready, who moved his family there from Jones in 1947, worked in Means' shop, logged, and did carpentry work. His brother, Orville, also came there. Mrs. Hollis McCready and Mrs. Orville McCready operated the Bonita Cafe.[71]

A new building replaced the old school around 1900. Built on the present school grounds, it was a brown two-story structure. This school only went through the ninth grade, and students had to go to surrounding towns to finish high school. A larger building that eventually replaced the first burned in the autumn of 1926, and classes met in several different locations for the remainder of the term. Some of the teachers in 1926-1927 were Nannette Pearson and Louise Rankin. By the beginning of the 1927 fall term, a new wooden one-story building was ready for occupancy. Becoming a high school at this time, the first graduating class of 1929 consisted of Mollye Herrington, Irena Crawford, and Louise Powers. A new high school was built in 1937 and continued in use until it burned in the 1980s. In 1958 the grammar school burned and was replaced by the present building.[72]

On August 31, 1891, I. F. Causey deeded land for the Bonita Cemetery to the Bonita Methodist Church. There is no record of this first church, but by 1899, the only parsonage for the circuit rider for the Bonita Circuit was in Bonita. The Bonita Methodist Episcopal Church, South, was built in 1904 and dedicated in 1906. Rev. A. S. J. Neill, a bricklayer, did the masonry work. In 1925 an annex was built to house the Sunday School classes. This church was destroyed by a tornado on December 8, 1951, and the congregation met in a vacant building until the new church was built the following year.[73]

Dr. Julian M. Stamper began practicing medicine in Bonita in 1896. Dr. William R. Knoefel arrived in 1900, and his twin, Dr. Eugene Knoefel, began a practice in nearby Bonne Idee Community the same year. Physicians arriving in 1904 were Sidney Legrand Williams, Robert L. Credelle, and E. W. Hunter. Dr. A. B. Gregory practiced there from 1913 to 1926 and from 1940 to 1943. Dr. E. L. Miller arrived in 1926, and Dr. M. W. Owens moved his practice from Jones to Bonita the following year. Dr. Owens died in 1942 and was the last physician in the town. Dr. Thomas Cleveland Richmond saw patients on Saturday afternoons in a backroom of Baggett's pharmacy.[74]

Young and old alike went to a swimming hole about two miles up from Lind Grove. The Walcott families "instigators of this project" began using this location in the 1920s and others followed. Around 1930 people began going to Clay Banks at the bend near Lind Grove. The steep bank invited daredevil jumps and a leaning tree anchored a rope for swings over and into the water. This popular spot stayed in use until the 1950s.[75]

The town of Bonita remains by the railroad that brought it into existence, but the trains no longer stop. The main part of Bobby and Gloria Abraugh's Bonita Hardware and Auto Parts store occupies the old Arthur Baggett drugstore building, and part is in the old 1925 bank building. A vacant lot adjoining it on the south brings back memories of the Village Theater. Doles Grocery stands vacant. Dr. Owens' office, moved to a different location, houses a small museum.[76] The oldest structure in town, the Dawson-Montgomery-Smith house built in 1857, still stands in a state of neglect. Also extant are the old homes of Winfield Scott (1892), Robert Hope (1895), and Jap Jones. These buildings serve as allusions to the history of this once thriving town – a place that a railroad conductor named Bonita for beautiful in 1890.

⁂

Plantersville

The bayou leaves Lind Grove and swings to the northwest for about a mile to pass under Cora's Bluff Bridge, the site of an old ferry crossing. (The actual site of Cora's Bluff is a little over a mile north of the bridge.) It then crosses under Knox Ferry Bridge, the site of another old ferry. A Mr. Britton, one of the earliest settlers, opened up a farm on the west bank. John Knox later owned a large farm on the east side of the bayou and was probably the owner of the ferry. Mound Cemetery, named for the large mound on which it was established, is located just above the bridge on the east bank. The earliest dates represented on markers are 1813, E. B. Wroten's birth year, and 1864, Bennett K. Wroten's death date. Other pre-1900 burials represent the families of Ashley, Bunckley, Haynes, Huff, and Naff. Early 1900 burials are Causey, Colbert, Overby, and Watt.[77] A hand-drawn map of the area "from [an] 1851 Morehouse Parish map" shows two tracts, owned by John B. Eddins and "heirs of B. Hemken," across the bayou from the cemetery. S. J. Harrell lived near there in 1909, and J. Howard Michie of Mer Rouge owned property nearby. Mound Landing was in this area.[78]

A mile down from Knox Ferry Bridge is the site of another steamboat landing known as Lightwood (also the name of a steamboat) and later as Twin Oaks. About two miles south of the bayou on the Old Bonita Road is the old community of Plantersville. Henry Phelps and James M. Lupo applied for and received a warrant for school land containing 263 acres in 1855. They sold this land the following year to William and Thomas H. Edwards. In 1859 Thomas Edwards deeded the land to Dr. John M. Hilliard who settled on it.[79]

In C. C. Davenport's *Looking Backward*, he mentions Hilliard's "neighbors" who were stretched out along the bayou from north of Point Pleasant to Jones. This "second crop of settlers" (coming in after the colonizers or descending from them) were: Colonel Aaron Livingston, Green B. Hopkins, J. W. Westmoreland, Wiley J. Ward, Jack Haggerty, John D. Moore Sr., James Pinel, Robert H. Ward, Wm. Shelton, Nathan Vester, William A. Rhimes, now the home of Sam Harrell; Dr. J. M. Hilliard whose home took the name of 'Plantersville;' Wm. J. Averitt, Robert J. Knox, W. H. Vaughn, Dr. A. S. Washburn, George D. Sharp, Noah Ford, Colonel Blunt, Walter R. Lassiter, Savory J. Knox, James and Joe Warnock, Lawrence Moore, A. K. Watt, George Beard, Dr. Tom and Dr. Wyatt Jones; two brothers – Cooper and E. D. Duckworth, J. H. and K. Overby, who were brothers, and George A. and Jesse Peterkin." The sole survivor of these settlers in 1911 was Aleck K. Watt.[80]

In 1795 William Edward Skanes and Jay Philip Stiles settled near the bayou at an undetermined location in the area. The following year Skanes initiated an effort to organize a Methodist Society and established a "crude meeting place." In 1804 construction began on a new building for the Methodist Society and a masonic lodge at Plantersville. The two-story structure was completed in 1807 and according to an old Bible notation was not dedicated until 1835. Methodist Circuit riders began coming to the Washita Circuit in 1806. The circuit extended fifty miles along the Ouachita River and Bayou Bartholomew with Monroe being in the center. Although it is likely others held services at the church, the first documented by name is John Griffing Jones in 1826. Lind Grove became the circuit name in 1871, and it was renamed the Bonita Circuit in 1897.[81]

Bartholomew Lodge #112, chartered in 1823 and disbanded in 1847, received a new charter in 1853. At the first organizational meeting in 1852, the members called for a plan to build a new lodge hall and church. Noah Ford, J. H. Blount, E. D. Duckworth, William J. Everett, and J. B. Eddins were on the new construction committee. The two-story building was completed the following year. The corner pillars were hewn from logs and penned together with wooden pegs. Round, peeled logs were used for rafters. Heart pine lumber from a sawmill at Point Pleasant and hauled by ox wagon was used for siding and floors. The boards, some of them measuring nineteen inches wide, were planed by hand and fastened with square-headed forged nails. The sills and joists were hand-hewn white oak, and the roof was made of cypress shingles. The second story was reached by a covered outside staircase that was penned together with wooden pegs. Two single doors about a yard wide opened into the interior. A slave balcony was at the rear of the sanctuary. Sam J. Harrell remembered "attending services in 1877 when candles glowed in brackets on the back of the old pews...[he] was always one of the hardy few who came and shivered around the wood heater or braved the summer heat." The building was renovated and restored in 1957 and some modifications were made. It is recognized as the oldest building in Morehouse Parish and as the second oldest Methodist church in Louisiana.[82]

The church was built two years before proper title was secured, and when Dr. Hilliard acquired the school warrant land in 1859, he deeded thirteen acres to the church and cemetery. The deed was never recorded, and the church finally received a deed when Hilliard sold the land surrounding it in 1860 to Ben P. Paton noting the exception of the thirteen acres. The cemetery across the road from the church contains the oldest graves with thirty-five markers dating from 1852. Seventeen markers on the church side date from 1880. The earliest marked grave is that of Soloman Vester, who was born in 1815 and died March 15, 1852. The first known burial was Jay Philip Stiles, one of the original founders. He died during the winter of 1806-1807. There are thirty-one marked burials up to the year 1900 with the family names of Arant, Brodnax, Brown, Bullen, Cammack, Carroll, Cheshire, Duckworth, Eddins, Edwards, Floyd, Ford, Gallagher, Greene, Haddick, Handy, Higginbotham, Hunter, Key, McCrory, Nash, Ogbourne, Perry, Phelps, Sisson, Thomas, Vaughan, Wilkins, Yeldell, and Young.[83]

The church was at one time called Plantersville Church. Plantersville was once a "flourishing little town" with "schools, a post office, several doctors, a pharmacy, Plantersville Store in a big red building, and of course, Bartholomew Church." N. S. Greenwood owned a store in 1860.

The first post office in the area was DeGlaize which opened August 16, 1848. Postmasters were Noah Ford (1848), Aaron H. Brewer (1849), John M. Hilliard (1850), Henry Curtis (1853), and Aaron H. Brewer (1853). Plantersville Post Office opened in 1853 with Brewer as postmaster and Hilliard succeeding him. This office closed in 1867, and on October 2, 1882, Brodnax Post Office opened nearby with Benjamin Brodnax as postmaster. The area population was from four to five hundred with no village but a "store and two dwellings."[84] Physicians who served the area were John William Staley (1841), Abner Standish Washburn (1850), N. J. Allen (1857), E. F. Finney (1860), William E. Pugh (1880), and Rae Byrd Levell (1917).[85] Another historic landmark is the home owned by T. C. Moore on Old Bonita Road. L. H. Hill, a resident of Honduras, was the first recorded owner of the land, and the Louisiana style plantation house was built before 1869.[86]

ﻞﻫﻼﻫ

From Mason Cave To Bonner Ferry

The bayou leaves Plantersville and soon makes a long northern loop forming Sam Harrell Bend. Bray Landing was situated before the top of the bend on plantation land owned by S. J. Harrell in 1909. Just before the top of Harrell Bend, the bayou passes by Mason Cave on the right-hand bank. Edwin F. Mason, in the business of transporting freedmen from the east to work on southern plantations, came to Morehouse Parish in 1875. He eventually became overseer of the I. L. Brown plantation near Mer Rouge where he met and married Brown's daughter, Jenny Rosalie, in 1883. After first renting farmland at Point Pleasant, Mason bought the Miller place in 1890. Nine years later he bought land at what would become Mason Cave. A daughter, Mariah Rosalie (Robertson), eventually homesteaded forty acres nearby, and another daughter, Bessie, and her husband, Bob Carter, lived on the Mason farm.[87]

Mason Cave, on the high bluff side of the bayou, was a popular recreational site in the early 1900s. A large, cold spring provided drinking water. Below the swimming hole a treacherous whirlpool threatened swimmers. Lonnie Hughes drowned while trying to rescue a girl from it in 1935. The site was being considered for a state park, but the whirlpool factor caused the park to be placed at Chemin-a-Haut instead. The "cave" is actually a large gully or ravine about fifty yards wide covering two or three acres. Gradual sloughing of the outer edges increased the area through the years. "Perhaps it started out as a cave where the spring runs out and then caved in," mused Gaston Harrison. Edwin Mason kept his mule in a fenced pasture on the top. "Grandpa went out to feed Old Jim one morning, and a washout had caused the fence to fall in. Old Jim had fallen in the gully and was killed," said Edwin Robertson. Huge oaks and other hardwood formed a canopy that kept down undergrowth. The timber was clear-cut, and the erstwhile natural park is now only an overgrown thicket. Steve Atkins, who frequented the site, said, "It used to be one of the most beautiful places I've ever seen. You could get lost in the beauty of it."[88]

Four miles north of the top of Sam Harrell Bend is the community of Tillou on the Old Berlin Road. When Tillou Post Office was established on April 24, 1891, with George W. Westbrook as postmaster, the outlying population was around four hundred with "no village." George Westbrook owned a small store and a groundhog sawmill. Tillou School, which went through the ninth grade, was in existence by the 1920s and closed upon consolidation with Bastrop. The Baptist congregation later used the building until they built a new church. Some families living there in the early 1900s were John Franklin and Sally Catherine (Kinnaird) Harrison, Pink Kennedy, Virgil Kitchens, John Barlow, Frank Jones, and Kelsie, Horrie, and Bussey Sawyer. Other families connected with this area were Kinnaird, Calahan, Crenshaw, Cain, Crawford, Grice, Sikes, and Jones.[89]

The bayou completes it southward loop around Harrell Bend and goes beneath Vester Bridge. Long known as Vesters Crossing, a ferry ran there until the first bridge was built in 1925.[90] The Vester field west of the bayou there is named after early settlers, probably Solomon and Wiley Vester, who are buried at Bartholomew Cemetery, or the Nathan Vester mentioned by Davenport. The 1851 hand-drawn map shows "Vester's Field" at this location, and up the bayou from there is "Heirs of B. Hemken." "The Vester place stretches all the way to the mouth of Chemin-a-Haut Creek," said Gaston Harrison.

Chemin-a-Haut Creek heads in Ashley County near Hamburg and empties into the bayou seven miles south of the Arkansas line. Seven Pines Landing, often called Miller Landing, was near the confluence. An early settler in the area was Chesley Johnston who came between 1839 and 1842. His son and daughter-in-law were buried in 1842 on the Johnston homeplace on the present Park Loop Road. In 1909 two plantations "divided by the high road" (the chemin-a-haut) were there with Mrs. T. O. Leavel of Brodnax, Louisiana, owning the northern one. T. E. Hudson owned a farm nearby that he purchased from V. N. Brodnax of Brodnax.[91] Chemin-a-Haut State Park, situated on 406 acres at the confluence of the creek, has trails that lead to high banks overlooking the bayou. The old swimming hole was just south of the park boundary.

The 1851 map shows "M. Blount's field" directly across the bayou from the mouth of Chemin-a-Haut Creek. The bayou drops south from Chemin-a-Haut for two miles before turning west to go beneath the Crossett Bridge on Highway 425. Just upstream from the bridge is the site of Wards Ferry. Having a rock bottom, this location was also a ford during low water. From there the road followed the bayou northward for a short distance and then looped west toward Beekman. This is the area of the old Ward Plantation that at one time encompassed around 1,300 acres. Davenport mentions Wiley J. and Robert H. Ward being on the bayou around 1858-1860, and the 1851 map shows "Wiley Ward's Field" at this location. Robert W. Ward owned a plantation in 1860.[92]

Jonathan Naff, son of Henry Hoss Naff, was born in Tennessee in 1831 and came to Morehouse Parish the same year. He became a farmer in the Beekman area. His son, John Henry Naff, also farmed at Beekman. Another son, James Ford "Jim" Naff established Naff plantation along the bayou south of Chemin-a-Haut Creek around 1915. Adjoining Naff to the south was Tom Day whose farm was just north of the bridge and on the southernmost part of the old Ward plantation. He purchased the farm from John Hope in 1906. Tom Day was the son of Robert Hamilton "Ham" Day who came to Morehouse Parish with his brother, Marshall, in 1870 on a cattle drive. After living in Arkansas and Texas, Ham Day settled near Beekman in 1892. Tom Day married Katie Naff, daughter of John Henry Naff, and Jim Naff's second and third wives were Addie Lee and Mary Ann Day, daughters of Ham Day. Mr. J. Weinstein of Bastrop owned part of the Ward plantation north of Day by 1909. Tom Day began running a ferry at the old Ward Ferry location in the 1920s and had a store on the west (north) side of the bayou. When the new Crossett Road came through in 1927, he moved his store to the roadside. A narrow wagon trail followed the bayou west to Wardville and parts of it are still visible. Church groups came to the ferry landing to hold baptizings.[93]

The bayou then makes a large southward bend near Wardville, an early settlement. Wardville Post Office was established on July 7, 1903, with Della Bezoni as postmistress. In October the following year, it closed with mail going to Bastrop. When the Arkansas, Louisiana and Mississippi Railroad came through in 1908, a hotel and depot were built at Wardville, and Frank Lumas opened a store. The train imported supplies and exported carbon black, which was produced from natural gas and used in pigments and rubber products. Parts of the foundation of the old carbon plant can still be seen. The railroad bridge across the bayou was a turning bridge to allow for steamboat passage, and the same bridge is still in use. Trains stopped at the bridge to get water from a water tank for their steam engines.

Leaving the bridge the bayou bends south to pass by Bussey Brake. International Paper Company began building this 2,200-acre reservoir in 1957 to provide a reserve water supply for the paper mill. After completion it was filled with water pumped from the bayou during the winter high water stage. The company pumps water from the bayou and, during low water periods, adds water to the bayou from the reservoir. One of the reasons IP located their mill in Bastrop was because it needed pure water for the papermaking process and the bayou supplied that. "We would not have IP if not for the bayou," said Benton Hunt. Bussey Brake is open to the public for fishing and recreation.[94]

A few miles to the south, the bayou runs under Bonner Ferry Bridge, the site of another old ferry crossing. Bonner family members buried in Old City Cemetery are Anna Hill (1859-1931), John Mushatt (1829-1900), Samuel L. (1854-1894), and William F. (1884-1960). Other settlers in Ward Two, west of the bayou, were Joe Hedge, Crawford Hamil and Chesley Johnson (1844), Andrew Cain (1848), Robert and S. M. Stevenson (1851), Joseph Kelley, James Humphrey, and Elijah Hughes (1853), Robert Haile and James Callahan (1855), Dr. J. E. Hope, S. Brown, and Frank Benson (1857).[95]

⚜︎

Bastrop

When Morehouse Parish was split off from Ouachita Parish in 1844, the first order of business was to select a site for the parish seat. An obvious location was at the intersection of the two main roads, Lind Grove, which ran from the state line to Monroe, and the Lake Lafourche to Point Pleasant road, which ran west from Prairie Mer Rouge. This intersection is believed to be at present Madison and Washington Streets. Already living there was a Mr. Gillespie who owned a blacksmith shop. Some of the commissioners and justices of peace were John Temple (parish judge), Aaron Livingston, S. F. Mains, W. A. Doles, James Woodburn, and J. B. Davenport. They chose to name the village Bastrop after the Spanish colonizer. Bastrop Post Office was created May 26, 1846, with Thomas L. Simpson as postmaster.[96]

A two-story courthouse and a jail, both built of hewed pine logs, were in place before June 1846. A brick courthouse replaced this log structure within a few years. The second courthouse burned in 1870 during the Reconstruction upheaval, and a new one was built the following year. The first sheriff was Colonel Aaron Livingston who also built the first hotel. Two saloons quickly went up. Andrew J. Hunter and Sylvester G. Parsons became the first attorneys to open practice. Augustus Stevens opened the first store. Within a few years R. C. Hendricks, S. Sugar, M. Levy, Wolf Silbernagel, and J. E. Emsewiler owned general merchandise stores. Robert B. Briscoe had the first drugstore. Early doctors were J. E. Matthews and William Maconchy. The first two ministers, who were Methodist, were J. L. Wright and Raynolds Trippett. Mr. and Mrs. Rolfe were managing a school for girls by 1850. Isaac T. Naff taught at the first coed school. A brick courthouse replaced the log structure within a few years.

W. A. Doles succeeded Livingston as sheriff in 1846. Following him were A. B. C. Winfrey (1848) and Thomas N. Barham (1850). Early mayors were E. K. W. Ross (1869), L. B. Trousdale (June 1871), Edward Starsney (November 1871), J. E. Emswiler (1872), Frank Vaughn (April 1873), D. B. Smith (June 1873), R. A. Phelps (1875), Frank Vaughn (1876), Samuel H. Stivens (1877), Frank Vaughn (1881), B. McFarland (1883), J. Lee Pettit (1886), James Campbell (1890), C. F. Baird (1894), S. E. Burwell (1896), J. E. Burwell (1897), W. M. Taylor (1898), Joseph Miller (1899), and David M. Evans Sr. (1903).[97]

In 1860 a roving newspaper reporter visited Bastrop and described it as a "very pleasant little town" with a "flourishing business." The prominent merchants were Bobo & Evans, Silbernagel & Company, M. Levy & Co., C. A. Williams, Friedham Brothers, and E. B. Pettes. Methodist and Baptist churches were in place, and F. D. Armstrong had a hotel. W. Prother was publishing the *Morehouse Advocate*, the only newspaper in the parish. R. A. Phelps was mayor and parish officers were A. J. Bobo, sheriff; James Bussey, clerk; J. F. Naff, recorder, and W. L. McMurtey, assessor. Population was 417. Among the occupations listed in the 1860 census were twelve carpenters, a brick mason, three shoemakers, four seamstresses, a butcher, three teamsters, two blacksmiths, a saddler, a wagon maker, two carriage makers, a gunsmith, two pilots (steamboat), two tailors, two dentists, five doctors, nine merchants, eleven lawyers, two teachers, one minister, two silversmiths, and one artist. Merchants received their goods and planters shipped their cotton by steamboats at Point Pleasant, less than two miles away.[98]

After the Civil War and a violent Reconstruction period, the town continued to prosper primarily from the surrounding agricultural base. The population in 1870 was 521. The arrival of the railroad in 1890 further boosted the economy. Bastrop National Bank opened in 1892 with Judge James Bussey as president. The discovery of natural gas in 1916 at the nearby Monroe Gas Field, which encompasses approximately four hundred square miles in Morehouse, Ouachita, and Union Parishes, profoundly altered the future of Bastrop. With low priced fuel available, new industries moved to the area. Carbon plants, brick manufacturers, lumber mills and paper mills moved in, and Bastrop boomed as an industrial center.[99]

R. J. Cullen and L. H. Fox built Bastrop Pulp and Paper Company in 1920. The mill not only provided employment for many but also bought logs from local suppliers. Constant streams of wagonloads of pulpwood arrived day and night from the surrounding pine forests. By 1930 the company, now Southern Kraft Corporation, part of International Paper Company, built a second mill, Bastrop Mill, for the manufacture of fiberboard. Both remained in operation until the older mill closed. IP eventually built mills for the manufacture of milk cartons and paper bags. Other industries in the early 1930s were Continental Paper & Bag Company, Frost Lumber Industries, Louisiana Chemical Company (alum manufactures), Boltz Manufacturing Company (turned wood products), Three Rivers Glass Company (glass containers), Edward Lumber Company, and Bastrop Brick Company.[100]

Hymann I. Seligman, son of Jake Seligman of Bonita, opened a store in Bastrop in 1923, and this business is currently in operation under different ownership. Snyder's Store and R. L. Thomas Hardware were open by the early 1930s. Prentiss Franklin and Louise Dunn founded Dunn Candy Company and Wholesale in 1928 and ran it until they sold in 1971. Bastrop General Hospital opened in the early 1930s with nineteen beds. The Felician Sisters began administrating it in the early 1940s and continued until 1952 when the city assumed management. The parish took it over in 1956, and at that time it became Morehouse General Hospital.[101] With a current population of around 14,000, Bastrop remains a stable industrial and agricultural center.

In 1926 George A. Winkler built a log cabin at the fork of the Crossett Highway and Old Bonita Road. He and his wife operated Log Cabin Service Station, which also carried groceries, until the early 1940s. The store later became Neel's Grocery.[102] The community still carries the name, Log Cabin.

✿❀❀✿

Point Pleasant

The bayou leaves Bonner Ferry Bridge to continue its route around Bastrop and next flows beneath Pleasant Drive Bridge. Below Anderson Lake the bayou passes by Douglas Cemetery on the east bank. A Baptist church and cemetery existed at this location by 1832. This church and three others in northern Louisiana were members of the Concord Association at this time. Bayou Bartholomew Baptist Church was "on the east bank [of the bayou] near old Point Pleasant." Jacob Hickman, a Baptist minister, settled on the bayou "near Point Pleasant" around 1811, and it is possible that Hickman was the founder of the church. Hickman eventually bought a parcel of land in the area known as the "Shaker tract" that contained approximately 4,000 acres. "Ballinger's Camp" was on this land at the time of purchase.[103] The Shaker tract is mentioned once more as being owned by Benjamin Scriber. Hickman bought land from George Hook in 1816 and "made settlement on it where Guice's dwelling is situated." In 1822 Hickman sold land east of the bayou to Phillip Hook. Hickman's daughter, Edna, who married Alexander Peck, received eight hundred acres from her father on the west side of the bayou in 1844.[104]

The Baptist church and cemetery were on property owned by the Newman family. William A. Doles acquired the land after the death of Mary Ann Newman and in 1836 donated a plot to the church. Lemuel Newman represented the church in the transaction. Doles sold the remainder of the tract to Asher Temple in 1844, and Temple eventually sold to Daniel B. Douglas. Alexander Nicholson Douglas was buried there in 1832, and Daniel B. Douglas and wife, Cynthia Paramore, were buried in 1882 and 1875 respectively. Samuel Newman was buried in 1832, and Mary Ann Lovett Newman in 1836. Edwin Brown Hutchinson, son of J. N. and Lizzie Hutchinson was buried in 1862, and James N. Hutchinson in 1864. Other burials are those of are Marie D. C. Langston (born in Bordeaux France in 1800 and died 1878) and Lizzie Starsney (born 1836 and died 1878, wife of Edward Starsney and daughter of Daniel B. and Cynthia Douglas).[105]

The bayou then reaches Point Pleasant Bridge less than two miles west of the center of Bastrop. The first permanent settler at old Point Pleasant was Francois Bonaventure who acquired a 2,000-acre land grant and established a trading post in 1775. Steamboats began coming up the bayou by 1833, and the Point became a major landing.[106] Isaiah Garrett, who later became a distinguished Louisiana lawyer, opened a small store around 1830.[107] Henry Hoss Naff Sr. arrived in 1831 and opened up a farm. Naff died in 1842 and was buried at Point Pleasant.[108] John R. Temple opened a second store, built a warehouse, and in 1840 built a steam-powered sawmill in partnership with William Lawhead, who operated it. Ben R. Temple, brother to John, went into business as a freight agent for the steamboat trade. The Weaks brothers owned a warehouse downstream from Temple.[109] More warehouses were built as steamboat trade grew. Point Pleasant Post Office, established July 27, 1837, with E. D. Garrett as postmaster, continued in operation until 1846.

Abraham Scriber bought the John McBride land grant consisting of 3,000 acres in 1818. After his death his widow, Lydia, married John T. Faulk who bought the Scriber estate and sold half of it to Benjamin Scriber.[110] A large marble obelisk stands in a heavily wooded area between the bayou and Levee Road about half a mile from Highway 165. "To the memory of Abraham Scriber" is engraved on the monument. In 1895 Alexander-Lawson AME Church and Cemetery was established at this location, and the pioneer's grave is in this cemetery, which is abandoned and overgrown. Also present at this location is a large pile of fired brick, a large above-the-ground concrete vat, and cable-scarred trees that were probably part of a gin or sawmill operation.[111]

Moses Guice rented a farm six or seven miles from the mouth of the bayou in 1841 and three years later bought a plantation on the west side of the bayou near Point Pleasant from Judge Ephraim K. Willson. Eli K. W.

Ross and Robert B. Jones were neighbors to Guice. A. D. Peck, who owned a large plantation, was the first to settle on the east side. He later sold to Hannibal Faulk who sold to Colonel L. P. Spyker in January 1857. Charles Polk settled on the east side, and Tom and Horace Polk established plantations on the west side about the same time.[112] The 1851 hand-drawn map shows Joseph Bonnaventure's large tract on the east side of the bayou extending from Point Pleasant upstream. Within the tract is Point Pleasant with six buildings and "B. Temple's house." On the bayou north of Temple are the houses of Dycer and Douglass. Due east of the Point is a tract owned by "Adam Pruett," and to the south are two tracts owned by Edna Hickman. South of there, within a large westward bend, are two tracts owned by Hannibal Faulk and Ephraim K. Willson. On the west side of the bayou from the northern half of the Bonaventure tract are three tracts owned by Edna Peck, Hannibal Faulk, and "Hannibal Faulk, Eliza S. Collier, heirs of Benjamin Scriber." Moses S. Guice is shown directly across the bayou from Point Pleasant with "Heirs of Needham Boone" adjoining his northern line. Within a large bend directly across the bayou from the Hickman properties is Ely K. W. Ross and wife. Below Ross and across the bayou from Willson is a tract owned by "heirs & Rep. of Mathias Dougherty location rejected." Beecham's field is partially within this tract, and Beecham's house is below.[113]

Colonel Leonidas Pendleton Spyker (pronounced Speaker) was born in 1810 in Virginia, the son of Dutch immigrants. He went to New Orleans as a young man and there met George Oglethorpe Gilmer, a large plantation owner from Bossier Parish. Spyker married Gilmer's daughter, Sarah, in 1844, and Gilmer's plantation eventually passed to the couple. In January 1857 Spyker moved his family and more than a hundred slaves from the Hard Times Plantation near Shreveport to begin anew on Bayou Bartholomew.[114] He named his place New Hope and immediately began improvements. He cleared new ground, planted Bois d'arc hedgerows, and built a slave hospital, brick kiln, and sawmill. The family lived in an existing house until a new one was built. The new home was furnished with goods brought up from New Orleans by steamboat.

A meticulous diarist, Spyker left a valuable record of people and activity at Point Pleasant and Bastrop during this time. The diary begins July 1, 1856, and ends October 31, 1860. It verifies the existence of a school. *After dinner went to the schoolhouse to hear the children...The children came from school while the snow was falling rapidly.* It tells of a church. *James Mason came to say there would be a sermon at the church tomorrow...Went to church to hear the Revd. Mr. Lacy who gave us a very good discourse...Parson Wright came to get Sunday School books at the church.*[115] This church was probably the Methodist church at Bastrop where James L. Wright and Thomas J. Lacy were pastors for the Bastrop

Circuit. Spyker was instrumental in the building of Christ Episcopal Church in Bastrop and bought adjoining land that he donated for a cemetery.[116] The diary reveals several general locations of homes and sites. Spyker mentions that he rode down to see Mr. Beachum, up to Mr. Mayo's, up to Colonel Ross's ferry, rode Waddell's ferry down to Tom Polk's, forded the bayou at Colonel Polk's gin house, and came home from Bastrop via Mr. Livingston's. He bought land in the bend above him from Mr. Emswiler and bought S. F. Heard's scrip for half of the land in the bend above known as the Copley or Bloody Bend. Mr. Naff evidently owned the other half. The Emswiler house was downstream. In Bastrop he did business with Mr. Todd and McLeish (a land transaction), collected money from Bobo on Mayo's draft, went to Briscoe's drugstore, and paid his accounts with R. M. Hinson and Sellernagle [*sic*].[117]

Spyker faithfully recorded daily events in the community. Tom Summerlin's twin children died of scarlet fever. Mr. Hart "passed" and Mrs. Mayo had twins. Mr. Elton, Andrew and Tommy put up a new gristmill. R. C. Cummings gave Spyker a Southdown ram. Doctors mentioned were Collier, McConkey, Martin, Armstrong (died), Cummings, Traylor, and Gray. Dr. McGraw came and plugged Spyker's teeth. Dr. McConkey lived in Bastrop but visited several times a week – usually right at dinnertime. Friends and neighbors visited daily and were well received, often staying for dinner. However, some were not so welcome. Peddlers stopped by occasionally and were hurried out. Once a "beggar woman" came. And then there was Mr. Hubbard who *came and billeted himself on us for the night.* The gracious host did have a limit to his hospitality. *A crazy man named Lee called to spend the night but we shipped him.*[118]

The Spyker family lived through the Civil War at Point Pleasant. Raiders ravaged the plantation near the end of the war, and Spyker rented it and moved to New Orleans where he entered the cotton commission business with Colonel Milton Sandidge, his brother-in-law. He died of yellow fever in 1867.[119] The original house no longer exists, but the site on Levee Road near Holley Farm Road is marked by a grove of pecan trees. Rank undergrowth consisting of wisteria, lilies, and shrubbery planted by the family almost conceals the brick walkways that once led to this plantation home. In the summer the old magnolias still permeate the atmosphere with their fragrant blossoms.

Point Pleasant became a ghost town after the drastic decline of steamboat trade in the first decade of 1900. C. C. Davenport wrote in 1911, "There is not a building left standing at the old landing and not once in a whole year does a steamboat tie up and discharge freight at it."[120]

Ouachita Parish

Island DeSiard (Old Sterlington)

From Point Pleasant the bayou continues on the last part of its journey to its juncture with the Ouachita River north of Sterlington. James G. Sandidge of Bastrop owned Keno Plantation, which stretched "for miles along the bayou," in 1909. At the same time Mrs. Clara Barber of Pine Bluff, Arkansas, owned a plantation at Sycamore Landing located on the east bank below Keno Plantation. Sycamore Landing was in a small bend just before the present junction of "Dead Bayou" and "Running Bayou."[121] Dead Bayou is a twelve-mile loop of the original bayou bed that was cut off when a shortcut channel was constructed in 1932. It is also called Bartholomew Lake or Cut-Off. The channel, which reenters the original bayou bed less than a mile from the mouth, is called Running Bayou. A steel span bridge, constructed over the channel to connect with the Ouachita City Road, washed out during a flash flood in later years.[122]

The area between the Ouachita River, the last section of the bayou, and Bayou DeSiard, and stretching to Monroe was called Island DeSiard or simply "the Island." Bayou DeSiard is shown on early maps variously emptying into Bartholomew or Bartholomew emptying into DeSiard. An 1850 article explains this unusual course. "The Bayou de Siard is a legitimate Bayou. At low-water it has two mouths, emptying into the Ouachita and Bayou Bartholomew. When the Bartholomew rises sufficiently, the water from her pour through the Siard; and at such times the Siard, if cleared out would be navigable all round to the Ouachita for steamers carrying 200 bales of cotton. This Siard, with the Bartholomew and Ouachita River, forms an island, upon which are situated some of the finest cotton plantations in Louisiana..."[123]

Some of the de Bastrop and Maison Rouge land claimants stayed in this area with their descendants intermarrying and becoming permanent citizens. George Hook, son-in-law of James Morrison, moved off the disputed Maison Rouge claim and bought 504 acres on the bayou by 1812. In 1818 he bought 1,000 arpents "located on Bartholomew across from old cabin" from John McBride, an original settler. After Hook's first wife died, he married Abraham Morhouse's widow, Eleanor Hook Morhouse, who was reputedly his cousin. Hook was sheriff from 1810 to 1814. M. J. Thomas bought the Hook plantation in 1820. Laurent (or Laurence) Cavet owned land east of the Ouachita River near the mouth of Bayou Bartholomew that he sold to Joseph Coupally in 1792. Maison Rouge bought the tract in 1795, and James W. Mason, Harriet Handy, John T. Sterling, John T. Faulk, James H. Brigham, and C. A. McLauchlin later owned parts of it. Cavet also owned 240 arpents on the bayou near DeSiard that Hugh Stephenson bought in 1814. Stephenson lived below Cavet and Joseph Pomet (variously spelled Pomer and Pomier) lived above Cavet in 1812.[124]

Henry C. Bartlett was living on the bayou by 1820 near the site of the future home of M. S. Dixon. He married Nancy Morrison, daughter of Sarah (Morrison) and James McLauchlin who settled there in 1793. Another McLauchlin daughter, Margaret Ann, married George Hamilton who bought 1,669 acres of land adjoining George Hook on the east side of Bartholomew in 1805. A son, Charles McLauchlin, married Julia Hook, daughter of Eleanor Hook Morhouse and George Hook. Jesse Collier bought bayou land in 1813 from Needom Reynolds, and in 1847 William F. Collier owned land at the junction of Bayou de Siard and Bartholomew "opposite Gen. Downs' Plantation."[125]

The first owner of the Collier plantation site was the Baron de Bastrop who granted it to Abraham Morhouse. Hugh Stephenson bought the two hundred acre tract in 1812. He died intestate and his wife, Nancy, bought the land back for seventy-five dollars. At her death the property was auctioned, and William F. Collier bought it for $195. Collier sold to Mrs. Mary Ann Neiman, widow of Peter F. Neiman. This lady also died without a will in 1851, and the land went into guardianship for her daughter, Mary Ann, who received it in 1861 at age nineteen. Mary Ann married W. W. Sloan the same year. The next owner was the Elder (or Elden) family. Living at the home in 1870 were J. D. Elder, L. T. Elder and wife, and Mose Elder. Mose Elder married Harriet Long and she sold the plantation to R. L. Moore Sr. Moore later bought the Scarborough Plantation and land near Guthrie Bend from Jessie Harmon Wilson. George Hamilton owned the Wilson land in 1805.[126]

The Downs plantation was south of the Cavet property near the junction of Bartholomew with Bayou DeSiard. Dr. William Weatherbee married Rebecca Downs and lived in this area from 1799 to 1820 and was coroner for Ouachita Parish, which included Morehouse at that time.[127] Guild Miller claimed a de Bastrop grant in 1797. His daughter, Mary Elizabeth, first married Benjamin "Benna" Scriber and then William F. Collier. Miller's son, John G. Miller, married Mary E. Scriber.[128]

In 1815 Robert James Knox married Elizabeth Ann Liles Hook, the fifteen-year-old daughter of George and Mary Morrison Hook. Andrew Allison Hill Knox, brother to Robert, married Martha Amanda Barlow in 1825. Their children were Robert, Savory, and Jane. Another brother, William O. Knox, first married Sarah Parker Anderson and then Julia P. Lewis. George H. Knox, son of Elizabeth (Hook) and Robert Knox, married Eleanor Ann Sterling, daughter of Eleanor Hook Morhouse and Robert H. Sterling and niece of John T. Sterling. Robert J. Knox died in 1826, and Elizabeth married John T. Sterling in 1828. The vast John T. Sterling plantation encompassed some of the Hook and Morrison grant land that was gained by inheritance from his wife's family. Sterling also purchased some of the Maison Rouge grant from Daniel Coxe. George Knox died in 1853 and Eleanor married Augustus Swan, overseer for John T. Sterling at that time.[129]

Upon the death of George Knox, W. W. Farmer bought his land. Farmerville was named in honor of this man in 1839. He died while serving as lieutenant governor in 1853, the same year he bought the Knox land.[130]   Elizabeth and John T. Sterling had no children who lived to adulthood, and her son, George Knox, preceded her in death. Upon the death of John Sterling in 1859, Elizabeth was left a wealthy widow. Upon the death of Augustus Swan, Elizabeth (Knox) and C. B. Routh bought the four hundred acre Swan plantation, Belle Hope, that Swan had purchased from John T. Sterling in 1856. Elizabeth Routh was Eleanor Swan's daughter by her fist marriage to George Knox.[131]

By 1870, A. D. and Elizabeth Ann Russell settled on the east side of the bayou at Russell's Bend where "Dead Bayou" curves away from "Running Bayou." An 1895 map shows a house at this location as well as two houses near the mouth of the bayou on the large Russell tract.[132] This land was part of the old Morrison grant. Living in the Russell household in 1880 was D. P. Selman. Buried in Bartholomew Cemetery are Dr. D. G. Selman (died 1867) and wives, Clara H. (died 1865) and Nancie D. Bartlett (died 1907). Nancie was the daughter of Henry and Nancy McLauchlin Bartlett. D. G. Fluker owned land near the junction of DeSiard and Bartholomew, and Dr. Esker N. Potts owned Pott's plantation by 1899. Pott's Landing was on the bayou near the M. S. Dixon home. In 1880 Potts was living with his father-in-law, Dr. A. S. Helmick.[133]

Arthur L. Smith married Laura Swan, daughter of Eleanor Sterling Knox and Augustus A. Swan, in 1879. At this time he was a bookkeeper for Ollie Steele, a merchant at Ouachita City. Laura Swan inherited half-interest in the Sterling plantation from her great-aunt, Elizabeth Sterling. When Laura died of malaria in 1886, her Sterling holdings were 1,041 acres. In 1888 Arthur Smith married Mary Ann Yongue, the daughter of Delaware (Jones) and Hugh Yongue, who were in Ouachita Parish by 1848. Their plantation, Loch Lommond, was near the mouth of Bayou Loutre on the Ouachita River.[134]

Smith continued to add to his holdings by buying the W. W. Farmer plantation and other parcels. As his children reached maturity, he divided the plantation among them. Children born to Mary Ann (Yongue) and Arthur Smith were Douglas Yongue (married Ella Creary Theus),

Josephine Hill (married Melville Sanders Dixon), Martin, and Marjorie May (married Harvey Lee Gregg). Smith remodeled and enlarged an old house for Josephine and M. S. Dixon on the Farmer place that Farmer had used as a hunting lodge. This house, probably built by one of the earliest settlers, was made of hand-hewn cypress boards and logs that were pegged together. The front walls were made of concrete and brick several inches thick with slits for gun portals. The original house contained four rooms with a dogtrot. The Gregg home was originally an overseer's house on the Smith plantation.[135]

John T. and Elizabeth Sterling built their plantation home on the bank of the Ouachita River and named it Sterlington. He owned a sawmill and kept the best cypress boards for the construction of the house. Built high off the ground, the one-story modified Georgian design contained seven large rooms with a center hallway. Each room contained large, open fireplaces. A fifty-foot wide gallery, supported by fluted columns of solid cypress with Doric caps and bases, extended across the front. Four wide windows, each containing twenty-four panes of glass, opened onto the gallery. The kitchen was a separate building. A. L. Smith bought this house upon his marriage to Laura Swan, and the home eventually passed to his son, Douglas Yongue Smith. The historic home burned November 4, 1944.[136]

A school existed before 1897. On July 3, 1897, Mr. Smith made a motion to discontinue the "DeSiard white school." The following year the school board minutes made reference to materials and labor for a new school. The second school, "Island DeSiard School No. 1," faced Bayou Bartholomew at its juncture with DeSiard. The building was a "cabin with a window on each side." Slate chalkboards were not in use when the school first started, and the blackboards consisted of wooden boards painted freshly black each year by the school board members. This school ran continuously from 1906 until sometime before 1913. Blanche Granary (Mrs. R. H. Oliver) taught there beginning in 1908. A third school was built in 1913 on land donated by L. M. Fairbanks. This one-room school, which went through the fifth and sometimes sixth grades, consolidated with the A. L. Smith Grammar School at Sterlington in 1930. Some teachers at Island DeSiard School were Mrs. Grayson Guthrie, Mrs. Mary T. Lundy, and Mrs. Margaret Hundley. Chrissie Hughes (Mrs. S. Willis Williams) served as School Supervisor of the Ouachita Parish School for thirty-five years. An early school for blacks, known as the Chambers School, was on land donated by R. L. Moore Sr.[137]

The most historic site in this area is Island Cemetery, also known as Dead Bayou or Bartholomew Cemetery. Located on the bayou bank on property owned originally by McLauchlin and later by Sterling, it contains the graves of some of the earliest settlers. Reportedly, Sterling slaves were buried in a separate cemetery adjoining it. It is estimated that the cemetery once covered about two acres and contained around 150 graves. A brick wall enclosed it originally but has since crumbled away. Many of the graves and markers have washed into the bayou, and other markers have been destroyed. Polly Morrison Hook, wife of George Hook, is the earliest marked grave, her death occurring on November 28, 1804. The next oldest marker is for Robert J. Knox who died in 1821. John T. and Elizabeth Sterling are buried there with unusual (for northern Louisiana) raised table tombs over their graves. An elaborate wrought iron fence encloses their graves, and other family burials also have iron fences. The most current marker is that of Margaret Ann Thomas, wife of J. T. Thomas, who died in 1919. Legend persists that during the Civil War a Confederate gunboat stopped there for the burial of a dead comrade. Another legend is that during the digging of one of the last graves, the remains of a Spanish soldier were uncovered.[138]

The town of Sterlington, situated on the Ouachita River about two miles below the mouth of Bartholomew, was described in 1924 as "merely a crossroads." The discovery of natural gas in the area in 1916 would, however, eventually cause rapid growth. At the time of its discovery, the North Louisiana or Monroe gas field was the largest in the world. Harvey Couch, founder of Arkansas Power & Light and Mississippi Power & Light, decided to turn from coal-fired plants to the less expensive natural gas for his power plants. He formed Louisiana Power Company, persuaded Westinghouse Electric and Manufacturing Company and the Aluminum Company of America each to give him a million dollar credit line for the purchase of generating equipment and conductors, and went to work. Construction began in December 1924, and the Sterlington plant began operation in November 1925. He also built a town for the forty-eight families who worked in the plant. "Grander than anything within miles," the town had "a sewage system, concrete sidewalks, graveled streets, electricity, water, and gas service." Single men stayed in a boarding house called the Club. Couch built a church and a school and employed a nurse for his people.[139]

Also taking advantage of the natural gas supply was a carbon plant, Thermatonic, which opened in 1925 manufacturing ink and carbon black. Dixie Ordnance located there and built Dixie Acres, a residential area, for their staff. This company now operates as Angus & Kock and manufactures nitrogen, ammonia, and racecar fuel.[140] Couch's plant continued to grow as part of Louisiana Power & Light and by 1929 was the largest generating station south of St. Louis and Baltimore.[141] One of the first gas wells in Ouachita Parish spewed forth on December 24, 1916, on property owned by Arthur L. Smith where Spanish colonizers previously settled. James Morrison, Laurence Cavet, James McLauchlin, and George

Hook would have looked on in astonishment. They used bear oil for light and wood for heating and cooking.

Union Parish

Ouachita City

Bayou Bartholomew empties into the Ouachita River directly across from the site of old Ouachita City in Union Parish. Previously called Parkers Landing, H. Bry wrote in 1847 that the village of Ouachita City was "lately formed." R. M. Bry visited the following year and wrote, "Here [at the mouth of Bartholomew] I crossed the river to 'Ouachita City,' a village of recent date, and the 'landing' for the freight to and from the parish of Union – its population yet small, is about eighty souls, but from its commanding situation, must soon be much greater."[142]

A steamboat landing and river town, this was one of the liveliest places in the area. There the boats turned into the bayou or continued on up the river, and the larger boats exchanged cargo with the smaller bayou boats. The bank was lined with large warehouses and saloons, and there was a large hotel. The 1851 hand-drawn map shows four buildings along the bank of the river with four others behind them. J. C. Wright, A. W. Davis, and W. E. Studly owned the larger buildings, which were probably warehouses. The road from Bastrop lead to the landing directly across from the village.[143]

An 1895 map shows a trail leading up from the river to the high outer bank. Two buildings are on the bank south of the road, and three more, perhaps houses, are on the bank north of the road. Seven more buildings are on each side of the road. Ollie B. Steele owned a mercantile store by 1879. His bookkeeper was Arthur Lee Smith who became a wealthy landowner. Smith was also a schoolteacher at Ouachita City and in later years donated land for white and black schools in Sterlington. Across the river there was also a big saloon on the "Point" (named Morehouse Point on the 1895 map) on the north side of the bayou mouth. Saloon patrons traveled back and forth in boats or used the ferry. Howard Nolan operated a ferry from the Ouachita Parish side and Dolly Stricklin ran one from Ouachita City with an agreement that they would not cross the river to pick up passengers. Stricklin sold out to Nolan and he then provided two-way service. After ferry service began at Sterlington, the Nolan ferry went out of business. Selma White and Joe Stokes owned ferries at Sterlington.

Bill Jones moved his family by houseboat on the Ouachita from Ashley County to Ouachita City in 1912. His son, Ed, remembered stores owned by John Peck, Howard Nolan, J. B. Brasher, Ida Mae Griffin, and Buck Bradley during the 1920s and 1930s. The post office was in the Peck, Brasher, and Griffin stores at different times. The Griffin store was in the old Griffin Hotel building, "a big and going hotel at one time." Elmer and William Nolan ran Bradley's hardware store. West of Ouachita City at the Spencer Community, Care Beth, J. B. Brasher, Lawrence Spencer, Arthur Simpson, Mr. Striplin, and Newt Mills owned stores. Newt Mills later served as a Louisiana congressman.

Steamboat trade was declining when the natural gas field was being developed and business activity became centered around the gas field work. The area bustled with activity as boats, ferries, and oxen-pulled wagons carried supplies and equipment to the sites. When a bridge was built at Sterlington in 1931 Ouachita City went out of existence.[144] Melburn Sullivan, who worked Ouachita boats, told his stepson, Jimmy Berry, about the first burial in the cemetery. Jimmy said, "This girl worked on a showboat. She died on the boat, and they buried her there."

Thus ends the long journey of Bayou Bartholomew through southeast Arkansas and Morehouse Parish. The 359 mile long bayou is truly a stream of history. It served the people who lived along it in various ways, the most important of which was as a transportation route. Bayou dwellers eagerly waited to hear the long resonating blast of a steamboat whistle and the cry, "Steamboat coming round the bend!

 Chapter Five

A Steamboat Thoroughfare

Canoes, Flatboats, and Keelboats

They drifted mostly, but sometimes they had to use poles to push the boat along or pull it with ropes

B. L. Beasley

The bayou served as the principal transportation route for the American Indians who hollowed out tree trunks with stone tools for their canoes. These dugouts, or *pirogues* as the French called them, were lightweight and fast, yet not very stable. A well-preserved cypress dugout with slightly incurved sides, flat bottom, and platforms (perhaps seats) at each end was discovered on the Red River in northwest Louisiana. The thirty-one foot long by twenty-two inch wide canoe dates to the second century A.D. In 1999 a fisherman found a similar dugout half-submerged in the Saline River near the mouth of Salt Creek in the Benton area. This canoe is twenty-three feet, eight inches long with two to three inch thick walls and appears to be made of yellow pine. Rope abrasions are evident on an anchor stone found nearby and on the bow of the boat. Made with stone tools, the dugout is estimated to be between 800 to 1,000 years old.[1] These canoes are representative of those used on the bayou in the same time period.

The early French trappers and hunters also used dugouts, but these were chiseled out with iron tools. The colonial French and Spanish used flat-bottom barges which were propelled by poling, rowing, or cordelling (towing with ropes), and, when conditions permitted, sails. A long rudder provided steerage with assistance from the oars. Each stream dwelling family owned a *voiture* (barge) or *pirogue*. The *voiture* had a partially enclosed roof over living and storage quarters. Still dependent upon water for a major transportation route, the earliest settlers used flatboats which were similar to the French barge. These were roofed and sided houseboats with an open area for stock and cargo. Some had brick fireplaces with chimneys, and others used boxes of sand or kettles for fire hearths. These usually downstream-only boats were propelled by the current and aided and guided by long rudders and oars. Obstacles such as sandbars or logs were overcome by cordelling, when ropes were tied to trees and then used to pull the boat across.[2]   When flatboats, which sometimes doubled as floating stores, took a year's harvest of pelts or other products downstream, they were usually broken up and sold for lumber. If the owners bought supplies, they loaded the boat and slowly, laboriously worked their way back upstream. If they traded for cash, they usually walked or rode horses back.

An example of arduous cordelling took place in 1806. Captain Josiah Davenport, a former sea captain, had traded his boat for money and slaves and was offering slaves for sale in New Orleans when Abraham Morhouse approached him.   Morhouse, needing manpower to pull a boat up the Mississippi and Ouachita to Fort Miro (Monroe), talked Davenport into using his slaves for that purpose. He also managed to arrange a loan. "Capt. Davenport loaned Mr. Morhouse the money and he used his savages – young Africans – to pull the pearogue [sic] to Monroe...tradition says that long ropes were made fast to the boat, the Africans on the banks with ropes over their shoulders, pulled the boat to its destination."[3]   The "pearogue" to which C. C. Davenport referred was presumably a flatboat or barge. In this type of cordelling, the towlines were carried by way of a skiff to trees on the bank and tied. The slaves then pulled the boat by walking on the bank on a footway. When the rope was pulled to the limit, it would be reset upstream and the process repeated. Benton Hunt said that his father told of seeing traces of the old "towhaut" (towpath) trail along the bayou near Zachary.

The development of the keelboat provided easier upstream passage as the shallow keel gave less resistance to the water. They were also propelled by poling, cordelling, rowing, and some sailing.   When boatmen encountered a channel with a dense growth of overhanging trees, they used "bushwhacking," a technique whereby each man gripped a limb at the bow, pulled on it until he reached the stern, and then returned to the bow to repeat the maneuver. Filhiol used this method of travel to explore the Ouachita to Ecore a Fabre in 1783, and Hunter and Dunbar used a keelboat and modified keelboat or barge for their exploration of the same river in 1804.[4]

Walter Havighurst described the hearty keelboatmen. "[They] had their own life and lore, even their own language – full of roaring oaths and exaggeration. They had their own costume – red flannel shirt, tanned leather cap, butternut trousers and faded blue jacket. They tapped barrels of cider and whiskey, cooked their meals in a box of earth on the cargo roof, took turns at the steering oars...They napped on the deck and jumped up to face the river hazards...Their life held the romance of extremes, blissful indolence and Herculean toil, the solitude of the river and riotous nights ashore, serenity and danger, frolic and death."[5] The legendary folk hero, Mike Fink, was a keelboatman.

Before the coming of the steamboats, farmers transported cotton down the bayou to markets in Monroe and New Orleans by rafts, barges, and flatboats. This provided an easier conveyance than ox carts on crude wagon trails struggling overland to destinations on the Mississippi or Ouachita. Dr. John Martin Taylor at Hollywood Plantation in Drew County had his gin on the bayou and loaded bales of cotton onto log rafts that he had constructed for this purpose. He carried his cotton down the bayou to the Ouachita and on to New Orleans where he sold both cotton and the logs from the raft. After purchasing supplies, he returned by steamboat up the Mississippi to Cypress Landing or Gaines Landing and then went by ox cart across the swamps to Hollywood. The mouth of Cypress Creek was nineteen miles from his home and Gaines Landing was thirty. Lloyd Smith of Garrett Bridge in Lincoln County and Betsy Rodgers of Dermott both remembered older folks talking of taking cotton down the bayou by barge or flatboat. B. L. Beasley of Bastrop reported flatboats still being in use around the turn of the century. He said, "Mr. Peter Poole had a flat boat and he'd take a crew of Negroes and go down to New Orleans to get supplies when the people ran out before the steamboats could run again. They drifted mostly, but sometimes they had to use poles to push the boat along, or pull it with ropes."[6]

The First Steamboats: 1833-1861

The next important river···is the Bartholomew···
Steamboats have ascended it for upwards
of two hundred miles from its mouth.
Hon. H. Bry, *DeBow's Review*, 1847

Although flatboats and keelboats continued to be used until well after the Civil War, a new kind of boat that the Indians called "Penelore" for "smoking canoe" soon took the lead on lower bayou commerce. Robert Fulton's *New Orleans* steamed down the Mississippi on its maiden voyage from Pittsburgh and arrived in New Orleans on January 8, 1812. The Fulton (and Robert Livingston) design was based on oceangoing vessels and proved to be unsuitable for upstream navigation in the swift currents above Natchez. A former keelboatman, Henry Miller Shreve, launched the small *Comet* the following year. In 1814 Shreve "took a little trip" by carrying a load of military stores on his *Enterprise* from Pittsburgh to New Orleans for General Andrew Jackson. After serving Jackson as a patrol boat and troop transport, the *Enterprise* became the first steamboat to successfully go up the Mississippi as far as Pittsburgh in 1815. He discovered on this trip that the keel was too deep and designed his next boat with a shallow draft and almost flat bottom. The *Washington*, a side-wheeler, left New Orleans and reached Louisville, a distance of 1,500 miles, in twenty-four days in 1817. During the 1820s and 1830s designs continually adapted to river travel, and longer and narrower boats with a flat hull and no keel or only a vestige keel evolved.[7]

The first steamboat on the Ouachita River was the *James Monroe*. In 1819 either Captain Nancarrow or Captain J. A. Paulfrey took a bold new step and piloted this boat through the Black and Red Rivers and up the Ouachita. The ninety-ton steamer, described as "a rough piece of work [with] a mast and sails," arrived at Fort Miro on May 1, 1819. In celebration of that great occasion, the four hundred inhabitants changed the name of their settlement to Monroe. (Dr. McGuire entered in his diary that he saw the boat at an unspecified location on April 3 and that the May 1 date was the second arrival.) A new town, Trenton, evolved on the west side of the river as a result of the coming of steamboat trade and became the most important cotton shipping center on the river.[8] The first steamboat to ply the Arkansas River, the *Comet*, arrived at Arkansas Post on March 31, 1820. Two years later the *Eagle* ascended to Little Rock, arriving on March 19, 1822.[9]

The bravery of these first captains and pilots venturing into unknown, unpredictable waters is not to be minimized. Treacherous currents, hidden shoals, overhanging trees, and snags required constant vigilance and instant decisions. Overhanging trees ripped off the high smokestacks. Running aground on shoals resulted in a hopeless grounding and a possible hull fracture. The dreaded snags fell into two classifications. "Sawyers" were submerged floating logs with an up and down motion, and "planters" were logs with their branches caught and buried ("planted") in the stream bottom with the log floating upwards. Despite these lurking hazards, the determined steamboat pioneers continued their daring excursions farther up the inland streams.

Captain Raspellier of the *Leopard* made at least two trips to Fabre's Bluff (near Camden) in the winter of 1822-23, and the *Nachitoches* served the area by 1824. Captain Johnston built the *Enterprise* at his sawmill at Saline Landing on Little River in Hempstead County and floated it down the Ouachita and Red Rivers to New Orleans where the boiler and machinery were installed. This boat plied the Ouachita for three seasons before it sank at Ecore a' Fabre. Jacob Barkman launched the small steamer, *Dime*, at Arkadelphia by 1830 and later, reportedly, owned a hundred ton capacity side-wheeler, the *Jim Barkman*. A boat of the same name, a sixty-five ton sternwheeler built in 1859, was owned by Capt. James R. Bangs of Arkadelphia and others. These boats exported hides, meats, furs, corn, cotton, and timber products.[10]

These early Ouachita captains passed the wide mouth of Bayou Bartholomew and heard of the large cotton plantations along the stream. Some cotton producers no doubt asked them to export their cotton. At some point before 1833 the first steamboat headed up the bayou. That year 125 citizens of Chicot County (which included all of present Chicot, Drew, Ashley, and part of Lincoln County) signed a petition asking for the construction of a canal between the Ouachita and Mississippi Rivers and for navigational improvement of the bayou. On November 18, 1833, Benjamin L. Miles wrote (with uncertain spelling and punctuation) to Delegate Hon. A. H. Sevier, "The improovements necessary on the Bartholomew to render it navagable for Steam Boats as high as the point where we would wish to intersect it with the canal would be but a light undertaking it is a large Bayou with a verry gentle courant has been navigated by fatboats Keel boats and Rafts and no drifts in it. a large portion of it is open and susseptable of Steam Boat navigation it is ferequently assended by Steam Boats thirty miles from its mouth from there up in places it needs some improvement."[11]

The petition called for a canal to be constructed between Townships 13 and 14 from the Mississippi to the bayou, a distance of eleven and one-half miles. (Within this range, the bayou is closest to the Mississippi at Dermott and about fourteen miles from Gaines Landing.) The bayou would serve as the connecting route from the canal to the Ouachita. In

1836 Congress passed a bill providing $3,000 for a survey of the bayou and for the canal route but this was never executed.[12] This kind of petition was not uncommon at the time. As early as 1818 Congress passed a resolution allowing it to appropriate money for the construction of roads as well as canals and for the improvement of waterways. Bills for river and harbor improvements followed in 1824. In 1826 many "River and Harbor" bills were passed to provide better transportation. Arkansas Territory Congressmen Ambrose Sevier and Edward Cross asked for appropriations for river and stream reclamation in 1830 but were refused. The introduction of steamboats created much speculation concerning shortcuts, levees, and stream diversion. A Mr. Kimball wanted to divert the Arkansas River into Bayou Bartholomew. An 1858 article in *DeBow's Review* said, "He [Mr. Kimball] is against both levees and cut-offs, but in favor of turning the Arkansas into the Bartholomew, and then into the Atchafalaya with Red River, and then directly into the Gulf."[13]

The most exalted feat that came out of these concerns was the partial clearing in 1833 of the infamous Red River raft by Captain Henry Shreve, who designed snagboats for this purpose and used them successfully on the Mississippi beginning in 1824. Dr. Charles McDermott met Shreve on a steamboat in 1828. His description of the trip gives some indication of the difficulties of travel at that time and attests to the popularity of Captain Shreve. "I was graduated from Yale in 1828 and started home [Louisiana] with Benjamine Bynusce of Port Gibson, Mississippi, one of my classmates. There were no railroads at that time; we went by stagecoach from Baltimore to Wheeling. The Ohio River was so low that the steamboats could not run. We bought a skiff and started down river. The sun was blistering by day, the current slow, and we were inexpressibly sore from pulling the oars. Cold rains fell at night as we camped on the bank. Selling our skiff and provisions...we took passage to Cincinnati in a little steamboat, which was half the time aground. The celebrated Captain Henry Shreve was aboard...."[14]

The notorious raft choked the river for 160 miles. "In places it was solid as a bridge; hunters and horsemen crossed it unaware of the stream beneath them," wrote Walter Havighurst. The confident riverman was awestruck when he first saw the task that lay before him. "The impenetrable mass...covered fully one-third of the surface for 100 miles. At places the jam was so dense it extended solidly to the bottom of the river, twenty-five feet deep." From April to July the resolute captain and his crew removed 1,976 snags from 80 miles of the jam. The appropriated funds became exhausted and Congress refused to expend more. In 1834 Shreve cleared 1,557 snags from the Arkansas River from the mouth to two hundred miles above Little Rock. With funds depleted again,

Congress refused Shreve's request for another appropriation for the Arkansas and sent him back to finish clearing the Red River raft.[15]

With matters of greater consequence pending, it is no wonder that Congress refused the 1833 petition from Chicot County calling for improving navigation on a lowly bayou. The "thirty miles from the mouth" indicates that boats were going as far as Point Pleasant at this time. Records are scant for this period, but Dr. R. F. McGuire, a physician and lawyer who lived on the Ouachita, noted the passage of steamboats in his diary. He traveled extensively and was gone for prolonged periods of time, which accounts for the extended time between the sightings. From 1827 to 1839 he recorded the names, *Decatur* (December 13, 1827, "first steamboat this fall"); *Cincinnati* and *Ontario* (1829); *Mariland* (1830); *S. B. Victory* and *Cincinnati* (1831); *Illinois, Reaper, Watchman,* and *Planet* (1833); and *Romeo* and *Chickasaw* (1837, "constantly running to this place"). In 1831 he wrote that three or four steamboats went to Black's Landing, indicating that these boats were going farther upstream. On December 23, 1839, he wrote, "Steamer *Columbus* here. Can't get up to Bartholomew." The matter of fact tone of the entry implies that some of these boats were routinely going to the bayou. They either went on up it or transferred their cargo to smaller bayou steamers. One such boat was the 102-ton side-wheeler, the *Clinton*, advertised in 1838 as going to Gerrad's Landing (unknown location) on Bartholomew. An 1841 advertisement for the *Columbus* announced in bold print FOR THE MOUTH OF BAYOU BARTHOLOMEW.[16]

At this time these bayou boats were being met by smaller upper bayou packets and by farmers with cotton barges from Arkansas. The 1833 canal petition reveals the interest of southeast Arkansas farmers and merchants in steamboat trade. Cotton was just beginning to emerge as a major cash crop, and farmers were acutely aware of the need for an expeditious method to get it to markets. Timothy Flint made an expedition on the Ouachita in 1835. He wrote, "Cotton plantations are supplanting all other projects. Steamboats plow up and down the forests. The numerous water courses connected with the Ouachita; as the Bayou Barthelimi, Bayou Macon, Rivier-au-Beouf; lakes of Sicily Island...are all beginning to experience the changes of cotton plantations forming on their banks. Probably thirty thousand bales of cotton are already upon these shores and the amount will soon be quadrupled." Steamboats were running on the Beouf River to Prairie Jefferson (Oak Ridge) by 1840.[17]

Point Pleasant was one of three settlements existing in present Morhouse Parish by 1830, the other two being Mer Rouge and Prairie Jefferson. Isaiah Garrett opened the first store in the area at Point Pleasant around 1830, and John R. Temple opened a second store and a warehouse before 1840. Weaks Brothers also owned a warehouse.[18] John Temple first arrived at Point Pleasant in 1833 at age twenty-one and apparently established his business that year.   At a friend's suggestion in New Orleans, Temple bought a stock of goods that he would use to begin a mercantile business on Bayou Bartholomew.   He arrived on the *Buckeye* and was amazed to find no one there to receive or take charge of his merchandise.   The boat was simply tied up to trees and the hands began unloading cargo on the bank.   After firing the cannon several times to announce its arrival, people began to come to the landing.

C. C. Davenport recounted the story of what happened next as told to him by Temple in 1859.   "The first to come to the boat were men on horseback, with guns on their shoulders, pistols and hack knives tied to the horn of saddles, and those men were dressed in every conceivable style. Nearly all of them wore caps made of coon skins, a few wore suits of buck skins and Indian moccasins.   The boat carried whiskey to be sold, and after a few hours the early comers to the boat were feeling good and noisy. Night came and free meals were served to everybody.   During the night there were several fights.   To set on a box, keep an eye on his merchandise, was the way he spent his first night at Point Pleasant.   Judge Temple had a slight stammer in his speech and when he had completed his well told story of that terrible night, he relieved himself by saying by—by—G-d I wished a thousand times during that night I was back in New Jersey."[19]

McGuire mentioned the *Dime* and *Buckeye* again in October 1843 and in August 1844 noted that the *Aid* and *Agnes* were not able to get to the mouth of Bartholomew.   On November 28, 1846, the *Laura*, "a very small steamboat," was the first arrival of the season.   This boat was a regular Bartholomew packet. McGuire recorded the *Dallas* going to the mouth of the bayou and returning on December 7, 1847.   In August 1848 the *Laura* "came down Bartholomew" and returned.   McGuire rode the *S. B. Downs* to Point Pleasant and on to Camden in May 1851 and went to Point Pleasant again in March 1852 on the *Swamp Fox*. The *Agnes* was a regular weekly packet for the mouth of Bartholomew in 1844.[20]

Recognizing the importance of bayou trade, George L. and John Kouns and William Tiley Scovell of Ohio bought the *Laura* in 1846 and put her into use on Bartholomew. (John Kouns and "Willie" Scovell, who were lifelong friends, married sisters.)   The next spring they began doing business as G. L. Kouns and Bros. and expanded their operation to include the Red River where they used their *Era* steamers number one through thirteen plus the *New Era*.   The *Era No. 7* and *No. 10* also ran on the Ouachita connecting with bayou boats.   Other Kouns brothers, Isaac Hunter Kouns and Benjamin Brown Kouns, soon joined the company. Captain Scovell's brothers, Noah and Matt, became captains in the Red River trade.   This company had the *Red Chief* (No. 1) built in 1857 specifically for bayou trade.   The *Ironton* [Ohio] *Register* announced the sternwheeler's debut. "A pretty little cotton boat for the Bayou Trade, called the *Red Chief*, length 116 feet, beam 30½, depth of hold 5-3, boilers 18 ft. long, 26 inches in diameter, 4½ stroke. It is said she will carry 1200 bales of cotton. J. G. Shute, Captain; C. H. Kouns, Clerk; Jesse Dillon, mate." Two years later Captain James G. Shute (a relative to the Kouns) and Jesse Dillon bought the *Red Chief No. 2*, an 86-ton sternwheeler that was 109 feet long and 24 feet wide.[21]

With steamboat trade penetrating the tributaries of larger rivers such as the Ouachita, the demand grew for the improvement of the smaller streams. The planters wanted the boats to come to their landings to export cotton as well as to bring in supplies. Walter Havighurst wrote, "Cotton depended on the rivers, and hundreds of steamboats depended on cotton. The river guidebooks thumbed by every clerk and captain listed all the plantation landings along the rivers of the South."[22] Bayou Bartholomew began to receive more attention as a navigable stream. The state boat, *Experiment*, began clearing some obstructions in 1847. In 1848 H. T. Williams, State Engineer, mentioned in his annual report that the bayou, navigable to Point Pleasant for larger boats, could be easily run by smaller boats to the state line if the points and bends were cleared. Engineer A. D. Wooldridge wrote in his 1852 report, "In this district Bayou Bartholomew has been cleared and made navigable as far as Point Pleasant, and considerable work performed further up. Several cut-offs have been made, one at the 'Big Round Turn,' by an excavation ninety yards long, shortening the navigation 90 miles." In 1855 Louisiana used fifty state-owned slaves to cut leaning trees, but the majority of those cut were left in the channel and thus became a hazard.[23]

Advertisements for boats landing at the mouth of the bayou from 1841 to 1861 reveal the interest in bayou trade. This is only a sampling as all the advertisements are not available. All the notices indicate that the boats landed at Ouachita City as well as at the mouth of Bartholomew directly across the river. Warehouses were on the bayou side as well as at Ouachita City. In March 1841 the bold print headline for the "superior steamboat" *Columbus* read **For Mouth of Bayou Bartholomew**. (C. C. Rhodes, master.) The ad for the *Agnes* in May 1844 stated she was "a weekly packet for the mouth" of the bayou. (W. M. Wilson, master.) The *Louisa* was making regular trips from New Orleans to Camden in 1854. Owned by Frank Keeling, the boat was advertised as being "elegantly fitted with modern improvement...having new furniture and carpets." In May 1856 summer arrangements for the *Atalanta*, "a very light draught [15 inches] steamer," included stops at the mouth on her way to and from Camden. (N. C. Briggs, master.) The *Comet* was making weekly landings at the mouth and Ouachita City in July 1859. (Len Moore, master.) The *Telegram*, a "new, magnificent and swift running passenger steamer" left every

Saturday in August 1859 for "Mouth of Bartholomew". (John W. Tobin, master.) The *Silver Moon*, "a light draught, fast running passenger packet steamer" was also a regular in 1859. (A. Greenlaw, master.) The *R. W. McRae*, a U. S. mail line steamer was making weekly trips from New Orleans to the mouth in 1860. (J. W. Tobin, master.) The *National* was a regular weekly packet to Camden with landings at Bartholomew in April 1861. (P. C. Montgomery, master.) Also in April 1861 the *J. F. Pargoud*, a regular weekly packet was meeting the *Red Chief No. 2* at the mouth. (J. W. Tobin, master of the *J.F.P.*) In addition the *Lizzie Simmons* and *Twilight* were landing at Ouachita City in 1860 and connected with bayou boats. The *Lizzie Simmons* advertisement indicated tributary trade.

Advertisements for boats going up the bayou from 1844 to 1861 include the following. In March 1844 the ad for the *Jo Nichol* read, "A Regular Ouachita Packet - **For Bayou Bartholomew**." (Davy Jones, master.) The *Elizabeth*, "a new and substantial packet" was a regular between New Orleans and Ecore Fabre in 1844. "She will also run up the bayou Bartholomew to Point Pleasant." J. W. White, master, purchased her "expressly for the Ouachita trade." In January 1859 the *Grenada* was advertised as a "Regular Ouachita, Bayou Bartholomew and Black River packet" going to Point Pleasant. (Cooper, master.) The *Homer* was landing at Point Pleasant, De Glaize (Plantersville area), Lind Grove, Cora's Bluff, and Arkansas line in 1860. (Levi Hopkins, master.) The bold print headline for the *Red Chief No. 1* announced her as a "Weekly Bayou Bartholomew Packet" in 1861. She met the *J. F. Pargoud* at Trenton to go to "for all landings on the Bayou as high as the State line...returning will leave the State line every FRIDAY. The transfer of cargoes from one boat to the other will be without delay or expense. Time through, FOUR DAYS." (G. L. Kouns and Bros; Jesse Dillon, master; E. F. Gilien, clerk.) In April 1861 the *J. F. Pargoud* was connecting "with the light draught packet *Red Chief No. 2*, and will take freight for all landings on Bayou Bartholomew with the privilege of reshipping." The January 1861 ad for the *Telegram* read, "**For Bayou Bartholomew, Arkansas Line.** Cora's Bluff, Lynd [*sic*] Grove, DeGlaize, Point Pleasant, Ouachita City...and all intermediate landings on Bartholomew." (H. F. Stewart, master.)[24] Lind Grove became a prominent landing and second turn-around. The steamer, *Lind Grove*, built in 1882 for the Ouachita trade with Campbell T. Sweeney as captain, was apparently named after the landing. The *Poplar Bluff* was another bayou boat that bore the name of a port. The *Josie W.* was named after Josie White of Monroe, and the *Addie* was named after Addie McCombs of Hamburg.[25]

In 1842 another petition asked the Chicot County Court "to appropriate the sum of $5,000 for the purpose of clearing out the Bayou Bartholomew, and for appointment of commissioners...." The citizens recommended the appointment of John P. Fisher, Franklin Stuart, and William H. Gaines as commissioners to "examine and enquire into the practicability of removing the obstructions complained of, the benefits which may result therefrom to the citizens of the Bayou and to the country at large...."[26] There is evidence that boats were coming to the Portland area before this date. John P. Fisher settled across the bayou from old Portland by 1833 and soon began construction of a large two-story house. According to a 1939 newspaper article based on an interview with a man whose father sold the land claim to Fisher, "Panes for the high windows, furniture for the home and provisions were brought up the Bayou from New Orleans by steamboat."[27]

By 1847 steamboats were navigating up the bayou approximately two hundred miles. Hon. H. Bry wrote, "The next important river [after the Saline, which he called a bayou] is the Bartholomew, which has its origins in hills near Little Rock, in Arkansas. Steamboats have ascended it for upwards of two hundred miles from its mouth...it could be made navigable at a small expense of labor much higher up in Arkansas." The distances were computed in water miles according to information Bry received from opinions of pilots and travelers. He pointed out that Bartholomew and River aux Beouf were about three times as long with their meanderings than they would be if they were in a straight line. His remark about the origin being near Little Rock was incorrect by approximately twenty-five miles depending on how close the hills were to Little Rock. Be that as it may, the 200 mile estimate places the boats going into Drew County as far as Baxter, which is now at the 185 mile mark. (Mileage distances vary in the Corps of Engineers' annual reports. In 1904 the distance to Baxter was given as 182.) R. M. Bry wrote in 1848 that Bartholomew was navigable for steamboats "upwards of 250 miles." This estimate indicates that boats could be going above Baxter. A report to Congress the same year gave the "probable extent" of navigable miles for steamboats as 150 for Bartholomew.[28]

From February 8, 1857, to April 7, 1860, Leonidas Spyker recorded the names of twenty-one steamboats that passed his home south of Point Pleasant. The busy plantation owner traveled frequently so his diary record is not all inclusive. These boats with number of sightings were the [*W. W.*] *Farmer* (10), *Sydonia* (3), *Fox* (3), *Red Chief* (35), *Silver Moon* (1), *Lucy Robinson* (17), *Young America* (6), *Sun Flower* (2), *Kate Dale* (2), *Tigress* (6), *Moreau* (1), *Gypsy* (3), *Louisa* (2), *John Ray* (1), *D'Arcy* (2), *Homer* (10), [*W. A.*] *Andrew* (2), *Jeannie Kirk* (4), *Red Chief No. 2* (5), *Erie* [sic, *Era*] and *Hetty Gilman* [sic, *Gilmore*](4). Two unidentified boats also passed in the night. The *Tigress* once stopped at his gin house to take on cotton. Spyker exported cotton, cottonseed, a cotton scraper, a carriage, corn, cement, trunks, and letters. Numbers of bales of cotton noted were

250, 18, 45, 199, 117, and 69. The boats brought him cotton seed, clothes, letters, window sashes, barrels of lime and pork, salt, apples, potatoes, oranges, limes, oysters, syrup, steel, iron, fruit trees, Bois d' Arc seed, bagging, rope, hats for Negroes, tin gutters, mill machinery, fruit cans, $30 in silver change, and five dogs. He also received a road scraper, big plow, music book, safe, saddle, mill mechanic, cotton scraper frame, shower-bath, and Southdown ram.

Spyker recorded other information. He traveled to or from New Orleans on the *Tigress, Sydonia, Homer,* and *W. A. Andrew* which landed at Point Pleasant. He also caught the *McRae* and *Persia* at the mouth. The trip to New Orleans on the bayou boats took five days, and the *McRae* made it in three days. The earliest boat to arrive for the season was the *Red Chief* on December 4, 1857, and the latest one arriving at the end of the season was the *Kate Dale* on May 18, 1857. The traffic peaked in February for these three years with thirty-eight boats. March was the next busiest month with twenty-nine listings. Traffic dwindled during the other months with eighteen recorded in January, fifteen in April, five in May, and sixteen in December. One day in January 1860, four boats passed in one day. The diarist also made note of a trade boat stopping by. This was likely a flatboat or keelboat. He mentioned that the *Red Chief* took cotton on her flatboat, which was a barge.[29] Spyker's diary ends six months before the outbreak of the Civil War, but it, as well as newspaper advertisements, indicates that steamboat activity on the bayou was becoming well established by this time.

The vast amount of cotton grown on the large bayou plantations was the contributing factor for enticing the steamers up the stream. A bumper cotton yield in 1859 caused an increase in steamboat traffic, and the 1859-1860 steamboat season saw a significant increase in traffic. The future looked promising. However, a drought in 1860 critically hampered cotton production and therefore steamboat trade.[30] The following year brought even worse disaster with the outbreak of the Civil War. Commerce by steamboats came to a virtual standstill. Some bayou boats, the *Jim Barkman, Jennie Kirk, Tigress, Red Chief, W. W. Farmer, W. A. Andrew,* and *Homer,* for example, were called into service by the Confederate government.

Steamboat Commerce after the Civil War

It is a navigable stream, and the boats come
nearly to the doors of the farmers.
Arkansas Gazette, May 2, 1875

Cotton production and steamboat trade resumed soon after the war even though labor was in short supply and the Reconstruction government had imposed a five dollar per bale revenue tax on all cotton shipped to New Orleans. At Camden the *White Cloud*, loaded with cotton, had somehow managed to escape destruction and took her cargo to New Orleans in early 1865. That year eleven packets transported 45,000 bales from Camden.[31] In 1869 a correspondent for a newspaper wrote, "We have on board now a large lot of plows of the most simple patterns, going up into Arkansas. They come thro' New Orleans, down the Mississippi, past all the cities on the big water, all the way from Pittsburgh. Their cotton pays for it all though. They raise enormous quantities of it...I found a cotton seed in my breakfast roll this morning."[32] In 1866 the *R. J. Lockwood, Coosa* and *Vicksburg* were landing at the mouth of the bayou. The steamer *Swan*, a bayou boat, met the *Cossa* and *Vicksburg* for reshipment on Bayous Bartholomew and D'Arbonne. The *May A. Brunner* was going "as high as the Arkansas line" in 1866. The *Big Horn* was making regular runs between New Orleans and Camden in 1868. *The Mayflower* was reshipping for Bartholomew in 1869. The following year the *Lightwood* was connecting with the *Garry Owen*, and the *Pioneer* was connecting with the *Wade Hampton* for bayou trade.[33]

Cotton production along Bartholomew attracted the interest of four steamship lines that built smaller boats specifically for bayou commerce. In 1867 Captain Elias B. Cryer of Trenton formed a steamship company that sent light draft boats to the upper Ouachita, Saline River, and Bayous D'Arbonne (to Farmerville) and Bartholomew. These packets met the larger boats bound for New Orleans at Trenton, transferred the cotton to them, and received freight to distribute into the smaller tributaries. The Cryer Line stayed in operation until at least 1896. Cryer boats known to operate on Bayou Bartholomew were the *Willie, St. Francis Belle, Sterling White, Tom Parker, D. Stein, Acme, Ora, Rowena, Frank Willard, Bastrop* and *Timmie Baker*. C. C. Honeycutt wrote that the *D. Stein* was "named for Daniel Stein, a wealthy Jew of Farmerville, La."[34]

The Blanks family, consisting of Jack, Fred A., Robert A., and H. Hanna Blanks, entered the Ouachita and tributaries trade in the 1860s. Over twenty-eight boats were in the Blanks Boat Line before they went out of business in the 1890s. The flagship of the line was the fast sternwheeler

Corona, owned by Captain Jack Blanks. Some other Ouachita boats were the *Ouachita Belle, Fred A. Blanks, Idahoe, Tahlequah, John Howard, John Wilson, Lotawanna*, and *John H. Hanna*. These boats connected with the Cryer boats, which received their cargo for shipment on Bartholomew. Blanks boats known to operate on the bayou were the *Josie W.* and *Hanna Blanks*.[35]

Captain Stoughten Cooley, who had been operating flatboats on the Mississippi since the 1840s, was coming down the river in a flatboat during a high water stage in 1868. Noticing a large flood moving through the right bank, he decided to follow it. He arrived at the Upper Tensas and went down it to the Black and Red and back into the Mississippi. Observing the many large plantations along the way, he decided to enter business in the area and built light-draft boats suitable for the smaller streams. His business eventually passed to his son, Capt. L. V. Cooley. In 1880 the Blanks boats began to enter the Tensas region, and the competition caused Cooley to enter the Ouachita and Bartholomew trade two years later. The rival firms eventually eliminated their competition when Cooley became a member of the Blanks company. They remained in partnership until Blanks dissolved in the 1890s.[36] Some bayou boats like the *D. Stein* and *Josie W.* are variously referred to as Cooley boats or Blanks boats. The *Leviere* (often spelled *La Vere*), a Bartholomew boat, may have belonged to Captain Cooley as his given name was LaVerrier.

The fourth company to enter Bartholomew trade was the Rabun Line, which began in 1880. At this time the merchants of Monroe and Trenton, on opposite sides of the Ouachita, were in strong competition for the tributary trade. The Monroe merchants were anxious to receive cotton and other products from Bartholomew and to export supplies on the return trip. A March 10, 1880, article in the *Monroe Bulletin* stated, "The best way to do this is by establishing a line of boats to run from Monroe into Bayou Bartholomew with Monroe as their 'port.' The valley of the Bartholomew is, as everyone knows, one of the favored regions in the South, and we think Mr. Vaughan's estimate of 30,000 bales as the amount of cotton raised in this region, entirely too low."[37]

In 1870 the *Gov. Allen*, a weekly New Orleans to Camden packet, was connecting with the *Pioneer* for the Bartholomew, the *Economist* for D'Arbonne, and the *Trenton* for Camden. The *John H. Hanna*, a Blanks boat, was connecting with the *Ora, Acme*, and *Timmie Baker* for Bartholomew in 1877. Another Blanks boat, the *Bastrop*, was on the Ouachita from New Orleans to Ouachita City by 1877. Captain F. A. Blanks was master of this weekly "U. S. Mail Packet." The *Bastrop* made her seventh trip for the year to Lind Grove on February 13, 1879. L. P. Delahoussaye, clerk, signed the bill of lading addressed to J. W. Bowe for freight expense and cost for a barrel of flour, box of sugar, bag of coffee, box of rice, caddy of tobacco, and plow. The total amount for these goods was $40.21. The New Orleans and Ouachita River Transportation Company owned this boat that sank in the bayou only two months later.[38]

Another company, the Merchants and Planters, also owned steamboats for trade on bayous and the Saline River. An 1877 advertisement announced: "BAYOU BARTHOLOMEW. Merchants' and Planters' Independent Packet. For Bayou Bartholomew. Leaves on Thursday, March 29 at 5 P.M. For POPLAR BLUFF, Point Pleasant, and way landings. The first class and fleet steamer *ELLA HUGHES*. Lew Rice, master. Will leave as above, positively, taking freights for all landings on Black and Ouachita Rivers as high as mouth B. B. Also connects with steamer *BERTHA BRUNNER* for Bayou d'Arbonne, and with light draft steamer for Saline River."[39]

Captain Cryer's Bills of Lading ledger reveals that he began shipping cotton in October 1875 and continued until July 1876 for a total of seventy trips using the *Tom Parker, Ora, Acme,* and *Bastrop.* The following season he began making cotton shipments on January 25, 1877, and made twenty-seven trips with the *Acme, Ora,* and *Timmie Baker* until July 19. On October 31, 1877, the season began again and continued until July 29, 1878. His *Acme, Timmie Baker,* and *Bertha Brunner* made sixty-one trips. The ledger skips to the 1880-81 season, which began October 31 and ended June 28. The *D. Stein, Clara S., and Laura Lee* made forty-eight trips with seven of these being from the Saline River and five from D'Arbonne. The next season began November 1, 1881, with the *D. Stein, St. Francis Belle, and John H. Hanna* making cotton runs. The ledger ends on April 14, 1882, with the last pages missing.[40] The *St. Francis Belle* went above McCombs Landing (the first two embarkations are illegible in Cryer's "Cotton Book") in March 1880, loading cotton from W. H. Nelson, H. D. Bell, M. H. Dean, Thomas Stanley, and R. Bowden before reaching McCombs downstream. After it made its last stops at Crawleys and Grants, it was loaded with 414 bales of cotton. The *Belle* returned in April, going as far as Poplar Bluff.[41]

The white bales accented the green water of the bayou during the cotton export season. The local newspaper carried the following announcements in November 1880: "The *Clara S.* arrived from the Bartholomew last Thursday with 140 bales of cotton...The *Fair Play* arrived in port Monday from the Bartholomew with over 300 bales and 700 sacks of cottonseed.... The *Rosa B.* arrived last Wednesday from the Bartholomew with 575 bales of cotton...." The tributary trade was so lucrative that it gained the attraction of merchants in St. Louis. An April 12, 1882, article stated, "The *David R. Powell*, from St. Louis, the fourth boat sent to the Ouachita by Scharff and Bernheimer, arrived Saturday morning with about 800 tons of freight, mostly for the tributaries."[42]

Bayou Bartholomew had become a steamboat thoroughfare. In 1881 the *Morehouse Clarion* carried advertisements for four bayou steamers. The clerk of the *William Fagan* announced that it "will enter the bayou on the first rise and will continue her trips throughout the season." Three other steamers, the *Willie, D. Stein,* and *St. Francis Belle,* would "make trips in the Bayou during the entire season, connecting regularly at Trenton with the Mammoth Sidewheel Weekly Packet *Fred A. Blanks,* of 6,000 bales capacity." The ad also noted that the *Willie* passed Point Pleasant going up on Saturday evening and returned going down Friday morning of every week.[43] The six-day span in return time conceivably indicates that the *Willie* was going beyond the state line. The *Water Lilly* made the run to the state line and back in twenty-four hours in 1883. On February 23, 1881, the *D. Stein* made her thirty-first trip for the season into Arkansas at least as far as Nobles Landing a mile below Poplar Bluff. A freight receipt for J. C. and A. C. Noble (*sic,* Nobles) from the Cryer Line advertised "Saline River and Bayous Bartholomew & D'Arbonne Packet from Trenton." The Nobles settled the account on June 14, 1882, and E. B. Cryer signed the receipt.[44]

An estimated 10,000 bales of cotton were transported down the bayou in 1881 as well as 70,000 sacks of cottonseed and 192,000 oak staves. Other down-freight items in 1881 for the Ouachita and tributaries included sugar, molasses, cattle (2,139 head), hogs (5,232 head), sheep (685 head), hay, and to a lesser extent, hides, wool, tallow, moss, and farm produce. In 1882 the *David R. Powell* out of St. Louis received 12,000 pounds of hides and 2,000 dozen empty glass bottles.[45] Oren Robertson said that at one time his grandfather, Edwin Mason, shipped his cattle from Point Pleasant.

Captain L. V. Cooley began running his *Tensas* up the bayou in 1882. The paper reported that year, "The Tensas has been entered in the Bartholomew trade as a through packet from New Orleans and will make regular trips as far as Lind Grove, touching at all intermediate points...." Advertisements in 1883 reveal the competition existing between the established Blanks line and the encroaching Cooley line for trade on Bartholomew. A January 6 *Ouachita Telegraph* announcement for Capt. L. V. Cooley's *Tensas,* termed her "The Independent Bayou Bartholomew packet." The same day the paper reported that the *D. Stein,* a Blanks boat, was "headed for Bartholomew." On January 27 the paper reported, "The *Tensas* and *H. Hanna Blanks,* both bound for the Bartholomew, also arrived Sunday...These two boats, being opposition packets, the one running in the Consolidated line and the other fighting it out on her own hook, are following each other like bloodhounds on the trail of a fugitive, and there doesn't appear to be an early date for any cessation of hostilities. The *Tensas* is carrying passengers at $5 and cotton...to New Orleans at 50 cents a bale."

Bartholomew was at the center of a trade war. The advertisements and notices of passages for 1883 read like a scoreboard for Blanks vs. Cooley. March 3 – The *"H. Hanna Blanks* passed up for the Bartholomew yesterday landing a quantity of corn, oats, etc." (The Hanna had entered the Tensas River trade in January 1881.) March 10 - Captain Cooley had gone up the bayou and was "highly pleased with the patronage." March 10 – The *Steamer 10* advertised as a through Bayou Bartholomew packet with L. V. Cooley, master. April 14 - "The *D. Stein* from Bayou Bartholomew arrived Saturday with a full load of cotton and cotton seed, which she reshipped on the *Fred A. Blanks*." April 14 – "The *Timmie Baker*, from Bayou Bartholomew, came in Saturday with a full load. She re-shipped 113 bales cotton seed on the *Tensas….*" The steamer was also carrying cottonseed consigned to oil mills in Meridian, Mississippi. May 12 - The *Tensas* was due "bound for Lind Grove and way landings on the Bartholomew; Capt. L. V. Cooley on the roof…." May 16 – "…the *Timmie Baker* recently brought 7,000 sacks of seed and 30 bales of cotton from the Bartholomew. The boat has delivered to the Bartholomew people about $2,000 worth of merchandise from Monroe merchants."

Other steamers entered the race for Bartholomew trade at the same time. The April 28, 1883, *Ouachita Telegram* reported, "The *Water Lily* [*sic, Lilly*] returned Friday night from Bartholomew whither she had gone under charter of the Cottonport saw mill. This little dinky made a run of 140 miles in 11 hours – 13 miles per hour coming down."[46] The 140 miles was the (then) distance to the state line. The *Water Lilly*, a sternwheeler, was built in 1880 and her "dinky" proportions were 112'x21'x3'.[47]

The season must have closed about this time as the next advertisement appeared October 11, 1883. The *Katie P. Kountz*, a New Orleans, Monroe, Trenton, and Bayou Bartholomew independent packet, "would enter the above trade as soon as the water would permit and would continue regularly throughout the season, connecting at Lind Grove with the packet for Upper Bayou Bartholomew." This boat made three trips in the 1879-1880 season carrying out 2,771 bales. The *Loretta May* was advertised on October 24, 1882, and November 15, 1883. The notice read, "Will ply as a trading and freight boat in the Bartholomew trade…making Monroe her headquarters…will deal particularly in cotton seed." On November 15, 1883, the following ad for the *Queen City* announced her as a regular New Orleans, Monroe, Trenton, and Bayou Bartholomew packet: "Will enter the above trade as soon as the water will permit and continue throughout the season, connecting at Lind Grove with packet for Upper Bayou Bartholomew."[48]

With more boats plying bayou trade, efforts to improve the waterway for navigation continued. An 1870 appropriation from Louisiana for $1,000 was used to clear the channel from the mouth to Point Pleasant, but

the intrepid little boats continued to run the upper bayou. An 1875 letter
from Hamburg to the *Arkansas Gazette* stated, "Through the eastern part
[of Ashley County] runs Bayou Bartholomew, upon and near whose banks
lie the richest corn, cotton and wheat lands in the state. It is a navigable
stream, and the boats come nearly to the doors of the farmers."[49] Col. W.
F. Slemons of Monticello (and father-in-law of Charles Duke of Baxter)
was elected to the 44th U. S. Congress in 1874. He supported public works
projects such as clearing Bartholomew.[50] The first federal consideration
came in 1879 in accordance with the provisions of the River and Harbor
Act of June 18, 1878. This work addressed the type of obstructions and the
cost of removal.   Another survey conducted in 1880 "dealt with the
navigable portion of the bayou, from Baxter Station, Arkansas [Drew
County], to the mouth, a distance of 184 miles." A report based on this
survey suggested the cutting of leaning trees and the removal of snags and
wrecks. The estimate for the improvement work was $26,862, but the
following year only $8,000 was allowed.[51] The *Monroe Bulletin* reported,
"Bartholomew has $8,000. Judging from the dilapidated condition of the
boats that ply its waters, but few streams could be in more need of
'repairs.' Trees overhang, logs jut out and snags point the course. The
most skillful dodger is regarded as the best pilot, and a successful trip is
claimed to be an accident."[52]
    Work began at Baxter in the summer of 1881 and continued through
December when the crew reached Bartholomew Post Office. (At this time
this post office was located two sections north of Wilmot.) An additional
$5,000 appropriation the following year allowed the work to resume, and
obstructions were removed from August through December as far as Lind
Grove. Obstruction removal by the contract method at seventy-five dollars
per mile began in 1884, but this was unsatisfactory and expensive. A
survey conducted in 1885 from Baxter to the Lincoln County line found
logs and shoals in the channel, snags, and leaning trees as well as a railroad
bridge at Baxter. The railroad bridge "formed a complete obstacle at all
stages," and the report recommended that improvement not be attempted
until the bridge could be changed to a drawbridge. A $5,000 appropriation
in 1886 allowed the snag boat, *Hooker*, to remove obstructions, and an
additional appropriation in 1888 permitted the work to continue. That year
Captain E. B. Cryer was quoted in the Chief Engineer's *Annual Report*,
observing that the improvement work extended the navigation season from
three to six months, cut trip time to one-third, and reduced freight rates by
thirty-three percent.[53]
    In an 1879 letter to the *Gazette*, Captain H. S. Taber of the Little Rock
Corps of Engineers reported on the "rivers navigated and improved upon"
within Arkansas. They were the Mississippi, Arkansas, Red, White, Black,
Ouachita, St. Francis, Saline, Petit Jean, Fourche Le Fevere, Little Red,

Little River North and South, Poteau, Cache, Bayou Bartholomew, Current, L'Anguille, and Little Missouri. Total navigable miles of waterways were around 3,470. The report said that boats were running on Bartholomew to Baxter during high water and that the bayou was navigable for six months of the year with recent improvements probably lengthening the period. Twelve thousand dollars had been expended for work on Bartholomew.[54]

Captain Taber also noted that according to the Chief of Engineers *Annual Report* of 1879 the bayou was navigable for 167 miles *in Arkansas* for six months of the year. Baxter is presently one hundred miles upstream from the state line, and even allowing for a reduction in miles by bends later being cut through, the 167 mile figure would place navigation upstream from Baxter. Mary Roane Tomlinson wrote that the bayou was once navigable for two-thirds its length, which would be around 240 miles and 55 miles up from Baxter by current length.[55] If this was correct, and if the first Little Rock, Mississippi River and Texas Railroad bridge (built in 1872) at Baxter was a turning bridge, steamboats may have been going up the bayou into Lincoln County. (There is no mention of a bridge obstructing navigation there until 1885.)

No documentation offering proof of steamboats going north of Baxter was found, but oral history attests to the possibility. Garvin Adcock, born in 1912, said, "I heard the old folks saying the steamboats went to Tillar Gin Company." This was one of the largest cotton producers in the area and was first headquartered in northeast Drew County at Winchester. Eddy Valentine told Curly Birch that he and his brother found an anchor in the bayou near Duncan Cemetery at the mouth of Four Mile Creek. This location is around eight miles south of Tillar. The size of the anchor attests to its having belonged to a steamboat. It was four to five feet long with three to four feet wide arms. Eddy and his brother cleverly used the six-inch wide flukes for plows. Valentine also stated that Eddy Miller said that he worked on a steamboat that pushed log rafts from Tillar to Dermott.[56] Charlie King of the Yorktown area was an old man when he told Robert Mitchell around 1983 that he heard of a steamboat being stranded on a shoal at Smith's farm. He said that it stayed there for two years waiting until the water got high enough for it to float again. The Smith place was near the present location of Crigler, east of Star City. Lois Baldwin Thomas was born in 1896 and moved to Tarry, in northern Lincoln County, in 1916. She said she heard the old folks talking about steamboats coming up the bayou. (A bridge at Yorktown was completed in 1878 that would have blocked boat traffic.) Murphy Brockman, born in 1919 southeast of Star City, also said that the old folks told about the boats coming up the bayou.

The improvement work successfully opened up the bayou for a lucrative cotton trade. The 1888 *Annual Report*, using Captain E. B. Cryer as the source, said, "It is stated that more cotton is brought out of Bartholomew than is shipped on the entire Ouachita River above Monroe, Louisiana." Cryer was a reliable authority; his accounts receivable book for June 1888 to September 1889 listed 352 clients. The *John Howard* was running to Lind Grove (possibly farther) in 1889. In 1890 the *Josie W.*, *Sterling White*, and *Sellie* made a total of forty-two roundtrips from the bayou to Monroe. They carried 17,839 tons of down-freight and 4,000 tons of return freight amounting to an estimated value of $492,700. A letter from Ashley County to the *Gazette* in March 1889 stated, "Our three navigable rivers, the Ouachita, Saline and Bayou Bartholomew, are now in good boating condition and our merchants are receiving groceries and other goods from New Orleans. Goodspeed reported in 1890 that the bayou served the eastern tier of Drew County townships as a direct transportation route to New Orleans.[57]

Captain Cryer's "Cotton Book" discloses the amount of cotton that he alone exported down the bayou during these lucrative years. During the 1887-88 season, which began December 13 and continued into April, the *D. Stein* made at least twenty trips up the bayou. (Some of the back pages may be missing.) The furthermost landings up the bayou were: Arkansas line, Osborne Place, Lind Grove, Upper Nobles Gin (up from McCombs), Green Goodwin and Ohio (around Wilmot), A. L. Anderson (around Point Pleasant), Womacks (Boydell), Normandy (north of Poplar Bluff), Elders (south of Point Pleasant), Womacks and Boyds (Boydell), Point Pleasant, and J. D. Hollaway (above Portland). Of these destinations, eight were in Ashley County and five were to Boydell in the extreme northern part of the county. The *D. Stein* shipped 4,241 bales of cotton and 21,499 sacks of cottonseed during the season. The charge for one bale of cotton varied from $2.50 to fifty cents with the average around two dollars. A small charge for insurance was also imposed. A sack of cottonseed weighed an average hundred pounds and the shipping cost was two dollars per ton plus insurance. Monroe Oil Mill, the consignee, paid for the shipping.

The "Cotton Book" also makes known a diversion from the standard procedure of boats going to the highest point upstream to begin loading cotton. The obliging captain of the *D. Stein* often reached a point downstream and then turned around to pick up more cotton at landings above. Out of the *D. Stein's* twenty trips in 1887-88, it made ten return trips, often backtracking two to four times. For example, in March the loading of cotton began at Womacks (Boydell) and continued down the bayou with stops at Boyds, McCombs, Portland, Alligator Bluff, Carlocks, Normandy, Green Goodwins, Ohio, and Lind Grove. It then proceeded back to Alligator Bluff and Normandy and then back to Portland with stops at Carlocks, Green Goodwins, Smiths, and the Curtis place. It then went back to Womacks where it began loading cottonseed and stopped for seed only at Nobles Gin, S. L. Moores, Clarks, Sol Carters, Portland, Sherrers, deYamperts, Carlocks, Normandy, and Harrels (in Morehouse Parish). The boat returned upstream to Crawleys and stopped at Bonners before leaving the bayou. They consistently took on seed on return trips after all the cotton was loaded on the first trips.[58]

In 1883 Ouachita River boats began carrying freight that forecast the doom of interior stream steamboats. The *Jennie Campbell* steamed up the river loaded with 53,000 bars of railroad iron. The next year two tugs arrived towing barges with 1,640 tons of the same, and the *Frank Henry* brought in six hundred tons that filled "the requirements of the railroad as far as Shreveport...and the remaining six miles of track will be laid without delay." By 1885 the Vicksburg, Shreveport and Pacific Railroad spanned the Ouachita River.[59] The completion of the Houston, Central Arkansas and Northern Railroad from McGehee, Arkansas, to Monroe in 1890 soon began to influence the lucrative steamboat trade on Bartholomew.

The bayou settlements moved to the iron rail. Old Portland left its long established bayou bank locale and moved two miles to the east to become a railroad town. Poplar Bluff turned its face from the bayou and became Parkdale. The small community at Lake Enterprise grew into Wilmot. Lind Grove folded up as business moved to Bonita and Bastrop, but the steamboats did not stop coming. They reduced their rates to compete with the railroad, and in turn the railroad had to reduce their rates during navigation season. The railroad leaders then began to oppose improvement projects for streams. On February 20, 1892, the *Gazette* reported that freight and passenger earnings for the current year at Portland was $15,000 *exclusive of steamboat business.*

Maintenance work resumed in July 1893, and the report gave a detailed account. A snag boat towed a quarter boat to Marble Place which was about twenty miles above the mouth. Since the water was low, the men cordelled the boat from that point. Progress was slow "on account of the swift current and numerous obstructions. At the following places the stream was blocked with fallen timber and drift, which had to be cleared away before the boat could pass, viz: Jones Place, Mound Place, Peterkin's, State Line, Riser's, Jim Smith's, Green Goodwin's, Normandy, Alex Arnett's, DeYampert, Marion, Bloomers, and Dr. Sherrer's. August 22, at the Perkins Place, Ark., about 2 miles below McCombs Landing, the boat stuck a snag and sank." The crew built a new boat from part of the wreckage and then dynamited the hull to keep it from forming an obstruction. "Successive high winds had passed over the bayou during the year, and Overseer Decker reported that never before in his experience had he seen a stream so badly obstructed by fallen timber throughout its entire length...Between Alex Arnett's and Normandy Landing, and at the Arkansas and Louisiana line were the most obstructed portions. Just below Arnett's a jam 150 feet long was removed...."

The 1894 report noted that the bayou was navigable from December 1, 1893, to June 1, 1894 in the past fiscal year. Boats going to McCombs Landing were the *Sterling White* (twenty round trips) and the *Marco* (one trip). The *Belle of D'Arbonne* made twenty round trips to undisclosed locations. Boats making one trip up the bayou were the *Helen Vaughan* (to Red Bluff and Elders), *Parlor City* (to DeSiard), and *H. W. Graves* (to Vester-land). They carried 2,434 tons of cotton, 2,991 tons of cotton seed, 159 tons of saw logs, 2,569 tons of staves, and 665 tons of miscellaneous products for a total of 8,818 tons. Return freight amounted to 3,469 tons.[60]

In 1894, four years after the coming of the railroad, many bayou farmers still favored steamboats over the railroad for shipping their products. The overseer of the improvement work said in his report for that year, "The greater portion of the commerce has been detracted by the Houston, Central Arkansas and Northern Branch of the Missouri Pacific Railway, running along the east bank, owing to the late period at which the bayou usually reaches a navigable stage. If there was navigation at the time the planters begin to move their crops the steamboats would control the greater portion of the trade. The above facts were learned from conversations with the planters along the stream, who do not seem to be satisfied with the railroad as a carrier."[61] Captain Cryer was still serving his bayou clients. His *Sterling White* made her first trip up the bayou for the next season on January 31, 1895, going as far as Vesterland. She continued running until July 1 for a total of at least (two destinations are not named) nine trips, five of which were into Ashley County with Wiggins being the highest destination for two trips. Also in 1895 the *Leviere* made twenty trips to Portland, and the *Parlor City* made one trip to Lind Grove.[62]

Captain Sam Ingram of Bastrop worked on steamboats from 1894 to 1898. During this period he made runs on the bayou to Parkdale aboard the *Stella*, *Parlor City* and *Sterling White*. Advertisements for the *Ouachita* in 1893 and the *Parlor City* in 1901 indicate that Ouachita River boats were still connecting with bayou packets. B. L. Beasley, who lived at Bastrop at this time, said, "I used to stay down at my uncle's sawmill at Ouachita City and watch those steamboats load and unload right across the river at the warehouses."[63] Table 1 reveals the amount of steamboat commerce on Bartholomew that continued for a decade after the coming of the railroad. Items usually listed as "miscellaneous" on freight reports are listed in table 2.

Table 1
Steamboat Commerce on Bayou Bartholomew from 1889 to 1900

Year	Cotton (tons)	Total value of all products
(1889-1890)	2,000	$492,700
(1890-1891)	3,971	826,000
(1891-1892)	2,372	515,000
(1892-1893)	1,000	136,000
(1893-1894)	2,434	564,000
(1894-1895)	1,390	243,000
(1895-1896)	1,235	561,000
(1896-1897)	175	97,00
(1897-1898)	1,206	284,000
(1898-1899)	2,125	382,000
(1899-1900)	385	129,000

Source: Hammond, "Abstract," 179-180. From *Annual Report, 1900.*
Note: The other products included cottonseed, cottonseed meal, saw logs, staves, miscellaneous, and return freight. The tons of saw logs and staves are given in the timber chapter

Table 2
Miscellaneous products shipped in 1889 on the Ouachita and tributaries

Cotton seed meal	sacks		6,145
Hides and skins	pkgs.	112	
Wool	bags	246	
Cattle	head	30	
Hogs	head	1,294	
Sugar	barrels		28
	Hogsheads	17	
Molasses	barrels	5	
Moss	bales	35	
Rice	sacks	795	
Seed cotton	sacks		14
Soap stock	barrels		30
Bones	sacks		51
Pecans	barrels		9
Apples	barrels		223
Potatoes	sacks & bbls		. 127
Peas	sacks & bbls.	192	
Poultry	coops		7
Eggs	boxes	4	
Rags	bales	18	

Source: Annual Report, 1889, 1,598.

Hides and skins, the first products brought down by the early trappers, were still coming down. The moss was Spanish moss, gathered by moss pickers and sold for use as a binder in mud clay or cement for building houses, packing material for breakable goods, and stuffing for furniture cushions. The notation that it was shipped in bales indicates that it had been dried and ginned in a moss gin. A bale of moss weighed from 125 to 150 pounds.[64] The amount of rice is interesting as it was not commonly grown in any large quantity at that time. The export of sugar from this area is also unusual. The bones were valued for their phosphate content in the manufacture of fertilizer, their use for this having been recognized in England more than three hundred years earlier. In the United States, buffalo bones from the Great Plains were collected and used for fertilizer. Slaughterhouses and butcher shops supplied bones for this purpose as well as individual "bone pickers" who salvaged bones from animal carcasses. Rags were used in the manufacture of paper and paper money – thus possibly the expression – "from rags to riches."

The drop to 175 tons of cotton in 1896-1897 and to 385 tons in 1899-1900 reflects on cotton production and drought conditions during the shipping season rather than on railroad competition. In 1900 the *Stella* went to the state line ten times, and the *Alice* made two trips a week on the lower bayou for a total of 104 passages. The *Alice* was powered by gasoline and only weighed twelve tons. In contrast the *Stella's* tonnage was 152. By 1905 the *Handy* and *Welcome* were the only steamboats reported on the bayou. The *Handy*, pushing a barge, made nineteen trips from Monroe to "local points." There were certainly more boats on the bayou than listed in the Chief Engineer's reports, as in some cases the masters simply refused to return the required paperwork. Scott Haddick of Bastrop worked as a mate on steamboats from 1906 to 1912 and during this time made runs up to Parkdale.[65]

Although the railroad was cutting into the steamboat freight business, improvement work continued on the bayou at irregular intervals through 1896. The report of a chopping party's work from May 22 to June 30 that year gives an idea of the staggering amount of obstacles removed.

Channel snags cut and destroyed	4,293
Stumps cut out and destroyed	1,043
Shore snags cut and destroyed	1,700
Logs cut and destroyed	2,729
Side jams removed	5
Leaning trees cut and destroyed	3,183
Trees girdled	26
Square yards willows and brush cut	1,904

The Chief of Engineer's 1896 report noted that before federal improvements, fourteen days were required to make the trip to Baxter because the boats had to stop and cut leaning trees and remove obstacles. He added that the work done had extended navigation to six months a year, allowed for the passage of boats with double the capacity of former ones, cut the trip time in half, and reduced freight rates by fifty percent.[66] The *Rapides* and *H. R. W. Hill* reportedly went to Gasters Landing, where Martin and Williams had a warehouse, two miles below Baxter. The *Rapides* was in the Red River trade in 1858-1860 and 1870 and was on Bayou Macon and Tensas in 1876.[67]

Work continued in 1897 from Baxter to McCombs Landing, which was forty-one miles south. From 1881 to 1897, $45,878.53 was spent on improvements. After 1897 no more improvement appropriations were made, but about $4,000 a year was granted for maintenance from McCombs Landing to the mouth, a distance of 141 miles. McCombs Landing became the official head of navigation at this time, but during high water boats could still reach Baxter. The improvement project allowed safer and easier passage during medium and high stages with the average width of the channel being about 225 feet with a minimum depth of about 8 feet. A railroad bridge near McCombs Landing was built south of present Highway 82 in 1898. Ashton McCombs told Junior Brooks that this swing span bridge never turned for the passage of boats.[68] The turning mechanism is still present on top of a concrete column in the middle of the bayou. There were also turning bridges at Parkdale and Portland.

The *Annual Report* for 1904 noted that maintenance work below McCombs Landing had continued since 1897 with $2,500 appropriated annually. From 1881 to the end of the fiscal year in June 1904, $45,873 had been spent for improvement work and $9,775 for maintenance. The report also summarized the volume of commerce on Bartholomew for the last fifteen years ending in 1903. The maximum reported was in 1891 with 49,299 tons valued at $826,000. The minimum was in 1903 with 2,080 tons valued at $171,000.[69]

A report of a survey made in 1915 in accordance with a new River and Harbor Act recommended that the improvement project be abandoned "for the reason that the cost of any useful improvement is regarded as greater than is warranted by the resulting benefits to general commerce and navigation." From 1897 to 1914, $77,705 was spent on improvements and maintenance; however, some maintenance work continued after this period. In 1920 a federal quarterboat did $1,500 worth of work. After 1925 no funds were available and no further operations were proposed. After 1931 Bayou Bartholomew was no longer included in the annual reports.[70]

Leroy Haynes, born in 1896, remembered seeing the snagboats. "We moved to the bayou around Gaines in 1911, and the boats had just about quit coming up by then. A small snagboat came in 1912, and a good-size one came after that. I would catch a 'possum or old coon or a squirrel and take down there and trade for a can of salmon. They wouldn't take money. The snagboat was a paddlewheeler and had seven or eight men and four or five johnboats. They were blowing logs and snags out with dynamite and that would kill a bunch of fish. They ate a lot of fish!"

In spite of the 1915 recommendation to abandon improvements, the bayou continued to serve as a freight avenue, but shipments dropped drastically. Only seven tons (approximately twenty-eight bales) of cotton were shipped that year. Other products shipped were cotton seed (445 tons), grain (11 tons), shingles (11 tons), hay (6 tons), and miscellaneous (53 tons). Total tonnage was 553 with a valuation of $22,582. The distance traveled was from seventy-five to sixty-eight miles, indicating that the boats were not crossing the state line.[71] Table 3 indicates the decline in bayou commerce after the coming of the railroad.

Table 3
Steamboat Commerce on Bayou Bartholomew from 1890 to 1925

Year	Tons	Value
1890	21,839	$492,700
1891	49,299	826,000
1892	15,155	515,000
1893	7,675	136,000
1894	12,287	564,000
1895	6,655	243,000
1896	17,660	561,000
1897	14,239	97,000
1898	8,075	284,000
1899	12,663	582,000
1900	7,131	129,000
1901	15,979	254,000
1902	13,514	193,000
1903	2,080	171,000
1904	2,789	285,000
1905	2,007	143,400
1906	2,865	245,501
1907	1,502	199,805
1908	4,152	24,937
1909	3,685	110,425
1910		[none reported]
1911		[none reported]
1912	400	7,200
1913	396	81,996
1914		[none reported]
1915	533	22,582
1916	1,150	2,675
1917	12,036	97,680
1918	9,014	60,070
1919	732	14,640
1920	1,575	28,350
1921	1,805	123,715
1922		[none reported]
1923		[none reported]
1924		[none reported]
1925	664	3,894

Source: U. S. Army, Chief of Engineers, *Annual Reports*, 1890 -1925.

Fires, Wrecks, and Superstitions

The boat was loaded with cotton and caught on fire···She said while it was burning all she could worry about was her new red dress.
Charles Naff

The packets used wood to fuel the fires for the steam boilers, and "wooding the boat" was required at landings. Bayou natives often sold wood to the boats. Spyker allowed his slaves to cut wood as a way of making their own money. On March 27, 1859, "The Steamer *W. W. Farmer* came up...Took all the negroes' wood." On April 7, 1860, "The Steamer *Homer* has just landed to take on the negroe's wood." Three days later they sold six cords to the *Red Chief.* Benjamin E. Harville of Ashley County sold wood to steamboats on the Mississippi just after the Civil War. He received $1 to $1.50 per cord. The J. Fred Crawley family at Crawleys Bend "always kept a stack of wood for the boats at their wharf," said Dr. Roy Grizzell. B. L Beasley of Bastrop supplied the boats with cordwood.[72] Gaston and Bealie Harrison told about George and Susan Westbrook selling wood to the boats. They collected pine knots and took them in a steel-wheeled wagon with an ox team to Oak Landing. "George would hear the whistle from Vester Bend at Tillou and have time to get to the bayou to meet it because of all the bends," Bealie said.

A seventy-five ton bayou boat burned around twenty to forty cords a day and usually made two wood stops a day. Pine was favored for its quick, hot fire. Hardwoods such as oak, ash, chestnut, and beech were also used. Cottonwood was not favored as it burned too fast and created a lot of ash. One captain said that using cottonwood was "just like throwing shavings into hell." When in a precarious situation, the boats also used bacon or side fat, which created a fast, hot fire. The supply was plentiful as they carried it by the barrels to their customers. Bacon was also used as a "racing fuel." When two boats came close together on the same course, they often engaged in impromptu races, and the crew broke up casks of bacon to add an extra boost to the already blazing fire.[73] This is probably where the terms "throwing the fat to the fire" and "adding fuel to the fire" originated. These races were not limited to larger streams. C. C. Honeycutt, a resident of Ashley County who worked on steamboats, wrote, "Back in the early seventies were the steamers, *Fair Play* and *Willie*, which belonged to competing companies. They used to run races up and down the bayou...."[74]

Fire and wooden boats and cotton simply was not a good combination. Even though the stacks were very high to carry off the blazing exhaust and to allow the sparks to burn out before landing on the cargo, live sparks did often cause fire. The height of the stacks created another danger as they would topple if they hit overhanging trees, and when they did, fire usually broke out. Nighttime brought on another hazard as the boats navigated by light emitted from pine torch fires in cast iron torch baskets hanging from the sides. The powerful steam boilers also contributed to the constant threat of fire caused by explosions. Before automatic steam escape valves were perfected, the only way to lower the pressure when landing was to "pull the fire" thereby releasing the pressure manually. The first steering lines were made of common rope that burned quickly, and the boat could not be steered to the bank for the expeditious abandonment of passengers and crew.[75]

Ed Jones related a story that attests to the longevity of a cotton fire. "One of the boats lost a cotton bale in the [Ouachita] river. A bunch of us boys got it and played on it for spell – they float over halfway up. Then we got tired of doing that and set it on fire. It burned for two weeks." Lottie Dean Bain (born 1873) of Portland went through the experience of a boat fire. Her great-grandson, Charles Naff, told the story. "She said that as a young girl she was going from Portland to New Orleans to have her teeth fixed. The boat was loaded with cotton and caught on fire. They managed to get it kicked into the bank and everybody got off. She said while it was burning all she could worry about was her new red dress."

A more serious account of a steamboat fire was recorded after the burning of the *Teche* near Vidalia, Louisiana, in 1825. The boat was heavily loaded with cotton, and about seventy passengers were aboard. At two o'clock in the morning, the boat weighed anchor and had just started downstream when the boiler blew up. "Every light on board was immediately extinguished, either by the escape of steam or the concussion of the air. An impenetrable darkness now hung over the scene of the disaster...until was heard a cry, the boat was on fire...Some were instantly killed by the explosion, others scalded, and not less than twenty or thirty were drowned."[76] One brave, unknown passenger unwittingly prevented a cataclysmic explosion. "One night a traveler on a Southern river was awakened by shouts of alarm. When he got dressed and out on deck, the crew had abandoned the boat and he was alone. Fire was spreading toward a barrel of turpentine but he snatched a bucket and drowned the flames. When the smoke cleared the crew came back aboard... Then the traveler saw three hundred kegs of dynamite under the charred deck."[77]

Bayou Bartholomew holds the remains of eight known steamboats that burned. On January 5, 1837, the 104-ton *Reindeer* burned at Point Pleasant with no loss of life.[78] The *Tippah* also burned at Point Pleasant on January 13, 1852, on a downbound trip. The only loss of life reported was that of the second engineer who drowned. The *Tippah*, built in 1851, was a 107-ton side-wheeler.[79] Union troops burned the *Jim Barkman*, a 65-ton sternwheeler, at Point Pleasant in 1865.[80] The *Lightwood*, a 156-ton sternwheeler, caught fire above the Louisiana line and burned to the water's edge on March 10, 1871. The 560 bales of cotton onboard was insured but the boat was not.[81] *The Big Horn* burned on April 10, 1873, in the Louisiana part of the bayou. The fire began when barrels of lime, used then for brick mortar, ignited in the hold. This 312-ton sternwheeler was built in 1865.[82] Fire consumed the *Bastrop*, owned by the New Orleans and River Transportation Co. on April 24, 1879. This boat was a 285-ton sternwheeler built in 1873. Capt. F. A. Blanks was master.[83] According to *Way's* fire destroyed the *Ollie B.* 120 miles above Monroe at Alexanders Landing on March 8, 1881. This small upper bayou packet had been connecting with the *Laura Lee* at the state line for points below. C. C. Honeycutt said the *Ollie B.* and *Ora B.* sank in Bayou D'Arbonne.[84] There are also conflicting reports on the loss of the *St. Francis Belle*. According to one account she was declared a total loss after burning at Point Pleasant on February 29, 1884. Scott Haddick said in 1950 that this boat was in the bend of the bayou by his home, and that its bell was hanging at the "St. John colored church right opposite the Jewish Cemetery." However, C. C. Honeycutt wrote in 1916 that this boat burned near Lind Grove. He wrote, "Her last trip was made in the spring of 1884, when she sank in Bayou Bartholomew, near Linn Grove. I was on her when she finished up her cargo of cotton and cotton seed at Moore & Dean's landing near where Wilmot now is. Her load consisted of 900 bales of cotton, 75 tons of cotton seed, and about 40 cords of 4 foot wood...There were several passengers aboard for New Orleans when she went down. No lives were lost, but all of the cotton seed and quite a number of cotton bales were lost...She was raised a few months later by the insurance company, but never made another trip up to this part of the country.[85]

Some sources list the *Big Horn* and *Bastrop* as foundered and sunk respectively, but when fire broke out, the pilot would deliberately scuttle the boat, if the water was deep enough to sink it, in an effort to keep it from completely burning. In this case, a burning boat became a sunken boat. The upper unburned decks occasionally floated off with the current and traveled until they became snagged or caught upon a shoal. When conditions warranted, the hull was sometimes raised and rebuilt.

When a boat rammed into a snag or onto a shoal, the resultant damage to the hull allowed water to quickly flow into the hold. A shoaled boat could occasionally be backed under its own power, but if it could not, the next passing vessel rescued it if the damage was not too great. When the boat snagged, if conditions permitted, the pilot would run the boat onto the bank or into shallow water to prevent sinking. Three boats are known to have sunk in Bartholomew. The *Louisa No. 2* snagged and was lost in

May 1859 in Louisiana with no loss of life.[86] This boat, built in 1856, was a fifty-seven ton sternwheeler. The *Mattie* sank at an undisclosed location in 1864.[87] In 1870 the *Economist* sank above Poplar Bluff and below Sandy Point on the east side of the bayou.[88] Described as "an odd looking specimen designed to float on 8 inches of water," this boat was built in 1868. Captain John W. Tobin purchased her in 1869 for Trenton to upper Bayou Bartholomew trade with S. A. Whyte as captain.[89] The aforementioned clearing of wrecks from the bayou in the 1884 report based on the 1880 survey indicates that there were substantially more sinkings than these three.

The remains of two boats can still be seen during periods of lowest water. Lodged on an east bank shoal within Spyker Bend, downstream from the Spyker house site, is what appears to be the bottom of a hull with a portion lodged on a cypress log. Paul Rawson examined the relic in 1980 and estimated it to be approximately 150 feet long by 20 to 30 feet wide. At that time the pointed bow was still intact. Rawson found blackened firebricks near the midship area that he proposed were from the boilers. He also discovered various pieces of iron, eyebolts, and cables. The structure exposed vertical planks on the bottom that were bridged on top by cypress crossbeams attached with hand-forged square nails about six inches long. Breadth-wise planking on top of the beams was sent to Louisiana Tech University where analysis determined this wood to be white oak. Billie Spyker told his descendants that he played on the sunken boat when he was a little boy. Other old-timers recalled having picnics on the boat. Jimmy Spyker told Rawson that at one time part of the wood looked like it had burned.[90] Winifred Day also saw this ruin and said that it appeared to have burned.

Tot Malone guided Jim Rider to the site in June 1988. At that time nearly the entire bottom was exposed. Rider estimated the ruins to be approximately 120 feet long by 24 feet wide. "Exposed bolt heads stuck up from the bottom cross timbers which appeared to be oak. The bottom planking is exposed in many places and [the boards] are approximately 12 inches wide," he wrote. Malone said that for several years sections of the sides were exposed, but people had carried off parts of the wreck.[91]

Ralph and Alvin Kinnaird were drifting down the bayou on a fishing trip around 1980 and noticed the structure. One exposed vertical plank was about two inches thick and sixty feet long. Ralph escorted the author to the site in August 1998. The exposed structure was approximately 100 by 25 feet. The "pointed bow" described by Rawson was no longer evident, but some of the horizontal planking was intact albeit much decreased in size from exposure. The crossbeams, nails, bolts, and vertical boards were the same as described by the earlier visitors, and part of the ruin was still lodged on top of the cypress log. Many of the bricks described by Rawson were found slightly downstream. Some locals speculate that the artifact is the remains of a cotton barge or wharf boat, but the earlier reports by Billie Spyker and Tot Malone indicate that it was a boat. Scott Haddick said in 1950 that the *Bastrop* "sank up at the bend behind Spyker's place" and that part of the hull could be seen during low water.[92] Five known boats sank in the area of Point Pleasant. They were the *Reindeer, Tippah, Jim Barkman, Bastrop*, and *St. Francis Belle* that went down in 1837, 1852, 1865, 1879, and 1884 respectively.[93]

The second relic is within Tatum Bend just above the Louisiana line. Sunken log retrievers, Joe Patterson and Donald Harris, discovered the structure in November 1999 when the bayou was extremely low. At the invitation of Mike and Pat Doles, who own the adjoining property, the author, Ed and Patsy White (certified amateur archeologists), several local residents, and Ralph Kinnaird (once again leading the way) investigated the site.[94] The remains are lodged near the west bank and under water varying in depth from six inches to three feet. The clear water afforded a good view of the structure which is sixty to seventy feet long. The boat obviously burned, and only the floor of the hull remains. The forward portion, in shallow water near the bank, clearly revealed the curving bow. Within this area were several different types of brick, some having the name Freeman on them.[95] Horizontal crossbeams and hogchains were evident as well as a vertical hogchain that ran the entire length. The aft section contained a small cylinder (the engine), two gears that drove the sidewheel, the paddlewheel shaft, and a long, curved iron belt approximately five inches wide that was part of the sidewheel. Stamped on one of the gears was "C. T. Dumont – Cin. O." Dumont was an Ohio based manufacturer of steamboat engines and boilers. This may be the remains of the *Ollie B.* which burned and sank at Alexanders Landing in 1881, according to one account as previously noted. C. C. Honeycutt described her, along with the *Ora B.*, as "two beautiful little steamers." The rains soon came, and the bayou rose to once again relegate the old steamer to its cloistered underwater grave.

Silt has engulfed the remains of other wrecks, but bayou residents have reported earlier sightings. Parts of the *Economist* north of Parkdale were exposed until around 1994. William deYampert's father salvaged a rope from a sunken boat near the swimming hole at Wilmot. Oren Robertson remembered seeing the frame of a boat at Haynes Bend west of Jones. Ralph Kinnaird, Bobby Abraugh, and Cecil Harp also knew of this site. Tom Harp wrote in 1960, "There was a steamboat that burned and naturally sank close to Coran's [Cora's] Bluff above Lind Grove. I was told that it had a lot of barb wire as freight...." Jim Sanchez told Lorraine Gregg around 1942 that he had seen the remains of a steamboat in Dead Bayou during low water. According to a story passed down, one bayou farmer took advantage of a sunken boat at his landing. Since it was on his property, he claimed the cotton, had his Negroes haul it out of the bayou, and sold it. Julia Huff Bryan confirmed this account. "The boiler caught fire and the boat sank. Jeff Haynes was a cotton buyer, and he had his hands put chains around the bales and drag them out of the bayou. The boat sank at Bois d'arc Bend – that was the first name of Modoc Bend," she said.[96]

Other bayou boats perished in different locations. The second *Buckeye*, built in 1837, collided with the *DeSoto* in Old River "on a beautiful moonlit night" March 1, 1844. Reports of deaths ranged from sixty to one hundred of the three hundred on board. The pilot of the *Buckeye*, Bob Klady, was charged with being drunk at the time of the collision.[97] C. C. Honeycutt wrote that the *D. Stein* "sank several times while plying our rivers, but was finally burned at Monroe in 1886", (see note) and the *Hanna Blanks* "was destroyed by fire near the mouth of Bayou Bartholomew in 1885." It is not clear if the latter boat was in the bayou or the Ouachita. He also said that the *Fair Play* burned at Monroe in 1876. A tropical storm destroyed the *Handy* while it was moored at Baton Rouge on September 20, 1909. "Hawsers holding the vessel snapped like pipestems. The boat was torn from her moorings and smashed beyond repair by waves in the river that rose to a height of 60 feet."[98] Most of the boats on Bartholomew eventually burned or sank. The average life of a steamboat was only four years.[99]

With all the perils associated with steamboat navigation, boatmen evolved into a superstitious lot. The *Franklin Pierce*, a Red River boat, developed the reputation for being an unlucky vessel. Her owner, Captain W. W. Wetherbury, felt so strongly about this that he brought suit to allow him to change the name. On February 22, 1855, the U. S. Congress passed a special act to allow him to change the name to *Texana*. It did little good as the ill-starred steamer burned less than two months later on April 18 in the Yazoo River.[100] Black cats did not make the boatmen turn their hat around or spit over their shoulder; it was white cats they considered unlucky, as well as a white horse or mule. Rats, on the other hand, brought good luck. Coffins containing corpses, a common freight on steamboats, were taken lightly by the crew. They reportedly used the flat box for a lunch or card table. (Bodies were packed in salt to preserve them during these final trips.) To play "There's No Place Like Home" on the calliope was considered unlucky. Although not necessarily a jinx, preachers aboard boats made some captains uneasy. The letter "M" being the thirteenth letter of the alphabet was taboo as the first letter of a boat's name.[101] The *Mattie* that sank in the bayou was, for some, proof of this bad omen. A six-letter name also forecast doom. Possibly the *Ollie B.* would not have burned if the last initial from her name had been omitted.

John G. Wilson expounded upon the subject in 1896. "Steamboatmen at that time were very much infected with superstition, especially the pilot and deckhands.   If a white horse was taken on board, they would commence to look out for high winds and stormy weather, and if a preacher accompanied the horse, why then the boat was in deadly peril, and it was only by the greatest luck that she would meet her destination. They had a proverb that if one boat meets with an accident, that there will others follow to the number of three. [This is similar to the adage, "Death comes in threes."] If rats are seen leaving the boat, it was very difficult to get a crew as they say that something is sure to happen. [The belief was that rats knew if a boat was going to sink.] Some boats seem to have a peculiar faculty for trouble.   They are always breaking in some part, getting aground, sinking until they are entirely lost or sent to the marine ways and are rebuilt, name changed to get rid of the enchantment. There are those who never commence anything, or start a journey on Friday, deeming it unlucky."[102]

A dismal factor connected with steamboat travel was very real and had nothing to do with superstitions. European immigrants arriving in major ports brought cholera, and the steamboats spread it from port to port. The first rampant outbreak erupted in 1832 and lasted until 1835. During a run from St. Louis to New Orleans in 1832, cholera broke out on the *Constitution* a few hours after leaving Natchez and "went like fire through the steamer." A passenger wrote, "I saw men perishing every minute about me and thrown into the river like so many dead hogs." Before reaching New Orleans, eighty were dead. A second epidemic occurred in 1848 with four thousand Europeans landing in New Orleans. By the following year it was said that all steamboats were infected and carrying the pestilence everywhere they went. The *Reindeer* propagated it up the Arkansas River. Robert F. Tucker of Hamburg traveled from Kentucky to Ashley County in 1850 and lost his wife and two children to cholera while aboard the *Baton Rouge*. Amanda Crawley's first husband, Thomas B. Tiller, left Pine Bluff on a steamer for a business trip to Natchez in 1852. She never saw him again; he died from cholera and was buried in Natchez.[103]

Steamboat Descriptions and Memories

It was a real treat to see that boat!

Gaston Harrison

Ninety-four boats were documented as being on Bartholomew, and the information given with some of them allows a composite examination. (See table four.) Bayou boats were of necessity smaller than steamboats on larger streams, but even their size varied greatly. Out of the fifty-two bayou boats with known tonnage, fifteen were under a hundred tons and four were four hundred or over. The tonnage stretched from the *Laura* at 26 tons to the *H. R. W. Hill* at 602 with the average being 191. Known lengths for thirty-seven bayou boats range from the *Addie* at 84 feet to the *Mayflower* at 212 feet with the average being 136. Widths varied from the eighteen-foot wide *Addie* to the thirty-eight foot wide *John Howard* (2) with the average being twenty-eight. Guards added to both sides to enlarge space for freight also increased the beam width. Depths ranged from two feet to six feet and three inches (the *John Howard* [2]) with the average being four feet and six inches. (The eight-inch depth of the *Economist* was exceptional.) In summary, from the information known, the average bayou boat measured 134'x28'x4'.6 with a 191 tonnage. By comparison, average Ouachita River boats, the *National*, a 379-ton side-wheeler, and the *J. Frank Pargoud*, a 522-ton side-wheeler, measured 184'x33'x6'.7 and 219'x36'x7' respectively.

The draft, the part submerged when loaded, was also significantly less on bayou boats. The depths given do not indicate draft; they are the distance from the main floor deck to the bottom of the hull. When a boat was fully loaded, however, the waterline often reached the main deck to the point of wetting the bottom bales of cotton. A light draft boat was especially necessary for streams such as the bayou and upper Ouachita. The *Sun Flower* and *Kate Dale* mentioned by Spyker in 1858 drew twelve and sixteen inches respectively, and the *Economist* drew only eight. Steamboat captains bragged that they only needed a heavy dew to get their boats through; others said they could navigate on spit alone.

Captain Dick Dicharry began his career in steamboating in Louisiana bayou trade and eventually owned two boats, the *Uncle Oliver* and *Tennessee Belle*. The latter, which burned in November 1942, was the "sole remaining steam packet on the lower Mississippi." The lessons and skills he learned while navigating the bayous benefited him when he began to navigate the larger stream. Ben Lucien Burman, who accompanied Captain Dick on many trips, wrote, "Bayou steamboating was steamboating at its worst. These wandering streams were even more unpredictable than the Mississippi. At times the bayou would be so thick with mud that the vessel seemed to be plowing through a sodden field...." Once when his boat went aground in the Mississippi he worked all afternoon and night to free her by grinding the paddlewheels in forward and reverse, shifting the cargo to the bow to lighten the stern, and digging away at the sand. He finally ordered his crew to use the firehose lines to wash the sand from beneath the hull, and the boat went free. At the next port downstream, the local rivermen were amazed to see the *Belle* approaching. A ferryboat captain, who the day before had taunted Captain Dick that he would be stuck until the following fall, said, "I might have known. I forgot he's a bayou captain, half alligator, half frog. You can't keep 'em grounded. When they can't crawl off a bar, they just jump over."[104]

Sidewheels had the advantage of allowing quicker turns to avoid the pitfalls of sharp bends, shoals, snags, and overhanging trees, but the disadvantage was that the wide guards necessary for them made the width much greater. Sternwheelers had the benefit of more power and a larger cargo area. The indication for side-wheeler or sternwheeler was given for sixty bayou boats. Out of these, only seven out of twenty-five were sternwheelers before the Civil War, and after the war, only two side-wheelers out of thirty-five were on the bayou.[105]

The railroad replaced the bayou and its steamboats as the principal form of transportation. An era ended, and a new one began. The distinct blast of the steamboat whistle reverberated for the last time around the bayou bends, and sunken ghosts of ships became mired in its depths. Few people are alive who can recall the wonder of steamboats on Bayou Bartholomew. Gaston Harrison, born in 1900, recollected his memories of the *Handy* in 1998. "I was around eight or nine. We were living at Pea Ridge farm at Hopkins Landing two or three bends down from Cora's Bluff. Best I remember it came up about once a month. You could hear the horn a long way off; it had a different tone than any other whistle. It was an exciting sound. When it came in, it would push a big wave of water up on the bank. It was the biggest boat I ever saw. It had a big square double deck. People came from all over to buy groceries off of it. A lot of them traded chickens for groceries. Papa and his brother always bought two stalks of bananas. Each stalk had several dozen bananas on it, and you could buy a stalk for seventy-five cents. They carried them on a pole between their shoulders. The boat brought whiskey by the barrel. Two or three families would go in together to get a barrel of it. Whiskey was also used for medicine, you know. They also brought blackstrap molasses by the barrel. It had a spigot on it, and you would take your container and fill it up. The boat pushed a barge and on the way back down, it would stop and load up cotton. All the gins on the bayou had a loading platform, or the folks would carry their cotton by wagon to the landings. There was another boat that came – the *Smith Brothers*. It was a smaller boat with mostly groceries and no cotton barge. But that *Handy* was something else. It was just like a little town. It was a real treat to see that boat!"

Buster Ford, born in 1915, also remembered the steamboats. "I saw one or two at Lind Grove when I was around seven or eight. I went with Grandpa on the wagon to take a load of cotton. It looked like a big old house, but it had a paddlewheel. They rolled the bales down the bank, and the crew manhandled them onto the barge that the boat pulled. You could hear the whistle all the way to McGinty and get in the wagon and be there before it got to Lind Grove." Bealie Harrison, born in 1907 at Tillou, remembered hearing the *Handy's* whistle from the bend at the Vester field. "People got in their wagons or rode horses to meet the boats. At Christmas everybody bought whiskey. The men would get together and make a list and give to George Westbrook, and he would get it off the boat for them. The only kind they had was I. W. Harper and R. B. Webb. Nine saloons at Monroe supplied the bottles. Virgil Kitchens ate breakfast on the boat one time and that was the first time he ever had light bread. He never forgot that."

The steamboat brought items that could not be obtained any other way. No wonder the arrival was such an exciting event in the backcountry! Newspapers arrived from New Orleans seven to ten days after they were published in the earlier days. "...it was a custom for the boats leaving New Orleans to provide several hundred of the latest New Orleans papers to be given out to all persons who would ask for a paper at every landing on the Ouachita river and on Bartholomew." Oysters were a welcome delicacy. "The only fresh oysters that could be obtained would be from the ice boxes on the steam boats. The barkeeper on every boat provided oysters freshly put up in hermetically sealed cans, that he would sell at every town on the river," C. C. Davenport wrote.[106]

Nancy Tharp, born in 1894, said, "My grandfather would go get groceries off the boat at Parkdale. When they came you could always see them getting in a hurry. They got barrels of lard and big sacks of sugar. They were just so glad when they came." James Bealer, born in 1894 on the McCombs plantation at Thebes, said his parents told him that they could not get groceries any other way. (However, the plantation did have a commissary.) Pawis Mayo (born 1877) told Buck Mayo that they looked forward to the basic supplies of sugar, salt, flour, and especially coffee beans. "They had to roast the coffee beans in the oven and then grind them," Buck said. Bananas were a favorite product, and most stories about steamboat memories include the mention of them. R. N. "Booster" Kinnaird told his son, Ralph, about getting bananas for twenty-five cents a stalk. Whiskey, a refreshing alternative to moonshine, was certainly a welcome import. Old store receipts, ledger sheets and bills of lading nearly always include whiskey. Robert Crawley explained, "Well, everybody had a lot of malaria back in those days and just didn't feel good. A little drink every now and then made them feel just a little better."

Cecil Harp remembered Robert and Kelley Harp talking about the steamboats coming. "It was just like Christmas. There was lots of drinking and jubilation and gambling – maybe even women." Ernestine Nobles Sprinkle said that her mother recalled that they could hear the whistle at Parkdale from Wilmot. "It was the first electric lights they ever saw. They never saw so many lights. They bought whole stalks of bananas. The boats brought up my grandparent's bed, surrey, and piano. I still have the bed." (The first electric lights on steamboats appeared in 1877.) An 1869 advertisement from a Monroe merchant names the goods brought up on the *Economist.* He received "a lot of new flour, Irish potatoes, fresh herring, dried green peas, split peas, mackerel, ginger preserves, cream crackers, cracknell biscuits, pecans, and raisins." James Dock Wolfe, born in 1920 on Long Prairie in southeast Drew County, remembered old-timers such as Will Chavis, Ed Chavis, Ash Wigley, Add Lagrone, and Dick Thurman talking about how they would go from the prairie to the bayou to get staples off steamboats for Will Chavis's store. "They got them from steamers somewhere down in the swamps," he said.[107] In 1888 J. S. Handy received his order for three cages containing five canaries. The Cryer receipt noted, "one canary bird dead."

Occasionally the bayou relinquishes curios from the steamboat days. Henry Austin's father was swimming in the bayou with some other boys near the landing at old Portland in the late 1890s. They found a wooden barrel under the water and managed to get it out and opened it. "It was full of pickled beef. It probably weighed around three hundred pounds. They took it home and ate it and it was good meat," Henry said.[108] J. D. Grice found two large ceramic whiskey jugs in the bayou at Parkdale. Inscribed on them is "Silver King Saloon, J. Y. Covington, Proprietor." (An 1888 receipt for two barrels and two half-barrels of whiskey, wine, and gin to be delivered to C. D. Covington was found in the Cryer Steamboat Line receipt book.)[109]

Page Webb was born in 1913 at the state line but never saw the steamboats. "But I could hear the whistle" he said. I just loved to hear that whistle." The history of the steamboat whistle goes back to the 1840s when Captain William H. Fulton heard a steam whistle on a factory roof. The A. Fulton shop in Pittsburgh then made a whistle for steamboats, and in 1844 Engineer J. S. Neal installed the first one used on western rivers on the *Revenue,* an Arkansas River tramp trader.[110] Congress created an act in 1852 that made the whistle mandatory on steamboats, replacing the bell system of signaling. Sir Charles Lyell, the English geologist, heard one of these first crude whistles described as "a wild and harsh scream, produced by the escape of steam" during his geological explorations up the Mississippi. He wrote, "[it] is a fearful sound in the night, and which it is hoped some machinist who has an ear for music will find means to modulate." His wish came true as future advancements in design produced dulcet three and five-tone models that could play notes and chords. The *Kate Adams*, a Mississippi side-wheeler familiar at Arkansas City, had a whistle with a full low-bodied tone that carried for over thirty miles. It had "a deep bass voice like a million bullfrogs on a summer night."[111]

The signaling system evolved into a universal steamboat language. One long, two short, and another long blast announced an approaching landing. This became known as the "begging whistle" as they were asking for passengers and freight. Customers at unscheduled way landings signaled the passing boats by white flags in daylight and lanterns at night if they had freight to ship. Three short blasts from the boat indicated it was stopping in response to the land signals. Several short, windy gusts signaled the actual landing. The boats also communicated with other boats by sounding the whistle, which is similar to the international system presently used.

The whistle helped in another unusual way. Some pilots were able to navigate on a foggy night by reading the echo off of a bluff, tree, or building. One could even use the barks of dogs in reaction to the whistle. The *Era No. 10*, a Beouf River boat, had one of the largest whistles among all boats. Once when she passed the *J. M. White* on the Mississippi, the pilot of the *White* said, "There goes a big whistle with a boat on it." Abraham Lincoln, a river pilot in his younger days, used to tell about a boat that had such a big whistle on it that when it blew, the boat stopped![112]

Each whistle had a distinctive sound that allowed local people to identify a boat by its resonating blast. Spyker wrote in his diary, "I thought I heard the Steamer *Homer's* whistle." When Mariah Mason (born 1885) was growing up at Mason Cave, she had a pet deer. "It paid no attention to the passing steamboat whistles, but a particular one would throw him into a fit," said Marion Robertson Doles. "One day when that one went off, he jumped on the porch and then jumped in the window and out again and left. He was gone for good."

The *Handy* was a typical bayou boat with measurements of 110'x22'x3'. The sternwheeler was built in 1903 for a cotton packet for the Monroe Railway and Navigation Company. Other boats put into service by this company at the same time on the Ouachita were the *Roberta, Bob Blanks,* and *Frank B. Hayne.* Driven away from trade at Camden by the construction of the Gurdon-Monroe branch of the Missouri-Pacific in 1909, the *Handy* began operating out of Monroe.[113] Cotton packets were designed, as the name implies, for carrying large loads of cotton bales. The main deck was extra wide and the boiler and cabin decks were very narrow. Guards, which were peripheral decks extending beyond the hull supported by stanchions or hog chains, were designed specifically for hauling extra freight and added more than a third to the carrying capacity. A fully laden boat would therefore be "loaded to the guards." By the mid-1800s boats measured their capacity by the number of bales they could carry. When fully loaded, the bales stacked on the guards often extended to the top deck, and a wall of cotton enclosed the passengers. The boats "resembled a block of cotton" with only a few feet of the top of the boat, the pilot house, and stacks visible.[114] Ed Jones remembered seeing steamboats coming down the Ouachita with cotton loaded on their barges so high the pilot could not see over. "So they came down backwards – pulling them in reverse instead of pushing them," he said.

Captain Stoughton Cooley described a fully loaded cotton packet. "The bales are stowed just about as children pile up their play blocks, and extend at first clear across the deck and from the extreme forecastle to the engine room…with a space in the middle for the boilers, and a small passageway at the bow. When the tiers are above a man's head the passageway is bridged over and the cotton piled up on each side and in front of the cabin, making a wall about it the thickness of two bales laid end to end, or ten feet, and rising to the hurricane deck, or top of the cabin, and sometimes several feet higher. Then it is that the cotton boat is majestic; when she is all hidden from the sight save texas, chimneys, and wheel, and the cotton on the guards dragging in the water, she is said to be loaded."[115]

Captain William B. Miller of the *Thompson Dean*, a Mississippi River boat, described a loaded steamboat in a letter to his children in 1875. He first explained that the bales were about five feet long, two feet thick, three feet wide, and weighed around five hundred pounds. Sacks of cottonseed weighed about 120 pounds. He wrote from Vicksburg, "We are now loaded, 5,000 bales and 10,000 sacks, and the cotton is twelve tiers high on our guards. If our passengers do get a peep of daylight they have to go on the hurricane deck or in the pilothouse. Our guards are dragging the water and our mates and our 100 men on deck are worn out with four days constant work day and night."[116] An 1857 advertisement for the *Eclipse* addressed the problem of nearly smothering the passengers between and under the cotton bales: "…and will never carry cotton above the boiler deck, she will afford particularly strong inducements to the traveling public…."[117]

Loading the huge bales by gangplank from the bank or wharf was no easy task. The roustabouts and stevedores were a robust breed. "They were rough. They didn't play," said Herman King. Mary Ann Dixon Johnston remembered watching cotton being loaded on the Ouachita. "The roustabouts were huge black men. They took a chain on each side of the five-hundred pound bales and pulled together. They sang wonderful songs all the time. The rhythm helped them stay in time." Roustabouts and deck hands were famous for their singing and provided much entertainment for passengers and onlookers. A passenger wrote in 1869, "The deck hands all carry cotton hooks (to roll the bales) in their waist-belts. These deck hands seem to be the gayest fellows in the world. When any boat leaves the levee at New Orleans, some one of them leads in a song, while the whole crew joins in the course, which consists in the long drawn, 'O-ho!' which sounds very pretty from a boat moving on the water."[118] Stephen Foster wrote many roustabout and steamboat songs, the most famous being "O, Susannah!" which was written in 1848. The fellow with the banjo on his knee was going to Louisiana aboard the *Telegraph*. The young songwriter was a bookkeeper in his brother's steamboat agent firm.[119]

Rousters received a little more than a dollar a day for their labor and were paid by the trip as all crew members were. On a six-day voyage to deYampert's Landing in March 1893, the thirteen rousters aboard received $6.00 to 5.50. Deducted from that was their bar bills, which ranged from $3.65 to sixty-five cents. Receiving less than the roustabouts were two cabin boys ($3.50 and $2.50) and a deck sweeper ($1.65). Two strikers and the cook received seven dollars each, and two firemen were paid $7.45 and $8.05. The wages for officers for this trip were: pilot ($20), second clerk ($8.05), watchmen ($7 and $10.50), engineer ($17.50), second engineer ($12), and bill clerk ($7).[120]

Local merchants generally bought cotton from the farmers or accepted it as trade for payment of merchandise. Some held cotton for speculation on the futures market and often doubled their money. When the cotton was shipped to New Orleans, a factor or agent then handled the transaction. The money was used to purchase goods that were shipped back upstream. If goods were ordered in late spring, they might not be received until the following winter. C. C. Honeycutt described the procedure. "There was bacon in 500 lb. boxes, pickled pork in 300 lb. barrels, hogsheads of brown sugar, great bags of rice and coffee and hundreds of barrels of flour...Nearly every planter had his merchant in New Orleans. He would make out his bill for supplies and send it to New Orleans...When the crops were harvested the cotton and cotton seed were shipped to the merchants and the proceeds applied to the planter's account, and a statement sent to him as to how he stood."[121] Plantation owners often went with their cotton to personally conduct this business. Ernestine Sprinkle (born 1918) told of her grandfather, James S. Nobles Sr., going on such a trip from Poplar Bluff. "That was the only way to ship cotton and seed. He would go to New Orleans in the fall with the cotton, sell it, and then buy supplies for a year. He always bought a barrel of whiskey." Oren Robertson said that his grandfather, Edwin Mason, also made trips to New Orleans to sell his cotton. William Pinkney Burks of Monticello made a trip to Memphis to buy his annual supplies. His niece, Marietta Webb (born 1878), said that he took several thousand dollars in gold with him. He went by ox wagon to Arkansas City where he caught a Mississippi steamboat. When he reached Memphis, "the city and all that gold went to his head and he got drunk and squandered all his money. He even washed his feet in champagne!"[122]

Although it is commonly accepted that the term "Dixie" originated from the Mason-Dixon Line survey in the 1760s with the slaveholding states being south of it, river tradition indicates that it derived from steamboat language. Banks issued their own notes that were often worthless, but the Citizens Bank of New Orleans was trusted far and wide. It printed its notes in English on one side and French on the reverse. The French side contained in large letters, DIX, for ten. These notes were "as good as gold" to the rivermen who pronounced the word as it was spelled. The notes were Dixies and the town they came from was Dixie's Land. "Going down South after Dixies" became a river phrase that soon expanded to include the entire Southland.[123] After Daniel Emmett wrote "Dixie, Land of Cotton" the term became as associated with the Old South as magnolias and mint juleps.

Bayou Voyages

The men would drink and play cards the whole
time.   They were all suffering from headache
and dehydration when they returned.

Jack Gibson

The crew may have had their superstitions, but this did not hinder passenger travel. The bayou steamboats offered a much more appealing mode of travel – the alternative was by horse, wagon, or buggy over crude roads.   Colonel Spyker often journeyed to New Orleans from Point Pleasant; unfortunately his diary offers no descriptions, but it does record the travel time. He went to the mouth of the bayou on Thursday morning, February 19, 1857, boarded the *Persia*, and reached New Orleans on Sunday. The voyage back lasted from March 6 to March 10, taking an additional day for the return trip upstream. In May 1858 an upbound trip from New Orleans lasted from Wednesday night until Monday.[124]

The arrival of the boats to the remote interior of bayou land naturally created a thrilling respite in an otherwise routine existence. N. Philip Norman described the dramatic ceremony of arrivals and departures in detail. "The mellow, sonorous tones of the organ-whistle blowing for landing; the silver-toned jingle of the signal bells in the engine room; the slow, deliberate, deep-throated groans of the 'scape pipes; the churning of the water by the huge paddle wheel; the clouds of black smoke belching forth from the tall, feather-crowned chimneys; the sharp commands of the captain or mate; the creaking of the blocks as the stage was swung outward over the guards preparatory to being lowered to the bank; the whine of the hemp 'hawse line' as it stretched to the breaking point to check the boat's momentum; the rush of visitors to board the boat; the chanting roustabouts, 'coon-jining' across the long stageplank; the boom tone of the roof bell notifying visitors and crew of the imminence of the boat's departure; the roar of the smokestacks which accompanied the stoking of the furnaces; the farewell gestures of those aboard and of those on shore; then again the creaking of blocks and the throb of the 'nigger-engine' while the stage was being 'histed' and swung into proper position; the jangling of the signal bells; the sighing of the 'scape pipes; the measured beat of the paddle wheel on the river surface and the disappearance of the boat around the bend were a combination of activities and events truly theatrical in content, because it brought a phase of metropolitan life to the planter's doorstep to momentarily break the monotony of his existence."[125]

Scott Haddick described the bustle at Point Pleasant that he witnessed around the turn of the century. "People would come from all around to buy supplies. They would set up camps there at the Point and wait for the boats to come in. Those who lived very far away from the Point would generally buy a year's supply of goods...Everyone traveled on a wagon pulled by mule teams. It was really quite an occasion when the family donned their best 'bib and tux' to come down to the trading center. It meant new clothes for all the family and all sorts of goodies for the children. Steamboats carried 40 to 50 Negroes for loading and unloading. Everything was done by hand then...The Negroes always went at a trot. They never walked when carrying supplies." Haddick said that there were seven warehouses at the Point and he had seen as many as seven boats tied up at one time.[126]

Spyker often took his wife and children for a boat ride from his house to Point Pleasant, and they would visit with friends onboard along the way. The boats occasionally sponsored dances and parties. Spyker wrote, "Tive and Morgan have gone to the Point to a frolic on the Steamer *Homer*." A notation in Cryer's Portage Book said, "May 13, 1893, To Spring Hill & Return Excursion – Colored." The day's voyage required only an engineer, fireman, striker (evidently an apprentice), and two rousters. Spring Hill was south of Marion in Union Parish. John Anderson Gibson moved to Morrell in 1874 at the age of eighteen. Charles C. Gibson Sr. said at that time his father was a farmhand "living in a shack with a dirt floor" and always looked forward to the coming of the steamboats. When the whistle sounded at Green Pugh Bend at the northern end of Lake Grampus, he would quit work and walk to the landing near Morrell and board the boat to join his friend Green Pugh for the trip on up to Baxter. The boat stopped and picked up other farmers along the way, and they would gamble as they rode to Baxter and back. "The men would drink and play cards the whole time," said Jack Gibson, a grandson. "They were all suffering from headache and dehydration when they returned."[127]

Lucie Nunn (born 1884, Bastrop) made a special trip to New Orleans before her marriage to William "Snig" Pugh. She not only went to purchase her trousseau, she also went to get her hair done for her wedding. "It took her a week to get back," said Virginia Harp. "The hairdo must have lasted for a long time!" Mrs. John William Morris Sr. of Parkdale took her children, Herman William (born 1885) and Johnnie (born 1882), to New Orleans by steamboat in 1895, five years after the railroad came. From there they went by train to enroll at Augusta Military Academy and a Catholic boarding school. "There was no other way to get anywhere from here then," said Mary Morris Foster.

Captain Cryer's Passenger Book, which begins in February 1888 and continues at irregular intervals through February 1896, lends some insight to travel on the bayou at that time. The first recorded voyage up the bayou was the *Sterling White's* roundtrip number four on January 29, 1890. Six passengers boarded at Monroe for Buffalo Landing, Ouachita City, and Poplar Bluff with J. W. Greer and A. C. Wolf bound for the latter destination. At Poplar Bluff Joseph Rand embarked for Monroe. Upon reaching Monroe six boarded for Poplar Bluff. G. P. George, an attorney, and H. C. Dade came aboard at Poplar Bluff for the trip down to Monroe. George and Dade returned on trip five on February 4. Fares ranged from five to three dollars to Poplar Bluff, five to Portland, five to two to D. M. Grants (below Wilmot), one to two to Ouachita City, and two to Lind Grove. Negroes, indicated by a c (for colored) by their name paid the three-dollar fares to Poplar Bluff. They rode on the deck while the others had cabins. A "Miller Negro" boarded at McCauly and paid for his fare to Parkdale with "wood." He either supplied the boat with wood or helped to load it. Helping to "wood the boat" was a common practice for those who could not afford the fare. During this time period the boat also carried passengers to and from Wiggins, Kittrells, Portland, Eatmans, Grants, Arkansas Line, Lind Grove, Wilsons, Masons, Point Pleasant, and Marble. Passenger numbers were small, ranging from an average of three to six each way.[128]

Around 1877 two teenage girls, Frances "Fannie" Harris and Code E. Swain, boarded a steamboat at Trenton and went up the bayou to Wardville to visit Mary and Dixon Moore, the parents of Ms. Harris's future husband, Robert A. Moore. Code Swain wrote a long poem describing their adventure. Following are several verses of *Our Trip Up The Bayou*.

The steamer *Willie* whistled
As it came sailing past
Towards us, she was ready,
So come along fast.

We dined at twelve
Had water without ice
And all we had for dessert
Was a little bit of rice.

In the evening, to the pilothouse
We were invited
And, of course, could
Not well feel slighted.
We enjoyed the scenery
On the Ouachita River

Though some of the snags
Made us shake and quiver.
After tea a game of cards was had
And Mr. R. and I were beaten bad.

I stole a bit of sleep
But was aroused from my slumber
By the tearing off of planks
And a great deal of lumber.
I raised up to see what was the matter
And the meaning of all the noise and clatter
But was gently laid down again by a tree
That came through the window of the little *Willie.*
We rose soon the next morning
The sun was shining brightly
The boat still plying up the bayou
Very quick and lightly.

The forty-five verses of doggerel also describe the captain, who was "pleasant with a mustache so gay/pretty blue eyes/and exquisite way."[129] C. C. Honeycutt wrote that steamboatmen were "well and favorably known to our people." He mentioned Captains Cryer, Bruner, Harding, and White, and pilots, John Gomillon ("one of the safest pilots that ever turned a steering wheel), John McClendon, and Harry Williams. "Frank Canady, Charlie Hanethorne, and Mike O'Connor were three mates that were very familiar characters to steamboat patrons...."[130]

Although some of the bayou boats made the round trip to New Orleans, others met larger boats at the mouth or at Monroe to continue to the Crescent City. The *Governor Allen* began making weekly runs from New Orleans to Camden in 1869. A passenger described his voyage aboard her the same year. "The boat is finely finished, very fast and carries 900 tons. I do not recollect ever hearing of the Ouachita (or Wachita) river when I studied geography, and when I learned I was to go up it, I painted, to myself, pictures of tedious days on such craft as the Sandy packets *Oil Hunter* or *Dexter.* My surprise was anything but disagreeable, therefore when I saw my boat, at the levee in New Orleans, lying beside, and forming not an unfavorable contrast with the Mississippi river packet, *Robert E. Lee.* Our staterooms are each furnished with washstand and furniture; the cabin is high and handsomely finished. During meals and at evening a string band entertains us with sweet melodies. Each day we are furnished with a bill of fare, from which we order our entrees, such as scallops of fowl, au gratin, cream sauce, calf's head a la royal, brain sauce; or braised roll of beef, a la Piedmontaise. Don't you wish you was me?

Perhaps you wouldn't if, like me, you had ordered pork cutlets a la Americaine, and gotten pig's foot." The *J. F. Pargoud*, a bayou boat, was described as "having rosewood furniture, lace curtains, chandeliers, silverware, bathrooms, and all other conveniences."[131]

A famous Ouachita River boat was Capt. L. V. Cooley's *America*, "an impressive cotton-style packet" two hundred foot long sternwheeler. Built in 1898, this belle of the Ouachita stayed in service from Monroe to New Orleans until around 1904 and often came to Ouachita City. After years of running from New Orleans to Vicksburg and Greenville, Captain Cooley returned her to the Ouachita where she ran until foundering at New Orleans in 1926. She was used in a 1924 movie, *Magnolia*, under the name *Winfield Scott*. Captain Cooley died and was buried in New Orleans in 1931. Over his grave hangs the roof bell of his best loved boat, the *America*.[132]

Captain Cooley owned four consecutive steamers named *Ouachita* that he ran from 1890 until his death. Mary Ann Dixon Johnston (born 1919) of Sterlington remembered joyous trips on the last *Ouachita*. "They would blow the whistle on the way up from Monroe and everyone would go to the landing. We would get on and go to Alabama Landing up from Ouachita City for a big dance onboard. They had the Bud Scott band and other good bands. I won a Charleston contest one time when I was around ten." Ed Jones (born 1912) of Ouachita City also remembered these boat dances. "When I was around fifteen they had a shore 'nuf band. It was an all black orchestra that would really make 'em shimmy. Whiskey was not allowed on the boat for these dances so some men would stash pints of it in mud along the banks and while the boat was loading up, they would paddle out in johnboats up to the side of the boat and sell it."

During a voyage up the Mississippi in the early 1800s J. F. Flugel recorded "regulations for the conduct of passengers aboard". Fines were levied for transgressions, and the amount collected was spent for after dinner wine for passengers. Smoking in cabins was prohibited, and gentlemen were asked to take off their shoes or boots before lying on a berth. Passengers were not allowed to speak to the helmsman, and all cards and games had to end at ten in the evening. No gentleman could descend the stairs to the ladies' cabins nor enter a lady's cabin without her permission, which had to be obtained through the captain. And lastly, "It is particularly requested that gentlemen will not spit on the cabin floors, as boxes are provided for that purpose."[133] The rule for cards and games (of chance) to end at ten was evidently never followed!

Bayou Bartholomew served as a steamboat passage into Morehouse Parish and the interior of the southeast Arkansas Delta for approximately seventy years. This egress for cotton and other products from the 1830s to the coming of the railroads in the 1890s allowed the Delta plantations and farms to flourish to their full potential. Steamboats also served as floating post offices, banks, brokerage firms, and stores. The bayou route provided for the import of goods that improved the quality of life for its citizens. The delivery of necessities such as basic food items and farm supplies was augmented by more exotic items not easily obtainable in any other way. Specialty cuisine such as bananas, lemons, oranges, oysters, mackerel, herring, and other delicacies came to the backwoods. Real whiskey and imported wine graced some of the fancier tables. Tobacco, tea, and coffee beans brought pleasant aromas to cabins and manors alike. Perfumes and fancy cosmetics gave welcome relief from homemade lye soap. Patent medicines and myrrh, camphor, calomel and opium assuaged swamp related illness such as malaria and ague. Newspapers, books, journals, and letters offered vicarious visits to other places. Household furnishings such as lamps, china, crystal, curtains, and furniture found their way across the ocean to bayou homes. Pianos also came to bayou land and their lyrical notes provided pleasure for all who listened. Little did the Italian, Bartolommeo Cristofori, dream in 1709 when he perfected his work on the first piano that his instrument would be played in America on the banks of Bayou Bartholomew.

The bayou participated in what is referred to in history as the "glorious Mississippi River steamboat era." Its part in this pageant has been overlooked or dismissed as a minor one, but it played a leading role for the people who benefited from it. C. C. Davenport wrote in 1911, "The arrival of a boat at Point Pleasant was announced by the firing of a cannon that was kept at the landing for that purpose. Just as far as that cannon could be heard farmers would hitch up teams, load the wagons with cotton bales and go to the steamboat and bring back supplies. The boat usually lay at the landing several days. Whiskey in the bar on the boat attracted all the lovers of strong drink...all classes of people would meet at the boat landing and the boats kept a table set, and furnished free meals to all who would occupy seats at the table. Occasionally the boats would announce a dance in the cabin of the boat; and young men and the girls for many miles around would go to that boat and continue to dance and have a good time...As a rule every planter made one trip during the boating season to New Orleans. Those were happy, happy days, and a trip to New Orleans and return, was productive of more genuine pleasure than a trip across the ocean on the finest steamer afloat...I would not give my recollections of the pleasure that I enjoyed on a Bartholomew boat crowded with passengers...eating three square meals a day, a dance on board every night, courting and flirting with the girls on board, for any other recollection of my life."[134]

Table 4

Steamboats Documented on Bayou Bartholomew

Name & Type* Dimensions	Tons	Year Built	Year/s on bayou	Lost
Acme	- -	- -	1877	- -
Addie Stw 84'x18'x2'	- -	1890	c. 1870-90	- -
Aid SW	137	1843	- -	abandoned 1848
Agnes SW	170	1842	- -	abandoned 1849
Bastrop Stw	285	1873	1879	Bayou Bartholomew LA 5-24-1879
Baton Rouge SW	241	1836	- -	abandoned 1845
Big Horn Stw 154'x33'.5"x4'.5"	312	1865	1873	Bayou Bartholomew LA 5-10-1873
Buckeye	170	- -	1833	- -
Clara S.	- -	1877	1880	Tehula Lake ? 12-27-1883
Clinton	102	1836	1838	abandoned 1840
D. Stein Stw 124'.4"x25'.8"x3'.5"	- -	1877	1878-1888	
D'Arcy	- -	- -	1860	- -
Economist Stw 8" depth	- -	1868	1870	Bayou Bartholomew 1870
Elizabeth SW 85'x22'x4'.8"	93	1842	1844	abandoned 1845
Ella Hughes Stw	212	1867	1877	New Orleans 3-17-1880
Era Stw 123'x23'.5"x3'	78	1856	1859	Red River 5-12-1859
Experiment(snagboat)	- -	- -	1847	- -

Name & Type* Dimensions	Tons	Year Built	Year/s on bayou	Lost
Fair Play Stw	- -	1877	1877-1880	Monroe LA c.1879 1880
Fox Stw	74	1855	1857,1859	Red River 3-28-1861
Grenada SW	217	1851	1859	Algiers LA 5- 10-1861
Frank Willard Stw	75	1873	- -	Still listed 1882
Gipsy SW	43	1858	1859,1860	Black Bayou LA 2-19-1861
H. R. W. Hill SW	602	1852	- -	Baton Rouge LA 10-31-1860
H. W. Graves	- -	- -	- -	- -
Handy Stw 110'x22'x3'	- -	1903	1905,1909	Baton Rouge LA 9-1909
Hanna Blanks Stw 155'x34'x5'.5"	- -	1880	c.1880-90	Ouachita River 12-29-1889 [or 1885]
Helen Vaughn	- -	- -	- -	- -
Hettie Gilmore Stw 110'x22'x3'.5"	- -	1859	1860	Out of service 1869
Homer SW	194	1859	1860	Ouachita River AR April 1864
Hooker (snagboat)	- -	- -	1886	- -
Jennie Kirk SW	91	1859	1860	Confederate Reg.1862
Jim Barkman Stw 93'x23'.7"x3'.3"	65	1859	1865	Point Pleasant LA 2-4-1865
Jo Nichol	- -	- -	1844	- -
John Howard Stw 180'x36'x6'	- -	1871	1889	See next listing
John Howard Stw 184'.6"x37'.8"x6'.3"	- -	1893	1889	Columbia LA 12-17-1898
John Ray Stw 100'x24'x4'	86	1859	1859	Pine Prairie LA 8-5-1860

Name & Type* Dimensions	Tons	Year Built	Year/s on bayou	Lost
Josie W. Stw	- -	1885	1890	Dismantled 1903
Kate Dale SW 136'x27'.3"x4'.7"	160	1858	1857,1858	Out of service 1862
Katie P. Kountz Stw	- -	1871	1883	Mississippi River 11-1-1883
Laura	26	1845	1846,1848	Ouachita River LA 11-8-1849
Leviere	- -	- -	1895	- -
Lightwood Stw 130'x26'x3'	156	1868	1870, 1871	Bayou Bartholomew AR 3-10-1871
Lind Grove Stw	163	1882	- -	- -
Lizzie Simmons SW 204'x36'.5"x6'.5"	454	1859	1860	Little Rock AR 9-10-1863
Loretta May	- -	- -	1882, 1883	- -
Louisa SW	394	1851	1859	Harrisonburg LA 3-2-1855
Louisa No. 2 Stw	57	1856	1859	Bayou Bartholomew LA May 1859
Lucy Robinson SW 21'x26'.7"x5'.6"	239	1851	1857, 1858	Dismantled 1859
Marco	- -	- -	1894	- -
Mattie Stw Mattie**	- -	- -	1864	Bayou Bartholomew 1864
May A. Brunner Stw	172	1865	1866	Red River LA 2-3-1866
Mayflower SW 212'x34'.5"x5'.5"	564	1867	1869	Dismantled St. Louis MO
Moreau SW 122'x24'.8"x4'.7"	132	1858	1859	Red River LA 2-8-1863
New York Stw 155'x33'x4'.5"	199	1862	1870	New Orleans LA 3-21-1870

Name & Type* Dimensions	Tons	Year Built	Year/s on bayou	Lost
Ollie B.	- -	- -	1881	Bayou Bartholomew AR 3-8-1881
Ora B.	- -	c.1872	1877	
Parlor City Stw 125'x25'x3'.7"	- -	1892	1895	New Orleans LA 10-1902
Pioneer Stw 102'.8"x20'.4"x3'.5"	50	1866	1870	Trenton LA 9-1870
Poplar Bluff	- -	1883	c.1886-90	- -
Queen City	- -	- -	1883	- -
Rapides Stw 153'.6"x37'.6"x5'.3"	415	1869	- -	Near Baton Rouge 2-28-1876
Red Chief Stw 113'x30'x5'	150	1857	1857-1861	Confederate Reg. 1861
Red Chief No. 2 Stw 109'x24'x3'.6"	86	1859	1859-1861	- -
Reindeer	104	1831	1837	Point Pleasant LA 1-1-1837
Rosa B.	- -	- -	1880	- -
Rowena	- -	- -	- -	- -
S.W. Downs SW 164'.8"x26'.7"x5'.7"	236	1851	1851	Off the lists in 1861
Sellie	- -	- -	1890	Bayou Bartholomew 1890
Silver Moon SW 24'x27'.5"x5'.5"	171	1857	1857	Bayou Goula LA 3-7-1858
Smith Brothers	- -	- -	1909	- -
St.Francis Belle	- -	- -	1881, 1884	Point Pleasant LA 2-29-1884
Steamer 10	- -	- -	1883	- -
Stella Stw	--	1886	1900	Columbia LA 7-24-1901
Sterling White 120'x30'x4'.5	117	1878	1890-1896	- -

Name & Type* Dimensions	Tons	Year Built	Year/s on bayou	Lost
Sun Flower SW 121'.5"x25'x3'.7"	105	1857	1858	Galveston Harbor TX 10-3-1867
Swamp Fox SW 162'x29'.8"x5'.8"	280	1851	1852	McDade LA 2-4-1857
Swan SW	36	1861	1866	Abandoned 1869
Sydonia SW 162'.5"x28'x5'.5"	235	1851	1857	Columbia LA 5-29-1857
Telegram Stw 158'x31'x4'.5"	205	1858	1861	Algiers LA 5-6-1861
Tensas Stw	333	1875	1882, 1883	- -
Tigress SW 178'x32'x6'	321	1858	1858, 1859	Vicksburg MS 5-22-1863
Timmie Baker Stw 100'x21'x3'	78	1875	1883	- -
Tippah SW 103'x24'.1"x4'.8"	107	1851	1852	Point Pleasant LA 1-13-1852
Tom Parker	84	1875	- -	Still listed 1882
Trenton Stw 130'x32'.2"x4'.2"	260	1869	- -	Still listed 1876
W.A. Andrew SW 132'x30'x5'.5"	229	1857	1860	Confederate Reg. 1862
W.W. Farmer SW 140'x32'x5'.1"	207	1854	1857-1859	Confederate Reg.1861
Wagner (snagboat)	- -	- -	1893	- -
Water Lilly	- -	- -	1883	- -
Welcome	- -	- -	1905	- -
William Fagan Stw 166'x34'.6"x4'.9"	- -	1879	1881	New Orleans LA 1-5—1881
Willie	- -	- -	1877, 1881	- -
Young America	- -	- -	1857-1859	- -

* SW indicates side-wheeler. Stw indicates sternwheeler.
** The second *Mattie* is documented by a photograph of her on the bayou in a later newspaper clipping.

 Chapter Six

A Watery Land

Overland Travel

As to the mud it was often pleasantly said that
the bottom was good wherever you could get to it.

Rev. John G. Jones, 1825

Steamboats offered a luxurious alternative to other methods of travel, and written accounts of early travel clearly illustrate this. John Smith and his wife, Sarah Bowden, came to the Dermott area from Louisiana before steamboat service was available. Goodspeed gave an account of their 1811 trip: "Mr. Smith and his wife and a number of slaves entered a boat made by himself, rowed them up Bayou Bartholomew to a point somewhere what is now [in] Chicot County, and with knives cut away the cane and selected a suitable place for the cabin. They opened up a settlement, and Mr. Smith returned to Louisiana for the rest of his property, leaving his family alone in the forest, far from human habitation, and was gone about twenty-one days."[1]

Even rowing up the bayou sounds less difficult than the overland trip that three Methodist circuit riders made in December 1825. John G. Jones and Alexander Talley were newly appointed to the Louisiana District and asked Ashley Hewit, who had made the trip before, to accompany them. They left Washington, Mississippi, for Natchez and continued to Vicksburg where they crossed the Mississippi River. Brother Jones described their journey. "We embarked in a small rowboat at the Vicksburg landing; and after coasting up for about three miles in the slack water near the shore to allow for drifting down in crossing, we were landed on the point opposite our embarkation. Our road from there to Lake Providence was a dim horse path...The banks of the river were covered with dense canebrakes and primeval forest, and often for fifteen or twenty miles there was unbroken wilderness." They reached Lake Providence after a two-day ride and spent the night with Harbord Hood. After resting a day, "Mr. Hewit informed us that the distance we would have to travel the next day through the swamp was forty-five miles, with but one cabin on the route, in which the ferryman lived on Bayou Macon, and that in order to accomplish the journey on a short December day we must start at daylight...after traveling a short distance through a dense canebrake, we entered the open swamp, crossed the Bayou Macon on a raft of logs pinned together, passed over a flat country called the Macon Hills just because it was a little above the high water mark, forded Beouf River...." They rode into the night to reach Prairie Mer Rouge "which threw us into an ecstasy." After spending the night with Col. Ely K. Ross, "Mr. Hewit kindly accompanied us through the Burnt Cabin settlement, on Bayou Bartholomew...and then on down the bayou to the [DeSiard] Island, where we preached our first sermon on the circuit at the house of Judge McLaughlin...We think it unnecessary to detail the many natural difficulties we met with in the way of mosquitoes and gnats, mud and water, bridgeless and ferryless bayous, etc. When the insects were out in full force we could bar them off by wearing a veil of mosquito netting attached to the rim of our hats. As to the mud it was often pleasantly said that the bottom was good wherever you could get to it; and as to the water, especially during the annual inundation, we took it as a matter of course and expected frequent wettings. We did not like to be plunged into deep water unexpectedly, as we sometimes were, but being a practiced swimmer, we took to the water, when necessary, as kindly as a water dog." This brave young preacher became "the first historian of Mississippi Methodism...and achieved more than any who preceded him."[2]

Others required to ride the wilderness trails in the line of business were attorneys going to the various outlying courts. Judge J. W. Bocage rode a circuit from Pine Bluff throughout south Arkansas from 1836 to 1840. He left a description of how he and others traveled. "To reach a point on a right line a distance of only twenty miles, often required the travel of thirty. There were no bridges, few ferries were established, often with only a canoe for crossing a stream, by the side of which the lawyer's horse swam. If a flat-boat, it was usually a small affair, carrying one horse and rider...The territory known as the second judicial district was a wilderness, showing to perfection nature's grand handiwork, replete with towering forest trees of every wood valuable in commerce, underbrush, tangled vines, interminable swamps, and dense canebrakes...his preparation and equipment must be of that character enabling him to surmount any difficulty; his horse must be a good swimmer as well as traveler. It was selected with great care...His horse must be the very best, strong and intelligent, must swim high and be well gaited for the road under the saddle. At the spring term [of court] the waters of the Bartholomew, Saline, Ouachita, Moros, the Lagles and numerous creeks and bayous were usually very high, with scarcely even a canoe to be had, and were crossed, the rider in the saddle, saddle-bags on his shoulders, while his steed was his boat and propelling power."[3]

C. C. Davenport described the Louisiana route used by the wave of emigrant wagon trains traveling westward from 1850 to 1860. They crossed the Mississippi at Vicksburg on a steam ferryboat, the only one operating between Memphis and Natchez. Following the riverbank to Lake Providence, they then proceeded west and passed through Prairie Mer Rouge. "During the fall months it was no uncommon sight to see and count as many as from fifty to seventy-five wagons each day. These emigrant wagons were pulled by teams of every description – mules, horses and oxen. Occasionally there would be an entire family, the man, wife and his children, all following a wagon pulled by one yoke of oxen. Every wagon had on it a cover of lowells or tent cloth. Nearly every wagon had tied to the back of it, the old-time spinning wheel and from one to six cur dogs would be following each wagon. The men, nearly all of them, carried on their shoulders a long barrel flint and steel squirrel rifle; and, fastened to a string around their necks they would have a cow's horn filled with powder...At Prairie Mer Rouge they struck the first settlements since leaving Lake Providence, a distance of fifty miles...Men not familiar with the peculiar soil, unmarked road between [the points] cannot conceive of the hardships and suffering endured by the emigrants that got caught in that miserable swamp country during periods of heavy rains. At times the roads became almost impassable for wagons. Often emigrant trains would not in an entire day get out of sight of the camping spot [of] the night before. It was miles between houses. There were two stretches of road, nine miles between houses. When wagons were broken and must be repaired and no repair shops, no tools, saws, augers...nothing could be done but remain in camp until the owners could go to the nearest settlement to make repairs. Several days of continuous rain meant a complete tie-up of the train for several days. When the trip across the swamp ended and the foot-sore, tired out men, women and children would see the open Prairie Mer Rouge, there would be shouts of joy and thanks to God." After the completion of the railroad from Monroe to Vicksburg in 1860, the road across that "dismal swamp" was abandoned.[4]

In the late autumn of 1849 Abel P. Wilson was moving his family to Arkansas. His wife became ill, and he left her in Mississippi. With three children, a number of slaves, household furnishings, teams and tools, they crossed the Mississippi River at Lake Providence. Before reaching Rough and Ready (near present Monticello), Abel wrote his wife a letter describing their progress. "...The rains set in before we left Lake Providence and we have been in mud and water nearly ever since. We were some 2 or 3 weeks going between 20 and 30 miles. We cut about 8 or 10 miles of road in the swamp there being a space of 20 miles where there was no house. We could only obtain a scanty supply for our selves and teams. From this and the severe cold we lost our gray mare and one or two other likely to die. We however have got to within some 4 or 5 miles of the hills and have stopped at a house to recruit our stock a few days, on the west bank of the byo Betholomew." Wilson left the family at the house and rode ahead to scout around. He spent the night at Thomas Denton's (near Fountain Hill) in Ashley County and wanted to return to the family, but his horse was "scarsely able to travel" and the twenty to thirty mile journey would take all day. "I expect...to try to bring my wagons forward though the roads is very bad and waters up so that we will necessarily make poore progress...[when I come for you] I must come by water and rail road."[5]

Others approached southeast Arkansas from the Mississippi River at Gaines Landing and trekked westward overland. The following description relates to the 1850s: "Most of them came by rail to Memphis where they boarded a boat and landed at Gaines' Landing, a place of two or three stores and one boarding house. Those who arrived in the winter had a most disagreeable time traveling literally in the mud, as the only mode of conveyance to Monticello was by ox wagon or horseback. They piled their baggage and children on the wagon and those that were able bodied plowed through mud above their shoe tops, some even walking for several days. It took three days from Gaines' Landing to Monticello."[6] The infinite number of mosquitoes made summer travel across the swampland even more miserable.

When Dr. William Alexander Noel moved to a plantation on the bayou south of Pine Bluff in October 1853, the family came on a chartered steamboat from Memphis. They brought with them their slaves, oxen, ox wagons, mules and wagons, carriage and carriage horses, and household furnishings. "When they arrived in Pine Bluff the fall rains had begun, and the roads from the river landing to the plantation were in fearful condition. Dr. Noel rode his horse ahead of the family carriage. The mud holes were so deep that five Negro men walked on each side of the carriage to lift and place the wheels on dry ground."[7]

Beouf Swamp (described in Louisiana by Davenport) was also a barrier that had to be crossed in lower southeast Arkansas. Cola (Cammack) Camak gave the following account to a reporter in 1939. "In the wet spring of 1867, the Whitesides family was migrating from Mississippi to Arkansas. Several covered wagons slowly trundled their household goods through the thick gum jungle that was the Beouf River swamp. When it was too dark to push any further through the dense undergrowth, the Whitesides decided to camp on the snowy white sands on the bank of Bayou Mason [*sic*, Macon]. He was awakened a short time later by the roar of rushing water, and suddenly his whole camp was deluged. Clinging to trees and wagons, the party yelled frantically for help. Luckily Mr. [Wylie J.] Cammack was out on the trail [hunting], heard their cries and discovered their plight. Plunging his plucky mare into the torrent, he made trip after trip until every member of the marooned family was safe. He directed and helped with the salvaging of their wagons and conducted them to his home [at old Portland] for the night."[8]

Fords, Ferries, and Bridges

We used the ferries to move cows across the
bayou during high water.
William deYampert

It was necessary to cross the lengthy, winding bayou at many points. Long before the first ramshackle bridges spanned the water barrier, people crossed on fords, footlogs, canoes, and makeshift rafts. Equestrians simply plunged in and allowed their horses to swim across. As travel increased on the primitive roads, ferries began to offer a drier alternative at the principal crossings. Many bridges that now extend over the bayou are at the old ford and ferry sites. Curly Birch attempted to document every bridge across Bayou Bartholomew in 1997; he found forty-seven plus three railroad bridges.[9] The first bridge across the bayou is on the Hardin-Reed Road south of Hardin, and the last is the Point Pleasant Bridge west of Bastrop.

A low water ford with a gravel bed near the bayou's source provides an accommodating crossing. "The Hyde family used to take their wagon across here to go to the springs to get water," Worley Jones said. Atkinson Ford was a low water crossing at Yorktown. The first bridge at Yorktown was ordered in 1872 and completed September 5, 1878. I. W. Cunningham constructed Atkinson Ford Bridge for a cost of $943. A steel bridge replaced this plank bridge in 1916.[10] Murphy Brockman remembered four bridges that have spanned the bayou south of Meroney. "They would all wear out and fall in. The first one was just flat, and a flood would stop you from crossing. After it fell in, the county built one. The WPA built the first good one in the 1930s. They used cypress pilings and it fell in 1961. The concrete bridge was finished in 1963." Shorty Lyle told about an entire train that fell through this bridge: "One time the trestle broke, and a train with twenty-one cars of gravel fell into the bayou."

Persons Bridge, south of Meroney and east of Star City, was named after the Person family who settled nearby in 1852. Sorrells Ferry, located near the mouth of Deep Bayou (south of Fresno), took its name from the Theodoric Finley Sorrells family who settled nearby in 1861 or 1862. Murphy Brockman remembered the old folks talking about this ferry. "Judge Sorrell's place was on the east side. The road went on from there to Varner. They left a rope on the bank to pull the ferry back to the other side." An 1860 map shows an unnamed ford in the bend south of present Persons Bridge. Nearby are Smith's mill and a cultivated field. Summerford Ford was on the east leg of the bayou bend south of Persons Bridge. It took its name from the Summerford family who arrived in 1866. Alvie Pugh said that his father told him there was also a ferry at this location. There was a ford in the bend "past the old Moore place" at Rose Hill. "That was the only place you could cross the bayou without swimming a horse," Edgar Norris said. Two "good" unnamed fords in this bend are shown on the 1860 map. Moore's place is shown south of the bayou at the bottom of the bend, and an Indian village is indicated about a mile upstream.

Batchelor Bridge crossed the bayou west of Avery. Named after the Batchelor family who lived at this site by 1850, it is now abandoned. "Mr. Batchelders Ford good" and a ferry are shown on the 1860 map about two miles upstream from the bridge site. Batchelor Bridge served as the bayou crossing on the Varner to Monticello road which went through Avery, Rose Hill, Tyro, and Coleman. Siegfried Johnson said Captain Avery told him that people used this road as an alternative route during winter months to haul supplies from steamers at Cummings Landing on the Arkansas River. The Gaines Landing Road with its buckshot land had to be avoided because it was virtually impassable during wet weather. The next ford was near Garrett Bridge. Brown's Ferry is due east of Tyro on the 1860 map with a primitive road leading to Tyro. Slightly downstream are a "Ford bad" and Jones Ferry near another primitive road leading to Tyro and Greenmount. Farther downstream near the present Lincoln and Desha line is a "Ford good" near Gibson's farm. The road follows the bayou downstream to a good ford at "Dr. Taylor's" where there is a large cultivated field. This location is in present Lincoln County and may have belonged to either Dr. John Martin Taylor or his double-first cousin, Dr. Charles Minor Taylor.

The 1860 map shows the road following the bayou to "Col. Taylor's Ford good" east of Florence. This is the home site of Hollywood Plantation in northeast Drew County. The Indians used this ford long before Peter Rives discovered it in 1818. Dr. Taylor constructed a floating bridge out of logs to use when the water was too high to ford. (Bayou bridges were built near Winchester and Tillar before 1894 as they were in need of repair that year.) The 1860 map indicates a road leading west from Hollywood to Florence. The bayou passes the home of Clayton on the east bank to come to "Pruitts Ferry" southeast of Selma. The next ferry is at the Hudspeth farm in T13S-R4W. The Military Road leads north from there to Selma. Below the Hudspeth farm is Bowden's, and below that is Miller's with a bad ford and steep banks noted. The Military Road ends and turns into a primitive road following down the bayou to connect with roads leading west to Monticello and Longview and south along the bayou to Gaster's house and farm (100 acres). Just below Gaster is the Humphrey farm (125 acres) with a bad ford noted. Farther downstream is a good ford at Colonel Belcher's house. The bayou then passes another Gaster field

and house.   By 1913 Hedge's Ferry was operating below Blissville
(Jerome.)[11]

Although Gasters Ferry is not indicated on the 1860 map, Stephen
Gaster did operate a ferry near his home south of Baxter.   The county court
granted him a license in 1848 "to run a public ferry across Bayou
Bartholomew, near his residence, the rates of ferriage being as follows:
Wagon and team, 50 cents; carryall or cart, 37½ cents; man and horse, 10
cents; footman, 5 cents; loose stock, 3 cents, all but lead horse, which was
5 cents. Their rates were to be doubled in high water."[12]   Gaster cut trees
on both sides of the bayou to allow uninterrupted operation during high
water. Located on the Gaines Landing Road, it remained in operation for
many years.[13]   The roadway leading from the old landing is still evident on
the west bank.

The first ferry location on the bayou in Ashley County was just above
Boydell. Ferguson's Ferry is shown there on a 1913 map. In 1907 the
county appropriated $6,000 to build a "handsome steel [bridge] of the
latest design" at Morrell and a like sum was granted for a bridge at
Portland.[14]   A low water ford was at Green Pugh Bend, north of Lake
Grampus, at the present location of the Jack Gibson Bridge.   Nobles
Landing Ferry was near the old Wiggins Cabin site north of the bayou
bridge on Highway 82 west of Montrose. An early newspaper article
quoted Emma Bierbaum: "Many's the time I forded the Bayou. Papa let
me have all the money I collected when I forded people across. It cost 15
cents for people on foot, and 25 cents for horsebackers, buggies and
wagons. Mostly we got horsebackers."[15]   An 1879 Corps of Engineers
map shows a ford below the Nobles place at the beginning of Perkins Bend
south of present Highway 82 as well as a ferry at the Perkins place. The
map also indicates ferries at Portland, below Portland at the Sherrer place,
at the beginning of Free Negro Bend at L. Bloomer's, a ford at Sandy
Point, and ferries at the J. W. Robinson place and Poplar Bluff.[16]   Joe
Miller, an early settler, also operated a ferry at Portland.[17]   James Bealer
remembered a later ferry at McCombs Landing east of Thebes. "I crossed
it a lot of times. You just pulled yourself across with a rope. People took
their cotton wagons across on it to the gin," he said.

In 1849 H. C. Dade petitioned the county court to license his ferry in
DeBastrop Township. His rates were a dollar for four horses and wagon,
fifty cents for a two-horse wagon, fifty cents for buggies or carriages, ten
cents for a man and horse, ten cents for a led horse, five cents for a
footman, and three cents each for any stock. Hunter Hollaway, born in
1895, remembered two ferries at Portland. He said that a Mr. Cain
(possibly Willis A. Cain) ran a ferry above Portland near the Hollaway
place and that a Mr. (Frank) Culpepper operated one at the old Portland
bayou location across from the Fisher-Moats house. The first bridge,

which turned to allow passage of boats, at Portland was just below the ferry. In later years a ferry was just west of Wilson Lake and was one of the last in operation. A Mr. Brooks operated a ferry in Free Negro Bend at Eddie Mitchell Bend. There was also a Wilson Ferry in the Bend near the old Chester Post Office site. John Wilson was operating a ferry (and another business along with it) in 1889. He left a note on it for his customers: "If ennybody cums here arter licker, or to git across the river, they can jes blow this hear horn, and if I don't cum when my Betsy up at the house heaers the horn blown, she'll come down and sell them the licker, or set them across the river."[18]

At Parkdale, Robinson Ferry provided transit across the bayou where the old road between Grand Lake and Hamburg intersected the road running north and south on the east side of the bayou. The location, known as Old Ferry, is near present Childress Chapel on Highway 8 west of town. A second ferry was near the present bridge. It became obsolete when the first bridge, a turning bridge, was built between 1908 and 1910.[19] Cecil Kelley found wooden piers, planks, and nails in a gully just north of the present bridge, indicating the probable site of the first bridge. Mark Hawkins said that his father told him Dr. Benjamin Holiday was driving a team of horses when they became excited and ran off the old bridge. The 1913 accident killed the horses and Dr. Holiday.

An 1844 map indicates one ferry on the bayou from the Wilmot area to the state line. It is shown just above the northern end of Lake Enterprise. A road leads from the ferry on the east side of the bayou to the Louisiana line and is the only road on the map.[20] Y. W. Etheridge wrote concerning the year 1841: "Phillip's ferry was operated on the road which led from Mer Rouge prairie in Louisiana across the Bayou, Overflow Creek bottom and on into what is now known as the Mt. Zion neighborhood...It also led east to Grand Lake on the Mississippi near present Eudora. Phillip's ferry was more recently known as Grant's ferry."[21] David Grant settled on the bayou south of Wilmot in 1851. When Fred Montgomery Sr. bought the Grant place, he continued the ferry operation, and it became known as Montgomery's Ferry. In later years Jim Smith had a ferry north of the present bayou bridge, and downstream were ferries known as Eatman and Bell. When the deYampert family bought the Bell place, they kept the ferry in operation. "We used the ferries to move cows across the bayou during high water," William deYampert said. Leroy Haynes said that Bell Ferry ceased to run around 1922 and was the last to operate in the area. In 1917 the Arkansas Legislature appropriated $8,000 for a bridge at Wilmot.[22]

When the Oscar Haynes family moved to the bayou east of Gaines Community in 1911, they found the old Crawley ferry in poor condition. Leroy Haynes said, "It was old and leaking so we built a new one out of hewed cypress logs covered with planks. It was twelve by thirty feet and would hold a wagon and team with a bale of cotton. When the bayou was low it was only about thirty to forty feet across, and my father would let me and Ellis pull it across. But when it was high it was two to three hundred feet across, and he would have to pull it then. We charged a quarter for a wagon and team, and ten cents for a horse or someone walking. Around 1921 it got to leaking so we just let it go down the bayou, and it sank somewhere. After that the folks all got together and built a low water floating bridge of Choctaw logs. When the water got too high we had to let it loose on one end and let it float downstream or the current would break it away. When the water started going down you had to watch it real close and move it back at just the right time."

A change of terminology takes place in Morehouse Parish where ferries are more commonly referred to presently as flats or rafts. William Penn McCain and his son, Jesse, built a ferry below the Arkansas state line in 1903. The ferry was "a few (100) yards up the (now) Ed Korjan Road made out of cypress and tupelo gum." McCain built a second ferry in 1909. While he was away, the ferry was left in the care of neighbors.[23] Frank Winkler, who lived at the present Marvin McKoin place, later owned a ferry at this location. His daughter, Florence, wrote, "...we, the Winklers, owned the old ferry. We bought it and a pontoon bridge, with Cammy [Commie] Hill's plow, when I was four and one-half years old. Papa sold the ferry to old man Lovette on Hopkins Hill at Deer Lick. I was eight years old and cried and cried. Old man Lovette went down the bayou with a mule on it in 1930. It used to be horses, wagons, and Model T's on their way to Wilmot. I rowed a boat 12 years to catch the bus to go to school at Wilmot."[24] Commie Hill later lived at the Winkler place, and a low water crossing there was called Commie Hill Ford. The pontoon bridge was still in use at this time.[25] Page Webb remembered a ferry at the state line owned by "Big Boy" Barnes.

Robert Zachary settled above the bayou on what is now known as Hopkins Hill before 1900 and operated a ferry at the foot of the hill. In later years, F. M. Hopkins, who also lived on the hill, ran a ferry at this location that remained in operation until a bridge was built around 1932. The sunken ferry remains in the bayou below the bridge and is visible about a foot under the water during low water. This was the last known ferry to operate across the bayou. The next ferry downstream was at Cora's Bluff where there was also a low water crossing. Gaston Harrison operated this ferry in 1925-1926. He said, "It was twelve by forty feet and we pulled it across by hand by the chains connected to each end. Oren Robertson remembered crossing this ferry around 1920. "I think this one held two cars; most of them held only one. When the old Model-T's got off on the bluff side they had to turn around and back up that steep hill.

The gas tanks were gravity fed, and that was the only way to get gas to the engine when going up a hill. If they got loose, they wound up down in the bayou." Cora Bluff Bridge replaced this ferry between 1928 and 1932. This bridge was closed in 1986.

Only a few miles downstream was Knox Ferry, which provided a major crossing between the Old Bonita Road and points north of the bayou. The present Knox Ferry Bridge marks the site. The next ford and ferry was at Vester's Crossing on the Old Berlin Road. Vester Bridge was built at this site in 1925. Robert W. Ward owned a large plantation on the bayou by 1860 and operated Wards Ferry just upstream from the present Crossett Highway Bridge. This site was also used as a ford during low water. Tom Day began operating a ferry there in the 1920s. He used two large cypress trees on each side to secure the cables, and these trees are still standing. Before the new Crossett Road was constructed in 1927, the road followed the bayou and then curved back toward Beekman. Part of the old bayou road toward Wardville is still evident on the bank. Ned Averitt operated a ferry near Wardville that provided passage between that community and Shelton community to the south. Bonner Ferry Bridge marks the site of another old ferry. Rocky Ford provided a low water crossing at the present site of Pleasant Drive (previously Van Avenue) Bridge.

Ed Jones remembered Scott's Ferry as the first ferry on the bayou up from its mouth. Mr. Scott lived on the Morehouse Parish side of the bayou. A tragic accident happened on this ferry when Ed was "a little boy" (he was born in 1912). "This old man told me and my daddy this. His Mama and Daddy lived in Arkansas and they were coming to visit them. He and his wife and a little crippled boy and another one of their kids went across the ferry with their mule and wagon to meet them. On the way back across it was a terrible current, and the flat turned over. He got the kids back up on and then saw his wife in the bayou. He jumped back in and got her to the bank. Then he looked back and the flat was turning over again. His Mama and Daddy and the two kids drowned. My daddy found them later when they floated up."

Earlier fords and ferries from the Point Pleasant area to the Ouachita River are mentioned in the Spyker diary (1856-1860). Spyker rode down to Gray Ferry Landing. He and his wife rode to Dr. Collier's ferry. He forded on horseback at Colonel Polk's gin house and once rode past Polk's to cross in a yawl boat. Once he crossed on the Ross ferry to go to Horace Polk's and returned by way of crossing at a gin house.[26] Mary Ann Johnston heard stories about a ferry at the mouth of the bayou soon after the Civil War. An 1851 hand drawn map of the area shows Boyd's Ferry south of Prairie DeButte

Pearl Etheridge Young crossed the bayou with her father in the early 1900s and left the following account:

The road was now a dark tunnel, grass grown and arched by the over-lapping boughs of the trees...It was nearly noon when we came to Bayou Bartholomew. A change in the quality of landscape had become apparent some miles back. The feathery cypress trees sank their stark, flaring trunks into black, stagnant pools...One feature of the landscape set the tone of the whole – a profusion of Spanish moss hanging in cloudy filigree from the boughs above us. [The bayou] had no bridge at this point and it was a watercourse of parts, not to be trifled with. We could not ford it. We drew up and looked for signs of human life...At last, peering through the trees, we saw a rope stretched between the opposing banks of the bayou and there at our feet, moored against the slippery descent, lay a floating wooden platform...my father's hallo brought no answer. "Everybody down in the bottom field picking cotton,"he said, and gave a mighty yodel. The response was long, musical, and reverberating...stillness reigned again until the ferryman came, an old negro with a grizzled head and wiry frame. The mare was coaxed onto the platform and the old man propelled us across by long rhythmic pulls on the rope. It seemed the right way to cross Bayou Bartholomew, the master bayou...In the swamp beyond the stillness deepened and the loneliness was unbroken.[27]*

Although some commercial fishermen had primitive houseboats, known as shanties, on the bayou, they were not a common sight. In 1909 William Penn McCain of Zachary heard that West Monroe needed carpenters and decided to use the bayou as the route to move his family to the town. With the help of his son, Jesse, he built a houseboat, which he named "The Little Star." He and his wife with five children then set out on their voyage down the bayou and on to West Monroe via the Ouachita. After living on the houseboat for a short time, the family moved into a rented house.

McCain's granddaughter, Dorothy Mack, continues the story. "Everything seemed fine for awhile. However, Grandma McCain found out that the previous owner had been a fisherman who was killed and was buried in the backyard not far from the doorsteps. Trouble began. Grandma had never wanted to move anyway, and the children became afraid to live there. Before long, Grandpa gave in to their wishes, and back up the bayou they came to Zachary. The Little Star was put up for sale, but there were no buyers. Finally someone bought the big motor, and the houseboat was anchored along the bayou bank. Time and weather took its toll. At last there was nothing left except a few rusted iron pieces which could still be seen along the sandy edges of the bayou as late as the 1960s."[28]

Mighty Floods

The water from the Arkansas River was
Coming in a heavy rush. It sounded
like a roaring in the woods.

Edgar Norris

When part of the Arkansas River flowed through the bayou bed, it created a larger channel that now makes the bayou an underfit stream, one that has sufficient carrying capacity to prevent overflow. The exception to this is the part of the bayou from its source to the old Arkansas channel entrance below Pine Bluff where the terraces begin. Floods are expected in any Delta landscape, but in Bartholomew country these floods usually come from the Arkansas and Mississippi Rivers.

In June 1867 the Arkansas River flooded from Little Rock to its mouth where high water from the Mississippi backed up for miles. The *Gazette* reported, "Below Pine Bluff, on the south bank, but little damage has been done as far down as the Jordan plantation. Here the water has entered through a bayou, covering some sixty acres of that place, and finding its way out at the Goodloe place. At Floyd Smith's the levee has broken and the water is pouring in through a crevasse several hundred feet in width. This inundates all the plantations on that side of the river, from the foot of South Bend to the mouth."[29] Chicot and Desha Counties were covered with floodwaters in 1874 for over two months. "The county of Desha [below the Arkansas River] and the entire county of Chicot have been inundated for several long weary weeks, with scarcely any lands out but fragments of levees...Chicot County has not 1000 acres of dry land...fully seventy-five per cent of the live stock of the county has either been drowned or starved to death...Their habitations overflowed and entirely swept away, our people are huddled together in attics, perched on roofs or scaffolds...."[30]

A superflood engulfed the Delta in March 1882. Two Little Rock men, W. L. Nelson and John King, visited the area and informed the *Gazette* of what they witnessed. "The water from Monticello [actually from the ridge east of the town at Collins] to Arkansas City is from five to fifty feet deep, and the trip could be made by no other means except a boat. All along the route could be seen colored people quartered in the lofts of houses, the water running swiftly through the main rooms, and cats, dogs, and hogs upon the roofs, while the cattle that escaped drowning were standing on narrow strips of ground or quartered upon rafts not far distant. They went to Monticello from Pine Bluff by rail, and for five miles the track could not be seen and was under water to the depth of four feet...The whole country

for many miles was one vast sheet of water...." Ten years later the area
flooded again. The *Gazette* reported in May 1892, "The [Arkansas] river
at this point [Pine Bluff] has already passed the highest guage ever known,
and is still rising...Many levees are broken below the city...Plantations
never before affected are today overflowed...The old Clayton levee is said
to have broken today, which will let waters into Bayou Bartholomew...The
trouble has just commenced from the overflow. The consequences cannot
be computed." Other major floods occurred in 1883, 1884, 1886, 1890,
1893, 1894, 1897, 1903, 1912, 1913, 1916, and 1922.[31]

Delta dwellers were aware of problem flooding from earliest
settlements days, and landowners with extensive holdings along the
Arkansas and Mississippi Rivers built low levees, a few feet high, to
protect their farmland from ordinary overflows. As high water repeatedly
washed over the embankments, the planters made them higher and higher.
Landowners began forming levee districts in the 1880s in an attempt to
connect and upgrade all levees to augment the flood control work that the
Mississippi River Commission in connection with the Army Corps of
Engineers began in 1879. These efforts resulted in higher and stronger
levees that contained the water during average flooding, but continued to
break in superfloods. Pete Daniel stated it simply, "The more complete the
system became, however, the more pressure the river exerted on the levees
– for there was no escape from the channel, no break or spillway in the
entire thousand-mile line from Cairo, Illinois, to the Gulf of Mexico."[32] In
1927 the rivers created an escape.

The Flood of 1927 was made more dramatic by the existence of levees.
John M. Barry explained this in *Rising Tide*: "Without levees, even a great
flood...meant only a gradual and gentle rising and spreading of water. But
if a levee towering as high as a four-story building gave way, the river
could explode upon the land with the power and suddenness of a dam
bursting."[33] The rains came in January. It rained and rained for months.
By early April the Mississippi reached the top of the levee and backwater
pushed into the already gorged tributaries from Cairo, Illinois, to the Gulf
of Mexico. On April 16 a crevasse opened in the levee at Dorena,
Missouri, and water gushed through flooding 175,000 acres. The Flood of
1927 had begun. Other Mississippi River levee crevasses followed in
Missouri, Illinois, and northern Arkansas. Then the levees of the
Arkansas, White, and St. Francis Rivers in Arkansas began to give way.
Floodwater reached Pine Bluff on April 19. On April 21 the strained
waters of the Mississippi broke through at Mounds Landing near
Greenville, Mississippi, and the Arkansas River levees gave way at South
Bend in Lincoln County and at Pendleton in Desha County. The race for
high land began.

As muddy water from the Arkansas surged across the southeast Delta, the terraces east of Bayou Bartholomew and the hills to the west became a refuge for thousands. Sue Gipson lived east of Tarry. She said, "We heard people talking about it was coming. I was so scared; I was afraid to go to sleep. We could see it coming out of the woods toward our house. It was slow, steady moving. We could walk the ridge to Tarry but not to Yorktown." At Tarry the water reached the doorsteps of the Thomas Store where it stayed for a week. "The sheriff rode up and down the bayou checking on people. They were running boats to the depot in Pine Bluff to get people out," Mrs. H. W. Thomas said. The area around Crigler and Meroney was flooded except for the bayou ridge. Siegfried Johnson said, "You could go from Meroney to Greenwood, Mississippi, in a boat."

Shorty Lyle, who lived at Todd, said, "The Arkansas River backed up into the bayou. We saw red water coming and we knew it wasn't our water. It got out in the low spots around there." At Batchelor Bridge the east bayou ridge was one of a few places above water. "People from Dark Corner brought their stock over here. The water from the Arkansas River was coming in a heavy rush. It sounded like a roaring in the woods," Edgar Norris said. Lloyd Smith said that at Garrett Bridge the water backed up to the hills. The Pickens area was flooded except for the east bayou ridge and the railroad embankment.

Desha and Chicot Counties were inundated; Drew and Ashley counties were flooded to the hills. Buildings in McGehee and Dermott rose out of three to four feet of water. The water washed out graves at Pounders Cemetery on the bayou west of McGehee according to Curly Birch. Charlie Bishop recalled the flood in Dermott: "...an airplane flew over and dropped little leaflets telling people to 'flee for your lives; the greatest flood in history is on its way down.' At that time folks were running a train from Dermott to Monticello and folks would get on that train to ride out there to find a place to stay. One man I know drove his car [to the depot] and left it on the street. He got his family on the train and went to the hills. When he came back the water had been up to the windows on his car. If he'd left it at home, it would have been safe because the water never got in his yard." The Bishop family took refuge in Frog Parker's house, and the boys waded daily to their home to check on a brood of chicks that stayed on the back porch during the flood. "One morning we went down and saw a log floating. That log had a rabbit on one end of it, and about middle-ways was a big old rattlesnake coiled up on it. Neither one seemed to be bothered by the other."

At Jerome the water covered the railroad track. "I heard folks talking about how they went in front of the trains probing to see if the track was still there," Von Greenway said. Boydell, Montrose, and Thebes succumbed to the rising water, which reached to Overflow Hill to the west.

Portland, on slightly higher land, became an island and a point of refuge for people who lived in the outlying area. Others fled to the hills. Ella Mae Herren Wells was twelve years old in 1927 and later described her experience. "Portland was like a cup turned upside down...that was all that was out of water for miles and miles around there...when they realized [the levee] wasn't going to hold, they started bringing the Negroes and the mules and the cattle and everything in town where it was a little higher...And just that little knoll that was Portland was all that stuck out, and I don't know how many thousands of people were there – just couldn't walk for people...We'd stand upstairs in the back bedroom. You could look out and see it coming...It was down in the schoolyard; that's how close it got...It was scary."[34]

The water from the east reached the railroad embankment at Sunshine. Herman King said, "We stayed in the second floor of the schoolhouse for two weeks. It was seventeen feet deep at our house east of the railroad. We put our chickens upstairs." Mark Hawkins said, "They always said Parkdale will never flood. The low bayou bank on the west lets the water go over the lower land to Overflow Creek." Ernie Sprinkle remembered the flood. "Parkdale did not get under water but it was surrounded. We could not go west because there was water to Overflow hill, so we went south to Bastrop and then to the hills to stay with relatives. There were tents of tenants everywhere, and Dr. Locke was giving typhoid shots. We stayed two weeks and then took the train from Hamburg to Montrose and on to Parkdale. The track was still under water. The Red Cross was bringing in supplies and food. The people of Greece sent some raisins, prunes, and salted mackerel. The blacks were saying they didn't like that old salty fish and shriveled up plums."

The Kitchens family lived on the Joe McGarry farm north of Wilmot. Earl Kitchens remembered the fateful day. "The boss man came and told us to get out and get out in a hurry. The water was coming across Dry Bayou from the west and four miles away. We took two wagonloads out and on the last one we were wading knee deep. We stayed about a week at Grandma's house in Wilmot." William deYampert said, "I was nine years old. We went to the present Highway 52 bridge to watch the water coming in. Every ten or fifteen minutes we would have to back up. My father had people building boats in a hurry to use for rescue. He took us to Monticello where we stayed. It took three weeks for the water to get off the farmland, and they had to replant the early crops. It damaged the ridges where it broke through around Dry Bayou and formed big holes. But it brought sand and topsoil and deposited it on the buckshot, and it is still good land. When the speed of water doubles, the capacity for carrying particles increases four times. When the water goes down the soil particles settle down." Wilmot, like Portland and Parkdale, remained above the flood.

Some families did leave Wilmot for the security afforded by the hills. Mildred Tilbury Edwards recalled the experience: "My father quietly gathered lumber, tar, glue, hammer, and nails beginning the building of a boat longer and wider than any of the boats owned by his fisherman friends...I, in childlike faith believed that Dad, like Noah, was building us an ark to sail the waters of the flood...And then, one day at dusk the news came...waters from the north were flooding southern Arkansas. We were to move out! We went by truck west of town to the flood waters of Overflow Creek where the boats were laden with food, water, family, friends, chickens, and pets. The boats were paddled over the water until we reached the hills. Here we set up housekeeping in a one room school house and a church...The men rowed the boats back and forth over the flooded miles to home to store the furniture on sawhorses and boxes out of the expected reach of the water. They brought back families, black and white, living on our rice farm as workers. Dad had bought tents which were set up. My older brother and another young man rode horses swimming in the water to drive the cows and horses through the flood waters to a dry pasture...Fifteen, or more, families camped for days...Cooking over bonfires, exploring the piney woods, sharing stories, singing, and worshiping, we wove together unforgettable happy experiences and unbelievable hardships to create enduring memories of the mighty flood...."[35]

Gaines Community on the east side of the bayou flooded. Leroy Haynes said, "It covered everything around Gaines. It got a foot deep in our house. My dad carried Mother and the little ones to the hills, but we stayed in the house. Had to get dressed on the bed. We went out and shot fish. You talk about snakes – they came in the house!" The Crawley family at Crawleys Bend escaped to the hills. "Dad got the cows up first and then took us to the hills. We camped out in tents for two weeks with lots of other folks. The water got up to the front porch at the Haynes place. It washed out whirlpool holes twenty feet deep near the bayou. They were still there in 1954 and then they leveled them," Ella Vail said.

Buck Mayo recalled the flood at McGinty. "Tom Bishop and Jasper Crenshaw were back of the Naff place cutting firewood on a pin oak ridge that had high palmettos on it. They kept hearing a rumbling, rattling sound. They walked back to see what it was and met the water. It was rustling leaves and chunks of wood. They hurried home and got Tom's bay horse and bridled him - didn't take the time to put on the saddle. He rode him bareback to the schoolhouse and stuck his head in the window and yelled, 'The overflow is coming!' We all left in a hurry for home. We were living on the Naff place then, and Daddy was in bed with typhoid fever. Robert Ward had an old coupe car and he came to the house and got Daddy and took him to Henry McCarty's in Bonita. Then Henry came out to get us and helped put things up in the house. Grandma Goodson lived on back of us, and she wasn't going to leave her turkeys. They waded in waist deep to get her. The Model-T drowned out, and we all got out and pushed it toward higher ground at Vernon Sawyer's. All of McGinty got under water except at Vernon's, and it was sloshing under the sills of his house. We paddled from Jones back out to the house to check on the hogs, chickens, and goats. We had to pull shingles off the top of the barn to get the corn out. We stayed about four weeks in Bonita."

Katie Bell Parker was living at Zachary. "We saw the water coming. Me, Mama, and my two sisters got in the wagon loaded with beds and cooking vessels and went to Hopkins Hill. There were around twenty families that stayed there in government tents. We cooked over a fire; it was fun for the kids. Daddy did not take his stock out. The water got out of the bayou and over the road all the way to Jones. It got in our yard but not in the house." The railroad embankment backed up water coming from the east at Jones and Bonita so the water was higher on the east side. Marion Doles described the flood at Bonita: "It came in washing like ocean waves." Oren Robertson said, "You could stand on our porch and see water all around." Cecil Harp, who lived south of Bonita, said that his family stayed at home but put their hay and corn on a scaffold. "The water got six inches deep under our house. We hauled hay to cattle in boats."

Eloise Means wrote, "When the flood came it was swift and fast. It soon had Bonita surrounded. They sandbagged the railroad culverts keeping most of the water across the tracks and from the town. Across the tracks [to the east], the water was really deep. Mr. Jim Harp had a two-story house and his daughter and son-in-law lived upstairs. She was pregnant and they needed to get her out. The water was deep enough that they rowed a boat into the house to the foot of the stairs so that her husband could put her in the boat. Water was about two feet deep around the Methodist Church and the children used the wooden sections of the sidewalk that floated up as rafts for fun. As the water continued to rise, families began to leave Bonita. Most from Bonita went to Spear Hill on Cooperlake Road to a schoolhouse. Some camped in buildings and others stayed in tents. Twin Oaks, at the corner of Bonita Road and Cooperlake Road, was known as 'tent city.' The tents were furnished by the Red Cross...The only road to Bastrop in those days was the old Bonita Road. About a mile out of Bonita the road was flooded and cars left the road and went into the fields, following turn rows until higher ground could be reached."[36]

Bastrop and the outlying hills became points of refuge. Around 10,000 people camped in the hill country around Bastrop, and others crowded into the town in tents and sheds. The Red Cross fed more than three hundred refugees daily in Bastrop and carried food to the hill camps. On May 4 the *Morehouse Enterprise* reported that Jones was inundated and Bonita had water within the city limits. Water from the bayou was spilling into the lowlands with an inch rise. Two feet of bayou water covered the railroad track for miles around Wardville. To prevent drift from breaking three bayou bridges, guards were stationed on them. On May 6 good news reached Bastrop – the water was beginning to recede with a twelve-inch fall reported at Jones.[37]

Finally the deluge ended and refugees returned to fetid, mud-soaked houses and eroded fields. It was almost too late to plant, but farmers persevered. Andrew Pickens said, "As a piece of land dried up everybody got their mules and worked that place. Everybody worked everybody's ground that year and split the shares evenly." Earl Kitchens said, "When we came back there was two feet of mud and snakes and frogs in the house. It ruined our early garden, but we made good field crops behind the water because it brought in topsoil." By May 11 refugees began to leave the Bastrop area for their homes. Finding the land too wet to cultivate, some "merely took a stick and poked the cotton and corn seed into the ground and made a fine crop that year."[38] Buck Mayo concluded his story, "It got up to the ceiling in our house. It was full of mud and the floors were buckled up. The cotton mattresses were wet, and we pulled the cotton out and dried it. The uncles helped us make a late crop, but the cutworms came behind the water and cut half of it down. We didn't have nothing." The Flood of 1927 was the worst natural disaster the United States ever experienced.[39]

There were to be other memorable floods, and they were exceptional bayou floods. Duke Shackelford recalled the flood of 1932. "From April 15th to the 17th it rained all the way to Star City. It rained ten or eleven inches on Friday and five inches on Sunday. The road from the state line to Bonita was covered. We had a plank walkway from the house to the railroad track and walked to town on the track. It stayed most of the month of April and was higher here than in 1927." Eloise Means said, "Bonita was surrounded by water. The highway was completed at this time and Robin Jordan built a raft with an outboard motor and rafted cars coming from the north across the water at the Bonne Idee to Bonita. Katie Bell and Roosevelt Parker married during the flood. Katie said, "We went in a boat from McGinty to the JP's house at Hopkins Hill. Water was all over the woods and roads. It was higher than in 1927."

In May 1958 the bayou overflowed its entire length. "We got ten inches of rain in twenty-four hours. The water flowed through the carport of our house. It ran over the ridge the house is on and then spread out," said Harvey Chambliss referring to the area south of Pine Bluff. Murphy

Brockman's father told him that the flood at Meroney was as bad as it was in 1927. "Everything was under water except the ridge where we lived. It went down in May or June, and we planted and made good crops," Murphy said. At Garrett Bridge the water was a foot lower than it was in 1927 according to watermarks Lloyd Smith's uncle pointed out. Lloyd said, "There was water all the way to the hills, and the roads were impassable. We had to leave." Amos Sledge recalled the flood in the Dermott area. "Everything around here [Grace Community] was under water. It was over the road three to four feet deep half-way to Baxter and most of the way to Dermott."

The last remarkable bayou flood was in January 1991. "It was over the road from Baxter to Dermott for two weeks," Amos Sledge contended. Morehouse Parish was inundated. "The bayou flooded Jones. It was the first time it flooded from the west. The bayou got higher than anyone can remember," Thelbert Bunch declared. Frank and Violet Day, living on the Bonner Ferry Road, vividly recalled the flood. "In 1958 there was a lot of land out; in 1991 there was no land out. It was way higher than in 1927. Our cotton field was out in 1927 and it wasn't in 1991." Violet never wants to experience another flood. "It was frightening. The levee was threatening to break and water was pouring in. The levee board said to evacuate, and we had to leave at night. The current was about to wash our one-ton, dualwheeled truck off the road. I was terrified. It got a foot deep in our carport." Frank continued, "It washed out holes in our farmland big enough to put a pickup truck in them." Winifred Day blamed the levee between the Ouachita and the bayou for causing the bayou water to back up. "Before the levee was built all the water around here ran into Ward Brake and then into DeButte Creek and on into the Ouachita. Now the levee cuts off that natural drainage and it backs up." Duke Shackelford concluded, "It got over the highway north of Bastrop and between Bastrop and Sterlington. At Point Pleasant you could not tell the Ouachita from the bayou."

Even though the watery land of bayou country often impeded travel and occasionally flooded, it did not discourage the residents in their endeavors. They trudged through the muddy trails, forded or swam their horses across the stream, enjoyed crossing on the ferries, and finally had the convenience of bridges and better roads. After the floods receded they proceeded with farming, often rejoicing in a new layer of deposited topsoil.

They were first and foremost farmers, and they accepted the disadvantages which were inconsequential when compared to the benefits of living on bayou land. They had rich soil, hardwood forests, abundant wildlife, and recreational opportunites provided by the bayou. The hardships created by overland travel and superfloods pale in comparison to other circumstances. Slavery, a civil war, and its aftermath are also a part of the bayou's history.

꙰

 Chapter Seven

Bondage, Rebellion, and Aftermath

Obey Your Master

Grandma was just about to be sold off to another family when freedom came.

Alvie Pugh

The first known recording of the name Bayou Bartholomew in written history pertained to a slave. On January 12, 1781, Balthazar de Villiers wrote to Governor Bernardo de Galvez, "An Arkansas Indian named Chalmet was hunting in the Ouachita region on Bayou Barthelemy and found, he says, a young black man who had a gun sitting alone in front of a little fire. The Indian wants to keep him, but I am going to make him give him up, in order to return him to his master when his master becomes known."[1] A simple yet somber tableau painted a description containing ominous words that would foreshadow events of the next eighty years. The Indian wanted "to keep him" as his own slave, but the commandant was going to "return him to his master." The lonely young black man shivering by a small fire on the bank of the bayou in the wilderness had run away and experienced "freedom" for a short while. This slave would never hear the word emancipation; perhaps his grandchildren did.

The importation of slaves to the American colonies began in 1619 when a slave ship landed twenty Negroes in Virginia.[2] Slavery reached the area that would become Arkansas in 1720 when German colonists brought the first slaves to John Law's colony below Arkansas Post. By 1798 black slaves numbered 56 of the total population of 393 at Arkansas Post. French colonizers also owned Indian slaves, but later Spanish dominion outlawed future ownership of Indian slaves. They were allowed to keep those they already owned when the law went into effect.[3] When Arkansas Territory was created in 1819, 1,617 slaves lived inside the borders. This number gradually increased through the years as more settlers came and additional farmland opened up. In 1827 slaves numbered 2,520, and in 1830 there were 4,567. The number increased to 9,838 in a total population of 52,240 in 1835.[4] The largest concentration of slaves was in the lowlands where most cotton plantations were located. Table 5 reveals the dramatic increase in slave numbers from 1850 to 1860.

Table 5
Slave and White Population in Southeast Arkansas and Morehouse Parish

County	Date	Whites	Slaves	Farms
Ashley	1850	1,409	644	
	1851	1,415	710	122
	1860	4,829	3,761	
Chicot	1850	1,112	3,984	
	1851	1,131	4,258	108
	1860	1,722	7,512	
Desha	1850	1,685	1,169	
	1851	1,759	1,173	119
	1860	2,655	3,784	
Drew	1850	2,361	915	
	1851	2,361	914	408
	1860	5,581	3,497	
Jefferson	1851	3,213	2,621	523
Morehouse Parish	1850	1,878	2,026	60
	1859	3,620	4,098	

Note: Lincoln County was part of Desha and Drew at this time.
Source: U. S. Bureau of the Census.   Ninth Census of the United States:1870. Population and Social Statistics, Vol. I, 13,14. 1851 census from *Arkansas Gazette*, April 4, 1851. Morehouse 1850 census from *The 1850 Federal Census of Morehouse Parish, Louisiana*, compiled by Faith White Nolin (Crossett: Southeast Arkansas Research, 1990), introduction. Morehouse 1859 census from Williamson, *Eastern Louisiana*, 140.

❧❦❧

New Orleans became a major slave trade center, and from there the new owners brought their chattel up the network of rivers or overland from landings on the Mississippi to the interior bayou land.   Slave markets operated at Monroe and Trenton, and reselling continued as slave buyers carried their investments farther up inland streams.   Some slave owner contractors, Captain James P. Clark of Ashley County for example, engaged their slaves in the clearing of timberland for others, particularly in the fertile swampland of the bayou.[5]

Leonidas Spyker made a detailed inventory of his "Negroes" in April 1859, and the account offers a realistic insight into slave holdings on a large plantation of that time. He grouped them as family units with twenty-five couples' names and the number of children. Old Dinah, age sixty, and Yellow Frank, age thirty-eight, had no children. The total number was 121 with 51 under age 15. Adult ages ranged from eighteen (1) to fifty (4), excluding Old Dinah. All other adults were from twenty to forty-five with the majority in their twenties and thirties. Only twelve were between the age of forty and fifty. Spyker also categorized the group into "black" and "yellow." Twelve adults were yellow and all of these except one couple were mated with a black. Children of these couples were mostly yellow. Part of the inventory was the notation that five males and two females died in 1859. The plantation yielded 580 bales of cotton and 7,500 bushels of corn. Stock included 50 mules, 3 horses, 90 cattle, and 170 sheep. (Spyker also mentioned oxen in several places.) Noted as "killed" were 65 hogs, 50 sheep, and 2 beeves.[6]

Cotton and corn production was the essential economic base of the plantation, especially the cotton. Some corn was sold, and some was kept for stock feed. Other crops mentioned in the diary were oats, sweet potatoes, watermelons, turnips, cantaloupes, and clover as well as plum and peach trees. Seventy adults (over age fifteen) and an unknown number of children toiled at many tasks to make the plantation produce. Work referred to in the diary included clearing new ground, log rolling and burning, breaking ground, subsoiling, preparing seed beds, planting, hoeing, picking cotton, ginning and packing cotton, and cutting cotton stalks. They planted the orchard and pruned and wormed the trees; they made roads, dug drainage ditches, cut rails, made fences, tended the coal kiln, worked at the sawmill, sheared sheep, and butchered animals for meat. Spyker rather simply wrote one day, "The hands made a good day's work." This was probably an understatement. Sally Jackson told Buster Ford that as men cleared land, the women piled and burned brush. The women hauled water from the bayou to do the laundry, fed stock, and "kept house for the old master."

Migrating families generally brought their slaves with them. Josiah Davenport, a sea captain, sold his boat in Savannah, Georgia, in 1806 to a man who kidnapped Africans for the slave trade. Part of his payment was in young slaves, which he brought to New Orleans to sell. It was there he met with Abraham Morhouse, accompanied him to what would become Morehouse Parish, and became a large plantation owner.[7] Spyker moved from near Plain Dealing, Louisiana, (twenty-eight miles north of Shreveport) to Point Pleasant in January 1857. The approximately hundred-mile journey took nine days. The entourage consisted of more than a hundred slaves, wagons loaded with farm equipment and supplies, farm animals, and a buggy. The diarist kept an account of the trip. The first day they covered about twelve miles and camped on Bayou Bodcau. The second day they crossed that bayou on a ferry and continued to Dorcheat Ferry. Snow and sleet began the next day. "The ground covered with ice and snow and a punching north wind blowing all night...." The fourth day they walked on frozen snow. "My boots collected balls under the heels so that I was obliged to cut it off every mile or so." Spyker went ahead the next day to Shilo to get the buggy mended (for the second time) and "was nearly frozen when I got there." The sixth day brought more sleet as the party trudged forward through Farmerville and crossed Bayou de L'outre. The following day they "had to build a bridge over another branch." On the eighth day they "reached the Ouachita River about sun-up and got everything across except the cattle by 1 p.m." Knowing his men would reach Point Pleasant the next day, Spyker left them and returned to Hard Times Plantation to bring his wife and children by carriage and a buggy over the same route to their new home which he named New Hope.[8]

Theodoric Finley Sorrells moved from Pine Bluff to a plantation already established on the bayou west of Varner around 1861. "He had eight Negro houses built in two rows on a high hill overlooking three bayous, Bartholomew, Cross and Deep," wrote his daughter, Mary Sorrells DeWoody. "The cabins were made of split logs of sassafras. Father's office, just a single room, was next to the last in the row and our family living quarters occupied the last. It differed from the others in that it had one big room and two smaller ones, used as dining room and plunder room The chimney was of dirt, and the fireplace was six or eight feet wide. The floors were made of planks split and smoothed as well as possible with a drawing knife...The kitchen was an unfloored cabin with a big dirt chimney and a pot rack, upon which was suspended an immense pot for boiling vegetables. We had trivets for the coffee pot, long handled waffle irons, skillets with lids. When you baked anything you had to put on the lid and heap coals on top of it. Lye hominy was made in a large wash pot. The negroes food was sent to the field in large wooden trays."[9]

When Dr. John M. Taylor and his bride moved to Drew County in 1844 they left half their slaves at their Kentucky tobacco plantation and sent the others on "river flatboats to Arkansas to work in the cottonfields." Mrs. Dillard Sanders, a descendant, wrote, "The slave quarters were on the west bank of the stream, about a 1/4 mile from the 'Big House', and the colored people had a church and a burying ground. The commissary was between the Quarters and the Big House."[10] The "burying ground" is still a well-kept and often used African-American cemetery. Stretching for approximately two acres on the bayou bank and containing numerous sunken, unmarked graves, the earliest marked date of birth is 1865 and the earliest marked death is 1907.

Thomas Sidney Smith migrated with a slave family to Lincoln County around 1853. His grandson, John I. Smith, wrote, "[I have] always thought that the reason our people came from Alabama was to flee from the slave and plantation conditions there. Their slavery desires were slight, and Grandpa may have purchased this family to protect them. A boy in this Thomas family was named Marion, and he and Pa were friends for life." John Smith's maternal grandfather, John Wesley McShan, moved from Mississippi to Collins, above the bayou in Drew County, in the 1850s. McShan did not believe in slavery and when he received a slave family through an inheritance, he told the authorities he did not want them. Smith wrote, "Since it was illegal to free them, Grandpa took them and said he would do the best he could for them. A young girl of this family was willed to Grandma as her personal servant. Grandma told the authorities that she did not want a servant, but in the end she took the girl, called Liza, and began to teach her."[11]

Archibald Nobles, who lived near Parkdale, owned seven slaves. "I believe a little cabin away from his house was the slave quarters," said Ernestine Nobles Sprinkle. Also at Parkdale was John Tillman Hughes whose wife took women slaves to the bayou to launder clothes. "I remember seeing three big iron pots behind the old house many years ago. They called them slave pots or sugar pots," said Mary Alice Cottrell Nelson. When William Benjamin and Lucius Webb deYampert settled on large plantations along the bayou in Ashley County, they "both brought boatloads of slaves with them."[12]

Murphy Brockman of Lincoln County recalled that slaves owned by Amanda Crow's father went by the surname Weaver. They were likely previously owned by Amanda's maternal grandparents, the Weavers, who had a farm on Bayou Bartholomew. Weaver slaves are buried at the Crow family cemetery. Sue Gipson of the Yorktown area said that her maternal grandmother, Sally York, was born at Tarry and owned by a man named York. Buster Ford's grandfather, Louis Ford Sr., was born near Jones, Louisiana, to parents who were brought as slaves from the West Indies. Buster's maternal grandmother, Sally Mays Jackson, said that her parents and her husband's parents, the Jacksons, were transported to South Carolina as slaves and then brought to Elon, Arkansas, by a Mr. Jackson. From Elon they walked for three days to a farm near Parkdale. Page Webb's maternal grandmother, Sealey Jackson, was born into slavery on the Pipes plantation near Collinston, Louisiana. Sealey lived to enjoy her eventual freedom for a long time; she died when she was 107 years old. Alvie Lee Pugh's grandparents, Alice (Jasper) and George Pugh Sr. were born as slaves in Virginia and Alabama respectively. Alice's father, Peter Jasper, was brought to Lincoln County in 1858. "Grandma was just about to be sold off to another family when freedom came," Alvie said.

Dr. Charles McDermott and his brother, Edward, who settled on the bayou at Dermott, owned slaves that they inherited from their mother. (Charles owned forty-six in 1850.) McDermott's journal reveals firsthand information about slavery. Referring to his boyhood memories in West Feliciana Parish, Louisiana, he wrote, "My father began planting indigo and sugar cane, as cotton was not yet planted there. He settled there about 1794. He brought his negroes from Kentucky and Virginia. Some he bought direct from the ships as they landed from Africa. The Africans were sold by the weight at $1.00 a pound. They were ignorant of our language or of French, and knew not how to plow or hoe. Often I have heard them talk about what part of the human body was the best to eat and how they fattened children for a feast. They were savage at times, when they were angry. One woman, named Lucy, was employed every day to boil corn in a kettle for hogs and oxen. She used a long wooden paddle to stir up the boiling contents and when any of the negro boys would come up to steal an ear of corn, she would strike at them with the paddle hard enough to break a bone if they did not elude the blow. She had large spots on her arms and breast as white as paper. An African man from the same coast [Congo] had his front teeth sharpened – he said by a nail – to make him bite well. He was a good natured creature, kind to the white children. His African name was Tosa...."[13]

It was of course up to the owners to provide medical care for their chattel. This was necessary to protect their investment and, perhaps for some, motivated by benevolence as well. C. C. Davenport, whose father owned 110 slaves, spelled out the importance of taking good care of them from a strictly economic point of view. "The average negro family consisted of the man, his wife and six children. Before the birth of any children, at marriage, in 1860, the man was valued at $1,500 and his wife at $1,000, equal to $2,500. After marriage and the family had grown to be six children, say three boys and three girls, the family...was valued at, customary price, $8,000. The natural growth of the family had added to the value of the family as profit, the sum of $5,500, and this was about the average profit from births from one family in the period of twelve to fifteen years." After explaining how one adult slave could work ten acres of cotton and five of corn and the good price for both products, he concluded his thesis. "From the statement made above, it can be seen that the opportunity to make big money at farming and taking care of the children, was good – excellent...In sickness, every slave was medicated and kindly nursed. I recall that he several times told me that during his life he never had a death among his negroes, [who were] field hand ages. I do not mean by this that there were no deaths from old age or children."[14]

J. Fred Crawley owned 156 slaves (including children) on his Crawley Bend plantation and built a slave hospital for their care. Robert Crawley said, "By the end of the 1920s we were still finding bricks from that old building." Dr. Charles McDermott's granddaughter wrote, "One room on the lower floor [of the home] was filled with cribs and beds for negro children, both sick and well. A negro nurse was always there to help Grandma give medicine and keep order. Every negro on the farm had his measure on her books and a certain number of articles of clothing were made and given each season."[15]

The Spyker diary gives a precise accounting for the medical care given to his slaves. He moved to the plantation in January 1857, and by March that year Mr. Dalrymple was "raising the hospital." He later referred to this building as the "sick house." He often noted their medical condition in his daily log: "Winney is quite sick. Something like scarletina." "Hall's child was sick last night." "Matty is some better. Boy is sick." The local doctors often paid medical visits to them. "Dr. Tive came to see . . .some of the negroes." Neighbors sent their slaves to Spyker to have their teeth pulled. Once Tom Polk "sent for a dozen leeches" which implies they were using them for drawing blood, a common practice at that time.[16]

In addition to these rather casual comments regarding the health care of his people, Spyker kept a separate medical log with specific instructions for issuing treatment. Remedies and recipes for preparing them leave a medical care record for the time. He prescribed for Eliza and Matilda "2 grs. Ipecca and ¼ oz. Squills to an oz. Water & to 2 oz. of the mixture add 1 teasp. of spts. of nitre. Dose adlt, 1 tablesp." For Milly's child, Ginney Bell, he directed, " 3 grs Calomel, 3 grs Rhub [probably rhubarb], 3 grs Soda, 1 gram Ipecac. Mix & make 3 doses - give at intervals of 3 hours until the bowels move. Then cease." Phillis needed snakeroot tea, poultices, brandy toddy and eggnog freely, carbonate of ammonia, Davis Powder, and Beef Essence for her ailment. More instructions for Phillis followed that included a mixture of ammonia, Blue Mass, and Davis Powders. She remained sick. "If the oil acts too much check it - If the hoarseness is not better by night, put a blister over the throat-& give Squills & 10 drops Spts Nitre 1 Tps of Squills at a dose -If a tonic is wanted give ammonia - if the sweat returns give ammonia."

Other prescriptions called for the use of opium, quinine, laudanum, morphine, tannin, Charley Oil, Mercurial Ointment (for blisters), Blue Mass (for measles), paregoric, and boneset (an herb). Since some of these mixtures acted as severe laxatives, he always counteracted this possibility with another remedy for the side effect: "If bowels start off give ¼ gr. Opium, 2 gr. Tannin or a starch and laudanum injection." In addition to beef essence (bouillon) and egg nog for nutriments, he suggested mutton tea and beef tea. The cure for a felon, an extremely painful tissue or bone inflammation, was a paste of soft soap and air-slacked lime.[17]

Ill treatment of slaves by their masters would likely not appear in plantation daybooks or published memoirs. Reminiscences by slave owners or their descendants usually portray a humane attitude. C. C. Davenport, who took charge of his father's plantation in 1858, wrote in his later years, "His treatment to his slaves was humane and kind...He had good frame cabins, brick chimneys, and the negro quarters were so arranged that a central well of water and a central wood pile, were convenient to every cabin home...The ration to the field working hands that was issued once each week, was, five pounds of salt meat to the men, four pounds of salt meat to the women, one quart molasses and one peck of corn meal to every working field hand." This amount of food hardly seems adequate although garden products supplemented it. The five pounds of salt meat when fried would yield only half that amount or less. A "good old mammy negro woman" cared for children in a communal nursery. Nursing mothers came three times a day to feed their babies, and all children went to their cabins for the noon meal. Between meals they ate "corn bread and clabber, or cold potatoes and pot liquor, or molasses and bread." The slaves had an allotted piece of ground where they grew their own cotton for which they received payment at Christmas. Slaves did not work on Sunday and had a week or two Christmas holiday. (The time off at Christmas would have been given only if all the crops were harvested.)

As for punishment, Davenport wrote, "There was no law against the whipping of slaves, but it was seldom done, and when done it was generally inflicted because of fusses-quarrels among themselves. All disagreements and troubles among the slaves were settled by the owners...It was a rare thing to see a negro in jail or in a penitentiary. As a rule, masters were kind to their slaves. Occasionally there were cruel masters and occasionally there were bad negroes that required severe punishment."[18]

Spyker had a peculiarity. He never referred to his people as slaves. He consistently called them his hands and on a few occasions referred to them as Negroes. The words slave nor slavery are not in his diary. There is no account of trouble from his slave community. One stoic entry alludes to a possible disturbance as well as to the absolute power of a master: "I went to field and settled with Frank and divorced him from Lydia." Slaves were not allowed the institution of legal marriage. There is no account of selling a slave and only one of buying one. "...went up to Col. May's place to see how the negroes would sell, but did not wait...Mr. Morgan says he must have $1700 for his boy Milo...Bought negro man Milo for $1700. He refuses to guarantee him running away unless I will increase the price."[19]

Masters sometimes freed their slaves in return for exceptional deeds. Mary Sorrells DeWoody wrote about a slave named Ishmael who belonged to her grandfather. "When he had completed his house [around 1833], save the doors, he left his family, making old Ishmael, the trusted servant, promise to sleep in the doorway at night, while he rode to Warren to buy hinges to hang the doors, and ammunition, for they were largely dependent upon wild game for meat. My grandfather was compelled to stay overnight; when he returned the old darkie presented him with a broken gun and his family with the marvelous account of how 'Old Daddie,' at the risk of his own life, had fought against a white man and an Indian, who had come will all [sic, ill] intent and had run them off. Later on, an Indian skeleton was found, proving almost certainly that he had received his death blow upon the head by an empty gun in the hands of this faithful servant. Old Ishmael was freed, and long years afterwards the broken gun upon the rack -- and Old Daddie's deserted log cabin on the hill, silently attested that all heroes are not inscribed on history's pages...."[20]

A strong religious belief in some kind of a caring, loving, delivering god provided some whisper of comfort to those held in enslavement. African and other theistic beliefs and customs gradually merged with the Christian ideology that some owners allowed to be taught. Other owners feared that strong religious convictions could give slaves enough strength to revolt and disallowed any kind of religious services or worship. Commonly repeated stories passed down in families of former slaves are that they put their heads under wash pots to pray and held secret services in the woods or their quarters. "They had to pray at night with their head under a wash pot," Buster Ford said. Alvie Pugh reiterated, "Some were allowed to go to church, but some were not allowed to pray. They had to put pots on the ground and put their heads under them to pray. Maybe the Lord would answer their prayers to have freedom."

Ironically, Dr. Charles McDermott learned to pray from a Negro slave. He wrote, "My first religious feelings were in 1818. My mother had bought an old negro from Virginia for $100 and had him to feed the horses and dogs. He would ask me to read hymns so he could memorize them. His name was Tartar. When I read to him from the Bible, he would exhort me never to be profane, nor help draw a fish seine on the Sabbath. From him, I learned to pray." McDermott built a church for his slaves upon his arrival at his bayou plantation. He wrote, "The hardest thing I ever did in my life was to call up my negroes and family on the first Sabbath we spent in Arkansas, to worship God. At one end of the long log house we were in, my brother, with his wicked friends, held to their own way. At the other end I called upon my family to worship God...I read and explained the Bible to them, had a prayer, and we sung several hymns. Oh, it was hard to do. But it broke the devil's head. My brother came to me the next day and said that if I wanted preaching on the place he would spend $100 to make a place. The worship of God was ever kept up – until I went to Honduras."[21]

The Davenports also allowed worship. Davenport wrote, "The religiously inclined held divine services once a week, in one of the cabins. Every plantation usually had one or more negro preachers."[22] Owners also used religious teachings to help control their slaves. "Obey your master" applied to the heavenly as well as the earthly master. Thou shalt not steal (thy master's chickens). Thou shalt labor for six days (long days). Thou shalt not kill, commit adultery, steal, bear false witness, covet thy neighbor's wife nor anything else. Why not teach such good rules? They followed one of the Hebrew judgments – the master could keep the wife (and the children she bore) and let the manservant go. They did not follow another judgment– if a couple was "married" when they came in, they must go out (be sold) together. Did masters read Exodus 21:20 to their slaves? *And if a man smite his servant, or his maid with a rod, and he die under his hand; he shall be surely punished.*

Religious fervor spread, however, and before the 1850s slaves were entrenched as members of white churches, especially Baptist and Methodist. By 1860 southern Methodist churches had 207,766 Negroes on their rolls with an additional 180,000 children taking catechism instruction. Many churches had slave balconies for a segregated seating arrangement. Others held separate services for slaves, and some owners allowed slaves to have their own church. Bartholomew Methodist Church near Plantersville had a slave gallery for slaves who attended church with their masters. The slavery issue split the Methodist Episcopal Church into north and south divisions in 1844. The northern churches wanted to alter the "General Rule in reference to buying, selling, and holding slaves," and the southern ones rebelled. Rev. John G. Jones of the Bartholomew Circuit wrote, "But our northern brethren, because they had it in their power, pushed us to the wall, and left us no alternative but separation or the defeat of our ministry in large portions of the slaveholding states. We were not willing to lose the fruits of our self sacrifice, labor, and toil among the slaves of the South or their owners, and accepted separation as much the better alternative."[23]

But as with all episodes, there was a dark side to give stark contrast to the only slightly brighter side. While some slaves may have been treated kindly, allowed to worship, given medical care, and clothed and fed sufficiently by their masters, others were mistreated. They were whipped with the lash, had salt put into the glistening wounds, overworked, underfed, and poorly clothed. Women were sold away from their mates. Children were sold away from their parents. Women were subject to the sexual whims and desires of their owners. With a brutal disregard for their rights as human beings, enslaved though they were, masters forced Negro women to bear their children. In this case a master's own children were also his slaves.

The slave woman had no choice in resisting the sexual advances made by her master. John W. Blassingame wrote, "The white man's lust for black women was one of the most serious impediments to the development of morality...Few slave parents could protect their pretty daughters from the sexual advancement of white men...The black autobiographers testified that many white men considered every slave cabin to be a house of ill-fame. Often through 'gifts,' but usually through force, white overseers and planters obtained the sexual favors of black women. Generally speaking, the women were literally forced to offer themselves 'willingly' and receive a trinket for their compliance rather than a flogging for their refusal and resistance."[24] Sexual submission had a distinct benefit for the Negress. F. George Kay wrote, "The slaves were not slow to see the advantages of a sexual liaison with their employers. It meant all the difference between working to exhaustion on the land and living in comparative luxury...a slave woman could consider nothing more desirable than that her daughter should attract a white man. Indeed it was the only chance for the child to evade physical labour as a slave."[25]

Alvie Pugh's father was born in 1887 to former slave parents, and they talked about it. Alvie spoke out: "I was told a many a thing about slavery, and I thought a lot about it then. My father was over a hundred years old and could tell everything. My grandmother and other old slavery people have told me things too. Some couldn't go to church or pray, and some were mistreated. The slaves in the north had more freedom and were treated better than southern slaves. In the south they would throw them in barns and feed them hay. They had to chew it as best they could. An old log barn – that's the way they kept them. Their names changed as their owners did. They took kids and tied them on blocks and auctioned them off like hogs or cows. They hauled them from Africa to here and made slaves out of them and treated them all kinds of ways. It was terrible."

Sally Jackson told her grandson, Buster Ford, about slavery. "She said sometimes they were treated pretty good and sometimes pretty bad. If two got into a fight in the field, the master would whip them at night. They were in division camps and the people couldn't talk to the ones in the other camp. They couldn't marry between camps either. Their master had all his babies by one woman, the cook in the camp. They all grew up as his slaves." James Bealer said that his grandfather was whipped. Thomas Y. Harp of Morehouse Parish wrote, "I can remember many old exslaves, but never had any discussion with any of them about their slave life except old 'aunt' Grace Moreau who lived on my place for more than 30 years. She once told me that she was owned by Bob Ward and he was mean."[26]

The states enacted laws regarding the treatment of slaves and other related issues such as marriage, runaways, punishment, and manumission. The constitution of the new state of Arkansas in 1836 obligated "the owners of any slave or slaves to treat them with humanity." It also provided for an impartial jury in slave cases, the same degree of punishment for slaves as whites, and the appointment of free defense counsel. The Revised Statutes and Digest of 1838 addressed more regulations for slaves and free Negroes. These issues basically instituted more control for the sake of control such as punishment for slaves being at large, having weapons, assembling, and drinking. Organized county patrols served as watchdogs. Infractions demanded severe and corporal punishment. Assemblage could mean revolt in which case the owner would be at the mercy of an irrepressible mob. Up to twenty lashes were allowed for such transgressions. The presence of free Negroes was especially intimidating, and they were highly regulated.

As the slave population increased, the regulation laws for both slaves and free Negroes became more severe. Free Negroes had to post a "good behavior" bond after January 1843 and by March the same year could no longer enter the state. More stringent laws pertaining to escape, crime, and punishment passed in 1849 and 1851. Slaves and free Negroes alike were subject to capital punishment for crimes against nature or assault to commit rape on white women. The same violations committed by white men were not capital. Punishment for the first offense of stealing a horse was "not less than fifty lashes well laid on." A second offense demanded death. Every Negro was considered a slave and the burden of proof fell upon the free Negro. Disregarding a statute defining a mulatto as a person with one-fourth or more Negro blood, the state accepted less than one-sixteenth as a guideline.

The abolitionist movement increased in intensity, and regulation laws increased proportionately. After February 1859 owners could no longer emancipate slaves by deed or last will. Imprisonment of slaves ended; they were simply given "no more than one hundred lashes, well laid on the bare back, in any one day." The number of lashes allowed had grown from twenty to fifty to a hundred through the years. After January 1, 1860, free Negroes were not allowed in the state and if found could be arrested and hired out for three months to earn money for their exportation. If they did not leave after that, they could be sold into slavery. Judge Jacob Trieber wrote, "It seems strange that no statute was ever enacted for the protection of slaves against cruel treatment, although the constitution expressly provided for laws 'to obligate owners of slaves to treat them with humanity.'"[27]

The Arkansas Supreme Court finally settled the mulatto issue (how much Negro blood constitutes a mulatto) on an appeal from an Ashley County case, *Daniel v. Guy et al.* In 1850 Abba (Abby) Guy (who lived on the bayou) appeared on the Union Township census as head of a mulatto family. Her occupation was listed as "spinstress" and her sixteen-year-old daughter's was "Belle of Hamburg Dance."[28] Abby socialized with white people and was apparently accepted as white. In 1855 William Daniel tried to claim Abby and her children as his slaves. Abby appealed to the county court, and even though Daniel produced a bill of sale showing he purchased her in 1825 at age thirteen and her mother, Polly, from James Condra, the court ruled on her behalf. The circuit court judge instructed the jury to decide the case on the consideration of race. If they were "less than one-fourth Negro," they were white and free. He allowed the jury to inspect them and instructed the jury to make their own judgment. Daniel protested saying that if Abby's mother was a slave, Abby and her children were slaves. The judge refused to instruct the jury on this premise, and Abby won the case. The Supreme Court overturned the decision ruling that a mulatto was considered a mulatto (and therefore a slave in this case) without regard to the grade of Negro and white blood mixture. Any intermixture, called the "one drop [of Negro blood] rule," constituted a mulatto. If Abby's mother was a slave with one-eighth Negro blood, then Abby and her children were also slaves.[29]

The colony of Louisiana, which included Arkansas, enacted similar laws known as the Black Code in 1724. Under the domination of the Catholic Church, these laws pertained to Jewish people as well as slaves. All Jews were to be expelled, and only Catholics could own slaves. Negroes could not carry "any kinds of weapons or big sticks." When slaves were executed for crimes, the state was to compensate the owners at market price. (This law may have provided a simple solution for the owner of an incorrigible slave: accuse him of a crime; have the state execute him, and get paid.) Negroes could not gather in crowds. A revised code issued in 1806 addressed the carrying of firearms, stealing, runaways, and required slaves to obey their masters' orders except for commission of crimes. A slave found on horseback without written permission was to receive twenty-five lashes. The code also gave some outlines for the treatment of slaves. They did not have to work on Sunday without fifty cents compensation. Owners had to furnish a monthly allotment of rations: a barrel of Indian corn or its equivalent in rice, beans, or other grain, and a pint of salt. Owners had to feed disabled slaves and give medical and "spiritual assistance" to the sick. Old and disabled slaves had to be sold with their children, and children under ten years of age could not be sold away from their mothers.[30]

Laws were made for the protection and welfare of slaves but they were generally disregarded. The owner was usually the judge and jury, and his slaves were at his mercy. It took a civil war to finally put an end to human bondage in the southern states.

Four Years of Pandemonium

We get plenty of Corn by crossing Bayou Bartholmue
for it. The plantations are all abandoned by their
owners & being now occupied by poor people⋯.
George Boddie, 1864

The diary begins: "*Home. May 20ᵗʰ, 1862. The above named day I started to Monticello to join Lieutenant Haynes squad of recruits for Capt. J. A. Owens Battery and left Monticello that day and camped the first night at Branchville. And the 21ˢᵗ at a church on Bayou Bartholomew below Pine Bluff. 22ⁿᵈ got to the Bluff and camped in the Court House and stayed until the 26ᵗʰ when we embarked from Pine Bluff on board stemer Kentucky for Memphis and got in the Mississippi River at Montgomerys point about 12 o'clock the 27ᵗʰ. 28ᵗʰ May landed at Memphis in the evening. Left Memphis the 29ᵗʰ for Corinth about 5 o'clock on locomotive Belle Kelso and got to Corinth same day about one o'clock and heared the first cannon booming....*"[31]

The unknown diarist from Drew County was one of 60,000 men from Arkansas who enlisted in the Confederate service after the April 12, 1861, assault on Fort Sumter and the state's ultimate joining of the Confederacy on May 20. Drew and Ashley Counties were among the first to raise companies in the state with Captain William H. Tebbs' Company A "composed of 87 men of the Bayou area" being one of "the first two companies raised in Arkansas," according to Judge Y. W. Etheridge. This company joined the Third Arkansas Infantry commanded by Col. Albert Rust.[32] Tebbs lived near the bayou southwest of Portland. Captain John G. Gibson of Tyro, above the bayou in Lincoln County, mustered a company on June 12, 1861, and left for Virginia. The following week Robert S. Taylor, who owned land on the bayou east of Selma in Drew County, organized the Selma Company (Company D) which also became part of the Third Arkansas. Lt. Col. Robert S. Taylor, a double-first cousin of Dr. John M. Taylor, was present at the surrender at Appomattox.[33] Louisiana voted for succession on January 23, 1861. Companies raised in Morehouse Parish bore such names as the Morehouse Avengers, Fencibles, Guards, Southrons, Stars, and the McKoin Rangers.

The area along Bayou Bartholomew in southeast Arkansas and Morehouse Parish saw little action except for raiding and reconnaissance by both armies. Guerrillas (organized groups fighting for either side), Bushwhackers (Confederate raiders) and Jayhawkers (locals not in favor of the war who preyed on their neighbors for supplies) added to the havoc.

Mary Sorrells DeWoody wrote, "We did not suffer, as many did, because we were off the regular line of the marching soldiers." Other bayou families, however, did receive visits from Union and Confederate troops and Bushwhackers. Mrs. C. H. Bohinger wrote, "The Yankees visited the Noel Plantation [on the bayou in Jefferson County], ransacked the dwelling house, then turned their attention to the smoke-house. They took all the meat they could carry and burned the rest."[34] Amanda Crow Brockman's father and brother, Matthew and Tom Crow, were killed by Union soldiers in Lincoln County in 1863. Mary Roane Tomlinson wrote, "As the war progressed, fear of the enemy's coming was an ever-present and increasing concern. The boom of the cannon when federal fleets attacked during the battle at Arkansas Post, miles away, was heard at Hollywood Plantation and it brought new terror to every heart. One day the Negroes ran in, saying, 'Marse John, the Yankees are coming.' Dr. Taylor's four-year-old daughter hid under the big poster bed and cowered in fright until a slave coaxed her out by assuring her that the soldiers had proved to be Confederates.

"When the 'Bushwhackers' actually did reach Hollywood Plantation they carried off everything portable. They crammed their saddlebags, they filled linen pillow cases with sweet potatoes, linen sheets and tablecloths with loot of every kind, and took all the livestock and poultry. Dr. Taylor had hidden his books, the family silver, portraits and other valuables for safety in a small house built deep in the cane brake. The enraged 'Bushwhackers,' baffled at not finding these valuables, set fire to the cane and in the resulting blaze were lost many family treasures that could not be replaced." Mrs. Taylor with her six children and some slaves were en route to their Kentucky home at this time. After the Emancipation Proclamation of January 1, 1863, Dr. Taylor called his slaves together and explained to them that they were free. He offered wages for those who elected to stay and work and allowed others to return to Kentucky. Mrs. Taylor left with her retinue in August by way of riverboats. After months of not hearing from her husband, she left Kentucky and secured permission to go by Confederate gunboat to Napoleon, a landing at the mouth of the Arkansas River, where she would then go overland to Hollywood. Accompanied only by her small son, she slept wrapped in a blanket on the deck. When the boat arrived at Napoleon, she was not allowed to disembark and had to return. Dr. Taylor did not see his family again until May 1865 when he finally was able to go to Kentucky.[35]

The Yankees paid a visit to the McDermott home. "At the outbreak of the Civil War, Charles McDermott was an outspoken secessionist and became widely known for his bitter denunciations of the Federal government. Near the close of the war, his life was saved by receipt of a message from a friend, warning that a company of Federal soldiers was approaching. He was very ill at the time, but his daughters got him into a wagon and into the woods in time to save him from hanging." "Before leaving the States, the Northern soldiers came to burn his home. The Commanding Officer saw Edward McDermott's picture, with whom he had been associated at Yale College, and refused to carry out orders. At that very hour, a Southern soldier (who had been sent to beat the Yankee Army in East Ark.) was hidden in the house by my aunt. The soldier was a friend of my father's who directed him to Grandpa's home. A romance budded between my Aunt and this man...but never flowered."[36]

Union strategy was to gain control of the Mississippi River which would separate Arkansas, Louisiana, and Texas from the eastern Confederate states. Northern Arkansas came under Federal control during the second year, and Little Rock fell in September 1863. The next move by Union forces was to take Pine Bluff, strategically situated on the Arkansas River. Union General Frederick Steele's command of 550 men occupied the city soon after the fall of Little Rock. In October Confederate forces attempted to gain control of the city. General Marmaduke planned a surprise attack for early Sunday morning. The day before, October 24, Col. Robert Newton marched his advance brigade from Princeton to the Bayou Bartholomew Road southeast of Pine Bluff where they spent the night. Col. Colton Greene's division followed, transporting heavy artillery over a muddy road and bivouacked to the southwest. A Federal patrol discovered Greene's forces the next morning, and the ensuing Rebel fire spoiled the surprise attack. The Confederates from both positions managed to push the Union forces back to the courthouse square where they had formed a breastworks of cotton bales. The battle broke out with heavy cannon fire and sharpshooters with the Rebels taking the greatest loss in the absence of protection. In retaliation the Confederates set fire to buildings occupied by the Fifth Kansas. Marmaduke arrived on the scene and made the decision to retreat to Princeton knowing that to continue would cause great loss of life to his men. The Arkansas River was under Union control.[37]

After the failure of the Union's Red River and Arkansas campaigns in March and April of 1864, the area south of Pine Bluff was relatively free of Union forces. The Confederate victories at Poison Spring, Marks' Mill, and Jenkins' Ferry made General Steele decide to withdraw to Little Rock, and after that Confederate troops in south Arkansas and northeastern Louisiana concentrated on guerilla warfare, stealing from Union supplies, spying, and cutting telegraph wires.

Another matter of concern was the illegal cotton trade whereby individuals sold cotton to the Federal government for gold and were under Union protection while behind enemy lines for this purpose. To avoid the illegality of these transactions, individuals set up mock companies that bought and resold cotton to the Union. The seller was not forbidden to sell to these companies, and the companies in turn were allowed to sell to the Federal government.

In May 1864 Colonel Colton Greene left Camden with eight to nine hundred men for Monticello and then "moved eastward across Bayous Bartholomew and Macon into the bottomlands along the Mississippi with orders to put 'an immediate quietus' on cotton trading with the enemy in Desha and Chicot counties." After seizing and burning a boat loaded with cotton near Gaines Landing, Greene's Rebel troops patrolled the Mississippi riverbank from Gaines to Lake Chicot "banging away at everything afloat." These actions led to the Battle of Ditch Bayou near Lake Village in June 1864 when the Confederates ousted Federal forces from southeast Arkansas.[38]

The Union army invaded northeast Louisiana during the winter of 1862-1863 as General Grant tried to approach Vicksburg from the south, his attempts from the east having failed. He began construction on a canal through DeSoto Point near Lake Providence to be used as an alternate route for Federal transports to evade the southern batteries at Vicksburg. The Mississippi River rose and stopped further construction, and the remains of this canal are still present. During this occupation the Federal government ordered the purchase of Confederate cotton and promised protection for individuals crossing Federal lines to sell.[39]

The Confederate government, (as well as individuals), was selling cotton to the Federal government. Colonel Osband described the system set up by the Cotton Bureau of the Trans-Mississippi Department with headquarters in Shreveport and a branch office at Monticello after his November 1864 scouting expedition. "A man by the name of Belzer had visited Shreveport in behalf of people living east of Monticello, and had perfected the following arrangement: The Confederate Government takes one-half the cotton at the gin. Previously have hauled it and hid it in piles, but now left it at the gin in care of the former owner; after the man has turned one-half to the Confederate Government he takes this certificate to Monticello and obtains [Col.] Polk's permit to ship upon paying Belzer the export dues, 60 cents per bale in specie. This being indorsed on the back of the permit, the man can bring his cotton to the river-bank for sale. The Confederate Government expects to sell this one-half of all the cotton to the Yankees, and a man by the name of Snyzer, or Snizer, has offered to buy it. Colonel Parkman, of Memphis, offered to buy it, and is in league with them in several operations. Four hundred bales of this cotton is on Gum Ridge, sixteen miles from Lake Village, and can be reached any time when it is dry...."[40] Gum Ridge stretched along the east side of Bayou Bartholomew from McGehee into Morehouse Parish.

The Third U.S. Colored Cavalry consisting of 940 men exclusive of its white officers arrived at Gaines Landing on November 8, 1864, on a scouting expedition.   After a reconnaissance to Bayou Macon, Col. Embury D. Osband, commander, returned to Vicksburg the following day. His report described the flood drenched Delta. "The swamps were full of water and knee deep in mud; the bayous were bank full, and if crossed must be swam; the whole country is so overflowed that it seemed folly to attempt any movement." He noted that no troops were in Monticello although Magruder had been there two months previously with 6,000 to 10,000 men before moving to Camden and "had eaten out the country entirely." J. S. Montgomery, who lived on Bayou Bartholomew, had met Parson's Regiment (a Monticello based Confederate troop), about eight hundred strong, going to Monticello from Gaines Landing.[41]

On January 28, 1865, 2,621 Federal cavalrymen, among whose numbers were the Third U.S. Colored Cavalry, arrived at Eunice, six miles above Gaines Landing. Colonel Osband was in command with intentions to "clean out the guerrillas and seize Rebel supplies." The troops marched southwest across Chicot County toward Bayou Bartholomew and reached it at "Judge Belzer's" the following afternoon. They took some corn, continued to the next plantation four miles down the bayou, and camped overnight "at Quindley, on Bayou Bartholomew." The next day they marched twenty-five miles down to "Holloway's Ferry" capturing some prisoners, horses and mules, and burning a "large steam grist mill" along the way. (This ferry was at the James Lee Hollaway home which was a mile and a half above old Portland.) A detachment crossed the bayou at the ferry, marched a mile and a half, and found "a supply depot, which contained, besides a considerable amount of commissary stores, about 100 stand of arms and a large amount of ammunition. These with the buildings were destroyed." (If this march was *down* the bayou, this would be at old Portland.) The following day (January 31), Osband heard that the Confederate transport steamboat, the *Jim Barkman*, was loading corn for the Camden troops ten miles down the bayou at Poplar Bluff (Parkdale). He "immediately sent a detachment...at rapid gait, to intercept and capture her, which was successfully performed." Placing an officer and twenty-five men on the boat, he ordered them to proceed to "Turner's wood-yard" with instructions to "take in tow all the ferry-boats he might find." The troops burned "a distillery and grist-mill, together with a large lot of cotton and corn" at Poplar Bluff.

The march continued down the bayou to Knox Ferry in Morehouse Parish. Ordering the officer of the *Barkman* to proceed and wait for him at Point Pleasant, Osband and his troops then left the bayou and marched to Bastrop. On February 2, "Foraging details brought in a large number of horses, mules, and negroes." The next day he sent two squadrons to Prairie

Mer Rouge to capture "all serviceable animals and negroes" and to then proceed up the west side of the bayou from Knox Ferry to Hamburg to rejoin the command. Osband advanced to Point Pleasant and "commenced ferrying across the bayou, using the steam-boat for that purpose...Completed the crossing of the command by 2 a.m. morning of the 4th. As soon as this was effected I burned the steam-boat and sunk her hull in a narrow part of the channel."

Osband then marched toward Hamburg and sent a small detachment "with orders to proceed north along the bayou, gather up all the stock they could find," and to meet him at Gaster's Ferry, which was south of Baxter. On February 7 Osband reached "Collins' Mill" (northwest of Gaster's Ferry). Two days later the troops reached "Shanghai" (present Selma) where they turned east to cross the bayou at "Taylor's Ferry" (at Hollywood Plantation). After they crossed the bayou they spent the night at "Hughes' plantation" and proceeded from there to Gaines Landing where they boarded a steamer for Memphis. The expedition captured 276 horses of "superior quality," 358 serviceable mules, "440 negroes, of whom 200 went into the service," and 44 prisoners. It also destroyed "large amounts of cotton, corn, and meat," and burned "several mills, distilleries, and store-houses, which were in the use of the Confederate Government."[42]

The troops burned distilleries because of the large amounts of corn required in the making of whiskey and that grain was badly needed by the forces. Two accounts, both Confederate, from the *Official Records* attest to this. General J. E. Johnston wrote from Virginia in 1862, "The War Department has directed the impressment of grain for military use when it cannot be purchased at fair prices. Let me suggest that whenever impressment becomes necessary the grain at the distilleries be taken first, because they generally control the grain market and less real oppression of individuals will be produced." Captain T. Reves was even more specific in 1863 when he wrote, "I wish to say to General Price that there are distilleries on the borders of Arkansas and Missouri that are consuming all the corn through this country (they pay $4 a bushel), taking the forage from our horses, and leaving the soldiers' families in a state of suffering, unless they pay $4 per bushel for corn for their subsistence. They sell their whiskey for $20 per gallon, making about $60 out of one bushel of corn."[43]

One Ashley County native left an account of his encounter with Osband's march down the bayou. Robert F. Tucker was on furlough from the Confederate army and traveling home on foot. After crossing the Mississippi by canoe under cover of darkness and going some distance, "he came upon Osborne's [*sic*] troops, 5,000 strong, on their march from the bottoms of Bayou Bartholomew, in Louisiana northward. He gave them the 'dodge,' however, and finally pursued his way home."[44] It was probably at this time that Thomas Felix Pugh's home on the bayou near Lake Grampus was raided. The following story about this event was told to Clifford Corder by J. W. Pugh: "The father had gone to the war, and the mother with her small children were at home alone. The Yankees came through and took everything she had. Her son, Green, was a young boy then. Mr. Ed Camak found out she was alone and starving with the kids and went out and brought them to Portland." This event perhaps influenced the young boy, Green, for the remainder of his life. He became a reclusive hermit and lived alone on the bayou for the duration of his life.[45]

Federal troops ravaged Colonel Spyker's plantation in February 1865 and were apparently members of the Osband expedition. Spyker's daughter, Mrs. Leonidas Spyker Wilkinson, was a teenager at the time and in later years gave a written account. She said that a thousand soldiers descended upon the plantation, and the officers used their home for quarters. Soldiers amused themselves by killing sheep, hogs, cattle, and by cutting off the heads of turkeys and chickens with their swords. The colonel ordered all buildings and provisions to be destroyed except "enough to feed the white family for a year." Spyker protested that he had more than sixty Negroes too old or too young to support themselves. One of the officers told him that he was in charge of carrying out the order as the troops left at night but that he had no intention of destroying as much as commanded. He set fire to a combined corncrib and carriage house to make it appear to the departing officer that he had set fire to the plantation, but the plan did not work. Soldiers returned from the troop demanding money and silver. Mrs. Spyker threw a sack containing seventy-five dollars, the only gold they had, into shrubbery outside a window. Ensuing threats forced the family to divulge where their silverware was hidden. The soldiers took all except a silver dipper, a spoon, and two forks that they overlooked. When morning came the family discovered that all their stock was killed or critically wounded and that all their able-bodied slaves had left with the troops. All cribs, granaries, and slave quarters were burned.[46]

Some Federal raiders in Morehouse Parish were not so successful. Tom Kinnaird told Bealie Harrison about four Yankees who were caught raiding. Bealie said, "The last seen of them, they were hanging from a tree where the Roy Gregory house now is – across from the Red Barn Station on Highway 165." A two-story house owned by William Fowles situated on top of Cora's Bluff served the area as a lookout station. When Union troops were in the area, the family would hang a white sheet from a designated window which was visible from the bayou and the surrounding countryside.[47]

Mary Sorrells DeWoody, whose family lived on the bayou in Lincoln County during the war, left a description of their life at the time. "I am attempting to write...what I remember of home life during that period...of our sacrifices, self-denials and loyalty to our beloved South; of our skill in making things with our hands the things we had been accustomed to and could not get because of the federal government blockading the rivers...We made everything we wore, our dresses were spun and woven at home, dyed with home grown dyes. For brown wool we used walnut hulls; for blue we found indigo weed...My grandfather John Harvie Marks made our sleighs, harness and shuttles for our spinning wheels...We also made our own handkerchiefs, towels, bridle reins, saddle girths, etc. Our hats were all home made, too. We would dig the palmetto...just as it would come out of the ground, scald it, and put it into the sun and dew to bleach, then strip it with a pine, and put it into water while we plaited it...it took about 20 yards for a hat...We knit, of course, all of our stockings, made beautiful hoods, shawls, gloves, suspenders and wristlets...out of just wool...There was no sale for produce in our section, labor was plentiful, no cotton raised; people were refugees and they would go off and leave what they had raised and gathered."[48]

Food and supplies for citizens as well as for Confederate and Union troops were major concerns. Pillage was rampant. Perhaps the worst kind of looting was from Jayhawkers, men described by Fredrick W. Williamson as "poor whites who were not so anxious to fight a war which had been made by rich men. Many of these men...succeeded in evading even conscription, by hiding out in the hills and swamps and preying on the farms in the neighborhood...." The story was told in Louisiana that General Liddell of Catahoula once brought a hundred soldiers home with him on furlough, rounded up Jayhawkers from the hills and swamps, and lined them up before a firing squad.[49]

The home-based Rebel army also ravaged the countryside. The letters from George Boddie, stationed near Warren in Bradley County, to his wife in Camden tell the sad story. "Feb 2, 1864, My Dear Mary...I do not think we will remain here long. The country is too poor and too many people have moved away hindering the support of the army...Though we have plenty yet, both for man and horse...We have made more enemies than friends by the indiscriminate <u>pressing</u> or rather <u>stealing</u> pursued by our Rulers in the country bordering on the Arkansas and Bayou Bartholemew. The people say we have nearly ruined them...." "May 23, 1864, My dear wife...Our whole command...have gone beyond Monticello...Sawthers' command had a brush with the Feds at a bridge on Bayou Bartholmew...This is very poor country and we might eat it out in a short time...." "[From a camp near Tyro.] June 27, 1864, My Dear Mary...I manage to swallow a little beef and bread each day...Mud Larks

[hogs] and Bacon have made their disappearance from these parts. We get plenty of Corn by crossing Bayou Bartholmue for it. The plantations are all abandoned by their owners & being now occupied by poor people....” Boddie mentioned a morose scene in a letter from Tyro dated June 11, 1864. “I came by the battle grounds and witnessed the disgusting sight of hogs and buzzards dragging the remains of <u>Feds</u> and Negroes from their shallow graves appearing to contend with each other for the <u>choice</u> pieces. Our dead are better cared for - having pole pins placed around the graves.”[50]

As the war lingered on, many deserted ranks and became fugitives. Ed T. Smith told the following story to his son, John I. Smith. An unknown soldier arrived at the home of Mrs. Amanda Youngblood, a young widow who lived on an isolated farm on the bayou near Garrett Bridge. He was young and attractive – and hungry. Amanda prepared a meal and during their conversation he told her he had deserted from the Confederate army. He gave his name as Samuel Jones and asked if he could stay as a farmhand. Needing help as well as protection, Amanda allowed him to stay knowing that harboring a deserter was dangerous. They agreed to tell no one and that he would never leave the farm. Samuel prepared a hiding place in a nearby almost impenetrable cypress swamp where he would flee upon a signal given by Amanda if someone should approach the house. They eventually fell in love, agreed to marry after the war, and began to live as husband and wife.

George W. Rowell, a teacher at nearby Greenmount and a “red-hot agitator for the Confederacy...became a Confederate officer of some kind and one of his duties was to run down deserters, of which there were plenty.” Rowell received word from a hunter that a stranger was living at the Youngblood farm and went to investigate. Amanda (pregnant now and showing plainly) rang the farm bell, and Samuel escaped to the swamp. When Rowell visited the third time, he figured out the signal system. He returned again with a helper who hid on the path to the swamp. Rowell slipped up on Amanda before she had a chance to ring the bell. She rang it as he questioned her as to the whereabouts of her “husband.” Samuel ran toward the swamp only to be met by a rifle leveled at his face.

“Rowell rode up and said, ‘You have come to the end of the road. It would have been better for you to have been shot down in battle. I guess you know the penalty for desertion.’ He began tying his arms and legs. Sam begged, ‘Just let me go and I will get Mandy to deed you the farm.’” Rowell replied that he would probably get the farm anyway if the south should win as he and his helper began making a large pile of dry timber.

Samuel Jones cried, “My poor Amanda! My poor baby!” “Amanda saw the smoke. When the fire was set, the end came among screams that did not last long.” Amanda gave birth to twin boys who became respected members of the community. Rowell somehow (probably by extortion) acquired the Youngblood farm and sold it to Ed T. Smith in 1900.[51]

Another deserter or else one avoiding conscription into service also used the bayou for a hideout in Lincoln County. "One man...a Mr. Dean, went down in the Bayou Bartholomew woods and built a cabin and lived out the War. His brothers brought him all the necessities. People knew about the arrangement but never told it to officers. They said, 'It is a rich man's war and a poor man's fight.'"[52] Lewis Gardner left his farm near Fountain Hill in Ashley County toward the end of the war "as a fugitive from the marauding of both Yankees and guerillas passing back and forth along the Monticello-Hamburg road." He went to the "swamp country of the Bayou Bartholomew" and farmed there until he died at Gum Ridge in 1865.[53]

The "rich" men were no longer wealthy. Confederate money was useless; gold and silver were scarce; slaves no longer held monetary value, and many plantations went out of production. A rumor spread throughout the south that slaves transported to Texas would not be freed if the Union should win. A significant number of plantation owners fled to the Lone Star State with their slaves. Escaped or captured slaves also went to Texas. George Boddie wrote from near Tyro on June 11, 1864, "Several Negroes told me they [had] seen several loads of Negro women & children going to Shreveport & Texas – captured in the Swamps after our men had left. A man by the name of Word living near Marks Mills having captured eight – Mostly fellows – Sold his claim to Macon of Warren for 4000 – who run them to Texas...I firmly believe that most of the missing Negroes from our neighborhood are in Texas."[54]

Able Wilson of Monticello sold his slaves to people migrating to Texas, "where it was believed they would be safe from federal intervention." One man who moved to Texas lost one of his slaves there. A public notice in a Jefferson newspaper read, "**Runaway** from the subscriber, a yellow boy, low in stature, a chronic sore on his leg, rather quick-spoken, some twenty-five years old. Bob is a very likely fellow. I moved from Ashley County, Arkansas, he may be trying to return...I will give One-Hundred Dollars reward to anyone who will catch him and lodge him in jail, where I can get him. [Signed] Jno. P. Duncan." The Sorrells family "fled to Texas" at the end of the war taking with them the freed slaves of John Harvie Marks, Mrs. Sorrells' father.[55] J. Fred Crawley left his bayou plantation during the war and went to Crockett, Texas, with his slaves.

Some bayou steamboats became involved in the war as they worked under contract with the Confederacy as troop and supply carriers, and others were captured and put into the Union navy. The importance of steamboats as a means of running supplies is revealed in a statement by the commanding general in New Orleans when Augustus L. Witherington, William S. Finch, and Robert "Bob" Withers attempted to enter service. The general accepted the company raised in Union County by Witherington but had other plans for the experienced steamboat men. He said, "We want provisions for this army. Men can't fight without food. Do you not own a boat? I want to tell you, Witherington, that you and your crew could do more for your South by becoming commissariat embargo runners. We need brave men for that post...You and Finch will help me a thousand times more. There are plenty of fighters, so far, but few I can trust to get food to my men. And they tell me you and Finch know the rivers to the mouth of the Mississippi, and even beyond to the Gulf, better than any men about." Hattie Witherington, daughter of Gus, wrote, "...they ran that embargo, slipping past spy boats, dodging into lagoons and hidden water contributory to the rivers, like river rats."[56]

On April 3, 1864, Major Isaac Brinker wrote orders to Withers, captain of the Morgan Nelson, "You will proceed with your Boat up Bayou Bartholomew with as little delay as possible and go up to where you can get Corn sufficient to load the Boat as near the Bayou as possible. You will load and return to this place with all possible speed." On May 17, 1864, Withers received similar orders from Camden: "You will depart with the steamboat Morgan Nelson,...near the mouth of Bayou Bartholomew to Tom G. Ferguson. There to receive a load of corn and bring it to this place without delay."[57]

General Kirby Smith addressed the crucial role of steamboats in supplying food for troops and stock in a letter to Lt. Gen. S. B. Buckner in February 1865. "The Fletcher and Morgan Nelson have...been ordered to Monroe, where they will be at the disposition of Major Buckner for the purpose of procuring corn. The Ouachita country above the Louisiana line is absolutely stripped of forage... General Magruder estimates that 30,000 bushels of corn will meet his necessities and enable him to maintain the line of the Ouachita until the coming crop can be gathered. The boats will be at the disposal of your officers, and I wish you would instruct them to use dispatch and energy in securing and removing corn from the Beouf...."[58]

The Lincoln Blockade prevented the sale of cotton, and as a result the port at New Orleans was virtually shut down. Soon after the war began the Union Navy instituted a blockade at the mouth of the Mississippi, and a year later a Union fleet arrived in New Orleans harbor to begin occupation of the city. Some courageous captains attempted to run the cotton blockade in an attempt to get cotton to Texas and Mexico, the only western outlets. For example, the *Governor Fletcher* (apparently the *Judge Fletcher*, a Kouns boat) left Camden with a load of cotton under Confederate guard. At Monroe they transferred the cotton to smaller boats that went through the Black and Red Rivers to Shreveport. The *Fletcher* served in this capacity and also transported troops for two or three months before laying up at Shreveport for the duration of the war. The steamers left the Red River at Shreveport to connect with Big Cypress Bayou which led to a port in Jefferson, Texas, the farthest inland port and the state's fifth largest city in the late 1800s. The Corps of Engineers eventually put the port out of business by dynamiting a beaver dam on the bayou, which caused the course to change.[59]

The Confederate navy converted the *Lizzie Simmons* into a gunboat and renamed her *Pontchartrain*. The U.S. gunboat, *General Price* destroyed her at Little Rock on September 10, 1863. Federal gunfire also destroyed the *Fox* on March 28, 1861, on the Red River. The *Sun Flower*, a Confederate boat, survived the war but wrecked in Galveston Harbor in 1867. The *Jennie Kirk* became a Confederate boat in 1861, but her fate is unknown. The remains of at least two boats that participated in the war are in the bayou. One is the previously discussed *Jim Barkman*, and the other is the *Mattie*, which sank in 1864.[60] It was common practice not to give the exact locations of wrecks in field reports in case the reports should fall into enemy hands.

The *Tigress* claimed special distinction during the war. Captured by the Union Army and renamed *USS Tigress*, she served as General Grant's dispatch boat during the siege of Shiloh. As boats continued bringing Union soldiers to Pittsburg Landing on the Tennessee River, Grant rode his horse daily aboard the *Tigress* to inspect troops. On one of these trips his horse fell on the muddy riverbank and caused injury to the general's leg. On Easter Sunday, April 6, 1862, the battle began. Walter Havighurst wrote, "Next morning was Easter, a bright sunrise and vireos and catbirds singing. Then came a rumble, from over the hill toward Shiloh Meetinghouse. Thunder grew in the cloudless sky. From the riverbank Marsh saw General Grant hobble onto the *Tigress*, an orderly bringing his horse. Marsh followed them aboard as the crew cast off. Hissing and rumbling, the *Tigress* charged up the river. On the way she met the steamer *John Warner* with a message from a desperate division on Owl Creek near the Shiloh churchyard. At Crump's Landing the *Tigress* swung into the bank beside the *Jesse K. Bell*, and speaking across the guardrails Grant instructed General Wallace to hold his division in readiness until Grant could assess the situation and send orders. Backing into the stream, the *Tigress* plunged on to Pittsburg Landing where cannon shells were crashing through treetops and the roar of musketry rose like a wall. When the landing stage touched down, Grant was helped onto his horse. He rode up the smoky hill toward Shiloh Churchyard." The next day the defeated Confederates withdrew toward Corinth. The *Tigress* witnessed one of the bloodiest battles of the war with 1,728 Confederate and 1,749 Union casualties and thousands more injured, many who died later.[61]

In November 1862 the *Tigress* was instrumental in the rescue of the crew of the wrecked *Eugene* on the Mississippi at Osceola, Arkansas. She saw her last action at Vicksburg on April 2, 1863. She was in the lead of five other transport boats running the batteries during the night when Confederate fire opened on them. Her portside was riddled with shots, and just as she passed the last battery a shot in her stern opened a four-foot hole in the hull. The *Tigress* limped to the Louisiana side and beached. One of the other boats rescued all crewmembers, and no lives were lost.[62] She would never return to her placid trips on Bayou Bartholomew.

The war gradually drew to an end. Only nine days before Lee's surrender at Appomattox on April 9, 1865, Captain John H. Norris, stationed with the Union army at Pine Bluff, led a scouting expedition composed of seventy-five men and two officers down the bayou into Lincoln County to "drive in all the beef cattle I could find." He wrote, "I proceeded out on the lower Monticello road twenty-three miles, took the Napoleon road, and marched twelve miles farther to Allison's farm, and camped...proceeded to Green Mount [near Tyro] on the same road...There I took the Auburn road and crossed Bayou Bartholomew at Brown's Ferry [present Garrett Bridge], and started back to Pine Bluff and commenced gathering up cattle. Camped at Price's near Bayou Bartholomew, on Sunday night, and at Doctor Stewart's on Monday night, and arrived at this post Tuesday...with 91 head of beef cattle, 13 prisoners, and 10 head of horses and mules, and a few firearms...I marched 125 miles going and coming."[63]

Guerrilla warfare continued after Lee's surrender. James Carter Watts of Pine Bluff told the story of the end of the war in Arkansas. General Powell Clayton's men at Pine Bluff first heard of Captain R. A. Kidd in January 1865. Telegraph lines were being cut, and replacement wire and other Union goods stolen. Lt. Charles Temple learned that the culprits belonged to a loosely formed band of insurgents led by Captain Kidd. It was not until March 4 that Captain John H. Norris encountered the group camped for the night southwest of Pine Bluff. After firing two carbine volleys, Norris ordered a charge, but the renegades quickly scattered into the woods. Of the twenty-four men, led by Kidd, Lt. Dixon, and Lt. Emillie, five were dead and two were taken prisoners. General Clayton ordered pursuit. On March 21 Captain Norris set out once more after the guerillas with 112 men and two officers. They rode through Cornersville in northern Drew County and reached Monticello the following morning. A few shots were fired, but once again the few Confederates in town vanished into the woods. Norris then learned that Captain Kidd was operating toward Bayou Bartholomew.

He headed toward the bayou and spent the night six miles away from it with a Mr. Helms. The next day, March 23, he returned to Pine Bluff still on the lookout for the elusive Kidd. In two more weeks the war was officially over, but the guerilla bands were slow to hear the news. On May 4 fifty men under Captain Ed Brown left Pine Bluff to go to the south side of Bartholomew to guard a crossing, and fifty more men under Captain George Suesberry proceeded down the north side in anticipation of capturing Kidd and his band. He arrived at the farm of a Mr. Harris twelve miles below Pine Bluff where he learned that Kidd had left the morning before. The next day Norris met Captain Brown at the home of John Rodgers eighteen miles south of Pine Bluff. Swimming their horses across the bayou they continued to Noble's farm and arrested Lt. Noble. The captain learned that Kidd and his gang was the only Confederate force left east of the Saline River.

General E. Kirby Smith surrendered his Confederate troops near the Arkansas-Missouri border on May 11, 1865, and that brought an end to the war west of the Mississippi -- but not for Captain Kidd. Captain Norris took out again with thirty men on May 15 still on the trail of Kidd and other renegade Confederates. At the Harris farm, Mrs. Harris told him that Kidd had taken her husband twelve days before. He learned that Lt. Dixon of Kidd's company was headed to Pine Bluff with eight to ten men and that Kidd was going there with twenty men. Captain Norris and Mallory stationed troops near the Harris house and others at the nearby bayou crossing. After hiding for an hour, Kidd came riding through with ten to twelve men. As he was crossing the bayou, he heard the Federals and began to gallop away, firing one volley. Wheeling his horse into a dense thicket, he reached the bayou again under heavy fire. Only one Confederate was captured.

Norris then headed down the bayou to Busby's Bridge and on to the Rodgers farm where he heard that "Kidd had passed by in a hurry." He then moved up the opposite side of the bayou back four miles to the bridge again in hopes of intercepting Lt. Dixon. After camping there for the night, he returned to Pine Bluff. Norris felt that Kidd and Dixon would reunite in the bayou bottoms and then fall back to Cornersville. He asked for 100 to 150 men to capture them but was allowed 60. The troop left Pine Bluff on May 23 and after combing the country for two days, arrived in Monticello late the second day. He established camp a few miles away and sent word to Captain Burks, the Confederate commander, that he was going to "remain there until they surrendered or until every corndodger and pound of meat was eaten and every ear of corn was properly disposed of to U.S. Cavalry horses." The next morning Confederates began sending flags of truce, and by the afternoon fourteen officers and seventy enlisted men surrendered. That number represented the entire Rebel force in the area --

all but one. Norris then received orders from General Clayton to end hostilities against Captain Kidd. Two days later Norris rode into Monticello for observation and upon his return to camp met the elusive Kidd who surrendered. This surrender marked the end of hostilities within the state on May 27, 1865.[64]

Col. John M. Sandidge, a neighbor and brother-in-law to Colonel Spyker at Point Pleasant, had the cheerless distinction, at the request of Governor H. W. Allen, of handing over the Louisiana State archives to the Federal army at the end of the war. Colonel Sandidge was serving as a U.S. Senator at the outbreak of the war and entered the Confederate service a month later.[65]

Although Lincoln emancipated the slaves in 1863, most were not freed by their owners until after the war. Ed Smith told the following story about a McShan slave. "During the latter days of the War, the slaves began to feel that they would soon be free, and they began to whoop and holler. The white folks decided to put a stop to the noise and organized a whipping crew. Grandma heard about it and told her Liza if any whipping began around where she was for her to run home. Whipping began and Liza fled home, the crew following not far behind. 'Get down behind my chair,' Grandma told Liza. The leader of the crew spoke, 'We come to whup yo' gal. She wuz on the gang makin' a lot of noise.' 'You are not going to do any such thing. When she needs whipping I'll do it. You men just go on.' The War was soon over, and the slaves were free. Grandma told Liza, 'You are free, and I think it best for you to join your family.' She replied, 'I don't want to be free. I want to stay with you.' 'But if you stay here you will never be free.' She did rejoin her family. I have heard my Mother and Aunt Cornelia ask, 'I wonder whatever became of Liza?'"[66]

꧁꧂

Reverberation and Hard Changes

Families scattered, fortunes wrecked, negroes freed.
Ida Crawley

The end of the War Between the States had no immediate effect on the resolution of social and economic problems for more than a decade. How were the large farmers to work their plantations with no labor? What were the freed slaves to do with their freedom? Whatever became of Liza and thousands more like her?

The farmers had to begin anew, and some simply gave up. Dr. Charles McDermott, a resolute Confederate, refused to live under Yankee dominion and moved his family to Honduras. With Charles Barrow of West Feliciana Parish he attempted to establish a secessionist colony, but climate, dysentery, and other hardships caused their effort to fail. Mrs. E. S. Smylie wrote, "The Catholics there warned him that he must quit expressing his religious views, or leave the country. [He had renounced Catholicism and become a Presbyterian.] So he came back to the States, a broken, land-poor old man. He spent the remainder of his days reading his Bible, the *Scientific American*, and abusing the Yankees." J. Fred Crawley, in Texas with his slaves, told them they were free to go. With heavy heart he returned to his now useless plantation on the bayou. Ida Crawley wrote in "The Doll," "Families scattered, fortunes wrecked, negroes freed. The repose of antebellum days of elegance and cultural luxury dwelt still in memory. The great columned porticos of the old colonial mansions stood sentinels of bygone days. Silent. Major J. Fred Crawley and wife with their family left their home on the bank of Bayou Bartholomew where the little steamer for over a week plied its way to New Orleans."[67] From New Orleans the family took a train. Major Crawley had no destination in mind, but when the train rolled into Sweetwater, Tennessee, he said, "We'll get off here." He bought land and built a house almost identical to the one he had left on Bayou Bartholomew. Eventually a son, Robert Page, returned to the bayou plantation and put it back into production. Two former slaves left Texas and rejoined the family in Tennessee.

Most of Colonel Spyker's fortune was gone at the close of the war, and he rented out his bayou plantation and moved to New Orleans. He entered the cotton brokerage business with his brother-in-law, Col. John Milton Sandidge, and reportedly made $90,000 during 1866. Spyker died from yellow fever the following year. Dr. John Martin Taylor joined his wife at their Kentucky plantation soon after the war ended. He struggled to keep both plantations running but finally sold the one in Kentucky after his wife died there in 1868. Some freed slaves stayed on at the bayou plantation but gradually drifted away. His cotton crop failed, and his fortune suffered heavily. Left with seven motherless children, he placed the younger ones with a housekeeper in Monticello where he visited them each week. The older boys attended colleges, medical school, and law school. One, Henry, lived with his father at Hollywood. The sons then managed the estate and were able to buy back much of the land lost during the war. Their holdings amounted to 11,000 acres.[68]

With the end of the war most southerners found their situation an abstruse one to accept. The 1866 Arkansas legislature refused to ratify the Fourteenth Amendment to the United States Constitution which extended civil and political rights to Negroes. It took a Reconstruction government to orchestrate an attempt at orderly transition. Abraham Lincoln designed a plan to limit whites' power over the blacks and to help the latter become responsible citizens. The Bureau of Refugees, Freedmen, and Abandoned Lands was formed in 1865 to administer the transition from slave labor to paid labor. The intention was to take over abandoned or confiscated land that would be rented in forty-acre plots to Negroes and white refugees for a three-year period with an option to purchase. The bureau also arranged labor contracts between freedmen and planters and endeavored to see that both parties fulfilled the contract agreement. Sallatheil A. Duke, a former Union army quartermaster, went to Fort Goodrich, Louisiana to administrate the Freedmen's Bureau's distribution of food and clothing to more than 2,000 freed slaves. It was during this time he became enamoured with the South and eventually bought a large tract of farmland along the bayou near Baxter in Drew County.[69]

A typical labor contract dated January 13, 1871, follows: "...The said Dick Smith agrees to live with the said J. C. Barrow and to do anything necessary to be done by or for the said Barrow, to either work on a Bayou Bartholomew farm or work here on this Calhoun County farm or stay and work at the Monticello place . . .that said Dick Smith here by agrees to take $120 [annually]...payable one half of the amount each month which is five dollars, (his wages being ten dollars a month...) and the said Dick Smith hereby agrees that if he quits, or leaves before the expiration of said year that he will forfeit the one half of his labor, or wages at end of the year." The remaining half wages owed were held until the end of the year, as an incentive to make the laborer stay in place the full year. The contract also determined that Barrow would be responsible for Smith's rations.[70]

Although the Freedmen's Bureau attempted to help the freed slaves, it was certainly not a smooth transition. Alvie Pugh explained the black man's dilemma. "With freedom they were supposed to get forty acres and a place to live. Some got it cleared up and then the owner would not give it to them; and then they would go clear up another place and they would take that away. There was nothing they could do about it. They still didn't have any freedom really. They could take your land away, and they would kill you if you didn't get off. You had to get off or they would bushwhack you. Some couldn't read or write or figure, and they would put their *X* on a paper and someone would get their land. The white folks would talk about what other whites were doing; they were mean to some white folks too."

Plantations remained in need of labor. Edwin Mason, who later settled at Mason Cave, was paid by planters in Morehouse Parish and southern Ashley County in 1875 to transport farm laborers. He brought freedmen from the Livingston, Alabama, area by boat up the bayou as far as Parkdale. The Callion family of the Jones area is descended from one of the freedmen brought by Mason.

After Lincoln's assassination Andrew Johnson carried on his proposals until radical Republicans passed an act on March 2, 1867, calling for more control over the government of the Rebel states. The era of Radical Reconstruction that followed was as deleterious in some areas as the war had been. Northern carpetbaggers, taking advantage of the disrupted conditions and seeking political offices, flocked south. Union troops, Freedmen's Bureau officials, and scalawags (southerners who were in favor of the Reconstruction government) added to the chaos. Many ex-Confederates refused to sign the Union loyalty oath and therefore lost their right to vote. The Radical Reconstruction government took control of Arkansas in 1867, and the following year Gen. Powell Clayton became governor.

In retaliation against the carpetbagger government, protestors organized the Ku Klux Klan. Freedmen's agents, scalawags, and outspoken Negroes received inhospitable visits from the hooded nightriders. Two of Governor Clayton's first acts were to attempt to suppress KKK activity and to place several counties under martial law for their vote against the proposed Republican constitution. Ashley County came under martial law in November 1868, and a militia arrived. Clayton had heard about the following incident when he sent the militia to the county.

Mrs. E. J. Camak of Portland recalled the years of Reconstruction as "bitter times." Interviewed in 1939 at age eighty, she said that homes and farms were ravaged and families broken up. "Terror reigned supreme and one never knew what new horror the next day would bring. Carpetbaggers and jayhawkers were eternally trying to incite race riots and colored uprisings. Women and children from miles around were guarded at the Jim Hollaway house [on the bayou] one night while the men wiped out the troublesome, Mosie Dean, a color inciter, about whom nothing was ever heard again."[71] Whatever became of Mosie Dean? The *Daily Republican* reported on November 25, 1868, "Moses Dean and his wife found since then hung in the woods...."

In another bayou related incident William Walker and Ben Tubbs were returning from Bastrop to their homes in southern Ashley County when the wife of a ferryman told them of trouble brewing. Her husband was going around the neighborhood "notifying the white people of a possible uprising of the negroes so that they might all get together and protect themselves." She asked them to stay with her until he returned, and while they were waiting, a black man rode up wearing a long sword. Walker leveled a gun at him and ordered him to drop the saber, which he did. They then decided to hang him and were tying a rope around his neck when he got away and jumped in the bayou. Walker shot at him but since it was dark, they never determined if he was killed. This man was never seen again.[72] Whatever became of him? Did the bayou become his watery grave?

James Madison Hudson of Jefferson County arrived home from service in the Confederate army in June 1865 and immediately took the loyalty oath. He intended to be "a good and loyal citizen, to obey the laws of the country and help to enforce them." He chased horse thieves and farmed. After the election of Powell Clayton and the ensuing carpetbag regime, Hudson noticed that the enfranchised Negroes "became very sassy and impudent...White ladies were forced from the sidewalks by them and they became almost unbearable." He joined the Ku Klux Klan, organized he said, "to protect Southern homes and our women and children. It aimed to conserve the peace of the community, to make the negro know and keep his place...[by] peaceable means, if possible, forcible means if necessary." He established a den in his neighborhood, but "never went on but one hike. The negroes of Bayou Bartholomew, under the leadership of a scalawag white man became unruly and we paraded among them, all masked, and the negroes were nearly scared to death. Some of them got down on their knees and swore they would always be true to white men."[73]

Ed T. Smith served as deputy sheriff in Lincoln County during the last years of Reconstruction government and was fair in his dealings with all people. A carpetbagger named Snyder moved into the "Bayou Bartholomew section" and attempted to become friends with the local people who refused to have anything to do with him. After unsuccessfully running for public office twice, Snyder decided to build a much needed modern cotton gin in another effort to gain favor with the community. Deputy Smith told him that feelings were still hard against him because he was a northerner and advised that he guard the gin day and night. Smith saw smoke soon after the gin was completed and went to investigate. He found evidence where a horse had been tied to a nearby tree and discovered tracks left by a galloping horse. One of the tracks indicated a broken shoe. Following the trail to Pine Bluff through the night, he found the sweating horse with the broken shoe in a livery and learned it belonged to a Mr. O'Neal of Lincoln County. He arrested the man and brought him back to jail where O'Neal implicated his accomplice, Ned Butler.

During the trial O'Neal testified falsely that he saw Butler burn the gin. Smith advised young Butler to tell the truth and told him that he would be treated fairly. The trial resulted in a hung jury, and before the next term of court, O'Neal jumped bond and fled to Texas. Butler went to trial again and was sentenced to a term in the penitentiary. Believing O'Neal to be the true culprit with Butler led astray by the older man, Smith felt this a harsh punishment. On the way to the prison, he allowed the young man to escape after telling him how to make his way to Texas. Three weeks later a letter arrived. "Dear Mr. Smith, I will never forgit whut you done for me... I am pickin' cotton and doin' good. Butler."[74]

Raiding by guerillas and jayhawkers continued. Mrs. A. J. Camak recalled the following encounter with jayhawkers. "Still a child, she was returning [on a steamboat] one night with her mother from a visit with relatives in Louisiana. The low element developed by the war was causing considerable trouble, and the captain received a tip that the boat was to be robbed at Lou deYampert landing where he was due to take on wood for fuel. Passengers were warned to be quiet and women and children to lie on the floor and all lights were extinguished, and the boat crept silently past the landing. But the horses of the waylaying jayhawkers sensed the approach of the craft and began to neigh. Immediately a barrage of bullets was directed at the boat. But the captain steamed up – burning freight for fuel – and set his passengers safely ashore."[75]

It took another "war" to finally terminate Radical Reconstruction in Arkansas. The Brooks-Baxter War had its beginning in 1872 when Elisha Baxter won a disputed election as governor over Joseph Brooks. Baxter, an Arkansas Unionist, was in favor of giving ex-Confederates the right to vote, and the majority of Democrats did not trust Brooks, a Radical carpetbagger. In April 1874 the Radicals influenced the Pulaski County circuit court to rule that Baxter was illegally elected and pronounced Brooks as governor. War ensued after the forcible removal of Baxter from office. Both sides raised militia and the federal government sent troops to Little Rock to prevent encounters. Around two hundred were killed during minor skirmishes before President Grant recognized Brooks as governor in May 1874. Sallatheil A. Duke, postmaster of Bartholomew Post Office, created a new community on the bayou in 1872 and named it Baxter as a token of his support for Elisha Baxter.[76]

Morehouse Parish reeled from violence wrought by Reconstruction. Federal forces, mostly Negroes, arrived by boat at Monroe in June 1865 and occupied northeast Louisiana for the next twelve years. Louisiana refused to ratify the Fourteenth Amendment "not on account of the negro vote but because the right of ex-rebels to hold office was threatened." The adoption of a "Republican-Carpetbagger-Scalawag" constitution in 1868 was countered by the formation of Ku Klux Klan dens throughout the state. Mary Ann Dixon Johnston's grandmother, Mary Ann Yongue Smith saw the klansmen when she was a child. "She told about peeping out of the windows at night toward the ferry landing at the mouth of the bayou and seeing men going by in white robes with torches on horseback," Mary Ann said.

Radicals and Negroes joined the Union League to combat the Klan. Formed in New York, the Union League Club sent organizers into the south "to create a solid block of Republican voters." They promised to give Negroes the white man's land, political offices, and social equality, and incited them to "assassinate white men and burn their houses." Terrorist extremists quickly invaded the Klan, and by 1870 it officially disbanded, although "some of the members refused to disband and degenerated into societies of the lowest type." The White League then organized to promote "openly organized and outspoken revolt" as opposed to the "secret and silent, sheeted horsemen riding in the night."[77]

A war for power continued among the various factions for over a decade. In 1876, for example, a Republican candidate for sheriff of Morehouse Parish, W. I. Law, defeated his Democrat opponent, Dr. Robert A. Phelps. On February 24, 1876, Phelps, then the mayor of Bastrop, was shot from ambush on the streets of Bastrop and died. Law was indicted by a grand jury and pled not guilty. Four months after his acquittal, Law received his "just rewards" as a "torchlight procession by the democracy" murdered the sheriff. No arrests were made. Another man, Mr. Zarr, a member of a "Democratic club" was indicted for the murder of Dr. Phelps, but he too was acquitted. A few weeks after the murder of Sheriff Law, Zarr was shot and killed. In 1870 the Democratic party began making serious attempts to gain control and was successful by 1876 in northeast Louisiana. After Federal troops withdrew the same year, the Democrats organized armed patrols to threaten remaining Republicans and Negroes who associated with them. Finally in 1881 the public was weary of violence and demanded resolution. By 1882 the Democrats were in full control, and the situation eased. Recovering from the effects of Reconstruction however took many more years.[78]

The economic and political upheaval evolved into a more progressive resolution, but the strained relationship between members of the white and black races continued. John I. Smith wrote that his father continued to play with black children, as he had always done, for a couple of years after the war. He blamed Carpetbaggers and the Reconstruction government for a change in attitude. "Then the carpetbaggers came and put new ideas into the heads of the blacks. Next came the federal soldiers with more ideas about social equality. First, the elder people separated from the blacks and then the boys and girls played entirely separate from each other...One development that brought ill feelings was the taking of voting rights away from the Confederate veterans and some of their friends, and giving the right to vote to the blacks. This resulted in many, or nearly all, of the offices being held by the carpetbaggers or blacks. No longer did white children and the black children play together."[79]

Klan activity did not diminish in some places after Reconstruction ended in the 1870s even though their actions were generally held in disrepute. In October 1892 the *Gazette* reported, "The good people of Drew County...have been terrorized for some time past by the depredations of white caps. These lawless desperadoes have been taking good men from their homes at night, tying them to the nearest tree and whipping them unmercifully, going so far as to kill three men. The Grand Jury...is now in session and...returned sixty indictments, a large number of them being against white-cappers, of whom there is a well organized band of forty-nine. One of them was for A. L. Hammell, who lives fifteen miles south of Monticello, who was arrested...for murder, as one of the white caps who had took Dan Baker, colored, from the jail at Monticello and killed him. Baker had been 'white-capped' in Ashley County, and killed one of his assailants, and was lodged in the jail at Monticello for safe keeping. A desperate effort will be made...to rid the county of this lawless gang." The following day the paper reported that two white-cappers, Bud Goodwin and George Hammill, were in jail and "charged with complicity in the mob who killed Calvin Reed...and also in the mob who took the negro from Sheriff Morgan and shot him to death in July."[80]

The fear instilled by the Klan and other vigilantes affected members of the black race for years to come. Alvie Pugh said, "Oh, yeah, I remember the Ku Klux Klan. After slavery they did all kinds of bad stuff, and it ain't all gone yet. I remember being mistreated by white folks when I was young. I knew they could bushwhack you. I had a fear of white men when I was young."

T. Y. Harp raised an interesting point in his memoirs. Harp was born in 1882 and knew an ex-slave, Rachel, who his grandfather, Thomas Harp, bought in 1829 for his wife. "It might have been that the slaves looked down on white people who did not own slaves themselves. Such non-slave owners were called 'po' white trash' but in a subdued tone. There was old Rachel...who had that attitude with my mother, although the family did own a slave. Rachel was quite impudent at times to my mother... As a boy going to school for two years I had to pass old Rachel's little cabin, not more than ten feet from the path leading to the school. On good or mild days old Rachel sat on her little porch smoking an old clay pipe. In all the days I passed her, she never evinced any sign that she knew I was cluttering up the scenery. She knew I was passing. The 'aversion' was mutual, you may be sure. I believe that loyalty to the former owner in such cases was much on the order of a 'one man' dog that will not accept overtures from outsiders."[81]

Some former owners attempted to help their freed slaves by giving them plots of land to work. Mary Roane Tomlinson wrote, "In Lincoln County on a gift bit of Taylor land there lives an aged widow of a Taylor slave, who cherishes her husband's Bible, a gift from Marse John." It contains in Dr. Taylor's handwriting a list of the births, deaths and marriages of the negro family, some born in Ky., the rest on Bayou Bartholomew. Some of the old slaves made annual pilgrimages to the homes of the Taylor family to get money, food and clothing which was always given them in memory of loved ones long gone with the Confederacy."[82] John L. deYampert of Ashley County gave his Negroes land and also sold plots to others in an area along the bayou that became known as Free Negro Bend. Glasco King's parents moved from Louisiana after the war and worked on the deYampert plantation at nearby Sunshine. When Glasco was nine, he lost his arm in a gin accident after which the deYampert family took him in and gave him an education. He became a teacher, preacher, storeowner, and farmer, and was the first black to be elected Justice of the Peace in Ashley County. His brother, Porter R. King, was also a teacher and preacher.

Other freed slaves eventually managed to acquire their own land. Peter Jasper of Lincoln County owned 280 acres which he farmed. George Pugh Sr. also of Lincoln County bought 160 acres in the early 1900s where he farmed and ran a sawmill. The Bob Jackson family, former slaves near Parkdale, homesteaded 160 acres at McGinty in the 1890s. Most freedmen, however, worked as sharecroppers, and it was not until later generations that some of their descendants were finally able to buy land. Josephine and Dock Gibson, children of slave parents, bought a three hundred-acre farm near Yorktown before 1913. Charles Tracy, a descendant of a Louisiana slave family, bought approximately a hundred acres near Yorktown in the first decade of the 1900s. His daughter, Ruth Teal, became a schoolteacher and principal. Lizza (Jackson) and Nick Webb, slave descendants, bought a sixty-nine acre farm near Jones in the 1920s. They paid $2,000 down on the total cost of $5,000 with $1,000 to be paid for the next three years. Nick died in 1927 leaving his wife and fourteen-year-old son, Page, to take over. "We had forty head of cows, four mules, and a saddle horse," Page said. "When he died he left nobody but me, Mama, and the Lord. I came off the rough side of the mountain." They were about to lose the farm when Jim Shackelford came to their rescue and helped them arrange a loan with the Federal Land Bank. "He was a good man," said Page.

The institution of slavery, a civil war, and its violent aftermath were at last over, but it would be many years before the wounds would heal. A progressive movement in state government instigated social reforms intent upon improving the quality of life from the late nineteenth century until the Great Depression of the 1930s. Whites as well as blacks were adversely affected during these trying years as most struggled to survive. A segregated South remained the status quo, however, until the struggle for equality finally began to make headway in the 1960s when the federal government exerted its power to achieve that end.

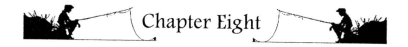

Chapter Eight

From Forests to Plantations

Early Sawmills and Log Rafting

I have wished···I had never seen a cypress tree.
Willie Skipper to his wife, 1896

Ancient bottomland hardwoods of oak, hickory, gum, and cypress encompassed the bayou. For the early settlers this vast forest was essentially an obstacle that had to be cleared for farming. The stately trees did provide the settlers, however, with material for houses, fuel, ox yokes, furniture, buckets, plow handles, gun stocks, wagon beds, boats, ferries, fence posts, caskets, brooms, and even musical instruments. As migration increased from the 1840s to the beginning of the Civil War, so did the demand for lumber. During the 1840s steam-powered sawmills came into use replacing the laborious whipsaw that was pulled by two men. With roads in a deplorable condition, it made sense to place these mills on the bayou, not only for the water supply, but also for transporting the logs by rafting to the mills. As early as 1836 people rafted logs down the bayou and on to New Orleans where lumber was in high demand. Judge J. W. Bocage saw John Buzzard and Buck Stephens on a steamboat trip that year and learned that Buzzard was "getting out a cypress raft on Bayou Bartholomew" and that Stephens was his partner "in rafting cypress timber to the lower coast market."[1]

Although rafting logs was a laborious and hazardous business, it afforded a good income and was commonplace. Y. W. Etheridge wrote, "...in those days [1850s] the finest logs one can possibly imagine were available without cost. The finest kind of cypress, gum, and oak logs were floated out down the Bayou during high water. These were cut down, rolled into the high water area, pegged together and floated down the stream to market." Leonidas Spyker noted in 1859 that rafts of logs were passing his house at Point Pleasant and that he had employed a raftsman to float logs to his sawmill. He wrote, "I went up to Judge Temple's to see about saw-logs. The Raftsman is not yet ready...I rode up to Majr. Ross's ferry to see the Raft, which got broke just below...Mr. Gill's large Raft passed down this evening."[2]

Steamboats also were used in log rafting. Eddy Valentine said that Eddy Miller told him about working on a steamboat that transported logs. Valentine said, "...[he] said he worked on a steamboat going from Tillar...to Dermott...pulling or pushing logs they tied together. He said they kept dynamite on there to blow logs and drifts out of their way. The sawmill was in Dermott...and they would go up around Tillar...where they had um banked up...He said that sometimes if they was way behind, they would light lanterns and run it twenty-four hours a day."[3] The steamboats pushed the log rafts which were positioned in front and beside them.

The first known sawmill erected on the bayou belonged to Peter Rives, who constructed a crude mill in 1819 on his land in northeast Drew County. A Mr. Culpepper had a mill near old Portland in the 1830s. John R. Temple and William Lawhead built a steam-powered sawmill on the bayou at Point Pleasant in 1840. "It was crude in construction and produced lumber very slowly. The mill was supplied with logs floated down the bayou from above." Spyker began making arrangements for a mill in March 1858. His neighbor was evidently a partner in the venture. Spyker wrote, "After dinner Major Ross called to settle the Steam mill matter, I gave him a draft for $1017.41, my half the amt. he paid for the mill, oxen, &c." One year later Spyker noted that the *Tigress* "brought my saddle but no saw mill." A few weeks later the *Red Chief* brought "a workman to put up my steam engine & mill."[4]

These small sawmills produced lumber for local use, but it was not until after the Civil War that the timber industry slowly began with the establishment of larger mills at Monroe. When C. M. Boyd returned to Ashley County after the war, he "cut a raft, hired some hands, and ran it to New Orleans, where he sold it." A Mr. Dardell and his nephew, Charlie Jenerette, rafted logs from the Tillar area in the early 1900s. Curly Birch wrote, "...in the early days, they would cut the huge cypress trees and in the springtime when the rains filled the bayou, they would float the logs south to the Ouachita River and sell them. After selling the logs they would buy horses for the trip home. He [Jenerette] said floating the logs was no easy task and that it took a long time."[5] Gaston Harrison, whose father worked as a raftsman, said, "Captain Jack Sisson owned a big farm around Galion with big cypress brakes in it. He cut the logs out of them and rafted them down the bayou." Local mills also employed rafting. Alvie Pugh said, "I saw them tied up and floating – going to different mills around here on the bank. When they got to the mill they would pull them out with teams of horses." Skipper and Lephiew had large numbers of rafts floated to their mill on the bayou north of Baxter.

Slavonian stave makers and bolt cutters also used rafts to get their products to export points. "Joe Stennis [of Lincoln County] floated his stave bolts on log rafts," Shorty Lyle stated. Dr. Corliss Curry wrote, "All winter [the Slavonians] cut staves, stacking them along the river banks, and when the annual spring floods began, they built barges of gum (...free for the taking), and loaded the staves aboard. The barges were floated to New Orleans, where both the barges and the staves were sold to exporters."[6] C. C. Honeycutt left a detailed description of stave barges. He wrote, "In 1891 I helped to build a stave barge on Bayou Bartholomew near Portland to carry out pipe staves...[It] was built to carry 45,000 of these staves. It was 125 feet long, 25 feet wide and carried 12 feet of water loaded. We got the great gunwale out of large pine trees; they were 30 inches wide, 15 inches thick and 25 feet long. We had to mortise holes in the sides and edge for the framework of the boat...it took 300 2-inch augur holes 8 inches deep to each gunwale, and there were 10 gunwales to the barge. The bottom and sides were made of 2x12[s] 25 feet long, with grooved seams and joints caulked with oakum...The bottom part of the barge was made out on the bank of the river, bottom side up, on land skids. When completed the props were knocked out and it slipped into the water, then we carried sand in small boats and loaded one side down until it stood at an angle of about 45 degrees; hitched our ropes and pulleys on the submerged side, from the opposite side of the boat and turned it over. Then we had the big job of bailing it out...We soon [were] ready to load staves. The sides and ends were built up as the loading progressed...."

Honeycutt described the trip. "We raised anchor on the 10th of February, 1891, and got to Monroe, La. on the 24th day of April. Our staves were stacked on the bank of the river for a distance of over a hundred miles. The largest amount we had at any one place was 5,000. It took us a week to load that pile of staves...We had a cabin to sleep in with upper and lower berths...It was built down in the bottom of the boat...We always tied up at night as we didn't have sufficient light to travel at night. We drifted with the current. The boat had a bow and stern oar which were made of pine logs 60 ft. long, balanced on the ends of the boat standing, in small boats siding up and fastened to the boat with iron pins, 2 inches in diameter. The end that went into the water had a piece 24 inches wide, 18 feet long, 3 inches thick at one end, run to a feather edge at the other [end], this was called the oar blade. It took 16 men to handle these oars...We also had 500 cribs of logs pinned together behind the barge, that was nearly a mile long . . ."[7]

Log rafts on the bayou varied in size. Gussie Turner of Portland found several sunken rafts that contained two to three hundred logs. Amos Sledge found one near Baxter that was about one-quarter of a mile long. Others reported that they were six to eight feet wide and "three logs long." The logs were held together by chain-dogs, two flat spikes or pins connected by a foot-long chain. One spike was driven into a log, and the other spike driven into the one next to it. Then a second spike and chain connected the second log to the next and so on until all the logs were attached. Curly Birch told Marvin Jeter of another method of fastening the logs. "[Sometimes] the bald cypress wood was too soft, and the pins would come out during the float trip. So, some bright person started boring holes in the logs and driving oak [also persimmon] pegs into them. When these moistened, they swelled and stuck tightly. Then they inserted the metal pins into the pegs, chained the logs together, and away they went."[8]

Getting the logs to the bayou was no easy feat. Buck Mayo described the process: "They used a Lindsay log wagon that had eight low but wide steel tires. There was a front and back bolster that was coupled together – that way the wagon could turn sharp corners in the woods. They used a bed chain to roll the logs up on them. The chain went under the wagon and was rolled around the log and connected to the team of mules that pulled it up. Sometime when it was real muddy, they had to use oxen that pulled mud boats like a mud slide loaded with logs. The ox had big spread-out feet and wouldn't sink in the mud like a mule. When they got to the bayou, they just dumped them in, and when they got a big ramp of them, they tied them together and took off to Monroe." Lloyd Smith said that he saw oxen pulling logs in mud that was waist deep.

The many cypress brakes enticed the lumbermen, who used an ingenious method to get the logs to the bayou. They dug canals – the hard way in the late 1800s and early 1900s. Lloyd Smith said, "They used a kind of fresno, a scoop about forty inches wide with two handles on the back. They were pulled by mules and the man had to bear down on the handles to push the scoop into the ground." One of the best known of these canals is the Ladd Canal, which was actually a series of canals, that stretched from the Avery-Garrett Bridge area to Walnut Lake (Pickens), where there was a sawmill. Other canals led to Bayou Bartholomew. Sam Williamson saw remnants of canals during a drainage survey on land south of the Jefferson Davis tract south of Pine Bluff. Harvey Chambliss noticed canals in the woods when he was hunting south of the Gibb Anderson place. This is approximately the same area, but on the opposite side of the bayou, where Mr. Williamson saw the canals. Amos Sledge said that when Willie Skipper cleared a brake on the present Lambert place, he drained it first and then floated the logs to the bayou. In Morehouse Parish timber men built a canal from the bayou to near the present Venoy Kinnaird farm.

Locally owned sawmills lined the bayou from Tarry in Lincoln County to Point Pleasant. The McGehee Brothers operated a steam mill in the early 1900s at Tarry where they used water from Thirteen Acre Lake. Two sawmills were at Yorktown around the turn of the century. E. P. Ladd owned a mill at Meroney, and V. L. Hill had one on the bayou south of Meroney. Bud Leal (or Lelg) operated a mill at Todd. There was a steam mill at Rose Hill around 1905. Jess Leatherman and Richard Jasper had mills near Batchelor Bridge. A steam shingle mill was on the bayou west of Tillar. Skipper and Lephiew's shingle mill was on the bayou north of Baxter. Bain Brothers owned a mill at Portland by 1893. W. H. Wells had a stave mill south of Portland by 1896. Rainer (and later Bowden) owned a mill north of Parkdale. McGarry and deYampert had a shingle mill on Lake Enterprise at Wilmot, and William B. deYampert and John Kidwell had groundhog sawmills. Ellis Doles, Thomas Yeldell, and Henry Jackson McCarty ran sawmills in McGinty in the early 1900s. George Westbrook had a sawmill at Tillou.

With the coming of the railroad in 1890, large timber companies from the north began large-scale exploitation of the forest. Shipment of logs and staves by steamboat continued as well, but the tonnage drastically declined after the 1890-1891 season. Table 6 not only illustrates the decline in shipment of timber products by steamboats after the railroad came but also attests to the large amount of products shipped.

Table 6
Timber Products Shipped on Bayou Bartholomew from 1889 to 1900

Year	Saw logs (tons)	Staves (tons)
1889-1890	11,839	
1890-1891	20,090	17,822
1891-1892	4,450	1,640
1892-1893	2,000	2,375
1893-1894	159	2,569
1894-1895		117
1895-1896	7,683	6,012
1896-1897	2,020	2,156
1897-1898	1,000	832
1898-1899	1,300	693
1899-1900	1,300	1,490

Source: Corps of Engineers *Annual Report* for 1900.

In 1892 the *Gazette* extolled the potential for timber harvest on Gum Ridge, which lay between the bayou and Beouf River from McGehee down into Morehouse Parish. "The ridgeland system...has a superficial area of approximately 500,000 acres, and extending from Morrell [Boydell]...to the vicinity of Monroe...and an average breadth of six miles...And, indeed, it would be injustice not to distinguish this region as among the heaviest timbered countries of the Mississippi Valley, the cypress in particular aggregating more than is today found in the remainder of the

State, and the hard woods, such as are adapted to manufacturing uses."[9]
The call did not go unheeded. The forests were ravaged by large timber
companies, most of which were from the north or financed by northern
capital.   Giant, virgin cypress trees were sliced into shingles; white oak
trees were shaped into barrel staves; hickory trees were carved into
handles; and red oaks were sawed into lumber.   Gum Ridge no longer
exists; it is leveled farmland.

Bayou Treasure: Sunken Logs

You never saw such good wood.

Garvin Adcock

If the logs were put into the bayou before they dried sufficiently, they (especially cypress) became waterlogged over a period of time and sank. Individual logs as well as entire rafts often submerged. It was too much trouble to attempt to pull them out, and there was no need for it – the supply seemed endless. These sunken logs rested on the bayou bed and were forgotten. In later years during periods of extreme low water, people discovered the logs and began to pull them out. They found that they were perfectly preserved and made superior lumber. In 1872 an article stated, "The wood, though light and soft, is of extreme durability. It has been asserted that cypress trees which have been buried a thousand years under the solid but always damp earth, now retains every quality of almost perfect wood." Willie Peter Brown of Portland searched the bayou for submerged logs which he pulled out and used to make shingles. "They are the best there is," he told Earl Cochran.[10]

The reason that these logs are "the best there is" goes back to their seedling environment, which for some was at least three hundred years ago. They sprouted under a canopy of mature trees that allowed only filtered sunlight to reach them. Competition for light, water, and nutrients was keen, and their growth was slow. This slow growth resulted in twenty to fifty rings an inch annually, which thereby produced an extremely dense wood. By comparison trees growing now generate only four to six growth rings a year. This slow and long growth created a fine-grained, hard, and beautifully colored wood. Another factor contributed to the exceptional wood quality. As the logs lay in their watery bed, another change took place. Instead of being exposed to oxygen-thriving bacteria and fungi that cause decay and deterioration, anaerobic bacteria invaded the wood and ate away the hemicellulose and starchy matter leaving only the cell walls. When waterlogged wood is recovered and dries, the cell walls remain open. By contrast when normal wood dries the cell openings close and deform.[11]

People have been retrieving sunken logs from the bayou for years. "We got some out at Lambert Bend and sawed them for lumber to build a barn. You never saw such good wood," Garvin Adcock stated. John B. Currie Sr. is proud of his bayou bed lumber. "Look at these boards in my den; some of them are twenty-two inches wide. They are made from red gum logs out of the bayou. There was a raft of them west of Jones. I got Benton Hunt to pull them out for me and had them sawed and kiln dried."

Benton Hunt described how he retrieved logs. "I took the grabs and went underwater and set them and then let out air bubbles so my brother would know when to tighten up on the cable. They were tied together with chains connected to spike drives. Nearly all of them were heart-figured gum."

In the early 1950s C. M. Hamilton of Point Pleasant needed a good supply of pecky cypress for his sawmill customers. (Pecky cypress contains small holes made by worms and is used in decorative woodwork such as paneling.) Jim Rider wrote, "He began walking certain stretches of the bayou and soon learned how to spot log rafts under the silt on the bottom...Hamilton roved the bayou for about two years, looking for log rafts, winching them out, and sawing them into salable lumber."[12]

This old, soaked wood has within recent times gained international attention for its unique qualities, and Bayou Bartholomew is yielding its ancient treasures to the world market. The wood is highly valued for woodcraft, sculpture, furniture, paneling, doors, flooring, and musical instruments. Around 1948 a young boy, Joe Patterson, moved with his family to Grace Community between Dermott and Baxter where they bought a farm on the bayou. On this farm on the bayou bank is the site of the old Skipper and Lephiew shingle mill with bricks from it still visible. Joe's father had been a tie-hacker in Missouri and knew his timber. One hot day in 1965 Joe shucked his sweaty clothes and jumped in the bayou for a skinny dip. He spotted a log under water and showed it to his father, who said, "That log is worth some money." Being too much trouble to get the log out, they let it lay, but Joe never forgot about it. In 1990 Joe finally decided to try to get it out. He dove under with a big set of tongs to hook to it and "danged near drown." After much difficulty he managed to get a cable around the giant and pulled it from the muck. The cypress log section was four and three feet in circumference at the ends and twenty-seven feet long.

During low water periods in the ensuing years, Joe discovered more sunken logs and rafts, many assumedly from the Skipper and Lephiew operation, along the bayou. After some investigation into marketing opportunities and legal considerations, Joe began a serious effort in log retrieval. He first experimented with and perfected an apparatus to facilitate hooking cables to the logs, and the bayou began to yield its treasures. A cypress butt cut that measures forty-two and twelve inches in diameter at the ends and is twelve feet long (800 board feet) carries a price tag of $2,400. Companies that market this lumber not only emphasize its quality, age, and uniqueness, but also the fact that it is environmentally friendly. "No trees are cut. No spotted owls are endangered. The forests are not being depleted. In fact forests are being preserved because this ancient wood is being preserved. It is estimated that for every log brought up...two trees are saved from cutting. Environmentalists love it."[13]

Bayou Mystery: Choctaw Logs

They are nature's styrofoam.

Duke Shackelford

The rafts of logs would not have sunk if the owners had used another bayou treasure – Choctaw logs. Log rafters often attached these logs to the outside of green log rafts to keep them from sinking. As opposed to the sinkers, these wonders of nature are floaters. They were highly prized by old-timers, and their utility is still recalled by bayou people. Leroy Haynes made the first mention of these logs in May 1998 on the first day of interviews for this research. "After the ferry quit running the folks built a floating bridge out of Choctaw logs," he said. "What is a Choctaw log?" Leroy replied, "It's an old, dead oak tree that turned into a Choctaw log. It's real light wood that floats real high. They used them as pontoons under the floating bridges." From that day on the answers to questions about Choctaw logs were varied yet similar. Ninety-eight year old Gaston Harrison said, "They used them to make rafts to cross the bayou on. They used two logs about two feet in diameter. The logs laid there a long time and dried up. It looks kind of petrified with big, open pores in it. All the sapwood is gone; it is all heart. They were covered with sand and then the sand washed away. All of them are oak."

Shorty Lyle said, "It's a lightweight, old, dried log on the bank. They floated in from the backwater when the bayou was up. People lashed two together to make a fishing raft called a Choctaw raft. Two black men caught a hundred-pound catfish on their trotline and went out on their raft and got it. It made a good raft because it wouldn't sink." Alvie Pugh verified their uses: "I've seen 'em; they are around here. We would get two and fasten them together and go across the bayou on them. Or get three or four and use them to carry our groceries and supplies across. Rafts were a common way to cross the bayou. You could haul most anything on them. They held more than a boat and they wouldn't sink or turn over. We also used them for a fishing raft that we would push with poles."

The varied uses and descriptions continued. Buck Mayo said, "It was mostly pecky oak. It was mostly heartwood and wouldn't sink. They used them under pontoons for houseboats." "I wish I had a dollar for everyone I had," said Ed Jones. "They float like a cork – don't weigh nothing. We made fish docks out of them to float our live-boxes on. People hunted in the woods in the backwater for miles for them. Only oak will choctaw." Benton Hunt used the logs. "I built a low water bridge across Hopkins Slough out of them. I used six logs spiked together and put plank runways on them. I hauled a cultivator and pair of mules across it – also a 110 John

Deere. Oak is the only wood that will choctaw. A Choctaw will be nothing less than eighteen inches in diameter," Benton said. "It has red lumber when cut and will last longer than white wood. We built a smokehouse out of it. Choctaw is red oak. Some logs swim high; some logs swim low. Choctaws swim the highest," Page Webb declared. There is an adage about the logs. Joe Cope said, "The old-timers say that when the moon is light, the Choctaws rise; when the moon is dark, they go down some. People who lived on houseboats that were on Choctaw logs noticed this and measured the difference during different moon phases."

Duke Shackelford said, "At the Winkler place they had a floating bridge made out of them that Model-Ts crossed on. Instead of rotting like normal logs, bacteria eat out the cell material leaving only the outer cellular membrane. They are nature's styrofoam." Cecil Harp explained, "Red oak is the only wood that will choctaw. The Indians used them for rafts. Years ago Orville McCready - he was part Indian - and I found one about twenty feet long. We sent a sample to the university and they said it was red oak and the only one that would do this. They could not explain how it choctawed."

People mentioned oak (particularly red oak), tupelo gum, "any hardwood," and cypress as wood that could choctaw. Benton Hunt said that cypress was "a lower form" of a Choctaw log. "If you can't find a Choctaw, you can use a pecky cypress," he said. The term, "Choctaw cypress," is documented in Iberville Parish, Louisiana, where old-timers once used it to build Joe-boats. Complaining that sunken solid cypress, when raised and used in boat building would eventually check (split), Gregory Dupre learned about Choctaw cypress from the old-timers. "Then you got the sinker lumber that does not make the best sides for a boat...being that it was the sinker type material, it was going to want to crack on you big time and it was better to use the 'choctaw' variety which was the floating type cypress. But nowadays you don't have any, and if you do have any, it is very, very rare."[14]

The term, Choctaw log, was documented in literature around 1875: "These impromptu rafts were known by the name of 'Choctaw Log,' the early settlers having learned their construction and utility from roving bands of Choctaw hunters." The term appeared again in the *National Geographic Magazine* during the Flood of 1927: "To save others [cattle], the owners built rafts, or 'choctaws,' as these craft are locally [Natchez area] called, and placed them on these floats. I saw one crowded with goats and pigs, and another, a 'double-decker,' filled with cackling poultry."[15]

The term is documented; the descriptions and uses are documented - but what is a Choctaw log? What happens to create such an unusual specimen? What causes a log to "choctaw?" Some familiar with the logs said that they fell into the bayou where they became covered with silt, perhaps for hundreds of years, underwent a change, and during a later flood the silt washed away and the logs "popped up." Others said that the choctawing process took place on land.

Cecil Harp gave the author a sample of his Choctaw log that had been sawed into lumber. It is extremely lightweight, resembles sponge or honeycomb, and floats almost entirely above the water "like a cork." Although it was pleasing to have this sample, an entire log would be much better. The word went out – "find a Choctaw log." Joe Cope, a commercial fisherman on the Arkansas River in Desha County, called in February 1999. "I've got one tied up," he said.

An excited crew launched from Wargo Landing the following day.[16] After a long, cold motorboat ride, the log came into view. Elation turned into disappointment when the chainsaw ripped through the end of the log for a test. The log was solid; it was a low-floating cottonwood "blue," highly valued by lumbermen for expensive paneling, but not by Choctaw log seekers. After many more miles on the choppy water and three more discouraging finds, a sinking heart leapt when Sammy Wells shouted, "I think that's one over there!" The boat turned and as it approached the log, the difference was notable. It was floating very high out of the water; two-thirds to three-fourths of the log was above the waterline. Once more the obligatory chainsaw cross-section test was performed. The saw easily went through the end of the log. It was a Choctaw! Bimbo Huskey and Buck Burton lashed it to the boat for its last ride down the river. After the log was loaded onto a trailer, it was measured. It was sixteen feet long and the circumference of both ends was close to five feet. Two men easily lifted the log. Another extraordinary characteristic was noted. An indescribable aroma emanated from the cut end, and after more than a year the sweet fragrance remains.

A section of the Harp specimen was already at the USDA Forest Products Laboratory in Wisconsin, where wood scientists determined that it was red oak. A specimen of the log proved to be the same. The scientists there had never seen anything like it, especially the massive deterioration. Dr. Carol Clausen, a microbiologist, wrote, "Though no one has witnessed this type of specimen before, there has been much speculation about the sequence of events that could lead to the condition of this wood...upon splitting the specimen, a few interesting things were noted. 1) the uniform size and shape of the cavities, 2) complete destruction of all anatomical structure in each cavity except for the vessels, which remain perfectly intact, as though they could not be digested." Dr. Jerrold E. Winandy of the same institution gave insight into the noted aroma. "Usually when wood is infected with anaerobic bacteria a distinctive odor is present."[17]

Samples of the log and/or descriptions were sent to other institutions where no one had heard of Choctaw logs. No definitive determination could be made concerning the manner of their deterioration. Dr. W. Ramsay Smith of the Louisiana Forest Products Laboratory at LSU wrote, "Not knowing anything specific about them, I would venture to say that the bacteria have reduced the specific gravity of the logs to have them float much higher, but normally with anaerobic bacterial deterioration the wood becomes much more porous and would more readily adsorb water, become waterlogged and sink. Somehow it appears a 'pocket' of air is trapped in the log to help maintain its buoyancy. Interesting problem." Dr. Terry L. Amburgey of the Forest Products Laboratory at Mississippi State wrote, "Choctawed wood likely occurs when a tree of a hardwood species (e.g., white oak) that had tyloses in its vessel elements becomes water-logged for an extended period of time (several decades). Bacterial and acid degradation over time would essentially remove all cellulosic material (rays, cell walls) and leave the lignin skeletin and tyloses. This would make the wood much lighter than normal and the tyloses would block water from entering many cells. Theoretically, this would result in 'Choctawed' wood that would float like a cork."[18]

Dr. Clausen later reviewed various opinions. "I thought it was a crustacean and definitely not a bacteria. Terry Highley [former FPL scientist] thought it was fungal followed by insect, but definitely not a crustacean. Terry Amburgey thought from a description only that it was a bacteria and not an insect. You have truly stumped the experts." Dr. Malcolm K. Cleaveland of the University of Arkansas wrote, "The wood is obviously in an advanced state of decay with much of the actual cell wall mass gone. No wonder it floats so high! The fungal hyphae may actually waterproof the wood to some degree, which would explain why it floats for a long time instead of waterlogging and sinking. On the other hand, maybe what is left has such a low specific gravity that it would never sink...Wouldn't it be interesting if it were hitherto unknown to science?"[19] The mystery of the Choctaw log remains unsolved.

※◎◎※

Such Fertile Land!

*In those bayou bends is some of the best
land on the face of the earth.*

Robert Crawley

Mary Sorrells DeWoody wrote concerning their antebellum bayou plantation, "I never saw such fertile land as that bayou place was! How well we did live, down there! We raised everything the soil would produce. In addition we had fish, all sorts of game, such as squirrel, rabbit, deer, quail, turkey, etc. Also scalybark hickory nuts, walnuts, pecans in profusion...When we left the bayou, we left great pens of pumpkins and hundreds of bushels of sweet potatoes."[20]

A farmer knows soil and the lay of the land as well as a pianist knows the nuances of musical notations. The migrating pioneers must have gazed in amazement when they reached the bayou terraces and bottomland. Coming from eastern areas where the soil was depleted from continual, non-diversified farming, they recognized good soil upon sight. They knew that the fine silty loam would make good cotton. They also realized that this land offered an unusual drainage feature that would be to their benefit. Because of the high banks most of the water generally drains away from the bayou instead of into it, thus preventing flooding. (The exception to this was and is from its source to below Pine Bluff where the shallow channel cannot carry excessive rainwater.) Creeks to the west, such as Ables, Cut-off, Bearhouse, Overflow, and Chemin a Haut, receive runoff from the hills first before they eventually empty into the bayou. Drainage from the east side of the bayou is generally to the east. With these advantages in mind, the pioneer farmer had to make a decision: risk subjecting his family to the malarial conditions in this mosquito infested swampland for the crops he could produce on this extraordinary soil or head on toward the hills. A. J. McShan chose the hills of Beech Creek in Ashley County out of consideration for the health of his family, but he realized the Delta produced better crops. He wrote to his brother, Feaster McShan, in 1855, "...I live five miles from Bayou Bartholomew the Lands on that make from 50 to 80 bushel corn to the acre & from one to two Bales cotton[.] I would Settle on that but I am afraid it ant healthy." He also noted that he hoped to make twenty bales of cotton from his twenty-five acre crop and twenty to forty bushels of corn per acre.[21] Those who decided to stay settled on the high banks and began clearing the bayou land. Some settled in the hills but farmed in the Delta. A letter published in a local paper in 1883 from the hill town of Collins stated, "Our cotton is very sorry except on the bayou bottoms...." The crops were good, but the malarial conditions continued. George W. Sawyer wrote from Hamburg on October 31, 1886, "There has been some sickness on the Bayou...and resulted in three or four deaths. All on the Bayou. John Allen, John Hudspeth, John Fork, and John Bell all died within the last two weeks with swamp fever and pneumonia."[22]

The settlers cleared land by sawing the trees down, rolling or pulling them to a pile, and burning them. Slave owners employed their slaves for this work while small farmers did it themselves, often with the help of neighbors. Clearing was no easy task. A family working alone could only clear a few acres a year. Farmers planted cotton in ground still studded with stumps. Poca Hunter of Morehouse Parish owned several hundred acres. He told Buster Ford that he was able to clear two to three acres a year using an ax and crosscut saw. Benton Hunt said, "My father had forty acres. It took four years [1932-1936] to clear seven acres. We finally cleared twenty acres. The Shackelfords had 2,200 acres to clear and they used labor all year round to get it done."

The early plantations began along the bayou and gradually moved outward. Ralph Kinnaird said, "The best land is from the bayou to the east about four miles." Within the curve of a bend was a choice location, for there lay deep deposits of the most fertile soil. The larger bends contain six to nine hundred acres. Some bayou plantations reached enormous proportions. The Avery plantation in Lincoln County contained 1,300 acres with 800 in cultivation. The antebellum Hollywood Plantation owned by the Taylor family in Drew County expanded to over 11,000 acres after the Civil War. The Pickens' holdings, begun around 1880 as a timber enterprise, reached over 14,000 acres with over 10,000 in cultivation. Tillar and Company owned around 24,000 acres, and a later division, Tillar Mercantile, had around 4,000 in cultivation. C. M. Boyd had 1,000 acres cultivated out of 5,000 in 1893 in the Baxter area. Charles T. Duke, also at Baxter, owned 9,000 acres with 3,000 in crops in 1907. The Waddell plantation at Boydell contained 1,900 acres. At Thebes the McCombs plantation encompassed thousands of acres from the bayou to Overflow Hill. In 1932 the J. W. Pugh plantation at Portland consisted of 7,000 acres with 6,000 in crops. The deYampert plantation at Wilmot had 4,000 acres of cotton and 1,000 acres of corn in 1924.[23]

In northeast Morehouse Parish, G. W. Naff established a 2,500 acre plantation, and Jim Shackelford's Hollyhurst Plantation grew to around 2,200 acres. Some large planters in the area were Demarquis Harp, J. T. Haynes, E. P. Zachary, and Jim Doles. Large plantations lined the bayou throughout the parish, and although ownership changed through the years, they are still in production.

George B. Gregory wrote from "Bayou Bartholomew" (in Ashley County) on July 18, 1845, "The crops in this country so far as I am acquainted is good or the best that I ever saw. I don't think you ever saw such cotton in all your life...My cotton is just as good as cotton ever gets to be...you can't see a man in it ten feet [away] and is a boling very well." Mr. Gregory was not aware that the Arkansas River once coursed through this land leaving in its wake the rich alluvial deposits most suitable for the growth of cotton and other crops. Goodspeed wrote concerning the Delta in Jefferson County, "The land...is...alluvial delta on the lowlands, of great and ancient depths, the same soil having been discovered to a depth of over fifty feet, where ancient shells and pre-historic remains were found. This...pregnant with potash and soda, and a wealth of organic matter, has made Jefferson County the equal of any agricultural region in the south, and second only to Washington County, Miss., as a cotton county." The chronicler also noted the bayou land "containing about 100,000 acres" in Drew County. "The lowlands along [the bayou] are free from overflow and are distinct from the lands of the rest of the county." In Ashley County he observed, "The bottom lands of [the bayou]...while of an alluvial nature, are distinct and separate from the Mississippi bottoms, and of a different character from the soil of the remainder of the county."[24]

This alluvial soil is composed of Portland silt loam (a very fine sandy loam named after Portland), Rilla and Hebert (both silt loam), and Perry clay. Alluvial sediments deposited by the Arkansas River formed all of these soil types and they occur in various combinations. Farmers "read" the soil and knew where to plant certain crops. The early farmers attempted to avoid a Perry clay type of soil known as buckshot or gumbo. Earl Cochran said, "The early farmers knew where the good land was and quit clearing. I think they could tell by the soil. They cleared to the buckshot and quit. The early fields were not squared because they quit clearing when they reached bad soil...It takes the pure in heart to work buckshot."[25] Thelbert Bunch related some lessons in soil quality: "If it grows good cockleburs, it is good cotton land. Blackberries indicate good, sandy ground and higher ground. They always cleared the sandy land first. Elm grows on stiff, white dirt that is mixed and not as dark as buckshot. Pin oak flats will be on buckshot." Mike Doles gave other examples: "They picked where gum grew for cotton, and oak for corn and possibly soybeans. Elm – don't bother clearing. It's crawfish dirt – worse than buckshot."

As more and more land was cleared, farmers did attempt raising cotton on buckshot fields but with poor luck. They eventually found that because of its poor internal drainage, it was good for rice, and that if it was drained and irrigated it would produce soybeans and corn. Joel Newcome wrote, "Catfish is the best 'crop' that has come along for buckshot. A tractor can work in buckshot if there is water standing to wash mud from tires. If the ground is wet, the mud will gum up on the tires so thick that the tractor cannot develop any power. If you walk across a wet buckshot field, your boots will become so heavy that it is impossible to walk. The general feeling is that the term came from the fact that when it is very dry, very hard pellets form at the surface that probably reminded the farmers of buckshot. They may have even loaded some in their shotgun shells – who knows?"[26]

Farming underwent a cycle of dramatic changes but still remains the basic infrastructure of Delta economy. The first major evolution occurred with the loss of slave labor and the ensuing tenant system. Whether a farmer previously used a hundred slaves or one, the labor required to work his land remained the same. Freed slaves and (later) poor whites became tenants in an arrangement that still bound them to the landowner. For example, R. A. Pugh of Portland entered into a contract with the Freedmen's Bureau for eight males, twelve females, and six children (who were exempt from labor). He was to "furnish land, teams, tools, and feed for teams & supply employee at cost & carriage & furnish medicine. Corn not charged to employees at more than 1.40 per bushel. Employee to furnish labor to make gather & receive the crop. To have all time not required to make & receive the crop. To pay for at cost & carriage feed, cloths [sic] & doctors bills for themselves & families and receive last fifths of all crop made by them."[27] Thus, the sharecropping system emerged.

Eventually the standard payment from sharecroppers to landowners became half of the crop plus reimbursement for the furnish to the commissary or designated store when the cotton was ginned. If sharecroppers could save enough to buy a team and equipment, they became tenant farmers and paid one-third of the corn and one-fourth of the cotton plus the furnish. This was commonly referred to as "thirds and fourths." The dream of all was to save enough money to buy their own farm. Very few of these dreams reached fulfillment. It was an endless cycle of work and debt. The trying times of the Great Depression followed by the war industry boom created a mass migration of tenants to northern factories. Paid day labor began to replace the tenant system. A 1940 editorial in the *Delta News* noted "almost revolutionary changes" in the bayou valley as more tenants were becoming "wage hands" or landowners.[28] Felix Pugh wrote a letter of recommendation for J. D. Wood, a former tenant, that succinctly expressed the changes taking place at this time: "The reason I am not keeping Mr. Wood is because I have rented the place he is now on to another party who is going to work the place with day labor and a tractor."[29]

The next consequential transformation revolutionized agriculture. With the labor force dwindling, farmers gradually gave up their mules and replaced them with mechanical equipment. Tractors pulling plows, discs, and other equipment slowly emerged in the 1910s, but their utility was mostly restricted to breaking land. The deYampert plantation, which used around a hundred mules, began the transition to tractors around 1936 although they used some steam tractors for breaking land before that time. By 1950 the transition was in full force, but day labor was still required for chopping, hoeing, and picking cotton.

The mechanical cotton picker came into limited use in the late 1940s. Wesley Bunch of Jones bought his first picker in 1948. He said, "Labor was getting hard to find, and I had to leave cotton in the field in 1947. Mechanical pickers were hard to get. A farmer had to put up money ahead to get one which had to be ordered. I went to Mr. [G. W.] Naff, and he gave me the rest of the money...that fall I picked 240 bales for myself and other farmers. The picker had cost $7,300 and it picked one row at a time. Today [1987] pickers are close to $100,000, but they pick two rows. Cotton pickers and machinery like that revolutionized farming – that and herbicides. These things just about did away with tenant farmers. And it helped because the kids could go to school and learn something that would help them make a living."[30] All of these transitions were gradual. Mark Hawkins reported that some were still picking cotton by hand in 1966. Page Webb never bought a mechanical picker for his small farm. "Why should I?" he said. "I could pick five-hundred pounds a day myself."

As mules left the farms, the production of corn decreased (although some was still grown for market), and other crops took its place. Some rice was grown in row crops for home consumption as early as 1850, and S. A. Duke experimented with the crop at Baxter soon after the Civil War. It was not until around 1925, however, that rice began to emerge as a commercial crop in the bayou section of the Delta. Henry and Dennis Tilbury of Wilmot first experimented with 150 acres of the grain and in 1926 added another hundred acres. Their brother, Floyd, entered the venture and raised six hundred acres with the bayou providing the water. Floyd Tilbury's son, F. N., said, "Rice farmers had to follow the bayou to get water for their rice. We had to have surface water available." Floyd moved to Bonita in 1935 and the following year planted the first rice in Morehouse Parish. In 1937 he raised a hundred acres of rice on the Ellis Doles place. The Tilbury brothers, Dennis, Henry, and Lloyd, also came to the parish to grow rice. Lloyd and Henry developed a farm on Prairie DeButte (north of Bastrop) where they put in two deep wells for irrigation. They also used water from the bayou by pumping it into DeButte Creek, which they dammed. Marion Doles wrote that Ellis Doles went to Stuttgart, Arkansas, to learn about rice production in 1937. He then hired Floyd Tilbury to grow rice on his land at the Vester place where they used water from the bayou for irrigation. The crop was successful, but it proved to be too costly to transport it to Stuttgart, the nearest market.[31]

At last the damnable buckshot land could be put into productive use; the poorly drained soil would hold the water needed for rice. "Garrard Mountjoy cleared Beouf Swamp and put in rice levees. He got Clifford Larrison, an experienced rice grower from Wilmot, to help him," Bobby Abraugh said. Around 1946 Pugh and Company of Portland entered into rice production, and Gus Pugh began in the early 1950s.[32] John Edd Curry credited Edgar Farmer as the first to grow rice in Lincoln County. "He started in the mid-1950s," he said. Presently rice production competes with soybeans as the second major cash crop after cotton. Large-scale cultivation of soybeans began during World War II, and by 1950 it was an established Delta product. Crops in order of income on the Pickens farm are cotton, soybeans, rice, and wheat. Harvey Chambliss divides his acreage into 800 for cotton, 800 for soybeans, and 600 to 700 for rice.

The Tilburys may have been the first (in 1926) to use the bayou for irrigation purposes. Irrigation did not become a common practice until the 1950s. Vernon Scott said that the Tillar farm began irrigating out of the bayou in 1948 and continues to do so. The Curry family at Garrett Bridge first used water from the bayou around 1945 when they siphoned water to irrigate pastureland. John Edd Curry installed his first relift pump in the bayou around 1951. The Pickens farm began pumping out of the bayou in 1954. "We later put in deep wells as they are more reliable. When you put a pump in the bayou, it will get too low and you have to move the pump or else the bayou will get high and flood out the pump," Andrew Pickens said. Lloyd Smith remarked, "My grandfather would have never dreamed that we would be pumping out of the bayou one day."

The last transition from farming to agribusiness centered around large landholdings and operating capital. Farming is now a very costly business. Equipment, seed, chemicals, and wells for irrigation require an exorbitant outlay. Harvey Chambliss said, "Cotton is an expensive crop to grow. It takes $150 dollars an acre just for poison and pumping water. You have to make two bales to the acre just to break even." The small farmer is out. Frank Day said, "Forty acres is not anything nowadays. You can't buy equipment to work just that much. So you rent out the land and make more." Two types of rent systems evolved to accommodate small landowners who could no longer afford to farm as well as large landowners who no longer cared to manage their farming interests. They simply rent their land to farming interests for a standard amount. Good cotton land rents for a hundred dollars an acre or more, and "lower class land" brings as little as thirty dollars an acre. Buster Ford is pleased with his rent arrangement. "I bought eighty acres in 1948 for $2,400 plus $100 interest. I paid for it by farming it with mules; then I bought a tractor. Now I rent it out for $6,000. I've been offered $90,000 for that eighty acres!"

Others who are willing to take a chance on having good crops let their land out on a share system. Ernie Sprinkle explained, "We furnish the land, wells, and water; they pay for the fertilizer and seed. When they make their crop, they pay us one-fifth." Mark Hawkins elaborated, "The one-fifth share is called eighty-twenty. The landowner also gets one-fifth of the government support payment. For example, if a product brings five cents a pound, the farmer gets four cents and the landowner gets one cent." Some landowners receive as much as a fourth share for cotton, rice, and soybeans.

Farming has always been an integral part of Delta life. Even for those who no longer till the land, there is a certain joy and excitement in observing the continual succession of seasonal tasks from the first spring plowing to the climatic harvest. Only those bound to the land fully know the fragrance of freshly turned earth, the marvel of new green sprouts, the delight of the first red and white cotton blossoms, the wonder as these flowers turn into hard green bolls, and the gratification as the bolls open to reveal their treasure of fluffy white cotton. They call it White Gold – another bayou treasure.

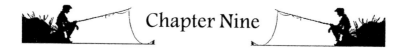

Chapter Nine

Living On The Edge

Desperadoes on the Bayou

I have heard all my life that Jesse James roamed this area.

Cecil Harp

Bayou Bartholomew flowed tranquilly along her course through the Delta but beheld in silence events contrary to her ordinarily peaceful disposition. The darker side of human nature played out its role along her banks. She witnessed violence, murder, hangings, and thievery, and watched as her waters became skillfully converted into moonshine. She heard agonizing screams, and her brown or green water became streaked with the crimson flow of blood. A screech owl flapped away from his watchful perch to avoid the spectacle afforded by leaning trees with sturdy branches as they were transformed into impromptu gallows. An old loggerhead turtle slipped off his resting log as the reflection of fire from burning crosses burnished the surface of the night water. Most of these events are buried in her shrouded mire, but some are proclaimed.

Judge J. W. Bocage wrote of the seditious element he observed in southeast Arkansas in 1836. "Others equally guilty of violating the criminal code in the [old] settlements flee to the new territory where seemingly out of the reach of arrest – they boldly present themselves at prominent points, or on the public highways, ever on the alert to evade recognition and arrest, they move back and forth on the fringe of civilization, seeking to prey on the innocent, unwary, and even their own fellows for want of easier conquests, adroit in the legerdemain of cards, and all other gambling devices."[1]

River pirates escaped through a network of streams across Desha County after raiding boats along the Mississippi. Cypress Creek led from the river to Possum Fork to Amos Bayou to Winchester, where there was a few miles portage to Bartholomew. The widely scattered settlers were subject to these marauding bands as they sought refuge in Delta canebrakes. One such group was John A. Murrell's gang who pillaged not only goods, horses, and money but also stole and resold the farmers' most valuable asset, slaves. These infamous outlaws were in southeast Arkansas as early as 1835. A local paper reported, "From 1835 to 1857, John A. Murrell and his gang of cutthroats rode and raided, robbed and terrorized the Delta Country. From all accounts, Murrell was the most daring and brazen robber who ever stripped a defenseless man or cut an innocent throat."[2] (John Murrell's gang, known as "The Mystic Confederacy" or "The Clan," numbered over 1,500 men who split into many smaller divisions and rode under Murrell's name. According to one source, Murrell was in prison in Tennessee from 1832 to 1842, but his devotees continued their pillage in his absence.)[3]

Judge J. W. Bocage of Jefferson County saw the gang leader's brother, Gilleam Murrell, during a steamboat trip to Columbia in Chicot County in 1836. The handsome, immaculately dressed, and bejeweled faro dealer dealt cards to John Buzzard, of Bayou Bartholomew, among others. The genial dealer was not so handsome the following day. As the judge toured the town he saw a dead man near the path "…lying in a pool of coagulated blood, his right hand nearly severed from the wrist. The diamonds, emeralds and rubies still adorned his fingers… The corpse pale as if every drop of blood had passed out through the many gaping wounds in his body inflicted with the terrible Bowie Knife." A short inquest found only that persons unknown killed him.[4] A "justice" system outside of the law was swift in those days.

The Murrell Gang came to Dr. McDermott's bayou plantation. McDermott wrote, "Chicot County at that time had quite a number of 'Murrellites' – men who lived by plunder, murder, gambling, and theft. About 8 of them lived near old man Fulton's house above Gaines' Landing. They would steal a horse or a negro. Once they got into a quarrel with one of their own members, a man named McReynolds. Seven of them came to his place and killed him with a gun. The names of this band were Fulton, Cooper, Johns, and James Forsythe. Once they took a barrel of sugar from my storehouse. I prudently made no complaint. When McReynolds persuaded some of my negroes to run off with him to Mobile, where he could sell them and divide the price with them, I kept silent and commanded the negroes to conceal my knowledge of his proposition. But there were other lawless men among the planters who seemed to fear neither God nor man. They were mostly from Kentucky. There were among them, the Gunns, Carters, Craigs, Campbells, and Fergusons. All they cared for was money, money, money, and whiskey."[5]

John Murrell had a hideout that became known as Murrell's Cave in Vernon Parish, west of Alexandria. According to T. Y. Harp's memoirs, he may have been en route to it when he stopped to visit a relative, Ben Murrell, a ferryman on Bayou Bartholomew in Morehouse Parish. Harp wrote that during this visit a party of trailing Mississippi horsemen captured the notorious miscreant, took him to nearby Bayou Bonne Idee, and hanged him. Harp said that he was the first white man hanged in Morehouse Parish. According to another source, Murrell died in Pikeville, Tennessee, on November 3, 1844.[6]

Another well-known outlaw gang rode the bayou trails and ridges during and after the Civil War. "One night during the war two strange men came to the hotel and stayed all night. No one knew who they were until the next day when someone found out that they were Frank and Jesse James." The hotel was at Collins, above the bayou in Drew County. The road from Collins south led to Line in Ashley County, where Dr. Jesse T. Young and his daughter, Cordelia, were riding along a narrow road going from Line toward Monticello when they saw a group of riders approaching. Dr. Young began to look for a place to pull his buggy over to allow them to pass when he saw the lead rider raise his hand to motion the riders off the road. They tipped hats in greetings and rode on. After several more miles the doctor encountered a second group of riders who stopped him and asked if he had met a group of men along the road. "Yes, we did, and a polite group of riders they were," he replied. The leader of the group then said, "Well, those polite riders were Jesse James and his whole gang."[7]

From Line the trail led to Thebes about a mile west of the bayou. James Bealer, born in 1894, was raised at Thebes and said he heard the old folks talking about the gang being around there. From Thebes a bayou trail led straight to old Portland where Mrs. T. R. (Jayne) Pugh used to tell about their staying overnight. Mrs. A. J. Camak remembered some strangers who visited their home near old Portland when she was around seven (1866). The W. J. Cammack home was "famed for its hospitality to travelers, and hardly a night passed without a number of overnight visitors." One night a peddler stopped in and just as the family was preparing for supper, a group of "rough men" rode up. They asked for lodging and her father invited them in. As the riders entered, the leader ordered them to disarm in a gentleman's house. "And so onto a spotless four-poster bed half a score of heavy pistols were tossed." The host calmly withdrew to the kitchen to inform his wife to set more plates for the new guests – Jesse James and his gang. The men were very courteous, and after supper one played the piano as others sang. The peddler was very nervous, however, and announced he was headed south the next morning. He waited until the other visitors left and then headed due north.[8]

From Portland they followed the bayou to the Wilmot area. Estelle Morris Jones told a story of their visit there. "My grandfather [Nathan Morris] always told us children that Jesse James had a regular path up and down the bayou. They would come by his home [near Wilmot] and spend the night and always leave money for food and bed. They would come once every two to three months. One time one of the men of the family had ridden off for a doctor or a midwife, and when he got back he was frozen to the saddle. One of the James boys told them not to pull him off the saddle. He took it off with him still on it and put it in a tub of water to get loose. Their hideout was in a church on lower Dry Bayou, which was east of Wilmot and down toward Laark." Nancy Tharpe, born in 1894, lived on Dry Bayou and remembered the old folks talking about Jesse James being around there. When a movie about Jesse James was scheduled to open in Wilmot in 1939, the local paper reported, "The famed outlaw is of special interest in and around Wilmot, as it is an old story in these parts how he used to hang out around Dry Bayou before this country was all settled up."[9]

The desperados continued riding on down into Morehouse Parish. Benton Hunt said that his father knew Jesse as a friend and that he stayed at a hideout where Overflow Creek runs into the bayou. Buck Mayo heard that they stayed at the Haynes place on the bayou west of Jones. "I have heard all my life that he roamed this area," declared Cecil Harp. "Folks were flattered if Jesse came by." A. K. Watt graciously received a stranger as his guest at his home at Lind Grove. Watt's niece, Mary Haynes Ober, daughter of Jeff Haynes, recalled the story in an early news article. She said that sometime between 1861 and 1865 a rider followed by a Negro man on a pack mule approached Watt's house. The rider handed Watt a note, and when he had read it, he invited the man into his home. He introduced him to his wife as Mr. Carter, a friend. The Negro was sent to the back of the house where he told the Watt servants that they had ridden all the way from Missouri.

"The next morning, Mr. Watt and his guest set out on horseback to find a suitable location for the young man to build a home. At the entrance of a very isolated place, known as Modoc Bend, already a steamboat landing of some importance...a suitable place was found. There Lex James, a first cousin to Jesse and Frank, established a place of refuge for these men." Watt was returning a favor. During the war Union forces in Missouri captured him, and his Negro manservant, Julius, sought help at the James homestead. The family helped him escape and gave him a mule to ride. Colonel Watt told them where he lived and that he would welcome an opportunity to return their hospitality and aid. The James brothers and their cousin used their bayou refuge for years. Although they used assumed names, all who knew them were suspicious of their identities.

"Mrs. Ober recalled hearing her father tell how the true identity of the James brothers became generally known in this section. It happened on a boat on Bayou Bartholomew tied up at Lind Grove. During a card game a card shark was discovered winning the game, and Jesse pulled out his pearl handle pistol with his name engraved on it. The card cheater, in a sharp tone demanded, 'To whom do I owe my disgrace?' The reply came, 'To Jesse James.'" The James brothers visited the area for around ten years, occasionally bringing their families down, with Lex operating and maintaining the farm. They then sold the place to Jeff Haynes, and Lex James went north.

Mr. Haynes remodeled the "very comfortable" house and discovered "a crudely fashioned, but efficient speaking tube from the first to the second floor and a trap door leading down the attic over the kitchen where one could leave the house unseen." The home burned in 1925, destroying many keepsakes, among which was a photograph of Frank James holding his little boy. Frank and Jesse later established a camp southeast of Bonita (in Beouf Swamp), but never stayed any long periods in Morehouse Parish again.[10]

Julia Huff Bryan said that Jeff Haynes sheltered horses for the James brothers as well as for Cole Younger. "Once Jesse held up a carpetbagger on the bayou and took everything he had except his team and buggy. He left him standing in his drawers," she said. T. Y. Harp also recalled stories about the James brothers "often" being in the parish. "About a mile south of Uncle Jim White's house there is still a place known as the James field. This is on the Cooper Cypress brake where Mr. Gabe Moss lived... An old darkie named Bob Owens...cooked for the James boys... Bob was a slave then. The James boys stole him in Tennessee on the way down here. They found Bob, a boy of about 12 years old, standing in the road...The late Newton Huff [of Lind Grove] used to sell the James boys groceries. Jesse had a mulatto son somewhere on Bayou Bartholomew. I was never able to learn what became of the boy. Cole Younger's mulatto boy was lynched in Old Floyd in West Carroll Parish for killing a white man with a butcher knife. Outside of taking U.S. Army horses I have never heard of the James boys disturbing the local people...It is my private opinion that the James boys were not here to hide out but to relax. And it is my public opinion that the sheriffs up in Missouri hunted the James boys about like you would hunt rattlesnakes in your bare feet."[11] They may have, but Bob Ford had his boots on when he shot Jesse James in the back of the head at his home in Missouri on the morning of April 3, 1882.

Lynching, Atrocity, and Murder

> *They all took him down to the bayou to hang him.*
> **Charles Bishop**

Jesse should have stayed at his house on Bayou Bartholomew – not that it was always a peaceful place. It was in fact a preferred place for lynchings and other atrocities. "They hanged a fellow across the bayou on the bank at Persons Bridge," Alvie Pugh said. "There was a hanging tree on the bayou at Rose Hill, and a man was burned at the stake by it at Gourd," said Lloyd Smith. Edward Williams was lynched at Baxter in August 1897.[12] A black man accused of attempted rape of a white woman was hanged on the bayou at Dermott, and another black man was hanged on the bayou between Parkdale and Wilmot for the same reason. Herman King said a big sycamore tree in Free Negro Bend was the hanging tree and that it is still standing. The charred remains of a black man were placed in a tub on the bank south of Wilmot. Two Crawley men hanged a man at Crawleys Bend. "Daddy took me and showed me the big oak tree," said Ella Crawley Vail. A black man accused of attempted rape near Jones managed to escape. He was captured the next day and hanged in Bastrop. Mildred Harrison heard about a hanging that took place on the bayou at Knox Ferry. Across the river from the mouth at Ouachita City, a large persimmon tree was the hanging tree. It still stands.

Charlie Bishop witnessed the Dermott hanging. "I was about fourteen at the time – 1926. I'd heard that a black man tried to rape a white woman, and some men in town caught him. But they didn't take him to jail…they took him out in the woods. And they held him there until about four o'clock in the afternoon while more men from town were rounded up. That's when I heard they had him, and I went out there too. They all took him down to the bayou to hang him. They tied the man's hands behind him and sat him on a horse behind another man who was sitting in the saddle. There was a ravine beside that hanging place, and when they had the noose around the black man's neck, the rider of the horse just rode off into that ravine causing the black man to be lifted off the horse and strung up. I had been watching all along, but once that rider took off, I could only watch for about a half a minute. The way it was done was awful. It hadn't broken his neck. He was a swinging to and fro, his hands tied behind his back, and he was making terrible gurgling noises. That was all I could take of it."

Chick Davis swung from a rope in Wilmot in July 1899. Several people remembered the lynching of Winston Pounds that took place near Wilmot on August 25, 1927.[13] Ernie Sprinkle explained, "This white lady's husband was gone, but two other ladies were in the house. A black man came in and was choking her, and the other ladies heard and ran in there. I don't think she was raped." Earl Kitchens told a different version. "My daddy told me about it. Piney [the man's nickname] was working as a yardboy on the place, and he got accused of peeping at the man's wife. They got up a posse and caught him and hanged him on the bayou close to George Porter's place. The tree is still there," Earl stated. Jack Gibson's father went out with the posse in his nightshirt. "They used bloodhounds to track him," Jack said. "I saw the body hanging in the tree the next day." William deYampert said that the man was accused of attempted rape, but that his father thought that the mob made a bad mistake and that the man was innocent. In this case the accused was a black man, but how easy it was in those days for a white man to commit a crime and then quickly blame it on a Negro. All he had to say was, "Old so and so did it," and off they went after him. From that point on, the man never had a chance to vindicate himself. How many innocent blacks swung from a rope as the real perpetrators smirked in the mob?

Leroy Haynes told the story of the washtub burial by the bayou. "There was a colored couple that lived out on the place where Fred Montgomery lives now. The man had killed someone on the place and the wife knew about it. They got in a fuss one day and she threatened to tell on him. They were out in the cotton patch and another woman and man heard them. So the man killed them all – his wife and the other two – with a chop axe in the head and then put a bullet in their head. Then he ran to his house and locked himself in. When they started coming after him, he set fire to the house and burned up in it. The men put his remains in a tin tub and carried the burnt body to the bayou. They just set it on the bank and left it. A gum tree grew up through it, and a little bit of that tub is still there."

Oral tradition tells of many murders taking place on or near the bayou. On an Easter Sunday a Mr. Silverspoon went in the Thomas store at Tarry. He bought an onion for chicken dressing and walked out the door only to be met by a fatal bullet. At the Yorktown bridge a riot was barely avoided around 1921 after a white posse killed a black man for telling a white lady that she looked nice. "We kept all the lights out and were ready to run to the gully in case they came to the house," said Nell Fullbright Lyle who was around six at the time. Mr. Burton, an old black man, was murdered by another black man near Todd. "There were some mysterious deaths on the bayou in the late twenties. They were three drifters, two blacks and one white, I believe," said Edgar Norris. "They were buried on Wells Bayou around the Avery place."

Stewart Condren and his wife, Mary, were murdered on or near the bayou in Drew County in 1851. This slaying remained unsolved, and the

Condren children, one of them a newborn, were taken in by neighbors.[14] A small notice appeared in the Gazette in 1871. "On the night of the 4th inst., on Bayou Bartholomew, in this county [Drew], Wm. Hoge [*sic*, Hogue] was killed by J. H. Moreland." On September 7, 1894, W. A. Jones shot and killed Harry Beltzhoover "near Tillar station." The perpetrator was "low, heavy set, black...with enamel teeth...a singing school teacher and barber by profession."[15]

These murders did not receive much public attention, but one in 1896 did. William F. "Willie" Skipper arose early at his Baxter home on the morning of May 13 for another day of work tending to his timber business, which included a shingle mill on the bayou upstream from Baxter. Frank McKay, a black man, came to his house to tell him that Alex Johnson, one of Skipper's hands, sent word that a log raft was threatening to break up and that he should come to check on it. Skipper walked to the site about a mile up the bayou where he met his hands (all black), Johnson, Jim Redd, Sam Lusk, and John Bradford. The next instant one stepped from behind him and demanded money. A scuffle ensued during which one man ripped off his vest while another put a cloth sack over his head and threw him into the bayou. Skipper floated down the current to log drift and caught hold. Redd then jumped into the bayou, grabbed him, and stabbed him in the throat. All the men dragged him to the bank, went through his clothes, and after finding no money, took his pocket knife and placed it in his hand to make it look like suicide. They hung his vest containing a gold pocket watch on an ironwood tree and walked away after tying pads around their feet to hide their tracks.[16]

Skipper's son, Walter, carried lunch to the mill for his father at noon and not finding him there, walked upstream looking for him. The boy continued looking and returned to Baxter around four in the afternoon. He told his uncle, J. S. Bulloch, that he could not find his father and Bulloch formed a search party. "The searchers soon came upon his dead body lying face down on the overflow bank of the Bayou in a pool of congealed blood. His throat was cut...." The inquest "rendered a verdict of suicide, the circumstantial evidence showing he had attempted to drown himself and failing in this had used his knife for the fatal effect." Family members and Skipper's business partner, William Henry Lephiew, refused to believe the suicide theory, and Lephiew launched his own investigation. In June the four men were arraigned and charged with murder before Justice Henry Lephiew (father of William Henry) at Baxter. Redd was held and the others discharged.

Bradford and Lusk left the country, and Redd and Johnson were convicted of first degree murder in September. After two appeals to the state Supreme Court and another trial, the two men awaited their third trial in the Monticello jail. On July 14, 1898, five days after the third trial was granted, Sheriff J. H. Hammock was out of town. At three o'clock in the morning a mob of men entered the jail, demanding custody of the prisoners from the jailer. He refused and they stormed into the cage where the men were being held with the intention of taking them out and lynching them. The *Advance* reported, "Redd and Johnson were confined in an iron cage, and the mob made a rush for it. The door was opened, but the doomed and desperate men defended themselves as best they could and it was closed. The mob surrounded the cage and a storm of death-ladened lead was poured in from all sides." Johnson was killed and Redd slowly died from wounds to the head. A coroner's jury ruled the same morning that they "met their death at the hands of parties unknown."[17]

R. H. "Butch" Dennington and Clifton Trigg grew up in Dermott and they recalled the rough and tumble days from the 1920s to the 1940s. "Those were wild times. Some of the men carried guns and there was some feuding going on. One time three blacks were robbing and causing trouble. Jim Bennett got on his horse and rode them down and killed all of them," Clifton said. "Charlie Skipper [deputy sheriff] and Tom Crook were tough. You heeded what they said. Once a family was accused of stealing hogs and they got up a posse composed of Charlie and Tom, and Louis Kirby's father, Charlie Bishop, Charlie Mays, Jim Bennett and others. They hid out at both ends of Skipper Bridge at the bayou, and when the family started to cross it, they let them get to the middle of it and then they all began shooting."

Several Chinese families came to Dermott as peddlers and eventually established grocery stores. The other town merchants felt threatened by the competition and trouble ensued. Around 1928 two businessmen carried a Chinese man to the back of their store, tied him over a barrel, beat him with a strap, and knocked out his eye. The Chinese Consulate came to investigate, but no one would talk. One of the merchants dynamited two Chinese groceries one night. The owners, Wahl and King, left town.[18]

From Dermott the bayou drifts down to Jerome, formerly called Blissville. Things were not so blissful on January 19, 1908. Deputy Sheriff J. Ed Chambers was preparing to go to bed when a Negro woman knocked on his door. Trembling and excited, she told him that Jim Dooley "was on a spree and waving a pistol" and she was afraid he would do her bodily harm. Chambers went to investigate around ten o'clock and demanded Jim to give up his pistol. Instead Dooley fired pointblank at the deputy. "Take me boys, I am killed!" he cried. His cry brought neighbors to the scene, but within two minutes he was dead. Dooley "took to his heels and sought refuge in the woods." A posse left Dermott early the next morning as indignation rose to "fever heat" in Blissville with speculation that "the negro's neck would be endangered if caught...." A little less than a month later, Nathan Reeves, alias Will Dooley, alias Jim "Goldy" (for his gold tooth) was hemmed in by a posse near Laconia on the Mississippi River. He defied arrest, and "the officers were forced to kill him."[19]

Portland was the site of at least five lynchings from 1891 to 1909. Henry Jones, a black man, beat his wife to death in 1891. A mob composed of both races, mostly black, took him from jail and hanged him from a tree. In June 1895 Frank King, a black man, shot and killed William Tony, a Negro preacher. "King was hung to the limb of a tree on the outskirts of town by a Negro mob...." A black man shot but did not kill A. J. Roddy, a white businessman in 1902. It was reported that Roddy had whipped the man's brother a few days before. "The Negro who did the shooting...was captured at Wilmot Tuesday evening, brought up to Portland on the midnight train and hanged to the nearest tree to the spot in front of the saloon where he fired the shot." A black man shot and killed Walter Cain, a deputy sheriff, when Cain attempted to arrest him. While bloodhounds trailed the murderer a mob hanged his brother from a telephone pole in town. Young Felix Pugh wrote to his cousin, "He is still hanging up there but mama won't let us go up to see him. It is so bad." A mob lynched Joseph Blakely in May 1909.[20]

In 1892 a farmer named Brazelton from Bonita arrived in Portland looking for two black tenants who had left his farm owing him money. Finding one, he shot but did not kill him. Brazelton refused to surrender to the local authorities as they were "all negroes" and took refuge in a store. The local blacks became incensed over the shooting and patrolled the town with guns keeping close watch over the store. A white deputy from an adjoining township arrived, persuaded the mob to disperse, and took Brazelton into custody. Word of the incident spread by train passengers into Louisiana, and about 150 men from Louisiana armed with Winchesters and side arms arrived in Portland at one o'clock in the morning aboard a chartered train. Brazelton made bond and left with his wounded Negro on the train the next morning. As the train passed through Parkdale, they celebrated their "bloodless victory" by firing "about a thousand shots."[21]

Earl Bishop related a hideous event that took place in Anthony Lake located in Free Negro Bend. "One of the several pools in King Tut Lake [a nickname] was called Whiskey Pool – this one had a large stump in the center. An old colored man's relatives believed he had a lot of money. One night they took him out and tied him to the stump. When he wouldn't tell them where the loot was buried, they poured hot moonshine down him until he died. They never found the money – it may not have existed."[22]

In June 1908 Louis Johnson, a black man, shot his wife in Parkdale. Another black man, Ernest Williams, probably wished that he had been mercifully shot as he gasped his last breath in June the same year. The man somehow provoked the wrath of the town's women of his own race, and they instigated their own vengeance. "A mob of enraged negro women dragged [him] to a telegraph pole on the outskirts of Parkdale...and lynched him...Negro women of the town are reported to have organized a league to enforce better moral conduct by their race, and to protect them from negro men. It is alleged Williams' conduct was offensive to some of them, and that they captured him one night and took his life...The lynching occurred between 8 and 9 o'clock at night...and the body was not discovered by officers of the law until the next day. The Coroner's Jury returned a verdict that the man had met death by being strangled with a grass rope at the hands of persons unknown." The *Gazette* reported, "This is probably the first instance in the history of the state where a man has been lynched by a mob of women...."[23] "They didn't mind killing one another back then," said 104 year old Nancy Tharp. "Rube Hill [a black] got killed in Parkdale by another man's wife. She had to kill him to keep him from killing her."

An ongoing animosity between H. C. Dade and two men, Ed Dunn (eighteen to twenty years old) and a Mr. Turnbow, all white, ended with fatal shots on the streets of Parkdale. Dade and his "about grown" son were walking when Dunn and Turnbow approached them in a wagon. They drew weapons immediately; Dade fired but his pistol snapped. Dunn jumped from the wagon and fired, "the ball from his pistol striking Mr. Dade just below the eye and passing through his head, causing almost immediate death. Seeing his father fall dead, Ivey Dade opened fire on his slayer and each party fired five shots to the other without effect." Dunn took one of the horses from the wagon and left. It was not known if Dade intended to shoot Dunn or Turnbow as enmity existed between him and both men.[24]

"Parkdale was terrible," said Mary Morris Foster. "There were a bunch of outlaws; it was a shoot-up town. People were always getting run out of town. There was a rough and rowdy white element here. It was wild." Y. W. Etheridge gave some explanation. He wrote, "With liquor voted in at Parkdale in the general election in 1896, the Missouri Pacific trains running, a sawmill or two in the community and an influx of new population, this was a boistrous community. It is said that a conductor on the north bound passenger train who had a drunk passenger on his coach during this period and did not know where the man wanted to go kept waking him up at each stop and asking him. The invariable answer was that he wanted to get off at hell. Finally the conductor said, 'Well, I'll just put you off at Parkdale.'"[25]

In 1898 R. N. "Jim" Ward shot and killed Dr. Charles Parkel as he drove his buggy down Parkdale's main street. "The horse began to run...The dead man was still sitting erect in the buggy holding the reins...."[26] Mark Hawkins told how his great-uncle was killed. "Around

1910 Cecil Dade and Will Brane were gambling in a house on the bayou. They got into it and Dade shot and killed and robbed Will Brane, who was my grandfather's brother. Dade then drug the body to the railroad track hoping the train would run over it to make it look like an accident. But when they found the body the next morning, Mr. Dade's dog was still sitting by it and they knew by that who killed him." Ernie Sprinkle remembered that Dade was sent to the penitentiary for the crime.

Ernie Sprinkle was raised in Parkdale and told about several murders. She said that John Turnbow Ralph witnessed a murder during a poker game. "Later on one night he got shot through a window in his home. I guess they killed him to keep him from telling. In the thirties Hawkins Barnes was drunk and the marshal told him to leave town. Hawkins tried to run over him with his horse so the marshal shot him. Around 1923 Mr. McDonald, the railroad agent, was in the depot at night and a man tried to rob the station. So he fought back and killed him." All this activity in Parkdale provided a good business for Brames Mercantile in Wilmot. Mark Hawkins said, "My mother said they had coffins upstairs. Every Sunday morning two to three people from Parkdale would be there to get coffins."

Sometime in the 1890s Aunt Caroline, a black lady, witnessed a stabbing during a fight on the John Sims Barnes place and had to go to court in Hamburg as a witness. Ernie Sprinkle's grandmother and her sister went along for the buggy ride and often repeated what happened during the trial. Judge Marcus Hawkins said, "I understand you are the only one who saw the fracas?" Aunt Caroline replied, "No, Judge, I didn't say the fracas. I said it was between the navel and the fracas." The court broke out in laughter and had to adjourn.

An early town marshal was no Wyatt Earp. Stories about Frank Barnes abound. Y. W. Etheridge told a story about him in 1959. Saying the anecdote took place in 1896 or 1897, he wrote, "Frank Barnes rode his mule into town, got more to drink than he needed and was running up and down the street 'popping off' both with his gun and his mouth. T. L. Atkin assayed to arrest him and called G. P. George in to assist him. Gun shots were exchanged between George, who emptied his gun at Barnes, and the latter who wounded George. George was given another gun by his brother and with it he wounded Barnes as he rode off. A local Baptist preacher went to see the wounded men, calmed them down and got them to agree that the one who got able to go see the other first would go and make friends. This they did, as it is said, and remained friends thereafter.[27]

Barnes was related to Ernie Sprinkle, and she told about him. "Frank Allen Barnes was the town marshal when he was young. He rode to town everyday on a gray mule. He drank all the time, and when whiskey was no longer legal, he drank antiseptic. He was the biggest liar in the country. I think when he was marshal he killed a man, an escaped murderer. He shot at my grandfather one time and the bullet went through his hat." Mary Morris Foster remembered him. "He rode a white donkey and was always singing and drunk. The kids were scared of him. I never heard of a marshal. I think they just fought it out." Mark Hawkins said, "He had a long white beard and rode a white mule. He hid whiskey all along his route." John Sumner Barnes is his nephew. He said, "His white horse was named Cal. One time he rode to Monticello and started playing Santa Claus with the children on the square and it was in the middle of July. Another time he caught a black boy stealing his apples. He made him get in the tree and eat apples until he got sick." Frank Barnes had a peculiar way of teaching a lesson. Charles Sidney Gibson remembered this tale that was told to him by a Mr. Hicks. "He knew a Negro was stealing his chickens, and one day one rode by with two live chickens hanging off the saddle. Mr. Barnes said, 'You like chickens, do you?' 'Yes sir,' the man replied. 'Well, you go ahead and eat them now,' Barnes said. 'But they ain't picked; they ain't cooked,' retorted the Negro. He made that man eat those chickens – feathers, guts, feet, and beak!" Beth Thurman heard a story about the white-gray donkey-mule-horse named Cal. "When Frank Barnes was dying, the horse came and stood with his head through the man's window all during his final hours." R.I.P., Mr. Frank Barnes, town marshal nonpareil.

There was a shooting at Crawleys Bend. "A Sutherland man shot Rufus Logan at the Haynes place. He had to shoot him two or three times. He was a crack shot, but it is hard to hit a running target in the back. The sheriff only came to our part of the country when he was running for office," Robert Crawley said. Zachary was a segregated community; only black day laborers were allowed to work there. Benton Hunt said, "One time a black moved into Zachary and my father and his friends went and shot into his house. The man came out and shot back. The next day the house was empty. It was ten years before another black moved in." In 1931 on a farm west of Bonita a tenant and his landlord got into an argument over some cotton sacks and farming implements. The landlord shot the tenant three times with a .38 pistol, but he recovered. The landlord was not so fortunate. Gunfire from the tenant's son-in-law proved fatal.

Ouachita City is reputed to have been the scene of many murders during its heyday in the last half of the nineteenth century. The details of the murder of John Benjamin Sims on Christmas Eve 1881 was told "over and over" in the family. Jimmy Montgomery of Bastrop was Sims' grandson, and he wrote the story for Sims' great-grandson, George Sims, who edited it for publication. John Sims went to a store, which had a saloon in it, to buy Christmas presents. In the back of the building the storekeeper was "getting on a black man," and Sims went back and separated them. "Grandpa was following the [black] man through the store and, as they passed a dry salt meat box, the storekeeper (who was a very high-tempered man) grabbed the [butcher] knife and stabbed John Sims clear through, the point of the knife coming out in front. A death blow to the heart. (Note: The storekeeper seems to have blamed the murder on the black man.)

"They carried him home and dressed him for burial, but they couldn't stop the blood from showing on his white shirt. The next morning, as Mamma [six years old] ran in to get her toys, she saw her papa in the coffin. She said that every Christmas as long as she lived she could see that spot of blood on his shirt. Later on Christmas day, the shopkeeper's wife and her children brought a buggy full of toys out to Mamma and her sisters and Brother George. On the storeowner's deathbed, he confessed to the killing. She [Mamma] never mentioned what happened to the black man."[28]

John I. Smith told about a rape case in the Garrett Bridge area. Sam Swift, a black man, was a tenant on the Ed T. Smith bayou farm. He was a good worker but spent all his spare time chasing after women. Another tenant, Ed Noland, "surprised Sam with his daughter in our pasture, but was unable to catch Sam, and he had Sam arrested for rape. The justice asked the daughter if Sam raped her. She answered 'yes.' Then he asked her, 'For how long?' and she said, 'Six months.' That, of course, ended the case. Ed [Noland] took his family and went to California."[29]

Bill Bishop remembered how Dermott boys were taught a forceful lesson in conduct at Skipper Bridge. "Marshall Snow Davis knew most of the teenagers who misbehaved were good kids, so when one would acted up, he figured the child just needed some extra attention. When that was the case, he would pick up the offender and take him to Skipper Bridge on Bayou Bartholomew. Once there, he would 'let' the teen bend over the bridge railing. Then he would take his belt - and after a brief working over with the belt, he would let him walk home. He figured by the time he had walked that distance, he'd had a chance to ponder his deed. The marshal almost never had to discipline the same child twice."[30]

Moonshine and Saloons

There were stills all up and down the bayou.

Leroy Haynes

"Yeah, they drank a lot in those days," said Robert Crawley. "Times were hard and they were sick a lot from malaria. It just made them feel better; it helped their attitude." Jack Gibson reiterated, "There were hardships on men and women. Everybody came in to town and blew off steam. Some women drank but not in the open. They would be glassy-eyed in the store." Charles Naff told about some ladies "sipping" in Jones. "My great-grandmother, Lottie Bain, took me with her to Jones to visit my great-aunt, Mary McDuffie Naff. The women had a little club that met at A's and Z's – that stood for Mrs. Adams and Mrs. Zachary who were sisters and lived together. They would have Bible study meetings and always had a very stylish decanter of sherry to serve. It never ran dry. They all got in great spirits and gloriously drunk." "My father always kept a bottle on the mantle and would serve anyone who came, but if he knew someone was coming who would drink it all up, he would hide it," Ernie Sprinkle said. Ella Vail said, "One time I was staying with my uncle during high water so I could get to school in Wilmot. I was in the second grade. He would fix us a hot toddy everyday before we went to school!"

Moonshine? "Oh, heck, everybody made whiskey back then – everyone was so poor. I knew a Methodist preacher who made it to sell; he was starving to death," Jack Gibson quipped. Leroy Haynes said, "Oh, Lord! In the thirties everybody was a moonshiner. There were stills all up and down the bayou. I drank some one time out of a dirty tin cup. It was so hot it liked to have burned my insides out. One time I was squirrel hunting on the bayou and found a neighbor's still. There were three barrels of mash uncovered and one of them had a dead buzzard in it. I guess he got to drinking it and got drunk and fell in and drowned." Leroy described the biggest still he ever saw. "It looked like a young sawmill," he said.

Stills were scattered along the entire length of the bayou, which afforded a hiding place as well as a good source of water. Harvey Chambliss, who grew up on the bayou south of Pine Bluff said, "A lot of our black help moonshined a lot. They made it on the bayou because they could drive a pipe down in the springs for water. I rode my horse a lot and knew where all the stills were. One time they forgot to pay the county deputy and he let the revenuers pick them up. They had to quit after World War II began because they couldn't get any sugar." Shorty Lyle said there were stills around Persons Bridge. "I went and watched them making it. One guy paid for his farm with moonshine money." Murphy Brockman knew this man as well. "He bought an eighty-acre farm for thirty-five dollars an acre and he sold the moonshine for a dollar a pint. They caught one guy making it, and he was using one of my old chemical poison barrels to cook it in. I doubt he even washed it out!"

Amos Sledge told about a big still at Five-Mile Brake (now Lake Wallace). "They were hid out in the brake in the button willows and had a plank boardwalk going into it," Amos said. Charlie Bishop discovered this still during a frog-gigging trip. "We got in [the boat] with the carbide light, and got out into that brake. And directly we came upon a bunch of logs tied together with brush and tar paper tied and wrapped in with the logs. So we held that light up and looked a bit harder. And even though none of us had ever seen one before, we knew what we were seeing was a whiskey still. And we also knew that if the owner of it saw us, we'd be having trouble. So that ended that frog gigging trip." Herbert Greenway said Jess Millard had a still near Jerome. "One day my uncle was walking down the road and Uncle Jess called to him to take a drink from his gallon of 'shine. He took one and Jess asked him how he was feeling and to take another one. After the third drink Jess told him that he had the jug hidden in the cotton patch and he just wanted to make sure that none of his kinfolks had found it and put poison in it."

"They made it on the bayou at Thebes," said James Bealer. "I used to get a hold of some. Four bits or a dollar." John Spivey was logging near Portland when he found a path leading up from the bayou. He followed it to a still on a high bank. "They were real ingenious," he said. "Instead of having to carry the water to put on the worm or condenser, they had rigged a rope to use to drop a bucket down to the bayou and pull up their water. I tell you one thing – that still sure didn't win any sanitary awards!" Herman King said his cousin had a still on Indian mound at Free Negro Bend. Nancy Tharp said, "Yes, people made it and got taken to jail. They called it shiny. J. R. Smith made it on the Sumner place near Parkdale. There was always a gang around his place of business." Mary Currie said that her grandmother, Vesta deYampert, said that some men used to make rum out of uncooked molasses around Wilmot. "They let the ribbon cane juice ferment. Some of the men around here died after drinking it." Some Wilmot bootleggers were caught. The local paper reported in 1912, "Last week some of the city officials and Deputy Sheriff Chesnutt got busy and took several negro bootleggers into custody.... The officers are determined that bootlegging shall become a very unprofitable occupation in Wilmot."[31] Ella Vail told of stills across the bayou from the Crawley place. "We would go pick berries and we could smell it cooking. Mama would make us be quiet and get out of there. She would say we could get shot."

"There were a lot of stills around McGinty," said Buck Mayo. "One of my first jobs was being a water boy for my uncle. I'd get water out of an old slough and put it in the fermenting barrel at night along with tadpoles, crawfish, and minnows. The ferment would kill them and they would swell and come to the top, and I would skim them off. When the mash got really ripe he would put it in a cooker and build a fire under it. When it started boiling, the steam with alcohol in it came up and went through a coil. The coil went through a container with about ten gallons of cold water in it. That cooled the steam and then it went into the thumper keg – it made a thumping sound. What steam hadn't converted back to alcohol converted to fluid and dripped out a pipe into a container. The first that came out was pure very strong and blue-looking. The longer it ran, the weaker it got. They let it run until the last part weakened the first part down to the proof they wanted. To test it for the proof they would put it in a pint bottle and shake it, and it would make a foam called a bead. They could tell by the way the foam and bubbles set about what proof it was."

The best made moonshine reached 180 proof or 90 percent. No wonder it was called white lightning! Ed Sanders told a story that attests to its potency. "My grandpaw visited his favorite moonshiner one afternoon. On the return trip, his Model T Ford ran out of gas. Grandpaw thought the matter over and decided that what he had just purchased was near enough 180 proof that it ought to make good fuel. He cautiously, so as to not pour too much, poured some in the fuel tank. A few twists of the crank and he was back in business."[32] Charles Naff also used moonshine for gasoline. "We found stills along the bayou near Portland in the 1950s. It was in galvanized barrels and would give you jakeleg if you drank it. We got some to take camping with us. If the car ran out of gas, it would run on moonshine. It did better in the car than it did in us. It was pretty volatile stuff!"

One of the best known moonshiners in Morehouse Parish was a black man named Jesse Harris. Bobby Abraugh loves to tell the story of Jesse and his famous Black Cat Saloon, which was near Jones. "During Prohibition and Depressions days he had his still out in Niemeyer-Darragh Brake less than a mile from the bayou. This was a large cypress brake, and he had to have all his raw materials – sugar, rye, barrels – carried across on a wooden walkway. The brake was filled with snakes and alligators. Then the finished product had to be carried out where it was taken to his house by car. There a long line of waiting and eager customers picked it up. His retail business was so good that he later constructed a night club honky-tonk on Highway 165 called the Black Cat. The institution stayed open for a number of years and was popular with the black and white community except for the preachers." Mike Doles interjected, "The Black Cat became the White Cat on Friday night!"

Bobby continued, "After Prohibition ended he continued making it and was arrested later by the Feds and sentenced to the pen for a year and a day. He had accumulated a lot of property but after he got out of the pen, he had to sell most of it to support his family. He had a lot of ventures – drilling for water, logging, sawmills, and farming – but none ever as profitable as his moonshining business. In the early fifties a Pentecostal minister showed up and had a revival at the Harris house. Mr. Harris and his family got saved and took religion seriously. He later built a Pentecostal church on the site of the old Black Cat Saloon. It was very successful with a large following and a competent minister. They later built a nice new church in Jones that is still going." When Oren Robertson was in high school he delivered groceries for Scott Buatt's store. His deliveries to the cotton house by the Harris place consisted of sugar and rye. He told how they sold the whiskey. "One time I was in their house and someone came to buy. They had four or five barrels on a rack. Mrs. Harris put a hose in a barrel and sucked on it to get it flowing and then put it in their jar."

Chuck, Winifred, and Frank Day visited several stills along the bayou and Chemin a Haut Creek where they found yellow jackets floating in the mash. "They didn't measure a good corn crop by bushels per acre in those days," Chuck said. "They measured it by gallons per acre!"

Of course legal alcoholic beverages were also available. In 1849 William Stephenson petitioned the Ashley County Court to sell "spirits" at or near his own residence on "barthalamew." After paying his six dollar fee, the clerk was "ordered to Grant the said Dram shop license to said Stephenson for the Term of six months...in the township of Debastrop."[33] One of the first trade buildings in Dermott after the railroad came was a saloon. The number grew to six or seven before the 1920 Prohibition. In 1896 two advertisements from Dermott appeared in the Drew County newspaper. Gasters Saloon offered "Pure Whiskey" that could be ordered by mail or telegraph with "Prompt Delivery" promised. J. F. Patton's ad read, "Order in the morning and take a 'smile' before supper."[34] Clifton Trigg told the story of one hapless saloonkeeper. "Mrs. Higgins' first husband, Mr. Jones, struck a match and put it in the bung of a whiskey barrel to check it. The barrel exploded and blew off his head." After Prohibition bootleggers kept the town supplied in whiskey.

Portland had three Blind Tigers (illegal saloons) in 1895. J. W. Pugh wrote that year, "Drunken people on the streets all the time." The following year a fourth saloon was in place. The county voted dry in 1896 with the exception of Portland and DeBastrop Townships, but by 1902 the county court was again licensing saloons. "...two at Portland, two at Parkdale, one at Wilmot, Montrose, and Morrell." Bob Pugh said, "At one time Portland had five saloons."[35]

"There were Blind Tigers on the bayou at Poplar Bluff," said Ernie Sprinkle. As it became a railroad town, joints and saloons lined the track, and "all the stores had a back room for drinking and gambling," said Mark Hawkins. "Tom Rowen had a well-known joint for blacks. People would come from St. Louis and elsewhere. There would be a hundred or more. They would have a barbecue, drink, and shoot craps. They played a dice and card game called cotch that would last for days," Mark said. Ernie Sprinkle remembered a black joint across the track. "It was called the C-Berg. You could hear the music all over town." Mary Morris Foster described the calaboose. "It was a little square wood building with four little windows with bars. The drunks wound up there and you could hear them begging, 'please give me a glass of water.'"

"There was beer and wine joints in Wilmot in the thirties," Earl Kitchens said. "Sometime it got pretty lively." It got lively in Jones as well, where Ed Bell owned a popular saloon. He opened it in the 1920s and maintained a flourishing business until the mid-1930s. Jack Gibson said, "That place was the center of things, and on Saturday nights there would be a keg of whiskey behind every store." The saloon building, later used for a post office, still stands by the highway. A saloon was in the Bonita area before it became a town. T. Y. Harp wrote that school was held in 1890-1891 "in an old abandoned jerry built saloon."[36] At one time there were four saloons in the town. The last building Bayou Bartholomew flowed past was a barroom. "There was a large saloon on the Morehouse Parish side of the point," said Ed Jones. "The men went back and forth across the river to it in boats."

The Invisible Empire

When I saw the Ku Klux, I turned the fan on 'em!
Herman King

The Knights of the Ku Klux Klan organized in 1915 as a successor to the Klan of the Reconstruction Period. This self-appointed vigilante league advocated patriotism, domestic safety, loyalty among members, and white supremacy. Although patriotism is a high-sounding term, in this case it meant intolerance of "foreigners," in other words, Catholics and Jews. Domestic safety, another amenable term, meant that members had an obligation to tend to the personal problems of anyone. The group advocated white supremacy in politics, society, and blood.[37] The nighttime spectacles of flaming crosses encircled by white-robed men in white, pointed hoods began to appear along the bayou around 1920. These gatherings were mainly ceremonial in nature and inspired loyalty and fervor among members; other times they were more ominous in nature. The real work of the Klan began in regular organized meetings and then was carried out by committees. The mode of operation was scare tactics with threats followed up by action if the warnings were not heeded. Targets were blacks, Jews, Catholics, men who abused their families, men or women accused of unseemly behavior, promiscuous women, and moonshiners. They also rallied to the support of their own members as well as to others (Protestant white only) in need.

Minutes of the Monticello Klan Number 108 from September 28, 1922, to October 6, 1925, reveal the secret internal structure and some of the activities as well as those of other local orders. The Imperial Wizard was the national director, and under him were the Grand Dragons, one over each state. Each local Klan was numbered, and the Exalted Cyclops presided over Klonklaves (meetings). Under him were the offices of the Terrors that included Klaliff (vice-president), Klokard (lecturer), Kludd (chaplain), Kligrapp (secretary), Klabee (treasurer), Kladd (conductor), Klarogo (inner guard ?), Klexter (outer guard), Klokan Chief (board of auditors, advisors, trustees and investigators), two Klokans (boards), and Night Hawk. Any person not a member of the Klan was called an alien. Dues were twenty-five cents a month (three dollars a year) and increased to a dollar for three months or four dollars a year. Special collections were taken when the need arose. Membership rose rapidly from 52 charter members in September 1922 to 124 reported in April 1923. Attendance at the meetings, which were held from once a month to three times a month, ranged from a high of sixty-four to a low of nine with around an average of forty. Although committee reports were given, the minutes seldom gave relevant detail saying instead "the matter was taken care of."

Only three committees were mentioned, the Klokan and an Emergency and a Shocking Committee. On March 23, 1923, the Shocking Committee was dissolved and another Secret Shocking Committee appointed "due to the Klan Secrets leaking into the possession of aliens." This committee was responsible for writing letters to "every man in Drew County whom we have reason to believe is making whiskey advising him to discontinue..." and to offer a reward of fifty dollars to anyone giving information leading to the arrest and conviction of any party "guilty of manufacturing or selling whiskey" excluding members of the Klan. It asked for the appointment of a secret committee "whose duty it will be to ascertain the names of young people who ride late at night" so that they could advise the parents of the "apparent danger of such amusements."

Benevolent gestures included raising sixteen dollars for two needy women, taking a collection for a widow of a klansman, sending groceries to a family whose head of household was in jail, and looking into the needs of the poor at Christmas. They investigated domestic matters such as a man reported to have whipped his mother, a man of twenty who wrote a letter to a girl of fourteen, a shooting, and a man who deserted his thirteen year old wife. A lady wrote asking for their help "to bring her son to the realization of his duty to her and the family." The Shocking Committee was "to write him a friendly letter."

In June 1923 the group accepted a motion to have the Klokan Committee "report on some women suitable to take up organization of a branch of the Womens K.K.K." The women did organize; in January 1924 a motion was made to offer them the use of their hall. Plans were being made in April of that year to establish a junior order of the KKK. Politically they worked together to help get Klan candidates elected for office. Other business included the appointment of a member "to build a large firey cross for the next meeting" and "to buy another Coleman lantern and ropes and pulleys for the firey cross." They often held large joint meetings where they paraded in uniform and had barbecue and watermelon. Other Klan orders mentioned in Drew County were at New Hope and Wilmar. Those mentioned outside of the county were at Hot Springs, Crossett, Warren, Dermott, and Morehouse Parish.[38]

Some minutes and a membership and dues book of Morehouse Parish Klan Number 34 dating from 1921 to 1924 give insight into this order. On November 1, 1921, the order "naturalized" forty-seven candidates. (After they were naturalized they were no longer aliens; they were citizens of the Invisible Empire.) This order appeared to have around 140 members from throughout the parish as well as from the southeast Arkansas communities of Crossett, Rawls, and Pugh. Bastrop had the largest representation followed by Bonita. Other members mentioned with addresses noted were from Jones, McGinty, Mer Rouge, Oak Ridge, and Collinston. As with the Monticello Klan, the membership list contained the names of merchants, other businessmen, physicians, ministers, and large and small farmers. George Patton summarized, "It appears that the Morehouse Klan set about to rid the parish of thieves, bootleggers, prostitutes, womanizers and other habitual lawbreakers or grossly immoral people."[39]

In December 1921 the Vigilance Committee of the Morehouse Klan distributed leaflets warning "white bootleggers, whiskey distillers and white men with concubines to repent. About 1:30 p.m. on Thursday Dec. 29, 1921, three automobiles came to Bastrop from the direction of Monroe. Each car contained four Klansmen in black robes and with faces covered. There was also a bootlegger held captive in each car. The three cars drove through Mer Rouge, Bonita, and Jones and to the Arkansas line...The 3 bootleggers were let out at the Arkansas line and told not to return." In March 1922 men in black robes captured a white man at Bastrop. He appeared an hour later with a sign on his back that read, "I was whipped for stealing hogs and cattle; and for bootlegging and distilling whiskey, and being an undesirable in general." He had forty-eight hours to leave the parish.[40]

In August some members of the Morehouse Klan became heinously violent. According to reports in the Bastrop newspaper, the events arose out of opposition by Klan members to an anti-Klan movement within the parish. Most local people think, however, that the entire affair originated from a personal vendetta by a prominent Klan member. After a baseball game in Bastrop the Klan, dressed in white robes, set up a roadblock on the road to Mer Rouge and captured five (white) men. The black-hooded abductors drove them to a wooded area and whipped four with a leather strap. They released three and kept two, who were never seen again. The fate of the two kidnapped men was not known until four months later when their mutilated bodies rose to the surface of Lake LaFourche after it was dynamited – probably in an attempt by the perpetrators to further destroy evidence.[41] Only then the true horror of their death became known. They were brutally tortured by being placed in a mechanical crushing device that broke rib, leg, and arm bones, and some organs were removed by a sharp instrument before death. Their heads were crushed and the brains removed. The examining pathologist said the mutilations were "due to atrocities for which medico-legal history...had no parallel." The Grand Jury began investigating the case in March 1923 and nine days later returned a "no true bill" for the kidnapping and murder charges. Lesser charges such as conspiring to murder, conspiring to assault, conspiring to compel people to leave the parish, and assault with a dangerous weapon were levied against eighteen men. Eleven were known Klan members, and others may have been.[42]

Several people remembered seeing the 1920s klansmen. Oren Robertson said around 1925 klansmen stopped his father in their car and searched them. Page Webb was driving one night to see his girlfriend when hooded, robed men stopped him. They recognized him and told him to go on home. "I saw them," said Buster Ford. "When I was quite young they paraded in Model-Ts in their white hoods and robes. They came down McGinty Road around 1925. Aunt Octavia told them her husband was being mean to her, and they got him and took him out and whipped him. But Aunt Octavia was mean herself." Edgar Norris remembered the Klan riding by the church and tossing in bags of money. James Bealer said, "They would scare me when they were coming around. I was around twelve years old. They would beat them with a buggy whip." Herman King had an encounter with klansmen. "They were laying in wait to kill my father coming home from St. Marion Church one night. Boy, they was a ugly thing with those white caps on. When I saw the Ku Klux, I turned the fan on 'em. We took off – what you talking about!"

Other people remembered Klan episodes told by their parents or grandparents. Garvin Adcock's grandfather was in the Klan in Drew County. He told Garvin that they swore on the Bible not to take a life and that they only punished people by hanging them by the feet and then taking them down. Chuck Day's grandfather said that they not only corrected blacks but also anyone who mistreated their family or would not work. Winifred Day said, "It began as a good thing and then turned into vigilantes." "In my father's early times the Klan tried to keep people in line," said Robert Crawley. "It was not a racial thing. For example, if someone was beating their wife, they advised him that it was not acceptable. If they kept on, they got a flogging." Ernie Sprinkle related that the Klan began "roving around" in the early 1920s. "So one of our Jewish merchants left Parkdale," she said. Klan activity peaked from 1920 to 1924 and then began to abate as public opinion turned against their conduct in the late 1920s. In the 1950s there was a minor resurgence of a new Klan. One man displayed the crisp, white robe worn by his sister in a Wilmot Klan of this period. Ruth Mayo Boone said, "I saw part of the last Ku Klux Klan in Bastrop around 1955. They were in their uniforms on horses parading down Highway 165."

These random examples of lawless activity along the bayou represent man's unfortunate inclination to follow an untamed course, but they pale in light of the wholesome daily life led by the majority. Bessie Fuller Green, born in 1912, said, "It was peaceful back then. I did not hear of police or jail until I was around fifteen. Our parents were our police." Estelle Kimbrell Works said, "It was not rowdy; there were no problems. We were all neighbors regardless of race." Guns did hang on the walls of most bayou homes, but they were for a useful and peaceful purpose. The area abounded in wild game, and bayou people loved to hunt.

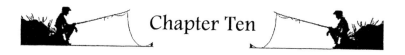

Chapter Ten

Hunters and their Prey

Alligators, Bullfrogs, and Turtles

We would catch alligators and play with them.
Then we started hunting them for food.

Buster Ford

The wilderness bayou and its adjacent brakes, swamps, canebrakes, and forest provided an ideal natural habitat for various aquatic and terrestrial creatures. Within this lush sanctuary the buffalo, elk, bear, deer, wolf, fox, cougar, bobcat, and lynx roamed on age-old trails. Beaver, otter, muskrat, raccoon, opossum, squirrel, and rabbit were plentiful. In and out of the water the alligator and turtle crawled, and the bullfrog hopped. Passenger pigeons, geese, and ducks blackened the sky with their numbers, and wild turkeys were profuse. Adding resplendent flashes of exotic elegance to the landscape were herons, cranes, egrets, and ibises. It was Eden made complete including even the serpent, for the cottonmouth moccasin made his home in the swampy haven. Surely Satan himself sent another critter - the mosquito that tormented both beast and man. Escaping the swarms of the stinging pest were the underwater dwellers. There swam huge gar, buffalo, drum or gaspergou, catfish, and their smaller relatives, bass, bream, perch, and crappie. Given the excusable exigencies of natural behavior in the fight for survival, this wilderness refuge was a serene place.

Of all the bayou creatures the alligator (*Alligator mississippiensis*) is the one most closely associated with it. The name is derived from Spanish for lizard, *el lagarto*, which became *alligarta* in South and Central America. The Spaniards and Frenchmen in Louisiana Territory called him by the name of his cousin, *cocodrile*, pronounced *ko-ko-dree'* in Spanish and *kro-ko-deel'* in French. The Choctaws referred to the tough-skinned reptile as *hachunchuba*, one without hair. They used his hide to fashion a musical instrument. After placing the fresh skin on a colony of ants that ate away the fleshly parts, they hung it in the sun to dry. The music came from scratching the dried hide with a stick. The meat from his tail was considered to be a "great delicacy."[1] This bayou denizen is the largest reptile in North America, and his ancestors walked this earth 160 million years past.

Bayou alligator stories are widespread. Sometime before the Civil War Mariah Hughes and her slave were washing clothes in the bayou below her Poplar Bluff home. Mary Alice Nelson told the story which was passed down through her family. "The slave woman had her baby lying on the bank. All of a sudden an alligator came out of the bayou and swept the baby into its mouth with its tail and went back in. The mother just stood there screaming and screaming."

In 1895 the *Gazette* reported, "Yesterday morning a negro by the name of Logan Clark was hunting on Bayou Bartholomew, near the place of Mr. Louis Cheek, five miles south of Pine Bluff, when he discovered on a log in the bayou an immense alligator. He shot and killed it...the saurian measures ten feet, five inches in length and one of the largest ever seen in this section of the south...Young alligators are frequently seen in the bayou near the place of Mr. Cheek." Reportedly the "largest alligator ever found in Arkansas" was captured on the bayou near Pine Bluff. He was named "Old Pine Bluff" and taken to the Arkansas Alligator Farm in Hot Springs where he lived for a number of years.[2]

Bayou dwellers reported alligator encounters along the bayou and its brakes from Pine Bluff to Wardville. Harvey Chambliss never saw one at his farm southeast of Pine Bluff until after they were stocked; then he ran over two with a disc when he crossed a mudhole. Mrs. H. W. Thomas said "one came up every once in a while" at Tarry. Robert Mitchell saw them in the bayou near Yorktown. "There were a lot around where Turtle Creek runs into the bayou near Yorktown," Murphy Brockman said. Alvie Pugh told about an alligator at Rose Hill. "When I was a little boy I would see them in certain places. One time my uncle was swimming and he got up on one's back. The 'gator tried to turn over and whirled around in the water trying to throw him off. After Uncle got out of there that alligator stirred up the place looking for him." In 1967 a bus driver killed a 9-foot, 175-pound specimen at Rose Hill. John Edd Curry of the Garrett Bridge area began seeing them "around twenty to twenty-five years ago." "The bayou is full of them," said Andrew Pickens of Pickens. Vernon Scott reported seeing many in brakes and sloughs in the Winchester-Tillar area. "I caught one in my net in the bayou at Baxter. We used to put carbide in the brakes to get rid of them," Garvin Adcock said. Earl Kitchens used to swim in the bayou at Wilmot when he was a young boy. "Then I saw two or three of them and I didn't swim there no more!" William deYampert of Wilmot told this alligator story: "There was a black man who was always prowling around with women at night. One night he came back to his house and went in. There were no lights on and he stumbled over something. It was an alligator! He shot it. I saw it; it was six feet long."

Robert Crawley said Arnold Vail shot one seven-foot in length at Crawleys Bend right after World War I. "I had a drowned one in my hoop net around 1948," Robert said.

Page Webb lived just below the state line. "I saw plenty of them. I would not eat them because they are wild and will eat you. You should not eat anything that will eat you," he said. Buster Ford ate them. "We would catch them and play with them. Then we started hunting them for food. We would track one to where he crawled up in a log and bust the log open and get him. I used to help Vernon Sawyer (not the same one here now) catch them. We would find their hole and run a cypress pole in it. He would bite on to it, and we would pull him out with two little mules. Sixteen feet is the biggest I ever saw. Vernon gave us the meat to eat and he sold the hides. We ate the tail first and then learned how to make sausage out of all the meat by mixing some pork in it. The tail tastes like gar." Benton Hunt also caught them. "You have to put a rope around their mouth," he said. "I had one and put a tire in its mouth and then touched the tail. He threw that tire out of his mouth and turned around and bit me. An alligator is safe until you get to his tail. He uses that to knock things in his mouth. Once I had a pet one that I kept tied up on the bayou. I tied turtles to a string to coax him out. Then someone came along and killed him. The largest one I caught was twelve feet. I gave him to the zoo at Monroe."

Cecil Harp caught a twelve foot, six inch alligator at Harp Brake. "It was ice and snow and I was walking over a floating log bridge when I saw one underneath the log with his mouth open. I went back and got a trace chain and put a loop in it and put it around his lower jaw. He clamped down on it and I tied him up. Three blacks came along and saw him. The next day he was killed and his tail gone. I believe they came back and got his tail to eat." This alligator may have descended from Old Lep, "the biggest in Louisiana, it is said." Old Lep lived in Harp Brake, and when the famous hunter, Ben Lilly, visited the Mark Harp home, he always rowed out to see him. He liked to poke him with a stick just to hear him roar, which was distinguishable from the roar of all other alligators. A particular roar forecast rain to fall about two days later. Once Lilly lassoed Old Lep on the bank, but instead of playing the line, he rolled over and over the rope causing Lilly's hand to be caught in it. Just before it seemed he was about to be drawn into the mouth, Lilly rammed his rifle into it and shot him.[3]

Bayou dwellers had little fear of the reptiles. In the late 1940s Bobby Abraugh and Dorman Mayo were grabbing for frogs in Graveyard Brake. "We were in water about waist deep, no hip boots, and a carbide light. We saw a little pair of red eyes and when he swam close to the grabs we grabbed him. That was a mistake. He squealed and here came a pair of *big* red eyes. We got to the bank in a hurry!" Jack Gibson was casual when he encountered the swamp denizens. "When we were frog hunting we would shove them away with our poles. We would wade right next to them when duck hunting. They would break into hog pens and eat them," he said.

The alligator almost disappeared and then reappeared several times along the bayou. Abundant in 1718 (they were crawling about on the streets of New Orleans), Don Juan Filhiol wrote in 1786 that they were thinned out above the Red River and were rare toward Arkansas Post. William Dunbar noted in 1804, "The Aligator [*sic*] goes no farther North than this," referring to a point on the Ouachita about fifteen miles north of "Bay Marau" (Moro Bay in Bradley County).[4] Randomly killed for sport and later hunted for their hides, the giant reptile found refuge in isolated brakes and swamps and some survived the human onslaught. Widespread hide hunting was affecting the population by the late 1920s but continued unchecked. Intensive land clearing for agriculture and wetland drainage efforts contributed to a decline in habitat. Between 1938 and 1958 Louisiana lost ninety percent of its alligators. They were finally given protection in the 1960s by Louisiana and Arkansas as well as by other states. Placement on the Endangered Species List in 1967 secured their future. From 1972 to 1984 Arkansas restocked 2,800 juvenile alligators procured from Louisiana, and the current population is stable.[5]

The alligator is generally a quiet creature except during mating season in early spring when the distinctive bellow (described as something between a moan and a roar) of the bull and the lower answering call of the cow echoes through the swamp. An amphibian, the mighty bullfrog, leads the chorus of nighttime bayou music. These masterful bass singers, using the bayou bank for their podium, begin their deep-pitched call at twilight, and are joined by their smaller kin, the throaty croaking leopard frog. The crescendo swells as petite treefrogs add their varied voices to the orchestra – the shrill click of the cricket frog, the resonating trill of the gray, the jingle bells of the spring peeper, and the rasping warble of the chorus frog. The symphony increases to Wagnerian grandeur only when the choir of several hundred *quanking* green treefrogs chimes in. The silver moon likely views the production with awe and demands an encore night after starry night.

Bayou folks delighted in the bullfrog's croak, but they also relished its delectable white meat. Men and boys hunted them as a sport with gigs, grabs, sticks, and .22s. "All we thought about was frogs," Bobby Abraugh said. "We would get fifty to a hundred a night by grabbing and sell them for twenty-five cents each." Before Bobby's frog hunting days, Shorty Lyle sold his frogs for even less. "My brother and I shot them with a .22 and sold them for a nickel. That would give us more shells to shoot more bullfrogs." Siegfried Johnson said, "We went bullfrogging in the daytime with a .22 single-shot Stevens. After we killed them all out on Wells Bayou, we went over to Bartholomew and got them. We would soak them overnight in salt water and have them fried for breakfast." Cecil Harp used a stick for his frog weapon. "We would go at night with a dim light, a candle, and kill them with sticks by the million." Mrs. H. W. Thomas said that her son, Wally, would go gigging at night and bring home a towsack full. Buster Ford practiced blind gigging whereby he waded waist deep in water thrusting the gig under logs. "When times were hard they let us make a living anyway we could," he said.

Charlie Bishop of Dermott remembered his bullfrogging days. "Another thing we boys enjoyed was catching bullfrogs, and the best place for that was...Five-Mile Brake [now Lake Wallace]. It was just a slough with a few fish in it, but there were millions of big old bullfrogs. My buddies and I would take a carbide light and head down there about dusk. After we'd caught as many as we wanted, we'd make a fire and fry up some of them in the iron skillet we'd brought along. And once in a while one of us would find a few duck eggs along the bank, and we'd fry them up too. But you need to remember, if you're gonna eat duck eggs, you gotta cook them till they are done through and through. Can't have any runny yolk. Otherwise, I'm telling you, you're not gonna want seconds."

Men and boys had their fun simply hunting bullfrogs, but they could also sell them. The Wilmot newspaper reported in May 1939, "Several of the men [at Gayland Plantation at Portland] are catching a lot of frogs. Frog buyers are usually around before breakfast." One of the buyers was evidently Louis Baer from Rayne, Louisiana. The paper said that he was shipping around a thousand frogs a day from Montrose "since last week" to restaurants and hotels all over the United States. He was also shipping "frogs, lizards, snakes, turtles, and aquatic plants to universities and research labs to be used in classwork and experimental purposes."[6] It is commonly said that there are not as many bullfrogs now. This was probably not caused by the seemingly overkill by hunting, but by the indiscriminate use of harmful chemicals by the timber industry and farmers.

Another creature closely associated with the bayou is the turtle, descended from ancient reptilians that appeared about two hundred million years ago. Most notable of the bayou turtles are the spiny softshell, snapping, and alligator snapping turtle. Most considered the softshell, which can reach eighteen inches in diameter, to be the best to eat, and the preferred method of preparing it was frying. Bessie Green liked to bake them. "If you fix them right they taste real good," she said. "Soak them in salt water then drain them and soak them in vinegar. Drain that off and boil in seasoned water. Then roll the meat in flour and put some strips of

bacon on it and bake it. Then pepper and vinegar season it real good."
Both snapping turtles were killed for meat. The alligator snapping turtle or
"loggerhead," as it is often called, is the largest freshwater turtle in the
world. It can grow to over twenty-six inches in diameter and weigh over
two hundred pounds. Often told tales attest to their size. "Gussie Turner
and Frank McKee sold them out of a wagon in Portland. They would be
the size of a number three washtub," said Charles Naff. Buster Ford said,
"I caught one as big as this desk [a standard size office desk]. Three of
them would fill up a wagon. We took a shell off one and made a horse
trough out of it." As for taste, Benton Hunt said, "The loggerhead makes
the best soup you ever ate." This turtle has a ferocious appearance and a
reputation for inflicting an excruciating bite. This led to his becoming a
favorite target for sport only. "We just shot them," said Shorty Lyle.

The loggerhead turtle was also hunted commercially for its meat.
Curly Birch said, "We don't have many loggerheads anymore; it took them
too long to grow. They fished them out of the bayous in Louisiana, and
then some men came up here in the early 1970s and got them out of Tillar
Brake. Five men in five boats went out at night with headlights. They
waited for two sets of bubbles to come up which meant they were walking
on the bottom. They caught them and hauled them in cattle trailers to
Baton Rouge. They hauled them on their backs with their feet tied and
shipped them alive in crates by air. At first the buyers paid fifty cents a
pound and then seventy-five cents. They weighed eighty pounds and were
two and one-half feet across." Curly also imparted some valuable
information. It has always been said that the snapping turtle will not
relinquish his painful bite until it thunders. That could be a long wait.
Curly said, "Shove Johnson grass up their nose to make them turn loose."

Fur, Feathers, and Scales

*He caught a six-foot gar that weighed over
a hundred pounds.*

Ralph Kinnaird

The bayou bottoms provided an ideal habitat for furbearers such as otter, fox, mink, raccoon, opossum, and bobcat. Men turned to trapping in the winter to supplement their income, carrying on a tradition that had its beginnings in the fur trade of the late 1600s. The pelt of the raccoon, whose name came from the Indian name, *arrathkune*, was used for currency just as beaver pelts were used in Canada and the northern states in the early days of the fur trade. (Widespread trapping of beavers continued until they were almost exterminated by the early 1900s.) The otter, which the Choctaws called *oshan*, produced the most valuable fur, a prime pelt bringing from fifteen to twenty dollars in the late 1920s. Following the otter in pelt value was the mink whose top value at the same time was nine dollars. The early French trappers encountered a comely creature that they called *Beta puante* for "stinking beast." Skunk fur brought only one dollar in the late 1920s.[7]

Ben Hunt was a professional trapper using from fifty to a hundred traps. "He set the traps and let the children check them before the school bus ran. We would come back and tell Mother where the varmints were, and he would go get them on horseback. He caught mostly possum, coon, and mink. We ate the possum and coon and sold the fur to the deYampert store in Wilmot," Benton Hunt said. Katie Parker said that her husband, Roosevelt, got five dollars for raccoon, seventy-five cents to a dollar for possum, and around fifteen dollars for a mink. "I made as much off of trapping as I did cotton," said Bealie Harrison. "A coon brought from five to ten dollars, and a skunk from three to four, and a possum a dollar. Papa's hog dog would tree a polecat, but when we got there he would sit down and not help. Them old dogs had lots of sense." With the recent decline in the fur market, created in part by the movement against using animal fur for clothing and the introduction of synthetic fibers, trapping is quickly becoming a lost craft.

Bayou Bartholomew is located along the Mississippi flyway and during migration the sky used to grow black with ducks and geese. Charlie Bishop told about a duck hunting episode near Dermott that took place in the late 1920s. The men left camp to take their five or six deer to town leaving Charlie and his father and a few others in camp. Charlie never had a full box of shells in his boyhood – "couldn't afford one." He wanted to go duck hunting, and a generous man gave him a box of shells. Charlie's father walked about three miles down and came back up scaring up the ducks. Charlie took a stand by a tree in a clearing and began calling them. "It wasn't long before I had what looked like a whirlwind of ducks over the top of me, coming right down through this opening and lighting in the water. And they kept coming and kept coming. And when there were so many that no more could find a place to light, I slowly picked up my gun and aimed and whistled so they'd stick their heads up. And I just shot through the thickest swarm of them. I wound up shooting until I ran out of shells. Then I grabbed me a hickory stick and I ran out through them ducks just hittin' them over the head." The young hunter picked up his ducks and counted as he strung them on wire to float them out. He had killed 152 ducks.

People flocked to the bayou to fish. Fishing was not only a pleasurable pastime, it also provided choice food, and for some, a supplemental income. Folks enjoyed catching crappie, perch, and bream with poles from the banks or from boats. Some gentlemen preferred to fly-fish for Kentucky, spotted, and small-mouth bass. Gigging was a preferred method for many. "We gigged at night. The water was so clear you could see fish on the bottom," Alvie Pugh said. The bayou is known for its gigantic fish. R. N. "Booster" Kinnaird fished the bayou all his life. "He caught six-foot gar that weighed over a hundred pounds. It was commonplace then," said Ralph Kinnaird. Bealie Harrison once caught on his trotline a fifty-pound appaloosa with a five-pound blue cat in its mouth.

Commercial fishermen used nets and trotlines to catch the delicious buffalo and catfish. "My father supported his family by the trade. He made his own nets. He took his fish in a wagon to Jones to sell, and he always had some in his live-box for folks coming by. During the Depression my mother started saving all the one-dollar bills from the fish money. She thought that all other money would become worthless. She put them in fruit jars and hid them in the smokehouse. On her deathbed she told the children to go look in the smokehouse. We found around 7,000 one-dollar bills! They had sweated and ruined, but the bank took them in," said Benton Hunt. Ed Jones fished commercially for many years. "My britches froze to my legs many times while running nets," he said. "I caught buffalo, catfish, and alligator gar. The gar weighed seventy to eighty-five pounds dressed. There's two kinds of gar – the alligator gar has a blunt nose and the scissorbill has a long, narrow nose. People liked to make garballs with the meat – you make them like salmon croquets. The favorite fish was the razorback buffalo and then the flathead or appaloosa catfish." Jess Millard fished in the Jerome area. "He put out hoop nets with wings on them and then got down the bayou and drove the buffalo into them. He got twenty-five cents a pound for undressed fish," Herbert Greenway said.

Estelle Works described the fish drives. "It was my Pap's job to catch the fish for the big fish fry at Panther Brake Plantation. He had a hoop net with wings on each side, and he would stretch it across the bayou downstream from the blacksmith shop. Papa would send all of us kids a ways up stream, and we would play in the water – wading, swimming, splashing, kicking, and making lots of noise which would run the fish downstream into Papa's net!" Another unusual way of catching fish was called "mudding the bayou." Falba Owens Core described the technique to Carolyn Haisty who wrote, "Falba says that she remembers as a child, when her family worked in the logging industry, the lumber company owners or those in charge would send the blacks into the Bartholomew with sticks, and they would stir up the water until it was so muddy that the fish would float to the top to get oxygen. Then those on the bank would grab the fish, and then everyone would have a big fish fry."[8]

Some engaged in outlaw fishing. Although there were some regulations, they were not as stringent as they are now. "We thought 'seasons' were salt and pepper," laughed Charles Adcock. Jack Gibson said, "The telephone came in, and the fish were slaughtered after World War II." "Calling up" stunned fish by electrical shock was not exactly legal. Buck Mayo became a game warden in 1953. He said, "The most complaints we had were about people using shocking machines to get fish." But the typical bayou fisherman was there for pure enjoyment. "We didn't have a boat and set out and checked our trotlines by swimming. If we caught a fish we would go borrow someone's boat to go get him," said Buster Ford. "We would paddle the boat way up the bayou and then float back down fishing," Bessie Green said. Charles Naff said, "The black women loved to fish more than anybody. If they weren't working, they were fishing."

Panthers, Wolves, Bear, Deer, and Hogs

I put two shots in his head, but he
got up and started coming after me.

Leroy Haynes

The animals inhabiting the great wilderness of bayou county lured the earliest hunters and trappers, the *coureurs de bois* who began roaming southward from New France (Canada) in the latter part of the 1600s. Spanish hunters from southern Louisiana began arriving in the 1730s. They hunted bear, deer, beaver and otter and entered into trade, along with the Indians, for hides, pelts, bear oil, and suet. The French and Spanish colonists also entered this trade, paying little attention to agricultural development. Settlers arriving in the early 1800s were more focused on clearing land for agriculture, but they also hunted avidly for food supply as well as for hides. The hunting tradition continued throughout the ensuing years and remains a part of bayou culture.

Buffalo were killed out by 1808, and elk were depleted by the 1830s. Bear and deer became the primary targets for early settlers. One of the first permanent bayou settlers was John Smith who settled north of present Dermott in the 1810s. Known as "Bear Hunter John" he was "a famous hunter and delighted in ridding the country of the wild animals with which it was overrun." Dr. Charles McDermott visited this area in 1834 and found "plenty of bears and deer." He noted the settlers established there among whom was "old John Smith" and wrote that they were "killing plenty of bears...I went bear hunting...and killed 3 bears, 1 wolf, 1 deer, 1 turkey and a fox."[9] The 1840 census lists Hardy Journigan as a hunter living in the John Fisher home on the bayou at old Portland. Several gave their occupation as bear hunter on the 1860 Ashley County census.

Camp hunts became traditional annual events. Groups of men, often accompanied by women and children, trekked on horseback with wagons loaded with paraphernalia to favorite hunting grounds. During these hunts they took any game they encountered with deer and bear being the chief target. Wylie J. Cammack moved to old Portland at the close of the Civil War. "He was a great hunter and famed as a scout...Camp hunts were common in those days, and it was great sport for little Cola [his daughter], who frequently rode right along with her beloved father. The cane in the brakes then was as high as house tops. With a pack of 25 or 30 dogs, [he] set his own hunting season as October 14 till March 14. He killed 90 bears in three seasons, some weighing as much as 500 pounds. Deer, too, were plentiful, and with firelights and his dog, 'Bulger,' [he] brought in many a fine kill. Frequently the deer he stalked turned out to be panther, and once he killed a cat measuring 13 feet from tip to tip."[10]

The bloodcurdling scream of the mountain lion echoed eerily across the swamps. Locally referred to as panther, this wild creature often strayed from his ordinary diet of deer and smaller mammals to domestic animals such as hogs, sheep, and calves. Farmers and hunters killed the big cat whenever they got a chance, not only because of the threat to livestock, but also because they were feared. Charles Naff said, "Lottie Bain said people talked about them jumping on people when going through timber." "My mother said Grandmother heard them screaming at night at Poplar Bluff," said Mary Alice Nelson. "Once she thought it was a woman screaming and answered. The panther came to an open window and jumped into the house. The varmint dogs killed it." Alvie Pugh recalled, "The old folks talked about them. They would get after hogs. They said if you didn't have a gun you better get a good, long stick to walk with for protection. If you stop walking, he stops. Never turn your back to him – just stare at him, and he will finally get tired and run off into the woods. As soon as he gets in the woods he takes a long jump and then hollers. Another one answers, and then you better get you a toehold and take off running."

Nell and Shorty Lyle said that when they were young panthers would migrate through in early spring and fall. John Edd Curry said his mother told him about hearing panthers at Garrett Bridge from the early 1900s to the 1930s. They would have to put the dogs in the house at night so the panthers would not get them. Panther Brake between Baxter and Lake Wallace was named for its inhabitants. "You could hear them screaming in there. No one ever went into that place," said Estelle Works who lived at Panther Brake Plantation from 1936 to 1939. Ella Crawley Vail remembered panthers at Crawleys Bend. "When they came through the stock would go crazy. That's the way we knew they were there. One night Daddy and Uncle Ed Franklin were camped out in the woods on the way home from Hamburg and they had been hearing them scream. Uncle Ed saw the reflection of the campfire in the iron wagon wheel and thought it was a panther and shot it. Uncle Ed was scary. You didn't go to his house at night unless you called out first or he would shoot."

Although bounty hunters took some cougars in the late 1800s and continued land clearing drove them into the swamps, the population managed to survive. Sightings continued in the 1950s. Murphy Brockman saw one chasing a rabbit in a cotton patch by the bayou. John Edd Curry was squirrel hunting on the bayou near Garrett Bridge. "He was climbing up a tree. He was coal black. I left out backwards," he said. Although black panther sightings are not confirmed by wildlife biologists, public reports insist that they are some black ones. Andrew Pickens said, "There are 'thousands' of them and they are all black. We once trailed one for three days and nights." Winifred Day told of one near Wardville. "A man killed a black panther at four in the morning near the railroad bridge. He took him to a taxidermist and had him mounted." Finally gaining protection as an endangered species, the mountain lion is making a comeback. Frequent sightings are now reported. William deYampert said, "I have seen three in the last ten years."

Competing with the scream of the panther in the stillness of the night was the haunting howl of the wolf. The red wolf, *Canis rufus*, whose color varied from tawny to gray to black, had a fondness for the meat of hogs, lambs, and calves that made him a much-hunted animal by farmers as well as bounty hunters. In 1871 the *Monticellonian* reported, "The wolves are getting very bad in the southern part of [Drew County]. We learned that one attacked a man last week and bit him so that he was compelled to call out for help." The same year the *Ashley Times* noted that two men had killed eight wolves for which they received forty dollars in county scrip.[11] "There used to be a lot of wolves," Gaston Harrison said. "I had some good hog dogs and they came up missing around Overflow Creek. When I found them they were dead with their entrails eaten out. The wolves did that. They had dens in hollows in the hills and stream banks. I've seen eight or ten in my life. Granddad "Big Daddy" Kinnaird had a pet one. He sold or gave it to Smith Brothers Boat Company."

"Oh, there were plenty of wolves. They were all around Holly Ridge [McGinty area] in 1941," Buck Mayo stated. By this time the number was greatly diminished on account of federal and state trapping programs and habitat mutation. Charlie Bishop of Dermott participated in trapping around 1928. "The game warden had sent for the trapper [Andy Ray], and since the warden couldn't go, he sent me to accompany the trapper...After a little we found an area where they'd been frequenting in a place where there was lots of cane growing...every now and then we'd find a trail going through...in one of these places the trapper set a couple of his steel traps. Three days later we returned to that spot, but his traps were gone...we looked a little further, and sure enough there was a female wolf in one of those traps with two little pups beside her. Those pups looked about six weeks old and were big enough to get around. So when they saw us, they started running...we took off after them and came upon a hollow log which was their den. And we found three more pups there. Well, Andy jumped down amongst them and managed to latch on to three of them. Here he was on the ground with one under each leg and holding the other by the neck. I grabbed the other two by their back feet to keep them from biting me. But those Andy had were biting him bad – just trying to eat him alive. I managed to tie the back legs of the pups I had and then helped Andy do the same thing with the three he had. Then he notched the ears of those pups saying that he'd know them the next time. After he shot the female in the trap we headed out of the woods with those pups. Once we got to town folks were coming up and wanting to buy them so Andy sold them for ten dollars each. But they were too old to be tamed so within a year everyone of them had found their way back to the woods, and Andy had to go out and catch them again."

By around 1947 the total population had been exterminated in Ashley County and presumably in the entire Gulf Coastal Plain.[12] The last known wolf, which had been killing goats, in Ashley County was trapped east of Montrose around this time. The trapper took the carcass to Alcus Burney, a taxidermist at Line, who mounted it. Still in fair condition, the wolf stands in Burney's old house, but its magnificent howl is silenced.[13]

Before the last wolves were killed out they were able to meet their close cousin, the coyote, who began arriving from the west in the 1940s. Some crossbreeding took place between the wolf and coyote as well as with feral dogs. This allowed some wolf characteristics to continue in the hybrid offspring, but these have virtually disappeared by now.[14] The coyote has thrived and his yipping bark and wolf-like howl still resound over the bayou. Curly Birch said, "The coyote will be the last thing on earth. Sly and wily, they will figure out a way to hang on when everything else is gone." Another clever and cunning creature, the fox, may be padding along with the coyote.

The canebrakes along the bayou provided an excellent shelter for the black bear, *Ursus americanus*. Although nearly hunted to extinction by 1900, some managed to survive, and bear hunting remained popular in the early 1900s. The *Ashley County Eagle* reported in 1901 that several men from Hamburg joined men from Portland to go on a bear hunt in the Beouf River Swamp. Charlie Skipper, born in 1882, hunted bear south of Baxter as a young man. Robert Crawley said one came through in the early 1940s and was killed near the bayou bridge at Wilmot. Ezell Moyers saw two sets of bear tracks along Bartholomew in the 1940s, and one was killed near the Ashley-Chicot line around 1950.[15]

Leroy Haynes killed a bear in 1926. "Tebb McCloud and his son, Harvey, spotted him in a cornfield south of Wilmot. They came and got me, and I put my three coon and deer dogs on the track. He headed toward the hills, and I followed on my horse. I ran off and left Tebb cause they were riding mules. I chased him through the woods on down into Louisiana toward Bastrop. At ten o'clock in the morning the dogs bayed him. I had five double-ought buckshot shells and a hand-pump gun. He killed one of my dogs. I put two shots in his head, but he got up and started coming after me. I shot him in the head two more times. I didn't have a hunting horn so I sat down on a log and started hollering for Tebb. When they finally caught up Tebb said, 'I bet you a damn dollar you let that bear get in the bayou.' Well, there he was lying there. He weighed

250 pounds and we had to dress him out – that was the only way we could get him home. We put the mule in a ravine and loaded the bear on him. Harvey led the mule, and Tebb toted the guns on the other mule, and I walked along holding and balancing the bear. It took us a half-day to get back – a little before dark. Folks came a running to see the bear, and then the mule looked back and saw it and tried to run off!"

With the large-scale land clearing in the Delta during the 1950s, the bear's habitat was essentially eliminated. Small remnant populations remained only in the Ouachita and Ozark Mountains and in the White River National Wildlife Refuge in Arkansas and in southern Louisiana. The Arkansas Game and Fish Commission began a restocking program in 1959, and the bear is once again seen along Bayou Bartholomew. Andrew Pickens said, "I have seen them through the years on this place. Around 1968 a coon dog bayed one in the cotton field. It had been eating watermelons in a nearby patch. The next night they turned the dogs on it and they bayed but would not go into it." Bear sightings along the bayou from the 1970s to the 1990s were reported from south of Pine Bluff to Wilmot. Once known as the Bear State, Arkansas has once more become the home of the great *Ursus*.

Many men enjoyed the pursuit of deer whose numbers were plentiful during the 1800s. Deer ate food and forage crops, and man ate deer. Mark Harp settled in 1880 near Lind Grove where "deer was so numerous that they had to be killed to save the crop on a twenty-acre field. Time and again [he] killed as many as five deer in one day around his field. He would load deer carcasses on his wagon and give them away to people in the settlement." Charles Naff said his grandfather had to send for a wagon to haul his deer to Portland. Hunting at night with fire pan lights was common practice. Buck Mayo described these early nightlights. "They were like a big skillet with a four-foot handle on it. They built a fire in the pan and carried it over shoulder with the light coming from behind. After that they used kerosene headlights with a reflector. Then the carbide light came in; it was a great improvement." Overkill, habitat destruction by continual land clearing, and nature's own system of checks and balances (disease from overpopulation) caused a decrease in the deer herd by 1887, when Arkansas passed a law to prohibit the killing of deer.[16] It is doubtful that hunters paid much attention to the restriction.

The traditional camp hunts continued. Oliver W. Jennings, a Church of Christ minister, visited Captain Henry Taylor at Hollywood Plantation in 1893 and accompanied him on a five-day camp hunt to Amos Bayou. Four gentlemen accompanied by Miles Jones, "an experienced hunter," and Julius, a "colored man" who served as "cook and general utility man" made up the party. On the first day of travel they bagged quail and squirrel. The first night out they set up a temporary camp where they feasted on "corn bread, baked in a pot-lid skillet, and rashers of bacon broiled on a spit." Arriving at their destination the following day, three men immediately set out "in quest of fresh game for dinner." They soon returned with several squirrels and a canvass-back duck that went into the camp stew kettle along with potatoes, onions, red pepper, butter, and flour dumplings. A second afternoon hunt by five men yielded seven ducks, two geese, and more than a dozen squirrels. No one hunted on Sunday morning as was customary. The last day of the hunt the minister at last saw his first deer and became "so agitated" that he was unable to shoot and interfered with Captain Taylor's shot. The captain told him he had a case of "buck ague," a term that lingers presently as buck fever. Miles Jones secured a "fine buck" and the cook used the heart to form the basis of the camp stew. The minister returned to Pine Bluff after realizing the dream of his boyhood – "to dwell for a season in a genuine forest."[17]

By 1920 deer were almost extinct in the area, and hundreds drowned during the Flood of 1927. During the 1930s it was a rare sight to spot a deer. Leroy Haynes' hounds jumped a "big buck" near Wilmot late one afternoon, and Leroy was determined it would not get away. He followed the yelping Walkers by horseback across the Beouf Swamp to the river where they turned south. Darkness fell as he crossed into Louisiana on his hot chase down the wind. The dogs finally ran out near Oak Ridge, twenty-five miles below the state line. They followed the rider back to camp near Laark where they arrived around ten that night. The buck went free.

Game refuges established and watched over by wardens during the late 1920s and 1930s were successful in an effort to begin to restore the deer population. In 1939 Arkansas regulations allowed only one buck to be taken during the October hunt. Only two men hunting in the Portland area bagged a deer – native Gus Pugh and a visitor from Little Rock, Victor Snyder, both hunting with the Portland Hunting Club. Victor Edwards was the only lucky hunter at the Claude Brooks Camp in the November hunt. Other hunting clubs participating in the Ashley Delta that year were El Dorado, John Barnes, Minor O'Neal, Gene Lawrence, Station Camp, Lou deYampert, and Ode Kidwell.[18] The hunters were there; the deer were not. It was not until around the 1950s that the deer population stabilized, and deer hunting remains one of the most popular sports of the area.

Hunting was a traditional activity for men and their sons. Boys eagerly pursued squirrel, rabbit, raccoon, opossum, and ducks, or as James Bealer said, "Anything I could get to shoot at." If anything represented a rite of passage signifying his entry into manhood in an adolescent's life, it was when he began to hunt. Nothing made him prouder than the day he was entrusted with his first gun. Willie Skipper of Baxter wrote to his ten year old son, Charles, in 1892, "Dear Son, I send you the Gun I promised to get for you by Mrs. Bulloch now. My Dear Boy, be very careful never have the muzzle pointed toward anyone while there is a load in it. Your Mama says she will not see any more pleasure until you boys are [a]long enough to know how to handle a gun...you had better look out when you shoot your gun. Bro's kicks like a mule."[19] Charlie Skipper hunted for the remainder of his life. Buck Mayo began hunting alone when he was twelve. "When my Uncle Dock shot his arm off he gave me his gun. I hunted for squirrel, rabbit, and deer," he said. Buck grew up to become a game warden.

Tom Harp was seven when he began hunting. He wrote about the year 1898, "I rode a mule [to school] and took a shotgun. When school dismissed at 4 o'clock I headed for Beouf Swamp to hunt squirrels...During the 30 days I think I killed 200 squirrels. Anyway there was enough every day for the family." Garvin Adcock said, "I hunted those bayou bottoms for squirrels barefooted. A few times I was close to stepping on a cottonmouth, but I never got bit. I didn't know you were supposed to have a hunting license until I was out of the army." Shorty Lyle grew up on the bayou at Todd. "I'd walk out of the house for fifty yards and I'd be hunting," he said. At Portland Charles Naff hunted quail, duck, and squirrel. "We hunted squirrel and duck by just drifting down the bayou in a boat. One time Billy Grimes was with me and we were camping out. All we had were .22s and we shot two redbirds for camp food. The next day we went and got a shotgun and ate better after that."

Fresh game was always welcome at the table – especially during the Great Depression. "Anything that was food for the family. They would shoot squirrel and rabbit and trap for coon and possum," Estelle Works said. "We made it during the Depression by rabbit hunting," said Buster Ford. "When we couldn't buy shells we would go possum hunting. We would climb the tree and knock them out with a stick. They were good to eat then, but I wouldn't eat one now." Earl Kitchens didn't need a gun; his dogs caught rabbits for him. "We rabbit hunted a heap. We had some good dogs and they would get six or seven. Then we had something to eat for our Sunday morning meal. My mother would parboil them, fry them, and make gravy with rice. We took the same dogs at night and got coon and possum." Benton Hunt said that his father would locate a hickory tree where the squirrels were cutting nuts. "He would come back and give us a number of shells, and we had better come back with that many squirrels." Chuck Day said, "During the Depression there was a law that if a rabbit ran across the road, you had to stop your car so you wouldn't hit the man chasing him."

Hogs relish acorns, and the various oak trees along the bayou provided an abundant supply. Farmers let their hogs run freely to "root hog or die," checking on them occasionally and rounding them up for marking, butchering, or market. Although the swine had some predators, mainly panthers and wolves, they flourished in the wild. Hogs penned near water were subject to being eaten by alligators. "As a ranger I had to remove lots of alligators from hog pens," Buck Mayo said. Bealie Harrison told of another predator. "There were worlds of eagles then and they would eat a fifteen to twenty pound pig. We always took a gun when checking on our hogs to shoot eagles." Pork was a mainstay food and market hogs provided additional income; consequently, owners kept careful check on them. A hog thief was considered to be the lowest of scoundrels. Ralph Kinnaird wrote, "My grandpa, Tom Kinnaird, rode his horse every day or two into the woods checking on his hogs and cows. One day he caught two men with one of his hogs on the end of their rope. His mark was in the ears. They got a little tough and threatened him. Then the one doing the talking noticed he had a .38 Winchester across the saddle pointed at him. So Grandpa said, 'Yes, the hammer is back and my finger is on the trigger; now turn my hog loose and get out of here.' "

The value of pork is evidenced by the following story told by Buster Ford wherein pork was used as payment. "I was working for David Doles clearing new ground. He paid seventy-five cents a day. When he paid up at the end of the week, he would give a dollar or a dollar-fifty and pay the rest in pork at five cents a pound." Some had herds of hogs amounting to large numbers. Gaston Harrison had "hundreds." He said, "My dog, Tizer, would run nothing but a hog. He would bay and wait for me. When I wanted to pen them that dog would get in front of them and make them run him and would back up toward the pen until he got into the gate. I spent many pleasant hours hunting hogs to vaccinate them or bring them in." Benton Hunt said that Mr. Hopkins had five to six hundred hogs. Dr. Ralph Douglas had four to five hundred on his Ashley County land. "One time I took a truck load of them to sell and they offered me ten to five cents a pound, so I took them back and turned them loose. There were wild hogs there for years until they drained and cleared the land," he said.

Feral hogs, descended from stock escaped from or abandoned by early settlers, roamed the woods. A man with a good hog dog could capture these to get his start. If hogs were not marked, they were considered to be wild and free for the taking, and hog hunting with dogs was a popular sport. These long-tusked wild hogs were vicious if cornered or surprised. Joe Craig swam in the bayou at Pine Bluff in the early 1920s. "There were lots of wild razorback hogs along the bayou and we always took a gun along," he wrote.[20] "Once I was picking blackberries and a hog came up and scared me up a snag. Then I realized it was just an ordinary hog – not a wild one," admitted Nell Lyle. Bobby Abraugh was not so fortunate. "My brother, Joe, and I were at the bayou swimming when the dogs started barking at some hogs. The more they barked, the more hogs showed up.

There was around a hundred of them. We climbed a tree and had to stay up there half a day."

Stock laws restricting free range began to be passed in the late 1920s for certain areas and continued until around 1970. The feral hog population slowly diminished almost entirely until the recent (beginning around 1980) reintroduction of domestic hogs and Russian boars into the wild by sportsmen for the purpose of hunting. One estimate is that four or five hogs will increase in number to 2,600 in a ten-year period.[21] They have multiplied to the extent of now being a nuisance to the timber industry and agriculture as well as competing with wildlife such as deer and turkey for food.

Ben Lilly: A Legendary Hunter

*There is a white hunter···who has joined us, who is really
a remarkable character. He literally lives in the woods.*
Theodore Roosevelt, Letters to His Children, 1907

The legend of an extraordinary hunter began in Morehouse Parish.
Benjamin Vernon Lilly was born in Mississippi in 1856 and at the age of
twelve ran away from home. He walked to the home of his uncle, Vernon
Lilly, who lived on Bayou Bonne Idee between Bonita and Mer Rouge.
The boy hunted for awhile, returned to Mississippi, and eventually wound
up in Memphis as a blacksmith. There the uncle found him and coaxed
him back, offering him his three hundred-acre farm if he would settle down
and marry. Farming did not appeal to Ben Lilly, but the vast swampy
wilderness filled with bear, panther, ducks, geese, turkey, alligators, and
wild hogs issued a clear call to the natural hunter instinct deeply instilled
within him. Ben only felt at home when he was in wilderness country, and
he became as much a part of it as the animals that lived there. He was
content using a hollow tree cavity for shelter. If it turned unbearably cold,
he slept by a burning log. It stifled Ben Lilly to have to sleep in a house,
and he rarely did.

His ability to read signs, track, and shoot as well as his physical
stamina quickly became local legend. He lifted a hundred-pound
blacksmith anvil straight out with one hand; he jumped flat-footed thirty-
six feet in three jumps; he jumped out of a barrel without touching the rim;
he ran at half-speed for ten miles. The well built, blue-eyed, handsome
man married Lelia Bunckley in 1880, but marital bliss was short-lived. His
hunting trips to the swamps lasted longer and longer. A trip to Ben could
mean walking or riding horseback for fifty to seventy-five miles in one
direction accompanied only by his hounds.

One day Lelia asked him to shoot a chicken hawk. Ben got his gun and
went out, but the hawk flew away. Ben followed the hawk, and more than
a year passed before he returned. He told Lelia, "That hawk kept flying."
He had been to the Sunflower Swamp in Mississippi where he killed sixty-
five bear, selling the meat and grease. Upon the death of their young son,
Ben divorced Lelia, giving her "a roll of bills that would choke a cow." In
1891 the woodsman married Mary Etta Sisson and settled in a home in
Mer Rouge where three children were born. Still disliking farming, he
supported the family by buying and selling cattle and cutting timber, which
he hauled to railroad sidings at Bonita and Mer Rouge. He also hunted
deer, waterfowl, alligators, and bear for the market. His greatest passion,
however, was the pursuit of the panther. Having heard many stories of

panthers killing humans in Mississippi and Louisiana, Ben, a religious man, felt it was his higher destiny to eliminate panthers from the earth.[22]

Ben Lilly loved his children but he could not tolerate living a normal home life. Mary told him if he ever left hunting again she hoped he would never return. In 1901 he transferred all his property to her (keeping five dollars for himself), affectionately kissed her and the children goodbye, got his hounds, and headed southeast for the swamps of the Tensas River. He logged timber, hunted wild hogs, continued his pursuit of bear and panther, and sent money to his family. After bear and panther became scarce there, he drifted to south Louisiana and wound up in the Big Thicket of Texas in 1906. The following year he was on a westward trek through Texas when he received a telegram summoning him to join President Theodore Roosevelt's bear hunting party on the Tensas River in East Carroll and Madison Parishes as a guide.

Ben arrived at the elaborate presidential camp on October 5 where he found too many people and too many (fifty) dogs. It was not his kind of hunt. Teddy Roosevelt was impressed with the man. He described him in an article for *Scribner's Magazine*, "I never met any other man so indifferent to fatigue and hardship...The morning he joined us in camp, he...had neither eaten nor drunk for twenty-four hours; for he did not like to drink swamp water. It had rained hard throughout the night...so he perched in a crooked tree in the beating rain, much as if he had been a wild turkey...He could run through the woods like a buck...though he was over fifty years old...He was particularly fond of the chase of the bear, which he followed by himself, with one or two dogs; often he would be on the trail of his quarry for days at a time, lying down to sleep whenever night overtook him; and he had killed over a hundred and twenty bears."[23]

The president managed to take a lean she-bear under the guide of Clive and Harley Metcalfe (from Mississippi) and their co-hunter and dog handler, Holt Collier, a former slave. Ben was off on the trail of another bear at the time. Someone on the hunt killed a cub, and the teddy bear fad increased to a craze. J. Frank Dobie wrote, "Representations of a bear cub became the chief American toy and doll as well as talisman for millions of adults." A railroad siding, first called O'Hara's Switch and later named Stamboul, east of the hunting area changed its name to Roosevelt, and Ben Lilly returned to Texas. He wandered on to Mexico and then to New Mexico and Arizona where he hunted bear and lion for ranchers for fifty to one hundred dollars a scalp. In 1916 he began working for the U.S. Biological Survey as a predatory hunter and sending specimens to them for a salary of one hundred dollars a month. Ben Lilly died in 1936 near Silver City, New Mexico, at the "County Farm," a private caregiver. Called the "last of the mountain men" and grouped among such notables as

Daniel Boone and Davy Crockett, one estimate is that Ben Lilly killed a thousand bears and lions.[24]

This great hunter is not forgotten in Morehouse Parish where a memorial to him stands in Mer Rouge. Thomas Y. Harp supplied much of the Louisiana material for J. Frank Dobie's book on Lilly. Harp's reminiscences include local people such as Mark, Doc, and Rube Harp; Bob and Cuba Causey; Jim Kelley, Jim Yeldell, Dr. Callaway, Billy Flowers, and John Naff. A local black man, I. H. "Tutt" Alford, accompanied Ben on his Louisiana hunts as cook as well as hunter. "My wife's grandfather, Walter Harris of Parkdale, hunted with Lilly. He took his dogs to the Roosevelt hunt. We used to have a bear hide that was killed on that hunt, but it ruined. My dad knew him; he would come through here," Benton Hunt said. Clyde Venable wrote that his wife's grandfather, Ichabod O. Brooks, of the Eudora (Chicot County) area, was a member of the Roosevelt Tensas hunt. Roosevelt referred to him in his *Scribner's* article as Ichabod Osborn (using his middle name for his last), who came with his son, Tom, and six or eight bear dogs.[25] Hazel Hawkins said that Red Burgess of Parkdale hunted with Lilly.

"He hunted around the Jones-McGinty area. Louis 'Buck' Wolf knew him. He said he carried his frying pan on his back. He had left his family by this time," stated Ruth Mayo Boone. Buster Ford's mother told him that Lilly hunted through the area. "She said he was a great hunter and a nice man," Buster said. Bealie Harrison recalled, "My mama said Ben hunted with Grandpa [James Robert] Kinnaird around Extra [Ashley County]. He came up several times a year buying and selling cattle or hunting and spent the night. He hunted with Grandpa and Mr. Maxwell. He told Grandpa about one time his dogs bayed a bear in the canebrakes and the bear hit one of the young dogs (he was not too well trained) with his foot and killed him. The bear slipped into the cane and Ben followed. The bear grabbed the end of the gun with his mouth and Ben shot him in the mouth."

Ben Lilly ventured up the bayou into Arkansas according to a story Bill Gooch told Curly Birch. "Across the bayou [from the Taylor house at Hollywood Plantation] was another house that had a dirt floor. An old black man lived there by himself. The only thing I can remember about him is that he 'swore and be damned' he was the camp boy for Ben Lilly, the famous bear hunter. He told me he and Ben Lilly hunted all over Arkansas, Louisiana, and half of Texas. They would go anywhere there were predatory animals...I feel like the old man was telling the truth...The old man, whose name was Bill Estus, said he had started out being Ben's camp boy when he was small."[26]

Ben Lilly had a particular and unusual fondness for Bayou Bartholomew. Buck Mayo said, "Grandpa Hayden said that Ben would go from Mer Rouge to the bayou to haul his drinking water. He probably went to Judge Lord's place on the Old Bonita Road. That was the only water he said was fit to drink."

The bayou wilderness was a haven for its creatures, but man invaded it to play out his age-old role as hunter and provider. The changing seasons evoked primeval impulses that beckoned him to answer the call of the wild. Early spring lured the fishermen to the banks for the appetizing fish, and they fished until summer's end. The first crisp days of autumn made their thoughts turn to lightload guns and squirrel hunting, and they returned to the woods in predawn darkness. As the days grew shorter and colder, the bucks began to hook saplings with hardened horns, and the hunting fervor rose to great intensity. Throughout the winter the hunters pursued various quarry, trappers walked their traplines, and commercial fishermen faced the cold water with their nets and trotlines. Hunting and fishing not only provided food, it also was a recreational activity which drew the people closer to nature and to each other through the special camaraderie shared by sportsmen.   Memories formed in those years were never forgotten. When any old man is asked about the first time his father took him squirrel hunting or fishing or when he claimed his first deer, his eyes will glisten, and he will give a detailed answer. These were good times, and they were coupled with more along the bayou.

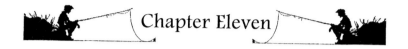

Chapter Eleven

Good Times on the Bayou

I used to just live on the bayou. I thought
it was the greatest place in the world to be.
Bobby Abraugh

"The bayou was the social thing in southeast Arkansas. Transportation was so bad, people didn't travel. That made the bayou the central area for social life," Jack Gibson said. J. W. Bocage, who arrived in Pine Bluff in 1836, wrote, "Those who survive the ordeal of pioneer life in the wilderness know full well, the angles of life were sharp, to round them required the grinding work of time...And yet – when memory brings the picture of 50 to 60 years ago...we are apt to look upon them as the golden days of our lives. The wild surroundings had for the true pioneer, a charm almost irresistible. Those who experienced the pleasurable commune with nature, if removed from the scene, longed for the enjoyment again." In 1845 George B. Gregory wrote to his brother from Bayou Bartholomew, "We had a pretty smart fandango on the Bayou on the 4th. A big barbacue and a few stump speeches and a big ball at night. I enjoyed myself finely." A newspaper correspondent from Dermott wrote in 1883, "There was quite a pleasant fish-fry on the banks of the bayou Friday last." In May 1912 the town of Wilmot hosted a picnic and barbecue attended by more than a thousand people from neighboring towns. The throng enjoyed two meals, races, pole vaulting, ball games, a shooting tournament, and a talent show. The Wilmot orchestra provided music for a night of dancing.[1]

The Fourth of July always called for a bayou outing. Leonidas Spyker wrote on July 4, 1856, "Independence Day – On this day 80 years since, our forefathers declared themselves free and independent of Great Britain. Long may the day be hallowed and kept in perfect remembrance...Hands have holiday this evening and tomorrow." The following day he wrote, "July 5. Negro Fourth of July. Have killed a beef, sheep and shote [shoat] for their dinner, which they are barbecuing." Slaves traditionally celebrated this holiday on the fifth as they were disenfranchised and the white populace felt that they should have no part in the Independence Day celebration.[2] Cecil Harp remembered seeing an African custom when he was young. "The blacks would roll up rags into softball size and soak them in coal oil. On a dark night they would get in teams and throw them at each other. These fireballs were absolutely beautiful. They had a big tail around five feet long like a comet."

Ernie Sprinkle said, "In the old days we had big barbecues at the Grove. They dug pits and barbecued on spits. The women brought the side dishes, and the politicians made speeches." William deYampert remembered when his family often went to Bells Ferry for a fish fry with all their friends. The Vester Kimbrell family lived on Panther Brake Plantation, south of Baxter, in the 1930s. Estelle Kimbrell Works said, "The overseer, Mr. Simms, gave plantation socials for the black and white tenants together every three or four months and on the Fourth of July. Aunt Lou Stonewall did the cooking for the fish fries and her husband roasted goats, pigs, or a calf on an open pit with a rod hanging over it." At Yorktown black families gathered on each Saturday as well as Independence Day at Shug Allen's place on the bayou. "He had a baseball field and they would play ball all afternoon. At night he would give a dance in his joint. Larkin Sanders played the guitar for the dances," Sue Gipson recalled.

The *Delta News* reported on the many Fourth of July activities in southeast Ashley County in 1939. At Portland four barbecues were held. Jake White served two sheep, two pigs, and a goat to seventy-five guests. H. M. Machen's company enjoyed chicken and mutton as "twin colored boys from the plantation sang, danced and played their uke for the guests." Sydney Herren had chicken, pork, and kid. "He also gave a barbecue for all the 'darkies' on his plantation." Bud and Mrs. Lizzie Machen barbecued mutton and beef. The townspeople of Wilmot picnicked on Lake Enterprise, and Parkdale turned out for a day of fishing in the bayou. E. V. Hinton had a plantation barbecue. The day concluded with many attending an all-night dance in Dermott. The following year the correspondent from Parkdale wrote, "While the white section seemed to be quieted by rain for the 4th activities, enjoyment season arrived on the bayou July 4 on the Callaway plantation with a grand picnic and a big ball game. Refreshments of all kinds were served. Three plantations were connected in this most elaborate affair. The refreshments were donated by the landlords of the plantations: Mr. Barnes, Mr. Callaway, and Mr. Henton."[3]

The Old Swimming Hole

How we loved playing in the bayou!
Estelle Kimbrell Works

Each community and many farms had a "swimming hole" that children as well as adults enjoyed. The first swimming hole on the bayou is at its source where a gravel bed holds a clear, deep pool of water surrounded by a sandy beach. "This was the only place to be in the summertime when we weren't in the cotton patch. There were two swimming places here called the big hole and the little hole. They also used the big hole for baptizing," Worley Jones said. Joe Craig swam at "McVey's hole" south of Pine Bluff in the early 1920s. Joe wrote, "We used to slip off from home and run all the way to the bayou about a mile and see who would jump in to chase off the scum on top of the water before anyone else jumped in. There was always about one-half inch of scum because there was no water flow in the summer. The McVeys had a slaughterhouse beside the bayou and dumped all the cattle remains [in it]. That was about one-fourth mile above the place we went swimming."[4] Harvey Chambliss swam near Hill's Acres (now Grider Field). "Me and the little black boys swam in it here. It was low and always muddy so we came out looking like we had hair on us from the dried mud," Harvey said.

The water was clearer by the time it reached the bridge, where people swam, at Yorktown. Murphy Brockman moved to the Meroney area in 1948. "The kids had a swimming hole half a mile down from the bridge. The water was clean and clear," Murphy said. There was also a swimming spot at Persons Bridge. Alvie Pugh swam behind the family home at Rose Hill. "The water was deep blue in the summer – you could see the bottom," he said. Edgar Norris and his friends swam below Batchelor Bridge. "We went to Garrett Bridge to swim and also a place on our farm. There were a lot of springs that threw up sand and made a good sandy bottom," recalled John Edd Curry. People from McGehee went swimming below the bridge on the Monticello highway. Curly Birch frequented this site. He said, "I would go swim and get out and lay on the bank looking up at the sky watching the buzzards ride the wind." Charles Adcock swam at Lambert Bend north of Baxter. "We would run to the water stripping our clothes off as we went and yelling 'last one in the hole is a rotten egg!' One time we jumped in and then saw some colored ladies fishing on the other bank laughing at us. We had to stay in until they left."

The Dermott swimmers went to Skipper Bridge and to a place behind the Buckner place. "The boys would play hooky from school and go swimming in the bayou," said Betsy Rodgers. The bayou bridge near Lake

Wallace was another frequented site. The swimming hole at Boydell was a half-mile downstream on the June Gibson farm. "It was in a curve where the water was swifter. The water was always clean until it rained," said Estelle Works. James Bealer swam at the bridge at Thebes. "We would get in and cool off. The water was so clear and clean," he said. Portland people swam at Alligator Bluff below the cemetery and at Wilson Lake. Residents of Free Negro Bend went swimming "near the Indian hill" according to Herman King. At Parkdale the swimming hole was at "Old Ferry" one and a half miles west from town on Highway 8. "The swimming hole was in its heyday during the late 1920s," Mary Foster remarked. "We went to it from the north side where there was a gentle slope and a spring nearby. There was another one at 'Round Turn' just for the boys without their suits," said Ernie Sprinkle. "The black folks swam at their baptizing place on H. S. Hill land out at the end of Grove Street," said Mark Hawkins. The Wilmot swimming hole was near the bayou bridge.

The McGinty and Jones people went to a site on the Shackelford farm near the commissary. "My father made a raft out of Choctaw logs for us to play on. The bathhouse was a big hollow stump with gin bagging for a door if there were girls around. Everyone from Wilmot and all around came," said Duke Shackelford. At Zachary folks swam below the bridge. "The old ferry was sunk there and we made a diving board off of it. We had to get above the springs or it would be too cold," Benton Hunt recalled. In the late 1920s Bonita residents began to frequent a place several miles above the Old Bonita Road. Marion Doles wrote, "There was a nice sandbar across the stream. At first those wishing to enjoy the sandbar had to be boated across. Later a steel cable was stretched across the bayou and, though the water was swift, participants would catch the cable, their bodies in the water floating downstream from the cable, and would maneuver their way across by using hand over hand. After this was used a time, a narrow footbridge was built on which to cross. In time this washed away during high water. Below this bridge there was a bend in the stream and a whirlpool there which was dangerous. All were warned to avoid this area. On most Sundays this area was filled with swimmers, many picnicking there. There were no dressing rooms. The trees and bushes provided the only privacy for dressing or undressing."[5]

Clay Banks, at the next bend, became a popular site during the 1930s. Boys gleefully jumped from the straight, high bank into the water. Bobby Abraugh said, "Downstream from there was a deep hole with a gravel bottom. A big willow tree leaned out over the water, and there was a cable with a towsack filled with dirt attached to a limb. We could swing all the way across the bayou on it and drop into the channel which was about ten feet deep." Ralph Kinnaird laughed, "Sometimes the girls would come and we would have to wear cut-off jeans." "One time we were skinny dipping and the girls showed up and took our clothes. We just about wrinkled up before they left and we could get out," Bobby continued. Mason Cave was another choice site. "The young folks would go there on Sunday afternoons," said Gaston Harrison. "It was a lively place with picnics, parties, and swimming." Frank Day remembered swimming at Hollaway Springs, just south of the mouth of Chemin a Haut Creek. "It was the main place to go. We would pass by Frank Cain's place and steal a watermelon and put it in the spring. We also swam at Frank Cain's Little Field. It had a good sandbar. Another good place was just above the Crossett Bridge at the old ferry site. People from Bastrop went to Rocky Ford out at the end of Van Avenue. We took a bath in the bayou everyday in the summer," Frank said. Estelle Works said, "One of our favorite times was in the afternoons when Papa would take us all for a bath and a swim in the bayou. How we loved playing in that bayou!"

With the coming of winter, the bayou and its oxbows infrequently afforded another kind of recreation. Murphy Brockman said older people told him that the bayou froze over enough to skate and walk on in the early 1900s. Susie Fuqua remembered skating on the frozen bayou. Gaston Harrison remembered that the bayou froze over twice in the 1920s. "Enough to skate on," he said. In 1940 the *Delta News* reported that people were skating on Lake Enterprise "a-foot, a-sled, or any kind of way they could skate without skates." The last time it had frozen enough to hold skaters was in 1933. Many recalled J. C. Kistler's walking across the lake in 1918. One remembered when the temperature dropped to eleven below zero in 1899 and the lake froze over.[6] Benton Hunt didn't need skates. "I hated shoes. I skated on ice barefooted," he said.

The bayou also provided a place for other kinds of recreation. "The bayou was the only place we had to play," said Buster Ford. Paolo Canulla grew up in Pine Bluff. He wrote, "We would play Huck Finn by running away from home, building a raft out of large limbs, and floating the bayou. Of course we would only last, at most five minutes, before deciding that this wasn't the day to float the bayou. But this didn't stop us; we would go home and plan for weeks. I think the closest we came to accomplishing our daring adventure was a day on the bayou and an overnight stay in the woods. I was around eight years old."[7] Paolo was not the only bayou rafter. Duke Shackelford reminisced, "We would build a raft and play Huck Finn. We would go down the bayou and camp for two or three nights. We had to sleep under a mosquito net and hide our food from the wood hogs."

Adults as well as children enjoyed bayou activities. In 1940 some Ashley County gentlemen organized the Bayou Club. The *Delta News* reported, "Speaking of boats – the Bayou Club has started up in good time...Charter members include 'Little Joe' Pugh, who we hear started it all, Gus Pugh, and Henry Morschheimer."[8] The Ray Thomas Robertson family of Bonita set up camp at Mason Cave. Marion Doles said, "We would go for two weeks and camp by the big spring where we kept watermelons cold. We caught fish and fried them for supper." Bobby Abraugh remarked, "The banks and woods were pristine - the cattle and hogs kept the undergrowth down. The kids ran and played in the big, open woods. We would shake muscadines off the vines or climb a tree and eat possum grapes till we were about sick. Everybody went to the bayou in those days."

One young Dermott lad slipped off to the bayou on more serious business. Dr. York Williams Jr. , president of Morris Booker Memorial High School and College, had a student with a terrible case of stuttering. Williams, perhaps remembering Demosthenes, advised, "Go down to the bayou and find you some rocks. Fill your mouth with rocks and talk with them in your mouth." The youth followed the advice, and Don Glover graduated from Howard University with a degree in jurisprudence and became mayor of Dermott and Circuit Court Judge.[9]

The Power of Love

*Married, on Bartholomew, in Chicot County···Mr. Reece Bowden,
late of Louisiana, to Miss Nancy Wiley···.*
Arkansas Gazette, May 8, 1833

With everyone going to the bayou, something else was destined to happen. As the adolescents matured, they began to experience enigmatic emotions that evolved into love. The courtship that followed often took place on the bayou. The editor of the *Lincoln Ledger* waxed mellifluously in 1919, "There are a great many old folk...who have not forgotten and who never will forget, the elm-bordered meadow, the moon-lit path and the murmuring stream along whose bright banks they wandered when they were first in love."[10] Katie Parker said, "We had no car so we just walked together to the bayou." "We had our dates on the bayou banks at Obers Bluff or Zachary Bridge. We would build a fire and sit around and talk," stated Jack Gibson. Many couples spent Sunday afternoons on a bayou bridge. Rev. Ralph Douglas said that George H. Richardson Sr. met Mattie Harvill while waiting for ferry between Tyro and Dumas, and this meeting led to love and marriage. Lillie McCain first met Tom Yeldell in 1903 when he delivered a load of lumber to be used by her father in building the Zachary ferry. She was twelve and he was thirty-six. Fifteen years later they married in Wilmot.

One couple chose to have their wedding on the bayou. Dorothy Mack wrote, "Daddy [Edward Chris Korjan] met Bell McCain and they planned to be married. It was Daddy's idea to have a secret wedding on the banks of Bayou Bartholomew. As he was known to be shy, Mama went along with his plan somewhat reluctantly. On March 14, 1914, Ben Staton, the Justice of the Peace, crossed the bayou on a barge near the old Reed place which was not far from Kimball, Arkansas. On his way he met a member of the Thompson family who lived nearby, and when asked where he was going, he told them – evidently forgetting his promise to keep things a secret. So when Mama and Daddy arrived at the wedding site, a small crowd had gathered to watch the ceremony – much to the embarrassment of the groom. Daddy was a bit upset with Ben Staton, but as the years went by, the incident became just another funny story to tell."[11]

Married life for the wilderness wife was often a lonely experience. Their husbands worked from daylight to dark, and neighbors were widely scattered. J. Fred Crawley spent the first few years of his marriage traveling about the state in search of more land to buy, leaving his farm on the bayou south of Pine Bluff in the hands of his wife and slaves. Martha Amanda Crawley wrote in 1856, "I am too lonely out here in the wilderness without him. It is only at intervals that I have visitors and they are such as do not interest me. I have not a single female associate out here and have not heard a sermon for nearly five months."[12]

After the couple moved to their plantation at Crawleys Bend, he traveled less and her writing reveals contentment. She described the happy domestic life of her neighbors in a "substantial hewn log-house" on Bayou Bartholomew in 1858. "The family has just supped and are now seated around a blazing log-fire, in the main room, which serves both for a sleeping and sitting compartment. The Father, a noble specimen of the Arkansas farmer, with slippered feet, is reclining before the sparkling fire, while the youngest, darling little Nellie, is rolling over him laughing joyously. The mother so delicate and refined, that you would wonder how she came to grace the dark, deep swamp, is reading aloud from an interesting book...What a cheerful glow pervades the room, what inward happiness and contentment are reflected from each face."[13]

One bayou couple, Launa Sawyer and Gaston Harrison, was happily married for seventy-five years. Their physician told them that only one couple out of two million has the opportunity to celebrate their seventy-fifth anniversary.

A Bayou Love Story

Julia Crawley, daughter of Amanda and J. Fred Crawley, was born in Tennessee in 1867, but frequently visited the bayou plantation, which was then owned by her brother, Robert Page. Julia wrote an ambiguous short story, "The Doll," about two ill-fated lovers. Family tradition holds that this story is actually a cloaked version of actual events. In the story, Julia, "just budding into womanhood," leaves her bayou home on horseback and meets her lover, Mr. Cox, at Jones Chapel. *Bayou Bartholomew borders in a curve a part of the chapel's grounds. Cypress trees form a grove so beautiful, the long gray southern moss hung and festooned from there...The little graveyard under the trees was all so silent. The chapel filled the scene, bearing a touch of Gothic elegance.* The parson quickly marries the eloping couple as they see her father and Rue Page galloping furiously toward them. *Young Page, with downcast eyes and muffled voice says to himself, "Too late. Oh God! Too late." They turn without a word and leave.* Julia instantly recognizes her foolish mistake; her heart belongs to Rue Page. She lives unhappily, keeping her tears in her heart. Once she meets Rue in the woods while riding, and they promise to marry if she is ever free. She is only freed by her death and is buried in the little cemetery by the bayou.

The great full moon shone through the fine clustering foliage of the cypress grove, letting in splashes of gray light that was akin in tone to the southern moss swaying silently in the moonlight gloom upon the real lover of Julia. Rue Page engulfed in grief upon her grave. To him alike, as unto her, no one had given courage. *And his great soul sought hers in elysian glory of heaven and wandered its way, leaving his body all neatly dressed for burial. There they are like Abelard and Heloise in Pier La Chase Paris, entombed together.*[14]

Bayou Baptizings

It was more like the real thing then.
Earl Kitchens

Being baptized in the bayou was a tradition that dated back to earliest settlement. Fred W. Allsopp wrote in *Folklore of Romantic Arkansas*, "On Bayou Bartholomew, in Ashley County...there was a favorite spot for baptizings much used before and after the Civil War...the accustomed spot for this religious ceremony was where the bayou made a narrow bend at a point of land covered with sand jutting out into the water, and where the water grew gradually deeper. The location was called 'Sandy Point,' and many were baptized there."[15]

The pure water of Bayou Bartholomew washed away the sins and restored the souls of multitudes of Christian converts, especially those of the Baptist and Pentecostal denominations. Amos Jones wrote in his biography of the well-known minister and educator, Dr. York W. Williams Jr., who grew up at Gourd, "The undisturbed setting on the banks of Bayou Bartholomew afforded him the rarest treat of all, to hear the very voice of God...The sylvan setting of the home place on the banks...offered an inescapable relationship with nature. The rumbling rhythm of the river, the whistling music of wafting winds, the rhythmic rustling and lyrical languages of leaf and limb, of trees...the concert of creatures...He was buried in baptism in the bayou's watery grave to rise and walk in the newness of life."[16]

Protracted meetings and revivals evoked religious furor that resulted in the conversion of many. Rev. W. T. Tardy described protracted meetings he attended in Drew County in the late nineteenth century. "The preaching I heard was superlatively Biblical and earnest to the point of boiling blood. The seeking note was prominent in all the sermons and the prophet did not cease to warn his hearers day and night...Their concentrated convictions forged a terrible bolt which they launched against sin with a deadly effect. I have seen audiences mightily swayed and entire platoons of strong men crowd the front benches and piteously cry for mercy. Sometimes the rough building would seem to rock as it was filled with the glory of God under the power of the preached word...The singing was old-fashioned, earnest, devotional, and weird. The music of the old hymns would break the heart of stone and start tears from every eye."[17]

Most of the swimming holes along the bayou were also baptismal sites, and congregations gathered to witness the baptism of the new converts. they believed that their salvation was not complete until immersed in water, and the moment created rapturous jubilation for all. Nancy Tharp said, "The preacher would get to preaching, shouting, and hollering, and then some would get the Holy Spirit and go into the water. I got it; it came over me and I went and jumped in." Alvie Pugh was baptized when he was twenty years old. "It would be people on the bayou the width and length from here to the road [a half-mile] to see it done. They would be singing and praying at the bank, and when one would come out of the water they would begin to shout. I had that good feeling before I went into the water, but when I came out I felt even better."

Bessie Green received baptism on her thirteenth birthday. "Oh, it was so enjoyable, and even though it looked liked people were having a good time, it was so spiritual, so spiritual. The singing fired you up, and then the Holy Ghost would really strike the people and just light them up. There was plenty of shouting. I tell you what – there was more shouting down on that bayou side than it is now for real. The people sang, shouted, and danced, and be so glad. I wanted to feel *different*, and after I was baptized and stood up to witness, it came to me. I was filled with love and care for everybody, and it is still mingling with me."

The baptisms were such a spectacle, especially those of the Negroes, that people not connected with the individual churches went to watch them. "I would go to Persons Bridge to watch. It was fun to see. They would throw those old black ladies in there and the singing and shouting would begin. They had fun; they would stay all day and sing, pray, preach, and eat," Shorty Lyle said. Earl Kitchens was baptized in the bayou north of Wilmot. "People would turn out in big numbers to come and watch the singing and shouting. It was more like the real thing then." Herman King said that when he was baptized more than 125 people were there. Buster Ford said, "Oh, they was a lot of fun. White people came to see all the playing, singing, and shouting down on the bayou bank. They wore white robes back then to be baptized in."

Herman King told of an unusual bayou conversion. "After you got baptized everyone would shake your hand. It was called mending; your soul had been mended. Then you would get the Holy Spirit and start shouting. One guy wanted to be baptized every year, and they got tired of him. He started shouting and he was hard to hold down so they turned him loose. He got swept downstream and caught in a drift and there was a snake in it. After he got through it there was no drift at all; he had cleaned it out! He was a gambler and joined the church every year, but after he got tangled up with that snake, he really got converted for the last time. He got saved for sure then."

Von Greenway related a similar "miracle" that took place at a white baptizing. "My mother told me this. She was at a baptizing one time, and a big cottonmouth came swimming down the bayou and the preacher grabbed him. The moccasin bit him on the wrist, and the preacher said, 'I rebuke you in the name of Jesus' and slung him in the bayou. The snake floated belly-up, and the bite did not hurt the preacher even though there were two fang marks with blood squirting out. A man of another denomination saw it and wanted to be baptized; it caused him to believe."

The white baptisms were more subdued but they were also accompanied by singing, praying, and some shouting. The Pentecostals were more likely to engage in shouting than the Baptists. Von Greenway described Pentecostal baptisms at Boydell and Jerome. "I was too mean to get baptized young, but I knew I was getting the Holy Ghost when I was four years old. Sometime after those old brush arbor revivals, people would want to be baptized that very night, so they would get a kerosene lantern and go down to the baptizing hole. People gathered on the bank and began to sing as they walked out in the bayou. Then when they came out the shouting would begin." John Edd Curry attended Baptist baptisms at Garrett Bridge. He said, "Every once in a while they would get the Holy Ghost and get pretty loud. The loudest I ever heard was when Mr. Sam Creighton was baptized. There was a lot of shouting that day, and he was doing quite a bit of it himself. One time there was a young preacher just out of the seminary – Ralph Douglas. He got out in the bayou and got stuck in the mud. He couldn't pull his feet out, so he had prayer and then dismissed the crowd but kept the deacons there to get him out."

Ruth Boone was fourteen when she joined the McGinty Baptist Church during a protracted meeting conducted by Rev. Thad Douglas. "It was in the early spring and I was afraid my father would not let me be baptized because it was cold weather. But I knew that the Bible taught that I should – that salvation was not complete until you were. I told Brother Douglas I wanted to be baptized right away, and he wanted me to wait till summer. But I insisted, and he came on a Sunday afternoon and baptized me all alone. The water wasn't cold to me – I was ready, no doubt."

The *Delta News* reported in 1940, "After a ten day revival at No. 2 Baptist Church [black] at Portland, eleven were baptized. The day's work began at eleven Sunday morning on the banks of Bayou Bartholomew. The highlight of the services was the conversion of nine year old Raymond Hill…the boy preached a short sermon on the water side. He amazed the huge crowd by discussing the Book of Revelations in a manner that no adult preacher could do without spiritual aids."[18]

Baptizing continued in the bayou until after World War II when some churches began to use baptisteries; however, during the 1950s the bayou was still being used. Even after churches had baptisteries, some still preferred to be baptized in the bayou. At least one bayou baptism took place in the early 1980s. Bessie Green lamented, "Those old baptizings are gone now, and it doesn't seem the same. It is not as spiritual now as it was back then. People's minds were more on the Lord then. The spirit was more evident in the old days."

The spirit was surely evident at the "all-day singings and dinner on the ground," which were church sponsored social events. Between eight and nine hundred people attended the People's Singing Convention at Zachary in 1940. Churches belonging to the convention were Upper and Lower Dry Bayou, Gaines, McGinty, and Zachary.[19]

Music from homes also drifted down the bayou. Mary Roane Tomlinson wrote of the Negroes singing at Hollywood Plantation. "...their singing makes a harmonious sweet sound which is echoed and carried far on the waters of this queer and fascinating stream." Dorothy Mack wrote, "In the years [my parents] lived on the bayou, Mama told me Daddy would go out in the late evenings and sit on the bayou bank and play his accordion. The neighbors along the bayou would sit on their porches and listen. It was a quiet way to relax after a hard day's work."[20] Susie Fuqua recalled one of her favorite bayou memories. "After dark we could hear singing coming up the bayou. It was so sweet and pure. Everything was pure back then."

Buried Treasure and Strange Events

They called her the swamp angel.
Susie Wright Fuqua

Persistent rumors of buried gold, silver, and money tantalized some into searching for an immediate yet elusive form of wealth. Gaston Harrison said, "John Knox was a wealthy farmer who lived on the bank of the bayou across from Cora's Bluff. Everybody said he had gold or money buried, and people were digging everywhere there." Bealie Harrison said that the rumor of the buried Knox fortune began when a Negro housekeeper told that Knox took a chest toward the bayou and never came back with it. A similar story persisted at Parkdale. "Alameda Dunnigan said that she heard my great-grandfather had gold buried under the walnut trees at the old homeplace. People looked and looked for it but never found anything," Ernie Sprinkle said. Gold was supposedly buried on the Skipper plantation at Baxter. Betsy Rodgers said, "People dug around there all the time. They did turn up gold pieces when they were plowing around the old Gaster homeplace."

Captain Perkins was a steamboat captain who owned a farm north of Portland. The story of his buried riches around Perkins Slough on the east side of the bayou led many to search for underground wealth. "I've seen a lot of holes where people had dug around Big Bend where he owned land," Junior Brooks said. Zeke Hawkins reiterated, "People dug up and down the bayou for money around Perkins Slough."[21] Charles Naff remembered people digging at Perkins Bend as well as at Green Pugh Bend north of Lake Grampus. Fortune hunters dug into a large Indian mound near the bayou at Free Negro Bend until it was nearly leveled. People reportedly found gold and silver in it as well as Indian relics. Herman King said, "They dug in that Indian hill a plenty." Benton Hunt acknowledged that money or gold was rumored to be buried on his place. "One guy got all excited when he hit something hard. All he dug up was a cast-iron stove that was buried after a house fire." Frank Day said that people dug on the Henry Day place in the 1920s.

"Uncle Jess Millard had a treasure map that marked a spot on Horseshoe Lake. He figured it was Lake Wallace because of the shape and looked around there for it," Von Greenway said. Amos Sledge was involved in digging for treasure. "They claimed some outlaws buried silver or gold in the little island in Townsend Brake. Around 1935 an old man came up from Louisiana looking for it. He had a big Geiger counter and found where he wanted to dig. He got my dad and my brother and me to help him out. We dug for two days and got a hole down six to eight feet deep. The next day the man had just disappeared. Three or four years later he sent for his things he had left." Amos also said that "word got out" that money or gold was buried where a railroad spur crossed the bayou north of Baxter.

There was a common legend among treasure seekers that nothing must be said while digging and that spirits often inhabited the burial site. Bryant Edwards searched ardently for treasure in Lincoln County. Murphy Brockman said, "He was looking in an old brake in front of my house near Meroney. Robbers had run in there and buried money. He said that monkeys would get after him when he started digging and a ghost would run him off." Buster Ford also dug for money one time. "When I was thirteen years old Uncle Harry Webb came for me. He said that the Lord had shown him where money was and told him to take me with him. He took me out there and told me, 'don't say nothing – no matter what happens.' We started digging and dug and dug. We found something; the shovel bumped the top of a pot. I heard something and looked around and a big, red bull came running, snorting at us. Fire was running out his nose. I screamed and the pot disappeared."

Albert Einstein once said, "Without mystery life is as meaningless as a snuffed out candle." People along the bayou witnessed or heard about occurrences that could not be explained in ordinary terms. Tales of apparitions, haunted houses, and bizarre events are part of bayou lore. "Whatever became of all the ghosts? People used to visit at night on the plantations and going home they would see things. The mules wouldn't go through Walker Brake [northwest of Wilmot] because they could see haints there," Bailey Sherrer said.[22] Page Webb saw "jack-o-lantern lights" above an old graveyard on his place. "They were coming across the field like a ball the size of hands flashing on and off. There were usually two together. The folks called them haints." Bealie Harrison saw peculiar lights at his place. "In the late 1910s a bright light like a spotlight snapping on and off came in here. You could see it moving from the ground to the top of the trees and back down. If you got close to it, around eighty yards, it would move away or go out. It was so bright you could count the limbs on trees. It just eased around like a balloon floating over the top of the ground or stand stationary four to five feet in the air. I saw it several times. It came two nights in a row when George Westbrook was on his deathbed." Mildred Harrison said her father told about seeing lights in the woods at night around 1870. "He said they would stay around for half an hour and then just leave. It stayed at the back of his field for a long time. It gave him a bad feeling."

Alvie Pugh encountered "something." "Me and a fellow was across the bayou one night coming in. The moon was shining bright, and I thought I saw a mink run in the road. I went running to it and was gonna kick it, but when I got close to him it was no mink. It was something with a shawl over its head and shoulders and had whiskers and great big eyes. It sat down and looked up at me. I didn't kick him. The other boy came up and wanted to know what was going on. I did not tell him - he would have run off and left me. I had to get across that footlog first before I told him!"

Some houses seemed to be haunted. The old Carlock plantation house at Free Negro Bend was notoriously haunted. Rosa Sims said, "It was built back in slavery times and was a big old two-story house. My aunt said that she heard her old slave master's voice calling to her there after freedom. My stepfather's sister also lived there. She said they could hear glass breaking."[23] Herman King also heard about this house. "My papa's sister stayed there. Four white men went there to go with her. She hit them in the head with a shovel and put them in the basement. She knew how to hit them in the temple and knock them out but not kill them. After she left things began to shake around in the house. The ghost came. People started saying they saw him."

Nancy Tharp said that a house on the Sumner place near Parkdale was haunted. "People died there and their spirits stayed. People would move in and have to move right out. They just couldn't stay there – it just scared them to death." Earl Kitchens said that long ago a house on the Ray Bird place out of Wilmot was haunted. "A heap of strange things happened out there. Every night folks would hear someone walking around in the house and see someone coming from the barn with a light." The old Avery plantation home above Batchelor Bridge created some excitement. "It was dilapidated for a long time and folks called it a haunted house. All the kids from Dumas would go there to see the haints flying out the windows. They dared not go in," Edgar Norris said. Cecil Harp said that people used to say the Lightwood Grocery on the Old Bonita Road was haunted. There was a way to keep ghosts out of houses. Mary Currie said, "I heard that people used to hang bottles around their house to keep them away."

Charlotte Hawkins became a recluse in her home in Parkdale after she was saddened by a divorce from Dr. M. C. Hawkins Sr. She wore black mourning clothes and stayed almost exclusively in her downstairs room until her death in 1949. Mark and Hazel Hawkins moved into the house in 1989 and not long afterwards began to notice something. Hazel described what happened. "We would just get a whiff like a brush of air and smell a musty odor like dead ashes in a fireplace. We noticed feeling cold air and smelling the odor in any season. Doors would close, books would fall, and little unexplainable things happened. Soon we began calling it the little ghost. We knew it had to be a friendly family ghost – there was never any bad feeling. We told our girls it was their great-grandmother. She could tell we loved the house and I think that made her feel good. We have all felt her at the same time. She is still there. Every once in a while we get a little whiff and then she is gone."

When Mrs. Lois Thomas of Tarry was four days from being 101 years old, she said, "My house has ghosts in it. It doesn't bother me a bit." Her daughter, Juanita Parker, who lived with her, said that was the first time she had heard her say that. Mrs. Thomas died the following year. Susie Fuqua lived on the bayou north of Garrett Bridge in the 1910s. She said, "I heard a lot of people say this: There was a girl with wings going down the bayou like she was walking on water – just drifting down the bayou. They called her the swamp angel."

An experience at Bartholomew Methodist Church near Plantersville scared the wits out of two men around 1917. Mrs. Emma Williamson told the story for a Bastrop newspaper many years ago: "Mr. John A. Williams and a friend made a trip to Bastrop by horseback and were on their way home when a storm came up just as they reached Bartholomew Church where they sought refuge from the rain. They tied their horses to a bush near the door and sat on a bench at the rear of the church looking outside waiting for the storm to abate. Lightning was flashing vividly and during one bright flash, they saw an apparition advancing toward them. It was a woman in a white dress with her long black hair flowing down her back. She moaned as she approached with hands outstretched toward the men, who sat petrified by fear as the ghostly vision came closer. She finally touched Mr. Williams' shirt with her open hand, leaving a bloody print on his white shirt. As she wandered on toward the pulpit, Mr. Williams and his companion leaped to their feet and fled out of the church in terror. They mounted their horses and rode at breakneck speed to Plantersville, the nearest village, where they told of their encounter with the ghost in the church. Shortly afterwards the mystery was solved when a hunter found a demented woman wandering in the woods living off berries. Her long black hair was hanging down her back and her hands were bloody from briar scratches when they took her away."[24]

Sometimes inexplicable events occurred. Eloise Means told the following story which took place in 1934: "Frank and Erie Brown, a black couple, worked for us. Frank also kept watch over Grandpa's boat that was tied up near his house, and Erie cooked and cleaned for Mother. The night Grandpa [Edwin Mason] died, Frank and Erie were there immediately. Frank told Daddy that he was awakened by Grandpa's voice telling him to look after the boat and that he just knew something was wrong with him."

The death of a loved one is always hard to accept, and the final goodbye at the burial a sad experience. A bereaved widow at Jones could not bear to part with her husband who died in 1906. Eloise Means related the story: "When he died she had a wooden vault like a mausoleum built behind her house. I think it was attached to it. She had his body put in there in a coffin with the whole top sealed with glass. She went out there daily to visit him and raised the coffin lid to look at him. She sat in her rocking chair while knitting and talked to him as if he were alive. When she died I think they buried him. The old house finally fell down."

John Edd Curry told two stories that took place in the Garrett Bridge area. "I had this old colored man working for me. He told me one night they were sitting up with a corpse. A ball of fire came out of the casket and went around the room and out the house and came back in and got in the casket. Another time they were having a funeral at the black church on top of the hill and the casket opened up. The body did not come up, but 'something' came up and everybody ran out of the church. I was teasing Percy Dancer about it. I said I bet they had to make a new door for the church house."

A WPA writer interviewed Leo King in 1939 and wrote his account of what he experienced in Ashley County.

Used t' row down Bayou Bartholomew long Free Nigger Bend. Only negro families farmin' th' lan' thereabouts, reason twuz so named. Thy wuz an ol' house 'bout ready t' go t' pieces, way on back in th' bend there. One o' th' farmers had it fer t' store cotton in. Weeds so thick an' heavy, growin' eight feet high, look like a swamp, an' mighty hard t' git through. Reason me an' John'd go there, well, uz a sugar cane patch nearabouts that ol' shack, you see. We'd go there an' git us some sugar cane an' go on in th' ol' place. We'd lay round on th' cotton bales, eatin' cane an' tellin' ghost stories, you know. Listen, one time we wuz layin' roun' like that. Well, we heard somebody beaten' in th' back wall. Noise soun' like somebody'd got a hammer an' wuz beatin' it on th' wall. First beat on th' wall John raise up. Said, "Whut's that!" We listen, an' there it go agin. Look like somebody tryin' t' scare us. Seen th' black wall boards tremblin, and dust asettin's been such a hard lick. Mus' be a ghost, didn' like whut ah tol.' John had been tellin' a tale, you know. Well, he gin t' git scared an' started t' go on home. Wanted me to come on with him, but ah said no, less'n he'd come with me roun' th' back an' fin' out who doin' that knockin'. Ah say when he lef', wouldn' do it nohow, say it wuz mighty still an' scary an' all. But ah did mean t' see if twuz reely a ghost chasin' us out a there er otherwise. Went on out th' front door an' stole round' th' corner an' seen a big black snake, look like a moccasin, shape of its head, abangin' away at th' wall with his tail. Jus' blammin' away, an' don' know why t' this day. Ten feet long if he wuz an inch. Well, ah felt some better, yet an' still ah lef' there in a hurry, an' unbeknownst t' that big ol' snake abangin' at th' cabin. Didn' have no stick er such fer t' take on a bugger like that. Well, knew twuz no ghost an' tol' John so, but jus' the same we ain't never gone back t' th' ol' house t' tell stories an' eat sugar cane after that happen. Ain' seared o' ghosts, but never did care t' tangle with snake size o' that one.[25]

Bayou People

When we weren't in school or working in the field,
we were on that bayou. It was the center of our lives.
Estelle Kimbrell Works

The ridge west of the bayou that separates the Delta from the "piney hills" also symbolically divided two rather distinct social classes or subcultures. The 1939 first edition of the *Delta News* defined its area and justified its name, "...so we started out looking for a five-letter word that would say the same thing as Bayou Bartholomew Valley and the only thing we got was Delta. Now anybody knows that Bayou Valley isn't what most of us think about when anybody says Delta. We think about the whole lower Mississippi River Valley from Memphis to New Orleans...The Bayou Valley is a miniature of what you get when you take a picture of THE Delta...when you looked [at a map] at Ashley County, you'd find that we're purple. The entire swamp country from the Chicot line...to where you go up Overflow Hill is colored purple. That makes us Delta. We're...alluvial...since there's a hill about twenty miles from Hamburg, the Hamburg section is positively the hills. That puts us down in the swamps...That...is your Delta. And this...is *Delta News*."[26]

There emerged from earliest settlement days a distinction between people who lived in the Delta and those who lived in the hills. Mary Roane Tomlinson acknowledged this difference in 1938: "The region which Bayou Bartholomew meanders is divided into two distinct types of land and soil, each with it equally attractive advantages, people, and industries."[27] Only those who braved malarial infested swamps in favor of some of the most fertile farmland in the world made their homes in the Delta. Hill people living on smaller, less fertile farms began to realize, however, that Delta farmers, large or small, were making more money. The Delta towns were smaller than hill towns, and Delta dwellers were considered rural whether they lived in town or not. The combination of wealthy and rural found expression in two derisive hillbilly nicknames for Delta dwellers - cornbread millionaires and bayou rich. They also called them swamp rats, delta rats, webfooters, flatlanders, bottomlanders, swamp babies, and swamp angels. The majority of blacks lived in the Delta, but those who did live in the hills even had a name for members of their race who lived in the lowlands. "They called us bayou coons," Alvie Pugh said.

Delta people described the attitude of hill people toward them. "We called them hillbillies and they called us swamp angels. I've heard that all my life. We have more in common with Chicot than with western Ashley County. There was even talk of us seceding from Ashley and becoming

Eastern Ashley County." (Mark Hawkins) "They called us cornbread millionaires or swamp rats. When we went to Hamburg, they would tell us to go back to the swamp. They think everyone down here has a lot of money." (Ernie Sprinkle) "People in the hills think we don't have good judgment to live down here. They used to look down on Delta people but not anymore." (Edgar Norris) "Hill people thought they were better than us." (Katie Bell Parker) "The hillbillies owned their small farms and thought Delta folks were just sharecroppers and tenants except for the plantation owners." (Bealie Harrison) "Hillbillies thought they were better. They resented outsiders and were more clannish. The hillbilly boys would not talk to hill girls who dated Delta boys." (Clifton Trigg) "If a Delta team beat the Monticello football team, they would throw rocks at them. There is still a barrier but not like it used to be." (Butch Dennington) "Yes, there was and is a distinction made by some. The Delta people were fortunate to have more fertile land with higher yields – one-fourth bale to an acre in the hills compared to three-fourths in the Delta. Actually there was a feeling of superiority among folks who lived in the Delta due to the advantage of more fertile soil." (Siegfried Johnson) "They resented us someway. They didn't mind us calling them hillbillies, but if they called us swamp rats, that's when the fight would start. We didn't like them coming down here and hunting and fishing in our bayou." (Shorty Lyle) "They called us [blacks] bayou coons. I would tell them, 'You hillbillies just come out of the hills down here to hustle something to eat.'" (Alvie Pugh)

Mary Dean Pugh elaborated on the subject of the class distinction. "Overflow Hill was the boundary. The hillbillies resented people in the Delta. Percy George [who lived in Hamburg] spoke of the Delta as the idle rich. They viewed us as prosperous. There was a great divisiveness, a distinct difference. The Delta was the haves and the hillbillies were the have-nots. A Delta person dealt with hill people with some trepidation. They thought we spent money foolishly on fancy clothes, food, and parties. They regarded the large tenant population as unfortunate and disregarded them – looked over them. The tenant farmers did not even go to the hills. Delta people associated more with Bastrop than the hill towns like Hamburg and Monticello. We were more at home there. Our Mainline parties included mostly people from Dermott to Wilmot and also some from Tillar, Dumas, Winchester, and Pickens. McGehee was not included because it was a railroad town; the other towns were centered around farming and farm-owned mercantiles."

Martha Amanda Crawley was aware of the superior attitude held by people who lived in towns. She wrote from her home on Bayou Bartholomew in 1858, "I sincerely pity the soul that can not appreciate the waving trees, the melodies of little birds, with the thousand and one of

Nature's beauties by which we are surrounded...we 'country folks' are aware that we are often laughed at by our Town and City contemporaries for our rusticity. But what care we for that? Our souls are not limited by a few dresses, ribbons, and dusty streets, but have room to expand by the exercise of the God-given principles of industry, benevolence and hospitality. Our time is fully employed in teaching our children...attending to our dairies, kitchens and other household affairs...We are no egotists...but would only inform those who ridicule our awkwardness, that we 'country folks' care not so much for outer adornment, as we do for that 'meek and quiet spirit which is in the sight of God above price.'"[28]

Robert D. "Bob" Pugh, a fifth-generation native of Portland, echoed Amanda's Crawley's motif 139 years later. He wrote, "Living with this geographic diversity in a rural setting enables one to become entwined in the beauty and spiritual renewal of the seasonal changes. When I was a child, Portland was the only place I had really known in the true sense of the word. Obviously, my world has grown considerably since those early memories, but my admiration of this community in rural Arkansas continues to grow as my experiences and horizons widen...Having a close appreciation of this environment, through rural small-town living, makes one's life more interesting than ordinary and enables a person to keep a sense of perspective. Life here is lived with consideration, concern, and generosity."[29]

Leo King was living in Chicago in 1939 when he told his splendid tale, but his thoughts were elsewhere: "Used t' row down Bayou Bartholomew." Bayou people had a close relationship with their environment, the center of it being the bayou, which they loved. Dennis Tilbury expressed this in 1940: "This old Bayou holds many a secret of hope, romance, defeat, and death to its breast...Beautiful, Beautiful Bayou, Beautiful Bartholomew, we know that our fathers fought the fight that they might live on its banks. We may now live on its banks to the east or the west, or down in the hills at its mouth, yet we live on the Beautiful Bayou, Bayou Bartholomew."[30]

Most everyone has their special place - a place where they had rather be; a place where the world seems most right; a place that simply "feels good" to be there. This place can be a mountain, canyon, forest, seashore, lake, or stream. For Henry David Thoreau, it was a pond. For people who lived along the bayou, it was the bayou. Lily Strickland sang of her bayou in 1938:[31]

> *Some folks they love the river,*
> *An' some folks love the sea;*
> *Some folks they love the mountains,*
> *But Bayou's the place for me!*

Shorty Lyle stated simply, "I would just get up and the bayou would be there everyday. It was just there." For Shorty and many others like him, the bayou was his enduring sense of place where he felt he belonged; it was a constant, fundamental factor in his life. It was always *there*. Material possessions and personal relationships can be transitory and ephemeral, but when one loves a part of the natural landscape, they are never alone. Lily Strickland continued her song:

> *Friends they come, an' friends they go;*
> *Noth-in' lasts for long, I know:*
> *You alone from day to day -*
> *Sing your song the same sweet way.*
> *Keep on singin' soft an' slow;*
> *Keep on singin' ol' Bayou.*

George Pugh was born and raised on Bayou Bartholomew and realized the impact it had on his life. He said, "I have strong ties here and I will never leave. When my life is over, I will end up on the bank of the bayou where I spent my childhood."[32] Lily Strickland ended her song:

> *When I reach my journey's end,*
> *I will know I had one friend.*
> *Sing on, Bayou, sing on!*

The flat Delta land was covered with forest during days of early settlement. A bayou gave relief to an otherwise dense landscape of trees, canebrakes, and swamps. After the timber was cut and some swamps drained, fields stretched to the east farther than the eye could see. To the west a protruding ridge broke the view. Within this monotonous vista ran a winding, glistening gem, a bayou that beckoned to all. It was an oasis that stretched for 359 miles with clean water, countless springs, sandy beaches, and shade trees. It was the center of life for its people. They swam, played, fished, and washed their clothes in it; they picnicked and hunted on its banks; they drank its water and the water of its springs; they came in solitude or great numbers; they were baptized in it; they lived and loved by it, and when they were dead, they were buried by it. Although their livelihood was primarily from the land, the bayou was the singular favored place to be. It was the *genus loci*, the place that made an enduring impression upon them; it was the "spirit of place." Bayou Bartholomew was home.

The Bayou Road

De souf road leads to New Awleans
Whah sum folks love to roam,
De norf road lead to Little Rock,
But de bayou road leads home.

De myrtle an de jassymine
Sweet as de honey comb,
Dey bloom beside de bayou road,
De road dat leads me home.

Awl dahkys sing in de cotton lan'
By de road ob sandy loam
De windin' road, de bayou road,
De road dat leads me home.

De bayou road's de road fo' me
De road dat leads me home.

J. A. Morris Sr.
Dermott (1869-1943)

Afterword

Sing on Bayou, Sing on!

Lament

It used to be such a pretty stream. It makes
me sick to look at it now.

Mary Morris Foster

The histories of the bayou and its people are inseparably interwoven. The history of a locale is irrevocably connected to the history of the people who share its milieu. Environmental historians pay particular attention to the relationship between man and the world around him. Thomas A. Woods wrote, "To understand the history of people, environmental historians study the interaction between the environment and human activity...people are clearly within nature and nature is within human history."[1] Sadly, human activity has caused significant aberration along this historical stream.

A 1994 report on water quality issued by the Arkansas Department of Pollution Control and Ecology stated that the entire length of the stream was suitable for the propagation of fish and wildlife; primary and secondary contact recreation; and public, industrial, and agricultural water supplies. It also stated, however, that 184.2 miles contained water degraded by nonpoint source pollution. (This is pollution caused by the movement of sediments, nutrients, and organic chemicals from diffuse sources to points of concentrations.) The report concluded that high sediment loads and turbidity caused degradation to the aquatic life. It also noted that pathogens, sediment/turbidity, and mercury levels impaired fish consumption, aquatic life, and swimming. The final analysis was that row crop agriculture appeared to be the major source of the nonpoint pollution.[2]

The bayou's joyful song is muted now; it has become a dirge. Throughout its history, people acclaimed its natural beauty, pristine purity, and usefulness. American Indians, Spanish colonists, and the earliest settlers recognized and valued its worth. Today people who grew up on it extol the bayou's virtues, but they also feel despair about its present condition. Mary Roane Tomlinson wrote in 1938, "To beauty lovers of the trees and flora this Bartholomew Bayou and swamp region give a breathless delight. There is nothing in all Arkansas more lovely than the hawthorn, wild plum and dogwood thickets mingled with redbud bushes all showered with bloom and mixed with the evergreen holly trees. These, with the towering cypress and the majestic oaks, make a landscape both beautiful and unforgettable, with a foreground of the peculiar reddish-green bayou water, covered with younquepins (the Arkansas lotus), water lilies, glistening swamp spider lilies, tall cattails, ferns and lush water plants." She also wrote the same year, "For a long period the beauty of the Bayou Bartholomew was unmolested."[3]

People became negligent in their role as caretakers of the earth and abused the beautiful, natural stream. The timber industry destroyed the magnificent hardwood bottomland forests that lined the banks and left tops of trees and wood scrap in the channel. This blockage caused silt backup and decreased the normal flow. With the lack of the natural barrier formed by the forest, topsoil washed into the bayou. Farmers cleared the abandoned timberland and transformed it into fields that also drained into the bayou through manmade drainage ditches. This runoff not only contained soil but in later years was inundated with befouling chemicals used in agriculture. With the advent of irrigation more topsoil and pollutants entered the stream. The final insult was that the bayou became a dumping ground. Dennis Tilbury wrote from Wilmot in 1939, "It makes me sad to see this stuff [rubbish, tin cans, old automobiles] gathered in town and dumped out on our county roads and lanes, and most especially on the banks of the beautiful, beautiful Bayou."[4] Alvie Pugh observed, "The Bible said man will destroy himself, and man has destroyed the bayou."

The bayou is now defiled by man's careless disregard. Impenetrable drifts of timber waste and fallen trees block the passage for boats. "You can't get a rowboat in at Lind Grove now," Cecil Harp declared. The barriers collect and hold indisputable evidence of the farmers' indifference. Fifty-gallon drums that once contained pesticides, herbicides, and other harmful chemicals float insolently in the debris among copious smaller containers. These bright yellow, blue, and green casks are grotesquely out of place where people once swam, fished and received baptism. Murphy Brockman said, "People use the bayou bridges and banks for dumping; poison barrels are everywhere in the bayou now." "I used to commercial fish in the bayou," said Garvin Adcock. "Now it is overflowing with agricultural chemicals."

The devastation of the stream is conspicuous in the permutation of its many springs that once flowed so freely. John Edd Curry said, "There are not as many springs now. Too many irrigation wells have caused the water table to drop." Amos Sledge echoed, "There are not half as many springs now because of all the irrigation. The water level in my well has fallen four feet in the last ten years." Thelbert Bunch admitted, "It's time to be

concerned about the water table because so many wells are going down."
Harvey Chambliss said, "The springs have stopped running now due to so
much sediment from the farms." Oren Robertson declared, "The springs
used to keep the bayou full. Now it is a drainage ditch." Edgar Norris
concluded, "Springs used to run all the time, but the bayou is now full of
silt and debris. It has aged from man's abuse."

Irrigation from deep wells not only drops the water table, but also the
excess water drains back into the bayou carrying soil and residue from
agricultural chemicals with it. "Around here a thousand acres of rice water
goes into the bayou. It ruins the fishing," Murphy Brockman observed.
"People do not realize that irrigation water drainage is putting their topsoil
back into the bayou and that they will never see it again. What makes the
bayou muddy is irrigation drainage and too much plowing," declared
Andrew Pickens. Farmers also dug drainage ditches leading to the bayou
to carry excess rainwater. Estelle Works said, "The bayou was clear and
free-running. Then they built drainage ditches for the buckshot land, and
when it rained the bayou became muddy." Murphy Brockman said, "It's
not as clear now because of so much agricultural drainage." Lift pumps
used in irrigation also invariably leak oil into the bayou.

A combination of all the factors caused the bayou to fill with silt.
Amos Sledge said, "In 1947 the bayou was much bigger and clearer. You
could see to the bottom. The fish holes are not as deep. Where there used
to be holes eight to ten feet deep, they are only four to five feet now. They
cleared the farmland too close to it and caused it to fill up." Murphy
Brockman observed, "It is not as clear now because the agricultural
drainage makes it muddy. In 1948 there were holes twenty-two feet deep
that are now only seven or eight feet deep. The silt came from cutting the
timber and drainage ditches." "Clearing land plus all the rice canals ruined
it," declared Frank Day. "At one time the runoff water filtered through
straw, leaves, and brush, and that cleaned the water. You used to could see
fish down through the water. It is ruined; it will never be the same."

Other molestations occurred. "It was clear except during high water,
but people would throw dead stock in it," Duke Shackelford said. Murphy
Brockman told of similar incidents. "Sometimes horses or cows would go
down to drink and they couldn't get turned back around in the cypress
knees. They would keep working and get bogged down and sink and die.
People would leave them there, and it would make filth in the bayou. It
happened with a lot of stock. Most farms had a place cleared out for their
stock to go down and drink." In more recent years a 2,000-gallon diesel
tank near Wilmot spilled its contents into the bayou through a canal.
Benton Hunt, who lives below the state line, said, "There were dead fish all
around here from it." Ed Jones remembered when a crop duster fell into

the bayou above Bastrop. "It killed everything from there to the Ouachita River."

Perhaps the consummate illustration of the bayou's near ruination is found in one of its previous uses. People used to drink its water. "The water was clear as a crystal. We drank out of it. Everybody did." (Winifred Day) "We drank out it, but they put poison in it now." (Earl Kitchens) "We drank from it in the autumn. It was clear and cool." (Alvie Pugh) "We moved to the bayou in December 1942 and had no running water or pump. We drank out of the bayou until June 1943. Lots of people did and no one ever got sick. It was fresh and running." (Bobby Abraugh) "We drank from it and its springs." (Buster Ford) "The bayou was cleaner then. We used its water to drink." (Bessie Green) "You could find a spring most anywhere along the bayou, but people drank water out of the bayou too." (Herman King) Duke Shackelford bluntly stated, "Good Lord! We drank water out of the bayou."

Cecil Harp summarized his view of the wholesale destruction of the bayou. "When I came back here in 1946 it was still a beautiful place. There was always a lot of water, and the fishing was always good. The water was clear and there were no chemicals in it to kill the fish and turtles. Then they logged too close to it and left scraps in it. Agricultural chemicals and too much irrigation messed it up more." Susie Fuqua lamented, "It was a clear, running stream and swift in the shallows. There's nothing to it now; it doesn't even look like the bayou anymore. They used to keep it cleaned out for boats to get through. Now people throw garbage in it. It looks like an old get-out. People don't take care of running water anymore. I am so sorry about how it looks now. It just makes me sick."

Steamboats were able to navigate the bayou only with the help of man who kept the channel cleared. The 1893 report of the Chief of Engineers stated, "Successive high winds had passed over the bayou during the year, and Overseer Decker reported that never before in his experience had he seen a stream so badly obstructed by fallen timber throughout its entire length. Many of the trees reached from bank to bank at the low stage of water, and there were from one to a dozen between all landings...At the State line a cyclone had passed, and for a distance of half a mile nearly every tree along the west bank had blown into the stream."[5]

Nature herself has an adverse effect on the bayou during catastrophic as well as normal events, adding to the corruption caused by humanity's dereliction. Leaning trees naturally fall into the channel. Tornadoes and high winds hurl large amounts of timber into the stream. Ice storms cause limbs and entire trees to break and fall. The devastating ice storm of 1994 left the bayou cluttered with fallen timber. The clogging timber drifts form impassable barriers, and more debris and rubbish from upstream backs up behind the obstructions. The bayou becomes filled with silt. It is constricted, retarded, congested, stifled, and strangulated.

Some people have wondered if the bayou was named after the apostle and saint, Bartholomew, who was flayed alive and is portrayed in art as carrying his skin in his hand or wrapped around him as a cloak. A bayou that carries his name has been flayed as well. Stripped and denuded of its once pristine, natural beauty, Bayou Bartholomew needs help.

Hope

Why doesn't someone do something about it?
Dr. Curtis Merrell

There is hope that the bayou will be restored to resemble its former natural state – to the way it was in 1900. It is estimated that it will take fifty years of concentrated hard work to overcome one hundred years of abuse and neglect. The hope lies in the hands of the Bayou Bartholomew Alliance with the cooperation of many state and federal agencies as well as the public. In the spring of 1995, Dr. Curtis Merrell of Monticello drove across the bayou bridge at Yorktown and once more made note of the muddy water and poor condition of the stream. He estimated that since he began commuting ten years earlier to his job as director of the Arkansas River Education Service Cooperative in Pine Bluff, he had crossed this bridge 6,000 times. Each time he crossed, the beleaguered bayou caught his attention. A nagging thought lingered in his mind: "Why doesn't someone do something about it?" At last it occurred to him that he would be the one to initiate the effort to "do something."

That spring he invited ten Monticello area residents to a meeting to discuss his concern about the neglect of the bayou and its appalling condition. He was pleasantly surprised to learn that the nine who attended shared his concern, and some told stories about the clear water of only forty or fifty years earlier when they waded, swam, and fly fished in it. With this encouragement, Merrell began to think hard about forming an organized effort to clean up and restore the bayou. Randall Mathis, Director of the Department of Environmental Quality, encouraged him to form an organization. In July, Merrell held a public meeting attended by the general public, bayou landowners, and representatives of the Arkansas Soil and Water Commission, Arkansas Game and Fish Commission, Corps of Engineers, University of Arkansas Cooperative Extension Service, Nature Conservancy, and other agencies. After speaking briefly of his vision to restore the water quality, provide more public access, educate the public about conservation, and coordinate with landowners on a voluntary basis, the agency representatives offered strong support. Only one person out of the sixty attending made any negative comments. The group decided to form an organization and incorporate as a non-profit. They elected Merrell president and gave him the responsibility of selecting the initial board membership.[6]

The board developed goals and by-laws, applied for and received a state charter as a non-profit corporation in October 1995, and received an

IRS 501-C3 designation as non-profit in 1996. The state charter established the goals of the Bayou Bartholomew Alliance as follows:

1. To improve the water quality of Bayou Bartholomew where it flows through Jefferson, Lincoln, Desha, Chicot, Drew, and Ashley Counties, Arkansas.
2. To restore and preserve the natural beauty of Bayou Bartholomew.
3. To educate the people including students in the public school districts of Arkansas about the esthetic and ecological value of Bayou Bartholomew, and its historical significance to the region.
4. To enhance the benefits of Bayou Bartholomew as they relate to wildlife and public recreation.
5. To improve the overall benefits of Bayou Bartholomew to the landowners adjacent thereto and for other such purposes.

A Technical Support Group was formed in July 1996 with a stated role to: (1) identify problems as related to the BBA objectives listed in the BBA by-laws; (2) develop solutions to the identified problems; (3) develop an overall plan with timelines for implementing the solutions; (4) assist in implementing the plan. Among the twenty-three members of the group were representatives from the following agencies: Arkansas Soil and Water Conservation Commission, Arkansas Game and Fish Commission, Division of Volunteerism, Bayou Bartholomew Alliance, Northeast Delta RC&D of Louisiana, USDA Natural Resources Conservation Service, University of Arkansas Cooperative Extension Service, Environmental Protection Agency, Arkansas Department of Pollution Control and Ecology (now the Department of Environmental Quality), U.S. NBS-TBC-7RP (UAPB), U.S. Fish and Wildlife Service, and Ducks Unlimited, Inc.

The Technical Support Group presented its findings in a booklet entitled *Short and Long Term Strategies for Restoring Bayou Bartholomew*. The introduction states, "Bayou Bartholomew is one of the few remaining large bayous that has not been channelized for improved drainage of cropland. Over 3,000 rural landowners live within the watershed boundaries [997,000 acres]. More than 50 percent of the watershed area is classified as prime agricultural land...Current land use is 20 percent cropland, seven percent grassland, and 73 percent forestland. Most of the forestlands are classified as forested wetlands. A large percentage of bottomland hardwoods are seasonally flooded. The Bayou is very important to fish and wildlife. The wetlands serve as a source of food and cover for fish and wildlife production. The area contains more than 250 species of fish and wildlife. Other wetland benefits are also important. They include benefits for water quality improvement, groundwater recharge, erosion control, fish production, and recreation. The Bayou is also a source of irrigation water. Because of these benefits, many interests compete for use of the Bayou water resource and adjacent land. In order to meet local needs, a balance must be reached. Improved water quality will benefit all land use objectives." A total of fifteen problems with potential sources or causes were identified as the following:

1. Sediment (cropland, riparian, streambanks, construction, bedload, silviculture, county roads)

2. Nutrients (points sources, agricultural practices, sediment, water from runoff and tailwater from irrigation, septic systems)

3. Dumping (lack of dump facilities, lack of recycling programs, lack of waste management services, lack of education)

4. Log jams (beavers, silviculture, ice storms, agricultural practices, stream flow)

5. In-stream flow (water use from surface and groundwater, land management, agricultural/industrial/municipal practices, urban development/industry, stream grading from channelization and tree cutting)

6. Habitat alteration (wetland drainage, land use change, development, channelization/maintenance, in-stream flow, logging, agricultural practices)

7. Diverse uses and interest (agriculture, public access, recreational activities, commercial fishing, point source discharge, dumping)

8. Lack of public access (private ownership, legal issues, funding, willing sellers)

9. Improper application of pesticides/herbicides (application mistakes/spills, lack of education, equipment, lack of enforcement of regulations, lack of erosion control, improper use of land or pesticides, improper calibration of equipment, improper application equipment, lack of scouting/consultation services)

10. Chemical barrels (see # 3, lack of dump sites, lack of regulation enforcement, lack of education, lack of recycling programs, lack of waste management services, cost factor)

11. Rock weirs (in-stream flow, irrigation needs for water control, lack of regulation/enforcement)

12. Improper management of irrigation water (lack of education, lack of technical assistance, lack of regulation/enforcement, mismanagement of irrigation and tailwater, lack of a water management plan)

13. Dissolved oxygen (nutrients, in-stream flow, lack of riparian vegetation area)
14. Lack of information exchange (lack of funding, lack of organization, lack of common data base, lack of cooperation, improper perception, lack of education, diverse interest groups)
15. Mercury (atmospheric, geologic)

The group formulated short term and long term plans to address each of the problems and the sources or causes. The booklet details specific strategies for solving all aspects of the problems and suggests possible funding for the projects.[7]

The Alliance operated out-of-pocket and on small donations until it received its first grant money, $9,000, from the McKnight Foundation through the Winrock International Foundation in 1996. Later that year the Weyerhaeuser Family Foundation conferred a grant of $25,000 for 1996, $15,000 1997, and $10,000 for 1998. Rick Weyerhaeuser, a resident of Massachusetts and chairman of the board at that time, said, "This is the first grant we have ever awarded without first making a site visit." In October 1996 the Alliance received a $25,000 grant from the National Fish and Wildlife Foundation. It was the largest grant given by the NFWF that year. In 1997 the Department of Pollution Control and Ecology awarded a grant which allowed the Alliance to employ its first full-time coordinator. Dr. Bill Layher, who had been conducting studies on the bayou for three years for the U.S. Geological Survey, assumed the coordinator's position in January 1998. The Three Rivers Audubon Society donated $1,500 which was used for materials which went into the building of over a hundred wood duck boxes.

In January 1999 the Arkansas Soil and Water Commission awarded a grant in the amount of $369,750 for services to be provided over a three year period in Jefferson and Lincoln Counties. The grant was used, along with other things, to place water quality technicians in the District Conservation Offices of Jefferson and Lincoln Counties. The technicians work with all landowners in the bayou watershed in these counties to make them aware of government financial incentives for conservation programs and to help those who want assistance in preparing conservation plans and applications. A no-till drill, at a cost of about $30,000, was purchased for loan or rent to farmers in those counties. A portion of the grant will be used to help the city of Pine Bluff develop and implement plans to reduce contamination of the bayou caused by pollution and contamination carried into the bayou from the urban area. Some monies from the grant were used to develop teaching modules for teaching conservation principles and needs to young people.

Other funds for restoration have been provided by ARKLA, International Paper Company, Tyson Foods, Arkansas Game and Fish Commission Stream Team Program, Environmental Protection Agency, private citizens, and landowners. Potlatch Corporation donated hardwood seedlings for planting in buffer zones. American Forests helped with funding to purchase 202,000 seedlings to be planted on 432 acres of previously farmed land along the bayou. The Alliance has applied for another multi-year Soil and Water Commission grant to address bayou problems in Ashley, Chicot, Desha, and Drew Counties.

Members of the Alliance and volunteers have completed several work projects along the bayou. They have restored riparian sites ruined by clear-cutting, planted 302,500 hardwood seedlings, and conducted three major trash removals at Highway 15 Bridge, Pinebergen Road Bridge, and Baxter. From these sites they removed such items as mattresses, grocery carts, furniture, rolls of carpet, newspaper vending machines, stoves, washing machines, tires, hot water tanks, television sets, 55-gallon drums, lawnmowers, a motorcycle, and a large metal safe. After the Baxter site was cleared of rubbish, workers completed a bank stabilization project by placing riprap, covering it with topsoil and erosion mats, and seeding it with grass. They returned to plant river birch and pecan seedlings on the fill. The material for this work was funded by a grant from the Arkansas Game and Fish Commission's Stream Team Program. The riprap, composed of chunks of concrete from a demolished bridge, was donated by the Drew County judge. The Alliance coordinated with the Department of Community Punishment to use female residents to clean up eight miles along the bayou near Pine Bluff. Male inmates from the Department of Correction have also been utilized.

When the Arkansas Game and Fish Commission began its Stream Team Program in 1997, the Alliance was named the state's first Stream Team. Bayou Bartholomew has now been included in the Nature Conservancy's list of streams in need of protection to maintain the nation's aquatic biodiversity. In an effort to make the bayou more accessible to the public, the Alliance is seeking to purchase (or have donated) small plots of land in each county for boat ramps.

Plans for the future are optimistic. Dr. Merrell wrote, "We plan to have a concrete boat ramp in at least four counties by the middle of 2001. We plan to realign logs or cuts swaths through log jams to make the bayou navigable by small boat throughout its length in Arkansas by the end of 2001. We plan to conduct numerous clean up days. We plan to step up the efforts to promote no-till or reduced tillage farming and winter water storage on rice fields, as well as promoting the construction of water reservoirs, planting buffer zones, et cetera. Look at the bayou now and watch it change for the better over the next five, ten, twenty, thirty, forty, fifty years! The bayou will once again have clean, high quality water, with public access, with buffer zones of hardwood and ground cover, with an abundance of edible fish and habitat for many animal species, a magnificent stream, unique to America, restored and preserved by thousands of concerned citizens."[8]

With the help of the Bayou Bartholomew Alliance, the many agencies involved with it, volunteers, and cooperation from landowners, there is hope that the bayou will be restored and that it can once more sing its song. David R. Brower's "A Credo for the Earth" eloquently pleads for mankind's conscientious treatment of and respect for the natural environment. His words speak of the universe, and they aptly fit a small part of it – a beloved bayou and a stream of history.

There is but one ocean though its coves have many names; a single sea of atmosphere with no coves at all; the miracle of soil, alive and giving life, lying thin on the only earth, for which there is no spare.
We seek a renewed stirring of love for the earth. We plead that what we are capable of doing to it is often what we ought not to do. We urge that all people now determine that an untrammeled wildness shall remain here to testify that this generation had love for the next.
We would celebrate a new renaissance. The old one found a way to exploit. The new one has discovered the Earth's limits. Knowing them, we may learn anew what compassion and beauty are, and pause to listen to the Earth's music.
We may see that progress is not the accelerating speed with which we multiply and subdue the earth nor the growing number of things we possess and cling to. It is a way along which to search for truth, to find serenity and love and reverence for life, to be part of an enduring harmony, trying hard not to sing out of tune.[9]

Sing on, Bayou Sing On!

Early Parkdale facing the railroad

Jerome Relocation Center, 1942

Wilmot City Hall, 1920

Captain J. B. Avery c. 1880

Steven Gaster (1800-1860)

Dermott Children at Viviene Skipper's seventh birthday party, 1927.
Front row, l to r: Annie Lang, Lois Grubb, Robert Grubb, Virginia Hoffman Hodges,
Ernest Crenshaw, Kate Hoffman Bynum, James Leeper,Joe Mercer Bennett, Eugene
Schnelz. Second row, l to r: Joe Dante, Helen Blanks Johnson, Scottie Courtney Evans,
Mary Wayne Mercer, unknown, unknown, Mabel Gregg, Viviene Skipper Morris,
Christine Kennedy, Blanche Neel. Third row l to r: Jennie Cohan Nunsbaum, Lillian
Gregg, Charles Schnelz, C. Johnson, Curtis Singleton. Back row l to r: Marie Bulloch,
May Berryman Jeffers, Marie Long, Mildred Mercer, Dorothy Anderson Lowe.

Tarry school group, 1913

Amanda Crawley (1827-1880)

J. Fred Crawley (born 1817)

Dr. Charles McDermott house

City Hotel, Dermott, 1910s

Wilmot, Track Meet, 1913

Dr. J. C. Chenault (right) in
front of his office, McGehee, c. 1914

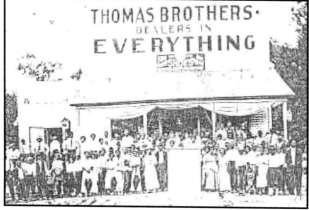

Thomas Brothers Store at Tarry. Left to right behind the podium
are owners R.L. and Wallace Thomas Sr., July 4, 1913

S.A. Duke House at Baxter

Main Street Portland, from postcard dated 1909

Hollywood Plantation House. Left to Right: Mildred Saunders Wood, Mrs. Dillard
Saunders, Jonathan Gibson Taylor, Mrs. Minnie Taylor, Garland Currie, 1914

St. Mary's Hospital, Dermott

William's Gin at Winchester, 1939

Pickens Commissary

Dermott Grocery and Commissary in the 1927 flood. Front, l to r: Harry Rose, L.W. McClenny, C.B Brevan, Mrs. Shemwell, R.C. McClerkin, J.H. Alexander. Back: l to r: S. L. Bowman, Herman Brown, Mrs. Clara Bulloch, and unknown

Jones Main Street from the north, c. 1910-1920. At this time the first building on the right was empty. Next to it is the Knox Nunn store with the gin stack in the background. The first building on the left is the Victor and Kay Sons store followed by Mr. Watt's store and the Methodist Church with the Masonic Lodge on the top story.

Wilmot Depot and Main Street, 1940s

North entrance to Tarry. Building on the right is the M.M. Taliaferro Store. The two story building on the left is the Colored Lodge, followed by the C.H. Clowers Store, c.1920s

McGinty Church group at the second church

Tom Day's store on the Crossett Highway north of Bastrop. Picture
l to r: unknown salesman, Frank Day, Sr., Tom Day, c. 1927

The steamer Mattie on Bayou Bartholomew or D'Arbonne.

The Water Lily, c. 1883

The Welcome, c.1905

The Tensas loaded to the guards, c. 1882

Bastrop bill of lading for J. W. Bowe at Lind Grove, 1879

Steamers Lily, ? Eagle, Saint Paul, and Quachita, probably at Quachita City.

John Howard bill of lading
for J.W. Boone at Lind Grove,
c. 1889

The John Howard, c. 1889

D. Stein bill of lading for J.C. and A.C. Nobles, who lived near Poplar Bluff, 1881

The D. Stein loaded with cotton, "in bayou country Louisiana," possibly at Point Pleasant, c. 1878

Captain Cooley's Ouachita, 1890-1926

The Handy, one of the last boats on Bartholomew, c. 1905 -1909

A ferry across Bartholomew in Morehouse Parish. Women l to r: Mary Jane Naff Day and Francis Moore Naff

A "half-wagon" in front of the McGehee-Thomas house at Tarry. N.M. Shell, plantation manager for the McGehee Planting Co. drives the wagon for Lizzie Goolsby, a local midwife and cook for the Thomas family, c. 1930

Building the bridge over the bayou at Baxter, 1916. Barkley White, foreman

The "Little Star" houseboat. Jesse McCain is in the pilot house. Pictured l to r: William Penn McCain, Bell McCain, Claude and Audie Mae McCain, Mattie and Jim McCain, 1906

The old Indian ford at Hollywood Plantation

Floating bridge at Zachary used by children to cross the bayou to school.
The boy in the boat is Jack Blanks and behind him is Caster Causey, 1925

Ferry south of Baxter, c. 1886. Men's first names are Will and Jim

Bonita school during the flood

Dermott in the 1927 flood. The caption reads, "On right looking to rear: Silbernagle Co. building, Dermott Grocery Co., Chicot Hotel, Exhange Bank. Across the railroad tract (line to Warren) on left is Dermott Bank. To the left is the two-story Dermott Hotel where Mary and I had a room during this flood. James Alexander"

A flood dilemma in Morehouse Parish

Raymond C. Hopkins poses in front of his Montrose home

A train reaches Montrose during the flood

Raging floodwater breaks through a crevasse in Morehouse Parish

Montrose residents adapt to the flooded streets

A house succumbs to the flood, Morehouse Parish

"Those who served" at Old Soldiers Day in Lincoln County

The Tigress, second from right, at Pittsburgh Landing during the siege at Shiloh

A thirteen-year-old farmer , (Dr.) H.W. Thomas, peddles his pumkin crop at Tarry, 1913

First rice combine at the McCloy farm at Baxter, 1929

Plowing with mules at Hollyhurst Plantation, Morehouse Parish

A Taylor man in the cypress swamps
near Hollywood Plantation

Detail of choctaw log retrieved from the Arkansas River

Farmhand lunch at the W.H. Lephiew farm near Baxter, 1915. Seated l to r: Peneo
Daniels, ? Sims, W. J. Splawn, Frank Etter, J. E. Leeper, W. G. Payne. Standing l to r: W.
H. Lephiew, W. Elvin Lephiew, Charlie Skipper, Ed Crenshaw, Milburn Austin

The Tank Saloon at Baxter

Willie F. Skipper

Parkdale Depot, scene to a murder

Deer hunting camp at Deep Elm near Jerome, c. 1938. Standing l to r: Roy Galloway, Byran Martin or Edgar Morgan, Curtis DeArmond, Chester Netherland of Bastrop, Ned O'Neill, unknown, Dewey Helms of El Dorado, Wesley Cruce, Bennie Hollingsworth. Seated l to r: Dolly Jolley, O. O. Axley, Gold DeArmond, John Hemphill, G. B. Colvin, Alex Carr. All men are from Bradley County except as noted.

Deer hunting camp near Dermott. Pictured l to r: L. Gordon, O. H. Mayes, C. F. Skipper, J. A. Bennett, Sidney Blythe (holding dog), C. J. Bishop, J. A. Morris, Ed Wagner (holding deer) O. A. Lowe, Peneo Daniels, Sid Jeffett, W. J. Splawn, Charley Carwford, T. H. Biggs.

Bluford Boone and dog, Blue, ready to check on wood hogs,
Jones-Bonita area, c. 1913

The Roosevelt camp in the Tensas Swamp, 1907. The
third man from the left is believed to be Ichabod Brooks

Edgar Morris and Dumas School students with alligator caught at the Moore place

Adam Withers with twelve-foot alligator at Baxter

Naff hunting camp with covered wagon. Pictured l to r: Ernest Brodnax, Allen Hausey, James Ford, "Big Jim" Naff. Standing, R. L. Vining, Herman Eubanks

"Big Jim" Naff at camp on the bayou across from the Naff Plantation near Jones

Dinner on the ground at McGinty Church. The tent in the
background served as the church before one was built in 1904

Waiting to be baptized in the bayou by Rev. Thad Douglas at Zachary

A bayou baptizing at Baxter. Note the bridge filled with spectators

R. N. "Booster" Kinnaird with six-foot plus
gar weighing over 100 pounds

Bennie Haynes (holding buffalo), Rev. A. S. Bradford, R. N. "Booster" Kinnaird
with catfish

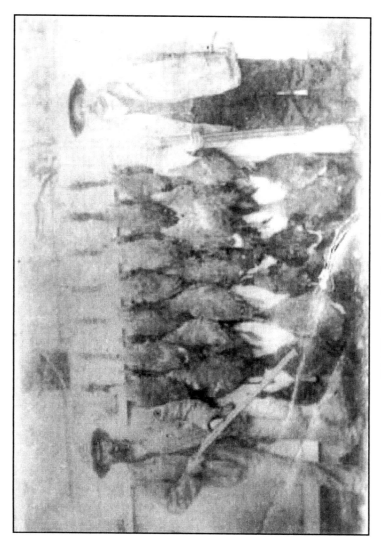

Ben Lilly and Theodore Roosevelt with turkeys

Bell McCain and Chris Korjan married on the bayou in 1914

Miss Williams, a teacher at Zachary School, rows merrily down the bayou in a pensive mood

Sunday afternoon on the bayou near McGinty. Pictured l to r: Bellita Causey McCain, unknown, Audrey Mae McCain

Roper family, c. 1926. l to r: Mode,
Jewel, Mary Tamzia Indiana (Sharp),
Mike, Jim Roper

Elmira (McCarty) Mayo and
Crawford A. Mayo I

McCain family, c. 1900. l to r: Oscar, age 7;
William Penn, age 36, Jess, age 10; John, age 4

Mary Butler Tipton (Born 1802),
wife of Henry Hoss Naff

Josiah Crenshaw family. Front row l to r: Willie (Jones) Crenshaw with Corene, Joe Crenshaw with Ida, Mary with Buddy and Anna. Back row l to r: Jack, Pearl, Jim, Sally, Bertha, Parlie, and Harvey. The child Irene was dead at this time, and Dollie Lee and J. C. not born.

Naff family members. L to r: Dora, William Elijah "Buck", Martha Ann, Frances "Fannie", John Allen "Jack", Lola Naff. Child is Robert Henry Day.

Dr. Charles McDermott (1804-1884)

Demarquis Ellis Harp (1845-1924) and
Willie Ann (Green) Harp (1855-1920)

James Jackson Keahey family, 1900. l to r: Martha,
George, Albert, James Jackson, Permilia (Campster),
Henry P., Lilly, Thadus (in stroller), Olla Keahey

Jennie Rosalie (Brown) and
Edwin Francis Mason on their
wedding day, April 18, 1883.
She was 32 and he was 39.

Author's Note

The family histories were obtained by the author during taped interviews with descendants of early bayou residents. The additional family histories were submitted by people who were also descended from bayou settlers. The summaries represent a joint effort for accuracy between the author and the submitters; however, the judicious genealogist should use the information presented here as a guide to primary sources for proper documentation. Some of the histories represent years of documented genealogical research, and others depict only what could be remembered by the respondents.

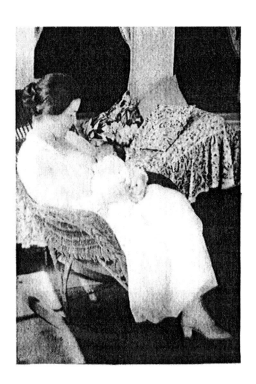

Part Two

Family Histories

*Those who do not consider themselves
as a link connecting the past and the future,
do not perform their duty to the world.*

Daniel Webster

Billy Bobby Abraugh

Billy Bobby Abraugh was born October 3, 1933, on the Jim Doles plantation near McGinty, the son of Hazel (Chandler) and Yeager Abraugh. Their other children were Joe William (m Alice Rea), Gladys Marie (m John T. Attaway), and Sandra Ellen (m Cecil Harp Jr.). Yeager Abraugh was born 23 Feb 1896, near Hebert, Franklin Parish, the son of Nettie and Sam Abraugh (b 18 May 1865; d 9 May 1932). Yeager moved to Jones in the late 1920s or early 1930s and worked on the Jim Doles plantation.

Hazel Chandler was born in 1911 at Pryor, OK, the daughter of Ellen (Evans) and Joe T. Chandler. Their other children were Ruth (m Roy Gray of Paris, AR), Freddie (m Mattie Lee Bunch), Joe Will (m Minnie Madison), Elmer (nev m), Velmer (twin to Elmer; m Lois Gillaspy), Elease (m 1st Charles Haynes; m 2nd C. J Courtney), and Dale Evan (m Jane Wing). Ellen Evans was born in 1892 at Russellville, AR, the daughter of Sarah (Jones) and John Thomas Evans. Sarah Jones was born in 1853 and died in 1900. John Thomas Evans was born in 1843 and died in 1899. The Evans father migrated in 1883 from Wales to Tennessee where he worked in the coal mines. After saving money, he sent for his family to join him. The passage took eleven days to New York. They then traveled by train to Tennessee. Upon hearing about coal mining being developed in Arkansas, they moved to Russellville in 1890.

Joe T. Chandler was born 9 Feb 1882 at Clarksville, AR, the son of Callie Isabella (May) and George William Tipton Chandler. Their other children were Jefferson Dewey, Charles Leon (m Martha Dobbs), and Katie (m Arthur Thomas). Callie Isabella May was born 24 Jul 1858 in Knoxville, TN. George William Tipton Chandler was born 3 Sep 1857 in Granger County TN. Joe T. Chandler moved from Ozark in 1931 to the Jim Doles plantation, where his brothers, Charlie and Jeff were working. Joe T. Chandler was a skilled bricklayer and stone mason. After the first crop was made, the family moved to the Naff farm.

Hazel Chandler and Yeager Abraugh eloped in 1933. They farmed for Kate Doles Taylor (Jim Doles' widow) and her husband, James Taylor, until 1934 when they moved to Baskin, LA. In 1939 they moved to the Naff farm and in 1940 relocated to the Walter Doles farm. They worked on the Roy Boone farm in 1942 and on the Lafayette Hopkins farm the following year. From 1944-46, Abraugh rented the James Taylor farm at McGinty. In 1947 he leased a farm near Jones from the Niemier-Darragh Estate.

Bobby Abraugh attended McGinty School through the sixth grade and then graduated from Bonita High School. He received a B.A. from Northern Louisiana University. Bobby married Gloria Hawkins, who was born at Bastrop, the only child of Minnie (Graham) and Johnny Hawkins. Minnie Graham's second marriage was to James Campbell Taylor, who adopted Gloria. James C. Taylor was born 1912, the son of Mary Dove (Allen) and Henry R. T. Taylor who were married in 1908 in Arcadia, LA. Their only other child was Mary Belle (b 1919; m Hollis Lock). James C. Taylor was first married to Kate (Madison) Doles, widow of Jim Doles.

Children born to Gloria (Hawkins) and Bobby Abraugh were Jennifer (m William E. Foster) and Julie Kay (m Dewey E. Weaver Jr.

Garvin Adcock

Garvin Adcock was born March 24, 1912, near Ladelle, the son of Dolly (Barnett) and Edgar Ernest "Eck" Adcock. Their only other child was Wesley (m Sarah Maddox). Eck Adcock was born in Alabama, the son of Charlie Adcock. Eck Adcock came to Arkansas with his siblings, Elsie Mae (m 1st Sam Barnett; m 2nd Holcraft from Line), Effie Mae (m Lena Rash), and Wade (moved to Oklahoma). Three brothers and three sisters stayed in Alabama. Dolly Barnett was the daughter of Nancy Catherine (Talley) and Ander P. Barnett. Ander Barnett was born in Mississippi and was a chairmaker by trade.

Garvin attended school at Shady Grove between Ladelle and Collins and then began to farm. He moved his family to the Skipper Bridge area near Dermott in 1940 where he rented land from R. T. Smith. Two years later he bought forty-four acres from Winford Wilson in Lambert Bend north of Baxter.

Garvin married Louella Maddox, the daughter of Catherine (Byrd) and M. F. Maddox. Children born to Louella and Garvin Adcock were Ernest Franklin (m Daisy Mae Marler), Erla Mae (m J. D. Ward), William (m three times), Ella Mae (m Robert Gorman), and Charles Edward (m Dovey Williams). Garvin said his father named his grandchildren "Mae" after his parents in Alabama. When asked how many grandchildren he had, he replied, "Oh, Lord! I don't know. There are over forty of them."

James Bealer

James Bealer was born August 29, 1894, at Thebes, the son of Susie (Larkin) and Andrew Bealer. James married Mary Wimberley and their children were Virginia, James Jr., Pearlene, and Lee Anna.

Ruth Mayo Boone

Ruth O'Lee Mayo Boone was born February 19, 1924, at McGinty, the daughter of Pearl Alma (Crenshaw) and Crawford Arnold Mayo II. Their other children were Hubert Arnold (m Flois Mae Wooden), Elsie Mae (m Calvin Rutherford Smith), Dudley Armstead (m Dorothy May Kelly), Joel Oliver (m Mary Louise Hudson), Lucille (m 1st Lowell Glendal Croom); m 2nd Bobby Ray Kennedy, Crawford Arnold III (m Billie Irene Fulcher Springman), and Dorman Edgar (m Sandra Warren).

Crawford Arnold Mayo II was born 13 May 1895 at McGinty, the son of Elmira Jane (McCarty) and Crawford Arnold "Dock" Mayo I. Their other children were Joel C. (b 20 Jan 1890; m Mattie Locke; d 28 Nov 1917), William Philip "Mack" (b 30 Mar 1893; m Lillie Mae Hayden), Goodrich Crump (b 5 Feb 1897; m Arrie Dee Manning), George Naff (b 28 Nov 1901; m Bertha Manning Boone), Vala Mae (b 20 May 1904; m Ray Crenshaw), and Dock Riley (b 26 Apr 1907; m Gladys Lee Crenshaw).

Elmira Jane McCarty, second wife of Crawford Arnold Mayo I, was born 15 Jan 1870, the daughter of M. R. (maiden name unknown) and William P. McCarty who were married c1853 in AL. Their other children were Henry Jackson (b Jun 1854 GA or AL; d 1913; bu Hamby Cemetery, Jones, LA; m c1883 Anna Eliza McClellan Locke), N. T. (b c1857), Theodocia (b c1870 LA), and Sarah (b c1873 LA).

Crawford Arnold "Dock" Mayo I was first married (c 1870) to [?] Elizabeth Ann (Crawford), and their children were Missouri (b 1871; m Matthew Y. McCarty, 25 May 1895), Dora E. (b Jan 1874; m John Turner 6 Jan 1893; d 1939), and Powis Armstead (b 22 Sep 1877; nev m; d 23 Dec 1927). Dock Mayo was living in LA by 1850. After his first wife died, he married Elmira Jane McCarty on 21 Jan 1889 in Morehouse Parish. Elmira was nineteen years old when she married, and Dock's daughter, Missouri, was eighteen. The family settled at McGinty before 1895. (The marriage of Elizabeth Ann (Crawford) and Crawford Arnold Mayo I has never been documented. Oral tradition is the source of his first wife's name. In 1870 he was living with his mother and a girl of 18 named Juel.)

Crawford Arnold Mayo I was born 30 Oct 1840, in AL, the son of Rebecca Jewell (it is not known if Jewell was a surname or given name) and John A. Mayo. Their other children, all born in AL, were Josephine (b c 1844), Joel D. (b c 1846; nev m; d 8 Aug 1887), and Sarah Eveline (b 17 Oct 1850; m Josephus Franklin "John" Howell; d 9 Oct 1911). John A. Mayo was born c 1808 in VA. Rebecca Jewell Mayo was born c 1815 and died 9 Sep 1879.

William P. McCarty married second (15 Feb 1875 in Lake Village, AR) Mary E. Simpson, and their children were Matthew Y. (b Apr 1878, Bayou Township, Ashley County; m 25 May 1895, Morehouse Parish, Missouri

Ann Mayo), Luke (b Jul 1888 AR; m 19 Sep 1915 in Oak Grove, West Carroll Parish, Della Sanders, H. [Henry?] (b Oct 1892 AR), and William Phillip (b Mar 1894 AR; m Rosie Evans Palmer). William P. McCarty was born Jun 1836 in GA and died after 1910.[1] The last reference to him is in the 1910 Ashley County census. M. R. McCarty was born in AL. Mary E. Simpson was born Aug 1856 in LA.

Children born to Missouri (Mayo) and Matthew Y. McCarty were Martha Ann (b 1897; d 18 Nov 1951; m Christual Lemuel Washington "Wash" Grice), William Philip "Bill" (b 23 Nov 1903); d 21 Aug 1984; m Mildred White), and Ella M. (b 14 Mar 1900; d 19 Jul 1991; m Ernest Leroy Bain).

Children born to Della (Sanders) and Luke McCarty were Precilla (b c1917; m ? Robinson), Othel (b 2 Sep 1919 West Carroll Parish), Ora (b 1929 Oak Grove, LA), and William James "Buddy" (b 25 Jun 1929 Oak Grove, LA).

Children born to Rosie Evans (Palmer) and William Phillip McCarty were Margarette, Audrey, Lucille, and Lavelle.

Children born to Anna Eliza McClellan (Locke) and Henry Jackson McCarty were Jesse J. (b 13 Jul 1885 LA; d 23 Jul 1962), William Henry (b Jul 1884 LA; m Ethel Yeldell), Ora Belle (b 11 Oct 1893, Jones; m Clarence C. Campbell), Claude L.(b 9 May 1895; d 20 Oct 1981; m Margaret Murphy), Maude M.(b c1897 LA), Mala M. (b c1899 LA; m Mock McKoin), Robert Leslie (b 13 Mar 1902; d 17 Apr 1982), and Myrtle Eva Leona (b 2 Oct 1907, Jones; m Romey Neal Snyder).

Children born to Ethel (Yeldell) and William Henry McCarty were Wilbur Douglas (b 23 Nov 1908; m Viola Ruth Robinson), Mattie Merle (b 24 Oct 1910), Henry Jackson (b 25 Sep 1913; m Erma Floyd), Mala Mabel (b 22 Feb 1917), and Ethel Leona (b 22 Jun 1922).

Children born to Ora Belle (McCarty) and Clarence C. Campbell were Ora Beatrice (b 15 Apr 1914, Jones; m C. H. Norris), Helen (b 14 Nov 1915, Jones; m Lester Leigh Eason), Clarence Mack (b 13 Jun 1919, Jones; m Aubrey Mae Hale), JoAnn (b aft 1925, Elaine, AR), and James Howard (b 1 Apr 1924, Elaine, AR; m Minnie Sneed). Clarence C. Campbell was born in LA, the son of Martha A. (Bilberry) and John Frank Campbell.

Children born to Mala M. (McCarty) and Mock McKoin were John Henry, Lucy, Gwendlyn, Kelly, and Julius Dair (b 11 Jul 1918; d 24 Apr 1971).

Children born to Myrtle Eva Leona (McCarty) and Romey Neal Snyder were Romey Neal Jr., Wallace, Mary Angela, Nan, Ann, Bobby Lee, Guy Arthur, Jackie Phillip, and Eva Isabel.

Children born to Martha Ann (McCarty) and Christual Lemuel Washington Grice were Eira Elva (b c1915; d 1931; bu Dry Bayou Cemetery near Wilmot), Henry (b 1917), David (b 1921), Christual Pouis (b 1919; d 23 Dec 1938; bu Dry Bayou Cemetery; nev m), William Benjamin, Edith (b and d 1925 Dumas, AR), Etta (b and d 1925 Dumas, AR), Ella Mae, Elma Jean, Ada Ruth, and Elva Jewel (b c1931; d 24 Dec 1938; bu Dry Bayou Cemetery).

Children born to Ella Myra (McCarty) and Earnest L. Bain were Bonnie Irene (b 2 Dec 1929) and Joyce Ann (b 7 Mar 1937).

For the children of Lillie Mae (Hayden) and William Philip Mayo, see Dan P. Mayo summary.

Children born to Arrie Dee (Manning) and Goodrich Crump Mayo Sr. were Versal Harold (b 1 Dec 1921; m Dorothy Broach), Ella Earlene (b 10 May 1923; nev m), Goodrich Crump Jr. (b 30 Apr 1925; m Martha Elizabeth Wyatt), Carl Harkness (b 6 Dec 1926; d 5 Jan 1935; nev m), Rose Marie (b 3 Sep 1929; m Edward Lee Golden), and Ruby Nell (b 7 Sep 1931; m Otis Eugene Bray). Arrie Lee Manning was born c1903, the daughter of Mettie M. (Hayes) and Walter Manning.

Children born to Bertha (Manning) Boone and George Naff Mayo I were Eloise (b 16 Oct 1927; m ? Johnson), Matalene (b 5 Jul 1930; m Fred Preston), George Naff II (b 13 Mar 1932), Derwood Crandal (b 3 Mar 1935), Mettie Sue (b 25 Jan 1939), Bettie Fay (b 21 Aug 1941), Billy Ray, and Eugene Russell (b 19 Sep 1943). Bertha Manning was the daughter of Mettie B. (Hayes) and Walter Manning.

Children born to Gladys Lee (Crenshaw) and Dock Riley Mayo were Dock Riley Jr. (m 1st Zelma Lee Roy), Clara Lee (m Renear Laurie Barthol), Harry O'Neal (m Billie Frances Jones), Ella Mae (m Robert Luke Crenshaw), and Bobby Ray (m Lena Carol Linsey). Gladys Lee Crenshaw was born 20 Jun 1913 at Jones, the daughter of Carrie (Jones) and Neal Crenshaw.

Children born to Sarah Eveline (Mayo) and John Franklin Howell were John Wilburn (b 12 Jul 1870; d 24 Dec 1905), William H. (b 8 Jan 1872), James Franklin (b Aug 1874); Mary Emily (b Jul 1876; m Frank C. Rogers; d Apr 1936; Martha Jane (b 24 Sep 1877; d 13 Aug 1887), Joseph E. Johnson (b 28 Oct 1879), George Washington (b 20 Feb 1882; m Bettie Bunch; d 1 May 1974), Grover Cleveland (b 19 Feb 1884; d 7 Nov 1892), Fannie Lue (b 7 Apr 1886), Ida (b 19 Feb 1889; d 24 May 1889), and Hatty May (b 2 May 1891; m Aussie Boone Naff; d 19 Jan 1978). John Franklin Howell was born 22 Aug 1850, the son of Eliza Ann (Naff) and Alexander Wilburn Howell. Their other children were Ann Eliza (b 27 Jul 1852); d 30 Jul 1852), Olive Augusta (b 17 Sep 1853; m Alfred Carter; d 27 Aug 1922), Willie (b 1855; d c 1860), and Jane E. (b 17 Sep 1856; m William Hill; d 28 Aug 1945).

Children born to Bettie (Bunch) and George Washington Howell were Dera Jane (m E. B. Floyd Jr.), Ezra (b 24 Feb 1922; m Maxine Cain), and Faye (b 25 Nov 1919; d 8 Feb 1930).

Children born to Dora Elizabeth (Mayo) and John Milton (or Manuel) Turner were Pruie Willie Ann Margaret Rebecca (named after her father's three sisters; b 3 May 1894; m Henry Clayborn Holloway), Henry Armstead (b 3 May 1896; m Fannie E. Porter), Alice L. (b 6 Aug 1897; m 1st James Sylvester Crenshaw; m 2nd Sherrod Morgan Crenshaw), Jessie Viola (b 11 Oct 1901; m 1st Guy Kennedy; m 2nd Floyd Huffins), and Velma Elizabeth (b 11 Jul 1904; m Alex Stewart Crawley). (For the children of the last couple, see the Robert Crawley summary).

Children born to Pruie (Turner) and Henry Clayborn Holloway were Vera Irene, David Douglas "Buck," Edna May, Donnie Dee, Isie Dee, Hattie Cecil "Tiny," Francis Virginia, and an unnamed infant son (b and d 4 Jul 1929).

Children born to Fannie E. (Porter) and Henry Armstead Turner were Nonie Pebble (d infant), Leva Armstead "Cat" (b 30 Jun 1920; m Wilma Hardgrave), Audrey "Rat" (b 1 May 1922; m Wayne McBroom), Robert A. "Man Boy" (b 6 Jul 1923; m Beatrice Kokia), Cubee A. "Nasty" (m Faye Chappell), Dotson "Stink," Irla Mae "Gal" (m Virgil Keirsey), Verletta "Bill" (b 16 Apr 1930; m 1st Grady L. Slack; m 2nd Pilgrim), Lavelder (b 16 Nov 1931; m Patsy Dale Murphy), Jeff B. (b 24 Oct 1933; m Bonnie Butler), and Jimmie Noe (b 24 May 1937; m Stanford Sivils). Fannie E. Porter was born 20 Mar 1898, the daughter of Ollie (Jones) and William Porter. Ollie Jones was born 30 Mar 1876 and died 11 Nov 1930. William Porter was born 5 Jun 1874 and died 27 Sep 1928.

Children born to Alice L. (Turner) and James Sylvester Crenshaw were Bert L. (b 26 Sep 1921; m Lonnie B. Blackwell), Jimmie Lee (b 12 Apr 1924; m E. E. Pettis), Dora May (b 12 May 1926; m James Wooden), and Bernice Jewel (b 20 Sep 1918; d Jan 1922). Children born to Alice L. (Turner) and Sherrod Morgan Crenshaw were Nonnie (m Geraldine Kilcrease) and Arlene (m Huff).

Pearl Alma Crenshaw, wife of Crawford Arnold Mayo II, was born 3 Sep 1899 at McGinty, the daughter of Willie (Jones) and Josiah Crenshaw. Willie Jones was the daughter of Mandy and Riley Jones who lived on the Frank Jones place west of the bayou.

Ruth Mayo attended school at McGinty through the sixth grade and then went to school at Bonita. She lacked three months finishing the tenth grade when she married Ethridge Wallace "E. W." Boone in 1942. E. W. Boone was born 26 Jan 1922, the son of Henrietta (Grice) and William Alonzo Boone. E. W. Boone died in June 1953. Children born to Ruth (Mayo) and E. W. Boone were Ethridge Alonzo "Speedy" (m Pricilla Colleen Fitzgerald), Linda Fay (m Carl Edward Wilson), and Daniel Lee (m Sandra Kay Anderson). Ruth has seven grandchildren and eight great-grandchildren.

Children born to Flois Mae (Wooden) and Hubert Arnold Mayo were Florence (m Grady Eugene Day) and Margarette (m John Albert Morris).

The only child born to Elsie Mae (Mayo) and Calvin Rutherford Smith was Barbara Gayle (m Steve Alexander).

Children born to Dorothy Mae (Kelley) and Dudley Armstead Mayo were Crawford Tilliman (m Sandra Elaine Saunders), Lavon Oliver (m Jeannie Lanell Brown), Versel Joe, Marilon Gail (m Ronnie Joe Kuykendall), Malcolm (m Barbara Jean Livesay), Rebecca Lynn (m Anthony Albert Hensley), and Tammy Lee (m George Allen Johnson).

Children born to Mary Louise (Hudson) and Joel Oliver Mayo were Janice Marie (m John H. Eswald), Teresa (m Robert Davis), and Sherrie Ann.

Children born to Lucille (Mayo) and Louwell Glendal Croom were Arthur Conley (m Julia Ann Houghton), and Glendal Eugene (m Helen Ruth Dougherty).

Children born to Billie Irene (Fulcher) Springman and Crawford Arnold Mayo III were Michael Ray and Patricia Lynn. Billie Irene (Fulcher) Springman's children from her first marriage were Carol Ann and Charlotte Rae.

Children born to Sandra (Warren) and Dorman Edgar Mayo were Carolyn Kay (m Charles Beech), Pennie Lee (m Gerald Lynn Sheets), and Terri (m 1st Calvin Stewart; m 2nd Herman Rushing).

(Additional information for this family was supplied by Glyn Pope.)

Willie Fount (Vick) and Murphy Brockman

Murphy Brockman was born December 12, 1919, near Star City, the son of Helen Lee (Edmonds) and Grover Brockman. Their other children were Zane (m Joyce Ross), Rebecca (m Richard Hendrickson), Grover, Jr. (m Linda Robertson) and Virginia (m Bill Adcock).

Grover Brockman was born 23 Jun 1894 at Butler Community southeast of Star City, the son of Amanda (Crow) and John Wilson Brockman. Their other children were Edgar Peary (b 5 Oct 1877; d 19 Oct 1878), Edward Wilson (b 17 Sep 1879; m Mildred W. ?; d 16 Dec 1965; their son: Edward Wilson Jr. (m Elizabeth D. ?), Donna Bell (b 21 Jan 1882; nev m; d 4 Mar 1965), and Edwin Ezra (b 5 Jan 1891; m Mamie Ollar; d 4 Aug 1970; their children: Marnell and Othnile).

John Wilson Brockman was born 5 Oct 1856 in Iberia, Miller County, MO, the son of Elizabeth (Castleman) and Henry Brockman. Their other children were Nancy Ellen (b 1853 MO; m Thomas Washington Johnson; d 1930), Eliza Susannah (b 1855 MO; m 1st 1871 Charles Summerford; m 2nd 1883 E. D. Lilly), Malinda Catherine "Cassie" (b 1859 MO; m John

Henley; d 1928), Henry Castleman "Seay" (b 1862 MO; m Alice Joyce; d 1928), Robert James (b 1869 Drew County, now Lincoln; m Molly Littlejohn; d 1899), Missouri Caroline "Callie" (b 1869 Drew County/Lincoln County; m O. C. "Neal" Joyce), William Ambrose (b 1871, Drew/Lincoln County; m Viola Matthews); d 1917), and Lewis Lycurgus (b 1878, Drew/Lincoln County; m Bertha Owen; d 1953). The Henry Brockman family moved to the Butler-Pleasant Hill Community in 1866. He served in the Confederate Army from 1862 until he was medically discharged in 1865.

Henry Brockman was born 1 Feb 1824 in KY, the son of Nancy (Elmore) and Rev. John Brockman. Their other children were John, William, James, Ambrose, Susan (m Wilcox), Annie, Sally (m Northrup), Malinda (m Shipman), and Susannah. The John Brockman family moved to Miller County, MO, sometime after their marriage in KY in 1818. John Brockman was born 12 Dec 1798 in Franklin County, VA, and in 1814 moved with his family to Barren County, KY. Rev. John Brockman was an ordained Baptist minister and served as the first moderator of the Osage River Association. He died in 1863 in Miller County, MO.

Nancy Elmore, wife of John Brockman, was born in 1797 in Rutherford County, NC, the daughter of John Elmore, a Revolutionary War soldier. She died in 1862 in Miller County, MO. Elizabeth L. Castleman, wife of Henry Brockman, was born in Monitor, MO, the daughter of Eliza Ann (Jones) and Abraham Castleman. Their other children were Mary Ann (b Nashville, TN; m Robert Reed), Caroline (b Nashville; m Obe D. Dyer), Catherine (b Monitor, MO; m Samuel Caulk), Ellen (b Monitor, MO; m 1st George Shelton; m 2nd Stiekenlike [sp?]), Manerva (b Monitor, MO; m Henry Dickenson), and Benjamin F. (b Monitor, MO; m 1st Nancy Hoskins; m 2nd Martha Burks). Abraham Castleman born in 1800 in Nashville, TN, married Eliza Ann Jones in Nashville in 1822, and died in Boliver, Polk County, MS. He was a Baptist minister and served as a colonel in the Muster Roll of Monitor, MO. He was the son of Louis Castleman, who served in the war of 1812. Eliza Ann Jones was born in Nashville and died in 1862 in Miller County, MO.

Amanda Crow, wife of John Wilson Brockman, was born 3 Aug 1855, near Selma, Drew County, the daughter of Luvenia Melvina (Weaver) and Matthew Madison Crow. She died 17 Dec 1939. Matthew Crow was born 1813 and died 10 Jun 1863. Luvenia Weaver Crow was born 3 Jun 1815 and died 27 Jul 1869. A handwritten note ["Grandma Crow's Bros and children"] in family history records suggests that the following were siblings of Luvenia Melvina Weaver: Othnill, Jacob, Eebin, Absalom, and Jeff. (Oral tradition also lists Tom and Randolph as brothers.) Children of Othnill Weaver: Jacob, Richard, Jonathan, and Daniel. Children of Jacob Weaver: Sophrona, Donna, Hirahm, and Netham. Children of Eebbin

Weaver: James, Mae, and Rebecca (m Daniels). The notation continues, "Brother Absalom Weaver who was in Ala. Luvenia Weaver Crow was my grandma. Mary or Polly Weaver Hutson. Wright Hutson Polly's husband. Uncle Jeff Crow staid [*sic*] in Alabama near Eufaula. Othnill Weaver & family, Wright Hutson & family, and Matthew Madison Crow and family came to Arkansas in 1854 from near Eufaula Alabama." Family oral history states that Amanda Crow's father, Matthew, and brother, Tom, were killed by carpetbaggers when Amanda was six years old and that the Crow family's slaves went by the name of Weaver. Murphy Brockman remembers that his grandmother, Amanda Crow Brockman, showed him the graves of Weaver slaves buried at Crow Cemetery when he was young. The Weaver family, parents of Luvenia Weaver, had a farm on Bayou Bartholomew.

Helen Leeice "Lee" Edmonds, wife of Grover Brockman, was born 10 Aug 1896, near Coleman, Drew County (now in Lincoln County), the daughter of Nancy Taylor (Henley) and George W. Edmonds. Their other children were Joseph Egleton (b 13 Aug 1879; n m; killed in gin accident, Kelso, 19 Sep 1928), Emma (b 1 Feb 1 1879; m Will Smith), Laura Louann (b 2 Aug 1886; m James Nichlos Fullbright), George (b 22 Nov 1888; m Beulah Morrison), Robert (b 6 Apr 1891; m Eula Tucker), Addie Mae (b 30 Jul 1893; m Doug Ligon), Bailey (b 15 Oct 1898; nev m; d 26 Oct 1949), William Cullen Bryant "Banny" (twin to Bailey; b 15 Oct 1898; nev m; d 26 Dec 1949; found dead at Edmonds' house), and Ray (b 27 Dec 1899; m Myrtle Pharr). George W. Edmonds had two children by a previous marriage, Maude (b 10 Apr 1872; m 1st ? Ferguson; 2nd Doc Tucker) and William Ludwall (b 17 Mar 1874; m Fannie Smith). Will Ferguson (b 17 Jun 1897), son of Maude Edmonds and first husband Ferguson, was adopted by Nancy and George W. Edmonds.

George W. Edmonds was born 4 Feb 1846 and died 3 Feb 1911. Nancy Taylor Henley was born 20 Mar 1858, died 15 Aug 1945. They are buried at Edmonds Cemetery in Lincoln County.

Children born to Maude Edmonds Ferguson and Doc Tucker were Alberta (m Will Thompson), Mamie (m T. J. Cox; their children: Frances Maude, Mamie Jane, and Joy), Walter Rea (m Brown Calhoun; their child: Lee Everett), A. O. "Bo" (m Alice Carter Tucker; their children: Walter, Kathleen, Doris, Glenda, and R. J.(m Margie Carter).

Children born to Fannie (Smith) and William Ludwall Edmonds were Gordie (m Mike Carter), Greta (m Duffie Seymore), Irma (m Little Tucker), Rena (m Miles Roberts), Johnnie (m Curtis Sawyers), Zona (m James Creighton), and Glen (m Floy Sawyer).

Children born to Emma (Edmonds) and Will Smith were Maggie (m Bennie Smith), Corma (m T. M Waters; their children: Laren and Troy Lynn), Jack (m Winnie; their children: Mike and Joe), Marvin, Tony (m

Evins Creighton; their children: Margaret Ann and Pam), Dennis, and Vance.

Children born to Beulah (Morrison) and George Edmonds were J. G., Herbert, Joe Grey, Marnell (m Haywood Green), Billy (m Wilda Witty), Mary Verlyn "Tootsie" (m George Allen "Pine Knot" Bradshaw), Charles Ray, and Mackie.

Children born to Eula (Tucker) and Robert Edmonds were R. L. (m Bessie Fern Lowery; their children: Patricia and Robert), G. T., Wallace, Harold (m Edith; their children: Mickey and Charles Burton, stepson), Paul Raymond, Bessie (m J. C. King; their children: Frances and Eddie Franklin "Sonny"), Nancy Maxine (m Houston McGehee; their children: Wrendell, Charlcie Nell, Billy, Linda, and Jackie), Carolyn, and Rayzell (m Jack Moren).

Children born to Addie Mae (Edmonds) and Doug Ligon were Angie Mae (m Paul Offutt; their child: Paul Ligon Offutt) and William Douglas, Jr. (his children: Barbara Kay and Douglas).

The only child born to Myrtle (Pharr) and Ray Edmonds was Garrett Laverne (m Van Harris; their children: Gregory Preston and Britt Van).

Murphy Brockman married Willie Fount Vick, who was born April 18, 1918, near Butler Community, the daughter of Mary Lee (O'Neal) and Elbert Lee Vick. Their other children were Dorothy Lee (m Adrian Martin), E. L., Jr. (m Inez Adair), Arie Jane (m Pat Elkin), and Fannie Pearl (m Jack Polk). Elbert Lee Vick was born ca 1892 on O'Neal Hill near Butler Community, the son of Amanda (Edmonds) and Fount Vick. Their other children were Bester (m Lily Belle Meyers), Elbert (m Mary Lee O'Neal), John (m ?), Ralph (m Reba _____), Houston (b 20 Oct 1896; m Katie Sides; d 28 Aug 1930), Marie (m Speedy Martin; m Stewart; m Brown), Ruth (m Eugene Snell), and Lela (m John O'Neal).

Fount Vick was born in 1866 near Butler and died there in 1936. His father came to the area about the same time as the Crow (1854) and Brockman (by 1856) families. Mary Lee O'Neal was born ca 1896 (she died 4 Apr 1992 at age 96), at O'Neal Hill, near Butler Community, the daughter of Fannie (Brown) and Henry O'Neal. Their other children were John (m Lela Vick), Wesley (m Evelyn Allen), Charlie Ben (m Alger Carter), Henry (m Mansfield Scott), and Mildred (m Russou Mathes). Henry O'Neal was killed when a mudcat chimney he was building fell on him.

Children born to Joyce (Ross) and Zane G. Brockman were Margaret Marie, Thomas Wayne, James Ray, and Johnny. Children born to Rebecca "Sister" Brockman and Richard Hendrickson were Dickie, Billy Grover, Don, Bob, and Joy "Sissy."

Children born to Willie Fount (Vick) and Murphy Brockman were Kenneth Wilson and Linda Doane.

Thelbert Bunch

Thelbert Bunch was born October 1, 1933, near Jones, the son of Ruby (Hayman) and Wesley Bunch. Their other children were Leonard (m Gayle Bingham) and Marilyn (m Doug Hudson). Wesley Bunch was born 21 Feb 1903 in West Carroll Parish, the son of Sally (Fleming) and Louis Bunch. Their other children were George Louis "Dick" (m Margie Floyd), Betty (m George Howell), Eunice (m Claude Thomas), Eunita (twin to Eunice; m Jackson Bennett), Dolly Bell (m 1st Ted McLemore; m 2nd Hamp Barfoot), Mattie Lee (m Freddie Chandler), Philip (m Erma Johnson), and Letha (m Vernon Scharfe).

Ruby Hayman was born 19 Feb 1908 in West Carroll Parish, the daughter of Mary and L. J. Hayman. Sally Fleming was born in West Carroll Parish. Louis Bunch was born in AL [?], migrated to West Carroll Parish, and moved to Jones in the early 1900s. His uncle, Millard Bunch, moved to Wilmot in the late 1800s. Louis Bunch settled at McGinty and rented land. Wesley Bunch began working for George T. Naff around 1930 and eventually rented the Naff farm. Around 1946 he became Naff's overseer.

Thelbert Bunch attended school at McGinty through the sixth grade and graduated from Bonita. He attended NLU for a semester and then farmed with his father until he entered the army in 1953. He returned from service in December 1955 and went into a partnership with his father, Wesley Bunch. After his father retired, he continued to farm until his retirement in 1991. In 1964 Thelbert and his father bought Slocum's gin in Jones from Union Oil Mill, the name becoming Bunch's Gin. Thelbert later built a new gin north of Jones, and when his brother and sister became stockholders in this gin, the name changed to Bunch Gin, Inc. The name changed again to Jones Producers Gin as more stockholders were taken in. This gin consolidated with the Bonita gin in 1997 and the name changed to Jones Producers Gin, Inc.

Thelbert Bunch married Janet Bolin, who was born 17 Feb 1936, in Shreveport, the daughter of Celia (Del Rio) and Melvin Bolin. Children born to Janet (Bolin) and Thelbert Bunch were Kenneth "Perry" (m 1st Becky Sims; m 2nd Carolyn Barthol West), Linda (m Farrell Hoskins), Andy Leon (m Sandra Tubbs), and Ryan. Janet and Thelbert have five grandchildren, two adoptive grandchildren, and five step grandchildren.

≈≈≈≈≈

Helen Byrd

Helen Byrd, who gives her birth date as "I am sixteen and I believe in Santa Claus," was born in Pine Bluff at what is now Byrd Lake Natural

Area, the daughter of Lois Ruby (Wilcox) and George Conlin Byrd Sr. Their other children were George Conlin Jr. (m Neva Blevins) and James Morgan Sr. (m Lorrene Raney). George Conlin Byrd Sr. was born at El Dorado, the son of Sara Gray (Cook) and Peter Paul Byrd Sr. Their other children were Nettie Letetia (m Hardee Cochran Kilgore) and Henry Boyd (nev m). Sara Byrd died and Peter Paul Byrd Sr. married second Martha Alphin. Children born to this marriage were Peter Paul Jr. (d 1918) and Ellen Doris (m James Crow Thompson Jr.)

Peter Paul Byrd Sr. was born 20 Oct 1855, in New Orleans, the son of Leinad (Speers) and John Henry Byrd, a well-known portrait painter. In the early 1890s, Peter Paul Byrd Sr. moved from El Dorado to Pine Bluff, where he was a cotton buyer. He bought land in the Byrd Lake area and developed a large farm and dairy.

Helen Byrd attended school at Miss Boyette's private school through the second grade and then attended Lake Side School in Pine Bluff. She graduated from Lake Side School at Lake Village. After several jobs in public work she accepted a position at General Water Works where she remained for thirty-five years. "Everyday was a new day," she said.

✦✦✦✦✦

Harvey Chambliss

Harvey Chambliss was born March 15, 1930, near Tarry, the son of Veva (Dixon) and Howard Beecher "H. B." Chambliss. Their other children were Glenny (m Albert Mack), Howard, Jr. (nev m), Joan (m Finnis Buckner), and Dan (m Martha Ann White).

Veva Dixon was born 18 Oct 1902, near Palmyra, Lincoln County, the daughter of Nancy Ethel (Fish) and Harvey Aaron Dixon. Their other children were Velma (b 1904; m Owen Barr), Jewel (nev m), and Grace (b 1908; m Nix.) Harvey Aaron Dixon operated steam gins.

H. B. Chambliss was born 25 Oct 1896, near Hickory Grove, Lincoln County, the son of Alameda "Allie" (Whitehead) and Lorenzo Dou Chambliss. Their only other child was Illa Belle (m Ray Ridgeway). H. B. located to Tarry as a young man and worked for C. H. Clowers County He eventually rented land on the bayou and farmed for himself. In 1932 he bought land west of Ladd on the bayou, moved to that location, and began a large farming operation. Other than farming, he continued to buy and sell farmland throughout the area. The family farm now consists of 2,200 acres in Jefferson County with an additional 1,300 in Cleveland County.

Alameda Whitehead was born 8 Apr 1875 in Lincoln County, the daughter of Nancy Jane (Mobley) and Edwin Whitehead. Lorenzo Dou Chambliss was born 3 Dec 1867 in New Albany, MS, the son of Frances Perlina (Freeman) and Joseph Kendrid Chambliss. Their other children were Gray (b 1860, Pontotac County MS; d young), James (b 1861, MS), Charley (b 1862, MS), Joel (b 1866, MS), Lucy Jane (b 1870, AR), and Henry Clay (b 1871, AR).

Frances Perlina Freeman was born 25 Dec 1839 in GA and died 15 Nov 1901 in Lincoln County. Joseph Kendrid Chambliss was born 9 Jul 1841 in AL and died 1924 in Lincoln County. He was the son of Nancy and Gray Chambliss whose other children were John (b 1838, AL), Matilda B. (b 20 Oct 1839, AL), Martha (b 1843, AL), Frances (b 1845, AL), James (b 1848, MS), Edney (b 1850, MS; d 1933), Lovinia (b 11 Oct 1856, MS), and Romond (b 1859, MS).

Nancy Chambliss (maiden name unknown) was born 5 Jun 1816 in GA and died 8 Oct 1888 in Lincoln County. Gray Chambliss was born 31 Aug 1808-12 in NC or SC and died Aug 1859 in Pontotac County MS. He was the son of Mary and William Chambliss whose other children were William, Sarah, Allen , Proscella, Henry, Elizabeth, Nathaniel, John, and Nancy.

William Chambliss was born 24 Dec 1761, Greensville County, VA, the son of Jean and Henry Chambliss. Their other children were Charles Thomas (b 10 Oct 1759; d 4 Jan 1778), David (b 4 Mar 1762), Mary Molly (b 15 Oct 1763), Bolling (b 1 Apr 1765; d 1842), Allen (b 1766; d 4 May 1801), Henry H. (b 5 Mar 1768; d 14 Dec 1857), Agnes (b 10 Nov 1769), Mark (b 25 Apr 1771), and Jeanne (b 6 Mar 1773).

Jean Chambliss died 16 Apr 1773, and Henry Chambliss married 2nd Mary and 3rd Lucy. He fathered twenty-eight children in these three marriages. Henry Chambliss was born 10 Aug 1734 in VA, the son of Agness and William Chambliss. Their only other son was William.

William Chambliss, father of Henry, was born c1702 in Prince George County VA, the son of Mary (Moore/Moor) and Henry Chambliss/Chamnis). Their other children, all born in Prince George County VA, were John (b c1690; d 1767-1770), Ann (b c1692), Nathaniel (b c 1694; d 1761), Mary (b c1696), Elizabeth (b c1698), Jacob b c1770), and Henry (b c1704). Henry Chambliss/Chamnis was born c1660 and died c1717-1719 in Prince George County. It is assumed that his father was John Chamnis.

Harvey Chambliss attended school at Hill Acres (the present location of Grider Field) through the ninth grade and graduated from Pine Bluff High School. Harvey married Margaret Jo Dean, who was born 13 Oct 1928 at Pine Bluff, the daughter of Carrie (Richardson) and Joe Dean.

Children born to Margaret Jo (Dean) and Harvey Chambliss were Harvey Dean (m Susanne Tortorich; their children: Allison and Lauren) and Jo Ellen (m Eddie Sanders; their children: Andrew, Ben, John, and Carrie).

Children born to Glenny (Chambliss) and Albert Mack were Daniel and Harvey. Children born to Jo Ann (Chambliss) and Finnis Buckner were

Jim Buckner and Bill. Children born to Martha Ann (White) and Dan Chambliss were Mark and Lewis.

❧❧❧

Robert Crawley, Ella (Crawley) Vail

Robert Arnell Crawley was born December 1, 1931, at the Ida J. Crawley Plantation at Tatum Bend in Ashley County, and Ella P. Crawley was born January 21, 1924, on the Naff farm, McGinty, LA, the children of Velma Elizabeth (Turner) and Alex Stewart Crawley. Their other children were Agness Earlene (b 20 Mar 1926, on the Haynes-Ober place, which was once a part of the J. Fred Crawley Plantation; m John Jackson), Jennisteen (b 12 Sep 1927, Haynes place; m Ben Washam), Avis Paulene (b 24 Jan 1929, Haynes place; m Hudie Harrelson), [all following children were born at the Ida J. Crawley Plantation] Clyda Fay (b 3 Jun 1930; d 25 Sep 1933 of "congestive chill"), Carolyn Sue (b 10 Jun 1936; m James Breazeal), unnamed infant (b 5 Jan 1934; d at birth), Elizabeth (b 28 Oct 1937; m George Sharp), and Alex Benard (b 25 Jul 1940; m Dixie House).

Velma Elizabeth Turner was born 11 July 1904 near Quitman, LA, the daughter of Dora Elizabeth (Mayo) and John Manuel Turner. John Turner was a section foreman with the railroad at Quitman. After his retirement they moved to be near the Mayo family near McGinty, LA.

Alex Stewart Crawley was born 22 Jul 1901, at Crawley Plantation, the son of Rebecca J. Genevia (Griffin) and Robert Page Crawley Sr. Their other children, all born at Crawley Plantation with the exception of Katie Genevia, were Robert Page Jr. (b 9 Sep 1888; m Nannie Hennington), Olga Irene (b 19 Nov 1890; m Ed Franklin), Mamie Griffin (b 10 Dec 1892; m Tom Evans), Willie G. (b 6 Apr 1894; d c1919), Freddie Bird (b 21 Oct 1896; m 1st Jean Hennington; m 2nd Tommy Evans, who was her sister's widower), Ida Bessie (b 22 Oct 1898; m Clyde Evans), Ella Lemmie (b 22 Sep 1902; m Wylie Pollock), and Katie Genevia (b 28 Nov 1905 at Griffin Plantation; m Floyd Huffine.) All of the above are buried at Bell Cemetery with the exception of Ella Pollock, who is buried at Mt. Zion near Berlin Community, Ashley County.

Rebecca J. Genevia Griffin was born 8 Feb 1865. Her parents owned Griffin Plantation, which was located north of Gaines Church. She had a sister who married Will Gaines, who owned a cotton gin at Gaines.

Robert Page Crawley Sr., father of Alex Stewart Crawley, was born 22 Aug 1863 at Crawley Plantation, the son of Amanda (Phillips) Tiller and J. Fred Crawley. (See Roy Grizzell summary.) J. Fred Crawley was born 1 Dec 1817, at Halifax County, NC, the son of Bird Crawley. According to Bird Crawley's will (15 Oct 1847, Tallahatchie County, MS), his other children were James D., Harrison T., Susan E. Chambers, Martha E.

Kinton [sp not certain], Martha Ann Page (m George W. Page), William G., and Benjamin C. Crawley.

Bird Crawley was the son of Aby and David Crawley Jr. of Halifax County, NC. According to his will (6 Jul 1828, Halifax County), their other children were David, Lemuel, Sandy, Benjamin, Joseph, John, and Sandy W. Crawley. Also mentioned in the will is a grandson, Marion Sandy Crawley, who is listed under the first Sandy.

David Crawley Jr. was the son of David Crawley Sr. According to his will (20 Oct 1773, Halifax County), his other children were Daniel, Betty Hall, and a daughter, Dolly Crawley. Also mentioned in the will is a grandson, John Crawley Johns, who is listed under Dolly Crawley.

J. Fred Crawley and his brother, William G. Crawley, moved to Jefferson County, AR, in 1853 and began buying land. J. Fred Crawley bought land in Ashley County in 1855-57 and established Crawley's Bend Plantation. After the Civil War he left his plantation and went to Tennessee. His son, Robert Page Sr., eventually traded land in Tennessee for a part of the Crawley Plantation and returned. J. Fred Crawley left the remaining portions of the plantation to his daughters, Mattie and Ida Jolly Crawley. The twenty-eight acres left to Ida is now owned by Robert Crawley, grandson of Robert Page Crawley Sr.

Children born to Nannie (Hennington) and Robert Page Crawley Jr. were J. P, Ouida (m Bruce Sanderlin), Nellie, Claude (m Marion McKoin), Viola, Matt (m Jean ?), Johnnie Maude, and Buford.

Children born to Olga Irene (Crawley) and Ed Franklin were Beuna Mae (m Arthur Barton), James (nev m), Leslie (m Dorothy Broach), and Esther (nev m).

Children born to Mamie Griffin (Crawley) and Tom Evans were Buck and Bessie (m Emmit Lee).

Children born to Jean (Hennington) and Freddie Bird Crawley were William Bean, Ernest, and Stevie Evans (m Eva Lou ?).

Children born to Ida Bessie (Crawley) and Clyde Evans were Marble Lee, Clydine (m Archie Parker), and Oscar (m Betty ?).

Children born to Lemmie (Crawley) and Wylie Pollock were James W. (m Geneva ?), Vernell, Mattie Jean (m Bobbie Lloyd), and Clayton.

Children born to Katie Genevia (Crawley) and Floyd Huffine were Margaret (nev m) and Fred (nev m).

Ella Perrene Crawley, daughter of Velma (Turner) and Alex Stewart Crawley, attended school at Wilmot where she graduated in 1941. Ella married W. A. Vail, who was born 28 Apr 1921 at Columbus, MS, the son of Ronnie Eula (Jeffcote) and W. Ed Vail. Children born to Ella (Crawley) and W. A. Vail were William Arnold Jr. (m Oma Nell "Tiny" Vonstory), Otis Don, and Janice Elaine (m Larry W. Walther).

Robert A. Crawley, son of Velma (Turner) and Alex Stewart Crawley, graduated from Wilmot High School and received a B.S. in agriculture and a M.Ed. from the University of Arkansas. He taught in public schools for fifteen years, was with the Arkansas Education Department for nineteen years, and taught at Capitol City Junior College for six years. Robert married Nell Howard, who was born 31 Oct 1932 at Fayetteville, AR, the daughter of Emma (Culp) and Jack H. Howard. Nell (Howard) and Robert Crawley had no children but adopted Tammie Jean (m 1st John Miles; m 2nd Allen Rauch) and Charles Floyd "Chuck" (m 1st Brenda Nelson; m 2nd Dana Gupton). Tammie Jean and Charles Floyd Crawley were brother and sister.

Children born to Agnes Earlene (Crawley) and John Henry Jackson were Ida Faye, Glen, and Terry. Jennisteen (Crawley) and Ben Washam had no children but adopted Bennie Jean Washam. Children born to Avis Pauline (Crawley) and Hudie Harrelson were Neva Beth, Kathy, and Steve. The only child born to Carolyn Sue (Crawley) and James Breazeal was Max Stewart. Children born to Elizabeth (Crawley) and George Sharp were Rhonda Elizabeth and Karen. Children born to Dixie (House) and Alex Bernard Crawley were Michael, Scott, and Jon Mark.

✻✺❧✺✻

John B. Currie Sr.

John B. Currie Sr. was born February 21, 1921, at Winchester, the son of Maysel (Walls) and Herman Carlton Currie Sr. Their other children were Jackson Daniel (nev m), Herman C. Jr. (m Laura Foss), and Thomas Trimble (m Dorothy Durkin). Herman Carlton Currie Sr. was the son of Belfield Ione (Mathis) and John Daniel Currie. John Daniel Currie was born in Brownsville, Tennessee, the son of ? (Shaw) and Dr. Shelby Currie. Dr. Shelby Currie moved from Tennessee to Jefferson County in 1853. He held a land grant on land that extended from east of Ladd to Bayou Bartholomew. John Daniel Currie bought a third interest in the Valley Planting Company at Winchester in 1890 and held it until 1920. Herman C. Currie was a cotton buyer at Winchester and later at Pine Bluff for R. A. Downs Cotton Company.

Maysel Walls was born in Lonoke County, Arkansas, the daughter of Molly (Robinson) and Andrew Jackson Walls. Molly Robinson was the daughter of ? (Swaim) and Dr. ? Robinson. One of their other children was U. S. Senator from Arkansas, Joe T. Robinson. Andrew Jackson Walls' grandfather lived next to Andrew Jackson's father in South Carolina and served as one of his pallbearers.

John B. Currie Sr. graduated from Pine Bluff High School and then attended Arkansas A&M College at Monticello in 1938-39. He then attended the University of Arkansas where he graduated in 1942 with a major in agriculture. He served in the Marine Corps from 1942 to 1946 and in 1946 moved to Wilmot to manage his wife's farming interests. John married (1944) Mary Elizabeth deYampert, who was born in Wilmot, the daughter of Vesta (Pyron) and William B. deYampert II. (See William B. deYampert summary.) Children born to Mary Elizabeth (deYampert) and John B. Currie Sr. were John B. Jr. "Johnny" (m Bland Shackelford), Mary (nev m; twin to Martha), Martha (m Larry Green), and William Jackson (m Anne Johnston). "Big John" Currie has seven grandchildren.

❧❦❧

John Edd Curry

John Edd Curry was born December 4, 1935, at Garrett Bridge, the only child of Iris (Anderson) and Les Curry. Les Curry was born at Tyro, the son of Manie (Wommack) and Bob Curry. Their other children were Detel (m Bernice Barnes), Bryant (m Ida Belle Jones), Vernon (m three times), Lillie (m Dennis Mooney), Lena (m Herman Hayes), and two or three who died in infancy. Bob Curry's father, name unknown, settled at Tyro in the 1850s. Les Curry moved from Tyro to the Anderson place at Garrett Bridge after his marriage to Iris Anderson.

Iris Anderson was born at Garrett Bridge, the daughter of ? (Mulligan) and E. C. G. Anderson Jr. Their other children were Ibbie (m Jack Brocuis) and John (m Helen Brewer ?). E. C. G. Anderson Jr. was born at Tyro, the son of Maria L. (Jones) and Dr. E. C. G. Anderson Sr., who settled at Tyro and farmed at Garrett Bridge before the Civil War. He eventually moved his family from Tyro to the bayou farm.

❧❦❧

Frank Day, Charles Day

Nathaniel Franklin "Frank" Day Jr. was born May 22, 1921, and Charles L. "Chuck" Day was born March 24, 1931 at Monroe, the sons of Thelma (Chappell) and Nathaniel Franklin Day Sr. of Beekman, LA. Their other children were Katharine Virginia (b 14 Apr 1923; m Franklin Robert Huber Jr.), Maurice Jerome (b 3 Sep 1926; m Martha Ann Elkins), and Marjorie Ann (b 13 Jan 1930; m Jennings Bryan "J. B." Huber).

Thelma Chappell was born 17 May 1900, the daughter of Susan Virginia (Moffett) and Hiram Samuel Chappell of Hattiesburg, MS. Their other children were Pauline (m ? Jones), Louise, Ella "Doll," J. D. "Bud," Roscoe (d young), Jewel and James. Hiram Chappell was in the logging business and moved his family to Beekman in the late 1910s. He was killed in an automobile accident, and his wife and children, except Pauline and Thelma, returned to Hattiesburg.

Nathaniel Franklin Day Sr. was born 12 Sep 1899 at Beekman, the son of Ida Katherine "Katie" (Naff) and Thomas Lynn "Tom" Day, who were married 18 Nov 1895. Their other children, all born at Beekman, were Luther Allen Sr. (b 21 Aug 1896; d 2 Dec 1980; m Mary Elizabeth Albright), Inez (b 13 May 1902; d 25 Nov 1998; m James Samuel Myrick Sr.), and Robert Henry (b 8 Mar 1904; d 17 Dec 1987; m Zelma Hughes). Katie Day died four days after the birth of Robert Henry, and Tom married Willa (Jones) Chancellor 11 Nov 1908. Children born to this marriage were Alma Beulah (b 7 Sep 1910; d 15 Nov 1922), Bernice (b 13 Mar 1913; d 21 Dec 1994; m 1st Samuel Plummer Johnston; m 2nd Colon Thomas Anders; m 3rd Johnny DeWayne Pamplin), John Fred (b 2 Nov 1916; d 18 Oct 1919), and Tom Ervin "Buddy" (b 10 Mar 1919; d 10 Mar 1936). Tom Day purchased a farm along Bayou Bartholomew from John Hope in 1906. The farm, part of the original Ward Plantation, was about a quarter of a mile north of the Crossett Bridge. He built a house on the northeast corner of the cultivated field, which was the location of an Indian burial. In addition to farming, Tom operated a ferry across the bayou and had a store at the landing. When the new road came through he moved the store to the highway. Tom Day died 28 Nov 1960 and was buried at Beekman Cemetery. After his death, his grandson, Luther Allen Day Jr., bought the farm from the heirs, and his wife, Doris, presently owns it.

Thomas Lynn "Tom" Day was born 13 Sep 1872 at Stevenson, LA, the child of Sarah Louisa (Johnston) and Robert Hamilton "Ham" Day. Their other children were Robert Chesley (b 6 Mar 1874; d 16 Jul 1962; m Annie L. Remore), Columbus Hawkins "Lum" (b 7 1877; d 15 Mar 1905; nev m), Sarah J. (d young), Addie Lee (b 1879; d 1899; m James Ford Naff), Mary Ann (b 1881; d 1950; m James Ford Naff), Eula Ross (b 1886; d 1910; m James Thomas Moore), Beulah Mae (b 1886; d 1965; m James Milton White), Willie Hamilton "Will" (b 1887; d 1974; m 1st Julia Ann Freeland; m 2nd Olivia Moore Kitchens), and an infant (b. 1892; d 1892). After the death of his wife, Ham Day married Louisa McGowan Moore (b 6 Nov 1860; d 10 Mar 1904). They had a son, Van, who married but had no children.

Robert Hamilton "Ham" Day and his brother, Robert Harmon, came to Morehouse Parish around 1870, driving cattle from Amite County, MS. Ham Day married Sarah Louisa Johnston 15 Jan 1872. She was born 2 Dec 1848, the daughter of Sarah Caroline (Russell) and Chesley Johnston whose home was located on the present Chemin-a-Haut Park Loop Road. The Chelsey Johnston family arrived in Morehouse Parish before the parish was divided from Ouachita Territory. One of Chelsey Johnston's sons, Jesse H., died 17 Sep 1842 and was buried at the homeplace. Sarah

Louisa (Johnston) Day died 18 Dec 1892 and was buried in Pipeline Cemetery. The Ham Day family first lived at Stevenson, near Beekman. Children born during this time were Tom, Robert, Columbus, Sarah J., and Addie Lee. Around 1880 the family moved to Nacogdoches, TX, where Ham farmed. While there four children were born, Mary Ann, twins Eula Ross and Beulah Mae, and Willie. (Willie was born at Melro, TX.) Louisa later became ill with cancer and was also pregnant. It is believed the family made a three-month journey by wagon from Nacogdoches back to Morehouse Parish in 1892. Louisa gave birth to a child, who died, in 1892 and she died 18 Dec the same year. Both are buried in the same grave in Pipeline Cemetery on Chemin-a-Haut Loop Park Road

Robert Hamilton "Ham" Day was born 10 Jun 1853 in Liberty, MS, the son of Lucretia Adaline (McGehee) and Robert Harmon Day. One of their other known children was Marshall Henry. Robert Harmon Day was the son of Nancy (McGehee) and Jeptha Day. Nancy McGehee was the daughter of Samuel McGehee, who served in the Revolutionary War. The McGehee family came to America from Scotland. Jeptha Day migrated from GA to MS. The Day family originated in Ireland under the names of O'Dea and Dea.

Children born to Eula Ross (Day) (dau of Sarah Louisa Johnston and Ham Day) and James Thomas Moore were Robbie (b 28 Nov 1906; d 2 Oct 1990; m 1st Wesley L. Martin; m 2nd Arthur Mulvey) and Alice Mae (b 24 Apr 1908; d 30 Apr 1990; m Sanford Elliot Harrison.)

Children born to Beulah Mae (Day) (dau of Sarah Louisa Johnston and Ham Day) and James Milton White were James Felson (b 11 Jul 1907; d 3 Mar 1970), infant son (b 1908; d 1908), Elsie Mae (b 5 Jan 1910; d 3 Mar 1911), Velma A. (b 27 Sep 1912; d 14 Apr 1913), Wilburn Odis (b 1 Oct 1913; d 16 Oct 1917), Edna Louise (b 6 Aug 1917; d 16 Apr 1995; m Joseph Armenio), Michael Watson "Buck" (b 31 Oct 1919; d 6 Jan 1998; m 1st Claudine Golden; m 2nd Claudia Rose Evans), John Milton "Bye Bye" (b 4 Feb 1921; d and bu TX; m Era Aline Barham), Bonnie Eloise (b 29 Dec 1929; m Donald Ford Joiner Sr.), Van Frank "Billy" (b 6 Jul 1926; d 20 May 1991; m Doris Brantley), and Vertie Sue (b 2 Jan 1930; m Charles E. Mills).

Children born to Julia Ann (Freeland) and Willie Hamilton "Will" Day (son of Sarah Louise Johnston and Ham Day) were Jack F. (b 15 Aug 1909; d 28 Jul 1969; m Annie Mae Johnson), Eula Rose (b 14 Dec 1911; d 22 Oct 1983; m Frederick Allen Day, no relation), Robert Louis (b 8 Jul 1913; m Nellie Jean McLeod), Columbus Hawkins "Lum" (b 6 Nov 1916; m Helen Kitchens), and Maxine (b 14 Mar 1922; m Delbert Eugene Swarthout).

Children born to Inez (Day), daughter of Katie (Naff) and Tom Day, and James Samuel Myrick Sr. were James Samuel Jr. (m 1st Sarah Hanna

Craig; m 2nd Mary Esther McCuen) and Thomas Day Sr. (m Ada Jeffus). Children born to Zelma (Hughes) and Robert Henry Day were Helen Patricia (m Hardy Gunter Sr.) and Robert Franklin (m Betty Sue Carpenter; div). For the children of Mary Elizabeth (Albright) and Luther Allen Day Sr., see the Winifred Day summary. The children of Thelma (Chappell) and Nathaniel Franklin Day Sr. are listed at the end of this summary.

Marshall Henry Day Sr., brother to Robert Hamilton Day, was born in Liberty, MS, July 16, 1864. After coming to Morehouse Parish around 1870, he eventually settled in Bonita. He married Estelle Easterling 31 Aug 1881. She was born 10 Oct 1860, died 21 Sep 1919, and was buried in Lower Bonne Idee Cemetery. Children born to Estelle (Easterling) and Marshall Henry Day Sr. were Marshall Jr. (m Bernice Jones; no ch; killed by a train May 1953; bu Desha County AR), Seaton (killed by a train in Desha County 1946), and Beulah Louetta (b 9 Sep 1888; d 18 Jun 1967; bu Bonne Idee; m 1st Henry E. Glossup; m 2nd Garland Alonza Doss). Marshall Henry Day Sr. married second Emma Peters who was born in 1889 at LaGrange, GA. Children born to this marriage were Catherine (b 8 Mar 1921; d 12 Feb 2000; m Odis Bagwell) and Marshall Emory (b 5 Oct 1922; d 12 Sep 1985; m Ethel Mae Pickett).

Ida Katherine "Katie" Naff, wife of Thomas Lynn Day, was born in 1878, at Beekman, the daughter of Frances "Fannie" (Moore) and John Henry Naff. Their other children were Annie Ophelia (b 1880; d 1943; m J. J. Denham), Ethel Zoula (b 1882; d 1957; m Ernest Brodnax), William Elijah "Buck" (b 1884; d 1909; m Dora Moore), Martha Jane "Mattie" (b 1886; d 1966; m Fred Harvey), Hattie Hulda (b 1888; d 1924; m Elmo A. Harvey); Gladys Hartland (b 1890; d 1965; m 1st Richard Grogan; m 2nd J. J. Pace), John Allen "Jack" (b 1892; d 1963; m Ruby Newman), and George Washington (b 17 Nov 1896; d 7 Sep 1903).

Fannie Moore was born 1 Aug 1861 in Union Parish, the daughter of Martha Ann (Day) and Peter Moore. She was fifteen years old when she married John Henry Naff on December 24, 1876 at Beekman. They homesteaded 160 acres of land in Section 32, Township 23 and gave an acre for the Little Compromise School. Their home was on present Lum Day Road.

John Henry Naff was born 5 Nov 1854 at Beekman, the son of Hulda Palestine (Hill) and Jonathan Lamar Naff. Their other children were Mary Jane (b 1856; d 1934; m Franklin Pierce Day), Nathaniel Franklin (b 1860; d 1901; m Mary Abigail Williamson), Jonathan Palestine (b 1863; m Ida Lanier), George Eakin, Isaac Tipton (d in childhood) and Hattie Zula (b 1868; m Leon Sugar). Hulda (Hill) Naff died in December 1868, and Jonathan married Martha Ann (Day) Moore on 31 Oct 1871. She was born 1 Aug 1840 in Dallas County, AL, the daughter of Winfred (Grumbles) and Marshall Day, who later moved to Union Parish. Martha Ann (Day) was first married to Peter Moore, who died in the Confederate service in 1863. It was their daughter, Frances "Fannie" Moore who married John Henry Naff. Children born to Martha Ann (Day) and Jonathan Naff were James Ford "Jim" (b 1872; d 1937; m 1st Annie Rebecca Hausey; m 2nd Addie Lee Day; m 3rd Mary Ann Day) and Winfred Hulda (b 1875; d 1914; m John Andrew White). James Ford "Jim" Naff first lived at Beekman and in 1911 purchased the Lum Ward plantation, consisting of around 300 acres along Bartholomew, from Jacob Weinstein. J. B. Levy sold the land to Weinstein in 1907.

Jonathan Lamar Naff was born in 1830 in Carter County, TN, the son of Mary Butler (Tipton) and Henry Hoss Naff Sr. Their other children were Isaac Tipton (b 1822; d 1884; m Emily Adaline Howell), Henry Hoss Jr. (m?), Catherine (m Levi Johnson), Franklin (d at Vicksburg), Amanda (m ?) Mayo, who died at Vicksburg), Jacob (d young), Sarah (m ?) Howell, who died at Vicksburg), Emaline (m ? Doles), and John Blair (owned a drug store in Bastrop and died at Vicksburg).

Henry Hoss Naff Sr. was born 26 Jul 1799 in Franklin County, VA, the son of Catherine (Hoss) and Jonathan Naff. Jonathan Naff was the son of Katherine (Flourin) and Jacob Naff Sr., who had eleven other children. Jacob Naff Sr., a descendant of Hans Naff of Switzerland, came to America in 1749. Katherine Flourin was the daughter of Joseph Flure (Flory, Flora, Fluery). Henry Hoss Naff Sr. migrated to Point Pleasant where he was a surveyor and clerked at a store. He died of yellow fever 9 July 1842 and was buried near the bayou at Point Pleasant. In 1966 Louise Naff Larsen, a great-granddaughter, learned that his marble tombstone was being used to hold a block of salt in a cow pasture, and she and a relative, Freddy Harvey, had the stone moved to Christ Church Cemetery.

Children born to Emily Adaline (Howell) and Isaac Tipton Naff were Henry Howell, Mary Letitia, Sarah (d age 16), and George Washington Naff. (See Mary Dean Pugh summary). Children born to ? and Henry Hoss Naff Jr. were Robert, Joe, Cordelia, John, Mattie, and Annie. Children born to Catherine (Naff) and Levi Johnson were Frank and Talitha. Franklin Naff had a son, Tom, who moved to Texas. Amanda (Naff) and ? Mayo had two daughters. Children born to Sarah (Naff) and ? Howell were Joe (lived near Jones) and Olive (m ? Carter). One of Emaline (Naff) Doles' daughters was Mary, who married Chesley Columbus "Lum" Johnston. Children born to Mary (Doles) and Lum Johnston were Benjamin, Franklin, William Columbus, Duran Lamar, Homer Chesley, Robert Lee, Floyd Walker, Annie Ethel, and Clara Irene.

Children born to Mary Jane (Naff) and Franklin Pierce Day were Mary Emma, John Henry, Franklin Pierce Jr., William Marshall, Sarah Jane, Winfred Hulda, and Lucinda Elizabeth. Children born to Mary Abigail (Williamson) and Nathaniel Franklin Naff were Joseph Jonathan (m

Blanche ?), Lillian Irene (m M. C. Cheshire), Oscar Lee (m Annie Albright), Cecil Lamar (m Jake Albright), Pearl Maude (m John Edwards), Mary Alice (m F. S. Stevenson), Hattie Hulda (m Ira Morgan), Thomas Watson (m Grace Sawyer), and Ella Abigail (m Leroy Bain Freeland). Children born to Ida (Lanier) and Jonathan Palestine Naff were Errice Leiton, Fred Palestine, David Ivy, Eva, and Horace. Hattie Zula (Naff) and Leon Sugar had no children.

Children born to Annie Rebecca (Hausey) and James Ford "Jim" Naff were Lola (b 1894; m Robert Washington Wallace) and Hausey. Jim Naff's second wife, Addie Lee Day, died during childbirth along with twin babies. Children born to Mary Ann (Day) (sister to Addie Lee) and Jim Naff were Lucille (m Jessie L. Westbrook), Addie Louise (m 1st James Henry Brown; m 2nd Will Bert Larsen), Dorris Ross (m Johnny L. Braswell Sr.), Harry Ford (m Ida Velma Harper), Mary Mildred (m Clarence Linzay), and J. B (m. Maggie Nell Coursen Peters).

Children born to Winfred Hulda (Naff) and John Andrew White were Beulah (m Asa I. Albright), Miller Clifton (m Alma Mae Washer), Ruth Vashti (m 1st Boatner Baugh; m 2nd Vernie Lee Plyant), Eva Ernestine (m Walter Caldwell Jr.), Cellestine (m Oscar Bates), Nathaniel Hawthorne (m Laura Boles), Keith Coleman (m Edna Heath), and Lela Esther (m Jack Cain). Winfred died a few days after the birth of Lela.

Frank Day, son of Thelma (Chappell) and Nathaniel Franklin Day Sr., attended school at Beekman through the seventh grade and graduated from Bastrop after the eleventh grade. After working for a few years, he entered the army in 1941. He returned to the Wardville area in 1945 and bought a farm on Bayou Bartholomew. Frank married Ethel Harrison and their only child was Frances Eileen (m James William Loyless; div). Ethel Harrison Day died in 1979, and Frank married Violet (Reeves) Glass in 1981. Frank and Violet Day live along Bayou Bartholomew on Bonner Ferry Road.

Charles Lynn "Chuck" Day, son of Thelma (Chappell) and Frank Day Sr., attended school at Beekman through the seventh grade and graduated from Bastrop in 1948. He served in the army from 1951-53 and then attended school in Kansas City where he learned the diesel mechanic trade. Chuck married Elizabeth LaBourde, and their children are Lisa Lynn (m Royce Walker), Sharon Rene (m 1st Russell Caraway; m 2nd Jimmy Edward Pope), and Charles Lynn (m Ellen Lena Brown). Chuck and Elizabeth Day have six grandchildren.

Children born to Katharine Virginia (Day) and Franklin Robert Huber Jr. were Barry Franklin (m Glenda Williams) and Karen Virginia. They have two grandchildren.

Children born to Martha Ann (Elkins) and Maurice Jerome Day Sr. were Lee Ann (m Martin Shell), Maurice Jerome Jr. "Jerry" (m Jane Elizabeth

Luscombe), and Thomas Elkins "Tom" (m Erin Denise Daniels). They
have five grandchildren.
  Children born to Marjorie Ann (Day) and J. B. Huber were Bryan (m
Marsha Ann Kaffka) and Maribeth (m Patrick Arthur Thomas). They have
three grandchildren.

❧❦❧

Winifred Day

  Winifred O'Neal Day Sr. was born June 3, 1921, at Beekman, the son
of Mary (Albright) and Luther Allen Day Sr. Their other children, all born
near Wardville, were Bunny (m Helen Polous), Margueritte (m Ozie
Edmond Hubbard), Muriel (m William Howard Johnson Sr.), Katharyn
Pennelope "Dooley" (m Cecil Harry Lilly Jr.), and Luther Jr. (m Doris
June Reed). Luther Allen Day Sr. was born 21 Aug 1896 at Wardville, the
son of Katie (Naff) and Tom Lynn Day. (See Frank Day summary.) Mary
Albright, wife of Luther Day, was born 10 Jan 1895 in Memphis, TN, the
daughter of Mary P. and Tom Albright. Their other children were Asa,
Jacob, Mary, Elizabeth, Charles, Felica, Bill, George "Tad," and Ann. The
Tom Albright family moved to Beekman c1895. They were of German
descent.
  Winifred Day attended Beekman School through the seventh grade and
graduated from Bastrop High School in the eleventh grade. He worked at
the old International Paper Mill at Bastrop and at plants in Sterlington.
Winifred married Vivian Westbrook, the daughter of Ozelle (Moore) and
William Westbrook. Children born to Vivian (Westbrook) and Winifred
Day were Winifred O'Neal Jr. (m Judy Jones; div) and Barbara Ann
Houston. Vivan (Westbrook) Day died 16 Mar 1996. Winifred, who lives
along Bayou Bartholomew on Wardville Road, has three grandchildren.
  The only child born to Helen (Poulos) and Bunny Day was James.
Children born to Mary Margueritte (Day) and Ozie Edmond Hubbard were
Mary Elizabeth (m Charles Wayne Moore Sr.) and Jo Ann (m Daniel
Norsworthy). Mary Margueritte Day's second marriage was to Sylvan
Enock Aycock, and they had one child, Muriel Marie (m John Baynard
Naff). Mary Margueritte (Day) Hubbard Aycock died 4 Oct 1979.
Children born to Muriel Marie (Day) and William Howard Johnston Sr.
were Bunny Samantha (m John F. Langston) and William Howard Jr. (m
Van Grigsby Wright). Children born to Katharyn Pennelope (Day) and
Cecil Harry Lilly Jr. were Katharyn Annette (m Joe Laing), Mary
Pennelope (m 1st Lewis Neal Elton; m 2nd William Murphy), and Cecil
Harry III (m Pamela Kay Knight). The only child born to Doris June
(Reed) and Luther Allen Day Jr. was Lynne Amber (m Richard H.
Anders).

Luther Allen Day Jr. died 13 Oct 1990. Marjorie Day Huber wrote, "Luther was a farmer. When he died, Morehouse Parish farmers quit work in their own cotton fields and took their equipment and employees to work for three days in the Day fields to get all the cotton to the gin. The farmers were Mike Costello, David McCarty, Tony Haynes, Jack Wallace Jr., Jeff McCain, Boyd Holley Jr., and David Daniels. David McCarty said, 'We knew that if it had been on of us, Luther would have been the first one in our fields harvesting our cotton. This was something we wanted to do for Luther and Doris.'"[2]

⚜︎⚜︎

R. H. "Butch" Dennington

Raymond Hadley "Butch" Dennington was born September 5, 1910, at Morehouse, Missouri, the son of Lucy (Holder) and Frank Herbert Dennington Sr. Their other children were Howard (d age 12), Cecil Marvin (m Louise Bishop), Carl Herbert (m Sue Thomas), Frank Hadley Jr., and Nettie Jean (m Ralph Waterson).

The family moved in 1913 to Dermott where the father was employed as a machinist with Bimel-Ashcroft Spoke Mill. After the mill closed he worked for the railroad.

Butch Dennington married Anita Lephiew who was born at Dermott, the only daughter of Mildred Anita (Johnson) and William E. Lephiew Jr. William E. Lephiew Jr. was the son of Martha Cordelia "Delia" (Bulloch) and William Henry Lephiew Sr. of Baxter. Their only other child was Ouida, who married Frank Johnson and had no children. Martha Cordelia Bulloch was the daughter of Ellen (Courtney) and Green Berry Bulloch.

William Henry Lephiew Sr. was born in Monticello, the only son of Ruth B. (Ferguson) and Henry H. Lephiew who were married in Monticello on 18 Sep 1853. Their other children were Sallie E. (m John H. Harden), Hattie H. (m Stephen R. Bulloch), Kate (m Dr. John T. Blanks), Lena (m C E. Singleton), Melissa, and Lizzie (d infant).

Ruth B. Ferguson was born in June 1831 in SC, the daughter of Sarah (Hyatt) and Jonathan Ferguson. Her parents were born in SC and moved to LA in 1864. Sarah Hyatt Ferguson died in Homer, LA in 1881.

Henry H. Lephiew was born 14 Nov 1830 in Marshall County, AL, the son of Edna (Johnson) and John H. Lephiew. Their other children were Benjamin F., James E., Newton, Robert M., George W., William J., Joseph P., John W., Elizabeth, Nancy O., and Sallie. Edna Johnson was born in Al, and John H. Lephiew was born in TN. The couple was married in LA. Edna Lephiew died there in 1849, and John H. Lephiew died there in 1865. Henry H. Lephiew moved in 1859 to Monticello where he established a grocery store which he kept until he entered the CSA Army in 1862. He was discharged in 1865 and resided in Colquit, LA, for a year before returning to Monticello where he opened another grocery store. In 1870 he moved to the Collins-Baxter area and engaged in farming.

William H. Lephiew Jr. was raised on the family farms and as a teenager went to work in S. A. Duke's store at Baxter. He then formed a partnership in a mercantile with W. F. Skipper and W. R. Taggart at Baxter. Skipper and Lephiew eventually bought out Taggart, and the firm became Skipper & Lephiew. In addition to the mercantile store, they bought timber and had cypress shingle mills. After Skipper's death in 1896, the business continued as W. H. Lephiew. Delia Bulloch Lephiew died in 1900, and in 1901 Lephiew married Skipper's widow, Malissa Bulloch Skipper. The following year they moved to Dermott where he established a large mercantile furnishing business and a gin.

Children born to Anita (Lephiew) and R. H. "Butch" Dennington were Lephiew (m Ann Archer) and Janet (m Swan B. Moss Jr.). After the death of Anita Lephiew Dennington, Butch married Lois Thomas Grumbles, daughter of Lois (Baldwin) and Wallace Thomas. (See Lois Baldwin Thomas summary.)

≈≈❦≈≈

William deYampert

William Benjamin deYampert III was born August 28, 1918, at Wilmot, the son of Vesta (Pyron) and William Benjamin deYampert II. Their only other child was Mary Virginia (m John B. Currie). William B. deYampert II was born in Suggville, AL or Ashley County, the son of Emma (Portis) and William Benjamin deYampert I. Their other children were Portis, Clifford, and May Belle. William B. deYampert I was born in Alabama, the son of Lucius Quintus Cincinnatis deYampert. L. Q. C. deYampert was first married to Anna Overton Wingfield, and some of their children were Francis Asbury (first child, b 1818), Julia Anna (fourth child, m Col. John Henry Webb), and Rev. John Lucius (sixth child, b 1830; d 1888; m Anna Judson King). Anna Overton Wingfield deYampert died in 1832, and L. Q. C. deYampert later married a Miss Glover and then Parthenie Webb. Some of his other children were Riddie (never m), Dr. Asbury Hayne (eighth child, m Miss Turpin), and Thomas Lucius Webb deYampert (ninth child [evidently the son of Parthenie Webb] m Anna Maria Turpin).[3]

L. Q. C. deYampert bought land in Ashley County before the Civil War for his sons, William I and Thomas Lucius Webb, who moved there. The following information was provided by Riddie deYampert in a 1939 interview. "Riddie deYampert's brothers, William Benjamin and Lucius Webb, were among the first settlers in bayou country. The father offered them a large plantation in Ashley County at the time of their marriages...Ben was given a plantation east of Portland, now the Wells place, and Louis was given one south of Portland which he named Sunshine. Both brought boatloads of slaves with them...After two of Ben deYampert's children died of swamp fever the mother insisted the family move to Hamburg. Lou [Lucius] deYampert remained at Sunshine in a large home called Alligator Bluff. He [a Methodist minister] and his wife had a church built there, bought a fine organ, and conducted services themselves".[4] A third son, Rev. John Lucius, a Methodist minister, also came to Ashley County. He died in 1888 and was buried at Portland.[5]

Lucius Quintus Cincinnatis deYampert was born October 1, 1792, in Georgia, the son of Mary (Ardis) and Dr. Jean deYampert. Dr. deYampert was a French physician of Huguenot descent and assisted in the American Revolution. L. Q. C. deYampert was an early settler in Perry County, Alabama, and a well-known Methodist minister.

William deYampert III married Anne Uzzle.

***

Marion Robertson Doles

Marion Robertson Doles was born October 23, 1913, near Camden, AR, the daughter of Mariah Rosalie (Mason) and Ray Thomas Robertson. (See Eloise Robertson summary for family history.) Marion attended Bonita School and graduated in 1931. She attended Dodd College at Shreveport for a year and in 1943 began substitute teaching at McGinty School. The following year she was hired as a full-time teacher and stayed there until 1949. In 1951 she returned to McGinty School and in 1951-52 began teaching at Bonita where she retired in 1971. She received her B.A. from NLU in 1954.

Marion married Frank Morris Doles on 31 Mar 1934. Frank Doles was born 31 Jan 1911 at Jones, the son of Willie Ina (Honeycutt) and Ellis Adrian Doles. Their other children were Willis Adrian (b 9 Feb 1908; d 31 Dec 1948), Mary Ellis (b 4 Aug 1913; d 17 Dec 1920), Howard (b 31 Dec 1915; d 26 Dec 1966; nev m), Jane (b 3 Sep 1919; m 1st Milton Lewis; m 2nd Ralph L. Pippins; their children: Mikal Ralph and Robert Lance Pippins), John Anderson (b 23 Dec 1922; m Thelma Wade; their children: Deborah Ann and Rebecca), Ina Katherine (b 15 Jul 1926; m Willis Bertrand "Bert" McCready; their children: James Ellis and Stephen Wayne), and William Tarrant (b 12 Feb 1928; m Billie Jean Kinnaird; their children: Linda Gail, Roy Kirk; and Mary Ina).

Ellis Doles and Ina Honeycutt were married 18 Dec 1906 at McGinty. They bought a farm on Lighter Knot Creek and later moved to Parkdale. They then moved to Pine Prairie near Mist, AR, where they ran cattle. The next move was to the Nunn place on Bayou Bartholomew (LA) where they farmed and bought and sold cattle. They eventually established a grocery and meat market in Bonita. Ellis served as town marshal in 1924. In the 1930s Ellis built some cabins in Bonita to rent to travelers. His brother, Will, came from Texas to run this business which flourished until the roads were improved around 1933. In 1940 their house at Bonita burned and they built a grocery store with living quarters in the back. Ina Doles ran this business until she broke her hip at age eighty-seven.

Ellis Adrian Doles was born 16 Dec 1883 at Shreveport, the son of Mary Frances (Jones) and Francis King Doles. Their other children were William Thomas (m Ruby L. Newman), Albert L. (nev m; d age 20), Myrtle Frances (nev m), Mamie Lee (m Arch L. Butler), Annie Birdy (m William Franklin Breathwit), and Tiny (m Emsley Harris).

Francis King "Frank" Doles was born 27 Nov 1851, the eighth child of Pheriba (Irvin) (also written as Ferriba Ervin) and William Adrian Doles Sr., who were married 8 Dec 1836. Their other children were James Robert (b 15 Jun 1838 GA; d Feb 1863 VA; enlisted in LA Infantry at Belview 10 Mar 1862), Jesse T. (b 23 Jul 1840; d 14 Jan 1842, Morehouse Parish), Patrick Mercer (b 14 Feb 1842; d 16 Oct 1913; served in LA 3rd Battery; m 17 Apr 1876 Fannie Elizabeth Rose (born 4 May 1854); their children: Mary Maude, William Walter, Willis Francis, James Robert, Bessie Belle, Fannie Rosa, Patrick Preston, David, and Annie Delone "Lonnie"), Emily Shells (b 19 May 1845; d 3 Jun 1877; m James A. Little; their children: two known daughters m Long and Fry), Nancy Ann (b 5 Aug 1847; d 3 Oct 1884), William Adrian Jr. (b 6 Nov 1849; d 30 Jun 1852, Bossier Parish), and Zachariah Taylor (twin to William A. Jr.; d 29 Jun 1852; bu in same grave with Zachariah). Frank Doles as a young man carried mail on horseback from Girad, LA to Bastrop and on to Hamburg, Elan, and Poplar Bluff (Parkdale), AR. He then moved to Texas where he met and married Mary Frances Jones. The family eventually moved to Bonita and lived with Ellis Doles.

William Adrian Doles was born 6 Dec 1807 in Southampton County VA, the son of Mary (Mercer) and James Willis Doles, who were married in 1804. Mary Mercer was born in Nansemond River, VA. William Adrian Doles began a term as justice of the peace in 1844 and was elected sheriff of Morehouse Parish in 1848. His wife, Pheriba Irvin (Ferriba Ervin) was born in 1819 at Bayou Bartholomew, LA, and died 8 Dec 1870 in Morehouse Parish.

Mary Frances Jones, wife of Francis King Doles, was born 27 Dec 1856, the daughter of Mary (Dickey) and William Thomas Jones, who were married in KY. She died 30 May 1907 at Jones.

Willie Ina Honeycutt, wife of Ellis Adrian Doles, was born 9 May 1886 at Hamburg, AR, the daughter of Ella Evelyn (Tarrant) and Morris

Osborne Honeycutt. Morris Osborne Honeycutt was born in 1858, the son of Mary Elizabeth (Neal) and William Whatley Honeycutt. William Whatley Honeycutt was born in 1818 and died 5 Jul 1852. Ella Evelyn Tarrant was born 19 Aug 1862, the daughter of Cynthia Ann (Farrar) and William Anderson Tarrant. She died 6 Apr 1940 and was buried at Dermott. Cynthia Ann Farrar was the daughter of Thomas Farrar.

Children born to Marion (Robertson) and Frank Morris Doles were Ellis Ray (m Barbara Jane Magee) and James Pat (m Carmen Elaine Booth). Marion has four grandchildren and six great- grandchildren.

≈≈◈≈≈

Dr. Ralph Douglas

Dr. Ralph Douglas was born April 7, 1906, at Springfield, Conway County, AR, the son of Martha Antha (Walker) and R. L. Douglas. Their other children were Allen Earl and Lela (m Doyle Deaver). He attended school at Springfield until he received an athletic scholarship from Morrilton High School. In 1927 he played baseball in an oil league in Seminole County, OK, and then entered semi-pro baseball. Upon receiving a football scholarship to University of the Ozarks, he attended there for two years. He then received a football scholarship to Ouachita Baptist where he graduated in 1933. At Ouachita he met Blanche Riley, and they married in the same year.

The couple lived in Oklahoma until 1934 when they moved to Lake Village, Chicot County, where he opened Douglas Wholesale & Retail Grocery & Mercantile and an Oldsmobile and Willis dealership. They bought farmland east of Sunshine and began farming, making their first crop in 1935. They rented the farm out in 1937 and moved to Pine Bluff, where Ralph worked for his father-in-law's Riley Butane Gas Company. Ralph accepted the pastorship of Gould First Baptist Church and later was pastor of churches Luxora and Truman. The couple then moved to Louisville, KY, where Ralph was pastor of a church and attended Southern Baptist Theological Seminary. There he received his master's degree in theology. He later graduated from Southern College with a doctorate in divinity. In 1954 Dr. Douglas became executive director of the Southern Baptist Convention in Little Rock, a position he held until his retirement in 1971.

Blanche Riley was born in 1911 at Montrose, the only child of Rosa Dell (Richardson) and Hunter Pryor Riley. Rosa Dell Richardson was the daughter of Mattie (Harvill) and George Henry Richardson Sr. Their other children were Mary Sue (m James Robert Riley), Terrell (m Iva Barnett), Georgia (nev m), and George Henry Jr. (m Catherine Bond). George Henry Richardson Sr. was the son of Susan Emily (Pascall) and ?

Richardson of Tyro. The father died during the Civil War. After his marriage in 1879, George Henry Richardson Sr. located to Milo in Ashley County and later to Hamburg where he established a mercantile business. He eventually owned stores in Thebes and Montrose and entered a partnership with his son, G. H. Jr., in Boydell.

Hunter Pryor Riley was the son of Georgia Carry (Taylor) and John Rutledge Riley Sr. Their other children were James Robert (m Mary Sue Richardson), John Rutledge Jr. (m India Olive Baker), Joe Pat (m Mammie Cone), and Columbus Allen (m Winnie Mae Craig). Georgia Carry Taylor Richardson died in 1889, and John Rutledge Riley Sr. then married Mrs. Martha Cone Sullivan. Children born to this marriage were Dr. Jesse Dean (b 10 Nov 1890; m Claudia Carpenter), David Cooper (b 8 Feb 1895; m Hazel Andrews), and Hattie Elizabeth (b 11 Sep 1896; m Claude M. Gregory).

John Rutledge Riley Sr. was born Nov 1852 at Berea, Ashley County, the son of Elizabeth Ann (Davis) and James Cooper Riley. Their other children were James Andrew (d young), William Alexander (twin to James Andrew; b 9 May 1853; d 4 Mar 1870), James Nathaniel (b 16 Jan 1855), Mary Ann (b 4 Apr 1857; m Thomas Miller Yelvington), Joseph Holmes (b 3 Mar 1860; m Eliza Thompson), Samuel Jackson (d young), Susan Elizabeth (b Feb 1866; m Tobe Linden), Robert Randolph (b 12 Nov 1868; m Eliza McDougal), Louisa Jane (b 9 May 1871; m John Powell), George Thomas (b 7 Jul 1873; m Effie Sullivan), and Patrick Joshua (d young). James Cooper Riley was born 1 Jan 1826, SC, and died Apr 1882 at Berea. Elizabeth Ann Davis Riley was born in 1833 and died in 1910. The couple was at Berea by 1857.

Children born to Blanche (Riley) and Dr. Ralph Douglas were Hunter Pryor Riley (m Martha ?), Rosalee (m 1st Joseph Dempsey; m 2nd Laron Scott), and R. L. III (d age 4 of said cause cerebral malaria).

⬥⬥⬥⬥⬥

James J. "Buster" Ford

James J. "Buster" Ford was born June 19, 1915, at McGinty, the son of Florence (Jackson) and Louis Ford Jr. Their other children were Evelyn, Kenneth "Ken Boy" (m Cleo Lemons), and Vernell Odessa (m Edward Mahone). Louis Ford married second Jessie Robinson and children born to this union were Elva Lee (nev m), Erma, Louis III (m Daisy ?), and Europe (nev m).

Louis Ford Jr. was born at McGinty, the son of Lucinda and Louis Ford Sr. Their other children, all born at McGinty, were Alice (m John Lindsay), Jennie (m Add Roan), Octavis (m Jim Caldwell), Polk, Porter (m Liza Jane Moore), Jesse, and Nunn (m Alice ?). Louis Ford Sr. was born in the Jones area. His parents were brought from the West Indies as slaves. Florence Jackson was born near Jones, the daughter of Sally (Mays) and Robert "Bob" Jackson. Their other children were Alice (nev m), Barbara (m Harry Webb), Lilly (m Pearl Bowden), Gertrude, Mitta (m Rev. Wright), William (m Littie Robinson), Webb (m Alberta Cunningham), and Erskine (m Johnnie Washington). Sally Mays Jackson declared that her parents and the Jackson family were brought to South Carolina as slaves and then transported to Elan, AR, by a Mr. Jackson. From Elan they walked three days to a farm near Parkdale. The Bob Jackson family moved to McGinty in the 1890s where they homesteaded 160 acres.

Buster Ford attended Hunter's Institute at McGinty for five or six terms and then completed the ninth grade at McGinty School. After two months in the tenth grade at Arkadelphia, he married in 1932 and began sharecropping on the Jap Jones farm. The next year he bought a pair of mules and rented land. In 1948 he bought an 80-acre farm and eventually farmed 150 acres.

Buster married Mildred Haynes who was born at Jones on Hollyhurst Plantation, the only child of Lillian (Parker) and George Haynes. Mildred Haynes' children were Lee Daniel and Jamie Mae Haynes. Buster's child before his marriage to Mildred was May Bell Ford (m L. J. McHenry). Children born to Mildred (Haynes) and Buster Ford were Lois Verdell (m Jesse Corbin), Florence (m L. C. Anderson), James, Jr. (d infant), Joyce Marie (m Jesse Chafel), Leotis (m Dessa Rea Britton), Thessolonia (nev m), Evelyn (m John Creighton), and James Albert (m Ethel Mae Martin). Mildred and Buster divorced, and Buster married Eula Mae Colbert, who was born at Jones, the daughter of Maggie (Payne) and T. L. Colbert. Children born to Eula Mae (Colbert) and Buster Ford were Margaret Ann (d infant), Earl Wayne (m 1st Linda Robinson; m 2nd ?), Earlene (twin to Earl Wayne; m Lee Arbie Jones), and Maggie Ann (m Melvin Thurman). When Eula Mae Ford died in 1983, they had ninety-six grandchildren. Buster states that he has not counted them since then.

⚜

Mary Morris Foster

Mary Morris Foster was born September 25, 1912, at Parkdale, the only child of Mabel (Ralph) and Herman William Morris. Mabel Ralph was the daughter of Viola Edward Rose Wimbish (Hill) and William Harrison Ralph. Their other children were Margaret "Mag" (b 6 Oct 1896; m James Howard Nobles Sr.; d 30 July 1954), Harrison (nev m; d age 32), and John (m Lena Burgess).

Viola Hill was born 17 Sep 1872, at Beech Creek, Ashley County, the daughter of Elizabeth Harriet (Wimbish) Wooldridge and James Edward

Hill. Elizabeth (Wimbish) Wooldridge Hill was born 8 Nov 1837, in Georgia and died 29 Jun 29 1909 at Beech Creek. James Edward Hill was born 10 Apr 1818 in Tuscaloosa County, Alabama, the son of Margaret (Stover) and John Hill. He died 3 Sep 1906 at Beech Creek. Margaret Stover was born c1795 and died in 1871 at Beech Creek. John Hill was born c1787 in Sevier County, TN died in 1862 at Beech Creek.

William Harrison Ralph was born 12 May 1869, the son of Sophronia (Donavan) and Harrison Adolphus Ralph. He died 26 Nov 1920 at Beech Creek. Harrison Adolphus Ralph was born 23 Feb 1841 in Drew County, the son of Emeline and Preston Ralph. Sophronia Donavan and Harrison Adolphus Ralph were married in Ashley County 21 Feb 1866.

Herman William Morris was born 6 Nov 1885 at Parkdale, the son of Mary Hadley (Hawkins) and John William Morris Sr. Their other children were Maggie May (b 25 Apr 1880; d 29 Jul 1883 Parkdale) and John William Jr. (b 6 Mar 1882 Parkdale; m William Thomas Files Sr.; d 30 May 1977 at Wilmot). The only child born to William Thomas (Files) –a female - and John William Morris Jr. was William Thomas Files (m Johnnie Caldwell). Children born to Johnnie (Caldwell) and William Thomas Files Morris were Mary Frances Files (m Nicholas Eugene Silitch) and Paula Morris Files (m 1st Robert Raiford Murphy; m 2nd James Ronald Twentey; m 3rd Martin Scott Flowers). Mary Hadley (Hawkins) Morris was the daughter of Harriet Eliza (Hadley) and Marcus Lafayette Hawkins. (See Mark Hawkins summary for Hawkins.)

John William Morris Sr. was born October 8, 1839, in Raleigh, Wake County, NC. He arrived at Poplar Bluff (Parkdale), probably by steamer, around 1855 at age sixteen and clerked in a store which was located on the bayou. He eventually established his own mercantile business and acquired farm land which he let out to tenants. By 1878 he had established Morris & Cohen (mercantile) with Isaac Cohen at Poplar Bluff. He died 30 Jun 1912 at Parkdale.

Mary Morris Foster attended Parkdale High School and after graduating from Galloway College returned to Parkdale to teach. She married Claude Lowe Foster who was born 2 Sep 1907 on the bayou west of Parkdale, the son of Mary (Sanders) and John Henry "Jim" Foster. Their other children were Lee (m Fronia Ralph), Roy, Beavery, and Clee (nev m).

Mary (Morris) and Claude Foster had one child, Ann (m Dr. Donald Lewis Stone). Mary has three grandchildren.

Susie Wright Fuqua

Susie Wright Fuqua was born August 3, 1904, near Bowser in Drew County, the daughter of Emile "Emma" (Mew) and Ed Wright. Their other children were Albert James "Shakes" (b Aug 6, 1908; nev m), Herbert Lemuel (twin to Albert; m Eddie Mae Donavan), Jessie (d age 3), Billy (d age 6), and a daughter, "Little Sister" (d young). Emile Mew Wright died and Ed Wright then married Minor Pascall. Their children were "Jack" Finn (m Margaret McGriff), Gibson, Adelle (m Harold Quimby), and Bernice.

Ed Wright was born in Crook Township, Drew County, Nov 10, 1873, the son of Sarah Virginia "Jennie" (Nelson) and ? Wright. Their other children were Florence (m Payton Lasiter) and Frankie (a daughter; d young). Sarah Virginia Nelson Wright's second marriage was to ? Taylor and their children were Joe, Elv, and Claude (m Mary Gibbs). The Wright family came to Arkansas from Georgia.

Emile Mew was born at Bowser in 1878, the daughter of Susan Abigail (Dunlap) and James Alexander "Jim" Mew. Their other children were John Henry (m Mary Elizabeth Hargis), Leonard (d infant), Frank Edward (m Easter Walthal), Hattie Sue (m Alonzo Tillman), and Abbe Sue (twin to Hattie; d infant). Susan Abigail Dunlap died in July 1885, and James Alexander Mew married her sister, Melissa Barbara, in 1888. They had no children. James Alexander Mew was born at Charleston, SC, 19 Jul 1848, the son of John Mew. The John Mew family also had a farm in Georgia and reportedly lived at Charleston during the summers. When James Alexander Mew was twenty-one years old, he moved to Baton Rouge, LA, and in 1875 moved to Drew County and settled near Bowser.

Children born to Mary Elizabeth (Hargis) and John Henry Mew were Annie Abigail (m 1st Wesley DeArmond, div; m 2nd Leonard Moss), Charles Leslie (m Geraldine Mosley), and James Turner (m Marie Stecker). Mary Elizabeth Hargis was the daughter of Nancy (Lewis) Barker and Charles W. Hargis.

Susie Wright attended school at Bowser until the family moved to Tyro, Lincoln County, in 1912. Ed Wright rented 112 acres north of Garrett Bridge from Buck Finn of Monticello. He placed his family at Tyro to escape the mosquito infested Delta and would commute to work. During winter the family would go and live on the farm. In 1915 the family moved to the bayou and used "mosquito bars," a netting draped over beds. Susie attended a country school on the farm until the family moved back to Drew County in 1920. She finished the eighth grade at Bowser.

Susie married Calvin Fuqua, who was born in Drew County, the son of Dee (Thurman) and Thomas Fuqua. Children born to Susie and Calvin

Fuqua were Ruby (m Herman Webb), William Calvin (m Dona Ray Dubay), Tom Ed (m Betty Burks), and Callie (m Sam Mays). Susie married second Perry Webb and their child was Martha Jo (m James Cross). Susie Wright Fuqua died 23 Aug 1999 and had 14 grandchildren, 25 great-grandchildren, and 8 great-great-grandchildren.

Jack Gibson

Jack Anderson Gibson was born March 3, 1920, at Boydell, the son of Johnnie (Barnes) and John June Gibson. Their other children were Mary Jane (m 1st Monroe Naron; m 2nd Percy Kenneth Boyd) and John Jr. (d young).

Johnnie Barnes was the daughter of Mary Jane (Nobles) and John Barnes. Their other children were Jim (nev m), Sally Jeff, John Sumner (m Tot Livingston), Mataline (m Max Broadnax), and Fannie Sue "Honey" (m Ed Bell).

John June Gibson was born in Drew County, the son of Mary Jane "Mattie" (Bulloch) and John Anderson Gibson. Their other children were Charles Clifford Sr. (b 20 Jan 1888, Baxter; m 1st Margaret Bynum; m 2nd Fannie Offuit Burkett), Frank Anderson (b 29 Apr 1892, Morrell; m Edna Bond), William Edward (m Annie Simpson), Sam (m Hazel Jennings), Eugene (m Lucille Logan), Steven Paul (m Exa Anderson), Robert Bonner (d young), Mabel Maude (m James Madison Waddell), and Gaston Pellam (m Nettie Winters McCollum).

Mary Jane Bulloch was born 1858 at Troy, the daughter of Milly Ann (Courtney) and William Wesley Bulloch. Their other children were Stephen Robert (b 1856, GA; d 1910, Ashley County; m 1st Millie Skipper; m 2nd Hettie H. Lephiew), Malissa Frances (b 1861, Troy; d infant), and Catherine Cinderella (b 1862, Troy; d 1948, Dermott; m 1st Benjamin Wilson Martin Jr.; m 2nd Samuel Howard).

John Anderson Gibson was born 1856 at Troy, the son of Frances Ann "Duck" (Gray) and Samuel Gibson. Their only other child was Thomas (m Patty Oliver). Samuel Gibson was first married to Winnie Gray and their children were William (b 1836, Meriwether Co, GA; killed in Civil War) and Mjr. Samuel (m Frances B. Finn). After Samuel Gibson died, Frances Gray Gibson married a Ferguson and their children were Sally (m Bailey) and Mary Frances (m Kidd). The Samuel Gibson family moved to Drew County in 1849 and settled near Collins. John Anderson Gibson settled at Morrell around 1874. He eventually bought the W. R. Roddy Mercantile, the firm becoming J.A. Gibson & Son, the son being Charles Clifford Sr. He farmed and ran a cotton gin.

John June Gibson, son of John Anderson Gibson, entered the cattle business and in 1924 moved from Morrell (Boydell) to Monticello where he established Gibson Meat Market. In 1927 the family moved to Wilmot where he continued in the cattle and horse enterprise. He moved his business in 1930 to Jones.

Jack Anderson Gibson attended school at Wilmot, Jones, and Bonita. He then entered NLU on a football scholarship and later attended LSU on a baseball scholarship. He signed with the Ben Johnson League for baseball and played for one season. His career was interrupted by a broken ankle and he moved to Boydell in 1940 where he worked in his father's gin. In 1941 he entered Mississippi State where he signed up for civilian pilot training. He entered the Navy in 1942 and flew fighter missions until the end of the war in 1945. He returned to Mississippi State for two years and then entered the farm and gin business with his father. In 1948 he bought Enterprise Plantation near Dermott with Billy and John Mitchell Baxter. When the Baxters went into the lumber business, Jack bought out their interest in the plantation. This plantation was originally owned by Mrs. Janie Dickinson and her sons. In 1971 Jack rented out his farm and entered the banking business. In 1980 he was appointed to finish the state senatorial term of his cousin, John Frank "Mutt" Gibson Sr. who died in office. Senator Jack Gibson served until 1993 and was appointed that year to head the Arkansas Livestock and Poultry Division, a position he currently holds.

Jack Gibson married first Sarah Kendrick and they adopted two children, June (m Lewis Gober) and John Anderson III "Brother" (m Deborah Jones). Jack married second Elizabeth Henigan, and they had a son, Andy. Jack also adopted Elizabeth's adopted daughter, Marcie.

Children born to Edna (Bond) and Frank Anderson Gibson were Edna Bond (nev m), Frank Anderson (m Barbara Minchew), William Grandy (m Ruth Short), Eugene (nev m), Joe (d infant), and Martha Ann (m Clyde Spoonamore). Children born to Annie (Simpson) and William Edward Gibson were William Edward (m Neva Buccanan) and Nancy Mary (m Lamar Eastham). Hazel (Jennings) and Sam Gibson had no children. Exa (Anderson) and Steven Paul Gibson had no children. Lucille (Logan) and Eugene Gibson's only child was Eugene Lee. Mabel Maude (Gibson) and James Madison Waddell's only child was James Madison Jr. Gaston Pellam and Nettie (Winters/McCollum) Gibson's only child was Gaston Pellam Jr. (m Gloria Worth). Children born to Margaret (Bynum) and Charles Clifford Gibson Sr. were Charles Clifford Jr. (m Helen Schultz), John Frank Sr. (m Juanita Watkins), and Robert Bynum (m Jean Toland).

Children born to Helen (Schultz) and Charles Clifford Gibson Jr. were Margaret (m Leonard Niven), Helen Marie (m John Robert Burks), Charles Clifford III (m Lisa Hartness), John Robert, and William Oren. Children born to Juanita (Watkins) and John Frank Gibson Sr. were John Frank Jr. (m 1st Judith Hardin; m 2nd Rebecca Nichols; m 3rd Renee Treadwell), and Charles Sidney (m Sherry Jones). Children born to Jean (Toland) and Robert Bynum Gibson were Robert Bynum Jr. (m Dolores Doty), Sam Toland (d 1983), and Brooks.

≈✺◈✺≈

Sue Gipson

Leanna Sue Gipson was born July 3, 1913, near Tarry, the daughter of Josephine (Smith) and Dock Gibson. Their other children were Ella, Alex, Fata, Henry, and Dock Jr. Dock Gibson was born in MS to a couple who were former slaves. He had two children, Willie and Mary, by a former marriage in MS. He left them with the maternal grandparents and came to the Yorktown area "after the surrender" with a white man, Bill Britley, who hired him to work. He married Josephine Smith in Lincoln County and managed to buy a 300-acre farm before Sue was born. He used five sharecropping families on the farm. Josephine Smith was the daughter of Sally (York) and Alex Smith. Sally York was born near Tarry as a York slave. Sally York Smith was a midwife.

Sue Gipson first attended school at Sweet Home on Tarry Road and then entered Morgan School which was on the bank of Bayou Bartholomew. She went to school seven months during the winter and two in the summer, walking the five-mile roundtrip. After she completed the eighth grade, she began working on the family farm. Sue married George Morgan in 1932 and moved to his place at nearby Phenix. She moved back to her homeplace after they divorced in 1957.

≈✺◈✺≈

Bessie Fuller Green

Bessie Fuller Green was born August 7, 1912, on Bayou Bartholomew near the Phenix/Yorktown area, the daughter of Melissa (Nelson) and James Fuller. Their other children were Ola (m Doc Hardin), Ruth (m David Green), Naomi (m Willie Allmon), Victoria (m Berry Rivers), and Samantha (m Buddy Hall; m 2nd Leander Christian). James Fuller was born 17 Nov 1885 in Cleveland County, the son of Louise (Bones ?) and Wyatt Fuller, who moved to Arkansas from Alabama. James Fuller moved to the Phenix area in 1908. Melissa Nelson was the daughter of Nettie and Mason Nelson of Tarry.

Bessie attended school at Mt. Nebo and then went to Merrill High School in Pine Bluff. She married William Green in 1932. William was born 12 Jan 1908 near Phenix, the son of Lular (Green) and Jack Crawl. He was raised by his grandmother, Florence Green. Children born to Bessie and William Green were Myrlee (m Junior Wright), Johnnie Mae (m Leroy Hamilton), James (m Katherine Summers), Eddie Joe (m Ella Johnson), Sippeio (drown in Bayou Bartholomew, age 17), Alsteen "Dimple" (m James Chapman), and Sharon Louise (m Clyde Mims). Bessie has 20 grandchildren, 25 great-grandchildren, and 8 great-great-grandchildren.

Herbert Lavaughn Greenway

Herbert Lavaughn "Von" Greenway was born November 10, 1926, at Picket Bend on Bayou Bartholomew near Jerome. He was the son of Iva Lee (Casteel) and T. H. Greenway. Their other children were Cecil L. (m Dorothy Rucks), Juanita (m G. W. Allen), Harold "Jim" (m Alice Kroger), Mickey (m James Reeves, div; m 2nd Everett Long), and Paulette (m Jim Murphy).

T. H. Greenway was born 9 Oct 1907 at St. James, AR, the son of Agnes (Murphree) and Jack Greenway. The Murphree family was of Dutch descent. Jack Greenway was the son of Newton Jack Greenway, whose wife was "full Cherokee." Iva Lee Casteel was born 2 Feb 1911 at Mountain Home, AR, the daughter of Ada (Cunningham) and J. R. Casteel. The Casteel family was originally from Knox County, TN.

The T. H. and Newton Jack Greenway families along with Bill Blackwell, who was married to Iva Lee Casteel's sister, moved to Picket Bend in 1925. Jack Greenway came by train with his cattle, mules, horses, and buggy. The others drove in a Model-T. Looking for better cotton land, they rented land from Hammond Waddell and began a farming operation which they continued until 1945.

Von Greenway attended school at Jerome through the ninth grade and then began farming full time. He married Jimmie Sue Shelby, who was born 25 Nov 1932 at Pansy, AR, the daughter of Johnnie (Lynn) and Walter Shelby. Children born to Jimmie Sue (Shelby) and Von Greenway were Sandra Kay (m Jackie Thompson), Judy Lennae (m Tim Fletcher), Paula Ann (m Randy Thompson), Cathy Sue (m Roger Herring), and Herbert Jr. "Buddy" (m Dorothy Kearney). They have eleven grandchildren.

Dr. Roy Grizzell

Dr. Roy Grizzell was born March 14, 1918, at Sweetwater, Loudon County, Tennessee, the son of Rena Bee (Williams) and Roy Grizzell Sr. Their other children were Rena (nev m), Ida (m Carl P. Elliott), and Julia (m Elliott Kyle). Roy Grizzell Sr. was born at Vergennes, IL, the son of Ida (Walker) and Charles Grizzell, M.D.

Rena Bee Williams was born 11 Apr 1892, at Sweetwater, TN, the daughter of Olga Irene (Crawley) and Jesse Edward Williams. Their other children were Olga and Jessie. Olga Irene Crawley was born 25 Apr 1872, Loudon County, TN, the daughter of Martha Amanda "Mattie" (Phillips) Tiller and J. Fred Crawley, who were married May 1, 1855, in Pine Bluff, AR. Their other children were Mattie Phillips (b 30 Jan 1856, Jefferson Co, AR; m 8 May 1877, John S. Lee; d 8 Jun 1935, Asheville, NC), Freddie George (b 18 Feb 1859, Ashley Co, AR; d 21 Nov 1859, Ashley County), Fannie Dora (b 03 Dec 1861, Ashley County; d 23 July 1864, Ashley County), Robert Page (b 22 Aug 1863, Ashley County; m Rebecca J. Genevia "Jammie" Griffin; d 05 Dec 1919, Ashley County), and Julia Ida (b 15 Nov 1867, Pond Creek, Roane, TN; nev m; d 15 Apr 1946, Asheville, NC). Julia Ida Crawley eventually went by the name of Ida Jolly Crawley. Family oral history reveals that she was in love with and engaged to a man whose name was Jolly. He had an injury and was never able to marry her. When he died, she assumed his name.

Martha Amanda "Mattie" Phillips was first married (23 Jul 1845) to Thomas Bridgeford Tiller and their children were William Oscar (b 21 Apr 1846, Marksville, Avoyelles Parish, LA; d 19 May 1848, Marksville), Ella Eliza (b 14 Oct 1848, Marksville; m John Ruffin Latimore, 4 Oct 1871; d 24 Feb 1926, Mountain Home, ID), Charles Monroe (b 12 Mar 1851, Marksville; d 11 Mar 1852, Pine Bluff, AR), and Thomas B. Jr. (b 03 Mar 1853, Pine Bluff; d 21 Oct 1854, Pine Bluff). J. Fred Crawley was first married to Melissa (surname unknown) and had a son, John Fred Jr. (b 03 Apr1854-5, Cohoma Co, MS; m Lulu Allen, 07 Aug 1879).

Martha Amanda Phillips was born 16 Jan 1827, at Huntsville, Madison County, AL, the daughter of Eliza (Martin) and William E. Phillips. She died 13 Jan 1880 and is buried at New Hope Church Cemetery, Philadelphia, TN. Thomas Bridgeford Tiller was born 27 Dec 1871, Frankfort, Franklin, KY, and died 07 Oct 1852 at Natchez, MS. He was on a business trip to Natchez from Jefferson County, contracted cholera, and died there. It was after this that Amanda married J. Fred Crawley.

J. Fred Crawley was born in Halifax County, NC, the son of Bird Crawley. (See Robert Crawley summary.) In 1853, J. Fred and his brother, William G. Crawley, migrated to Jefferson County, AR, and began to acquire property, some of which was located near Tucker. Deeds from 1854 reveal that they were buying government offered swampland. In 1855-57, J. Fred Crawley bought land at Tatum Bend on Bayou Bartholomew in Ashley County and moved there. He built a large two-story home on the bayou which was the center of Crawley's Bend Plantation. This home burned "about a hundred years ago." (The family

Bible record reveals the last birth at Crawley Plantation on 22 Sept 1902. The next birth on 28 Nov 1905 took place at Griffin Plantation, so it may be assumed that the home burned between 1902-1905.) After the War Between the States, J. Fred Crawley moved to Sweetwater, TN, and built a similar home. (See Robert Crawley Summary.)

Julia Ida Jolly Crawley, daughter of Amanda (Phillips) and J. Fred Crawley, studied art at the Corcoran Museum in Washington, D.C. for five years under Johaneas Oertel, Lucien Powell and other noted artists. She then studied in Paris under Sir Frederick Massey. Embarking then upon a tour of Europe, Africa, and Asia, she collected art, antiquities, geological specimens, and archeological artifacts. In 1919 she bought the Deemon-Rumbough-Williamson house in Asheville, TN, which was built c1872 by the builders of the Vanderbilt's Biltmore. She filled its sixteen rooms with her collection, including her own paintings, and opened the Crawley Museum of Art and Archeology. She died there in 1946.

Roy Grizzell Jr. graduated from Richmond High School in Augusta, GA, received his B.S.F. from University of Georgia and his M.F. in forestry and Ph.D. in biology from University of Michigan. He came to Little Rock in 1960 as state biologist for the Soil Conservation Service. After retirement in 1978, he moved to Monticello. Roy married Virginia Roe, who was born in Takoma Park, MD, the daughter of Ella (Neill) and Glenwood C. Roe. Children born to Roy and Virginia Grizzell were Linda (m Chuck Baker; children: Amy, Justin, Ginny) and Diane (m David Thompson; children: Abbie, Ben).

Children born to Ida (Grizzell) and Carl Elliott were Carl P. and Rena B. Children born to Julia (Grizzell) and Elliott Kyle were Elliott Grizzell and Julie Ann.

≈≈◎≈≈

Cecil Harp

Cecil Dreher Harp was born August 8, 1918, near Bonita, the son of Belle (Dreher) and Daniel Robert Harp. Their other children were Willie Belle (m Louie Rankin), Anne Vivian (m Carnel Edward Evans), Robert Paul (m Mildred Estelle), Charles Ellis (m Mary Andrews), Mary Louise (m Isaac Lafayette Hopkins), and Virginia Ruth (m Charles Gilman White).

Belle Dreher was born 17 May 1884, near Clinton, East Feliciana Parish. Belle met Daniel Robert Harp during a visit to Bonita with her half-sister. Daniel Robert Harp was born 25 Dec 1878 on Bayou Bonne Idee east of Mer Rouge, the son of Willie Ann (Green) and Demarquis Ellis "Mark" Harp. Their other children were Rufus Green (b 17 May 1873; d 2 Jul 1876), James Franklin (b 3 Feb 1875; m Ella May Carter; d 10 Dec 1950),

Tina Ann (b 26 Feb 1877; d 26 Apr 1886), Demarquis Kelly (b 17 Dec 1880; d 18 Jan 1890), Thomas Young (b 10 Feb 1882 near Lind Grove; m Flora Alberta Degelow), Grover (b 31 Dec 1884; m Josie Belle Hewette), Charles Weiss (b 18 Apr 1887; d 25 Dec 1916), Ora Ethel (b 8 Jan 1889; d 5 Oct 1898), William E. (b 18 Jul 1890; d 17 Aug 1890), and Foster (b 1 Dec 1892; d 19 Aug 1897).

Willie Ann Green was born in the Green Community four miles south of Oak Grove, the daughter of Elizabeth (Roberts) and Daniel Green. The family lived on the Beouf River near Goodwill on a farm later owned by Travis Green. Willie Ann Green and Mark Harp were married 15 Feb 1872 on the bank of Beouf River at Russell Ford under a large bitter pecan tree. Mark Harp died 1 Nov 1924 and is buried at Harp Cemetery on the old Methodist Church grounds located on the bank of Bayou Bonne Idee east of Mer Rouge with his wife and children except James Franklin who is buried in Bonita.

Demarquis Ellis "Mark" Harp was born 28 Sept 1845 in Marshall County, MS, the son of Prudence (Masoner) and Thomas M. Harp. Their other children were Mary Ann (b 3 Sep 1821 TN; d 3 Dec 1863; m Jonathan D. Cain), Elizabeth Jane (b 21 Jun 1823 TN; m Thomas Gilbreath), William T. (b 1824 TN; m Ann Ester Morris), Adeline (b 3 Feb 1827 TN; m Eli Merritt; d 6 May 1898 MS), James Nathan (b 1830 Rhea County TN; m Elizabeth Humphrey, 16 Sep 1854, Morehouse Parish; d 10 Jul 1885 on Bonne Idee), Harriet Prudence (b Rhea County TN; m Henry Washington Scoggins; d 1875), Martha (b Rhea County TN; m Joseph S. McKay; d 1861 MS), Thomas Young (b Rhea County TN; m Sarah Angeline Stevenson, 1 Dec 1865, Hamburg, AR; bu Stevenson Cemetery in 2nd Ward, no marker); Isaac C. "Doc" (b 1837, Meigs County TN; d in Confederate Army, Camp Moore, Tangipahoa Parish); Lee Ann (b 1839 MS; d 1840 Marshall County MS), Anderson Wisdom (b 1840 Marshall County; d 7 Dec 1862, battle of Prairie Grove, AR), America Missouri (b 1840; m Warren Alexander Montgomery; d c1918, Bonita), and Rufus Kelley (b 24 Sep 1847; m Eliza Ann Green, 16 Nov 1876 on Bonne Idee; d on Bonne Idee 2 May 1913.

Prudence Masoner, wife of Thomas M. Harp, was born 29 Aug 1802, presumably in Greene Co, TN, the daughter of Massie (Runyon) and John Masoner. Their only other known child was Isaac (b 1797, VA; m Mahala Templeton, Rhea County TN). Thomas Marion Harp was born 15 Aug 1798 NC. He married Prudence Masoner in Overton County TN in 1820. They eventually settled in Marshall County MS where he died 1 May 1850.

Six children born to Prudence (Masoner) and Thomas M. Harp settled in Louisiana: Mary Ann Cain (Vernon Parish), James Nathan (Morehouse Parish), Isaac C. (d Tangipahoa Parish), America Missouri Montgomery (d

Bonita), Demarquis Ellis (Bonne Idee), and Rufus Kelley (Bonne Idee). Thomas Young Harp settled in Ashley County. Dates given in the family history indicate that this migration occurred before the Civil War.

Children born to Mary Ann (Harp) and Jonathan D. Cain were William Columbus (b 12 Sep 1837, Marshall County MS; m Rebecca Chaddick, 1856, in now Vernon Parish [formed 1871]; d 19 Nov 1908), Mary Jane (b 1 Jan 1840, Marshall County; m Benjamin Franklin Miller; d 28 Jun 1875, Vernon Parish), Thomas Madison "Mat" (b 17 Jan 1842, Marshall County; m Mrs. Craft) Cryer; d 11 Dec 1900, Vernon Parish), Sarah M. (b 31 Oct 1844, MS; m 1st Thomas Jefferson Miller; m 2nd Uriah Chaddick; d 18 Dec 1899), Jonathan James (b 14 Jan 1847; m M. J. Craft, 1867 in Newton County TX; d 1870s Morehouse Parish while on a visit), Emily Rebecca (b 13 May 1847, MS; m Solomon D. Cole in Newton County TX; d 1866 Vernon Parish), Martha Leeann Prudence (b 13 Nov 1852, Vernon Parish; m Alford Cryer; d 23 May 1873 Vernon Parish), Robert Demarcus (twin to Martha Prudence; m 1st Melvina Chaddick; d 3 Oct 1931), and Margaret Harriet (nev m).

Children born (all in Morehouse Parish) to Elizabeth (Humphrey) and James Nathan Harp were Thomas (b 21 Oct 1855; d 9 Oct 1861), James W. (b 14 Oct 1857; d 9 Jan 1862), America "Annie/Sissy"(b 7 Mar 1858; m Zeph Boudreau Sisson; d 1 Feb 1899), Dock Young (b 17 May 1862; m Katie S. Williams; d 1 Feb 1899), Benjamin R. (b 13 Jan 1865; d 4 Mar 1884), Anderson W. (b 27 Sep 1869; d 29 Dec 1893), Lula Belle (b 29 Feb 1872; d 4 Dec 1904; m Robert Walter Hope at Bonita 27 Dec 1893; Robert W. Hope b on Bayou Bartholomew, 2nd Ward, Morehouse Parish, 6 Jun 1870; d 26 Dec 1927), and Harriet Prudence (b 15 Mar 1874; m Robert W. Hope, 27 Dec 1905; d 8 Feb 1956).

Children born to Sarah Angeline (Stevenson) and Thomas M. "Young Harp" Harp were Tina (d infant) and Oliver Young "Ollie" (b c 1868; m Cornelia Burns). Young and Angeline Harp died before 1873 and their son, Ollie, was cared for by Prudence Harp until her death in 1877, at which time he was put under the care of Rufus Kelley Harp.

Children born to America Missouri (Harp) and Warren Alexander Montgomery were Jeff Davis and Charles Warren (d 1865). Children born (all on Bonne Idee) to Eliza Ann (Green) and Rufus Kelley Harp were Jesse Clay (b 30 Aug 1877; d 12 Dec 1877), Kelley Bowman (b 5 Mar 1890; m Florence Alice (Bosshammer) Clements), and Robert E. Lee (b 1 Sep 1895; m Anna Kirkpatrick).

Demarquis Ellis Harp entered the mercantile business and owned several thousand acres of farmland. His son, Daniel Robert, attended LSU where he majored in agriculture, and then entered farming.

Cecil Harp attended Bonita School and graduated in 1936. After a year at LSU, he worked in Texas until he was drafted into the army in 1940.

Cecil received the Purple Heart for action at Manila under General MacArthur. He returned to Bonita in 1946 and went into partnership with his father. Cecil married Virginia Frances Henderson who was born 29 Sep 1923, at Humble,Texas, the daughter of Zelia Mae (Hodges) and Joseph Perry Henderson. Children born to Virginia (Henderson) and Cecil Harp were Cecil Dreher Jr., Diana Louise, Linda, and James Milton. Cecil Harp died October 7, 1999.

The only child born to Willie Belle (Harp) and Louie Rodney Rankin was Diane. Children born to Annie Vivian (Harp) and Carnel Edward Evans were Norma Jean (m Clifford Walker King), Dan Harp (m Joanne Gillen), and Charles Edward. Children born to Mildred O'lene (Estelle) and Robert Paul Harp were Paul Ramon and Paulette Estelle. Children born to Mary Inez (Andrews) and Charles Ellis Harp were Charles Ellis, Robert Patrick, Kathleen Mary, and Kerry Lee (m George Joseph Kramer). They also adopted two children of Mary Inez Andrews from a former marriage: Sylvia Ilene and Steve Michael Harp. Children born to Mary Louise (Harp) and Isaac Lafayette Hopkins were Faye Louise (m Arthur Hope Baggett), Travis Dreher, Ronald Francis, and Maribelle. Children born to Virginia Ruth (Harp) and Charles Gilman White were Charles Gilman Jr., Walter River, Ann Townsend.

≈≋◉◠≈

Bealie and Mildred (Sikes) Harrison

Bealie Harrison was born November 12, 1907, at Tillou, the son of Sarah Anne Nancy Lavinia "Sally Catherine" (Kinnaird) and John Franklin Harrison. (See Gaston Harrison summary.) Bealie attended school at Tillou through the seventh grade and then went to Bastrop. He farmed and worked in timber and in 1952 opened a store on the Old Berlin Road which he operated until 1972. In 1994 he purchased the Kinnaird homeplace there.

Bealie Harrison married Mildred Sikes who was born September 29, 1924, at Blaine, Sunflower County, MS, the daughter of Lula Elizabeth (Andleton) and Charles Edward Sikes. Their other children were Artie Logan, Alpha (m M. J. Fancher), Eula (m Bealie Parker), Katie (m Russell Bryan), Alma (m Walter Sims), Elizabeth (m Walter Peede), Charlena (m Harrie Sawyer), Ruth (nev m; d age 19 of appendicitis), and Margaret (m Ben Martin). This was a family of ten girls; a boy was stillborn. These births occurred over a thirty year period. Charles Edward Sikes was a blacksmith. The Sikes family moved to Jones in 1929 and sharecropped at Robertson Bend on a farm managed by Ellis Doles. Two years later they moved across the bayou and sharecropped for Willis Doles. In 1934 they moved to Tillou and began farming for themselves. Mildred attended

Zachary School through the third grade, Bonita in the fourth grade, and graduated from Bastrop High School.

Mildred Sikes and Bealie Harrison married 12 Sep 1942. Children born to them were Mikel Rodger (b 11 Apr 1944; d 17 May 1944), Shirley Faye (m Gary Warner), John Edward (m Betty Gayle Bryan), and Deborah Kay (m 1st Michael Johnson; m 2nd Gary Hughes, div). Mildred and Bealie have eight grandchildren and two great-grandchildren.

✦✦✦

Gaston and Launa (Sawyer) Harrison

Gaston Harrison was born August 14, 1900, at Extra, Ashley County, the son of Sally Catherine (Kinnaird) and John Franklin Harrison. The family lived at Tillou, LA, at the time, but the mother went to her mother's house for the birth. Their other children were Herbert (m Zellie Riels), Lee (nev m), Bealie (m Mildred Sikes), Bertie (m Leonard Kitchens), and Zelma (m Tom Harbor).

Sally Catherine Kinnaird was born c1873 (she died 1965 at age 92), the child of Amanda (Smith) and James Robert "Big Daddy" Kinnaird. Their other children were Bob (nev m), Tom (m Emma Westbrook), Will (m Henrietta Harrison), Jim (nev m), Joe (m Bess Loving), Jack (m Lessie Riels), Fred (m Emma Moorer), Matt (m William Langford), and Ella (m William Folds). It is said in family oral history that Amanda Smith Kinnaird bore twenty-three children. Amanda and James Robert Kinnaird are buried at Extra Cemetery.

John Franklin Harrison was born c1870 (he died in 1922 at age 52), near Tillou, the son of Martha (Westbrook) and James G. Harrison. Their other children were Jimmy (m Jo Ann Gee), Bascon (m Ida Crawford), Norward (m Lula Jones), Henrietta (m Will Kinnaird), and Verna (m John Johnson). John Franklin Harrison had a brother, Nathaniel (m Jo Smith; moved to Corpus Christi, TX). Martha Westbrook was a sister to George (m Susan Vaughn) and Napoleon (m Sielie Bailiff). Martha and James G. Harrison were married at Cora's Bluff and are buried at Cora's Bluff Cemetery.

Launa Sawyer Harrison was born July 16, 1901, at Extra, the daughter of Neta Mae (Bailiff) and Steve Oren Sawyer. Their other children were Willie Mae (b 5 Nov 1896; d 16 Feb 1985; m Erby Byrd), Percy O. (b 28 Nov 1898; d 18 Jan 1988; m Emmie (Maxwell) Jones), Bennie (b 15 Nov 1903; d 19 Feb 1967; m Ruth Salters) Chester (b 16 Feb 1907; d 12 Jan 1924 of pneumonia), Verdelle (b 13 Mar 1914; m Arlie Williamson); Helen (b 3 Jul 1917; d 8 Jun 1920), and Kelsie (b 15 Feb 1919; m Ona Jones).

Neta Mae Bailiff was born 14 Jan 1879 at Mt. Zion, Ashley County, the daughter of Sarah Josephine (Waters) and

William Parks Bailiff. Their other children were Mary Julia (b 1870; d
young), William Owen (d young), John Arthur (nev m), Ben Hunter (nev
m), and Willie Pearl (b 23 May 1882; m John White). The parentage of
Josephine Waters (b 22 Oct 1847; d 12 May 1897) is unknown; her father
was a brother to Sam Waters. William Parks Bailiff was born 11 Feb 1836
and died 28 Jul 1895. This couple is buried at Mt. Zion Cemetery.

Steve Oren Sawyer born 13 Oct 1871, in Ashley County, the son of Mary
Ann (Rushing) and Henry Isaac Sawyer. Their other children were Robert,
Jackson, Elmo (m Lucy Smith), Augustus "Gus" (m Ella Herrington ?),
Henry (m Lizzie Westbrook), Tom (m Vennie McCloud), Alla (m William
Allen), Zelia (m Eugene Moorer), Betty (m Tebe McCloud), Lena (m Roy
Segars), and Lucian (m Lennie Vinson).

Mary Ann Rushing was born 30 Sep 1833 in AL, the daughter of
Elizabeth (Gay) and Bryant Rushing. Their other children were William
H. (m Mary D. "Polly" Sawyer), John, Bell, Robert R. "Fox" (b 11 Nov
1820 AL; d 3 Jun 1865; m Sophia Caroline Sawyer), Emily (b c1825; m
Samuel McClanahan), Elizabeth Ann (b c1827 AL; m Elbert H. Sawyer)
Susan (b c1830; m Dr. Alfred M. Caldwell; m 2nd James W. Perkins), and
Washington Key (b c1830-31; m Sara Post; moved to Union Parish after
the Civil War; d 1879).

Henry Isaac Sawyer was born in 1826 in AL, the son of Sarah (Wooley)
and William Early Sawyer. Their other children were Nancy Ann, Irene,
Louisa, Ransom B. (m Olivis ?), Mack E. (b 1830 AL; m Martha Helin
Kinnaird), John W. (b 1832 AL; m Mary E. ?), Holeman (b 1834 AL; m
Martha J. ?), Martha (b 1836 AL), Elnora (b 1838 AL), Andrew (b 1840
AL), and Sarah (b 1843 AL). The William Early Sawyer family moved to
the Berlin area of Ashley County between 1844-50. Henry I. Sawyer
moved to Berlin in 1861. Others who came to the area by 1860 were
Reason, Mack, Holeman, and John W. Sawyer.

William Early Sawyer was born in 1796 in SC, the son of Elizabeth
(Bird/Byrd) and George Sawyer. Their other children were Benjamin (m
Sallie Johnson), Anselm (m Sarah Norris), Henry (m Elizabeth Warren),
Memona (m Richard Williams), Esther (m R. H. Holstein Jr.), Nancy (m
Edward Warren), Rachel (m Dailey), Sebenah (m Dawson), Hellender (m
Steadman), Elkanah (m Celia Holstein), and Elizabeth (m James M.
Norris). George Sawyer married a second time to Mary Jones Gunter.
Children born to this marriage were George R. (m Mrs. Matilda Lovelace
Williams), John Vardell (m Clariet Cullum), Rev. Stannon Butler, Lucinda,
Deborah, Stanmore, Mary, Matilda (m Martin Kinnaird), and Epsy (m
Frank Thrailkill).

Gaston Harrison grew up in Tillou near Bayou Bartholomew. He
attended Tillou School through the ninth grade and then worked at the
Fairbanks gas field for two years. Launa Sawyer Harrison attended school

at Extra through the ninth grade and then boarded in Hamburg to attend school there through part of the ninth and tenth grades. The couple who had known each other "every since we were kids" were married on 29 Apr 1923. They lived in Bastrop and then Bonita, where Gaston was in business with Gee Perdue at Gee's Grocery Store. In 1925 they moved to Cora's Bluff where they tenant farmed for a Mr. Lloyd for two years. In 1928 they bought forty acres of the Tom Maxwell place near Tillou. F. Marion Hopkins awarded the young couple their start with their own land. He came by one day and told them that the place was for sale and they ought to buy it. Gaston replied that he would like to but that he had no money. Hopkins replied, "I got some," and loaned them the payment. A month later he returned and told them another forty was up for sale and bought it for them. The price was eight dollars an acre. "You can pay for it anyway you want to," he said. "We paid if off pretty quick," Launa said.

Children born to Launa (Sawyer) and Gaston Harrison were Mary Kathryn (m Raymond Jenkins) and Dorothy Lorrane (m Jack Atkins). Children born to Mary Kathryn (Harrison) and Raymond Jenkins were Morris (m Alice Wells), Mark, and Jeffrey (d age seven in a car accident). Children born to Dorothy Lorrane (Harrison) and Jack Atkins were Steve (m Dona Johnson), Jim (m Renee Perkins), and Unake (m Kelly Pugh).

Children born to Zellie (Riels) and Herbert Harrison were Venoy (m Barbara ?) and Maycelle (m Warren Hanni). The only child born to Bertie (Harrison) and Leonard Kitchens was Omie Jean (m Ben Roberson). The only child born to Zelna (Harrison) and Tom Harber was James (m Dorothy Priest). (See also Bealie Harrison summary.)

Gaston and Launa Harrison were married for seventy-five years. Launa died October 31, 1998. They had five grandchildren and ten great-grandchildren.

<hr />

Mark Hawkins

Mark Lafayette Hawkins, Jr. was born August 4, 1938, at Searcy, the son of Frances (Brame) and Mark Lafayette Hawkins Sr. of Parkdale. Their only other child was a son who died at birth. Frances Brame was born October 14, 1912 at Wilmot. Mark Lafayette Hawkins Sr. was born Nov. 1, 1902, in Parkdale, the son of Charlotte (Burks) and Dr. Martin Cassetty Hawkins Sr. Their other children were a son (b,d 8 Jun 1898), Dr. Martin Cassetty Jr. (b 16 Nov 1900; m Marion Lee Alexander; d 2 Nov 1978), Charlotte Burks (b 28 Jun 1907; nev m; d 5 Jan 1988), and Marie Theresa (b 6 Feb 1919; m Arthur Rood McCleary; d 11 Oct 1982). Dr. Martin Cassetty Hawkins Sr. moved to Parkdale in 1895 and began a medical practice there which continued for 61 years.

Charlotte (Burks) and Dr. Martin Cassetty Hawkins were divorced, and he then married (27 Mar 1933) Gladys (McMurray) Barnes who was born April 29, 1905, in Marianna, AR. They had one child, Hadley Holmes (b 22 July 1940; m Barbara Anita Cordel; m 2nd Jeaneane Daniels; m 3rd ?). Charlotte Burks Hawkins was born Feb 17, 1879, at Monticello and died May 29, 1949, at Parkdale.

Dr. Martin Cassetty Hawkins Sr. was born March 20, 1869, in Hamburg, the son of Harriet Eliza (Hadley) and Judge Marcus Lafayette Hawkins. Their other children were Mary Hadley (b 17 Mar 1860; m John William Morris), Margaret P. (b 20 Mar 1864; m Ransom M. Moore), Kate (b 11 Jul 1866; m Robert W. Ward, Jr.), Marcus Lafayette, Jr. (b 3 Jul 1872; d 14 Oct 1901), Gertrude (b 4 Feb 1876; d 15 Aug 1883), and Benjamin Thomas (b 13 Jun 1879; m Mabel Moore; m 2nd Ida Gregory; d Feb 2, 1937).

Children born to Mary Hadley (Hawkins) and John William Morris are listed in the Mary Morris Foster summary. Children born to Margaret P. (Hawkins) and Ransom McCann Moore Sr. were Marcus Hawkins (m Lillian Kiel), Sampson Levi (m Hattie Davidson), Ransom McCann Jr. (m Fannie Julia Hill), and Morris Joline (b 17 Oct 1892).

Children born to Kate (Hawkins) and Robert Wilkins Ward Jr. were Robert Hawkins (b 1886; d 1893), Hattie Gertrude (m Henry Vaughn Stillwell; bu Waco, TX), Robert Wilkins (m Eva Catherine Adam, who was b 1899, Waco, TX), and Cassetty Marcus (m Jennie Mae Johnston).

Harriet Eliza Hadley was born March 4, 1858, in Ashley County, the daughter of Hannah (Holmes) and James Hadley. Marcus Lafayette Hawkins, Sr. was born March 29, 1934, in Talledaga, Alabama, the son of Millie (Hosea) and John C. Hawkins. Their other children were John T. (b 1832 AL; m Margaret E.), Rebecca J. (b 1834 AL; m William F. Trammel), Sarah Elizabeth (b 1836 AL), Thomas P. (b 1838 AL; m Marietta ?; moved to Fannin Co TX by 1871), Adelia (b 1842 AL; in Fannin Co TX by 1870), Virginia P. (b 1844 AL; m Nion T. Moore; lived in TX), James H. (b 1846/50 AL; m Ariah E. ?; in Fannin Co TX by 1876); Paraline (b 1848 AL), Musadore (b 1850 AL); and Martha A. (b 1850 AL; m Robert Johnson; in TX by 1880). Marcus Lafayette Hawkins Sr. read law in Mississippi and after being admitted to the bar, he moved to Hamburg in December 1855 and began a law practice and engaged in farming.

Melissa B. "Millie" Hosea was born in 1812 in Georgia. She was one-fourth Choctaw Indian. John C. Hawkins was born in 1810 in Georgia, the son of Lucy (Colbert) and Thomas P. Hawkins. Their other children were Elizabeth (b 14 Sep 1799, Shelby Co AL; m Thomas H. Brasher), Missouri Minerva (m Henry Brasher), Tabitha (m 1821 in AL John Andrew Jackson Brasher), Thomas M., Harrison P., Pinckney C., and Rebecca (m William

Hubbard). Lucy Colbert was born in North Carolina, the daughter of William and Miriam Colbert. She died in 1838. Thomas P. Hawkins was born in 1837 in North Carolina. He died in Warren County, North Carolina. He was of Welsh descent and his ancestors settled in Virginia and North Carolina before the Revolutionary War.

Mark Lafayette Hawkins Jr. attended Parkdale School and graduated from Wilmot High School. After graduating from the University of Arkansas with a degree in agriculture, he returned to Parkdale and entered the family farming business. After farming for 25 years, he rented the farmland out and established Parkdale Chemical. Mark married Hazel Jean Barksdale. Children born to Hazel (Barksdale) and Mark Hawkins were Charlotte Leigh (m Floyd Jay Odell; div) and Carol Ann (m James Rushworth; div).

Leroy Haynes

Leroy Haynes was born January 30, 1896, near Berlin Community in Ashley County, the son of Azzie (Braughton) and Oscar Haynes. Their other children were Jeff (d age two), Ellis (m Edith Evans), Ada Belle (m Reuben Smith), O. T. (m Velma Chadwick), Ozelle (m Claude Thompson), Bennie (m Minnie Armstrong), Vesper (m Charlotte Chambers), and Preston (d age two).

Oscar Haynes was born in Alabama or Georgia, the son of Ada (Kinnaird) and Henry Haynes. Henry Haynes entered the Confederate Army near age sixteen. Azzie Braughton was born in Drew County, the daughter of Dora (Dennard) and Jake B. Braughton. The Oscar Haynes family moved from Berlin to Gaines near Wilmot in 1911.

Leroy Haynes married Belle Sawyer, and their children were Mary Frances (d age two), James (m Ouida Yates), DeWayne (m Mary Schultz), Ruth (m Elgin Ward), and Clayton (m 1st Margie Jones; m 2nd). Leroy Haynes died June 30, 1999, at age 103.

Benton Hunt

Benton B. Hunt was born December 12, 1926 at Zachary, the son of Minnie (Foster) and Ben Hunt. Their other children, all born at Zachary, were B. M. (b 1918; m Charlie Mae Jackson), Exa Lee (m William Smith), Myra (nev m), James (m Rose Pardo), Herbert (m Trixie Whitman), and Bevin (m Ernestine Sammons).

Minnie Foster was born 22 Jun 1892 the daughter of Mary Ada and James Robert Foster. Ben Hunt was born 26 Apr 1888 near Poplar Bluff,

MO, the son of Rachel (Oakley) and Billy Hunt. Billy Hunt died and Rachel then married a Mr. Burkett. The family left Missouri and settled at Zachary where they began sharecropping for J. B. Blanks. In 1932 Ben Hunt moved his family onto a forty-acre plot on the Blanks plantation and began clearing land. By 1936 they had cleared seven acres and began farming. The father supported his family by trapping and commercial fishing during these years and continued that trade after he began farming. They eventually cleared twenty acres of farmland.

Benton Hunt attended school at Zachary through the sixth grade and went to the seventh grade at Bonita. He went to work in the pipeline trade and then worked for International Paper in Bastrop. He served in the army from 1945-48 and in 1951 began farming for himself on land purchased from Mrs. Marian Day. In 1964 he bought 300 acres at the Blanks homeplace. His farm acreage eventually increased to 1,200 acres plus 4,000 acres of rented land. Benton Hunt married Mary Lovett, who was born 1 Jun 1930, near Parkdale, the only child of Mittie (Simms) and Ed Lovett. Mittie Simms was born 12 Dec 1891 at Parkdale, the daughter of Addah (Moore) and Jessie Simms. Their only other child was A. P. (m Minnie Morris). Addah Moore Simms married second Walter Harris and they had one child, Charles Harris. Ed Lovett was born 16 Apr 1895, the son of Mary "Mollie" (Taylor) and William Lovett.

Children born to Mary (Lovett) and Benton Hunt were Mary Ann (m Mike Satori) and Mike (m Susie Sims; div). They have four grandchildren, Jason Michael, Mary Denise and Christopher Paul Sartori, and Andrew Seth Hunt.

⚜

Siegfried Johnson

Hans Siegfried "Sieg" Johnson was born September 17, 1917, at Pine Bluff, the son of Hattie (Culver) and John Bates Avery Johnson Sr. Their other children were John Bates Avery Jr. (b 1910; m Ethel McNulty) and Kenneth Culver (b 1912; m Helene Brown; m 2nd Yvonne Brantley; d 1987). Hattie Culver was born 1887 in Leavenworth, Kansas, the daughter of Ida (Hamblin) and Fred M. Culver. Their other children were Fred (m Arrah Hargis) and Edward (m Zeralda ?). Fred Culver was associated with the Cotton Belt railroad and moved his family to Pine Bluff in the 1890s.

John Bates Avery Johnson Sr. was born 18 Jun 1887, at Star City, the son of Octavia A. (Dyer) and Hans Siegfried J. Johnson (originally Jensen). Their other children were Joe W. (b 1883; m Ellen Mac Reynolds) and Charles H. (b 1885; m Ruby I. Givens). Octavia Johnson died 5 Dec 1887 when her son, John Bates Avery, was near six months old. The father took this child to Octavia's sister, Josephine (Dyer), who was married to Captain

John Bates Avery. The couple raised their nephew as a foster son. The other children, Joe and Charles, were raised by Octavia's brother, Charlie Dyer, and his wife, Hettie (Knapp), who lived near Star City and later moved to Pine Bluff. Hans Siegfried Johnson died in 1889. He and Octavia are buried at Holly Springs Cemetery.

Octavia Dyer was born 2 Jul 1857 near Chickamauga, GA, the daughter of Jane Roslyn (Thomson) and John W. Dyer. Their other children were Josephine Ann (b 9 Dec 1853; m Capt. John Bates Avery; d 1939), Joel Mitchell (b 5 Apr 1852; m Belle Issacs; d 21 Apr 1920), John William (b 25 Nov 1855; m Ada ?; d 7 May 1931), Edwin R. (b 7 Nov 1858; m ? Watson; d 6 Oct 1912), and Charles Henry (b 2 Nov 1860; m Hettie Knapp; [their child, Avery]; d 1926). John W. Dyer died during the Civil War and soon after the war, his widow moved with her six children to St. Charles, AR, where they arrived by boat. She eventually located in Stuttgart where she supported her family as a seamstress. Her burial place is not known. Jane R. (Thomson) Dyer was born 30 Apr 1830 in Athens, GA. John W. Dyer was born 5 Jul 1820 in GA. They were married 2 May 1851.

John Bates Avery, husband of Josephine Dyer, and foster parent of John Bates Avery Johnson, was originally from Ohio. A soldier in the Union Army, he came south after the war was over. He arrived in Pine Bluff around 1867 and eventually established a mule barn on Barraque Street which was later named J. B. Avery & Son. He was managing Rob Roy Plantation for John M. Gracie near Altheimer when he met Josephine Dyer at a social gathering at Arkansas Post. They were married in 1877. The same year he bought 160 acres in Lincoln County at the junction of bayous Cross and Wells. This was the beginning of Avery Plantation which eventually consisted of 1,300 acres. Captain Avery died 1931 and is buried at Graceland Cemetery in Pine Bluff.

Hans Siegfried J. Johnson (Jensen) was born 1845 in Denmark, the son of Hansine Elsemine Abelone (Lund) (1813-1880) and Wilhelm Edinger Balle Jensen (1818-1868). He left Copenhagen in 1867 and arrived at Charleston, SC. He eventually migrated to Lincoln County and was working at Round Lake Plantation when he met and married Octavia Dyer.

Siegfried Johnson attended Avery School for two years, Wells Bayou School for two years, and entered Lakeside Elementary at Pine Bluff. He graduated from Pine Bluff High and entered Louisiana State University where he received a degree in business commerce. At LSU he was a member of the National Guard band and played at Huey Long's funeral in 1935. He returned to Avery Plantation in 1938 and ran the farm with his father for two years. In 1940 he received training in the Army Air Corp and was promoted to 2nd lieutenant. After leaving service in 1945, he and his father rented Round Lake Plantation. Avery Plantation was under lease to Andrew Hirt at this time. In 1951 Siegfried entered the G. R. McSwine Lumber Company, which was formed in Pine Bluff in the 1940s. He married Nathalie McSwine, the daughter of Mercedes (Gill) and Griffith McSwine.

Children born to Nathalie (McSwine) and Siegfried Johnson were Ross Culver (nev m), Siegfried Sigmund (m Sherry Oxner) and John Bates Avery III (m Nancy Smith, div). They have two grandchildren, Page and Juanita Ashley. The only child born to Ethel (McNulty) and John Bates Avery Johnson Jr. was Jerrilyn. The only child born to Helene (Brown) and Kenneth C. Johnson was Kenneth, Jr. Children born to Yvonne (Brantley) and Kenneth Johnson were John Richard and Greg Brantley.

Mary Ann Dixon Johnston

Mary Ann Dixon Johnston was born August 13, 1919, at Monroe, the daughter of Josephine Hill (Smith) and Melville Sanders Dixon. Their other children were Charles (b 1919, Sterlington; d 1919), Melville Sanders (b 22 May 1923, Sterlington: m Jean Junot), and Joe Hart (b 12 Aug 1925, Sterlington; m Theo Adele Kramer; d 2 Mar 1970). Melville Sanders Dixon located to Sterlington upon his marriage to Josephine Smith in 1918.

Josephine Hill Smith was born 24 Aug 1896 at Sterlington, the daughter of Mary Ann (Yongue) and Arthur Lee Smith, who were married 2 Feb 1888 in Ouachita Parish. Their other children, all born at Sterlington, were Douglas Yongue (b 13 Jan 1893; m Ella Creary Theus; d 13 Nov 1956), Martin H. (b 19 Nov 1891; d 15 Feb 1947), and Marjorie Mae (b 12 May 1894; m Harvey Lee Gregg; d 1976). Arthur Lee Smith was first married (1 Jan 1879) to Laura Swan and their children were Walter (d 24 Jul 1919), Victor E. (b 23 Mar 1881; d 24 Jul 1912), Eula Lee (b 20 Mar 1883; d in CA), and Ollie Steele (b 13 Mar 1885; d 11 Aug 1911).

Children born to Ella Creary (Theus) and Douglas Yongue Smith were Arthur Lee and Douglas Yongue Jr. Children born to Marjorie Mae (Smith) and Harvey Lee Gregg were Harvey Lee Jr. (killed in WWII), Bruce Frizell, and Jerry Baird.

Arthur Lee Smith was born 5 Nov 1856 in Marengo County AL, the son of Dialtha Perry (Lee) and Martin Hancock Smith. Their other children were Walter (b 1858; m Emma Hickey; bu Monroe), Eula (b 1859; m William F. Prioleau), Charley (d infant), and Rupert (d early childhood). Dialtha Perry Lee Smith died 27 Jan 1860 in Marengo County and Martin Hancock Smith married Hermoine England.

Children born to this marriage were Martin (d 1894) and Robert (m Eugenia Wilson; bu CA). Martin Hancock Smith was born in 1826,

Franklin County VA, the son of Ann E. (Carmichael) and William F. Smith. William F. Smith was the son of Isaac Smith. Ann E. Carmichael was born 4 Oct 1797, VA, the daughter of John Carmichael.

Arthur Lee Smith arrived in Ouachita City by 1879 and began working in a mercantile store owned by Ollie B. Steele, who was a cousin and guardian of Mary Ann Yongue. He married Laura Swan, a niece of Mrs. John Sterling, and began a large farming operation on the Sterling Plantation, which Laura probably received from the Sterling family. Smith also taught school at Ouachita City. Laura died of "swamp fever," and he then married Mary Ann Yongue.

Mary Ann Yongue was born 20 Jun 1862 in Ouachita Parish, the daughter of Delaware (Jones) and Hugh Yongue. Their other children, all born in Ouachita Parish, were California (b 1850; d 27 Aug ?), Nina (b 20 Jun 1858; m Alexander George Hamilton; d 17 Jul ?), and Hugh (b 9 Jul 1866; d 8 May ?). Hugh Yongue was born 9 Jul 1826 in Fairfield County SC, the son of Esther (Winn) and Jonathan Yongue. Their other children were Emeline (b 1821 SC; d 1837 AL), Juliet (m William Parks; bu Union Parish), James L. (b 1829 SC; d 1837 AL), Harriet Caroline (b 1831 SC; d 1837 AL), Elizabeth Susan (b 1834; d 1837 AL), and Mary Ann (b 7 Feb 1840; m Thomas Christian Seltzer; d 1898 Rehoboth, AL).

Jonathan Yongue was born 5 Mar 1793 in Fairfield District, SC, the son of Rosanna and Hugh Yongue. Hugh Yongue was born 25 Dec 1777 in Fairfield District, the son of Margaret and Hugh Yongue (R.S). Hugh Yongue was born in 1733 in Ireland. Esther Winn was born 2 Aug 1800 in Fairfield District. Rosanna Yongue was born in 1777. Margaret Yongue was born in 1733 in Ireland. The Yongue name is often spelled Young. By 1848, Hugh Yongue and his wife, Delaware Jones, along with his sister, Juliet, and her husband William Parks, had migrated to Ouachita and Union Parishes and bought land.

Melville Sanders Dixon was born May 1894, in Monroe, the son of Jessie Lee (Hart) and Charles Tillman Dixon. Their other children, all born in Monroe, were Helen Juanita (b 22 Jul 1894; m Nelson D. Abell), Hortense (b 16 Jul 1899; m H. Kirt Touchstone), Lady Bird (b 6 Jul 1896; m Herbert Breard), Harold Hart (b 14 Oct 1901; m Margaret Atkins), and Charles T. (b 21 Feb 1898; m Louise Breard). Jessie Lee Hart was born 18 Mar 1868 in Minden, LA, the daughter of John Lee Hart (b 1835; d 1875, Minden, LA).

Charles Tillman Dixon was born 15 Oct 1860 in Monroe, the son of Rachael Louise (Meridith) and William Sanders Dixon. Their other children were Harriet W. (m Wade Hampton Hough), Pauline (m Tom Lilly) Lace (b 5 Oct 1864; m H. L. Stewart), Emma Louise (m W. A. Bazone), and Mary or Minnie (d infant). William Sanders Dixon was first married to Ann Holloway, daughter of Daniel Holloway, and their children were William Henry (b 15 Jan 1845; m Mary Francis Hough), Ann, and Daniel.

William Sanders Dixon was born 8 Apr 1817 in Clinton, East Feliciana Parish, LA, the son of Nancy (Sanders) and William George Dixon. Their other children, all born in Clinton, were Mary Eleanor (b c1815; m Orlando W. McKneely), Thomas Ferguson (b 13 Aug 1818; m Sarah Ann Simms), George Llewellyn (b c1820; m Mary Morris), Benjamin Franklin (b 9 Sep 1821; m 1st Jane E. S. Norwood; m 2nd Aletha A. Jackson), Louisiana (b c1824; m 1st Frank Yarborough; m 2nd Joseph L. Sizemore), James (b c1827), Jared Young (b c1829), and Ann (m William P. Flynn).

William George Dixon was born 1783-4 in Camden District SC, the son of Ann (Ferguson) and Thomas Dixon. Thomas Dixon was born in Ireland. Ann Ferguson was born in SC. Nancy Sanders was born 1793 Chester County SC, the daughter of Mary (Young) and William Gunnell Sanders. William Gunnell Sanders was born 16 Feb 1769 in Loudon County VA, the son of Mary (Gore) and James Sanders, and died 1825 in Wilkerson County, MS. James Sanders was born in VA and died 20 Apr 1797 in Natchez, MS. Mary Gore was the daughter of Elizabeth and James Gore (R.S.). James Gore was born c1705 in Prince George County MD, the son of Mary (Burke) and James Gore/Goore. Mary Young was born c 1774 in Wilkerson County MS, the daughter of Eleanor (McClerkin) and William Young (R.S.). William Young was born in Ireland and died 1826 in Trigg County KY. Eleanor McClerkin was born 1775 in Ireland, the daughter of James McClerkin, who was born 1725 in Ireland and died 1797 in Chester County SC.

Rachael Louise Meredith, wife of William Sanders Dixon, was born 1837, the daughter of Mary Ann "Polly" (Faust) and James Meredith. Their other children were Sarah (b 15 Jul 1818, MS; m John Gray), Wyatt O. (b 1818, MS; m 1st Elizabeth Wooten; m 2nd Melvina Cuday), James M. (b 1820; m Josephine Larch), Iverson A. (b 1827; m Axie E. Brown), Cicero Christopher (b 10 Jan 1832; m Amantha Louise Blanks), and Martha Ann (m 1st Robert L. Slemons; m 2nd William I. Hanna). James Meredith was born 1784 in SC, the son of Abigail (Naley/Neely) and Thomas Meredith. Mary Ann Faust was born 1796 SC, the daughter of Nancy A. and William James Faust. Mary Ann Faust and James Meredith were married in MS and died in Caldwell Parish, LA.

Mary Ann Dixon married John Bishop Johnston Jr. who was born 18 Aug 1912, in Monroe, the son of Julia Elizabeth (Barns) and John Bishop Johnston Sr. Their other children, born in Monroe, were Elizabeth (b 20 Oct 1909; m Dr. Claud Bernard Wright) and Jane (d infant).

John Bishop Johnston Sr. was born 10 Mar 1885 in Monroe, the son of Maggie Pugh (Bishop) and John Washington Johnston Jr. Their other children, all born in Monroe, were Maggie Estelle (b 14 Aug 1881), Katie

Lou (b 6 Feb 1883; m Byron Cann), David Andrew (b 16 Feb 1887; m Dorothy Yuille), Minnie Cordelia (b 1888; m Frank B. Chase), Mittie Key (b 5 Dec 1891; m Charles Speed), and Edward Ball (b 9 Jan 1893).

John Washington Johnston Jr. was born 10 Jan 1851 in Eufala, AL, the son of Louise (Ball) and John Washington Johnston Sr. John Washington Johnston Sr. was born 15 Mar 1822 in GA, the son of Mary (Rawls) and Andrew Neel Johnston. Andrew Neel Johnston was born 23 Feb 1798, the son of Mary (Walker) and John O. [?] Johnston. He died 6 Apr 1840 in Leon County FL. John Johnston was born 1767 in Colleton District, SC and died 1807 probably in GA. Mary Walker was born 1770 in Colleton District, SC, the daughter of Isham Walker. Mary Rawls, wife of Andrew Neel Johnston, was born 1798, the daughter of William Rawls.

Elizabeth Barns, wife of John Bishop Johnston, Sr., was born 3 Jan 1886 in McComb, MS, the daughter of Isabella Louisa (Flemming) and George Alonzo Barns. George Alonzo Barns was born 18 Jul 1857 in Detroit, MI, the son of Julia Jane (Moore) and Alonzo Theodore Barns. Alonzo Theodore Barns was born in Auburn, NY, the son of Theodore Barns. Louisa Flemming was born 26 Jan 1864 in New Orleans, the daughter of Jane Elizabeth (Lanier) and William Flemming. William Flemming was born 1824 in Fermanagh County Ireland. Jane Elizabeth Lanier was born 10 Jul 1843 in St. Tammany Parish, LA, the daughter of Pamelia Elizabeth (Robertson) and Hillary Jones Lanier.

Maggie Pugh Bishop, wife of John Bishop Johnston Sr., was born 2 Jul 1860 in Delhi, LA, the daughter of Phoebe Cordelia (Benton) and John Bishop. Their only other child who lived to adulthood was Minnie Lou (b 7 Oct 1870; m Frank G. Hulse). John Bishop was born c1820 and married Phoebe Cordelia Benton 5 Nov 1856. Phoebe Cordelia Benton was born 23 Mar 1837 in KY, the daughter of Adeline Pitts (Woolfork) and Thomas Hart Benton. Thomas Hart Benton was born c1801 and died 26 Apr 1866. Adeline Pitts Woolfork (Woolfolk, Woolford) was born c1804, probably in Scott Co, KY, the daughter of Elizah Woolfolk, and died 18 Mar 1845.

Louise Ball, wife of John Washington Johnston Sr. was born 6 May 1827 in SC, the daughter of Margaret Sara (Mulligan) and William Robert Ball. William Robert Ball was born c1796 in Beaufort District, SC, the son of Margaret (Shields) Laurens or Lawrence, widow, and Sampson Ball. Sampson Ball was born c1750 in SC, the son of Catherine (Burrows ?) and William Ball, Jr. William Ball Jr. was the son of Margaret (Sampson) and William Ball. Margaret Sara Mulligan was born 1804 in Beaufort District, SC, the son of Catherine (Merry) and John Mulligan. John Mulligan was born 1776 in Ireland and died 1840. Catherine Merry was born 1776 in Boston [?], the daughter of Sarah (Davis) and Captain Merry. She died 1876 in Spartanburg, SC.

Children born to Mary Ann (Dixon) and John Bishop Johnston were Jo Elizabeth, John Bishop (m Dorothy Jo Biedenharn), Jay Dixon (m Billie Knox Reynolds), Mary Ann (m William Jackson Currie), and Nina Marie (m George Stancil Pate).

❧❀⊛❀☙

Ed Jones

Ed Jones was born June 8, 1912, at Hamburg, the son of Hattie (White) and Bill Jones. Their other children, all born at Ouachita City, were Mae (m Calvin Gillette), Annie (m Luther Ford), Della (m Sid Bales or Bails), Hattie L. (m Skitter Aarons), Mary (m Maurice Holly), and Oliver Doss (killed age 18 during an argument over a boat on the Ouachita River).

Bill Jones was born in Arkansas. His father died when he was young. His mother was Susan Jones who lived in the Hamburg area. Their other children were Sam (m Carrie Striplen), Maggie (m Dave White), Minnie (m Henry Mormon), and Allie (m Lee ?). Bill Jones came to Ouachita City when he was seventeen, married Hattie White the following year, and moved back to Hamburg. When their son, Ed, was three months old they put the family on a houseboat on the Saline River and moved to Ouachita City. They first lived on land owned by Hattie and eventually built a home on the main road (now the Old Ouachita City Road) from the landing. Hattie White was born at Crossroads, LA, the daughter of Callie and Young White. Their other children were Lawrence (m Willie Thomas) and Dave (m Maggie Jones). The family moved from Crossroads to Ouachita City. The father died before Hattie was born. Bill Jones was a commercial fisherman, farmer, and logger. Ed Jones married Irene Hatcher, and their children were Raymond (m Betty Joiner), Eloise (m 1st Henry Gill; m 2nd Johnny Nunez), Ronnie (m 1st Myrtle Wilson; m 2nd Trinkey Smith), and Marilyn (m Robert Davis). They have twelve grandchildren.

❧❀⊛❀☙

Herman King

Herman King was born February 21, 1910, at Sunshine, the son of Nancy (Smith) and Glasco King. Their other children were Mary (m ? Hart), Abraham Lincoln, Leonard (d young), Frankie (m ? Harris), Elsie (m ? Washington), and Love (m Beedie Brooks). Nancy Smith was from Fountain Hill (Ashley County), and Glasco King was born in LA. The King family moved to Sunshine after the Civil War and worked on the deYampert plantation.

When Glasco King was nine his arm was caught in the gin on the plantation and blood poisoning ensued. The arm had to be amputated, and deYampert took the boy into his house. He eventually sent him to Corbin School in Pine Bluff. Upon King's return to Sunshine, he began a teaching career which lasted his lifetime. He was also a store owner, farmer, and Baptist preacher, and was the first African-American to be elected justice of the peace in Ashley County. His brother, Porter R. King, was also a teacher and preacher. Glasco's children, Mary and Love, also became teachers.

Herman King attended school at Sunshine through the eighth grade and transferred to Portland where he received enough credits to enter Corbin School. He graduated from AM&N College (now UAPB) and taught agriculture at schools in Conway and Calhoun Counties for two years. He then joined his brother, Abram, in his real estate business in Chicago. Herman married Margaret Hayes, but the marriage soon ended in divorce. They had no children.

❦

Ralph Kinnaird

Ralph Kinnaird was born December 4, 1934, at Jones, the son of Kate (Dew) and Robert Neadam "Booster" Kinnaird. Their other children were Alvin (m Lorene Mixion), Ramona (m Harold Crabtree), and Sue (m Leroy Watts).

Kate Dew was born in 1911 at Beech Creek, the daughter of Sue (Hudgens) and Jess Dew. Their other children were Mildred (m Chester Fogle) and Mort (m Ruby Ogden). Jess Dew's children from a previous marriage to Sarah Ann Carter were Luna (m Frank Dew; their children: Virgil, Annie Mae [married Floyd Riles]), Bertha (m Jack Perry; their child: Helen), Reavie (m Easter Kinnaird), and Roy (m Etoil Cannon; their child: Roy). Jess Dew died when Kate was three, and Sue Hudgens Dew then married I. V. Holland. The only child born to this marriage was Preston (m Berthaney Smith; their child: Dyeann). Sue Holland was born in 1876 and died in 1966. I. V. Holland was born in 1876 and died in 1942.

Robert Neadam Kinnaird was born 9 Jun 1904 at Hopkins Hill, the son of Emma K (Westbrook) (b 1878; d 1940) and Tom Kinnaird. Their other children were Easter (b 1897; d 1982; m Reavie K. Holland), Bonney (m Dave Doles), Lois (m Sherman Grubbs), Roy, Julian (m Mildred Brodnax), Newton (m Ardale Hunt), Red (m Lavern Barlow), Neter (d young), Dorothy (d young), and Cora (d young).Tom Kinnaird was born in 1870 at Extra, the son of Amanda (Smith) and James Robert Kinnaird. (See Gaston Harrison summary).

Ralph Kinnard attended school at McGinty through the sixth grade, graduated from Bonita, and entered the mechanic trade. Ralph married

Edna Snyder who was born in 1938 at Rasco, TX, the daughter of Mavis and Lewis Snyder. Children born to Edna (Snyder) and Ralph Kinnaird were Roxann (m Bill Tull) and Robert (m Carean Wilson). Edna Kinnaird was killed in an automobile accident in 1973, and Ralph married Wanda Kegle Johnson who was born at Fairdealing, MO, the daughter of Pearline and Bearnest Kegle. Wanda was first married to Gaylon Johnson and their children were Gayla (m Kerby Adams) and Terry (m Christena Baugh). Ralph and Wanda have eight grandchildren.

Earl Kitchens

Earl Kitchens was born October 13, 1922, in Wilmot, the son of Minnie (Davis) and Jim "Pete" Kitchens. Their other children were Annie (m James Goree), Inez (m Ed Freeman), James (m Gertrude Johnson), Maggie (m Thomas Liggens), Otis (m Grace Joiner), Minnie Lou (m Leon Shelton), J. M. "Jim" (m 1st Skinny Steveson; m 2nd Gladys Lucky), Luther (m Lee Holman), and Dorothy (m Edward Filmore).

Pete Kitchens's parents moved from Houston, TX to Wilmot around 1913. Minnie Davis was born 1896 in Mer Rouge, LA, the daughter of Annie (Smith) and Felix Davis. Annie Smith was the daughter of Fanny and Will Smith. Fanny was later married to a Turner.

Earl Kitchens married Ernestine Parker who was born 9 Sep 1926 at Parkdale, the daughter of Miley and Delee Parker. Children born to Ernestine (Parker) and Earl Kitchens were Rocky and Billy. They also have an adopted son, Cleveland Parker. The only child born to Annie (Kitchens) and James Goree was Berneice (m 1st Willie Patterson; m 2nd Carl Mackie.)

W. D. and Nell (Fullbright) Lyle

W. D. "Shorty" Lyle was born September 13, 1915, at Star City, the son of Lenoice "Lee" (Jenkins) and John Kirk Lyle. Their other child was John Carlos "J. C." (m Pearl Ross). John Kirk Lyle was first married to Mattie McPherson and they had a daughter, Roulede Stewart (b 1902; m Z. T. Stone, son of Z. T. and Sarah Collins Stone.) His third marriage was to Averile (Throneberry) Rogers and they had no issue. Lee Jenkins was born 30 Jan 1897 at Star City, the daughter of Nancy (Harvill) and Henry Tucker Jenkins. Mattie McPherson was born 10 Aug 1882 at Coleman, the daughter of Bettie (Henley) and John W. McPherson. Averile Throneberry was born 1896 at Butler Community, the daughter of Dolly (White) and Willis Throneberry. She was the widow of Will Rogers. The John K. Lyle family moved to Bayou Bartholomew across and down from Person's Bridge around 1925.

John Kirk Lyle was born 16 Apr 1881 at Lyle, the son of Harriet "Hettie" Cornelia (Nichols) and William Henry Lyle. Their other children were Sarah Martin (b 16 May 1883 at Lyle; m William Mark Rogers), Leona Madura (b 16 Dec 1874; m Ocie Marks), Franklin Carlos (b 28 Mar 1876; m Mildred I. Kersh, b 15 Nov 1879 at Lyle, dau of Mildred G. [Watson] and Napoleon b. Kersh), William Donan (b 18 Sep 1877; n m), Henry Dellmon (b 25 Jun 1879; m Ethel Mauney, b 12 Dec 1884, Coleman, dau of Ida Eudora [Johnson] and John Watson Mauney), Mary Euist (b 13 Aug 1885; m John Elvie Knox), and Cullen Waterson (b 31 Aug 1887; m Inez Bush).

William Henry Lyle was born 9 Jun 1846 in Chester County, SC, the son of Sarah Martin (Knox) and Thomas Lyle, who were married 17 Dec 1840. Their other children were John Knox (b 16 Nov 1841), David Franklin (b 4 July 1843), Martha Jane (b 5 Jun 1849), Elizabeth Caroline (b 12 Oct 1850), Mary Paulina (b 2 Mar 1852; m George Washington Thomas), James Martin (b 24 Oct 1855; m Nettie Gammil), and Thomas Brown (b 15 Jan 1859; m Linnie DeWoody). The Thomas Lyle family left SC in 1851 and settled in Tipton County TN. In October 1854 they migrated to the Montongo area of Drew County and had a large farm on Bayou Bartholomew. William Henry Lyle served in the CSA, first as a substitute for his father in the "Old Men's Company and later joined the 2nd Arkansas Cavalry. He died 15 Jun 1922 and was buried at Mt. Zion Cemetery at Relf's Bluff.

Sarah Martin (Knox) Lyle died 2 Mar 1862 of consumption, and Thomas Lyle married second on 22 Jan 1863 Jane Minerva (Boyd) Duncan, widow of William Roddy Duncan of Johnstown, Bradley County, AR. Children born to this marriage were Jane Isabella (b 23 Apr 1863) and Tallulah Irene Adelaid "Lula" (b 26 Sep 1865; m James Abner Bishop). (See Bishop family history.) Thomas Lyle was born in Antrim County, Ireland 1 Nov 1817, the son of Jean (Stuart) and David Lyle. The family migrated to South Carolina in 1817 aboard the ship *Elizabeth.* He died 25 Jan 1892 and was buried at Mt. Zion.

Shorty Lyle attended school at Persons School near Todd through the eighth grade and then entered high school at Star City. He then attended Coynes Trade School where he received training in the electrical trade. Shorty married Virginia Nell Fullbright, who was born March 9, 1915, at Star City, the daughter of Laura Louann (Edmonds) and James Nichlos Fullbright. Their other children were Ann (m William Buck Blythe), Harry Earl (m Mary Burrous), and Paul Edmonds (m Jennie Fea McGehee).

Laura Louann Edmonds was born 2 Aug 1886, near Coleman, Drew County, (the site of the Edmonds' home now being in Lincoln County), the daughter of Nancy Taylor (Henley) and George W. Edmonds. (See Murphy Brockman summary.) Laura Louann Edmonds Fullbright died of typhoid 15 Jul 1916 at age twenty-nine. James N. Fullbright died of pneumonia while in service in 1917 and was buried by his wife in Edmonds Cemetery, Lincoln County. Their children were raised by their grandmother, Nancy Edmonds.

James Nichlos Fullbright was born 2 Aug 1886 at Star City, the son of Sally [?] (Hooper) and Philip Winston Fullbright. Their other children were Norman A. (m 1stIrene Young; m 2nd Maye McCarty), Zula Bell (m David Lafait Hooper), Bunello "Nellie" (m A. Murphy), William (m Rosie McEntere), Sarah Edith (m Walter Calloway), and Audrey Lud (m 1st Sarah Hooper; m 2nd Nora Price).

Children born to Mary (Burrows) and Harry Earl Fullbright were James Earl (m Marilyn; their child: Moya Elizabeth) and Jana Lynn (m Lloyd Kuhn). Anna Lee (Fullbright) and William Buck Blythe had no children. The only child born to Paul and wife Fullbright was Jimmie Nell (m Norman Nichols; their adopted twins: Paula Louann and Nickey). Children born to Virginia Nell (Fullbright) and W. D. Lyle were Katie Jean (m Vernon Blake; their children: Vernon Lyle and Jonathan Stuart) and W. D. Jr. "Mickey" (m Mollie Lynn Tribble; their children: Susan Bethany and Sarah Catherine).

≈୨◎୧≈

Dan P. Mayo

Dan Phillip "Buck" Mayo was born May 3, 1917, at McGinty, the son of Lilly (Hayden) and William Phillip "Mack" Mayo. Their other children, all born at McGinty, were Bessie (m Cecil Hayman), Odell (m James Gilbert Sr.), Jimmy D. "Red" (m Bernice Poke McCain), William Norris (m 1st Marie Mashaw; m 2nd Eunice ?), George Everette "Pete" (m Martha Bray), Dorothy (m Jimmy Blackman), and Mack Newt (m Virginia Dare Thompson).

Lilly Hayden was born 27 Feb 1898 in Morehouse Parish, the daughter of (Exie Neeley) and Sam Hayden of McGinty. Mack Mayo was born 27 Feb 1898 at McGinty, the son of Elmira Jane (McCarty) and Crawford Arnold Mayo I. (See Ruth Mayo Boone summary.)

Buck Mayo attended school at McGinty through the sixth grade and "then became a regular plowboy." He bought a forty-acre farm near Laark in 1941 and in 1953 became a ranger for the Louisiana Game & Fisheries Commission. In 1968 he was appointed district supervisor of enforcement over the district that included the parishes of East Carroll, West Carroll,

Morehouse, Richland, Ouachita, Union, Lincoln and Jackson. He held this position until his retirement in 1978.

Buck Mayo married Helen Brewster who was born at McGinty, the daughter of Mary (Johnson) and ? Brewster. Children born to Helen (Brewster) and Buck Mayo were Verlene (m 2nd Johnny King; m 3rd Charles White) and George Alton (m Mary M.). Buck's second marriage was to Helen (Boone) Montgomery. Buck Mayo died 1 Nov 1999 leaving two grandchildren.

The only child born to Bessie (Mayo) and Cecil Hubert Hayman was William Eugene (m Catherine Yvonne Smith).

Children born to Odell (Mayo) and James Mason Gilbert Sr. were James Mason II (m 1st Julie Lee Hamby; m 2nd Julie Flemming) and Sandra Ann (m William Donahoo).

Children born to Bernice (Polk) McCain and Jimmy D. Mayo were Shirley June (m Willard Kelly) and Jimmy D. Jr. (m 1st Freddie Jean Chandler; m 2nd Judy Faye Shuff).

Children born to Marie (Mashaw) and William Norris Mayo were Patricia Ann (m 1st Billy Morgan; m 2nd Scotty Meadow) and Kathy Jean (m Terrell Trichell).

Children born to Dorothy Ann (Mayo) and Jimmy Blackman were Judy Monica (M Freddy Joe Stewart) and Janet Sue (m John Harrell Harper).

Children born to Martha Lou (Bray) and George Everette Mayo were Tommy Mack (m Jeanetta Lee Anderson), Cynthia Odell (m Jerry Lynn Jones), Jerri Dian (m Jeffery Thomas Wilmore), and Jamie Bray (m 1st William Wayne Owens Jr.; m 2nd Ladd Michael Gentry).

Children born to Virginia Dare (Thompson) and Mack Newt Mayo were Tanya Lynn (m John Pauly), Ceanne Renee (m Heidi Lynn Schofield) and Angela Dawn (m Steve Darling).

⚓

Eloise Robertson Means, Edwin Robertson, Oren T. Robertson

Eloise Robertson Means was born May 4, 1920, at Bonita, the daughter of Mariah Rosalie (Mason) and Ray Thomas Robertson. Their other children were Edwin Benjamin (b 20 Dec 1910, Camden, AR; m Georgia Bliss Berry), Marion Bernice (b 23 Oct 1913, Camden; m Frank Morris Doles), and Oren T. (b 8 Feb 1917, Tillou; m Lois Clement Young Smith).

Mariah Rosalie Mason was born 25 Aug 1885 at Point Pleasant, the daughter of Jennie (Rosalie) Brown and Edwin Francis Mason. Their only other child was Sarah Elizabeth "Bessie" (b 5 Aug 1892, Tillou; m Robert C. Carter). Children born to Sarah Elizabeth "Bessie" (Mason) and Robert C. Carter were Louise (m Ray Forest), Lionel Wellington (m Annie Mae

Farrar), Hugh Darrol (m Rose Stanley), Roy (m Ethel Elizabeth Wyatt), and Troy (m Peggy Marie Richards).

Edwin F. Mason was born 22 Sep 1844 in Livingston, AL, the son of Sarah Ann (Hutcherson) and Robert Mason. Their other children, all born in Sumpter County, AL, were George Washington (b 1839; m Anna Farrar), Robert Saunders (b 1840; m Ann Kennard McConnico), and Elizabeth E. (b 1842; m Henry R. Foss). Robert Mason was born 9 Sep 1816 in VA, the son of Millicent (Saunders) and George Mason. George Mason was born 1777, the son of Rebecca (Waggoner) and Charles Mason. Charles Mason was born 1735 in VA and died 1818 in SC. Millicent Saunders (d 1834) was the daughter of Nathaniel Saunders. Rebecca Waggoner Mason died 1791 in VA. Sarah Ann Hutcherson, wife of Robert Mason, was born 6 Sep 1817 in VA, the daughter of Elizabeth (Lancaster) and George Washington Hutcherson. George Washington Hutcherson was born 1783 in VA, the son of Sarah (Reid) and William Hutcherson Jr. William Hutcherson Jr. was the son of Ruth and William Hutcherson (d 1775). Elizabeth Lancaster was born 1787 in VA, the daughter of Johanna (Singleton) and Richard Lancaster (d 1815).

Edwin F. Mason entered the Confederate Army in 1863 and served until the conclusion at which time he was made a prisoner of war. He was paroled May 1, 1865. He married Jessie Bolton in 1871 and they had a child, Edwin Bolton. Jessie died 15 Mar 1874, and Edwin was grief stricken. He placed his seventeen month old son under the care of his wife's mother and in 1875, upon hearing that families were needed on plantations in Morehouse Parish, entered the business of transporting farm laborers to the area. Eventually he accepted a position as overseer on the I. L. Brown plantation near Mer Rouge. There he met Jennie Rosalie Brown and married in 1883. He rented land at Point Pleasant until 1889 when he homesteaded forty acres on Bayou Bartholomew near Tillou, an area that became known as Masons' Cave.

Jennie Rosalie Brown was born 12 Jun 1851 at Mer Rouge, the daughter of Maria Head (Spain) and Isaac Lawrence Brown. Their other children were Thomas Jefferson (b 11 May 1841, Hamburg, MS; d 1863, Iuka, MS), Sarah Ann (b 27 Nov 1843, Hamburg, MS; m William Albert Harrington; d 5 Oct 1907, Bastrop), James Spain (b 14 Nov 1844; m Sarah Jane Elizabeth Knox; d 28 Sep 1875, Bastrop; Sarah Knox Brown m 2nd Robert Stuart Nunn), Albert Isaac (b 3 Nov 1846; d 21 Dec 1868), William Brice (b 19 Sep 1848; m Mrs. Emma Smith), Francis E. Woodworth (b 13 Apr 1855, Mer Rouge; d 3 Jun 1869), John Malcolm (b 23 Jul 1857, Mer Rouge; m May Compton; d 8 Jan 1892), and Amelia Cornelia (b 26 Mar 1860; m James Walter "Jim" Jones; d 24 Feb 1902).

Isaac Lawrence Brown was born 3 Jul 1814 in Franklin County MS, the son of Sarah Elizabeth (Kennison) and Elijah Woodworth Brown. Elijah

Woodworth Brown was born in Franklin County MS and died 19 Sep 1835 in Mer Rouge. Sarah Elizabeth Kennison was born in Jefferson County MS. Maria Head Spain, wife of Isaac Lawrence Brown, was born 20 Mar 1819 in Jefferson County MS, the daughter of Nancy (Head) and James Spain. She died 13 Mar 1876 in Mer Rouge.

Ray Thomas Robertson, husband of Mariah Rosalie Mason, was born 4 Jun 1888 at Camden, AR, the son of Margaret Anna (Reynolds) and Benjamin Willis Robertson. Their other children, all born at Camden, were John David (b 30 Jan 1875; m 1st Ollie Woods; m 2nd Mary Frances Bradshaw), Minnie Eva (b 23 Dec 1876; m Julius Harvey Linebarier), Mary Adda (b 9 Sep 1879; m William F. Pierce), Hugh Benjamin (b 4 Oct 1881; m Bertha Sutton), Tarver Ernest (b 28 Jan 1884; d 26 Oct 1903), Richard Orland (b 7 Jul 1886; d 26 Oct 1891), Claude Henry (b 4 Oct 1890; m Idell Ross), and Thadeus Hoyt (b 7 Jan 1893; d Jun 1893). The parents both died in 1893 of la grippe (a virus similar to influenza), and the children were taken into the homes of aunts and uncles.

Benjamin Willis Robertson was born 5 Jun 1850 near Bastrop, the son of Martha Ann (Davis) and Willis Tarver Robertson, MD. Their other children were John William (b 26 Sep 1851; nev m; d 18 Mar 1874), James Henry (b 22 Sep 1853, Locust Bayou, AR; m Mattie Melvina Mitchell), Pauline Winny (b 22 Sep 1855; m James Nason Reynolds), Robert Thomas (b 3 Dec 1862; d 11 May 1864), Martha Priscilla (b 5 Sep 1865; d 22 Feb 1878), and Mary Sarah Charlotte (b Locust Bayou, AR, 5 Sep 1868; m Thomas Hugh Reynolds).

Willis Tarver Robertson was born 20 Apr 1826 in Montgomery, AL, the son of ? (Tarver) and Willis Robertson (b 13 Sep 1786, NC; d 17 Nov 1863 AR). While studying medicine in Mobile, he met Martha Ann Davis on a house call. She was visiting relatives there and contracted measles. They became secretly engaged and after he finished medical training, he moved to Bastrop where they married in 1848. Two years later they moved to Locust Bayou, AR.

Margaret Anna Reynolds, wife of Benjamin Willis Robertson, was born 7 Aug 1854 at Starkville, MS, the daughter of Mary Miranda (Nason) and Hugh Montgomery Reynolds. Hugh Montgomery Reynolds was born 18 Jan 1818, in Fairfield District SC, the son of Elizabeth Jane (Montgomery) and William Reynolds. William Reynolds was born in SC, the son of Nancy Elizabeth (Montgomery) and Benjamin Reynolds (b Ireland). Elizabeth Jane Montgomery was born in SC, the daughter of Margaret and Hugh Montgomery Sr., who were born in Ireland. Mary Miranda Nason was born 12 Jan 1822 in Athens, GA, the daughter of Margaret Eurena (Montgomery) and James Nason. James Nason was born 1782 in Ireland, the son of James Nason. Margaret Eurena Montgomery was born 23 Oct 1788, the daughter of Margaret (Reynolds) and Charles Montgomery Sr.

Charles Montgomery Sr. was born in 1748 in Ireland and died in 1820 in SC. Margaret Reynolds was born in 1752 in Ireland and died in 1818 in SC.

Mariah Rosalie Mason attended public school until the age of sixteen and then took classes at a business school in Bastrop. When she was eighteen she homesteaded forty acres of land adjoining her father's place at Mason Cave. Her sister, Bessie, also homesteaded land there. In 1907 while working at Heart's commissary near Galion, Mariah Rosalie Mason met Ray Robertson who was working in the area. They married 12 Jan 1910 and moved to near Camden, AR. In 1916 they moved to her father's farm and worked there until 1918 when Ray went to work as a rural mail carrier in Bonita. He continued in this position for forty years. Ray and Rosalie divorced in 1959. Rosalie died 9 Apr 1960 and Ray died 18 Jan 1971.

Edwin Robertson, eldest son of Rosalie (Mason) and Ray Robertson, attended Bonita School and graduated from Mer Rouge in 1928. He received a Radio Phone License from Coyne Electric and Radio School of Chicago in 1935. After working as a pharmacy assistant, he opened a grocery store in Bonita in 1940 and ran it for twenty years. Edwin and Georgia Bliss (Berry) adopted two children, Thomas Edwin (m Denise (LaCompe) Chartrey) and Nancy Lee (nev m).

Marion Robertson: see Marion Robertson Dole summary.

Oren T. Robertson attended Bonita School, graduating in 1935. He attended NLU for a year and public worked several years before joining the Navy in 1941. He returned to Bonita and opened a theater there in 1946, sold it in 1951, and opened a variety store. He began teaching at Bonita in 1956 and eventually earned a B. A. and master's degree. Oren married Lois Clement Young Smith, who was born 11 Dec 1919 in Apollo, PA. Children born to Lois (Smith) and Oren Robertson were John Thomas (m Velma Melissa Moore), Rebecca Ann (m 1st David Wayne Mayfield; m 2nd William Melvin Mix), and William Oren (nev m).

Eloise Robertson attended Bonita School and graduated in 1937. She then attended Northeast Louisiana Junior College and Louisiana Tech for three semesters. Eloise married Louis R. W. Means who was born 27 Dec 1916 at Mound City, IL. His father was working at the heading mill in Bonita and Louis joined him there. The couple lived in Bonita, Indiana, and Florida before retiring to Bastrop in 1980. They had no children.

<hr/>

Mary Alice Cottrell Nelson

Mary Alice Cottrell was born December 30, 1930, at El Dorado, the daughter of Mattie Ella (Hughes) and Jesse Jewel Cottrell. Their other children were Raymond (d. infant 1919), Kermit Keith (m Bernice Lucille

Andress), and James Oliver (m Eula Frances Clark). Jesse Jewel Cottrell was born 9 May 1898 in Union County, the son of Nancy Alice (Dumas) and Elijah Washington Cottrell.

Mattie Ella Hughes was born 9 Sep 1901, near Mount Holly, Union County, the daughter of Mary Jane (Morgan) and Andrew George Hughes. Their other children were Linnie Reca (b 17 Feb 1892; m David Buren Kennedy), Maxie Onizine (b 26 Jul 1893; m Nora Zelma Thompkins); Temmie Tillman (b 21 May 1895; m Carrie Ruth Lewis), Odies Lemuel (b 17 Sep 1896; m Lera Lola Martin), and Ora Lou (b 20 May 1899; m 1st James Miller Roach; m 2nd William Franklin Ritchie. Mary Jane Morgan was born 19 Mar 1862 in Mount Holly, Union County, the daughter of Beatrice Almeda (Cockerham) and Isiah Onizine Morgan.

Andrew George Hughes was born 27 Nov 1858 at Poplar Bluff (Parkdale), the son of Mariah Louisa (Cole) and John Tillman Hughes. Their other children, all born at Poplar Bluff, were William Dolphus (b 13 Apr 1857; m Prudence Emily Hays; d 20 Dec 1920), Sarah Ella (b 1860; nev m; d 22 Sep 1884), John Lewis (b 4 Mar 1864; m Mattie Idell Rodgers; d 28 Mar 1928), Jessie (b c1867; d before 1880 in Poplar Bluff), James Carr (b 12 Jul 1873; m 1st Della Lee Carter; m 2nd Cora Maude Carter; d 6 Feb 1924), Jarrott Tillman (b 20 Oct 1875; m Ida Grace Pedron, dau of Virginia(Perry) and Theodore Louis Pedron; d 8 Jan 1961), and Mattie Lou (b 30 Jan 1878; m Albert Lewis "Bob" Harson; d 25 May 1947). ("At age eighty 'Uncle Bob' was a night watchman in Gurdon; he was a strong and healthy man. It was believed he was searching one night for three hijackers who were thought to be on a certain train and that he might have attempted to arrest them. His body, cut to pieces, was found on the track soon after the Missouri Pacific train had passed." From "Backward Glimpses: The Story of George D. Hughes and Mary Johnson" by Dorothy White. Date of his death was 17 May 1931.)

Mariah Louisa Cole, wife of John Tillman Hughes was born c1839 in AL, the daughter of Nancy (Barrett) and William G. Cole. Their other children were Thomas J. (b c1842 in AR; thought to have died in Civil War), William L. (b c1844, supposedly in Ashley Co; not in census after 1860), Jessie M. (b c 1847 in Ashley Co; m P. A. Scoggins in Ashley County 15 Jul 1868; no children), Robert M. (b c1851 in Ashley or Union County [the Cole family listed in Union County in 1850]; m Virginia Wilkins 21 Feb 1872 in Ashley County; d before 1880; three children: Willie G., Louisa M. and Robert W.), and John W. (b c1853 Ashley or Union County). One of Mariah Cole's nephews is reported by family tradition to have been "Doc Cole," who rode with the Cole and Younger brothers, along with the James gang, as Confederate guerrillas with W. C. Quantrill. A lock of his hair has been passed down in the family. William G. Cole, father of Mariah, was born c1810 in Holstein, Denmark. Nancy

Barrett was born c1818 in SC. The William G. Cole family lost their fortune during the Civil War.

John Tillman Hughes was born c1826 in Talbot County GA, the son of Mary (Johnson) and George D. Hughes. Their other children were Laban (b 10 Feb 1807, SC; m 7 Mar 1839, Elizabeth C. Beech, dau of Thomas G. and Sarah W. Hamil Beech; died in McKinney, Collin County TX), Elizabeth (believed to have been a twin to Laban; m 15 Feb 1829, Littleton Hooton in Talbot County GA), Mary (b c1810 SC; m 1st 27 Sep 1840 Elisha Bustin in Talbot County; m 2nd Jesse Baily 1850-56 Union County AR; separated), James W. (b 8 Mar 1814, SC; m 1st 28 Nov 1843 Mary Elizabeth Hays in Talbot County; m 2nd 15 Oct 1886 Mrs. Mary E. Churchwell in Ouachita County AR; d 11 Jun 1897), Lucretia "Creesie" (b c1817 SC or GA; nev m; death and date unknown; may be bu at Parkdale), William Johnson (b 25 Jun 1820 Jasper County, GA; m 1st 3 Jan 1839 Sarah E. Clark; m 2nd 30 Jun 1863 Lavinia Deets in Union County, AR; d 26 Dec 1894 in Saint Maurice, LA), Martha (b 22 Jun 1825 Talbot County; m 12 Jul 1849 John Stephens Graham in Union County; d 12 Feb 1901), Freeman (b 27 Apr 1829 Talbot County; m 1st 17 Nov 1853 Eliza Ann Sewell in Columbia County AR; m 2nd 6 Dec 1865 Martha Dees Bird in Columbia County; d 20 Nov 1915), Henry Jordan (b c1832 Talbot County; m 1st 22 Jul 1850 Sarah McCullock in Union County; m 2nd Mrs. Mary A. Mitchell in Ouachita County AR; div; "In 1880 Henry was in Archer County, Texas, with a wife and two small children. Where and when he died are not known. Henry's son, James Marion, changed his family name to Huse in Rockwall County, Texas." [Dorothy White]), and Sarah (b c1834 Talbot County; m 1st 28 Nov 1855 James E. Hays in Union County; m 2nd 22 Dec 1858 E. L. Barnett in Union Co; d 27 Oct 1860 of "fever").

John Tillman Hughes settled at Poplar Bluff. He married Mariah Louisa Cole in Ashley County 26 Jul 1856. In 1857 he built a mercantile store, the first, at the steamboat landing. He was appointed postmaster 18 Jul 1860. Mariah and John Tillman Hughes took into their household and store John W. Morris when he was sixteen. This young man learned the mercantile trade from Hughes and went on to become a leading citizen of Poplar Bluff/Parkdale.

George D. Hughes, father of John Tillman Hughes, was born between 1780-1790 in SC. At first a farmer, by 1840 he was engaged in a manufacturing business which engaged four slaves in Fairfield District SC. His wife, Mary Johnson, was born c1790 in SC. The couple migrated to Georgia Indian Territory having a child in Jasper County in 1820 and settling in Talbot County before 1830. Living close to them in Georgia were Willis, Solomon, and Zophiah Hughes. The couple eventually moved westward and were in Union County by 1857 with 360 acres of land and four slaves. George D. Hughes died 10 Feb 1859 and is thought to have been buried near Lisbon northwest of El Dorado. Mary Hughes died 10 Sep 1864 and may be buried in an unmarked grave at Antioch East Cemetery in Columbia County. [All information provided by Dorothy White in her book "Backward Glimpses: The Story of George D. Hughes and Mary Johnson."]

Mary Alice Cottrell, great-great granddaughter of George A. Hughes, married Maxwell Henry Nelson, who was born 21 Jan 1925 in Calion, AR, the son of Catherine Margaret (Kiger) and Amos Elliott Nelson. Children born to Mary Alice and Maxwell Nelson were Daryl Rockfield (m 1st Elizabeth Ann Dyess; m 2nd Regina Carol Langley) and Gregory Clayton (m Sheila Jean Turner; div). They have five grandchildren.

⋙⊙⋘

Edgar Norris

Robert Edgar Norris was born December 14, 1923, at Wells Bayou Community, the son of Martha (Chance) and Enoch Edgar Norris. Their other children were Homer Ravanel (b 5 Oct 1912; m Beulah Eastman; d 7 May 1977) and James D. (b 9 Sep 1915; m Winona Hinch).

Enoch Edgar Norris was born 12 Jan 1871, at Elizabeth, MS, the son of Lina (Terry) and Marshall Norris. Their other children were Perry (b 1869; d 1889), Lula (b 1873; d 1895, Humphrey, AR), Ada (b 1876; m Lonnie Leonadus Reed; d 1899, Price place, Lincoln County), Oscar (b 1878; d 1883), Ola (b 29 Mar 1880; d Apr 1927, Marianna, AR), and Billy Bob (b 22 Aug 1883; m Lula (Chance) Paschall; d 18 Jun 1968). Marshall Norris died in 1884 in Elizabeth, MS, and in 1887, his widow departed by train with her six young children to Reedville, AR. From there they continued their journey by walking to the Marion Hudson place in Lincoln County, where they made a crop the following year. Subsequent years found the family at the Godfrey place at Avery (1889-1890), Batchelor place (1891-1892), Avery place (1893), Tom Johnson place at Wells Bayou (1894), Ed Haygood place at Tyro (1895), Morgan place near Tyro (1896), and to the Price place at Wells Bayou (1896-1905). Enoch Edgar Norris and Billy Bob Norris bought land near Batchelor Bridge around 1905 and began farming as Norris Brothers.

The only child born to Ada (Norris) and Lonnie Leonadus Reed was Grace (b 30 Apr 1895; m Idell Chance; their children: Glynn Thaddaeus, Norris, and Jack). Children born to Lula (Chance) Paschall and Billy Bob Norris were Perry Lamar (b 8 Apr 1907; d 22 May 1908), Harry Curtis (b 14 Dec 1908; m Edith Mae Gibson), Robert Lina (b 28 Dec 1920; nev m; d 7 Aug 1920), Nophlet Brown (b 17 Feb 1912; m Ava Carter), Ralph Donald (m Mae Summerford), Ruth Louise (b 7 Apr 1920; m Grover Smith), Lois Nell (b 8 Aug 1918; d 7 Aug 1920), Edgar Gene (b 26 Dec

1920; m Peggy Brown); their children: Michael Nolan, and Mary Frances (b 3 Jan 1924; m Oscar Ginnett).

Lula Chance, wife of Billy Bob Norris, was first married to Fred Paschall and they had one child, Willie L. (m Johnnie Wilson). Fred Paschall died 9 Feb 1904. Martha Elizabeth Chance, mother of Edgar Norris, was born 12 Jun 1892, near Crigler, the daughter of Julia (Brown) and Luther Chance. Their other children were Odis (d infant), Mary (b 1881; d 1920), Lula (b 1884; d 1955), George (d infant), Idell (b 1888; d 1918), Elva (b 1894; d 1952), Nettie (b 1897; d 1963), and Freddie (b 1905; d 1965). Luther Chance was born in 1858 (in NC?) and died in 1933 in Lincoln County. Julia Brown was born in 1860 in NC, the daughter of Louise N. and Edom Brown. She died 18 Oct 1942 in Lincoln County. The Chance, Brown, and Plemins families were all from NC. Robert Edgar Norris married Mary Emily Wigley who was born in 1929, at Fountain Prairie, Ashley County, the daughter of Vernice (White) and Ashley Wigley. Children born to Mary Emily (Wigley) and Edgar Norris were Ronnie Edgar (m Linda Burns), Robert Ashley "Sluggo" (m Mary Katherine Petty), and Darnell (m Scott Osbrooks). They have six grandchildren. Children born to Beulah (Eastman) and Ravenel Norris were Homer Eastham and Douglas Ed. Children born to Winona (Hinch) and J. D. Norris were Martha Sharon and Ross Alan.

⚬❦⚬

Katie Bell Parker

Katie Bell Parker was born January 22, 1916, at Parkdale, the daughter of Mattie (Matlock) and Bunyan Bell. Their other children were Jimmie Dean (b c1911; m Joel Nugent) and Ethel (b 28 Feb 1918; m Wilbur Wyatt). Bunyan Bell was first married to unknown and had the following children: Foster (m Mary Ingram), Alfred (m Zella Cunningham), Billy (d age 8 of epilepsy), and Ellen (m Philip Brown).

Bunyan Bell was born 20 May c1873 at place unknown and died at age seventy-five in 1948 at Jones. He and his siblings came from AL to Wilmot c1910. It is not known if the parents came. He had nine siblings of which seven are known: John Robert (m Adelia ?; lived at Wilmot), Billy (m 1st ?; m 2nd Emma ?; lived at Wilmot); George (m Johnnie ?; lived at Wilmot), Greenlee (m ?; moved to TX), Elisha (m ?; lived at Wilmot), Anna (m Henry Hill; lived at Eudora), and Charlie (lost in Civil War).

Mattie Matlock was born c1874 (she was a year older than Bunyan Bell), probably in LA, of unknown parentage. She appeared to be nearly full-bloodied American Indian. Her mother died when she was twelve and her father was blind from the Civil War. She and her siblings were placed in an orphan's home in Monroe upon her mother's death. She had two sisters and a brother, who because of their younger age, were adopted. Mattie never heard from them again. Mattie got out of the orphanage at age sixteen and soon married Will Holt. He died a year or two later and their baby died six months after his death.

The Bunyan Bell family moved to Zachary in 1921 where they sharecropped for Tom Bannister. The following year he bought a mule and rented land from Jessie Zachary. Katie attended school at Zachary through the sixth grade and then went to Bonita through the tenth grade. In 1932 she married Roosevelt Parker, who was born 9 Feb 1911, near Greenwood, MS, the son of Mattie (Moore) and Willie Parker. Their other children were Bealie (m Eula May Sikes), Dora (m Joe Franklin), Bell (nev m; afflicted), and J. W. (m Florence Strange). Willie Parker died and Mattie married Louis Washam. Children born to this marriage were Ben (m Jennisteen "Jennie" Crawley) and Inez (m Wyatt Strange). The Willie Parker family moved to Zachary around 1912.

Katie and Roosevelt Parker sharecropped for Joe Franklin their first year of marriage and the following year bought a mule and rented land from Mr. Adams, a brother-in-law to Mrs. Zachary. In 1935 the family moved to Bastrop where Roosevelt went to work for the highway department. Roosevelt Parker died in 1994. Children born to Katie (Bell) and Roosevelt Parker were Albert Leonard "Bo" (m Linda Harris), Billie Jean (m 1st Pete Vail; m 2nd Ray Herrington), Von (m Sue Rudolph), and Judy (m Kenneth Wells). Katie has nine grandchildren and fifteen great-grandchildren.

⚜

Andrew Pickens

Reuben Andrew Pickens was born February 25, 1941, at Little Rock, the son of Madeline (Smith) and Reuben Adolphus "R. A." Pickens II of Pickens. Their other children were Madeline (m Joe Ashman) and Rebecca Jane (m John Lambi; div). R. A. Pickens II married second Margaret Downie Hutchins on July 5, 1969. His third marriage was to Carol (McCaleb) Blackwell on August 24, 1972.

Madeline Smith was born 26 Jan 1914, at Wheatley, St. Francis County AR, the daughter of Ella (Lyons) and Henry King Smith. Their other children were Eloise (m W. L. Horner; their child: W. L. Jr. "Jack"), Nannie Clark (m J. E. Allman of Dumas; their children: Nan [m Dr. Art Squire] and J. E. III), Henry King Jr. (nev m), and Rayford (d age 20 from head injury received in a horse accident at age 4). Ella Lyons was an orphan and her parentage is unknown except for the Lyons name. She had a sister, Mamie Lyons, who never married and lived with Ella throughout her life.

R. A. Pickens II was born 7 Jan 1915 at Selma or Walnut Lake (family Bible record indicates Walnut Lake whereas he always said he was born at Selma), the son of Ollye (Cox) and Burton Cecil "B. C." Pickens Sr. (m 3 May 1906 in Malden, MO). Their other children were an infant son (d 24 Jan 1913) and B. C. Jr. (b 3 Oct 1917; d 16 Jan 1927 of appendicitis; bu Oakland Cemetery, Monticello). They also had an adopted daughter, Barbara Pickens (m Peter E. Stanley). Her parents are believed to have been Williamson from the Sheridan, AR area.

B. C. (named Bertie Cecil; he changed his name to Burton Cecil) Pickens Sr., father of R. A. Pickens II, was born 27 Dec 1878, at Selma, the son of Susan A. (Potts) and Reuben Andrew Pickens I (m 3 Jan 1878 in Selma). Their other children were Edie Stanley (b Feb 1882; d 1 Nov 1882) and Katie May (b 24 Apr 1880; m Arthur Walker Mills; their child: Catherine Pickens m Billy Belamy). Susan A. (Potts) Pickens was born 22 Jan 1854 in Claiborn Parish, died 8 Mar 1883, and was buried at Selma. Reuben Andrew Pickens I married second Lucy B.? (b 2 Sep 1859; d 13 Nov 1910; bu in Oakland Cemetery). B. C. Pickens Sr. died 17 Mar 1932 of appendicitis and is buried at Oakland Cemetery. Ollye Cox Pickens was born in 1884, died in 1979, and is buried at Oakland.

Reuben Adolphus Pickens I, father of B. C. Pickens, was born 14 Oct 1852 in Fayette County TN, the son of Susan (Stanley) and William Alexander Pickens (m 30 Sep 1849, Fayette Co). Their other children were William S. (b 6 Dec 1859; d 5 Mar 1923), Martha D. (m R. S. Wright) and Lucy Kitty (m Sam M. Killiam). William Alexander Pickens brought his family to Selma, AR after the Civil War. It is not certain if he came to Arkansas from Tennessee or from Vicksburg, MS. He established a sawmill business at Selma. William Alexander Pickens died in 1868.

William Alexander Pickens, father of R. A. Pickens I, was born in 1822 in Mississippi, the son of Sallie (Rutledge) and Rev. Israel Sidney Pickens, who were married in TN in 1818. Their other children were Andrew G. (b 1821 MS; m Elizabeth F. Botts, 19 Jan 1842, Fayette County TN), Sarah C. (b 1825 MS; m Moses McKinley, 1871, Fayette County), Margaret E. (b 1827, MS; m Francis M. Griffin, 28 Dec 1847, Fayette County), Charles Lauderdale (b 19 Dec 1829 [cemetery record book has 1825], Fayette County TN; m Anna Eliza Shorter, Mar 1858), Israel McGrady (b 1832 TN; m Harriet J. Churchill, 24 Sep 24 1852, Fayette County; died 1862 in Civil War), Susan A. (b 1834 TN; m Hugh S. Rogers, 26 Nov 1867; moved to TX), and Robert P. (b 1839 TN; killed accidentally when young).

Andrew G. Pickens, Sarah Pickens McKinley, and Margaret Pickens Griffin stayed in TN. Susan Pickens Rogers moved to Texas. Israel McGrady Pickens' widow, Harriet Churchill Pickens, moved to

Independence County AR after the Civil War where her brother, James Churchill lived. Her children were Charles P. (m Emma C. McDonald), John William (m Joe Anna Summers), James M. (m Lula Bennett), Lula A. (m E. F. Baker), and Cora C. (m A. T. Best. Ira Pickens of Newport, AR, is descended from the Israel McGrady Pickens line. Charles L. Pickens moved his family to Drew County and settled near Florence. His children were Annie Eunice, Charles Henry (m Kitty Bass Prewitt), Lillian Sue, Edward Sidney, Sallie Ada, Minnie Olivia, Jessie May (d infant), Robert Shorter, and Annie. Charles L. Pickens died at Florence 1 Nov 1905 and was buried at Mount Tabor Cemetery.

Rev. Israel Sidney Pickens, father of William Alexander Pickens, was born 5 Jun 1799 in Abbeville County SC, the son of Margaret (Gillespie) and Andrew Pickens, who were married 1790 in SC. Their other known children were James H. (d 1825, Giles County TN; most of his children went to Hempstead and Sevier Counties AR), Andrew (a missionary to Chickasaw Indians in MS; d 1824 of fever there; m and had six children; widow moved to Fayette County TN; children later moved to AR), and Robert B. (lived in Monroe County MS; moved to Fayette County TN in 1831; m twice; two sets of children; the older set moved to Independence County AR c1860). Andrew Pickens was first married to unknown. In his two marriages he fathered eight sons and four daughters. Rev. Israel Sidney Pickens moved from SC to Fayette County TN in 1827-28 and was pastor of Shiloh Cumberland Presbyterian Church for thirty years. He served for a few years as a missionary to the Chickasaw Indians in MS at the same place his brother Andrew had died. He died 12 Dec 1876 and was buried in the Shiloh Church Cemetery.

According to research compiled by Rev. E. M. Sharp in 1961, Andrew Pickens, father of Israel Sidney Pickens, was born in 1753 in Augusta County VA, the son of Zerubiah and Gabriel Pickens of Abbeville County SC. Their other children were William (settled in Maury County TN in 1807), Abraham (settled in Maury County; d there in 1834), and Jonathan (d in Hardin County TN after 1830). Gabriel Pickens was the son of Margaret and William Pickens who came from Ireland to Burks County PA by 1718. Some of their known children were Israel (Lunenberg County VA 1749), John (m Eleanor; d 1770, Abbeville County SC), Andrew (m Nancy Davis; d 1756 Mecklenburg County NC), and Robert (m Mirian Davis; d in Anderson County SC).

Reuben Andrew Pickens, son of R. A. Pickens II, graduated from Dumas High School and then attended A&M College and University of Arkansas for two years. He married Catherine Buckley and their children were John Marshall (m Karen Dancer; their child: Stephen Andrew), Kendall Lynne (m Roy Tiner; div), and Andrew Buckley "Drew" (m Elizabeth Pugh Newcome). Andrew married second Debbie Rockenstien, and they had one child, Luke Eli.   Andrew's third marriage was to Peggy Jean Kendricks.

Madeline (Pickens) and Joe Ashman had no children.   Children born to Rebecca Jane (Pickens) and John Lambi were Madeline Elizabeth, Katherine Alexander, and Daniel Pickens.

❧❦❧

Alvie Lee Pugh

Alvie Lee Pugh was born March 9, 1912, on the King place (now the Pugh place) near Person's Bridge, the son of Pearlie (Dunlap) and Andrew Pugh. Their other children were Murray (m Audrey ?), Mulvie, Arlee (m 1st Walter Tatum; m 2nd ?), Norma, Hiawatha (m Willie Mae ?), Vercie Lee (m Willie Fowler), Mattie B. (m Otta Wise), and Justine (m ? Fowler).

Pearlie Dunlap was born on the Perry place (the site of the Old Soldiers Park at Star City), the daughter of ? (Perry) and Oliver Dunlap. Their other children were Gussie (m ? Tatum), Jennie Bell (m ? Gardner; m 2nd ?)), Lizzie (m 1st Charlie Blackman; m 2nd Shannon ?), Lettie Bell (m Will Haygood), and Thomas.

Andrew Pugh was born in April 1887, near Rose Hill, the son of Alice (Jasper) and George Pugh Sr. Their other children were George Jr. (m Rosie Owens), Rachel (m Leroy Gipson), Emma (Henry Maxwell), and Alvie McKinley (m 1st Eva Bell Tatum; m 2nd Mary Alice Nails; m 3rd Lena Bell Easter). In the early 1900s George Pugh acquired 160 acres of land in the Rose Hill area and began farming.

George Pugh Sr. was born into slavery, place unknown, in January 1851. His father was originally from AL. "As far as I know, he was a Pugh slave," Alvie stated. Alice Jasper was born into slavery in VA in January 1851, the daughter of Annie (Burks) and Peter Richard Jasper. Their other children were Billy (b VA; m 2nd Rosie ?), Charlie (b AR; m Eliza ?), Peter Richard II (b AR; m 1st Susie Dale ?; m 2nd Marger Jones [Jasper ?]), Mattie, and Sanders. The Peter Jasper family left Virginia in 1858 and lived near what is now the Avery place. After the war the family established themselves on a 280 tract of land, farmed, and raised their family.

Alvie Pugh attended school at Rose Hill through the fourth grade. "But I kept on learning a lot after I quit," he said. He then entered the family farm and sawmill business. Children born to Alvie Pugh were L. C. (m Polly Rochelle), Herman (m Sally Witherston), Lillian (m Edward Lewis), Gloria (m Lee Vel Dawson), Shearlean (m John Perry), Roy, and Andrew (m Willie Anna ?).

❧❦❧

Mary Dean Naff Pugh and Charles Naff

Mary Dean Naff Pugh was born October 8, 1922, at Portland the daughter of Eula Dean (Bain) and Henry Huffman Naff. Their only other child was Henry Leroy (b 20 Sep 1918; m 1st Patsy Bell; m 2nd Frances (Cornell) Streeter; m 3rd Oma Lee Elton; d 9 Feb 1975). Charles Henry Naff was born 14 Dec 1940, at Little Rock, the son of Patsy (Bell) and Henry Leroy Naff of Portland.

Eula Dean Bain was born 7 Oct 1895 at Portland, the daughter of Lottie D. (Dean) and Dolphus Leroy Bain. Lottie Dean was born 1 Dec 1873 at Hamburg, the daughter of Virginia (Jackson) Lambert and Matthew Henry Dean. Matthew Henry Dean was the son of Charlotte (Horn) and Dr. James Dean. Dr. James Dean brought his family from TN to Ashley County before the Civil War and settled on a plantation near Wilmot. Dolphus Leroy Bain was born 7 May 1866 [?] in MS, the son of Nancy Elmira Stell and Samuel S. Bain. He was accidentally shot and killed 27 Jan 1912 while turkey hunting near Parkdale. He was mayor of Portland at the time and was a member of the mercantile firm of D. L. Bain & Company.

Henry Huffman Naff moved to Portland upon his marriage to Dean Bain in 1917. He and his wife were killed in a private plane accident near Portland on 31 May 1949. He was vice-president and cashier at Peoples Bank, partner and co-owner of Naff-Pugh Gin Company, and a farmer. Henry Huffman Naff was born 24 Apr 1895 at Bastrop, the son of Caroline Irene (Huffman) and George Washington Naff. Their other children were Mary McDuffie (b 23 Apr 1898, Bastrop; m 1st Oliver Kent Ludlum; m 2nd William Shelton Gray; m 3rd John Clyde Morris Sr.) and George Tipton (b 11 Nov 1900, Bastrop; m Myrtle Adeline Johnson).

Caroline Irene Huffman was born 5 Jul 1869 at Oak Ridge, LA, the daughter of Zarilla Irene (McDuffie) and Col. Jno. Huffman. Their other children were Mary (name was Kate Read; father changed to Mary; b 30 May 1872; m Charles Kidd Lewis), Jonas W. (d 22 May 1884), and John M. (b 28 Feb 1875; d 1 Nov 1891). Col. Jno. M. Huffman was born 6 Feb 1832 in Shelbyville, Spencer County KY, the son of Catherine (Smeltzer) and Joseph Huffman. He moved to Collin County TX in 1855 and served with General Sam Houston as a ranger for two years. During the Civil War he served with the 3rd Kentucky Regiment under J. H. Morgan. After the war he relocated to Morehouse Parish where he became a successful planter.

Zarilla Irene McDuffie was born 4 Jun 1845 in Hinds County MS, the daughter of Euphemia "Effie" Caroline and George McDuffie. Their other children were Mary Jane (b 6 Nov 1882; d 13 Jul 1944), Ida Leone (b 20 Sep 1848; d 9 Jul 1923; m 1st Jack P. Myers; m 2nd Litter Huffman), Kate (b 1 Jun 1850; m 1st Jno. J. Read; m 2nd Walter S. White), Nancy (b 18 Dec 1852; d 14 Feb (854), Caroline (b 18 Dec 1852; d 7 Nov 1861), Georgia (b 23 Apr 1865; d 10 Apr 1926); m Robert Bruce Traylor), and Fannie (b 26 Jun 1860; d 3 Jan 1877).

George Washington Naff was born 9 Mar 1862 in Bastrop, the son of Emily (Howell) and Isaac Tipton Naff. Their other children were Henry Howell (m Mollie Wright), Mary Letitia (b 24 Aug 1856; m W. A. Collins; no children), and Sarah G. (b 2 Mar 1859; d 4 Nov 1875). George Washington Naff became one of the largest landowners in Morehouse Parish but devoted most of his career to public service. At age eighteen he became deputy clerk of the district court and held that office until 1916 when he resigned to become cashier at the Bastrop State Bank & Trust Company. He served as Morehouse Parish sheriff from 1924 until 1932 and died 13 Sep 1933.

Isaac Tipton Naff was born 12 Apr 1822 at Green County TN, the son of Mary Butler (Tipton) and Henry Hoss Naff Sr. Their other children were Henry Hoss Jr., Catherine, Frank or Franklin, Amanda, Jonathan Lamar, Jacob, Sarah, Emmaline, and John Blair. Five of these children were born in TN and five were born in Morehouse Parish. Mary Butler Tipton was born 26 Apr 1802. Henry Hoss Naff was born 26 Jul 1799 in Franklin County VA and died 9 Jul 1842 in Bastrop. He settled in the area of what would later become Bastrop in 1831 and farmed. Isaac Tipton Naff taught at the first coeducational school in Bastrop. His wife, Emily Howell, was born 23 Jun 1826, the daughter of Lettitia (Harold) and William Howell. (See Frank Day summary.)

Mary Dean Naff attended Portland School through the ninth grade and then entered Abbott Academy, at Andover, MA. She later attended Vassar and Sarah Lawrence Colleges. While in New York she met and married (1944) Howard Henry, who was killed in WWII in 1945. She married second Hampton Pugh, who was born 9 Sep 1915 at Hamburg, the son of Maude (McCorvey) and Frank Norwood Pugh. The only child born to Mary Dean (Naff) and Hampton Pugh was John Tipton (m Suzanne Russell). Their grandchildren are Mary Ann (m Andrew Cash Stallings), John Tipton Jr., and Clarke Hampton.

Charles Henry Naff was raised at Portland by his great-grandmother, Lottie Dean Bain, after his grandparents, Dean (Bain) and Henry Naff, were killed. Charles Naff married Gerri Lee Garner, the daughter of Christine (Overby) and Cleo Brown Garner. Children born to Gerri Lee (Garner) and Charles Naff were Priscilla Dean (m Lloyd Medina) and Todd Bain.

Martha Morris Rodgers

Martha Louise "Betsy" Morris Rodgers was born March 25, 1927, at Dermott, the only child of Viviene Louise (Skipper) and James Alfred Morris Jr. James Alfred Morris Jr. was born 10 Feb 1900, at Iola, Kansas, the son of Grace Lilliace (Crawford) and James Alfred Morris Sr. Their other children were Ellen Ruth (m Henry C. Clanton), May (m Charles W. Tillman), Elizabeth (m S. Laron Offutt), and Charles Frederick (d age 18; fell under a train while attempting to board south of Parkdale).

Grace Lilliace Crawford was born 24 Feb 1869 at Twinsburg, OH, the daughter of Caroline Elmina (Chamberlain) and A. W. Crawford. She died 6 Sep 1947 at Dermott. J. A. Morris Sr. was born 7 Aug 1869 at Frankfort, KY and died 14 Aug 1943 at Dermott. He moved to Warren, AR, as a railroad master for the Iron Mountain Railroad and in the early 1900s moved to Dermott where he was employed by Missouri-Pacific Railroad. His home was located at the southwest corner of Speedway and Freeman Streets.

Viviene Louise Skipper was born 14 Jun 1920 at Baxter, the daughter of Maude Mae (Grubb) and Charles Floyd "Charlie" Skipper. Their other children were William Curtis "Deacon" (b 25 Jan 1910; m Agatha Cook; d 1971) and Bruce (b 13 Dec 1904; d 25 May 1907). The Charlie Skipper family moved from Baxter to Dermott in 1904. Maude Grubb was born 3 Oct 1883 at Huran, SD, the daughter of Ellen (Dare) and Samuel Curtis Grubb. Their only other child was Bruce Cody (m Maude Bulloch). Samuel Curtis Grubb was born 5 Apr 1850 in Sangamon Co, IL, and moved his family to the Baxter area around 1884. He was involved in a sawmill operation there and was a millwright. He died 1 May 1900 at Baxter. Ellen Grubb related that she insisted they move after she was marooned in a blizzard with her husband away. She told about having to hold on to a rope to make her way to the barn. After the death of her husband, Ellen Grubb moved to Dermott and managed a hotel. She eventually married Rev. N. C. Denson, a well-known Baptist minister.

Charles Floyd "Charlie" Skipper was born Feb 1 1882, south of Baxter, the son of Malissa "Lissie" (Bulloch) and William Franklin "Willie" Skipper, who were married 22 Jul 1879. Their only other child was Walter (m Fannie Wilkinson). Children born to Fannie (Wilkinson) and Walter Skipper were Lucille (m 1st ? Edwards; m 2nd Paul Nahlen), and Walter Jr. (m Elizabeth ?). Fannie Wilkinson Skipper later married Green Calvin Bulloch. Children born to Lucille (Skipper) and ? Edwards were Gloria Jean and Francille. Known children born to Elizabeth and Walter Skipper Jr. were Jan, Tommy.

Willie Skipper was murdered on Bayou Bartholomew on 13 May 1896. On 14 Feb 1901, Malissa Bulloch Skipper married William H. Lephiew, who had been in business with her husband, and moved to Dermott. William H. Lephiew's first wife was Martha Cordelia "Delia" Bulloch, a daughter of Ellen (Courtney) and Green Berry Bulloch. She died in 1900.

William Franklin "Willie" Skipper was born in 1856 south of Baxter, the son of M. S. and Everett Skipper, a merchant and farmer. Their other children, as listed by the 1860 Drew County Census, were CLA (dau; b 1854 AR), ML (dau; b 1856), HM (son; b 1858), and M (dau; b 1860). M. S. Skipper, wife of Everett Skipper, was born in 1827 in GA. Everett Skipper came from AL, his home being within sight of Warm Springs, GA. He joined the Confederate Army in Monticello.

Martha Louise "Betsy" Morris graduated from Dermott High School in 1944 and attended Louisiana Tech at Ruston. She began working for Delta Production Credit Association in Dermott in 1951, retired in 1989, and continued to work part-time until 1998. Betsy married Edwin Cantrell Rodgers, who was born 23 Aug 1922 at Dermott, the son of Rosa (Harkins) and William C. Rodgers. Their only other child was William Duell Rodgers. Rosa Harkins was born 10 Aug 1888 in Pope County AR and died 31 Mar 1979 in Dermott. William C. Rodgers was born 23 Oct 1897 in Conway County AR and died 11 Aug 1969 in Dermott.

Betsy and Edwin Rodgers had one child, Jane Ann (m 1st Joe Moreland; m 2nd James Diemer). Edwin Rodgers died 17 Feb 1988. Betsy has two grandchildren, Anne Christie Moreland (m Durwood Eugene Johnston III) and Michael Ray Diemer. She has two great-grandchildren, Abbie Frances and Zakry Christopher Johnston.

✦✦✦

Vernon Scott

Vernon Scott was born March 1915, at Eupora, MS, the son of Frances (Willingham) and Thaddeus Scott. He graduated from high school at Eupora, received the bachelor's degree in vocational education from Mississippi State University, and did graduate work at Louisiana State University. In 1936 he accepted a position teaching vocational agriculture in Forest, LA. In 1938 he went to work for the Farm Security Administration in West Carroll Parish. After six months, he was promoted to county supervisor in Lincoln Parish, LA, and was later transferred to the office in Little Rock, AR, where he worked as a farm management specialist until 1943, when he enlisted in the Navy. He was assigned to a PT boat squadron in the South Pacific.

After the war Vernon moved to Tillar as general manager of Tillar & Company where he assisted with the closing out of Tillar Mercantile Company. He continued as general manager of Tillar & Company until his retirement in 1987. He is currently living in Tillar where he manages his family's Coon Bayou Farms operation.

Vernon and his wife, formerly Marjorie Glenn of Batesville, AR, reared three children in Tillar: Sharon, John and Sarah.

≈⊙≈

Duke Shackelford

Henry Duke Shackelford was born May 30, 1926, on Bayou Bartholomew near McGinty, the youngest son of Gladys (Parks) and James Barnes "Jim" Shackelford. (The parents could not agree on a name so Dr. Crandall, the attending physician, finally just put "Henry" on the birth certificate. They eventually named their son Duke.) Their other children were John Francis (b 10 Jul 1914; d 4 Jun 1970; m 1st Marvin Wright; m 2nd Rachel Nettles), James William "Bill" (m Adele Bergholm), Walter Draper (b 25 Oct 1918; d 23 Feb 1968; m 1st Narene McGough; m 2nd Bettye Jones Dye), and Louis Craig (b 14 Aug 1921; d 15 Sep 1977; m 1st Frances Devany, div; m 2nd Clotene Jackson, div; m 3rd Mildred Ware).

Gladys Parks was born 2 Nov 1891 in Mechanicsburg, Yazoo County MS, the daughter of Josie (Duke) and Charles Parks. Jim Shackelford was born 5 Aug 1887, at Anding, Yazoo County MS, the son of Anna Nora (Seale) and John Francis Shackelford. Their other children were May (nev m), Gladys (m Green Clay Walker), Louis (m Laura Dalton), Dave Seale (m Gladys Zachary of Jones), and Edna (m C. C. Crim).

Jim Shackelford moved to the McGinty area from Sunflower, MS in 1918. He bought property which included about 800 acres of land, a country store, and a steam-powered cotton gin that had been owned by Arthur Wooten. He moved his family into "a residence of sorts," began farming the property, and operating the store and gin. He continued to buy small tracts of land and leased a farm from Wolf & Sibernagle Company. In the winter of 1936-37, he acquired Hollyhurst Plantation at Jones. This was a tract of about 2,400 acres originally owned by the Jones family for whom the town was named. In the 1940s he acquired the Richmond and Bunckley farms, and in 1950 he bought the Kellers Bend farm from the Willie Wilhite heirs. The home on the bayou burned in 1934, and the family moved into a house in Jones. In 1939 he built a new home on Hollyhurst Plantation. Jim Shackelford died 27 May 1956, and Gladys Parks Shackelford died 12 Aug 1991.

Duke Shackelford attended public school at Bonita and graduated in 1943. He attended LSU for two quarters before enlisting in the U. S. Navy in May 1944. He returned to LSU in 1946, graduated with a bachelor's degree in agriculture in 1949, and returned to Jones to work in the family business.

Duke married Susan Davenport Madison on 24 Nov 1951. She was born 25 Apr 1930 at Bastrop, the daughter of Frances (Davenport) and George Thomas Madison. Their only other child was Mary Moss Henderson. Children born to Sue (Madison) and Duke Shackelford were George Thomas Madison (nev m), John Francis III (m Lucy Lacey), and Parks Davenport (m Julie Anna Potts). Sue Madison Shackelford died 19 Jun 1996. Duke has three grandchildren by Lucy (Lacey) and John Shackelford. They are Lucy Parks, Susan Davenport, and Elizabeth Lacey.

≈≈⊚≈≈

Amos Sledge

Amos Andrew Sledge was born May 14, 1914, at Damascus, Faulkner County, AR, the son of Mary Matilda Elizabeth (Palmer) and Andrew Cornelius "Neal" Sledge, who were married in Faulkner County on 5 Nov 1907. Their other children were Hebert (m Zora Atkinson), James (nev m), Earl (m Ovie Stevenson), Leona (m Arie Stevenson), Cynthia "Trig" (m Phillip Brannon), and Hubert "Goob" (m Jewell Cash). Mary Palmer was born 11 May 1892 the daughter of Susan Elizabeth "Lizzie" (Hartwick) and Harphey P. Palmer. Lizzie Hartwick was born 6 Dec 1870, the daughter of Mary J. (Lee) and Jacob Hartwick who were married in Van Buren County 24 Jun 1869. Jacob Hartwick was the son of Matilda (b c1825) and Leonard H. Hartwick (b Oct 1832). Leonard H. Hartwick was the son of Delila and Leonard Hartwick who were both born c1775 in NC. Harphey P. Palmer was born 15 Oct 1870, the son of Elizabeth P. "Betsy" (Holland) (b 1834; d 1918)and William Hosea Palmer (b 30 Nov 1829; d 1890).

Neal Sledge was born 30 Sep 1883 at Morrilton, AR, the son of Mary M. (Hogue) and James Franklin Sledge. Mary M. Hogue was born 21 Apr 1862, the daughter of Rose Etta (Sledge) (b 16 Jan 1833; d 5 Feb 1904) and John Pryor Hogue (b 5 Feb 1820; d 8 Mar 1882). James Franklin Sledge was born in 1849, the son of Martha [?] and Thomas Sledge (b c1825). (Recent research indicates that Martha Sledge may have been a later wife of Thomas and not the mother of James Franklin.)

Amos Sledge attended school at Damascus through the eighth grade and then "continued to work in the field." In November 1930, the family moved to the Bob Finn place near Bellaire and rented land. In 1947 they moved to Lake Wallace and rented land owned by Charlie Head. Amos bought land at Grace Community from Harrison Moglothin in 1958. Felix Rodgers previously owned this tract. Amos began truck farming for which he was acclaimed. On 21 Sep 1987, Amos married Beatrice Brooks who was born 23 Jun 1924 at Vina, AL, the daughter of Cynthia (Aldridge) and

Newt Brooks. Amos and Beatrice had no children but had a host of nieces and nephews. Amos Sledge died 20 Mar 1999.

Children born to Zora (Atkinson) and Hebert Carl Sledge were Hebert Andrew (m Mabel Pace), Harold Junior (m Wanda Roberts), Shirley Virginia (m Loy Dean Hicks), Shelby Earl "Buddy" (m Donna Kolb), Loyd Amos (d young), Sylvia Marie (d infant), Ronald Lynn (m Janice Nolan), and Margaret Elaine (d young).

Children born to Ovie (Stevenson) and Earl Cecil Sledge were Virginia Earlene (m R. V. Pierson) and Jerry Don (m Carolyn Mangum).

Children born to Leona Elizabeth (Sledge) and Arie Stevenson were Carl Lee (m 1st Cretel Alice Shelton; m 2nd Helen Beverly Gadpaille), Patricia Ann (m 1st Tommy Ellis; m 2nd Floyd Baughman), Mary Lois (m Carl Edward Lee), and Steve Brian (d 1984).

Children born to Cynthia (Sledge) and Phillip Brannon were Michael Dale (m Sheila Ann Farrell), Phyllis Gail (m 1st Robert Miller; m 2nd Brian Smith; m 3rd Michael George Flory), and Charles Roger (m Brenda Joyce Cox).

Children born to Jewell Etta (Cash) and Hubert Sledge were Hubert Fay Jr. (m Wilma Johnson), Judy Ann (m William Brisby), Cheryl Darlene (m Jimmy Allison), John Andrew (m Sharon Smith), and James Randall).

❦

Lloyd Smith

Lloyd Smith was born March 16, 1928, at Pine Bluff, the son of Cora (Woolf) and Judge Henry Waterson Smith. Their other children were Edward Tucker II (b 1922; m Barbara June Dry) and Henry Kenneth (b 1924; m Nannette Wells). Cora Woolf was born at Houston, Perry County AR, the daughter of Louana (Harrington) and Thomas Edwin Woolf. The Woolf family moved from Alabama to Arkansas after the Civil War.

Henry Waterson Smith was born in 1888 at Greenmount, Lincoln County, the son of Martha "Mattie" (McShan) and Edward Tucker Smith. Their other children were Adelia (b 1880; d 1935; m Jesse Thomas Peacock), Mary Susan (b 1882; d 1967), Laura Lee (b 1884; d 1925; m Luther Vick), Thomas Wesley (b 1886; d 1973; m Sallie Lee Wakefield), Clay King (b 1891; d 1965; m Alma Starling), Carl McShan (b 1891; d 1973), Ollie Maude (b 1893; d 1910), Mattie Cornelia (b 1894; d 1944; m Hiram Heartsill Ragon), Edward Roland (b 1896; d 1976; m Gladys Dunning), Sam Otis (b 1898; d 1943), and John Ira (b 1900; m Ruth Lee Bellwood). Mattie McShan was born 3 Aug 1861 in Collins, the daughter of Susan Roland (Tarrant) and John Wesley McShan. Susan Roland Tarrant was born 19 Feb 1827 in Jefferson County, died 10 Feb 1909 in Drew County, and was buried at Collins. John Wesley McShan was born

25 Sep 1811 in KY, died 8 Dec 1903 in Lincoln County, and was buried at Tyro. (See McShan family history.)

Edward Tucker Smith was born in 1856 at Greenmount, the son of Mary Elizabeth (King) and Thomas Sidney Smith. Their other children were Mary Claywell (b 1846; d 1921; m John Styles), Martha "Mattie" (b Holly Grove, MS; m Doc Tiner), John King (b 1851; d 1928; m Iola Payne at Tyro); Sam (m Hattie Williams); Medora (d infant), William D. (b 1858; d 1863), Susania (b 1862; d 1863), Thomas Sidney (b 1863; d 1877), and Rhoda Lee (b 1870; d 1965; m Benjamin Payne).

Thomas Sidney Smith was born in 1813 in GA or TN, the son of Mary and John Smith. John Smith was born c1790 and died in 1857. John and Thomas Sidney Smith lived in TN and MS before moving to Collins and soon thereafter to Greenmount around 1853. They crossed the Mississippi River at Gaines Landing en route to Collins. John Smith was postmaster at Greenmount and Tyro. Thomas Sidney Smith received at least two land grants from the U. S. General Land Office, one in 1856. Edward Tucker Smith later located at Tyro where he farmed. He eventually moved to Monticello so that his twelve children could receive a better education. The family moved to Dumas c1933. In the early 1900s, Clay King Smith moved his family to the Garrett Bridge area, where Lloyd Smith presently lives. The family farmed and during the 1920s ran a small general store on the property. His brothers and his father stayed with them during farming season, returning to Tyro on the weekends.

Children born to Adelia (Smith) and Jesse Thomas Peacock were Nannie Lee (b 1905; d 1972; m John William Staudinger), Elizabeth (b 1907), Mary Ruth (b 1909), Jesse Thomas, Jr. (b 1913; m Mary Pearce), Henry Edward (b 1915; m Viola Borchert), and Herman Paul (b 1917; m Lucille Srygley). Children born to Laura Lee (Smith) and Luther Vick were Mattie Elizabeth (b 1915; m 1st F. A. Smithers; m 2nd William Sheley), Mary Sue (b 1917; m Edward Park), Luther Edward (b 1920; d 1928), and Laura Frances (b 1921; d 1953; m Harold Splawn). The only child born to Alma (Starling) and Clay King Smith was Clay King Jr. (b 1916; m 1st Tommie Carter; m 2nd Velora Danly). The only child born to Mattie Cornelia (Smith) and Hiram Heartsill Ragon was Hiram Heartsill Jr. (b 1917; m 1st Paula Lemley; m 2nd Bertha Heiskell; m 3rd Pauline Self). The only child born to Ruth Lee (Bellwood) and John Ira Smith was Morrison (b 1936; m Mary Matthews).

Lloyd Smith graduated from Pine Bluff High School and then entered University of Arkansas. After enlisting in the army, he returned to the university, and later was sent as a reserve to Korea. After returning he again attended the university. In 1956 he began a farming operation at Garrett Bridge. Lloyd married Marise Emerson Chastain, the daughter of

Mary Lee (Emerson) and Garvin Chastain of Ranger, TX. Marise and Lloyd Smith had one child, Stephen Henry (nev m).

≈⊛≈

Ernestine Nobles Sprinkle

Ernestine Nobles Sprinkle was born July 16, 1918, at Parkdale, the daughter of Margaret Lee "Mag" (Ralph) and James Howard Nobles Sr. Their other children were James Howard Jr. (b 24 Nov 1914; m Eulalie "Lee" MacFarline), Margaret Sue (b 10 Dec 1916), and William Ralph (b 3 Nov 1920; d 11 Nov 1920). Mag Ralph was born 6 Oct 1896, at Beech Creek, the daughter of Viola Edward Rose Wimbish (Hill) and William Harrison Ralph. (See Mary Morris Foster summary for Ralph and Hill family history.)

James Howard Nobles Sr. was born 14 Dec 1885, at Poplar Bluff, the son of Susan Rebecca (Barnes) and James Samuel "Jim" Nobles Sr. Their other children were Willie May (b 7 Dec 1881; nev m), Mollie Neal (b 6 Nov 1883; nev m); Archibald "Archie" Crawford III (b 27 Feb 1889; d 31 Jan 1906), and Houston Samuel (b 20 Oct 1891; d 20 Oct 1952; nev m).

James Samuel "Jim" Nobles Sr. was born 28 Nov 1850 in Barbour County AL, the son of Eliza and Archibald Crawford Nobles I. Their other children were Mollie (nev m), Lawrence (m Elizabeth Cockrell in Ashley County 17 Nov 1859; served in Confederate army; never returned); Martha A. (b 13 Aug 1837; m James Newton Murry; d 10 Aug 1910), Celia (m Jo Cockrell 22 Oct 1865), Eliza (nev m; d Jan 1928?), Annie (m Richard Brooks); and Archibald Crawford "Arch" II (b 13 Apr 1856; m 1st Nannie Gill; one child, Linnie d age 2; m 2nd Ella Sue Wolf; no ch; d 10 Feb 1889).

Archibald Crawford Nobles I was born November 15, 1808 in NC. He came from Barbour County AL to Poplar Bluff around 1858 and settled on the bayou one mile south on land now known as J. S. Nobles and A. C. Nobles. His first wife died and on 5 Jul 1857, he married Nancy Ann Murry. He died August 5, 1875.

Susan Rebecca Barnes was born 13 Jun 1861 at Poplar Bluff, the daughter of Martha Ann (Lacey) and John Sims Barnes. Their other children were John Sims (b 1854), William Evans "Willie" (b 1859; m Mag ?), , Frank Allen (b 1856), Fannie Julia (b 1864; m Price Hill; their dau, Fannie Julia m Ransom Moore; their dau Harriet), Jeffie (b 1869; m ? Bell), and Lucy (b 1871; m ? Morris). Children born to Mag and William Evans Barnes were John K., Harry O., Evan, James Nobles, Willie Kathryn, and Frances Jennet.

John Sims Barnes was born in 1825 the son of Susanna (Sims) and Daniel T. Barnes. Their other children were Swepson, Gabriel (b 1819; m Eliza Jordan), Francis, William, Charles, Robert, Leonard, Thomas,

Granville "Gran," Edward "Edwin," Daniel W. L. "Wash," and Lucy. Susanna Sims was the daughter of Jane Merriweather (Lewis) and Swepson Sims. Daniel T. Barnes was born in 1794, the son of Lucy Ann (Stow) and Gabriel Barnes. Gabriel Barnes was born in 1765, the son of Susannah and Henry Barnes (d 1787). Lucy Ann Stow was the daughter of Susanna and Joel Stow.

The only [?] child born to Eliza (Jordan) and Gabriel Barnes was Daniel (b 1848; m Mary Jane Hill). Their daughter was Bessie May (b 1881; m James Otis Lindsey). Children born to Bessie May (Barnes) and James Otis Lindsey were Halbert, Mary Lou, Allen "James", Flora, and William H. Mary Jane Hill was the daughter of Margaret (Miller) and James Hill (b 10 Apr 1818). James Otis Lindsey was born in 1878, the son of Flora Dale (Halbert) and James Lindsey. James Lindsey was the son of Parmelia (Martin) and Toliver Lindsey (b 1818 KY). Flora Dale Halbert was b in 1853, the daughter of Julia Ann (Brown) (b 1826) and Ira Halbert. Ira Halbert was the son of Willie (Eddins) and Xenophon Halbert. Willie Eddins was the daughter of Rebecca (Green) and James Eddins. Xenophon Halbert was the son of Margaret (Harper) and John Halbert. John Halbert was the son of Elizabeth (Hill) (b 1714 VA) and William Halbert (b 18 Sept 1747).

Martha Ann Lacey, wife of John Sims Barnes, was born 8 Jun 8, 1831, in Elyton, Jefferson County AL, the daughter of Rebecca (Harmon) and Joshua Lacey. Rebecca Harmon Lacey was born in 1790 in KY and died 1882 in Montevallo, AL. Joshua Lacey was born in 1780 in SC, the son of Jane Harper (b SC; m 1766; d 1813 Livingston County KY) and Joshua Lacey (b Sep 1742, Cumberland County KY; d 20 Mar 1813, Livingston County KY).

Ernestine Nobles attended Parkdale High School and graduated from the University of Central Arkansas. Ernestine married Ralph E. Sprinkle, who was born in NC. Children born to Ernestine (Nobles) and Ralph Sprinkle were Margaret Patricia and James Ralph. Ernestine has three grandchildren.

≈≈❀❧≈

Ruth Tracy Teal

Ruth Tracy Teal was born February 17, 1901, in Holly, LA (De Soto Parish), the daughter of Kitty (Johnson) and Charles Harpton Tracy. Kitty Johnson was the daughter of Fannie (Green) and Anthony Johnson. Ruth said of her grandparents, "My grandfather [Tracy] was three-quarters Indian and hunted extensively. He wore his hair down to his shoulder like Frederick Douglas. By the time my father was around nine years old, he was the man of the house because grandfather would go off for long periods of time. My mother's father, Anthony Johnson, was evidently an old white man - very light skinned. He had other children who would come to see Mama. He worked on a boat and had straight hair and a long handlebar mustache." Kitty (Johnson) Tracy died when Ruth was around three years old, and Charles married her sister, Nettie, as Kitty had asked her on her deathbed to take care of her children.

Charles Tracy left De Soto Parish to join a Mr. Blow who had left the parish earlier. They worked on farms around Pine Bluff and Star City, and Tracy eventually bought a hundred-acre farm on the bayou near Yorktown. Before he left Louisiana, the black children could only attend school for three months a year. Tracy organized a "Home Industrial Society" to raise money to pay the teachers for another five-month term. The teacher, as well as a preacher, boarded with the Tracy family. The preacher told Tracy, "Send your children to college." Ruth was sent to Bishop College, a white institution, in Marshall, Texas, as a special ward to C. H. Maxon, the president. There she obtained her high school diploma and in May 1924 received a B.S. degree. She went to Baton Rouge to teach at McKinley High School, "the first black school in Louisiana." She taught French, English, Latin, and Van Toole's arithmetic.

Around 1930 Ruth moved to her father's farm and began teaching at Lincoln High in Star City. After five years there she returned to Louisiana to teach and later went back to the school at Star City, where she was principal. In 1945 she began teaching at Bright Star near Tarry and then taught at schools in Marion, Rison, and England, AR. She retired from the England school in 1973. During her seven-year tenure at Marion she met and married Lawrence J. Teal.

Nancy Oberton Tharp

Nancy Obertson Tharp was born June 9, 1894, near Wilmot, the daughter of Ella (Robinson) and James Oberton. Ella Robinson was born on the upper Carter place near Wilmot, the daughter of Cora and John Robinson. James Oberton was born in LA and came to the Wilmot area after the Civil War. The Oberton and Robinson families were descendants of slaves. John Robinson was a sharecropper on the deYampert plantation (upper Carter place).

Nancy attended school at Walnut Grove for a few years but had to discontinue her education to help out with the family. She married Norman Tharp who was born in LA. After their marriage they worked on the Currie plantation (Sumner place) near Parkdale. Children born to Nancy (Oberton) and Norman Tharp were Eulavee (m Odel Bankston), Annie Mae (m "Devil" ?), "Baby Sister" (nev m), Pearlone (nev m),

Freddie (nev m), Sammy Lee (nev m), Frank (nev m), and four who died young. Nancy has a "room full" of grand and great-grandchildren.

~~~~~~~~

Lois Baldwin Thomas

Lois Arkansas Baldwin Thomas was born July 19, 1896, at Brooks, Grant County AR, the daughter of Mary Elizabeth (Chadick) and Charles William Baldwin. In 1906 the family moved to Rison (Cleveland County), and in 1914 Lois began teaching at Sherill in Jefferson County. In 1915 Lois moved to Tarry in Lincoln County to teach. There she met Henry Wallace Thomas, and they married the following year on 30 Nov 1916.

Henry Wallace Thomas was born 12 Jan 1873 at Relfs Bluff Community in Lincoln County, the son of Mary Paulina (Lyle) and George Washington Thomas. Their other children were Thomas Alpha (m 1st Ada Calhoun; m 2nd Mae McEntire), Joel Lee (m Virgia Mays), Robert Leron "Bob" (m 1st Paulina Calhoun; m 2nd Lillie Stephenson), George William (m Evie Ross), Pearl Adelia (nev m), Edna Gladden (Thurmon T. Ross), Nova Ethel (m Clay Ross), Jennie Olive (m Garland Ross), and May (m Charles Russell). Mary Paulina Lyle was born 2 Mar 1852, the daughter of Sarah Martin (Knox) and Thomas Lyle. In 1854 the Thomas Lyle family moved from Tennessee to Montongo (Drew County) and established a large farm on Bayou Bartholomew. (See W. D. Lyle summary for Knox and Lyle family history.)

George Washington Thomas was born 26 Feb 1840 in Barbour County AL, the son of Foeba (Hagler) and Joel Thomas. The couple had four girls and five boys. Joel Thomas was born 4 Mar 1804 in Scotland or Holland and married Foeba Hagler in Holland. Foeba Hagler was born in 1801. The family came to America and settled in NC. By 1840 they were living in Barbour County with seven children. In 1851 they began a move to Arkansas, and Foeba died en route of influenza. She was buried in Barbour County or near Liles, MS. Joel Thomas settled at Relfs Bluff (then Drew, now Lincoln County) near the Mt. Zion Presbyterian Church. He married a widow, Nancy Burr, who had two sons and a daughter. It is not known if Joel and Nancy had children of their own. On 5 Aug 1869 Joel Thomas deeded two acres of land for the Mt. Zion Presbyterian Church. He died 9 Feb 1886, and Nancy Burr Thomas died 1 Feb 1893.

George Washington Thomas enlisted in the Confederate Army on 10 Jul 1861 and was assigned to Company A, 9th Regiment of the Arkansas Infantry. He was sent to Mississippi where he was seriously wounded at the Battle of Corinth . After being hospitalized for six months, although he was crippled he returned to active duty as a wagoneer. Taken prisoner during the battle of Nashville, he was held at Camp Douglas in Illinois for six months. Released on 15 June 1865, he returned to the farm at Relfs Bluff. He was an active member of the UCV Ben McCullough Camp in Lincoln County. He married Mary Paulina Lyle 16 Nov 1870. In addition to farming he operated a country store in front of his house at Relfs Bluff. His son, Alpha, operated a steam gin and gristmill at some nearby springs. George Washington Thomas died 26 May 1928 and Mary Paulina (Lyle) Thomas died 20 Sep 1934. Both are buried in Mt. Zion Cemetery.

Henry Wallace Thomas, son of George Washington Thomas, attended Fryar School, also known as Red Hill Academy, and later went to James School of Business in both Wilmar and Pine Bluff. He and his brother, Robert Loren "Bob," bought the McGehee Brothers mercantile store at Tarry and operated it as Thomas Brothers. Henry Wallace eventually went into business for himself, owning H. W. Thomas General Merchandise. The building burned and was rebuilt in 1933. Henry Wallace Thomas died 2 Oct 1947, and his wife continued operating the store until 1986. He was also postmaster, a position his wife assumed upon his death. Lois Baldwin Thomas died 26 Dec 1998 at age 102.

Children born to Lois (Baldwin) and Henry Wallace Thomas were Dr. Henry Wallace Jr. (m 1st 5 Jan 1941 Virginia Allen of Dunnellon, FL; m 2nd 8 Jan 1983 Jessie "Cissy" (Ferguson) Knoll), Mary Juanita (m 30 Jan 1943 William Woodrow "Woody" Parker), and Lois Evelyn (m 1st Dr. Thomas Harold Grumbles; m 2nd 26 Dec 1973 Raymond Hadley "Butch" Dennington).

Children born to Virginia (Allen) and Dr. Henry Wallace Thomas Jr. were Wallace Allan "Al" (m Carolyn Grisham) and David Ronald "Ronnie" (m Carolyn Kay Patterson). Children born to Al and Carolyn (Grisham) Thomas were Brad Allan and Greg Wallace. Children born to Carolyn Kay (Patterson) and Ronnie Thomas were Tanya Carol and Candice Rochelle.

The only child born to Juanita (Thomas) and Woodrow Parker was Rebecca Ann (m Parker Hill). Children born to Rebecca Ann (Parker) and Parker Hill were Sarah Ann, Paul Andrew, Joshua David, Rachael Lynn, and Mary Leigh. They also adopted as their daughter, Ly Nguyen.

Children born to Lois Evelyn (Thomas) and Thomas Harold Grumbles, DDS, were Thomas Harold Jr. (m Rita Rebecca Thweatt) and Judith Lynn (m Phil Phillips Jr.) Children born to Rita Rebecca (Thweatt) and Thomas Harold Grumbles Jr. were Andrew Thomas, Rebecca Thweatt, and Robin Toll. The only child born to Judith Lynn (Grumbles) and Phil Phillips Jr. was Thomas Rhett Lashlee.

Clifton Trigg

Clifton Trigg was born August 17, 1914, at Caglesville, Pope County Arkansas, the child of Mittie May (Tyler) and Thomas Philip "Tom" Trigg. Their other children were Minnie (b 7 Sep 1907; d 8 Aug 1908) and Rheba May (b 11 Nov 1910; d 8 Sep 1915). Mittie Tyler was born 29 Feb 1888 and died 2 Sep 1959. Tom Trigg was born 14 Feb 1884 in Pope County, the son of Armenda (Hamilton) and Pink Trigg. Their other children were Henry (m Jeannie Richardson) and Dora (m Connie Barham).

Tom and Henry Trigg sold their farms in Pope County and moved to Dermott in 1919. Henry rented a farm known as the old Smith place on the bayou at Grace Community. Tom bought a farm across from Skipper Bridge at Dermott and farmed for three years. The land was not well drained, and he went broke. He and David A. Gates then bought Gum Ridge Plantation from Judge McDonald, but after three years that venture also failed. Tom then leased the Renley farm at Bellaire and farmed it, with help from J. B. Griswood, until 1929. He then bought a dairy on the north side of Dermott, and Henry ran a dairy on the south end of the town.

Clifton Trigg worked on the farm and at the dairy and completed twelve years at Dermott although he did not graduate. He married Maxine Elliot, who was born 1 Jul 1914 in Nashville, TN, the daughter of Barbara Lee (Chambers) and Holderness D. Elliott Sr. Their only other child was Holderness D. Jr. Holderness D. Elliott Sr. was a pharmacist and owned Central Drug Store in Dermott. He was forced to close during the Depression and went to work at Delta Drug and later at Perry Drug.

In 1944 Clifton Trigg went into business with Chester Courtney as Courtney-Trigg Company. They had a dry goods store, grocery store, and a drug store. Y. L. Tow bought the grocery business, and the Courtney-Trigg partnership dissolved with Courtney taking the drug store and Trigg taking the dry goods store. In 1952 Clifton opened Trigg's Department Store in Dermott and Crossett. The Dermott store was replaced with a new building in 1958. Clifton entered the banking business with the opening of his First State Bank in Crossett in 1964. He later served on bank boards with Union National in Little Rock and First State in Sherwood and Magnolia.

Children born to Maxine (Elliott) and Clifton Trigg were Teresa (m 1st Larry Reynolds; m 2nd Charles Faulk III) and Toni Lynn (m 1st Leroy Higginbotham III; m 2nd James Soucchi. Maxine Trigg died 27 Jan 1997. Clifton has four grandchildren and eight grandchildren.

Page Webb

Page Webb was born July 9, 1913, at Collinston, LA, the son of Lizza (Jackson) and Nick Webb. Their other children were Katie (m Mack Haney), Lizzie (m Jim Kidd), Ruth (m Bennie Adams), William (m Priscilla ?), and Pice (d young). Nick Webb was born at Collinston of parents who were former slaves. One of Nick's brothers was Lemroy, who was born into slavery. The parents died when Nick was still young and he eventually located at Ryan, AR. Around 1929 he and Lizza bought a sixty-nine acre farm north of Jones on the state line. Lizza Jackson was born during slavery on the Pipes Plantation near Collinston, the daughter of Sealey Jackson. Sealey Jackson lived to be 107 years old.

Page Webb attended school at Wilmot through the third grade and then began farming. He was fourteen years old when his father died, and he took over the farm. He and his mother worked the farm and finished paying it out. Page married Frankie May Moore who was born in Wilmot, the daughter of ? and Frank Moore. Children born to Frankie (Moore) and Page Webb were Page Jr. and Alversa. Page has three grandchildren.

Ella Mae McDermott White

Ella Mae McDermott White was born August 29, 1912, at Dermott, the daughter of Mary Leota (Honeycutt) and Arthur Remzen McDermott. Their other children were Elwood (d infant), Arthur Floyd (m Rosella Hunter), and Llewellyn Baker (b 11 Jun 1918; d 1 Feb 1998; nev m). Mary Leota Honeycutt was born 18 Nov 1887 in Ashley County, the daughter of Ella Evelyn (Tarrant) and Osborn Morris Honeycutt. Their other children were Ethel Leaton (b 11 Mar 1883; m Walter E. Farrar; their children: Emmett Osborn [d infant], Lois Virginia [nev m], Ella Avon [m W. Fort Rawls], and Thomas Morris [m Mary Cathcrine Middlebrooks]), Leora (d infant), Willie Ina (b 22 May 1886; m Ellis Adrian Doles; their children: Ellis Adrian [nev m], Frank Morris [m Marian B. Robertson], John Anderson [m Thelma Wade], Jane [m Ralph Pippin], Ina Catherine [m W. Bert McCready], Mary Ellis [d young], William Tarrant [m Jean Kinnaird], and Howard [nev m]). (See Marian Robertson Doles summary.)

Ella Evelyn Tarrant Honeycutt was second married to John Robert Neal (previously spelled Neel) and their children were Nora Tarrant (m Charles Bishop), Daisy Bell (m Fred Beal), Robbie (nev m), Terry (nev m), and Ronnie Blanche (m Jess Montgomery). (See Bishop family history.)

Osborn Morris Honeycutt was born 1859 in AL, the son of Mary Elizabeth (Neel) and William W. Honeycutt. Mary Elizabeth Neel was born 1 Nov 1833, Tuscaloosa County AL, the daughter of Nancy (Snider) and William R. Neel. She came to Ashley County with her parents in 1850 and died there 22 Mar 1917. Nancy Snider was born ca 1815 and died 9 Feb 1896 in Ashley County. William R. Neel was born in 1810 and died 5 Dec 1860 in Ashley County.

Ella Evelyn Tarrant was born 19 Aug 1861 in AL, the daughter of Cynthia Ann (Farrar) and William A. Tarrant who moved to Ashley County c1878. She died 6 Apr 1940 in Dermott. Cynthia Ann Farrar was born 10 May 1830 in Perry County AL and died in Ashley County. She was the daughter of Judith (Webb) and Thomas Farrar. Judith Webb died 1 Mar 1846. Thomas Farrar was born 1 Mar 1793 and died 22 Sept 1859. William A. Tarrant was born 1823 in AL, the son of Mary Caroline (Walker) and George Tarrant.

Arthur Remzen McDermott was born 14 May 1878 in Dermott, the son of Ella (Jenkins) and Philander McDermott. Their other children, all born in Dermott, were Ada (b 28 Jan 1880; m Edward Jones; d 1938), Benjamin (b 13 Mar 1881; m Phoebe Evans,; d 1919), Hester "Hetty" (b 16 Jan 1885; m Elwood Baker; d 10 Apr 1912), Emma (b 18 Apr 1887; m Frederick Ellis; d 30 May 1971), Stinson (b 2 July 1888; m Laura ?), and Isador Angus (b 18 Apr 1890; m Walter W. Williamson). Arthur R. McDermott died 30 Aug 1922 and is buried with his wife, Leota Honeycutt McDermott, in the Dermott Cemetery. Ella Jenkins McDermott died 14 Nov 1893 and is buried in the McDermott Cemetery.

Philander McDermott was born 11 May 1846 at the present town of Dermott, the son of Hester Susan "Hettie" (Smith) and Dr. Charles M. McDermott. Their other children were William (b 1835; d West Feliciana Parish LA), Benjamin (b 1836 LA; m Isabelle Hurd, 1858; d 1871), Emily (b 1838, West Feliciana;), Edward (b 1840 West Feliciana; d 1861, Dermott), Charles O. (b 1841 West Feliciana; d 1842, West Feliciana), Susan "Hetty" (b 1842 West Feliciana; d 1851, Drew County), Jane (b 9 Mar 1844 West Feliciana; m Rev. M. W. Shaw; d 21 Apr 1923, Amite County MS), Annabelle (b 1848, Dermott; m Joseph Robert Anderson), Catherine Van Court (b 11 July 1850, West Feliciana; m R. Elbert Lambert; d 25 Sept 1910, Monticello, Drew County), Charles A. (b 1852 LA; m Sallie C. Mason; d 1937, Santa Monica, CA), Margaret "Maggie" (b 27 Aug 1854, LA; m Joe Bennett Mercer; d 3 Apr 1889), (William P. (b 1856 AR; d 1880), John Scott (b 1856 AR; d 1871), an infant (b/d 1858), and Edward Ozan "Ned" (b 1862, Monticello; m 1st Nannie Wood; m 2nd Lula Kinabrew; m 3rd Phoebe Evans McDermott, the widow of his nephew Benjamin McDermott, who was the son of Ella (Jenkins) and Philander McDermott; d 13 Feb 1940, Wilmot; bu McDermott Cemetery).

Charles and Hettie McDermott also raised the orphaned children of his brother, Edward. They were Hettie (b c1847), Alice E. (b 1848), Susan (b 1848), and Eddie (b 1856).

Children born to Isabelle (Hurd) and Benjamin McDermott were Matthew (b 1863; d 1894; m Ellen Dupree; their children: Benjamin Harry, Russell, and Matthew Angus), May (b 1860; m W. Dixon Trotter), and Lena (b 1868; m Burnes Mason; their children: McDermott, Wyatt, Willie Mae, and Bernice).

Children born to Jane (McDermott) and Rev. Matthew Shaw were Matthew Alex (b 1862; d 1863), Emaline Irene (b 3 Feb 1864; d 5 Apr 1957; m Rev. Nathaniel Smylie; their children: Theodore, John, Janie Margaret [m Stark], and Matthew), Charles (b 1870; m Mattie Hearing), Ethelene (b 1867; d 1869), Hettie (b 1872; d ?), Mary B. (b 1874; m Lee Kiblinger), Benjamin Edward (b 1876; d 1876), Annabelle (b 1879; d 1880), and Ethel (b 1882; m a Mr. James).

Children born to Annabelle (McDermott) and J. R. Anderson were Janie (b 1871; m H. Hughes; their daughter, Annabelle, m Mr. Payne), Benjamin (nev m), Smylie, Charles Gordon, and Gurvin.

Children born to Catherine Van Court (McDermott) and Elbert Lambert were Nona (b 1871; m E. O. Cornish; their children: Ruth [b 1893; d 1897], Joseph [b 1895], Edith [b 1896], and Winna [b 1897]), Lucy (b 1872; nev m), Scott (b 1873; m George Knox), Cecil (b 1884; nev m), Annabelle (m Dr. M. C. Crandall of Wilmot; their daughter: Marguerite, m William Mart), and Kenneth (b 1890).

Children born to Maggie (McDermott) and Joe B. Mercer were Kate (b 1876; m V. Bordeaux, 1897; their children: Mercer [b 1899;d 1900] and Hazel [b 1901]), Eula (b 1877; m James Bennett; their children: Robert Hilton [b 1899] and Joe Mercer [baptized 1905; d 1964; nev m]), Mary Annie (b 1879; d 1880), May Wayne (b 1881; d 1882), Ethel (b 1883; d 1887), Charlie (b 1885), and Ethel (b 1887; m Carl Helmstater; their children: Carl Jr. [d 1942] and Mary [d age 11]).

Children born to Lula (Kinabrew) and Edward Ozan McDermott were Harry Edward (b 1896; d 1973; m Elizabeth Lewis; b 1903; d 1990) and Rosa (b 1894; d 1985; m Roe Hollis; no children). Children born to Elizabeth (Lewis) and Harry Edward McDermott were Harry E. Jr. (m Mary Alice McClellan) and Mary Rosalind (b 1922, Wilmot; d 1990; m James C. Lawson). Children born to Mary Rosalind (McDermott) and James C. Lawson were Suzanne (m Castle), James Jr., and William.

Charles M. McDermott was born 22 Sept 1808 in West Feliciana Parish, LA, the son of Emily (Ozan/Ozenne) and Patrick McDermott. Emily Ozan/Ozenne, mother of Charles McDermott, was the daughter of Marguerite (Decuir) and Jacques F. Ozenne. She died 1832 at Pointe Coupee, LA. Marguerite Decuir was born 17 Dec 1743, the daughter of Genevieve (Mayeux) and Jean Francois Decuire who were married 5 Nov 1743 in New Orleans. Genevieve Mayeux was born in New Orleans, the daughter of Marie (Sellier) and Pierre Mayeux, who died 1747. Jean

Francois Decuire was born c1704 at Mirge (Diocese Treves) France, the son of Marie Catherine (Tomes) and Albert Decuire, who was born c1662 and died Oct 1750.

Jacques F. Ozenne, maternal grandfather of Charles McDermott, was born at New Orleans, the son of Charlotte Julie (Moreau) and Jacques Ozenne, who were married 10 Nov 1727. Charlotte Julie Moreau was the daughter of Jeanne (Damourette) and Joseph Moreau. Jacques Ozenne was born in New Orleans, the son of Marthe (Damoulin) and Phillipe Ozenne.

Patrick McDermott, father of Charles McDermott, was born 23 May 1803, in Doun County, Ireland, the son of Agnes (Lauvage) and Guilaume McDermott. He died c1813-14 at Pointe Coupee, LA. Guilaume McDermott was born in Doun County, Ireland.

Ella Jenkins, wife of Philander McDermott, was born in 1853 in Amite County, MS, the daughter of Sarah A. (Daniels) and Remzen P. Jenkins. Sarah A. Daniels was born 1830 in Amite County, the daughter of Eliza (Jackson) and John M. Daniels, who were married 13 Jan 1825. Remzen P. Jenkins was born 25 Jul 1825 in Amite County, the son of Janet (Perkins) and William Jenkins, who were married 2 Sept 1824. Janet Perkins Jenkins was born 22 Feb 1802 and died 12 Mar 1870. William Jenkins was born 1797 and died 30 Sept 1875.

Hester Susan Smith, wife of Charles McDermott, was born in 1818 in Adams County MS, the daughter of Anabelle (Scott) and Benjamin Smith. Annabelle Scott was born 1793, the daughter of Susanna (Miller) and John T. Scott Sr. She died 18 Jul 1886 at St. Francisville, LA. Benjamin Smith was born 19 Jan 1792 in Natchez Territory, the son of Esther (Brashear) and Philander Smith. He died Jun 23 1826 in St. Francisville, LA. Esther Brashear was born 1765 the daughter of Catherine Lucy (Belt) and Benjamin Brashear. She died 21 Oct 1801 at Natchez, MS. Catherine Lucy Belt was born 18 Mar 1729-30 in Prince George's County MD, the daughter of Margaret (Queen) and John Belt. She died there in 1773. Margaret Queen was born 1709 and John Belt was born 13 Mar 1707.

Philander Smith, grandfather of Hester Susan (Smith) McDermott, was born 11 Jan 1765 in Granville, MS, the son of Sarah (Cook) and Rev. Jedediah Smith. He died 29 Jun 1824 at Second Creek, Natchez District. Sarah Cook was born 31 Oct 1731 at Windsor, CT, the daughter of Mary (Brooks) and Nathanell Cook Jr. Jedediah Smith was born 1 Jan 1726-27 at Suffield, CT, the son of Christiana (Owen) and Ebenezer Smith II. He died 2 Sep 1776 at Natchez District. Ebenezer Smith II was born 1699, the son of Sarah (Huxley) Barlow and Ebenezer Smith. Sarah Huxley was born at Suffield, CT, the daughter of Sarah (Spencer) and Thomas Huxley. Sarah Spencer was born c1646, the daughter of Sarah (Bearding) and Thomas Spencer. She died 24 Aug 1712 at Suffield, CT. Thomas Spencer was born 29 Mar 1607 and died 11 Sept 1687. Ebenezer Smith was born

1668 (baptized 1669, Hadley, MA), the son of Mary (Ensign) and Samuel Smith. He died Sep 1728. Mary Ensign was born c1636 at Northhampton, MA, the daughter of Sarah (Elson) and James Ensign. She died 2 July 1723 at Suffield. Sarah Elson was born c1611 and died May 1676. James Ensign was born c1607 and died Nov 1670. Samuel Smith was born 27 Jan 1638-39 at Wethersfield, CT, the son of Dorothy (Cotter) and Rev. Henry Smith. He died 10 Sep 1708 at Hadley, MA. Dorothy Cotter (second wife of Henry Smith) was born 1611 in England and died 1676 in CT. Henry Smith was born 1588 and died 1648.

(Philander Smith's brother, Luther L., married Anna Eliza Davis, eldest sister of Jefferson Davis, the president of the Confederacy. Jefferson Davis married Sarah Knox Taylor who was the daughter of General Zachary Taylor. A story passed down through time alleges that "Old Rough and Ready," as the general was fondly known, passed through the present town of Dermott while surveying a route for the Indian removal. Following the Gaines Landing Road, which led from Gaines Landing on the Mississippi, he paused to rest under a large oak and blazed it with an axe. Located at the corner of Gaines and Pecan Streets near the Golden house and in front of the store once there, the tree was known as the "Zachary Taylor tree" for many years. The tree still stands although the mark is no longer evident. Luther Smith's plantation, Locust Grove, was near St. Francisville, LA. Buried in Locust Grove Cemetery, preserved in 1937 by the Louisiana State Parks Commission, are several people of historic interest: Sarah Knox (Taylor) Davis (died in 1835 of malaria during a visit to Locust Grove), General Eleazor Wheelock Ripley, (a hero of the War of 1812 who was married to Luther Smith's niece, Aurelia Smith), Dr. Ben Davis (a brother to Jefferson Davis and the first husband of Aurelia Smith), and Anna Eliza Davis Smith.)

Ella Mae McDermott, daughter of Arthur McDermott and great-granddaughter of Dr. Charles McDermott graduated from Dermott High School, earned a B.S.E. from Arkansas A&M, a M.S.E. from Arkansas State Teachers College, and taught in Arkansas public schools for thirty-two years. Ella Mae married Austin White, who was born 21 Aug 1916 west of Portland, the son of Alma Coleman "Colie" (Howie) and Jacob Ferrel "Jake" White. Children born to Ella Mae (McDermott) and Austin White were John Austin Jr. (m Mary Elizabeth Quarles) and Linda Carole (m Donald Kent Switzer). They have four grandchildren and four great-grandchildren.

Children born to Rosella (Hunter) and Arthur Floyd McDermott, son of Arthur McDermott, were Rosalie (m Lee E. Johnson), James Arthur (m Marilyn McKee), and Floyd Hunter (m Nina Abernathy).

C. S. Williamson

C. S. "Sam" Williamson was born in 1918 at Pine Bluff, the son of Esther Dunlap (Triplett) and C. S. Williamson Sr. Esther Dunlap Triplett was born at Pine Bluff, the daughter of Estelle (Holland) and Charles Hector Triplett Jr. Their other children were Charles Hector III (m Elizabeth Hearne), Gerald (m Pearl Stroude), Arthur (m Vashti ?), and Frank (m ? Hearne, a sister to Elizabeth). Estelle Holland was the daughter of Hannah and W. H. Holland.

Charles Hector Triplett Jr. was born in 1850 at the Triplett home, Morven, about a mile north of Tucker (Jefferson County), the son of Esther Ann (Dunlap) and Charles Hector Triplett Sr. Their other children were Sarah Lindsay (b 4 Nov 1833; m John Leonados Buck; d 2 Jan 1911), Margaret Ann (b 11 Nov 1836; d 18 Aug 1837), Jane Richards (b 18 Jul 1838; d 24 Jul 1839), Marion Dunlap (b 10 Apr 1840; m William W. Lindsay; d 4 Feb 1910), Virginia (b 3 May 1842; d 7 Dec 1842), Charles Hector (first son so named; b 17 Oct 1843; d 10 Aug 1849), and John Edward (b 18 Jan; d 16 Jul 1849). Charles Hector Triplett Sr. and Esther Ann Dunlap were married in VA on 7 Feb 1833.

In 1846 the couple with their surviving children, Sarah (age 13), Marion (age 6), Charles (age 3), and John (an infant), "left Virginia in a covered wagon, drawn by oxen...travelled across the Allegheny Mountains to a landing on the Ohio River. There they boarded a steamboat and journeyed down the Ohio to the Mississippi River, down it to the Arkansas River and up it to a landing near the present site of Rob Roy, about 13 miles northeast of Pine Bluff, which was then a small village. Then they continued overland to a bluff on the west side of the Arkansas River about 3 miles east of Redfield. Old maps name the site Triplett Bluff, which is now included in the Pine Bluff Arsenal."[6] They later moved onto a plantation north of Tucker.

Charles Hector Triplett Sr. was born August 18, 1809, at Round Hill, Fairfax County VA, the son of Sarah "Sally" (Lindsey) and George Triplett, who were married in December 1805. Their other children were George William (b 28 Jun 1807), John Thomas (b Jan 1812), William Walter (b 2 Jun 1814), Helen Marion (b 19 Sep 1817), Francis Frederick (b 29 Mar 1819), and Catherine Ann Sarah (b 5 Jul 1821). George Triplett died 6 Oct 1821 and Sarah Lindsay Triplett died 29 Apr 1837. It is believed, but not substantiated, that George Triplett was descended from William Triplett of England.

Charles Hector Triplett Jr. entered the business world at age eighteen as a clerk in Pine Bluff. After four years, he began a real estate venture that proved to be remarkably successful. One of his most interesting real estate purchases occurred in 1909 when he bought 2,100 acres along Bayou

Bartholomew from the heirs of the Jefferson Davis estate. (See historical text.) He bought the assets of the failed Bank of Pine Bluff and established the National Bank of Arkansas of which he was president. In addition to his business associations, he also served as a public official holding the offices of county treasurer (1888-1892) and sheriff (1894-1898). His election to sheriff in 1894 was notable as it marked the first Democrat to be elected after Reconstruction. The C. H. Triplett Company (farming interest) consisted of the children of Charles Hector Triplett Jr., and all land is still currently owned by their heirs.

⚜

Estelle Kimbrell Works and W. A. Kimbrell

Estelle Kimbrell Works was born June 8, 1926, at Big Bend in Cleveland County, and W. A. "Dub" Kimbrell was born October 1, 1930, at Bellaire, the children of Virgie (Payne) and Vester "Vess" Kimbrell. Their other children were Leon (m Virginia McGarity), Grady (m Janice Ashcraft), D. H. "Dee" (m Marjorie Pruitt), Hughey (m Shirley Ezell), Gene (m Emma Gibson), Dolores (m Larry Williams), Birdie (m J. T. Sims), and Carmen (m Edward Walls). Vess Kimbrell was first married to Minnie Slayton, and they had one child, R. C. (m Marie Works).

Vess Kimbrell was born 28 Jan 1889 at Herbine, Cleveland County, the son of Adderianne "Addie" (McKinney) and Harrison Kimbrell, M.D. Addie McKinney was born at Herbine, the daughter of Mary E. (Tucker) and Norman Augustus McKinney. Virgie Payne was born 23 Feb 1910 at Big Bend, the daughter of Carrie (Nichols) and William Payne. Vess Kimbrell moved his family to Panther Brake Plantation, located on Bayou Bartholomew between Baxter and Lake Wallace, in 1936. He was employed by the plantation, which was owned by the Sterling Hartwell/Henry Hennegin Tucker family of Little Rock, as a blacksmith and also farmed. The children attended school at Baxter. In 1939 the family moved to the June Gibson plantation near Boydell.

Estelle Kimbrell married Bertis Works, the son of Effie (Maroney) and Leroy Works. Children born to Estelle (Kimbrell) and Bertis Works were Barbara (m J. D. White), Patricia Ann (m Charles Witcher, div), Danny (m Phyliss Spakes), and Ronny (m Linda Cook). They have six grandchildren and three step grandchildren. Dub Kimbrell married Martha Cornett, the daughter of Madelyn (Utter) and Clyde Cornett. Children born to Martha (Cornett) and Dub Kimbrell were Karen (m Jeff Loveless) and Angie (m Steve Gentry). They have three grandchildren.

⚜

Additional Family Histories

Chester Arrington
Related by Loyce Arrington Armstrong
and submitted by Dorothy Mack

Chester Arrington was born around Crossett or Hamburg and had no brothers or sisters. He was orphaned at the age of two and went to live with his grandfather. Chester Arrington married Jeanette "Nettie" Franklin, and their children were Loyce, Ruby, Lucille, C. W., Cecil, Clyde, Vernon, and Jeanette. The Arrington family moved to the Blanks place at Zachary around 1920. Later they moved to the other side of the bayou across from the school.

Loyce Arrington married George Armstrong 28 Nov 1928. Their children were Clay T. (child: Samantha), Bobby (children: Pam and Rod), and Ella Dean (m Vining; children: Theresa, Marty, and Keith).

※③⓪④

The Bishop Family of Dermott
Submitted by Amy Bishop Flowers

Charles J. Bishop was the fourth of twelve children born to James Abner "Ab" and Talullah Irene Adalaide "Lula" (Lyle) Bishop, his worldly entrance being on 1 Feb 1888 in Rock Springs, Drew County AR. After his mother's death in 1905, his father married a second time to Emma Norton, and to this union three children were born. The other fourteen sons and daughters of Ab Bishop, in their order of birth, were: Thomas Fred, Carroll Wood, Earnest B., Verda May, Roy Fennard, James Gervis, Guy, Ouida Bell, Harry Will, Barcey Abner, Jay L., Elizabeth Theresa, Curry Abner, and Major Van.

Ab Bishop, born 19 May 1858 in Jefferson County AR, was the son of Elizabeth (Bassett) and John J. Bishop. His siblings, three older and three younger, were: Nancy, Della, Jabus Lafayette Monroe Currey, Thomas J., Charles J., and Jonathan. Ab's parents moved from Bibb County AL to Jefferson County in 1857 along with some of his mother's family. After his father's death in 1864, his mother moved the family to Drew County to be nearer relatives.

John J. Bishop, father of Ab and grandfather of Charles, was born 11 Feb 1829 in Madison County AL. His father, John W. Bishop, b 1792 in TN, held the office of AL state senator in 1841 and served in the AL legislature from 1853-55. John J. Bishop's mother was the former Sarah Hamblin (b

1792; d 1849, Talladega County AL), daughter of John and Margaret Hamblin. John W. Bishop was born 1792 in TN, the son of Elizabeth (Wilson) and Joseph Bishop. Elizabeth Wilson was the daughter of Samuel Wilson Sr. Joseph Bishop was born 1760 or 1761, in Hawkins County TN by 1787, and died in Morgan County AL March 1828.

Charles J. Bishop moved from Monticello to Dermott about 1908. He was a painter and paperhanger by trade. He married Nora Tarrant Neel in Hamburg, AR, on 10 Jul 1910. She was born 2 Oct 1892 in Jones, LA, the daughter of Ella Evelyn (Tarrant) and John Robert Neel. Nora's mother had previously been married to Osborne Morris Honeycutt, and after his death she married his cousin, J. R. Neel.

Charlie and Nora Bishop made their home in Dermott where they both died in 1974. Their children were:

1. James Carroll, b 2 Jun 1911; d in Dermott on 31 Dec 1924 when the school bus accidentally ran over him.
2. Charles Ernest, b 22 Aug 1912; m Hariett Mackrell Wilson; two children: Fred Carroll (b 1939; m Stella Pugh) and Kay Charlene (b 1942; m Bill Lantz). Charles Ernest Bishop later married Donna Kay Adcock of Dermott, and they reside in IL.
3. Louise, b 22 Sep 1913; m Cecil Marvin Dennington; three children: Cecil Herbert "Denny" (b 1938; m Katherine Crabtree), Christine (b 1948; m 1st ? Lincoln; m 2nd Richard Brister), and Irene (b 1950; m Richard Wooten).
4. Robert Abner, b 20 Nov 1914; m Eddy Marion Joyce of Wilmar, Drew County; child: Bob Edd (b 1942; m 1st Marcia Weidmyer; m 2nd Pat Harding.
5. Martha Anne, b 20 Jun 1916; d 16 Apr 1999; m John Sylvester Chandler; children: Cynthia (b 1946; m 1st Donald Ramsey Walker; m 2nd Gerald Dean) and Rilla Sue (b 1953; m Robert Anderson Graham).
6. Mary Nell, b 2 Nov 1917; m Theron Allen Crowder; children: Carol Louise (b 1939; m 1st Bobby Wray Herren; m 2nd Robert Kenneth Evans) and James Lewis (b 1940; m Tommie Joe Johnson).
7. Paul, b 26 Oct 1918; m Maysie Jeanice Oxford; children: Beverly Jane (b 1950;) and Elizabeth Ann (b 1955).
8. Mildred, b 14 Jan 1920; m Roscoe Vernon Bates; children: Nonie (b 1946; m Melvin Carpenter) and Sherry Beth (b 1950).
9. Evelyn, b 2 Oct 1922; d of pneumonia 30 Jun 1923.
10. William Carl "Bill," b 13 Sep 1927; m Edna Earle Bordeaux of Monticello; child: Amy Eileen (b 1955; m 1st Philip Anthony Belin, div; m 2nd James Edward Flowers; children: Philip Anthony, William Christopher, and Kelly Amanda Flowers. Amy Eileen Bishop Flowers died 16 Jul 2000.

Reese Bowden
Submitted by Geneva Clampit and edited by the author

Reese/Reece [the name is spelled Reese and Reece in court records, Reese in census records, and both ways in the family Bible] Bowden was born in Franklin Parish LA in 1809 according to his tombstone. However, he was 37 in 1850 according to the census and age 35 when he married in 1847, which indicates he may have been born 1812-13. His sister, Martha "Mollie", married Stephen Gaster. Other of his siblings may have been Jesse, Lemuel, John, James, Elizabeth, and Sarah. Sarah Bowden married John Smith, who settled on the bayou between Dermott and Baxter in the 1810s. (According to Mildred Bowden Oglesby, Jesse Bowden married Martha Ann Wiley, who was the daughter of Dovey (?) and Edward Wiley. The 1850 census lists Jesse Bowden, age 28, in his household with Katharine, age 26, born in LA; Mary E., age 8, born in AR; James, age 10, born in AR; Martha , age 6, born in AR; and Katharine, age 2, born in AR.) By 1830 Stephen Gaster and Edward Wiley were also living in the area. Reese Bowden arrived in 1831 or 1832, and in 1833 married Nancy Wiley, the daughter of Edward Wiley.

Elizabeth Bowden married first George McDermott and their children were Loula, Annie (m Wiley Cruce), and Charlie (b 10 Feb 1870). Elizabeth's second marriage was to Bob Riley, and their children were Jim, John, Willie, Walter, and Tom.

Children born to Nancy (Wiley) and Reese Bowden were Edward (b 23 Aug 1835; d 23 Jun 1911), Jesse (b 10 Jun 1837), Miranda (b 15 Dec 1839), and Sarah (b 15 Oct 1844; evidently m Ferguson Gilliam; see court record below). On 30 Jan 1847, Reese Bowden (age 35) married Diantha Louise Hall (age 18). She was born 1 Nov 1829 in Canton, Wilcox County AL, the daughter of Elizabeth (Bartell) and Elizur Hall, who were married 25 Dec 1828. Children born to Diantha (Hall) and Reese Bowden were Lemuel Henry (b 10 Sep 1848; d 1850), Mary Elizabeth "Lizzie" (b 24 May 1850), Katie/Kate (b 23 Dec 1854), Reece/Reese (b 15 Feb 1856), Montriuele Taylor (b 10 Sep 1862; d 28 May 1869), William Edward "Will" (b 13 Feb 1864; d 5 Jun 1937), Ida Bell (b 21 Apr 1867; d 8 Dec 1934; m ? Murphy), Maude Louisa (b 23 Apr 1872; m Tom Biggs), and Missouri (b 3 Jan 1874; d 12 Sep 1882). Reese Bowden died in 1883 and was buried in Old Troy Cemetery.

Will Bowden, son of Nancy (Wiley) and Reese Bowden, married Amanda Grant on 17 Aug 1887. He was 22 and she was 18. Their children were Ruth (oldest ch; bu at New Troy Cemetery), Willie Bell (b 12 Oct 1891), Claude (b 13 Jul 1894; d 5 Aug 1940), Rita Maude (b 2 Oct 1897), Everett (b 4 Jan 1901; d 18 Jul 1905), and Howard Clifford (b 31

May 1904; d 4 Nov 1975). Will Bowden died 5 Jun 1937, and Amanda (Grant) Bowden died 29 1913. Both were buried at Old Troy Cemetery.

Amanda Grant was born 29 Sep 1869. Drew Grant was born 15 May 1864, died 27 May 1926, and was buried in McArthur Cemetery. John Grant, dates unknown, was possibly buried in Graves or Jordan Cemetery. Mollie Grant was buried at Ebenezer Cemetery in Bradley County.

From Chicot County, Book of Deeds and Records, Book B, page 396: "Bond Lewis Johnson to Reece Bowden land on Bayou Bartholomew, range 14. Oct. 28, 1834."

From Drew County, Book of Deeds and Mortgages, Book B: "Before Aug. 18, 1860 – Guardianship of Bowden heirs. Comes Reece Bowden, guardian of Edward Bowden, Jesse Bowden, Miranda Bowden, Ferguson and Sarah Bowden Gilliam, and presents to the court showing his petition that he as such guardian has received from the estate of Edward Wiley (father of Nancy Wiley Bowden, deceased) in right of his said children and now in his possession as their property the following slaves, names Tom, a negro man, Lewis, a negro man, and Judy, a negro woman and her increase, that said slaves have never been divided or distributed between his said children, and they have arrived at the age that entitles them to the control of their property and are desirous of having said slaves divided among them according to their respective shares and praying the court to appoint three discreet persons to value and divide said slaves among his said wards, and upon consideration of said petition, the court appoints Benjamin Collins, W. R. Smith, and Everett Skipper to make said division. E. R. Haynes, Judge."

❦

Campster, Keahey, Jackson, Tubb, Williams
by Frances Permilia Moffett Lawrence Campster

Samuel Roswell Campster, was born August 2, 1827, in Catahoula Parish, Louisiana, and died June 27, 1898 at Garnett, [Lincoln County] Arkansas. Samuel was the son of Henry and Mary (Townsend) Campster and the grandson of George Campster from France. Samuel's mother Mary Townsend was from Ireland. Samuel Roswell Campster married Catherina Permilia Williams, born September 7, 1828 in Hinds County, Mississippi, on August 30, 1850 in Drew County, Arkansas. Catherina Permilia Williams was the daughter of Jacob Peter and Rebecca (Tubb) Williams. Catherina died on the 19th day of March, 1913 in Drew County, Arkansas.

During the Civil War, Samuel Roswell Campster served under Yell as a Private in Company A, 26th Regiment of the Arkansas Infantry. Civil War Pension records reveal that Samuel's wife Catherina Campster filed application number 6570 for Civil War Veterans Benefits. Samuel and Catherina lived in the Garnett, Arkansas area where records show Samuel owned land, and paid taxes on that land from 1859 through 1894. During their marriage, Samuel and Catherina Campster had nine children: 1. Mary Josephine Campster; born July 25, 1851; died November 25, 1851. 2. Elizabeth Jane (Betty) Campster; born February 20, 1853, married Able Brown January 9, 1871 (no other information available). 3. Lilla Ann Campster; born February 14, 1855, died July 17, 1856 in Drew County, Arkansas. 4. Permilia Theodocia "Docia" Campster; born March 25, 1857; died October 1930 in Arkansas; married January 3, 1874 in Drew County, Arkansas to James Jackson Keahey, born July 17, 1849 in Jackson Parish, Louisiana; died August 2, 1905 at Garrett, Arkansas. He was the son of George Pleasant and Susanna (Berry) Keahey. 5. John W. R. Campster; born October 7, 1858, died July 16, 1874 in Drew County; never married. 6. Francis Marion Campster; born October 7, 1860; died November 3, 1944; married in 1886 to Elizabeth Townsend. 7. George Washington Campster; born February 7, 1863; died July 23, 1908; married to Artelia Beulah Jones. 8. Martha Catherine (Dolly) Campster; born July 11, 1867; died August 8, 1954; married Charles Little Chambless February 17, 1884. 9. Emily L. Campster, born April 5, 1868; died September 9, 1868.

⁂

James Jackson Keahey

James Jackson Keahey, son of George P. and Susanna (Berry) Keahey, was born in Jackson Parish, Louisiana, July 17, 1849. James was married in Drew County, Arkansas on January 3, 1874 to Permilia Theodocia "Docia" Campster. Permilia was born in Drew County March 25, 1857, daughter of Samuel R. and Catherina Permilia (Williams) Campster James Jackson Keahey died at Garnett, Arkansas, on August 2,1905, followed by his wife Permilia, who died 1930 in Drew County. James Jackson Keahey was a farmer, and he and Permilia were the parents of ten children. The children were:

1. Henry Putnam Keahey, born November 17, 1877; died April 11, 1911;married first April 7, 1901 at Star City, Arkansas, to Lois Martin. Lois was born in 1876, and died July 8, 1904. Henry and Lois had two children, a son Coy Keahey, born February 1, 1902, and a daughter Lois Keahey, born July 8, 1904. Lois Keahey, wife of Henry died July 8, 1904. Henry's infant daughter Lois died in December of 1904. Henry's son Coy died September 16, 1908. Henry Putnam Keahey married second in Warren, Bradley County, Arkansas on May 24, 1905 to Lena Cobb, daughter of J. and Clara (Harris) Cobb. Lena Cobb was born October 19,

1882, and died January 19, 1925 at Hodge, Jackson Parish, Louisiana. Henry and Lena had two daughters prior to Henry's death in 1911. Firstborn was Clara Permilia Keahey on May 12, 1906; died February 13, 1973 in Monroe, Ouachita Parish, Louisiana. Clara Permelia was named after her two grandmothers. Clara married in Jonesboro, Jackson Parish, Louisiana August 14, 1924 to Francis "Jake" Lee Moffett, who was born August 22, 1898 in Jackson Parish, Louisiana. Francis Moffett died in Vinita, Oklahoma on July 28, 1962, and was buried July 31, 1962 at Jonesboro, Louisiana. Francis was the son of Jerry Y. and Mary "Mollie" E. (Taylor) Moffett. The second daughter of Henry and Lena Keahey was Willie "Bill" Oma Keahey, born September 26, 1907; died May 12, 1976 at Alexandria, Rapides Parish, Louisiana. Willie married in January of 1927 at New Orleans, Louisiana, to Charles Austin Gray. Charles was born February 7, 1907, son of Charlie B. and Lyndie (Reynolds) Gray, and died February 1, 1973, at Ruby, Louisiana. Willie and Charles were the parents of five children: a. Charles Henry Gray, named after his two grandfathers, was born January 28, 1928, in New Orleans; died April 1970 at Amite, Louisiana. b. Roy Marvin Gray, born June 8, 1929, in New Orleans; died October 1988 in New Orleans. c. Aubon "Billy" Oren Gray, born May 19, 1933, at Ruby Louisiana; died May 1978 at Amite, Louisiana. d. Gerald Neil Gray, born November 1, 1934; died January 16, 1987, at Corpus Christi, Texas. e. J. Roline Gray was born July 21, 1937, at Ollie, Louisiana.

2.   Martha Susana Keahey, born December 2, 1879, at Garnett, Arkansas; died July 20, 1965. Martha married William "Will" Alexander Goins on July 28, 1901, at Star City, Arkansas.

3.   James Albert Keahey, born March 1883 in Arkansas, died 1926 at El Dorado, Union County, Arkansas. James married Franky Chambless in 1903.

4.   George Samuel Keahey, born July 4, 1886; died June 3, 1943, in Drew County, Arkansas. George was a farmer, married first to Alice Gray, daughter of Jesse and Minnie (Fawn) Gray, and second to Ivey Graves.

5.   Pearl Keahey, 1888 – 1900.

6.   Olla Mae Keahey, born November 26, 1891, died May 18, 1972 at Camden, Ouachita County, Arkansas. Olla married Aaron Pledge on July 21, 1916, at Star City, Arkansas.

7.   Lilly Keahey, born December 1895; married John New.

8.   Thad Keahey, born March 1899; died February 1981, at Dumas, Arkansas. Thad married a widow Tabor, and the couple had no children of their own.

9.   Beatrice Keahey, born and died 1900.

10.   Velma Keahey, born and died young.

Jackson-Keahey Settlers of Garnett

Early settlers of Garnett, Arkansas, included the daughters of two Jackson sisters, who married two Keahey brothers. The Jackson sisters, Martha and Mary Jane, were daughters of Samuel and Christiana (Seals) Jackson, who married John and James Keahey, sons of William and Margaret Keahey of Scotland.

It is interesting to note that Samuel Jackson was an uncle of President Andrew Jackson. Samuel's brother was Andrew Jackson Sr., father of the president. Samuel and Andrew Sr. were sons of Hugh Jackson of Bonnybefor, Ireland; their lineage has been traced back to 1540 in Yorkshire, England. Christiana Seals Jackson was the daughter of William and J. (Winifred) Seals, whose lineage to Middlesex County, England has been recorded from 1636.

The first of the Jackson-Keahey marriages was in Moore County, North Carolina, about 1780 between James Keahey, born November 28, 1749, and Mary Jane Jackson. Mary Jane died during 1813 in Richmond County, North Carolina, followed by James who died September 18, 1823, in Wayne County MS. Margaret Keahey, daughter of James and Mary Jane, married George Jackson Keahey (her first cousin) on September 19, 1816. George was the son of John and Martha (Jackson) Keahey. John Keahey was born in 1750 and died October 26, 1823, in Wayne County MS. He was married in 1780 to Martha Jackson, who died April 1, 1824, in Wayne County.

George Jackson Keahey was born April 12, 1789, in Richmond County NC and died April 3, 1878, in Scott County MS. Margaret Keahey, born May 5, 1799, died May 1847 in Scott County. They are buried in Hillsboro Cemetery in Scott County. A large granite monument marks their graves, and inscribed on it is a list of their children and their spouses' names.

Their son George Pleasant Keahey, born October 17, 1825, in Scott County, married Susanna Berry February 12, 1845, in Scott County. Susanna was born in MS on August 30, 1828. Both died and were buried in Lincoln County AR; George on October 12, 1872, and Susanna on January 6, 1898. They are buried on the old Smith plantation east of Star City, Lincoln County.

Susanna Berry was the daughter of Stephen Berry and his first wife, who was born in Scotland. Stephen Berry was the son of German and Susanna (Bails/Bayles) Berry. German was the son of John Berry from Scotland. Susanna Bails/Bayles was the daughter of William Bails/Bayles of VA.

George and Susanna did a lot of traveling before they settled in the Garnett, Arkansas area. They were the parents of eight children:

1. William Abraham, born in MS, married Isador McGraw.
2. James Jackson, born in Jackson Parish, LA, married Permilia Theodocia Campster.
3. Margaret Keahey, born in TX, married J. C. Green.
4. Christian Keahey, born in TX, married James Chance.

5.　George Keahey, never married.
6.　John Keahey, born in TX, married Annie Summerford.
7.　Martha Keahey, born in AR, married Abner A. Hill.
8.　Andrew Keahey, born in AR, married Anne Throneburry.
(The Keahey Bible records, census records, and the Jackson and Seals research was by Emma B. Reeves. The Berry research is the work of the author, Frances Permelia Moffett Lawrence.)

≈≈⊚≈≈

Tubb, Williams, Campster

Garnett, Arkansas is a long way from England. However long the distance, settlers did make the trip, although indirectly, ending up in a small Arkansas community. John Tubb was born in 1700 in England and in 1725 married Rebecca (maiden name unknown.) Although John, a mariner, died at sea at age 35, prior to his death he and Rebecca had two sons that are known. William Tubb, son of John and Rebecca, was born in 1729 and died in SC in 1804. In 1752 William married Elizabeth (born 1730; died 1800 in SC) in NC. William Tubb was a Revolutionary War patriot who served in NC. George Tubb, older brother of William, was born in 1727 and died in 1802 in SC. In 1748 George married in NC to Mary (maiden name unknown), who was born in 1729 and died in 1802 in SC. George Tubb Sr. was also a Revolutionary War patriot, serving by furnishing horses to the army in NC. While George Tubb Sr. and his wife Mary had nine children, this article will focus on the line that came to the Garnett, AR area. George Tubb Jr. was born in NC in 1774 and died in 1833 in Perry County AL. George Jr. married in 1792 in SC to Elizabeth Jane Floyd, born 1777 in SC and died July 31, 1851, in Noxubee County MS. Her estate papers there list fourteen children. Her father, William Floyd, was also a Revolutionary War patriot who died in 1821 in Franklin County TN. His estate papers are located there. Of the fourteen children of George Jr. and Elizabeth, their oldest daughter, Rebecca Tubb, was born July 21, 1793, in SC. She was named after her grandmother, Rebecca Tubb, as was the custom. About 1811 Rebecca Tubb married Jacob Peter Williams, born 1783 in Jamestown, VA. Jacob died at Garnett, AR in 1849. His wife, Rebecca, died sometime prior to the 1860 census. Jacob Peter Williams was in the War of 1812, serving under General Andrew Jackson at the Battle of New Orleans. Rebecca and Jacob P. Williams were in Hinds County MS as early as 1811 where all eight of their children were born. The children were:
1.Susan Williams, born 1816, died May 20, 1850, at Hinds County MS. Married Carroll C. Tabor on December 25, 1834 and had four children.
2.Mary A. Williams, born 1820 and appeared on the 1850 census at Drew County AR. No other information.

3. Samuel Williams, born 1825, died before 1900 in Oklahoma Territory. Married Cynthia (maiden name unknown).

4 Isabell "Isias" Williams, born 1826, died before 1900 in Oklahoma Territory. Married in 1844 to Franklin "Frank" Cogbill.

5. Catherine Permilia Williams, born September 7, 1828, died March 19, 1913 in Drew County AR. Catherine married on August 30, 1850, in Drew County to Samuel Roswell Campster. (See Campster family history.)

6. George W. Williams, born 1831, died during Civil War.

7. C. W. Williams, born 1835, died before 1900 in Oklahoma Territory. Married Eveline (maiden name unknown).

8. Loucinda S. Williams, born March 8, 1836, and died March 1, 1920, in AR. She married Francis Marion McGraw, a half-brother to Samuel Roswell Campster. (See # 5, Catherine Permilia Williams.)

This information is from Bible records, estate papers, Revolutionary War papers, and the National Society of the Daughters of the American Revolution papers.

<hr />

Crute Lineage
Submitted by Dorothy Groh

Richard Crute Sr. (d 11 Aug 1746) married Mrs. Rebecca (maiden name unknown) Blincoe (b c1685-1690; d 17 Nov 1756). Their children were Frances (b c1728), Robert (b c1730; d bef 1756), Richard Jr. (b c1732; d bef 28 May 1767), and Catherine (b c1734). Richard Crute Jr. married (c1750) Hanna Lampkin who was born 21 Dec 1734 and died after 11 Feb 1805. Their children were John Lampkin Crute (b 1 May 1756; d 6 Oct 1840; m Rebeckah Smith 27 Oct 1785, Amelia County, VA), Catherine "Catey Dyke" (b c1758; d 1808), and Mourning (b c1767). Rebeckah Smith was born c1767 and died 17 May 1836.

Children born to Rebeckah (Smith) and John Lampkin Crute were Willis Richard Venable, M.D. (b c1786; d bef 1854; m 1st 12 Sep 1808, Prince Edward Co. VA, Susannah T. Watson {b c1788; d bef 1843}; m 2nd 20 Mar 1843, Mecklenburg Co. VA, Nancy T. {maiden name unknown} Dortch {b 1806; d aft 1870}), Mary "Polly" (b c1790; d aft 1854; m 18 Oct 1814, Prince Edward Co. VA, Thomas Ellington), Clemmonds (b 1793; d 8 Jan 1858; m 21 Dec 1816, Amelia Co. VA, Sally "Sarah Ann" Miller {b c1795; d bef 1858}), John Thomas (b c1795; d 10 Jan 1853; m 30 Nov 1815, Mecklenburg Co. VA, Martha A. Ligon {b c1799; d Dec 1858}), Samuel Smith (b c1797; d aft 1870; m 1st 5 Dec 1820, Prince Edward Co. VA, Nancy W. Lockett {b 1800; d bef 22 Jan 1833}; m 2nd c1830, VA?, Martha A. Pierce {b 1800-12; d bef 1870}),

Nancy (b 1799; d bef 19 Dec 1831; m 23 Mar 1820, Prince Edward Co. VA, Willis Armes {d bef 20 Aug 1821}), Venable (b c1800; d bef Oct 1880; m 25 Sep 1823, Prince Edward Co. VA, Louise V. Vaughan {b c1804}), Nelson K. (b c1802; d bef Jul 1854; m 20 Dec 1823, Cassandra G. Lockett {b 1803; d aft 1842), and Maria Martin (b c1811; d 19 Mar 1883; m 4 Oct 1831, Prince Edward Co. VA, Nathaniel M. Mottley {b c1810; d 29 Jul 1854).

Children born to Samuel Smith Crute (son of Rebeckah (Smith) and John Lampkin Crute) and second wife, Martha A. Pierce, were Henderson Pierce (b c1830; m Ellen S. ?), Isabella S. (b c1832; m 14 Aug 1845, Lowndes Co. MS, Alexander V. Winter M. D.), Edward S. (b c1834; d c1870; m 23 Sep 1858, Madison Co. AL, Sallie J. Spotswood {b c1839; d bef 1880}), Victoria C. (b c1836), Algernon Sidney (b 1838 probably in Columbia Co. GA; d aft 1901; m 8 Dec 1866 Hettie Susan McDermott {b 1 Jan 1848; d 30 Nov 188?}), and Ida (b c1840; d aft 1870; m Charles Childress).

Children born to Ella S. (?) and Henderson Pierce Crute were Katie B. (b c1863), Frank S. (b c1864), Ida (b c1869), and William (b c Jan 1870).

Children born to Sallie J. (Spotswood) and Edward S. Crute were Ida Belle (b 1859; m c Oct 1885, Madison Co. AL, James Gillespie), Carter Spotswood (b c1861; d 1899; m 1880, Mary Catherine Wagner {b 12 Jul 1865; d 22 Dec 1947}), Robert E. Lee (b c1866), Elliot C. (b c1869), Irene S. (b c1870), and Emma S. (b c1870).

Children born to Hettie Susan (McDermott) and Algernon Sidney Crute were John Owens "Buck" (b 5 Mar 1870; d 12 Sep 18??), Algernon Sidney "Babe" Jr. (b Feb 1871; d 1933; m Sally Flood), Henderson Pierce (b Jun 1873; d 1934; m c1902, Martha Cunningham {b 1874; d 1958), Edward Harrison "Punch" (b 1875; d 1940; m 1919, Cora Bulloch {b 1875; d 1940), and Hettie Elizabeth (b Jun 1880; d 1947; m Seborn William "Will" Crook {b 5 Oct 1878; d 11 Jan 1947).

Children born to Ida (Crute) and Charles Childress were Charlie (b c1862), Maggie (b 1865), Henderson (b c1867), and Adda (b c1868).

Children born to Mary Catherine (Wagner) and Carter Spotswood Crute were Robbie Lee (b 1881), Sallie Louise (b 1883), Emma (b 1886; d 1886), Anna Mae (b 1886; d 1886), John Spotswood (b 1889), and Birdie Lynn (b 9 Nov 1893; d 17 Jan 1958; m 25 Sep 1912, Kansas City, KS, John Harrison Swartz {b 10 Nov 1889; d 23 Sep 1967}).

Children born to Martha (Cunningham) and Henderson Pierce Crute were Hulbert Pierce (b 13 Sep 1903; d 23 Jan 1984; m Luna Belle Owens {b 31 Jan 1904; d 14 Jan 1988}), Mary B. (b c 1906), Kathleen (m Herburt Boothby) and Louise.

Children born to Cora L. (Bulloch) and Edward Harrison "Punch" Crook were Mary Ophelia (b 14 Jul 1911; m Harry W. Pickering {b 14 Feb

1910; d 17 Apr 1975}), Elizabeth Hettie (b 30 Mar 1916; d 22 Dec 1983; m J. C. Barnes {b 9 Jan 1910; d 2 Jul 1977), and Robbie Jeanette (b 7 May 1927; m Benjamin C. Turner Jr.)

Children born to Hettie Elizabeth (Crute) and Seborn William "Will" Crook were Daphne, Ruby, Ethel, Libby, Vivian (b 1912; d 1989; m Joseph G. Crook {b 1902; d 1982), Harold, and Henry.

Children born to Birdie Lynn (Crute) and John Harrison Swartz were Katherine Louise (b 9 Jun 1913), Martin Grant (b 30 Oct 1914; d 14 Mar 1980), John Carter (b 2 Oct 1918; d 27 Jun 1944), Carl Henry (b 7 Sep 1920; d 3 Dec 1980), Carleen Harriet (b 7 Sep 1920), Pauline Marjorie (b 8 Sep 1921), Robert Lee (b 27 Jun 1925; d 6 May 1926), Harriet Lynn (b 30 Jan 1927), Billie Joyce (b 14 Jul 1930; d 3 Jan 1984; m 1st 1946, Dwight, KS, Lowell Edwin Hoch {b 25 Sep 1928}; m 2nd 24 Dec 1949, Dwight, KS, James Lee Anderson Sr.{b 28 Jun 1925}; m 3rd 24 Aug 1972, Franklin Edward Sullivan {b 24 Aug 1920}), and Nora Ann (b 19 Jul 1935).

The only child born to Luna Belle (Owens) and Hulbert Pierce Crute was Norma Jean (m George Banks Collins).

The only child born to Mary Ophelia (Crute) and Harry W. Pickering was Jackie (m Leonard Soper).

The only child born to Elizabeth Hettie (Crute) and J. C. Barnes was Michael Crute (b 27 Feb 1945; d 25 Jan 1986).

Children born to Robbie Jeanette (Crute) and Benjamin C. Turner Jr. were Deborah Ann and Linda Gale.

(Additional information on this family supplied by the author from her book, Old Times Not Forgotten: A History of Drew County.   This information was obtained from Robbie Crute Turner.)

Hettie Susan McDermott, who married Algernon Sidney Crute, was the daughter of Elizabeth (Fairchild) and Edward McDermott. Their only other child was Edward Ann. Edward and Elizabeth McDermott both died when their children were young, and Edward's brother, Dr. Charles McDermott, raised the girls. Edward Ann McDermott married Robert Watkins Finn of Monticello, and their children were R. W. Jr., Charles, Tracey W., W. H., Mrs. Sam Cole, Mrs. M. E. Shewmake, and Mrs. V. B. McCloy.

John Lampkin Crute served in the American Revolutionary War. The Samuel Smith Crute family was living in Columbia County, GA, in the 1830s and later moved to Loundes County, MS, where he had large landholdings during the late 1840s into the 1850s. The family moved westward to AR, leaving some of the older children in MS. Samuel Smith Crute bought the "old Smith plantation," located on Bayou Bartholomew, from Charles McDermott. This land may have previously belonged to John Smith, an early settler and once a neighbor to Dr. McDermott.

Samuel S. Crute's children, Algernon Sidney Crute and Ida (Crute) Childress, settled in Drew and Chicot Counties. Algernon Sidney and Hettie (McDermott) Crute are buried in Rough and Ready Cemetery (at Monticello) in unmarked graves. Algernon Sidney Crute's sons, John Owens "Buck," Algernon Sidney Jr. "Babe," and Edward Harrison "Punch," all owned farms along the Old Troy Road south of Collins in Drew County.

✦✦✦

John Buford Daniels Family 1821-1963
From material compiled and written by Alma Daniels Barnett in 1963 and additional information submitted by Marian Daniels. Edited by the author.

William Allen Daniels was born in MS c1821 and died 25 Mar 1868. He married Caroline L. Buford who was born 7 Jan 1829 in Amite County MS. Children born to this marriage were Adella S. (m Robert Lowery of TX), John B. (m Annie Cannon), Ida I. (m N. S. Anderson of MS), Lily A. (m J. B. Krisel of Chicot County AR), William P. (moved to Chicot County), Coral L. (m W. S. Adams of Chicot County), Ernest W.(moved to WA), and Robert J. (d 1854 MS). The William Allen Daniels family moved to the Dermott area in 1858 where they bought land that ran from Bayou Bartholomew to Big Bayou. This area includes the South Trotter Street part of the town. The old Daniels Cemetery is behind Heritage Manor and contains the grave of William Allen Daniels. His wife, who died 7 Mar 1910, is buried in the Dermott Cemetery.

John B. Daniels, son of William Allen Daniels, married Annie Cannon in Dermott 29 Oct 1885. She was the daughter of Mary (Smith) and John Quincy Cannon of Shelby County TN. John Quincy Cannon was born 1820 in SC and died 1876. Mary Smith was born 1839 in TN and died 1884 in TN. Upon the death of Annie Cannon's mother, Annie moved to Dermott to make her home with her aunt, Mrs. Mattie Parish. Children born to Annie (Cannon) and John B. Daniels were Bertie Carrie (b 7 Sep 1887; m William J. Splawn), Robert Julius (b 30 Aug 1889), Alma (b 2 Jul 1891), John Buford (b 29 Dec 1895), and Erwin (b 15 Dec 1899; d Jun 1900).

Alma Daniels Barnett wrote, "That fall Mr. Daniels moved his family to the town of Dermott where he bought a house. At this time he gave up his farming interests and became County Surveyor and dealt in real estate. In 1910 he built a large house in the west end of Dermott on property he had acquired and which he divided and sold in town lots." John B. Daniels died 13 Feb 1913 and his wife died 27 Jul 1939.

Bertie Carrie Daniels, daughter of Annie (Cannon) and John B. Daniels, attended Hinemon University High School in Monticello and

Arkansas College in Batesville. She married 27 Jun 1911 William Splawn, son of Ann (Brooks) and William E. Splawn. William J. Splawn served as treasurer of Chicot County for eight terms. Children born to Bertie Carrie (Daniels) and William J. Splawn were John Erwin "Jack" (b 17 Jul 1912; killed in an automobile accident at Dyess, AR 4 Dec 1937; nev m), Annie Lois (b 29 Apr 1914; m Wilbur Ray North), William J. Jr. (b 11 Mar 1916; m Zelma Falls), Harold Blair (b 29 Apr 1919; m 1st Laura Frances Vick; m 2nd Rena {James} Carmack), and Roy D. (b 18 Feb 1919; m Mildred Thomas).

Robert Julius Daniels Sr., son of Annie (Cannon) and John B. Daniels, married Neva Kennedy. Children born to this marriage were Robert Julius Jr. (b 24 Jun 1916) and Harry David (b 18 May 1920). Robert Julius Daniels Sr. was a farmer and also worked as an overseer for others. Robert Julius Daniels Jr. married Jane Bulloch, daughter of Cora (Bird) and William Bulloch. Children born to Jane (Bulloch) and Robert Daniels Jr. were Danny (b 15 Feb 1946; d age 3 days), Donna (b 18 May 1948), and Carol Jane (b 6 Apr 1952). Harry David Daniels married Marian Myer of McGehee. Their children were David Allen (b 22 May 1950), Dinah Lynn (b 16 Aug 1952), Dale Edward (b 17 Nov 1958), and Donald Lamar (b 24 Aug 1965; killed in an automobile-bicycle accident 16 Jun 1974). The Harry Daniels family lives on the old Robert Daniels Sr. homeplace, which Robert bought around 1929. This location is about a half a mile from the original Daniels' land.

Alma Daniels, daughter of Annie (Cannon) and John B. Daniels, married Uzal Conditt Barnett, the son of Amanda (Phipps) and Robert Emmit Barnett of Hartford, KY. Uzal Conditt Barnett was teaching at the College of the Ozarks at Clarksville, AR, when he first married Frances Foster. Children born to this marriage were Ellis Foster (b 11 Apr 1905; m Thomas Lemuel Stanford) and Frances Victor (b 12 Nov 1908; m Alice Morin). Frances Foster Barnett died a week after the birth of the last child. Children born to Alma (Daniels) and Uzal Conditt Barnett were Robert Julius (b 17 May 1913; m Mary Bentley Spikes) and Charles Conditt (b 14 Aug 1915; m Mary Lee Mitchell). Uzal Conditt Barnett died 19 Dec 1958 at Dermott. John Buford Daniels Jr. married Florence Owen. Their only child was Betty (b 17 Feb 1925; m Turner C. Feezor). Children born to Betty (Daniels) and Turner Feezor were Betty Cole, John Daniels, and Robert Milton.

Elijah Ferguson Descendants
Submitted by Jessie "Cissy" (Ferguson) Thomas

John Ferguson, who was born 1722 and died 20 Dec 1794 in Culpepper County VA, is assumed to have been the father of Jesse, Alexander, Elijah, James, Samuel, William, John, Lewis, Elizabeth, Catron (m ? Coones), and Martha (m ? Pain).

Elijah Ferguson was born c1775 in VA and died c1840 in MS. He married Elizabeth Jackson, who was born 1786 in SC, the daughter of Thomas Jackson, a Revolutionary War veteran. (See below for Jackson lineage.) Elijah bought land on the Amite River in East Feliciana Parish LA. Children born to Elizabeth (Jackson) and Elijah Ferguson were Joseph W. (b 1807; m 23 Apr 1833 Mary Ann Hatchell), Aaron (b c1809 LA; m 1st Elizabeth Robinson; m 2nd Elizabeth Taylor), John Harvey (b 1812; m 10 Jul 1834 Lucinda Lee; m 2nd Sarah Haskew; d 6 Dec 1859), Eliza (b c1816; m Felix B. Collins), Matilda (b c1818; m 9 Sep 1836 in Carroll Co. MS John W. Lewis), Margaret (b 1823 LA; m 1st 31 Dec 1844 in Drew County AR, Elbeit A. Emmons; m 2nd 15 Jun 1853 in Drew County, Albert McCall), Elizabeth (b c1824; m 19 Nov 1844 in Carroll Co. MS, David D. Bain), Thomas F. (b 1828 LA), John Jackson (b 1828 LA), and Ann (b c1830; m Pleasant D. Robinson).

The 1860 Drew County census gives the following information on some of the children of Elijah Ferguson. Living in the household of Elizabeth (Ferguson) and David D. Bain (age 40) were Jinnetty (age 14; b MS), Jackson (age 12; b MS), and William (age 10; b AR). Living in the household of Martha J. (McCate ?) (age 22; b MS) and John Jackson Ferguson (age 40) were Thomas T. (age 2; b AR) and ? (age 6 months; female; b AR). Living in the household of Mary (Robinson) Ferguson (age 27; b AL; seamstress; widow of Thomas F.) were Charles O. (age 6; b AR) and Pleasant L. (male; age 2; b AR). Living in the household of Margaret (Ferguson) McCall (age 37; b LA) was Josephine (age 13; b MS). Elizabeth (Ferguson) Collins was evidently deceased by this time as her children were living with other members of the family: Martha (age 15; b MS; living with her aunt, Elizabeth Bains); Jane (age 13; b MS; living with her uncle, J. W. Ferguson); Bahannon/Rohannon (age 10; b AR; living with grandmother and uncle, Thomas Ferguson). (Mary (Robinson) Ferguson, wife of Thomas Ferguson, was listed as a widow in the census.) Living in the household of Ann (Ferguson) Robinson were James H. (age 11; b MS), Preston K. (age 5; b MS), Elizabeth C. (age 3; b MS), Mary I. Douglas (age 15; b MS), and Rufus (age 13, b MS). (It appears that the last two children were not her own.)

Joseph W. Ferguson, son of Elijah, moved with his family to Carroll County MS and then to Drew County AR. Children born to Mary Ann (Hatchell) and Joseph W. Ferguson were Edwin R. (b 1837 MS; m 29 Mar 1857 in Drew County, Victoria E. Rodgers), Martha J. (b 1843 MS; m 23 Jan 1861 in Drew County, William H. Baldy, who was b 1841), Leonidas (b 1848 MS), and Mary Ann (b 1850 Drew County; m 20 Dec 1860 in Drew County, George Hyatt Galor).

Eliza Ferguson, daughter of Elijah, married Felix Collins and their children, according to research by Ann Elizabeth and William Richard Ferguson, were Martha Jane (b 1837 MS), Rohannon/Bahannon (b 1840 AR), and Jenetta. According to the 1860 Drew County census, "Jinnetty" was in the household of Elizabeth (Ferguson) and D. D. Bain, and Bahannon/Rohannon, listed under Elizabeth (Ferguson) Collins, was living with his grandmother and uncle, Thomas F.

Margaret Ferguson, daughter of Elijah, married Elbeit A. Emmons and their only child was Josephine (b 1847 Carroll County MS). James Harvey Ferguson, son of Elijah, married Lucinda Lee, the daughter of John and Nancy Lee of East Feliciana Parish. Children born to Lucinda (Lee) and James Harvey Ferguson were William Jasper (b 3 Oct 1835 MS; m 11 Jul 1859 in Drew County, M. C. Rogers; m three more times), Benjamin Newton (b 21 Mar 1838 in Crystal Springs MS; m 15 Jan 1861, Susan E. Meyers; d 15 Jan 1861), Mary Louisa (b 1840 MS; m 6 Mar 1859 in Carroll County, Clayton Easterling; m 2nd James Cooper Merriweather), Wiley Worth, and John (b 1842; d young). James Harvey Ferguson moved to present Drew County in 1835. A mill owner, he died "from overheat and worthless doctor," according to a memoir by Benjamin Newton Ferguson.

William Jasper Ferguson, son of James Harvey, settled at Morrell in Ashley County. His sons by his first wife, M. C. Rogers, Guy and Worth, eventually moved to Texas. His first wife died and he then married Martha (Rorex) Davis, who was divorced from a Mr. Davis. She had two sons by Davis, and a daughter, Frances "Fannie," who married Robert P. Miller. Children born to Frances (Davis) and Robert P. Miller were Jessie Edna (m Sidney W. Ferguson), Willie Cleo (m Sam Ferguson), and Samuel G. (See below.) Jessie "Cissy" (Ferguson) Knoll Thomas, daughter of Jessie Edna (Miller) and Sidney W. Ferguson, wrote, "My father went to Morrell (Boydell) in the late 1880s to visit his relative, William Jasper Ferguson, who was by this time married to my grandmother, Martha Rorex Davis Ferguson. While Sidney was on this visit he met my mother, Jessie Edna Miller, and his cousin, Lee Ferguson, also of Clarendon, met her sister, Willie Cleo Miller. Sidney wed Jessie, and Lee wed Willie, and they both went to Clarendon. Jessie's mother, Frances, and brother, Sam, followed. Soon after this, Jessie's grandmother, Martha Rorex Davis Ferguson got a divorce from William Jasper Ferguson, and he married a sister-in-law of Martha who had been married to Martha's brother, Jim (?) Rorex, then deceased. She [the sister-in-law] was much younger than Martha and took William away from Martha. Martha then went to Clarendon to live with the other kin. William Jasper Ferguson sold his Morrell farm (now the Jack Gibson farm) and took his new wife to around Monticello to live."

Mary Alice, daughter of Mary Louisa (Ferguson) and James Cooper Merriweather, married Enoch Simmons Guice. Their son, William W., married Bertha Lee Stinson, and their only child was Mary Alice (married Charles Bridewell). Bertha Lee Stinson was born in 1898 at Morrell, Ashley County, the daughter of Nellie Esther (Newton) and Simon Thomas Stinson. Simon Thomas Stinson was the son of Eliza Turquan (Bickley) and Micajah Stinson. The Micajah Stinson family migrated from Union Springs, AL, in 1880 and settled near Troy, Drew County. They later moved to Morrell and established a farm on Bayou Bartholomew.

Benjamin Newton Ferguson, son of James Harvey, was raised by his grandmother, Elizabeth (Jackson) Ferguson, after his mother died when he was young. Children born to him and Susan E. Meyers were S. Alpha (b c1861 Drew County; d 1891 at Bell, TX), Willie Roy (b 6 Apr 1875; m 20 Dec 1898, Mary Elma Childs; d Apr 23 1974), Nora (b 1878 Old Troy, Bell County TX; m Dr. J. D. Mickie; d 1934), Lillie (b 1880 Old Troy; m Dan Hooks; d 1958), and Pearl (b 16 Sep 1882 Old Troy; m Frank Boyd; d 1961). Benjamin Newton Ferguson went into partnership with a Mr. Johnson in Drew County, and they owned a dry goods and grocery store. He enlisted in Captain Wolf's Co., Monroe's Regiment of Cable's Brigade, leaving Susan and baby Alpha at home. During the war, the farm was lost, and Susan and Alpha ended up following the camp of Confederate soldiers. She then gained employment with a family in Cairo, ILL, and after they war the couple returned to the site of their lost farm in Drew County. In June 1870 the family left Drew County for Texas with three horses, a wagon, and $632. They traveled through north Louisiana and stopped in Waco, TX for five years where he worked as a carpenter. They then bought 1600 acres at Old Troy, TX and later sold it and bought three sections at Burk Station (now Iowa Park). It turned out that this land contained oil. Willie Roy Ferguson, son of Benjamin Newton, would become the first president of the Wichita Falls Bank.

Aaron Ferguson, son of Elijah, married Elizabeth Robinson and their children were John Ashford, Mary A., Margaret Caroline (m S. S. Heneningway), and Jesse B. Aaron married second in 1850 in Carroll County MS Mrs. Elizabeth Taylor, a widow. Her children by Taylor were George, Elizer J., and Sarah Caroline. Children born to Elizabeth Taylor and Aaron Ferguson were William P., Andrew Jackson, and Benjamin K. Listed in the Aaron Ferguson household in the 1850 census for Carroll

County MS were Aaron (age 33; b LA; farmer), Elizabeth Taylor Ferguson (age 28; b AL), John (age 11; b MS), Caroline (age 9; b MS), Elijah (age 7; b MS), George Taylor (age 11; b MS), Elizer (age 6; b MS), and Caroline (age 2; b MS). Aaron Ferguson died of black lung in Drew County in May 1860. Living in the household of Elizabeth Taylor Ferguson (age 36; b TN) were John Ashford (age 22; b MS; farmer), Mary A. (age 21; b MS), Caroline (age 20; b MS), Jesse B. (age 16; b MS), Elizer J. (age 15; b MS), Sarah C. (age 12; b MS), William P. (age 10; b MS), Andrew Jackson (age 6; b AR), and Benjamin K. (age 2; b AR). (There is a discrepancy in the birthplace of Elizabeth Taylor.)

Andrew Jackson Ferguson, son of Elizabeth (Robinson) and Aaron Ferguson married Luna Sutherland. Children born to this marriage were Sidney Walker and Minnie L. Luna Sutherland Ferguson died, and Andrew Jackson Ferguson then married Joanna Sutherland, said to be no relation to Luna. Listed in the household in the Monroe County AR 1880 census were: A. J. (age 26; b MS), Joanna Sutherland (age 24; housekeeper), S. W. [Sidney Walker] (son; age 4; b AR), M. L. (dau; age 2; b AR), and Wm. P. (brother [to Andrew Jackson]; age 28; b MS).

Sidney Walker Ferguson, son of Luna (Sutherland) and Andrew Jackson Ferguson, married Jessie Edna Miller, the daughter of Frances (Davis) and Robert P. Miller. Children born to Jessie Edna (Miller) and Sidney Walker Ferguson were Zola Mae (m Parker Henderson), Willie Andrew, Lena Cleo (m Richard Trice), Verna (m J. W. Mullins), Lillie Virginia (m John Boutwell), Sidney W. Jr. (m Norma Curry), Robert Lee (m Dorothy ?), and Jessie Frances "Cissy." Cissy Ferguson married Joseph Franklin Knoll and their children were Frances Jo (m Martin Roy Waltman Jr.) and Elizabeth Ann "Libby" (m Jerry Gill). Cissy Ferguson Knoll married second Dr. H. W. Thomas. She has three grandchildren and three great-grandchildren.

Elizabeth Jackson, who married Elijah Ferguson, was the daughter of Frances (Richardson) and Thomas Jackson. Thomas Jackson of Ann (?) and Thomas Jackson Jr. Thomas Jackson Jr. was the son of was the son of Mary (Miller) and Issac Jackson. Issac Jackson was the son Dorothy (Mason) and Thomas Jackson Sr. Thomas Jackson Sr. was the son of Margaret (Keete) and Richard Jackson. Richard Jackson was the son of ? and Anthony Jackson. Anthony Jackson was the son of Ursula (Hildyard) and Richard Jackson. Ursula Hildyard was the daughter of Jane (Thrvege) and Richard Hildyard. Richard Hildyard was the son of Emma (Rudson) and Sir Martin Hildyard. Emma Rudson was the daughter of Anne (Wooton) and Robert Rudston.

Frances Richardson, wife of Thomas Jackson, was the daughter of Hannah (Mitchell) and Arthur Richardson. Arthur Richardson was the son of Armarenthia (Smith) and John Richardson Jr. Armarenthia (Smith) was the daughter of Sabana (Smith) and Thomas Smith.

(Some of this information is from "Genealogy of the Descendants of Elijah Ferguson" which was compiled by William Richard Ferguson and Ann Elizabeth Ferguson in 1976. Other information is from *Genealogy of Wilkinson and Kindred Families*.)

꧁꧂

Grant, Stanley, Fuller
Submitted by Sandra Fuller Fisher

David Milton Grant and his wife, Nancy A. Waitts, moved from GA to DeBastrop Township lying west of Bayou Bartholomew in 1851. This township was named after him in 1889. David Grant started buying land and became a progressive farmer, raising corn, cotton, and wheat. He was the largest taxpayer in the township. His family consisted of Mary Frances, Elizabeth A., Joseph Pinckey, and John Milton. John Milton Grant was killed in the Civil War, and Joseph Pinckey married Alice Dean, both of whom died in their twenties. Elizabeth married Samuel Watkins. David Milton Grant (b 10 Jan 1818; d 15 Jul 1903), Nancy A. Waitts Grant (b 18 Jul 1821; d 5 Sep 1903), Elizabeth Grant Watkins (b 9 Jun 1846; d 23 Feb 1926), and Samuel Watkins (b 8 Jan 1841; d 15 Apr 1914) are buried approximately seven miles west of Wilmot at the old Montgomery place. Also buried there is Althena Beard (b 18 Jul 1871; d 23 Feb 1926), daughter of Mary Frances (Grant) and Thomas Stanley and wife of W. B. Beard.

Mary Frances Grant married Thomas Stanley in 1860. He enlisted in the Confederate army, suffered a gunshot wound through his face, was captured, and imprisoned by the Union army in Indiana. Mary Frances followed Thomas to the prison camp and later gave birth to their first child, a son Thomas M. "Purdy" Stanley. Their other children were six girls. Thomas and Mary Frances (Grant) Stanley are buried at Wilmot. One of their daughters, Mary Elizabeth "Johnnie", married William Sanford Fuller in 1886.

Mary Elizabeth (Stanley) and William Sanford Fuller lived at Parkdale where they owned land and raised their family. Their children were Kenneth (b 23 Jan 1887; d 8 Nov 1888; bu Parkdale), Leonard (b 28 Jan 1888; d 31 Oct 1888; bu Parkdale), William Lavell (b 15 Oct 1890, Parkdale; d 15 Dec 1972; bu Wilmot; m Mabel Evelyn Keene), John Wyatt (b Jun 1894, Parkdale; d Dallas), and Mary Frances (b Aug 1896, Parkdale; d Dallas, TX). William Lavelle Fuller attended school at Parkdale and Hamburg. When he was sixteen he entered the University of Arkansas, which he attended for two years. He enlisted in the U.S. Army in 1917 and served in France during WWI. In 1919 he married Mabel Keene in Dallas, TX, and returned to Wilmot to work on his father's farm.

Children born to Mabel Evelyn (Keene) and William Lavelle Fuller were Blanche Lorraine (m Bernard Lewis Goldstein), Kenneth Wyatt (m Marion Joy Wilson), Marian Francene (d young, 1926), Frances Lanell (d young, 1928), Virginia Jo (m 1st William Hurren; m 2nd Guy Dickey), William Lavelle Jr. (m Marlene Borman), Richard Lee (m Florence Smith), Joyce Raye (m 1st Charles Malone; m 2nd Kermit Carter), John Sanford (m Rochelle Bosivert), Donald Keene (nev m), James Larry (m Janie Rabb), Gloria Ann (m James Buckley), and Sandra (m Robert M. Fisher). Mabel Evelyn (Keene) and William Lavelle Fuller are buried on the old homeplace, now owned by Caine Wilder, across the bayou from the Grant Cemetery.

❦

Haisty, Harvey
Submitted by Carolyn (Haisty) Haisty

The Three Brothers: Matthew, James, and John Haisty

"At some point prior to 1848, three young men from NC made their way to Drew County AR and settled in Selma. The first evidence of their presence there is the marriage of Matthew to Mary 'Mournin' Sawyers on 30 Jan 1848. It appears that Mary was a widow with two children. Those children were listed in the 1850 census and have been identified as Sawyers. Other children found in that household were not Matthew's either. The family was in Springhill Township. The 1850 census shows John Haisty in Marion Township as head of household. Living with him was his brother, James, and a lady, Sarah, born in 1790 and presumed to have been their mother.

"Mary Sawyers Haisty died 5 May 1853, and on 25 Dec 1853 Matthew married Delaney Shumake Simmons, widow of Edward Simmons. Their child, Mary Emeline, the only known surviving descendant, was born in April 1857. By 1860 Matthew, Delaney, Mary Emeline, and two Simmons sons, Jesse M. T. and Alexander B., were living in Conway County AR. Stories about the rift in the Haisty family circulated for years, and the main one proved to be true. Matthew became a Union soldier, whereas his two brothers were Confederates. James died in Rock Island Prison in Illinois, where he was buried in a marked grave, and John was buried in Selma Cemetery in Drew County. His grave is marked with a Confederate tombstone, although no record has been found of his service. After Matthew left Drew County for the nest of Union sympathizers in Conway

County, the rest of the family lost all contact with him. Other families who apparently traveled with them were those of Shumake, Vaughn, and Cherry. Alexander B. Simmons, stepson of Matthew, became a prominent merchant in Solgohachia. Mary Emeline Haisty married William Fielder Scroggins there on 7 Dec 1890. No record has been found on their family.

"John Haisty remained on the Selma property that he had settled on by the 1850s for the duration of his life. His only son, Samuel Phillip, lived there and the land is still in the possession of some of his great-grandchildren. John Haisty donated land for the Selma Cemetery as well as for a black church and cemetery.

"On 27 Aug 1859, John Haisty married Permelia J. or I. Bartlett, the daughter of Rebecca (Hawks) and Churchwell Bartlett of Warren County, NC. Permelia's brother, Richard, and her sister, Mildred, also migrated to Drew County. Mildred married Ransom Smith Breedlove, nephew of John Harding Breedlove who brought a wagon train from GA that included the Peacock clan. Children born to Permelia and John Haisty were Sarah Rebecca "Sallie," Lucy Alice, and Samuel Phillip. Sallie and Phil married brother and sister, Thomas Brooks and Jessie Ida Harvey. They were the children of Mary Ann (Hamlett) and Jesse Sherwood Harvey who owned land adjacent to the Haisty farm at Selma. The Harvey family was from Halifax County NC and Hardeman County TN before moving to Drew County. Lucy Alice "Sook" married Booker Harper of Florence.

"On 20 Oct 1859 James Haisty married Harriet Elizabeth Peacock, daughter of Jared Peacock and his wife, Martha, who was the widow of Jacob C. Davidson. James and Harriet were the parents of twins, Matthew Randell and Martha Louise, and John Wesley. James died when the twins were four years old and John Wesley was near age two. Harriet later married Jennings D. Crowell, a widower with two children. The family moved to Gravelly, AR, leaving the Haisty boys with Jennings' daughter, Molly, who was married to Pearson Bond. John Wesley Haisty stated as an adult that he (and most likely his brother as well) was virtually an indentured servant to Pearson Bond. Apparently Martha Louise lived at least part of the time with her mother. Harriet had two children by Crowell, Lula Leticia (m George Carter Hunkapillar) and Harriet Elizabeth "Lizzie" (m Thomas M. Piercy). Harriet died 6 Oct 1872 soon after the birth of Lizzie, who Molly (Crowell) and Pearson Bond also raised.

"It is believed that all Haisty/Hasty families in the U. S. came from a James and Elizabeth Haisty who were in Southampton County, VA in the 1700s. The Haisty family originated in Ireland. James O'Neill Haisty of Australia, his brother, John Patrick, and a cousin, Annette Caswell, both of New Zealand, attended the Haisty reunion in Arkansas in 1998. Neill Haisty (his mother was an O'Neill) found the grave of his great-grandfather, who was born in Kilrea, Ireland, in No Town, New Zealand. While the relationship between the "Down Under" Haistys has not been established, it is believed that the families are related. There are many of the same names in both families - John, James, Matthew, and Samuel, for example – as well as physical resemblances, including red hair. In all the world, no other Haistys can be found." (By Carolyn Haisty)

Children born to Rebecca (Hawks) and Churchwell Bartlett were Permelia Isabel (b 1823-28 NC; d 2 Oct 1870 Selma; m 27 Aug 1859 at Selma, John Haisty), Caroline (b c1830), James Richard (b c1831), Dionitia (b c1833), Leonidas J. (b c1837), Mary W. (b c1838), Cinthie E. (b c1839), Thomas (b c1841), Susan (b c1843), and Mildred O. (b c1846; m 23 Mar 1872 in Drew County, Ransom Smith Breedlove). Churchwell Bartlett was born in Warren County NC in 1801, the son of Elizabeth and William Bartlett. Rebecca Hawks was born in Warren County in 1801, the daughter of Sally (Hicks) and Jeremiah Hawks.

Born to Sarah and unknown Haisty were Matthew (b 1814-19 NC; d 5 Oct 1903; m 30 Jan 1848 Drew County, Mary Sawyers; m 2nd Delaney Shumake), John (b 1818-20 NC; d 9 Feb 1893; m Selma AR, 27 Aug 1859 Permelia Isabel Bartlett), and James (b 2 Nov 1825 NC; d 31 May 1864 Rock Island Prison IL; m 20 Oct 1859 Selma AR, Harriet Elizabeth Peacock).

Descendants of John Haisty:

Children born (all at Selma) to Permelia Isabel (Bartlett) and John Haisty were Sarah Rebecca (b 31 Jan 1862; d 4 Sep 1935; m 28 Feb 1883 Thomas Brooks Harvey), Lucy Alice (b 1864; d 1946; m 11 Oct 1882 Booker Harper), and Samuel Phillip (b Jul 1869; d 2 Jan 1944; m 7 Mar 1894 Jessie Ida Harvey).

Children born (all at Selma) to Sarah Rebecca (Haisty) and Thomas Brooks Harvey were Edgar Lee Brooks (b 29 Nov 1883; d 23 Nov 1972; m 25 Dec 1907 Maggie Lee Spivey), John Melvin (b 13 Dec 1885; d Nov 1979; m 24 Nov 1918 Pearl Etta Hall), Benjamin Ingram Sr. (b 16 May 1888; d 10 Oct 1976; m 19 Jun 1921 Coy Rogers), Lenna Estelle (b 2 Sep 1891; d 16 Mar 1974; m 24 Dec 1916 Charles Delmas Appleberry), Jesse Stanley (b 11 Aug 1894; d 19 Jun 1970; m 31 Dec 1927 Ina Mae Groce), and Lois Lucy (b 13 Oct 1903; m 7 Sep 1933 Floyd Monroe Reep).

Children born to Maggie Lee (Spivey) and Edgar Lee Brooks Harvey were Jesse Stanley (m Dorothy Redmond), Fletcher Brooks (m Bernice Fish), Sarah Estelle (m Victor Romaine Boyd), Catherine Ruth (m William S. Padgett), and Ed Lee Jr. (m Nora Elizabeth Longacre). The only child born to Pearl Etta (Hall) and John Melvin Harvey was Mildred Lois (m Gayle Martin Smith). Children born to Coy (Rogers) and Benjamin Ingram Harvey Sr. were Merle Louise (m. Louis Peter Linneman) and Benjamin Ingram Jr. (m Betty Beard). The only child born to Lenna Estelle (Harvey) and Charles Delmas Appleberry was Sarah Olivia (m James Teeter Rogers).

The only child born to Ina Mae (Groce) and Jesse Stanley Harvey was Terry.

Children born to Claudia Isabel (Harper) and Joseph Benjamin Graves were Nina Bess (m Talbot Lee Cooper), Jeff Edward (m Iva Lee Watts), Floyd Lafayette (m Mildred Coneal Felts), and Ira Hilton (m Willie Faye Huie).

Children born (all in Drew County) to Lucy Alice (Haisty) and Booker Harper were Bessie May (b 25 Jul 1883; d 27 Jan 1963), Don (b Sep 1887; d 19 Oct 1958), Bill, Parse, Bob, Claudia Isabel (b 5 Apr 1885; d 15 Dec 1972; m Joseph Benjamin Graves), Sallie Viola (b 6 Mar 1892; d 15 Aug 1970; m James Earl Hoover), Otis, Katie Alice (b 26 Jan 1897; d 23 Apr 1981; m Robert Ezma Crain), and Jack (b 5 Aug 1906; d May 1984; m Marie Howard). Booker Harper was born in 1853, the son of Darius Marion Harper, and died in Drew County in 1916.

Children born to Sallie Viola (Harper) and James Earl Hoover were Mignon (m Tom Edd Henley), Lorraine (m George Washington Hays), and Royal (m Opal Lack). Children born to Katie Alice (Harper) and Robert Ezma Crain were Lawrence Eugene, Marnette (m ? Bennett), Evelyn (m ? Underwood), and Robert Ezma Jr. (m Betty Jane Hogue). Children born to Marie (Howard) and Jack Harper were James Booker (m Sue Pounders) and Terry Barton (m Monique ?).

Children born (all at Selma) to Jessie Ida (Harvey) and Samuel Phillip Haisty were Anna Lora, John Sherwood (b 14 Feb 1895; d 13 Feb 1963; m 14 Sep 1920 Grace Barton Brown), Willie Phil (b 17 Nov 1899; d 4 May 1943; m 9 Jun 1927 Lucy Mae Owens), Shirley Emmett (b 1902; d 1966 Germany; m Esther Beasley), Myrta Isabel (b 1905; d 1910-11), Jesse Brooks (b 1 Jan 1908; d 14 Jan 1983; m 19 Sep 1935 Inez Barrett), and twin to Brooks (b and d 1 Jan 1908).

Children born to Grace Barton (Brown) and John Sherwood Haisty were Reba Avanelle (m Joseph Hilman Poff), Sherwood Ellsworth (m Betty Jane Harshaw), Marian Jeanette (m John Alfred Glen Stanford), Paul Vernon (m Mary Jane Swancy; in 2nd Xiu), and John Dale (m Betty Lou Hogue). Children born to Lucy Mae (Owens) and Willie Phil Haisty were William Delbert (b 1929; d 1949) and Carolyn Mae (m John Stanley Haisty, son of William Preston, grandson of John Wesley, and great-grandson of James Haisty). The only child born to Esther (Beasley) and Shirley Emmett Haisty was Robert Winston (m Christa Renata Ossadnik). Children born to Inez (Barrett) and Jesse Brooks Haisty were Gwendolyn (m Owen David Stanford), Brooks Barrett (m Barbara Ann Akin; m 2nd Vikki Marie Colvert), and Linda Pauline (m Willie Earl Grant; m 2nd Lee Hays).

Children born to Carolyn Mae (Haisty) and John Stanley Haisty were Linda Carolyn (m Ronald Quentin Skelton), Brett Stanton (m Marilyn Rose

Carmody), Kimberly Susan (m Clay Rodney Farris) and Philip Preston (m Teresa Kay Walker).

Descendants of James Haisty:

Children born (all at Selma, Drew County) to Harriet Elizabeth (Peacock) and James Haisty were Matthew Randell (b 4 Oct 1860; d 1947; m 9 Oct 1884 near Collins, Drew County, Caldonie Langston), Martha Louise (b 4 Oct 1860; d 13 Apr 1898; m 17 Jul 1879 in Drew County, Noah Phillips), and John Wesley (b 8 Nov 1862; d 23 Sep 1941; m 26 Nov 1882 in Drew County, Martha Mahala Phillips.

Children born to Caldonie (Langston) and Matthew Randell Haisty were twins, Fronnie and Dona (b 12 Aug; d 28 Aug 1885 Drew County), Maudie Elizabeth (b 8 Jun 1894; d 11 Sep 1980; m Edward Collins; m 2nd Herbert H. Lemley), Minnie Mae (b 24 Aug 1896 at Haw Branch, Drew County; d 4 Feb 1978 at Dermott; m James Dennis Smith; m 2nd Reber Nathan Donaldson Sr.), Mattie (b 4 Jan 1900; d Sep 1989; m Jeff E. Duckworth), Verly (b 6 Aug 1902; d May 1987; m Clarence D. Wren), Lettie Lee (b 21 Jul 1906; d 26 Aug 1907), and Annie Lou (b 6 Jan ?; d 16 Jun ?). Caldonia Langston was born 1 Dec 1866 at Collins, AR, the daughter of Elizabeth (Biggs) and W. S. Langston, and died in Dermott, AR in 1954.

Children born to Maudie Elizabeth (Haisty) and Edward Collins were Bonnie C. (m Lillian Irene Jarrett) and Paul (m Doris Graves). Children born to Maudie Elizabeth (Haisty) and Herbert H. Lemley were Herbert Duane (m Dorothy Marie Griffin) and Donie Elon (m Robert H. Campbell; m 2nd unknown), m 3rd Francis Nung Lee). The only child born to Minnie Mae (Haisty) and James Dennis Smith was Elzie Lawrence (m Myrtle Marnett Ellington). Children born to Minnie Mae (Haisty) and Reber Nathan Donaldson Sr. were Dorothy May Jean (m Arlice Ray Douglas; m 2nd Herschel Acord; m 3rd Odes Calvin Herring Sr.), William Nathan (m Norma Ruth Abshire), Reber Nathan Jr. (m Thelma Joyce Gladden; m 2nd Laura Eugene Hoover), and Henry Matthew (m Vonnie Allen).

Children born to Martha Louise (Haisty) and Noah Phillips were Ophelia (b Jul 1880; m 27 Oct 1895 in Ashley County, John Henry Gilliam), Hattie Mae (b 1882; d 20 Nov 1904; m Oliver P. Miles), Catie F. (b 21 Mar 1889; d 21 Apr 1894), Ritchie May (b 24 May 1889; d 5 May 1900), S. K. (b 26 Apr 1892; d 19 Jun 1970; m 25 Dec 1916 in Cooper, LA, Wynona Jane Craft), and Matthew Wesley (b 26 Mar 1895; d 4 Aug 1982; m 30 Mar 1913 in Womack, LA, Mary Effie Harvey). Noah Phillips was born 5 May 1860 in Drew County, the son of Rhoda (Shepherd) and Chesley P. Phillips. Noah Phillips was later married to Frances Murray and Maggie (Marler) Burrough.

Children born to Ophelia (Phillips) and John Henry Gilliam were Henry P. (b May 1897), Mattie Eliza (b 30 Mar 1903; d 22 Sep 1985; m Bonnie T. "Scrouge" Towles; m 2nd James Melton Kellum; m 3rd Fred Dugger), Joseph (b 25 Mar 1905; d 21 Jan 1948; m Mary Estelle Pace), Alpha (b 24 Oct 1908; d 3 Jan 1974; m Goble Turpin), Alice Orell (b 29 Oct 1909 Hamburg, AR; d 16 Feb 1998; m William Milas Jackson Lemley), John Claude (b 17 Aug 1915; m Amy Jewel Pace), and Preston (d infant). John Henry Gilliam was born Feb 1871 in AR, the son of Anna Eliza "AnnE" (Green) and Joseph Guyger Gilliam, and died in 1928.

The only child born to Hattie Mae (Phillips) and Oliver P. Miles was Lavanna Mae (b Nov 1904; m ? Snow). Children born to Wynona Jane (Craft) and S. K. Phillips were Emry Alton (b 17 Mar 1918 in Almadane, LA; m Johnye Marion Green) and Emogene (b 10 Sep 1925 Pickering, LA; d 11 Mar 1990; m William Ray Buckliew). Children born to Mary Effie (Harvey) and Matthew Wesley Phillips were Cleo Effie (b 3 Jan 1915; m James Arthur Halbert), Virginia Eddie Mae (b 20 Jul 1918 Rosepine, LA; d 9 Jan 2000; m William Claud Montgomery), Daniel Matthew (b 30 Mar 1921; d 20 Sep 1948; m Marion Spivey), Harvey Eugene (b 9 Apr 1924; d 28 Jul 1978; m Nancy Jane Findley), Martha Louise (b 21 Mar 1933; m Thomas Herald Partridge), and Mary Ann (b 21 Mar 1933; d 24 Mar 1933). Mary Effie Harvey was born 23 Dec 1898 in AR, the daughter of Missouri Melissa (Wilson) and James Arthur Harvey.

Children born to Martha Mahala (Phillips) and John Wesley Haisty were Jesse New Year (b 1 Jan 1884; d 1962; m 1st Sarah Jane Carpenter; m 2nd Kittie Williamson), Carroll Wesley (b 21 Aug 1886; d 29 Mar 1922; m Nora Carpenter), Lucy Annie Elizabeth (b 21 Jun 1889; d 9 Dec 1890), John Quintin (b 20 Aug 1891; d 29 Aug 1975; m Alma Rial), Henry Erastus (b 3 Jun 1893; d Jul 22, 1900), William Preston (b 4 Dec 1896; d 10 Nov 1983; m Ecil Christina Wells) and Virgil Lee (b 20 Jun 1902; d 4 Feb 1936; m Winnie Estelle Scifres). Martha Mahala (Phillips) was the daughter of Rhoda Shepherd and Chesley P. Phillips.

Only child born to Sarah Jane (Carpenter) and Jesse New Year Haisty was Vera Juanita (b 23 Nov 1904; d 23 Mar 1983; m Ira "Tex" Gabbert). Only child born to Kittie (Williamson) and Jesse New Year Haisty was Nonie Maxine (b 14 Jun 1909; d 5 Oct 1981; m Duffy C. Lites). Children born to Nora (Carpenter) and Carroll Wesley Haisty were John Byron (b 1 Jun 1907; d 18 Apr 1969; m 1st Mary Louise Rash; m 2nd Emma Lou Phillips), William Erastus (b 23 Jan 1910; d 14 Aug 1955; m 1st Ora Mae Gates; m 2nd Lela Jacks; m 3rd Bertha), Martha Lou (b 19 Feb 1913; d 11 Oct 1956; m John D. Rogers), Pauline (b 3 Jul 1916; d 12 Aug 1982; m Emmett Elijah Tilghmon), Margaret (b 19 Sep 1919; d 11 Aug 1999; m Rodman Samuel McQuiston) and twins Evelyn (b 23 Mar 1922; d 26 Mar 1922) and Everett (b 23 Mar 1922; d 31 Mar 1922). Only child born to Alma (Rial) and John Quintin Haisty was Conrad Leopold (b 6 Aug 1918; d 21 May 1986; m Donna Sue Hunnicut). Children born to Ecil Christina (Wells) and William Preston Haisty were Wesley Kenneth (m Mona Earl

Clymer), Edna Bernice (b 12 Sep 1918; d 10 Jan 2000; m Robert Walter Durham), LaBonne Willene (b 26 Jul 1920; d 14 Aug 1989; m 1st Franklin Pierce Barrett; m 2nd Glenn E. Jordan), Carroll Wood, Dorothy Nell (m Eugene William Byrne) and John Stanley (m Carolyn Mae Haisty). Children born to Winnie Estelle (Scifres) and Virgil Lee Haisty were Vonnie Aileen (b 25 Aug 1924; d 21 Nov 1981; m Lionel Borden, Jr.) and Frances E. (b 20 Nov 1926; d 15 Jan 1927).

Descendants of Jesse Sherwood Harvey:

Jesse Sherwood Harvey was born 25 Apr 1828 in Halifax Co., NC and died at Selma, AR 16 Dec 1905. He married Mary Ann Hamlett 5 Aug 1855 in Hardeman County TN. Mary Ann Hamlett was born 9 Sep 1833 in Halifax County NC, the daughter of Frances W. (Harvey) and William Hamlett. She died 13 Dec 1927 at Tillar, AR. Children born to Mary Ann (Hamlett) and Jesse Sherwood Harvey were John Robert (b 30 Nov 1856; d 15 Apr 1880), Thomas Brooks (b 24 Mar 1860; d 13 Apr 1944; m Sarah Rebecca Haisty), William Hamlett (b 24 Mar 1863; d 17 Mar 1870), Mary Frances (b 9 Feb 1866; d 22 Nov 1943; m George Washington Stroud), Adelaid Etta (b 19 May 1869; d 23 Feb 1953 Drew County; m 1st John David Barrett; m 2nd Andrew Marshall Weatherall), Jessie Ida (b 7 Feb 1873 Selma, AR; d Apr 1953; m Samuel Phillip Haisty), and Kara Ruth (b 6 Nov 1876; d 7 Nov 1905). The William Hamlett family left Halifax County NC in December 1842 and reached TN eight weeks later in January 1843. There Mary Ann Hamlett married Jesse Sherwood Harvey in 1855. The couple moved to AR in 1861, moved back to Shelby County TN in 1864, and returned to AR in 1870. Jesse Sherwood Harvey served in the Civil War and sustained an injury that crippled him for life. His service record has not been found.

Children and grandchildren born to Thomas Brooks Harvey and Jessie Ida (Harvey) Haisty are covered in the Haisty family history. Children born to Mary Frances (Harvey) and George Washington Stroud, b 1861; d 1943 were Joseph Hilliard (b 1902; d 1974; m Marion McKinney, b 1905; d 1998) and Gertrude (b 1899; d 1985; m Horace G. Boyd, Sr., b 1901; d 1961). Children born to Adelaid Etta Harvey and John David Barrett, b 1868; d 1897 were Fannie Lula (b 1892; d 1983; m Hiram C. Birch, b 1874; d 1956), Ida Mae (b 1894; d 1995; m Hernando Staten) and John Robert (b 1897; d 1965; m Marie Lucile Brown, b 1900; d 1986). Children born to Adelaid Etta (Harvey) and Andrew Marshall Weatherall, b 1861; d 1949 were James Columbus (b 1902; d 1990; m 1st Henri Erba Owens; m 2nd Alberta (Sawyer) Lawn), Flora Holmes (b 1905; d 1989; m David Sapp) Kara Elizabeth (m Richard C. Burdge) and Willie Helen (b 1910; d 1998; m Ernest C. Maxwell).

Children born to Marion McKinney and Joseph Hilliard Stroud were George Hilliard (m Madie Evans), Joe Hinton (m. Kathleen Fojtik) and

William Harvey (m Jamie Bigham). Children born to Gertrude Stroud and Horace G. Boyd, Sr. were Martha, Horace G., Jr. (m Billie Fay Dickson) and Mary Grace. Children born to Fannie Lula (Barrett) and Hiram C. Birch were Travis (m Virginia Youngblood), Shirley (m 1st John Wood; m 2nd Charles "Chuck" Childers; m 3rd Garlon Midgett), Lynette (m Harold Glossup), Gertrude (m Dwaine Godfrey), David (m Vera Gortney) and Calvin (b 1924; d 1983; m May Dell Phillips). Children born to Marie Lucile (Brown) and John Robert Barrett were Dorothy Louise (m William Joshua "Billie" Seamans), Mary Idelle (m. 1st William H. "Duck" Adams; m 2nd Ray Gibson; m 3rd Billy Wilson), Helen Lucile (m 1st William Clifton "Speck" Shepard; m 2nd Jim Wood) and John Robert, Jr. (m Helen Joyce Pharr).

Other children born to Frances W. (Harvey) and William Hamlett were Elizabeth (m William Columbus Tindall, who was born in Ireland), William R. (b 3 Dec 1837 Halifax County NC; d 31 Jan 1905 Hardeman County TN; m 27 Feb 1863 Eliza C. H. Powell), and Addie W. (b 30 Dec 1840 Halifax County NC; m 12 Dec 1865 in Desha County AR, Chesley C. Clayton). Descendants of William Hamlett:

Children born to Elizabeth (Hamlett) and William Columbus Tindall were Robert Barnabas (b 1873; d 1945; m Jewel Dickson, b 1882; d 1945), William Columbus Jr. (b 1877; d 1952; m Linnie Mason, b 1883; d 1927; m 2nd Irma (Blythe) Erwin, b 1877; d 1972). The children of Mary Ann (Hamlett) and Jesse Sherwood Harvey are listed above. Children born to Addie W. (Hamlett) and Chesley C. Clayton were Sebastian Cabot (b 1867; d 1932; m Cecelia Elizabeth A.Cusick), Stinson V. (b 1871; d 1939; m Bertie Poe), Graland or Garland (b 1873; d 1895), Willie C. (b 1874; d 1904), and Lee Arthur (b 1875; d 1929; m Maggie Mae Duncan).

Children born to Jewel (Dickson) and Robert Barnabas Tindall were John Robert (b c1906; m Willie Barnett; m 2nd Jean ?), Katherine Ruth (b 1908; m Elmo Daniels), Lawrence William (b 1911; m Ida Pearl Mullis), Marshall Marvin (b 1915; m Eddie Mullis), and an infant (d 1919).

Children born to Willie (Barnett) and John Robert Tindall were Catherine, Edwin, Jerry Lee and Bruce Allen. Children born to Katherine Ruth (Tindall) and Elmo Daniels were Wayne Elmo (m Geraldine Harvey), an infant (d at birth), Robert Lamar (m 1st Margaret ?; m 2nd Katie Pace) and Marsha Sue (m David Miles). Son of Ida Pearl (Mullis) and 1st husband Glen Whitaker was Billy Glen Whitaker Tindall (adopted by 2nd husband Lawrence William Tindall). Children born to Eddie (Mullis) and Marshall Marvin Tindall were Bobby, Jimmy and Carolyn.

Hopkins, Heflin
Submitted by Martha Hopkins Smith

Joseph Pickens Hopkins was born 12 Aug 1845 in TN and arrived with his family in Jefferson County AR in the mid- 1800s. He married Millie Woodel, daughter of Rebecca (Grumbles) and Robert Woodel, in 1873. By 1880 the couple had moved to Smith Township in Lincoln County and had two sons, William Thomas (b 3 Mar 1874) and James (b 19 Oct 1878; m Myrtle White). Their other children were Waterson (b 24 Feb 1889), Fannie (m Jesse Bailey, Minnie (b 1880), and Zemma (b 7 Sep 1898; m James Milton Heflin). Joseph and Millie Hopkins spent their lives in Lincoln County and were buried in Heflin Cemetery at Star City as were James, Waterson, and Minnie.

William Thomas "Tom" Hopkins attended school through the eighth grade and then went to work. He met Minnie Louetta Heflin at church. She was the daughter of Frances Jane (Wilson) and James Franklin Heflin. Both the Heflin and Wilson families had lived in the area since the mid-1800s. Minnie Heflin was born 24 Mar 1881 at Star City. Her siblings, all born in Star City, were Mary Catherine "Mollie" (b c1874; m Alex Boyd), twins Callie (m 1894 Henry Russ) and Calvin (b 1876), John F. (b c 1879), James Milton (b 1883; m Zemma Hopkins), Agnes (b 1887; m 1905 J. W. Bailey), Luther (b 1891; m 1913 Lula Sturges), and Clifton (d young). The Heflin family lived on farmland that had been in the family since the arrival of Minnie's great-grandparents, James Heflin and Nancy Thurman, from MS to AR in the 1840s. It was located about a mile north of Star City along Cane Creek which flows into Bayou Bartholomew further downstream. Minnie's grandfather, Milton Edward Heflin (b 1825; m 1850 Vernetta McLemore), who died in the 1870s, was buried on his property along Cane Creek, and his grave, which is planted with daffodils surrounding the border, can still be seen when the flowers are in bloom.

Minnie Heflin and Thomas Hopkins were married in Star City 6 Oct 1901. Minnie was twenty and William Thomas was twenty-seven. They had four children: Willie Myrtis (b 1903; m 1922 Donald Lambert), Floyd Watson (b 1905; m 1939 Nedra Dodd), Thomas Veo (b 1907; m Thelma Nall), and Raymond James (b 1916; m Mildred Roberts).

Thomas Hopkins began studying to become a minister through a correspondence course and began serving as a Methodist minister in his community in his early thirties. In 1919 he joined the Little Rock Annual Conference which assigned him to churches in Hermitage, Monticello, Montrose, Roe, Carthage, and Doddridge. He was in Montrose from 1924 to 1928 and experienced the 1927 flood. He retired from the ministry in 1935 at age sixty-one and moved to Little Rock where he died in 1950.

⚜

Lambert
Submitted by Eleanor R. (Mrs. Russell) Lambert

1 James Andrew Lambert of Burke Co. GA, was born c1730, died 1802, Burke Co., and married unknown. Issue:

2-1 Andrew Lambert (see following)

2-2 John Lambert b c1767/8, m Catherine Chambers.

2-3 James Lambert b 1770/1, m Ester ?

2-4 Robert Lambert b 1778 d 1859 at Perdue Hill, AL; m Winny Davis, who was b 1782 and d 6 Nov 1855, the dau of John Davis of Perdue Hill, AL. Issue:

3-1 Andrew M. Lambert b 1810; d 1895; m Martha Jane Dumas. Issue: 15 children.

3-2 Elias Lambert m Elizabeth Dumas (sister to the above   Martha Jane Dumas).

2-5 Isaac Lambert b 1780/5 in Burke Co. GA; m Abigail ?

2-1 Andrew Lambert (James 1) was b probably in Burke Co. GA, and d 1846 at Mt. Pleasant, Monroe Co, AL. He m c1789 Anna Lewis, b 1768; d 1845; bu near Mt. Pleasant, AL. Issue:

3-3 James Lambert b c1790 GA

3-4 William Lambert b c1792; murdered while young

3-5 John Lambert (see following)

3-6 Andrew Lambert II b 27 Jul 1795 Monroe Co. AL; m Rebecca Hurst, who was b 1804 and d 1875. Issue:

4-1 Caswell Lambert b 1825; d 1890; m Mary C. Jackson

4-2 Christiana Lambert b 1827; d 1890; m Joseph F. Boyles

4-3- Andrew Jackson Lambert b 1829; d 1911; m Josephine Shaunfield

4-4-Barthena Lambert b 1831; m Joseph L. Carson

4-5 Mary Ann Lambert m the above Joseph L. Carson, as his second wife

4-6 Frances E. Lambert b 1839; m Thomas Hestle

4-7 Calvin W. Lambert b 1843; d 1868; m Ella Solomon

4-8 Marion DeKalb Lambert b 1846; d 1896; m Harriet Victoria Sawyer

3-7 Isaac Buck Lambert b 22 Mar 1798; d 8 Sep 1880; m Eleanor Thompson

3-8 Polly Ann Lambert b c1800; m ? Thompson. Issue:

4-9 Joanna Thompson

3-9 Mary Ann Lambert b 1802/3

3-5 John Lambert (James 1, Andrew 2) b 1794 GA; d bef 1846, Monroe Co. AL; m c1816 Sarah Gathright, dau of Miles Gathright and Mary Hargrove. Sarah Gathright b 1794 GA; d 1853 Drew Co. AR, Issue:

4-10 Perry Lambert (see following)

4-11 Cypean Lambert; b GA; m Nancy ?

4-12 Dora Ann; b GA; d 1887 Drew Co. AR; m Richard Francis Withers, son of John Withers and Mary Bowen. Issue:

5-1 Crelia Withers m ? Moore

5-2 Liza Withers m ? Whiteside. Issue:

6-1 Fletcher Whiteside

5-3, 5-4 Male Withers; d in Confederate Army

5-3 – 5-8 Male Withers

4-13 Roana Ogburn Lambert b GA; d AL

4-14 Sarah Ann Ferrell Lambert b GA; d AL

4-15 Andrew Milton Lambert b 23 Nov 1827 AL; d 27 Aug 1910; bu Greenhill Cem., Drew Co. AR; m 4 May 1854 Martha E. Berryman. Issue:

5-9 Henry T. Lambert b 1854/5

5-10 William M. Lambert b 1859

5-11 Andrew Lambert b c1862

5-12 Camilla Lambert b c1863; m ? Jordan

5-13 Daniel Webster Lambert b 8 Aug 1867; d 1 Jan 1944; m 27 Sep 1902 Aribelle Mhoon in Drew Co. AR. Issue:

6-2 Nettie Lambert

6-3- Ollie Bell Lambert b 12 May 1911; d 3 Sep 1980; m 31 Jan 1931 Melvin H. Green. Issue:

7-1 Evelyn Green b 1932; d 1935

7-2 Myrtis M. Green b 7 May 1936; m 8 Jul 1960 William E. Grable b 17 Sep 1936. Issue:

8-1 Sheree D. Grable m ? Villegas

8-2 Penny E. Grable m ? Krodel

4-16 Polly Ann Lambert b 1831 AL; m John Bussey

4-17 George Washington Lambert b 1834 Monroe Co. AL: d Drew Co. AR; m Mary Virginia Jackson

4-18 Eliza Ann Lambert b 1836 Monroe Co. AL: d Bastrop, LA; m James T. Bussey

4-19 William Henry Lambert b 1840 Monroe Co. AL; d Drew Co. AR; m Elizabeth Ann Jackson, a sister of the above Mary Virginia Jackson who married George Washington Lambert. See above # 4-17.

4-10 Perry Lambert (James 1, Andrew 2, John 3) b 9 May 1817 GA; d 9 Nov 1877 Drew Co. AR; bu Prairie Chapel Cem., located on Drew Co. Road #1, about six miles west of Lacey, surrounded by land the Rev. John

Withers (his father-in-law) settled in 1848. He m 5 Dec 1844 Carolina Virginia Withers, dau of John Withers and Mary Bowen. Carolina Virginia Withers b 25 Feb 1825 Lexington District SC; d 6 Jul 1898 Monticello, AR; bu Oakland Cem., Monticello. Perry Lambert moved his family from AL to Longview, AR c1847, where he and William Hardy owned a store. They later moved to Monticello so the children could receive a better education. Issue:

5-14 Perry Elbert Lambert b 12 Oct 1845 Monroe Co. AL; m Catty McDermott

5-15 Alice Eugenia Lambert b 13 Apr 1847 Monroe Co. AL; d Drew County AR

5-16 Charles Wesley Lambert b 13 Mar 1849 Monroe Co. AL; d 1913 Drew Co.; m Caroline Hardy

5-17 John Milton Lambert b 31 Dec 1850; d Drew Co.; m Willie Jeter

5-18 Walter Lambert b 25 Feb 1853; d Drew Co.; m Cordelia Hardy. Issue:

6-4 Rebecca "Rebie" Lambert b 7 Jan 1891; d 2 Oct 1983

6-5 Elbert Anderson Lambert m 1st Lola Parker; m 2nd Frances Kelton

6-6 Florence "Floy" Lambert; unmarried

6-7 Lola Naomi Lambert m Fitzhugh Marshall

6-8 Walter Hardy Lambert; unmarried

5-19 Julia Lambert b 1 Oct 1855; d Drew Co.; m Harry Hankins

5-20 Theodosia Lambert b 19 Jan 1857; d 21 Sep 1936 Drew Co.; m James B. Pyron, who came to Ashley Co. AR in 1856. Issue:

6-9 Vesta Pyron b 15 Jul 1888 Drew Co.; d c1986; m 24 May 1917 William Benjamin deYampert II. He was b at Suggville, AL, son of William Benjamin deYampert I and Emma Porter [or Portis]. Issue:

7-3 William Benjamin deYampert III b 28 Aug 1918; m Ann Uzzle

7-4 Mary Virginia deYampert b 2 Oct 1920; m John B. Currie; d c1990

6-10 Esther Rhea Pyron b 18 Sep 1889; d Drew Co.; m Harry E. Street

7-5 Mary Virginia Pyron b 28 May 1895; d 1918

5-21 George Washington Lambert (see following)

5-22 Virginia Lambert b 21 Jun 1863; d Drew Co.; m 1st John Herndon; m 2nd Moses Coleman

5-23 Emma Lambert b 4 Jun 1863; d Drew Co.; m Moses Hill

5-24 Travis Lambert b 25 Aug 1865; d TX; m Mary Carmmack

5-21 George Washington Lambert (James 1, Andrew 2, John 3, Perry 4) b 8 Apr 1859 Drew Co; d 10 Nov 1940 Drew Co.; bu Oakland Cem. Monticello; m in Drew Co. 28 Sep 1885 Marion Jefferies (later known as

Mary Tagart, adopted dau of W. R. Tagart and Nancy Eugenia Prewit).
Marion Jefferies b 24 Jun 1866 Stourbridge, Worcestershire, England; d
Drew Co. 5 Feb 1921. She was the dau of Mark Jefferies and Anna Maria
Purchase of Stourbridge, England. Mark Jefferies came to Galveston, TX
from England and from there to Jefferson, TX via steamboat. He arrived
with one dau, Marion, and his second wife, his first wife having died in
England some years before. Also arriving with him was a step-daughter,
Agnes ?, who was 14 years old in the 1880 census, which made her born in
1866 in England. (Name of father and mother unknown.) Her (Agnes) birth
mother (Mark Jefferies second wife) d 13 Jul 1874, and Mark Jefferies also
d in Jefferson in Aug 1874. Thus the step-daughter and her step-sister,
Marion Jefferies, both of whom were born in 1866, were left orphans at the
tender age of 8 years. In the 1880 census of Marion Co. TX, under Tagart, is
one, Marion Tagart, white female age 14, orphan, born in 1866 in England,
with both parents listed as having been born in England also. So Marion
Jefferies was probably adopted by the Tagarts six years before the 1880
census. W. R. Tagart and his wife, Nancy Eugenia Prewit Tagart, must
have come to Drew Co. AR about this time, as he died in Drew Co. in 1890.
Marion Jefferies came to Drew County with her adoptive parents and took
the name of Mary Tagart.

The Centennial History of Arkansas Vol 3, p 1080, by Dallas T.
Herndon says of George W. Lambert, "...[he], who is numbered among
Monticello's foremost businessmen...[his parents] in the late 40s came to
Arkansas [from AL], casting in their lot with the early pioneers of Drew
County, who were known as 'canebreakers.' The father followed the
occupation of farming, and also engaged in merchandising, operating a
chain of stores in southeastern Arkansas and becoming widely known
through his mercantile activities....

"Mr. Lambert [George W.] acquired his early education in one of the
primitive schoolhouses of the early days, the structure being built of logs,
while slabs were made to serve as benches. Later he attended the public
schools of Monticello for a few months, but his educational opportunities
were very limited. His father met with financial reverses previous to his
demise, and the son was obliged to fight life's battles unassisted."

According to Herndon, George W. Lambert took up farm work until he
was twenty-five. After "conducting a grocery store for some years" he
entered the mule business, and later became a cotton buyer. He continued
his farming operation during those years and in 1913 became one of the
organizers and vice-president of the Commercial Loan and Trust Company,
which opened 10 Apr 1913. He was elected president in 1917 and was still
serving in 1922. He purchased stock in the Southern Compress Company of
Monticello in 1907 and was serving as president in 1922. In 1908 he helped
to organize the Exchange Bank of Dermott and was on the board of

directors in 1922. He became associated with the Drew Cotton Seed Oil Mills about 1915 and was director in 1922.

6-11 Estern Russell Lambert (James 1, Andrew 1, John 3, Perry 4, George 5) b Monticello 31 Aug 1889; d Pine Bluff 31 Jan 1970; m Theola Simmons, dau of John Franklin Simmons and Emma Hunter. Emma Hunter b Sardis, MS 8 Sep 1896. John Franklin Simmons was a physician, a director of the Citizens Bank of Pine Bluff, and the first president of Simmons National Bank in Pine Bluff, later known as Simmons 1st National. Theola Simmons Lambert d Pine Bluff 3 Mar 1982. Estern Russell Lambert was reared in Monticello and attended Ouachita Baptist College, Cornell University, and the University of Arkansas, Fayetteville. He served in both world wars. Issue:

7-6 Estern Russell Lambert Jr. (see following)

7-7 Mary Louise Lambert b Pine Bluff 1924; m 1945 James A. Ter Keurst, a native of Holland, Mich. Div 1974. Issue:

8-1 – 8-3 John Simmons Ter Keurst; Ann Theola Ter Keurst m ? Whittington; Valerie Ter Keurst, unmarried.

7-6 Estern Russell Lambert Jr. (James 1, Andrew 2, John 3, Perry 4, George 5, Russell 6) b Pine Bluff 6 Aug 1922; m Memphis TN Eleanor Lindsey Rucks, b Memphis 8 Mar 1924; dau of Dr. Walker Lee Rucks and Clifford Lindsey. Issue:

8-4 Estern Russell Lambert III b Memphis 9 Dec 1945; m Ann Elizabeth Holaday, dau of Charles Austin Holaday and Ann Hollingsworth Russ. Issue:

9-1 – 9-2 Lindsey Elizabeth, Katherine Austin Lambert

8-5 Richard Stockton Lambert b Pine Bluff 7 Jul 1948; m Sandra Ann McLeod; div. Issue:

9-3 Carolyn Ainslie Lambert

8-6 Robert Alexander Lambert, M.D. b Chattanooga, TN 1 Apr 1954; m Tonya Lynne Shirey. Issue:

9-4 – 9-8 Amy Elizabeth, Emily Rebecca, and triplets, William Arthur, Eleanor Grace, and Joseph Alexander Lambert.

Eleanor Lambert wrote, "Russell's family never actually lived on the bayou at all; true, they have farmed the land for many years, but the family lived in either Monticello or Pine Bluff. ...Russell's grandmother inherited the land on the bayou from her adoptive parents...Since Mr. Tagart died in Drew County in 1890, he must have come to Arkansas between 1880-1890 and purchased the land on Bayou Bartholomew. (Unless he had purchased this land on the way to Texas some time before. He seems to have owned quite a bit of land in Texas, and still did, when he left there to come to Arkansas.) (He was born in North Carolina and was 33 years of age in 1860 with personal real estate worth 90,000 dollars; Marion Co. TX; wife 29 years old and born in TN.) [Author's note: There was a Taggart family

living in northeastern Drew County before the Civil War. See Old Times
Not Forgotten: A History of Drew County, p 219.]
"...Russell and his good friend, the late Walter Trulock III, enjoyed
many happy bird hunting trips to this farm with Mr. George Lambert,
Russell's grandfather, when Russell and Walter were young men. Our
children spent many a summer afternoon down there, when Russell was
going back and forth farming the place. I knew that at the time our sons
were building a tree house out over Bayou Bartholomew. Many years later
when I had the opportunity to go down there, and when I looked up at the
remnants of the 'tree house,' I almost had a heart attack – it must have been
300 feet above the bayou!"

≈≈≈≈

William Penn McCain
Submitted by John C. Yeldell and Dorothy Korjan Mack

William Penn McCain was born 30 April 1865 at Alamo, TX, the son of
Mary Parizade "Parry" (Moore) and John Anderson McCain Sr. Their other
children were Marion Monroe (b 1 Jul 1853 Webster County MS; d 3 Apr
1899 Indianola, MS; m Darthula "Katie" ?), Mary Jane (b 24 Jun 1855
Webster County MS; d 22 Jun 1879; nev m), Louisa L. L. (b 24 Aug 1863
TX; d 27 Nov 1877; nev m), and John Anderson Jr. (b 7 Sep 1867 Sabine
County TX; d 12 Apr 1899; m 1st Alice ?; m 2nd Mary Mollie Smith).
    John Anderson McCain Sr. was born 19 Jul 1823 in GA or SC, the son
of Naomi (Neely) (b 1800; d 1874) and Alexander Hamilton McCain (b
1736; d 1838). By 1863 he was a soldier in Texas, where he was assigned
as a border guard on the Rio Grande. He died in 1868 in Sabine County,
and the family returned to MS. Mary Parizade Moore was born 28 Aug
1831 in AL, the daughter of Mary "Polly" (Rankin) and Bennett Wright
Moore. She died 24 Dec 1898.
    Children born to John Anderson McCain Jr. were Mary Parizade (b 5 Jul
1891), Callie (b 2 Oct 1893), Katie Dean or Catie Deen (b 5 Sep 1896), and
John Anderson III (b 9 Nov 1898). Zora and Alice McCain may have also
been his children.
    William Penn McCain married Martha Jane Mitchell on 20 Oct 1887.
She was born 20 Jan 1872 in Webster County MS, the daughter of Mary
(Farris, b TN), and John Mitchell (b MS). Children born to Martha Jane
(Mitchell) and William Penn McCain were William Jesse (b 4 Aug 1889
New Port, MS; d 26 Nov 1965; m Dollie Mitchell, his first cousin), Mary
Lillie (b 14 Aug 1891, New Port, MS; d 22 Dec 1967 Bastrop, LA; m 1918
Thomas Asberry Yeldell), George Oscar (b 16 Sep 1893 Newport, MS; d 19
Nov 1920 Wilmot, AR; m 1913 Willie Reid), Ludie Bell (b 14 Feb 1895

Warren, AR; d 21 Jul 1987 Jones, LA; m 1914 Edward Chris Korjan), John (b 20 Nov 1896 Jones, LA; d age 7), Claude Vernon (b 29 Jun 1900 Wilmar, AR; d 25 Aug 1982 Corona, CA; m 1920 Annie Bellita Causey), Audrey Mae (b 8 Jul 1904 Mer Rouge, LA; d 1 Jul 1968 San Jose, CA; m 1926 Clarence Burgstrom), James Aubrey "Jim" (b 6 May 1907 OK; d 21 Jan 1943 Oakland, CA; m Mildred ?), Lawrence Edward (b 4 Oct 1910 Kern Falls, AR ; d 2 Jan 1962 San Bruno, CA; m ?; no children), Velma Lee (b 7 Apr 1912 Jones, LA; d 14 Feb 1994 Twin Falls, ID; m Frank Patton), and Theodore Edward (b 7 Jul 1914, Jones, LA; d 14 Feb 1975 Oakland, CA; m 1935 Dorothy O'Neil). The William Penn McCain family first moved to the Jones, LA, area in 1895 or 1896.

Children born to Mary Lillie (McCain) and Thomas Asberry Yeldell were Thomas Eugene (b 12 Aug 1918 Jones, LA; m 1945 Phyllis Graham), Etta Mildred (b 3 Jun 1921 Drew County AR; m 1936 George Evans), Margarite (b 1923; d at birth), and John Calvin (b 30 May 1925 New Hope Community, Drew County AR; m 1934 Mary McDaniel). Thomas Asberry Yeldell died 6 Jan 1925 and was buried at Union Ridge Cemetery, Monticello, AR.

Children born to Ludie Bell (McCain) and Edward Chris Korjan were Edna (b 4 Mar 1915; m 1944 Adam Duff Cockrell), Eugene Buddy (b 11 Jul 1917 Wilmot, AR; m 1946 Carla Moore), and Dorothy L. (b 31 Jan 1927, Jones, LA; m 1949 Donald Mack).

Children born to Annie Bellita (Causey) and Claude Vernon McCain were Verna (b 27 Apr 1924 Portland, AR; m 1947 James Stevens), Irma (b 28 May 1925 Lake Village, AR; m Orrin Chance), Elmer (b 19 Jun 1926 Jones, LA; m 1925 Dorothy Danforth), Davie L. (b 21 Apr 1928 Jones, LA; d 5 Jul 1989; m 1958 Juanita Beasley), Ralph (b 22 Apr 1930 Jones, LA; m 1958 Claudette Barrack), and Lincoln (b 22 Jul 1933 Jones, LA; m 1962 Sabina Piatt).

Thomas Asberry Yeldell was born 4 Oct 1867 in Mer Rouge, the son of Alice (McDonald) and Willis Asberry Yeldell. Their only (?) other child was Berry Oscar. Albert Monroe Yeldell was a brother to Willis Asberry. Both served in the Civil War. Albert Monroe Yeldell was married to Veleria M. ? and they had a son, John H.

Edward Chris Korjan was born 27 Aug 1885 at St. Louis, MO, the son of Katherine (Willard) and Christian H. Korjan. Their other children were Christian Jr.(b 1875; d 26 May 1909), Margaret "Maggie", Emil (b 1883), Edward Chris, and Fred. Katherine Willard was born 1855 in IL and died 31 Oct 1893. Christian H. Korjan was born 1842 in Hanover, Germany, and died 4 Aug 1894.

Dorothy Korjan Mack wrote, "In 1893, at the age of 40, my father's mother died, followed by his father's death in 1894, and in 1895, his grandmother died, leaving the children orphans and not able to make a living for themselves. My dad was eight at the time. The three younger children, Emil, Edward, and Fred were placed in an orphan's home, but soon family members took them in. Emil, who was about fourteen at the time, joined the army, pretending to be older than he was. Daddy was taken in by an uncle who owned a big farm out from St. Louis, and Fred went to live with an uncle who owned a drugstore. Christian Jr. was about twenty by 1895 and was working as a commercial artist in St. Louis. Margaret was perhaps sixteen or seventeen years of age.

"We know very little about the children after Daddy left St. Louis in 1910 and came to Wilmot, Arkansas and began farming. His sister, Margaret, corresponded for awhile. Through her, he found out that Fred, the youngest, by then a young man, left St. Louis for California. In the year 1909 Daddy's oldest brother, Christian Jr. was a victim of foul play. His body was found floating in the Mississippi River, the mystery of his death was never solved. It wasn't until the late 1930s that we heard once more from Daddy's side of the family. His brother, Emil, who had been in the military service all those years since he was fourteen years old, spending much of the time in the Philippines, contacted him."

Emil Korjan had one child, Jean, who lived in New Jersey and exchanged letters with the family. The grandmother who cared for the children until she died is believed to have been Louisa Dickbreider, who was residing with the family in 1880. She was born in Prussia and died 4 Mar 1895 at age eighty-two.

Anita Belitta Causey was the daughter of Hardie and Burl Causey (no relation). Their other children were Castor, Lizzie Mae, Gaines, and Lucille. Hardie Causey was raised by the Jesse Burl Sadler family of Ashley County. Jesse Burl Sadler's parents were Mattie B. (Causey) and Andrew Jasper Sadler.

John Calvin Yeldell married Mary McDaniel who was born 13 Sep 1935, the daughter of Ludie and Jesse McDaniel. Children born to Mary (McDaniel) and John Calvin Yeldell were Pattie Renee (m Tommy Dugas) and Donna Renel (m Billy Burge).

Dorothy Korjan married Donald Richardson Mack who was born 11 Aug 1923 at Holden, LA, the son of Florence (Richardson) and Columbus Mack. Children born to Dorothy (Korjan) and Donald Mack were Deanna (m Harry King) and Ginger (m Donald Thompson).

John H. McCready
Submitted by Virginia Lois McCready Nightingale

John H. McCready was born 5 Dec 1871 in Golconda, IL, the son of Ebyyan [or Elizabeth Ann] (Holderfield) and Nathan McCready. Their other children were Nancy or Vaney (b 1869), and Ovelia Montre (b 1872; m 7 Dec 1887 George Hall in Livingston County KY; children: Emma C., b Sep 1891, m Bloodworth; Effie M., b Aug 1893; and William J., b Nov 1899).

Nathan McCready was born in 1843, the son of Esther Clarinda "Hetty" (Fox) and John McCready. Hetty Fox was b 1824, the daughter of Rebecca (Galbraith) and Nathan Fox. John McCready was born c1825 and died 26 Oct 1863 in Pope County, IL.

John H. McCready married Jessie Tempie Trammel 2 Feb 1893 in Livingston County KY. Their children were James Hollis (b 21 Jun 1897; d 13 Mar 1978; bu Bonita; m 7 Jan 1919 Lela Ramage, b 26 Jan 1904; d 13 Oct 1971; bu Bonita), Flossie (b 30 Mar 1902; d 1 Jan 1991; m Vernon Woodard), Orville Cooper (b 8 Jul 1909; d 22 Nov 1981; m Ozelle Winfrey), Josephine (b 13 Apr 1911; d 13 Jun 1984; m Frank Randolph Stamm), and Ethyl (b 21 Apr 1917; d 1976; m Ross Lane).

Lela Ramage was the daughter of Mattie (Dukes) and Silas Ramage of Smithland, KY. Children born to Lela (Ramage) and John Hollis McCready were Mary Lela, David Earl Willis Bertrand, James Ralph, Hazel Louise, Jolene Faye, Kenneth Louis, Orville Lee, Virginia Lois, and Melba Arnell. Children born to Flossie (McCready) and Vernon Woodard were Virginia and Gary. Children born to Ozelle (Winfrey, daughter of John and Essie Winfrey of Jones) and Orville Cooper McCready were Billy Wayne and Margaret Joan. Children born to Josephine (McCready) and Frank Randolph Stamm were Edward Vandall and Betty. Children born to Ethyl (McCready) and Ross Lane were Don Trammel and Elizabeth Ann (m J. T. Tyson).

In 1922 John H. McCready with his wife and five children and a daughter-in-law, Lela Ramage McCready, left Paducah, KY and went to LA to work in the logging industry. After working in Tallulah and Sondhiemer, the family moved in 1838 to an area north of Jones and farmed. In 1947 the Hollis McCready family moved to Bonita where he logged hickory and persimmon for the Eugene Ware Handle Company. His wife, Lela, and Orville McCready's wife, Ozelle, operated the Bonita Café for many years. Orville McCready lived in Bonita and worked for the County Department of Transportation. He pursued his hobby of collecting Native American artifacts, and one of his collections is held by the Snyder Museum in

Bastrop. The McCready family claims Native American status through Cherokee ancestors.

⚜

McShan
Submitted by Jane Duke McAshan

John Wesley McShan was born 25 Sep 1811 in KY, the son of Frances and John McShan, died 8 Dec 1903 in Lincoln County, and was buried at Tyro. He married Susan Roland Tarrant in Jefferson County 15 May 1845. She was born 19 Feb 1827 in Jefferson County, died 10 Feb 1909, and was buried at Collins in Drew County. Children born to them were Florence Ann (b Jun 1846 AL; d after 1910; m Francis Marvin Skipper), Cornelia (b 1848 MS; m Alonzo A. Moss, b 1847 MS), Mary Remala (b 1850 MS), John R. (b 1855 MS), Mary (b 1858), Sarah (b 1860 Drew County), Martha (b 3 Aug 1861; d 1940; m Edward Tucker Smith), Laura (b 10 Dec 1863, Drew County; m 1st Basley Carl Graves; m 2nd Charles S. Faucett), and William Henry (b Jul 1867; d 1933; bu Collins; m Fannie Neal). Fannie Neal was born 28 Mar 1877, died 7 Oct 1962, and was buried in Rash Cemetery, Drew County.

Florence Ann (McShan) and Francis Marvin Skipper's children, all born in AR, were Adelia (b 1867), Caddie (b 1870; m ? Wood), Ida (b 1874; m ? Smith), and Henry Marvin (b Sep 1888; m 1909 Katie R., b 1891 AR). (See also Skipper genealogy submitted by Sara Neeley.) Children born to Cornelia (McShan) and Alonza Moss were Victor (b 1871), Lelia (b 1873), Fannie (b 1875; m ? Fuller) and Lizzie (b 1877; m ? McCoy), and Nettie (b 1882; m ? Frey). For the children of Martha (McShan) and Edward Tucker Smith, see the Lloyd Smith summary. The only child born to Laura (McShan) and Basley Carl Graves was Ella Mae (b 5 Nov 1889 Florence, Drew County; d 27 May 1977 Shreveport, LA; m George Houston Lawler (b 13 Jan 1880 Pine Bluff AR)). Children born to Laura (McShan) and Charles S. Faucett were Joseph Muncie (b 7 Apr 1898; d Sep 1985), Clyde (b 28 Jan 1900; d Dec 1970), and Lara Gladys (b 1902; m ? Holt). The only known children born to Fannie (Neal) and William S. McShan were Elvine (b May 1899; d bef 1906) and Grace (b 1905).

The McShan name also appeared early in Ashley County. In 1860 Andrew J. McShan, who was a first cousin to John Wesley McShan and the son of Alice (Feaster) and Hundley McShan, was living there with his family and apparently some other relatives. The 1860 Ashley County census lists Andrew (farmer; age 38; b SC), Mary C. [his wife] (age 37; b AL), Florence [his dau] (age 14; b AL), Thomas W. [his son] (age 9; b AL), Elizabeth G. F. Coleman [his sister] (age 60; b SC), David T. Hamilton (age

20; b SC), John W. Sanders (overseer; age 21; b GA), James M. Clinton (teacher; age 24; b KY), and William H. Simpson [Mary McShan's brother] (farmer; age 45; b SC). William H. Simpson's family consisted of his wife Harriett A. (age 37; b SC) and children William E. (age 16; b AL), Thomas W. (age 14; b AL), Elizabeth B. (age 12; b AL), and John M. (age 8; b AL). Andrew J. McShan was born 1822 in SC and died 1866 in Ashley County. He married Mary C. Simpson who was born in 1823 in AL and died after Feb 1862. Their children were Florence Missouri (b 1846; m William J. Price 6 Jun 1865 in Ashley County) and Thomas Walton (b 1851).

Another early Ashley County McShan family was that of James Chambers McShan, who was an uncle to John Wesley McShan and the son of Nehemiah Mackshan. He was born 1787 in VA or NC and died Jan 1860 in Calhoun County AR. He married Susannah Slaughter who was born 1792 in NC and died after 1850. The marriage took place on 6 Jan 1824 in Lawrence County MS. Their children were George Washington (b 13 Sep 1824 MS; d 31 Oct 1908 LA; m 1st Elizabeth M. Anderson 15 Jan 1849 Drew County; m 2nd Mary Louise Martin 11 Mar 1851 Ashley County; m 3rd Sarah A. Nicelson 8 Jan 1874; m 4th Anne Greenwood), Nancy Jamenia (b 2 Feb 1829 MS; d 8 Jun 1907 Tahoka, TX; m James Broswell Everett 2 Mar 1851 Ashley County), Carolina (b 1830; m 1st James L. Martin 18 Jun 1853 in Ashley County; m 2nd Samuel Griffin Finklea 11 Nov 1855 in Ashley County), Robert Francis (b 7 Sep 1833 MS; d 26 Feb 1886 Cleveland TX; m Elizabeth Catherine Gillespy 31 Aug 1854 Drew County), and James Chambers Jr. (b 21 Jul 1835 MS; d 5 Jul 1895 San Jacinto County TX; m Nancy J. Gillespy 17 May 1857 Drew County).

Ezekiel Brooke Owens Family
Submitted by Carolyn (Haisty) Haisty

"Ezekiel Brooke Owens was born in 1806 in Bedford County, TN to Hunter Owens who was born in Scotland. The name of Hunter's wife is not known. A brother to Ezekiel was John H. who was born in NC in 1801. John's middle name was most likely Hunter. Family history tells us that Hunter Owens was in the Revolutionary War. We have not found records to bear this out. This history also tells us that he died in NC of an accidental gunshot.

"According to Goodspeed, Ezekiel Owens reportedly settled along Bayou Bartholomew in Drew County in 1834, although his land records do not confirm that. Perhaps his first home was along the bayou, but he eventually settled in the Rose Hill Community. According to the places of birth of his first three children, he was not a permanent resident until some time between 1836 and 1839.

"On September 29, 1832, Ezekiel married Adelia Pendleton Payne in Shelby County TN. Adelia was the daughter of Dr. Nathaniel West Payne, a prominent physician in VA, and Catherine Wilson (or Willson) Alexander. Catherine was the daughter of Ann (Austin) and Robert Alexander. Adelia Pendleton Payne was a descendant of many families from the Old Dominion. She was related to Martha Dandridge Custis Washington (wife of George Washington), Dolley Payne Madison (wife of James Madison), and Dorothea Dandridge (second wife of Patrick Henry). She was a direct descendant of Governor Alexander Spotswood of VA, Nicholas Martiau, George Reade, Augustine Warner and Thomas, Lord De La Warr West for whom Delaware was named, as well as other notable families. Some of her family has been traced back to the 400s through lords, kings, and emperors.

"The first child of Ezekiel and Adelia, William Nathaniel Owens, was born 12 Mar 1834 in Shelby County TN. Their second child, James A. Owens, who became the leader of Owens Battery during the Civil War, was born in Hinds County, MS 5 Nov 1836. Their third child, Catherine B. Owens, was born 21 Feb 1839 in Drew County AR.

"Ezekiel was a learned man and had been a school teacher. He apparently was an adventurer as evidenced by his moves and the fact that he went on at least one trek to the gold fields in CA, returning via a ship that sailed around Cape Horn to New Orleans. He then traveled up the course of rivers to the Saline River and to his home in Drew County. Family lore says that he went on two of these journeys, be we have found solid evidence of only one as he left a journal of that trip. One story says that he made the first trip as a wagon master and went back on a second trip as a doctor. His son, William Nathaniel, made the trip with him as chronicled in the journal." (By Carolyn Haisty.)

James Hunter Owens, son of Hunter Owens, was born in 1801 and married Selina Gabbie in SC before 1825. Selina Gabbie was born in Yorkville, SC in 1805, and she and her husband died in Drew County AR after 1880. Children born to this marriage were William E. (b 1825 SC; d 1882 Drew County; m Caroline V. Wells, b 1830; d 1880), John A. (b 8 Jun 1829 SC; m 1st Margaret Carroll, b 1856; m 2nd Catherine Gaster), James M. (b 1831 SC; d 1874; m 1860 Margaret Spencer), Robert E. (b 1833 TN; m Jane A. Gabbott), Thomas W. (b 1836 TN; m Julia Ferguson), Mary E. (b 1838 TN; d 7 Jan 1883; m 1866 Marmaduke E. Ferguson in Drew County), Marion (b 1843 TN), Leander Dan (b 24 Apr 1844 TN; d 22 Aug 1911 Drew County; m Mary V. "Mollie" Tippin, b 1858; d 1926), and Albert H. (b 14 Oct 1845 AR; d 17 Feb 1925 Drew County; m 1st Maranda L. Oslin, b 1848; d 1890; m 2nd Melissa Oslin, b 1844; d 1926). John A. and James M. Owens were both physicians. John A. Owens practiced in Monticello and

Pine Bluff, Arkansas while James M. Owens was in practice in Hamburg and Monticello, Arkansas.

Children born to Caroline V. (Wells) and William E. Owens were William Walter (b 1854), Charles H. (b 1857; d 1920; m Christibel Harrison), Edward (b 1861), Frank (b 1864; m Nancy Payne), Rene (b 1866), Samuel (b 1869; d 1943; m Catherin Octavia Gulley) and Katherine (b 1874; d 1943; m George Austin). The only child born to Margaret (Carroll) and John A. Owens was Willie H. (b 1854; m ?). Children born to Catherine (Gaster) and John A. Owens were Clarence (b 1856), Charles William (b 1858), Lizzie May (b 1860), John Harvey (b 1862), Warren Stone (b 1866), Minitta (b 1868), Carl Eric (b 1870), Claude Bernard (b 1874), Ida, and an infant (d young). Children born to Julia Ferguson and Thomas W. Owens were Fannie, Tommie, Hunter, Charlie, Henry, Smyle, Lillian, and Hattie. (Julia Ferguson was born 10 Feb 1843 in Chester Co., SC). Children born to Mary E. (Owens) and Marmaduke E. Ferguson were Hyder (b 1867), James L. (b 1868), Edward (b 1870), Minnie (b 1872), Theresa (b 1874), and Bettie R. (b 1876). (Marmaduke E. Ferguson was born 5 Nov 1839 in Chester County SC, the son of Sarah "Sallie" (Hyatt) and Jonathan Ferguson. He was a brother of Julia Ferguson who married Thomas W. Owens). Marmaduke's second wife (m 23 Oct 1884 was Josephine (Tomlin), widow of B. Glosup.) Children born to Mary V. (Tippin) and Leander Dan Owens were James Edward (b 1882; d 1960; m Maggie Belle Pevey, b 1893; d 1975), Werner Hall (b 1894; m 1st Flora ?; m 2nd True Thompson), Dennis (m Minta ?), Lena (m Martin Stewart), Corrine (b 1887; d 1958; m Grover T. Owens, b 1885; d 1964), and Allene (m Ben Erwin). Children born to Maranda L. (Oslin) and Albert H. Owens were Elza Drew (b 1870; d 1962; m Elizabeth Catherine Campster, b 1888; d 1974), Carl C. (m Leota Turner), Lillie (m ? Gulledge), and Nettie (b 1878; d 1950; m Don Henry Echols).

Ezekiel Brooke Owens, son of Hunter Owens, married Adelia Pendleton Payne 29 Sep 1832 in TN. Children born to this marriage were William Nathaniel (b 12 Mar 1834 TN; d 27 Sep 1892 Drew County; m 1st Ellen F. Patterson; m 2nd Frances E. Scrieber), James A. (Alexander) (b 5 Nov 1836 MS; d 15 Dec 1891 Barkada, Drew County; m Martha J. "Mattie" Goyne), Catherine B. (b 21 Feb 1839 Drew County; d 13 Jan 1844), Albert P. (b 22 Nov 1841 Drew County; d 20 Jul 1844 Drew County), Mary Wilson (b 17 Sep 1844 Drew County; d 12 Apr 1877; m William Joseph Echols), Milton Hubert (b 23 Dec 1846 Drew County; d 18 Nov 1933 Drew County; m Martha Caroline Hankins), Lycurgus Bruce (b 4 Feb 1849 Drew County; d 19 Sep 1909; m Sallie Agnes Steadman), Lewis C. or Luke (b 6 Jan 1852 Drew County; d 24 Jul 1938; m Ester McKay), and Adelia Celestia (b 25 Jun 1854 Drew County; d 19 Dec 1937; m John Branch Blankenship; b 1853; d 1883).

Children born to Ellen F. (Patterson) (b 4 Jan 1835; d 20 Mar 1869) and William Nathaniel Owens were Flavius E. (b 21 Oct 1855; d 15 Jan 1879), William Walton (b 26 Apr 1857; d 2 Feb 1933; m 17 Jan 1886 Eliza Jane McQuiston), Charles Cabell (b 26 Mar 1859; d 26 Mar 1860), Logan Wilson (b 8 Nov 1861; d 18 Aug 1880), and Emma Lee (b 4 Sep 1864; d 25 Apr 1946; m 2 Jan 1889 Andrew Washington McQuiston).

Children born to Martha J. (Goyne) (b 26 May 1837; d 4 Jan 1884) and James A. Owens were Walter S. (b 16 Dec 1859; d 30 Apr 1889), John R. A. (b 2 Nov 1862; d young), Charles W. (b 13 Nov 1866), William Spotswood (b 25 May 1867 Drew County; d 17 Nov 1936 Wilmar, AR; m 1st Ora Belle Daniel; m 2nd Willie E. Stewart), Jesse E. (b 12 Dec 1869; d 10 Jan 1906; m Zula Hooker), Henry Elmer (b 12 Jul 1872; m Ida Reviere), Mary Ella (b 12 Jul 1872 Drew County; d 18 Mar 1929 Drew County; m 11 Oct 1893 Richard Henry Howell), Fanny Adelia Jane (b 30 Mar 1874 Barkada, Drew County; d 29 Dec 1966 Barkada; m Horace L. Rhodes), and Effie Beatrice (b 19 Aug 1877).

Children born to Mary Wilson (Owens) and William Joseph Echols (son of Rebecca Malley and Thomas Echols; b 1845 Carroll County MS; d 1928 Drew County) were George Ezekiel, Ellen, and Henry.

Children born (all in Drew County) to Martha Caroline (Hankins) (dau of Sarah S. Albright and Robert W. Hankins; b 15 Nov 1849 Drew County; d 3 Sep 1928 Drew County) and Milton Hubert Owens were Leona May (b 7 Sep 1868; d 13 May 1956; m John T. Thompson), Robert Wilson (b 28 Feb 1870; d 7 Mar 1959; m Laura Alice Jones), Florence Iva (b 10 Dec 1872; d 13 Mar 1957 Wilmar, AR; m Samuel Dunn Dickson Jr.), Henry Monroe (b 14 Nov 1874; d 25 Oct 1964 Wilmar, AR; m Mattie Lou Miller), Jo Anna "Jodie" (b 2 Feb 1879; d 4 Mar 1935; m Joe E. Smith), Lois Ethel (b 22 Jan 1882; d 13 May 1938; m Jay Bennett Hogue), Ben Ingram (b 25 Jul 1884; d 27 Oct 1964; m Jessie Merritt, Mary Almeda (Gurley) Merrill, Ruby Mae Culbert), Milton Neil (b 2 May 1886; d 11 May 1970; m Hallie May Rabb), and Virginia Gertrude (b 28 Sep 1889; d 27 Dec 1977; m James Gill McCone).

Children born to Sallie Agnes (Steadman) (dau of Mary Isabell Fee and John Franklin Steadman; b 23 Sep 1853; d 23 Dec 1923) and Lycurgus Bruce Owens were Frank Romain (b 8 Dec 1869; d 26 Aug 1925; m 18 Feb 1893 in Drew County Catherine Miller; m 2nd Ruth Johns), Mary (b 24 Nov 1872; d 1973 TX; m Oct 1889 W. F. Matheny), Grace (b 5 Oct 1875 Hot Springs AR; d 1957 TN; m J. W. McDonald), Ella (b 4 Jul 1878; d 24 Apr 1962; m ? Newton), Graves (b 4 Jul 1878; d 29 Sep 1933 CA), Myrtle (b 20 Jul 1883 Monticello, AR; d 7 Oct 1980 TN; m 19 Nov 1913 Dr. Oscar Hughes Looney), Leah Fern (b 26 Jan 1887 Monticello AR; d 3 Jan 1993 Pine Bluff AR; m Bester Arvin Owen), and Wycliff (b 13 Sep 1892 Monticello AR; d 25 Jan 1897 Monticello).

Children born to Ester (McKay) and Lewis C. or Luke Owens were Olive H. (b 1877; d 1955; m Charles Gill Landers), Ella May, Robert Ezekiel (b 15 Aug 1883 Drew County; d 27 Jun 1961; m Della Rosa Allen), Wylie Clifton (m Ida Mae Hamilton), William Victor (d 1940), Paul, and Ray.

Children born to Adelia Celestia (Owens) and John Branch Blankenship were William Horace (b 4 Oct 1876; d 26 Mar 1961; m Mona Welch), Annie Pendleton (b 29 Dec 1879; m 3 Feb 1904 Paul Hartwell Greeson), and Mildred Pearl (b 25 Dec 1881; d 3 Nov 1922; m Julius Wrightman Smith).

The following are descendants of Ellen F. (Patterson) and William Nathaniel Owens:

Children born to Eliza Jane (McQuiston) and William Walton Owens were William McQuiston (b 1888; d 1888), Edward Everett (b 1889; m Norma Clair Rutherford), Ruby (b 1899; m Augustus Carnes Swindler), and Ruth Isabel (b 1902). Children born to Emma Lee (Owens) and Andrew Washington McQuiston (b 1863; d 1941) were Ethel (b 1890; m William Thurman Evans), Mary Ellen (b 1892; d 1944; m C. C. Minatra), Charlie Clifton (b 1894; m Fern Wylie), and Willie Gertrude (b 1896; d 1945; m Ruben Archibald Little).

The following are descendants of Martha J. (Goyne) and James A. Owens:

Children born to Ora Belle (Daniel) and William Spotswood Owens were Curtis, Alvin (b 1898; d 1906), Fred McClure (b 1901; d 1960; m Laura Mae Butler), and an infant (b 1905; d 1906). Children born to Zula (Hooker) and Jesse E. Owens were Lamar Williamson (b 1898; d 1972; m Ruth Ethelyn Bird), Bund, Fred, Ovid Edward (b 1902; d 1961; m Rebecca Thankful Sasser), and Lucille (b 1905; d 1994; m Barney Gumpert). Children born to Mary Ella (Owens) and Richard Henry Howell were Sherwood Scott (b 1895; d 1971; m Dorothy Kojetsky), Hattie Bell (b 1897; m Joseph Fry; m 2nd Marvin Powers; m 3rd Hadley R. Morse), and Richard Harris (b 1903; d 1968; m 1st Sylvia Evelyn White; m 2nd Margaret Rose Sampson. The only child born to Fanny Adelia Jane (Owens) and Horace L. Rhodes was Tennessee "Tennie" (b 1906; d 1992; m Charles Hiram Stafford).

Children born to Laura Mae (Butler) and Fred McClure Owens were Margurite (m Charles Lee White), McRae (m Patty Ragar), and Robert Butler (m 1st Charlotte Ann Key; m 2nd LaWanda Faye West). The only child born to Ruth Ethelyn (Bird) and Lamar Williamson Owens was Lamar Williamson Jr. (m Wilma ?). Children born to Rebecca Thankful (Sasser) and Ovid Edward Owens were Geraldine (m Morris Parker) and Ovid Edward Jr. (m Jean ?). Children born to Lucille (Owens) and Barney Gumpert were Rosemary (m J. D. Edwards; m 2nd Newt Bynum) and

Barbara Owens (m Breen). The only child born to Tennessee (Rhodes) and Charles Hiram Stafford was Charles Hiram Jr. (m Betty Jo Chambers).

The following are descendants of Martha Caroline (Hankins) and Milton Hubert Owens:
Children born to Leona May (Owens) and John T. Thompson were Linwood H. (m Maude L.?), Robert Harrell, Marvin, Thomas Ray, and Ellis (m Virginia ?). The only child born to Laura Alice (Jones) and Robert Wilson Owens was Travis. They also had an adopted daughter, Mary Elizabeth (m Hughes Lee Buerger Sr.). Children born to Florence Iva (Owens) and Samuel Dunn Dickson Jr. were Karl (m Lettie Loraine Hilliard), Verner (m Myrtle Clower), Vesta P. (m Marion Oliver Taylor), Mittie Belle (m Chester Arthur Franklin), Florence (m Kirk Coil), Joya (m Bert Gaster), Robert Wilson, and Joe Clarence (m Meryl Christine Scott). Children born to Mattie Lou (Miller) and Henry Monroe Owens were Henri Erba (m James Columbus Weatherall), Lucy Mae (m Willie Phil Haisty; m 2nd Latham Ephriam Wright Sr.), Luna Belle (m Hulbert Pierce Crute), Albert Davis (m Reenie ?; m 2nd Rose Mary Myron), Ralph Miller, and William Monroe (m Ruth Ann Gill). Children born to Jo Anna (Owens) and Joe E. Smith were Thelma (m Braxton Lamar), Lois (m Bert Morgan), Hobson, LaDell (m Jerry Ashcraft), and Margaret Caroline (m Walter E. Datz). Children born to Lois Ethel (Owens) and Jay Bennett Hogue were Helen Gray (m Ernest Valentine Wolfe) and Jay Bennett Jr. (m Dorothy Aylor). The only child born to Jessie (Merritt) and Ben Ingram Owens was Carroll Lee (m Elizabeth Chitwood). Children born to Mary Almeda (Gurley) Merrill and Ben Ingram Owens were R. W., Henry Sylvester "Bill" (m Louise Finey), Edward Earl (m Thelma Merritt), Lena Almeda (m Oscar Lee Boatright Sr.), Jodie Belle (m Asa Duke Carter; m 2nd John Irvin Johnson), and Gladys Christene (m Spence Byrd). Children born to Ruby Mae (Culbert) and Ben Ingram Owens were Laron "Big Boy," Hugh Chester "Chet" (m Mary Lee Vaught), J. D. (m Rubye Gertrude Smith), and Homer Lee (m 1st Maude; m 2nd Joyce Staton). Children born to Hallie May (Rabb) and Milton Neil Owens were Lavenia, Virginia, Alco (m 1st Edwin McKinzie; m 2nd Charles Ottis Dahme), Dorothy Lynn (m Jay D. Calhoun), and Sandra DeMaris (m James Delbert West). Children born to Virginia Gertrude (Owens) and James Gill McCone were H. Wayne and James Thomas (m Jane English).

Children born to Mary Elizabeth (Owens) and Hughes Lee Buerger were Hughes Lee Jr. (m Dorothy L.?), Mary Jean (m Dale Whitten), Annie Laurie (m 1st Hal Johnstone); m 2nd Leroy Kunetka), Edith Lou (m Hank Gottard), Breymann (m Roberta Dee Harlan), Robert Wilson, and Theodore Charles. Children born to Lettie Loraine (Hilliard) and Karl Dickson were Mary Katherine (m Jack Taylor), Florence Isabel (m Walter Rasch; m 2nd John S. Witulski), and an infant (d 1918). Children born to Myrtle (Clower) and

Verner Dickson were Frances (m Robert Lee Howard) and Helen Marie (m 1st Wesley Wood; m 2nd Howard Newton). Children born to Mittie Belle (Dickson) and Chester Arthur Franklin were Marcella Mae (m James Jackson Stone), Lois Eva (m Hugh Curry Moyers), Mary Alice (m Donald Foster Dace), and Charles Hugh (m 1st Rita Sims; m 2nd Ann Brooks). The only child born to Florence (Dickson) and Kirk Coil was George Kirk. Children born to Joya (Dickson) and Bert Gaster were Walter Dickson and Joann. Children born to Meryl Christine (Scott) and Joe Clarence Dickson were Robert Dunn (m Carolyn Ann Rainey), Jerry Gordon (m Betty Dean Moran), and Paul Allen (m Martha Nell Cherry). Children born to Lucy Mae (Owens) and Willie Phil Haisty were William Delbert and Carolyn Mae (m John Stanley Haisty). Children born to Luna Belle (Owens) and Hulbert Pierce Crute were an infant (d infant) and Norma Jean (m George Banks Collins). Children born to Rose Mary (Myron) and Albert Davis Owens were Barbara Jean (m James Michael Portman), Linda Diane, and Nancy Lou (m Robert Jerome McClure). Children born to Ruth Ann (Gill) and William Monroe Owens were Janey Lou (m Douglas E. Fisher), and Arthur David (m 1st Linda Green; m 2nd Roxanne; m 3rd Nancy). The only child born to Thelma (Smith) and Braxton Lamar was Norma Jean (m Bunny Bloodworth). Children born to Lois (Smith) and Bert Morgan were Martha and Robert. Children born to Margaret Caroline (Smith) and Warren E. Datz were Edwin Louis and David Warren. Children born to Helen Gray (Hogue) and Ernest Valentine Wolfe were Martha Loraine (m Joe William Cline) and Ernestine (m Hal Nichols). Children born to Dorothy (Aylor) and Jay Bennett Hogue Jr. were Larry Bennett, Ronald, and Deanne. The only child born to Elizabeth (Chitwood) and Carroll Lee Owens was Milton Chipman (m Judy Jane Yadon; m 2nd Barbara June ?). Children born to Thelma (Merritt) and Edward Earl Owens were James Edward "Jamie," Mary Ann, Bert Franklin (m 1st Jane Isom; m 2nd Joann Fortenberry; m 3rd Mary Emerson), Joe Merritt (m Virgie Wilson), and Pamela Kay. Children born to Lena Almeda (Owens) and Oscar Lee Boatright were Imogene (m C. B. Miles; m 2nd Andrew Vincent Greco), Billy Charles (m Anna ?), James Floyd, Lillian Almeda "Polly" (m 1st Gerald Stuart; m 2nd Reggie Harvey Sullivan Jr.), Helen Virginia (partner to William Frederick Litzius; m 1st Ben Franklin Guess; m 2nd Larry Lee Hight;), Brenda Joyce (m 1st Larry Dean Calhoun; partner to Ronald Ray Wood; m 2nd Victor Evans), Bessie Mae (m ? Olsen; m 2nd Richard Gott), Barbara Ruth (m 1st William Henderson Tait; m 2nd Rolland Dale Johnson; m 3rd Richard Eugene Robinson), Jane Ellen (m Zeke Whitwing), and Oscar Lee Jr. (m Linda Gail Alexander). Children born to Jodie Belle (Owens) and Asa Duke Carter were Betty Jo (m Richard Allen Crawford), Elizabeth Ann (m Gilbert Alfred Calderon), Nannie Sue (m Edward Michael Lawrence; m 2nd Paul Emmanuel Tanga), Acel Dewaine (m 1st Marlen

Eugene Austin; m 2nd Charles Delmar Carpenter). Children born to Gladys Christene (Owens) and Spence Byrd were Thomas Edwin, Sheila Marie (m William Thomas Summers), Virginia Sue (m David Dee Crum), Don Lee (m Martha Robinson), Grover Wayne (m Verna Lea Ledford), Sherry Dale (m William Henry McAlister), Sybil Gail (m Allen Leroy Skinner Jr.), and Sharon Kay. Children born to Mary Lee (Vaught) and Hugh Chester Owens were Shirley Jean, Chester Lamar, Charles Edward, Doris Gail, Billy Carroll, and Patricia Annette. Children born to Rubye Gertrude (Smith) and J. D. Owens were Marvin Albert, Sandra Kay, and Bobby Ray. Children born to Joyce (Staton) and Homer Lee Owens were Benny Lee and Vickie Lynn. Children born to Dorothy Lynne (Owens) and Jay D. Calhoun were Elizabeth Anne (m Steve Byron Hollinger) and Lisa Lynne (m Ronald Allen Martin). Children born to Sandra DeMaris (Owens) and James Delbert West were Deborah Lynne (m Harold Bernard Brooks) and James Neil (m Julie Michelle Smith). Children born to Jane (English) and James Thomas McCone were Jane English, James Thomas Jr., Peyton Gill, Majen (m ? Gibson), and Julia.

The Following are descendants of Sallie Agnes (Steadman) and Lycurgus Bruce Owens.:

Children born to Catherine (Miller) and Frank Romain Owens were Venice (b 1896), Travis, and Elvin L. (b 1895; d 1900). Children born to Ruth (Johns) and Frank Romain Owens were Allene (m Sam Mosely) and Arthur. Children born to Myrtle (Owens) and Dr. Oscar Hughes Looney (b 1868; d 1938) were Agnes Steadman (b 1915; d 1961; m Russell Ward McGlothlin), Polly Ann Hughes (b 1915; m Haywood Clark Cole), and Myrtle Owens (b 1917; m Richard B. Pelton). Children born to Leah Fern (Owens) and Bester Arvin Owen were Walter Wycliff (m Lucille Rankin), James Reuben (b 1909; d 1991; m Geraldine Parsley), Bester Arvin Jr. (b 1915; d 1982; m Madelyn Russell), and Fern (m Thomas Bentley Stone). The only child born to Allene (Owens) and Sam Mosely was Mary Sam. The only known child born to Arthur Owens was Nora Lee. Children born to Agnes Steadman (Looney) and Russell Ward McGlothlin were James Hughes and William Steadman. Children born to Polly Ann Hughes (Looney) and Haywood Clark Cole were Polly Ann (m Mike Pitts), Sarah Lee (m William R. Blank), and Carolyn Clark (m Paul V. Guagliardo). Children born to Myrtle Owens (Looney) and Richard B. Pelton were David William (m Sandra Bridges) and Pamela Owens.

The following are descendants of Ester (McKay) and Lewis C. or Luke Owens:

Children born to Olive H. (Owens) and Charles Gill Landers were Hunter, Ewell, and Mary. Children born to Della Rosa (Allen) and Robert Ezekiel Owens were Falba Arlene (m Robert Walker Core) and Robert Ezekiel Jr. Children born to Ida Mae (Hamilton) and Wylie Clifton Owens were Wylie Clifton Jr. (m Ella Lee Brown) and Virginia (m Quentin Derryberry). Children born to Falba Arlene (Owens) and Robert Walker Core were Falba Anne (m Everette Cloid Walker III) and Roberta Lynn (m Clyde Phillip Angle).

The following are descendants of Adelia Celestia (Owens) and John Branch Blankenship:

Children born to Mona (Welch) and William Horace Blankenship were Raymond Owen (m Mabel Hunt) and Frank Welch (m 1st Frederica Vogelman; m 2nd Ilene Mountain). Children born to Annie Pendleton (Blankenship) and Paul Hartwell Greeson (b 1878; d 1956) were Joseph, Myrtle, James (m Margaret Carmen Miller), Mary Elizabeth (m Lee Roy Hankins), and Martha Lois (m Roy S. Bensinger). The only child born to Mildred Pearl (Blankenship) and Julius Wightman Smith (b 1880; d 1960) was Dorthea Dandridge (m Claude L. Casey). The only child born to Frederica (Vogelman) and Frank Welch Blankenship was William Frederick. Children born to Margaret Carmen (Miller) and James Greeson were Philip Hartwell (m 1st Joyce ?; m 2nd Ruth Mae Connolly), Anna Margaret (m Paul Coffman), Deborah Louise Greeson (m Gary Barton Gentry), James Timothy, and Bruce Riley. The only child born to Martha Lois (Greeson) and Roy S. Bensinger was Roy Edward. Children born to Dorthea Dandridge (Smith) and Claude L. Casey were Dorothea June (m Dale Edward Slessman) and Luisita Mildred (b 1924; d 1924).

⚜

Roper, Adams
Submitted by Betty Adams Kinney

Betty Marie Adams McKee Kinney was born 8 Jul 1936 in Wilmot, the daughter of Alice Jewel (Roper) and Muriel Leon Adams who were married 25 Feb 1933 at the home of William J. Bell in Ashley County. Their only other child was C. L. (Crawford Leon) (b 17 Jan 1934; m 1st Betty Roberts; m 2nd Callie ?; m 3rd Annette Hilburn).

Muriel Leon Adams was born 13 Sep 1912 in Como, MO, the son of Maysie Nevada (Paxton) and Andrew Crawford Adams. Their other children were Inez (m Albert Tilbury), Crawford Paul (m Lessie Walters), and Laverne (m Verner Forbes). The family moved to Wilmot sometime prior to 1933. Maysie (Paxton) Adams was born 1 Feb 1893 in New Madrid, MO and died 3 Feb 1958. Andrew Crawford Adams was born 25 Nov 1886 in Johnson County IL and died 18 Sep 1977. They were both buried in Wilmot. Andrew Crawford Adams was the son of Martha Jane (Newlin) and George Washington Adams. Their other children were Rose, Ophelia, Flossie, Lyles, Georgia (b 4 Oct 1895 Sterling, UT), and Harold.

George Washington Adams was born 26 Jul 1853 in Pulley's Mills, IL, and died 14 July 1897 in Sampth, IL. A Mormon, he took his family to Manti, UT for a few years to assist with the construction of the Manti Temple. On the return trip they traveled in a covered wagon across Utah and by train to IL. The Singer sewing machine that they took with them is still operable today and will adapt to a modern buttonhole attachment.

Leon Adams worked for the deYampert Trust, his principal job being to run the cotton gin. Sometime after WWII William deYampert III and Leon made a business trip to Chicago where Leon first saw a manually operated cement block machine. Knowing the gin workers needed year round employment, he came up with the idea to manufacture concrete blocks during the off-season. At that time most of the buildings in Wilmot were constructed of wood or brick, but when the machinery arrived in town, a new era of building began. He built several buildings for the deYamperts including the present deYampert store, William's home and swimming pool on Lake Vesta, and a medical facility. Just prior to his death in 1969, he had built a restaurant on the northern edge of town and was beginning a motel, which was never completed.

Alice Jewel Roper was born 14 Jul 1916 near Fountain Hill in Ashley County, the daughter of Mary Tamzia Indiana (Sharp) and John William Roper Sr. Their other children were John William Jr. (b 28 Sep 1906; d 2 Apr 1982; m Cara Bonner), Tamzia (b 2 Sep 1908; d 11 Mar 1972; m Linville Holland), James Nathaniel (b 13 Nov 1910; m Sue Anna Allison), Mode Franklin (b 12 Oct 1912; d 9 Sep 1966; m Bernice Hughes), and Mike Gilbert (b Sep 1918; d 14 Oct 1997; m Margie Haynes). John William Roper was previously married to Ellie Burchell, and their children were Sarah Bell (b 6 Apr 1901; d 16 Apr 1991; m Willie Goodwin), Icey Jewel, and Ellie. John William Roper Sr. was born 29 Jan 1865 and died 2 Sep 1924 at Wilmot. His wife died 18 Oct 1961 at Wilmot.

John William Roper Sr. was the son of Nancie A. (Matheny) and James D. Roper. Their other children were Margaret (b 1857; m Will Morris), James (b 1860), Mary (b 1862), Moses S. (b 1867), Georgie A. (b 1870 DeBastrop Twsp, Ashley County), Alice (b 1873 DeBastrop Twsp; m Nathan L. Morris), Rosa Elizabeth (b 1875 DeBastrop Twsp; m Ivan Morris), and Gilbert Morris (b 1878 DeBastrop Twsp). Nancie A. (Matheny) Roper was born 1833 in AR and died Feb 1880 in Ashley County. James D. Roper Sr. was born 1831 in SC. He and his brother, Thomas A. (b 1824 SC; m Sarah ?) both farmed near Wilmot and served in the Confederate Army. James D. enlisted in Co. G, 37th AR Infantry on 10 May 1682 at Hamburg. They had one sister, Margaret (b 1832 SC). They were the children of Martha (b 1803 SC) and Dana W. Roper (b 1795 SC).

Mary Tamzia Indiana (Sharp) Roper was born 18 Feb 1903 in Neshoba, MS, the daughter of Tamzia (Clark) and William Ferdinand Sharp. Their other children were Frank, Lee, Joe, Mike (b 1 Apr 1885; d 9 Feb 1933 Lubbock, TX), Columbia, and William Hiram (b 15 Mar 1881; d 10 Dec 1902 Crossett, AR). William F. Sharp received a grant for a homestead for 119.92 acres in Ashley County on 20 May 1862.

William F. Sharp was born in 1853 in Neshoba County, MS, the son of Sarah L. (Harrison) and Henry R. "Rice" Sharp who were married 9 Nov 1843 in Lawrence County TN. They had eight other children. According to the 1818 List of Taxable Property, Polls, and Census of Lawrence County, David Crockett lived in the county and participated in the taking of the census where Henry and his brother, Groves, lived.

Sarah L. Harrison was born c1825 in VA. Henry R. Sharp was born in 1820 in Lawrence County, TN, the son of Henry Sharp. Henry Sharp was born in 1779 in Southampton, VA, and married Keziah Gurley in 1801 in Johnson County NC. He was descended from Groves Sharp who was born in 1779 in VA. Groves Sharp's father was Francis II and his grandfather was Francis I. Henry Sharp was a justice of the peace in Lawrence County.

Mary Tamzia (Sharp) Roper would never talk about her Indian ancestry until she was accidentally burned over a large part of her body. During the following illness, she would ramble and talked about her mother wearing her hair in long, black braids. She said that her mother (Tamzia Clark) was "full blood" and her father (William F. Sharp) was half-Indian. (This has not been verified by research.) She was short in stature with a medium dark complexion and wore her very coarse graying black hair in a coil on the top of her head. Everyone called her Aunt Mary.

Children born to C. L. Adams and Betty (Roberts) were Tracy Jamar and Muriel Leon "Buddy." Children born to C. L. Adams and Annette (Hilburn) were Michael Eugene, Crawford Lee, and Stacy Marie. He also adopted her son, Kelly Joe. C. L. Adams died 9 Oct 1988 and was buried at Dry Bayou Cemetery near Wilmot.

Betty Adams graduated from Wilmot in 1954 and married Joe Frank McKee on 14 May 1954. Joe Frank McKee was born 22 Oct 1929 at Portland, the son of Frances Dell (Hunter) and Frank McKee. He died 20 Sep 1989 and was buried at Portland. The only child born to Betty (Adams) and Joe Frank McKee was Alice Marie (unmarried). Betty's second marriage was to Roland T. Kinney Jr. of Monroe.

⚜

Skipper
Submitted by Sara Neeley

James Skipper received four land patents in Drew County from 1857 to 1860. On 1 Jul 1857 he bought 200 acres in T14S-R7W; on 3 May 1858 had bought two parcels of 80 and 120 acres, and on 1 Sep 1860 he bought 40 acres. The 1860 census for Drew County lists James Skipper (b c1794 NC; $5,000 real estate; $5,000 personal property), Martha (wife; b 1807 NC), Mary (b 1836 AL), Civil E. (b 1838 AL), and Francis M. [Marian] (b 1843 AL). The 1870 census for Drew County lists Moriah Skipper (b 1849 GA), Frances [Francis Marian?] (b 1846 AL), Adelia (b 1867 AR), Better (female; b Aug 1870), and Mariah (black; b 1863 AR). It is likely, but not proven, that James was related to William Franklin "Willie" Skipper of Baxter.

Living in the household of James Skipper (b c1796 in NC) in 1850 in Henry County AL were: Martha (wife, b c1808 NC), Comfort (dau, b c1829, ? NC), Mary Farmer (dau, b 15 May 1836 AL), Civil (dau, b c1840 AL), and Marian (son, b c1843 AL). Other Skipper households represented in the 1850 census were:

1. Daniel (b 1811 SC), Nancy (b 1800 SC), Elizabeth (b 1829 FL), and Jonathon W. (b 1816 GA).

2. P. M. (b 1815 SC), Elizabeth (b 1823 Al), James (b 1844 AL), Nancy J. (b 1845 AL), Mary A. (b 1847 AL), and Charlotte (b 1848 AL).

3. P. B. (sheriff; b 1820 SC), M. S. (female; b 1833 GA), male (b 1847 AL), A. B. (b 1848 AL), and male (b 1849 AL).

Mary Farmer Skipper, daughter of James and Martha Skipper, married William Daniel (or Daniels). After William died, Mary married Henry A. Hall (b 1845 MS) in Drew County on 29 Jul 1873. In 1880 Mary and Henry Hall were living in Van Buren County AR. With them were Merron (Marian), Martha (b 1876 AR), Oscar (b 1878 AR), Zedock Daniels (b 1865 AR), and Florence William Daniels (b 1866 AR). William Daniels, born in TN, was the father of the last two children. The Henry Hall family moved to Bowie, TX in 1881.

The will of James Skipper, dated 11 Feb 1862, mentions the following children: James M. and his children, James William and Mary Jane; Everett (possibly the Civil E. mentioned in the 1860 census); Francis Marian (listed in the 1850 and 1860 census); Mary Farmer; Elizabeth Ann, wife of James Irwin Murphy (also spelled Murphey; m in Henry Co. AL); and Martha Jane, wife of Hugh T. Murphy (also spelled Murphey). Subscribing as witnesses to the will, which was handed to Samuel Gibson, clerk of probate court, were William H. Harrison, John West, and Samuel Gibbs. James Skipper was deceased when the will was delivered on 1 Nov 1862. Francis Marian Skipper is buried at Collins, Drew County. He was born 29 Mar 1842 and died 1 Dec 1896. See McShan family history for his marriage and children.

John Smith
Submitted by Karen Groce

According to Goodspeed, John Smith, known as "Bear Hunter John," was born in MS and married twice. His second wife was Sarah Bowden who he married in her native state of LA. About 1811 the couple with a number of slaves rowed up Bayou Bartholomew in a boat he had built and settled near the present town of Dermott. He extended his land holdings and eventually moved up the bayou to a point 25 to 30 miles south of Pine Bluff, where he died in 1862, and Sarah (Bowden) died c1867. John Smith served in the War of 1812 and was with Andrew Jackson at New Orleans.

The couple had twelve children, one of whom was James Smith, born in 1836 in what is now Lincoln County. When he was 16 he became manager of his father's plantation. He married Mary Rogers, a native of GA, in 1855. [Goodspeed's date of 1847 is in error.] She was the daughter of James and Matilda (Thornton) Rogers, natives of NC, who moved from GA to Drew County. James Rogers died there in 1863 [Goodspeed's date of 1852 is in error], and Matilda Rogers died in 1861. [Goodspeed says her death occurred 11 years after James's death, which is in error.] Both are buried in Mt. Pleasant Cemetery. James and Mary Smith had nine children, of which two sons and five daughters were living in 1890. James Smith joined Company F, Ninth Arkansas Infantry in 1861 and served as a captain until the surrender at Vicksburg. He returned to the Lincoln County plantation for a number of years before moving to Star City, where he was in the liquor and merchandising business for about twelve years. Fire destroyed his building in 1883, and he relocated to Kingsland in Cleveland County where he built and operated Smith Hotel. The hotel was still in business in 1890.

Stone, Turnage, Riley
Submitted by Clif Turnage

Stone – William Benton Stone was born 18 Dec 1830 and died 22 Oct 1880. He married Artimisa Jane Waldrop, and their children were Mary Susan (b 29 May 1854; d 18 Oct 1859), John Benton (b 25 Apr 1857; d Nov 1923; m 1st Matilda Carlin Seymore 19 Sep 1878; m 2nd Eleanor Wallington 23 Dec 1880), David Samuel Rawleigh (b 6 Jun 1859; d 14 Aug 1860), Marguerite Ann Francis (b 2 Feb 1861; d Sep 1865), Tabetha Cumy (b 28 Nov 1862; d Dec 1908; m James Harper 28 Dec 1880), Nancy Jane

Basdel (b 29 Jan 1865; d Sep 1869), Robert Marion (b 16 Feb 1869; d 6 Feb 1888), Jackson Vanburen Waldrop (b 17 Nov 1870; m Anna Riley), Amanda Carolin (b 15 Dec 1872; d 25 Dec 1962; m W. E. Brown), and William Norman (b 23 Feb ?; d 14 1896).

Children born to Anna (Riley) and Jackson Vanburen Stone were Robert Marion (b 17 Nov 1893; m Ruth M. Douglas 13 Mar 1915), Julia Fidelia (b 3 Oct 1895; m Thad D. Douglas Feb 1915), Carney O. (b 11 Feb 1902; m John Edward Bailey 7 Dec 1924), Vonnie Ann (b 12 Sep 1903; m James R. Bailey 30 Dec 1925), Helen Elizabeth (b 11 Feb 1905; m Charles Wisner 5 Dec 1924), Gladys Josephine (b 19 Nov 1906; m 1st Cecil Turnage 21 Jan 1925; m 2nd Zack Boykin 2 Apr 1953), Charles Henry (b 23 Nov 1908; m Mary Wilcoxon 27 Jan 1934), George D. (b 4 Oct 1910; d Dec 1911), Irene (b 29 Jan 1913; m Harry Smith 20 Dec 1941), James Jackson (b 28 Jan 1916; m Marcella Mae Franklin 2 Sep 1939), Agnes (b 9 Oct 1917; m Thomas Adair 17 Jan 1937), and Anna Winnimay (b 5 Aug 1923; m Cecil Riley 28 Nov 1946).

Artimissa Jane Waldrop, wife of William Benton Stone, was born 7 Nov 1834, the daughter of Susan and Sam R. Waldrop. Their other children were Francis Marion (b 18 Oct 1835), Jackson Van Buren (b 2 Apr 1837), Benton Zachariah (b 12 Feb 1839), William Lee (b 1 Aug 1840), Elizabeth Ann Hasseltine (b 28 Dec 1841), Hester Caroline (b 7 Dec 1843), Nancy Henrietta (b 15 Jan 1846), Susannah Mandaline (b 14 Aug 1848) and John Samuel Dunwooda (b 28 Nov 1852).

Turnage – The Turnage family came from Wales in the 1600s and settled in VA. Some migrated to SC and from there some went to southern MS in the 1700s.

Alcus Thomas Turnage was born 10 Mar 1877 in MS, died 10 Sep 1939 at Hamburg, AR, and was buried at Trafalgar. He married Susan Laura Barnes, who was born 22 Jan 1881 in Ashley County, died 10 Sep 1959, and was buried at Trafalgar. Their children, all born in Ashley County, were Marvin Dewey (b 22 Oct 1899; m Doris Mary Harkey), Frank Lee (b 1 Oct 1901; m Walta Aline Baker), Viola (b 8 Feb 1903; m George Hitch), Cecil (b 1904-07; m 1st Gladys Stone; m 2nd Mildred Stephens), Pell Burney (b 27 Jul 1908; m Mildred B. Johnston), Mabel (b 11 Apr 1910; m William Olen Martin), Brooksey Mack (b 13 Feb 1913; m Maude Elsie Stotts), Daphne Alton (b 17 Feb 1915; m Frances Pamplin), Claudia (b 16 May 1917; m William George Schwind), Opal G. (b 8 Apr 1919; m Layton H. McAfee), and Merle G. (b 2 Jul 1923; m Edward F. Smith).

Children born to Gladys (Stone) and Cecil Turnage were Edward M. and Charles L.(m Marlys Cashion). Children born to Cecil Turnage and second wife, Mildred Stephens, were Michael Robert and David Patrick. A child born to Marlys (Cashion) and Charles L. Turnage was Clif.

Children born to Marcella Mae (Franklin) and James Jackson Stone were Linda Gail (m Harry Shiver) and Carola Ann (m Billy Raymond Carpenter).

Cathryn Turnage wrote, "Alcus [Turnage] was 41 years old, a farmer residing in the Trafalgar community when he registered for the draft during WWI, in 1918. Marvin D. Turnage [son of Alcus] was born in 1899 in Arkansas. Family tradition states that Alcus rode horseback from Nacogdoches, Texas to Ashley County AR in the 1890s after his parents died. Alcus' father is believed to have been John or William Turnage, living in Monticello, MS, prior to moving to Nacogdoches, Texas around 1875. Susan Barnes was the daughter of John Barnes and Sophronia White."

Riley – James Cooper Riley (b 1 Jan 1826) married 1 Jan 1851 Elizabeth Ann Davis (b 11 Nov 1833). Their children were John Rutledge Sr. (b 12 Nov 1851; m 1st Georgia Carry Taylor; m 2nd Martha Cone), James Andrew (b 9 May 1853; d 3 Jan 1854), William Alexander (twin to James Andrew; d 4 Mar 1870), James Nathaniel (b 16 Jan 1855; m 1st Julia Fidelia Taylor; m 2nd Mattie Yelvington), Mary Ann (b 4 Apr 1857; m Thomas Miller Yelvington), Joseph Holmes (b 3 Mar 1860; m Eliza Thompson), Samuel Jackson (b 15 Mar 1863; d 1 Jan 1878), Susan Elizabeth (b 27 Feb 1866; m 1st James Henry Rodgers; m 2nd Francia Marion Linder; m 3rd L. W. Elkins), Robert Randolph (b 12 Nov 1868; m Eliza McDougal), Louisa Jane (b 9 May 1871; m John T. Powell), George Thomas (b 7 Jul 1873; m 1st Effie Sullivan; m 2nd Laura Stanley), and Patrick Johnson (b 25 Sep 1876; d 9 Aug 1877).

The only child born to James Nathaniel Riley and first wife Julia Fidela Taylor was Anna Elizabeth (m Jackson Van Buren Stone). Children born to James Nathaniel Riley and second wife Mattie Yelvington were John Clark Sr.(b 30 Aug 1888; m Inez Locke), Ira Green Sr. (b 25 Oct 1890; m Lula Bell Stanley), Kitty Virginia (b 20 Feb 1898; m Velma G. Clark), James Samuel (b 30 Oct 1899; d 12 Jul 1905), James Henry (b 27 Sep 1884; d 25 Feb 1885), Hettie Liev (b 30 Nov 1882; d 16 Oct 1887), Catty Polly (b 13 Feb 1884; d 20 Dec 1897), and Frank Davis (b 13 Oct 1894; d 4 Aug 1904).

Children born to Lula Bell (Stanley) and Ira Green Riley were Claude Willis (m Mary Marie Judkins), Ira Green Jr. (m Margaret Ann Higginbotham), Harold Fredrick, and James Clark (m Jimmy Gail Masters). Children born to Kitty Virginia (Riley) and Velma G. Clark were Samuel James (m Dorothy Lee Kelley), Carroll Huey (m Iral Sue Finnell), and Mary Sue (m Levi Clark). Children born to Inez (Locke) and John Clark Riley Sr. were John Clark Jr. and Elizabeth Beth (m William North).

Gladys Stone Turnage was fond of saying, "I lived halfway between Promise Land and Paradise at Mt. Olive on the banks of Jordan Creek on the road to Troy." Jordan Creek empties into Bearhouse Creek which joins with Bayou Bartholomew near Thebes.

꙰꙰꙰

Dr. Charles Martin Taylor
Compiled by the author from
information in the Drew County Museum

Charles Martin Taylor was born July 23, 1819, in Winchester, KY, the son of Mildred E. (Martin) and Samuel Martin Taylor. Their other children were Jonathan Gibson (b 15 Mar 1811), Mary Ann (b 3 Jul 1813), Sarah Elizabeth (b 29 Sep 1816), Samuel Francis (b 1821), Robert William (b 1823), Rachel Mildred (b 1826), Susan America (b 1828), Hetty Hawes (b 1830), and George Edward (b 1833). Mildred E. Martin was born 9 Jun 1793, and married Samuel Martin Taylor 21 Feb 1810. Samuel Martin Taylor was born 30 Jan 1785, the ninth child of Ann "Nancy" (Berry) and Jonathan Taylor. They were married in 1764 and had thirteen children. Ann Berry Taylor died 18 Mar 1809, and Jonathan Taylor died 26 Jun 1803. They were buried at Basin Springs Cemetery in Clark County, KY. Ann Berry was born 7 Aug 1749, the daughter of Mary "Mollie" (Pryor) and Major William Berry of Gloucester and Caroline Counties VA. Mary Pryor was born 15 Nov 1730, the daughter of Prudence (Thornton) and Colonel Samuel Pryor of Gloucester County VA. Prudence Thornton was born 31 Mar 1699.

Jonathan Taylor was born in 1742, the son of Rachel (Gibson) and Colonel George Taylor of Orange County VA. Their other children were James (b 1738; m Ann Pendleton), George (d 1761), Edmund (b 1744; m Sarah Stubbs), Francis (nev m), Richard (b 1749; m Catherine Davis), John, William Berry (b 1753; m Lucy Hord; m 2nd Eliza Courts), Dr. Charles (b 1755; m Sarah Conway), Reuben (b 1757; m Rebecca Moore), Benjamin (b 1760; m Susan Courtney), and George (b 1769; d 1805). Richard and Catherine Taylor's grandson, Edmund Haynes Taylor, was "Old Taylor" of distillery fame.

Rachel Gibson was the daughter of Jonathan Gibson. George Taylor was born 10 Feb 1711, the son of Martha (Thompson) and James Taylor II of King and Queen County VA. Their other children were Frances (b 30 Aug 1700; m Ambrose Madison), Martha (b 17 Jan 1702; m Thomas Chew), James (b 30 Mar 1703; m Alice Catlett; m 2nd Elizabeth Lewis; m 3rd Mrs. Mary Gregory), Zachary (b 17 Apr 1707; m Elizabeth Lee; m 2nd M. Blackburn), Tabitha (b 2 Mar 1713; m T. Wild), Erasmus (b 5 Sep 1715; m Jane Moore), Hannah (b 15 Mar 1718; m Nicholas Battaille), and Mildred (b 11 Dec 1724; m Richard Thomas). Frances (Taylor) and Ambrose

Madison had a son, James, who married Nellie Conway. Born to Nellie (Conway) and James Madison was James who became the president of the United States. Elizabeth (Lee) and Zachary Taylor had a son, Richard, who married Sarah Strother. Sarah and Richard Taylor's son was Zachary, who also served as president.

John Martin Taylor married Mary Elizabeth Robertson 4 Jul 1843 in Union County KY. She was born 9 Aug 1824 in Nashville, TN, the daughter of Martha Eliza (Goodloe) and Benjamin Franklin Robertson, who were married 30 Sep 1823. Benjamin Franklin Robertson was born 4 Mar 1799, the son of Addy (Davis) and Jonathan Franklin Robertson, who were married 1 Dec 1791. Addy Davis was born 30 Dec 1773, the daughter of Fanny and Frederic Davis. Jonathan Friar Robertson was born 18 Jun 1769, the son of Charlotte and General James Robertson who was known as the "founder of Nashville."

Martha Eliza Goodloe was born 15 Jun 1807 in Maury County TN, the daughter of Elizabeth (Jelks) and John Minor Goodloe, who were married 12 Nov 1805. John Minor Goodloe was born 1771 or 1789, the son of Sarah and Robert Goodloe. Sarah was born 1745, and Robert Goodloe was born 24 Apr 1741. Martha Eliza Goodloe Robertson married second (5 Nov 1826) General William Arnold, who died 1 Jun 1833. She married third (17 Mar 1836) Peter Rives, who was born 24 Oct 1793 in VA. Peter Rives claimed land on Bayou Bartholomew in Drew County and well as land in Desha, Lincoln, and Crittenden Counties in 1818. He settled on the bayou and built a cabin. By 1836 he was in Crittenden County where he died in 1852. Martha Eliza Goodloe Rives died there 4 Jan 1881.

Dr. John Martin Taylor and his wife, who was Rives' stepdaughter, purchased the Rives land in Drew, Lincoln, and Desha Counties and settled on it in 1844. Dr. Taylor was a graduate of Transylvania University Medical School at Lexington, KY. Children born to Mary Elizabeth (Robertson) and Dr. John Martin Taylor were Franklin Robertson (b 22 Dec 1847; d 2 Sep 1852), Henry Robertson (b 27 Jul 1849; d 6 Jun 1900; nev m), Samuel Mitchell (b 1 Sep 1851; d 1 Sep 1900; m Plunkett Elvira Paschal), Jonathan Gibson "Gip" (b 17 Sep 1853; d 20 May 1929), John Martin (b 23 Jul 1855; d 15 Dec 1904), Robert Edward (b 2 Oct 1857), Eliza Mildred (b 14 Sep 1859 in KY; d 29 Mar 1931; m Henry P. Bradford), an infant daughter (b and d 1861), Benjamin Hawes (b 21 Apr 1863; m Lizzie K. ?; d 4 Oct 1915), Goodloe Rives (b 22 Jan 1868 in KY; d 18 May 1943), and Minnie (d infant).

Dr. Samuel Mitchell Taylor and Plunkett Elvira Paschal had a daughter, Belle Robertson, who was born 9 Sep 1894 and died 15 Mar 1936. Belle married Oliver Jennings on 23 Nov 1872. Plunkett Elvira Paschal was born 4 Sep 1857 and died 5 Jan 1898. Eliza Mildred (Taylor) and Henry P. Bradford were married 5 Apr 1882. Their daughter, Mildred Taylor, was

born 1 Dec 1886. She married Dillard Saunders, and their daughter was
Mildred Percy.
Buried in marked graves at the old Taylor Hollywood Plantation near
Winchester in Drew County are: Dr. John M. Taylor (d 30 Oct 1844), Dr.
Samuel Mitchell Taylor (d 1 Sep 1900), Elvira Plunkett Taylor (d 5 Jan
1898), Franklin Robertson Taylor (d 2 Sep 1852), Henry Robertson Taylor
(d 6 Jun 1900), infant Taylor, daughter of Benjamin H. and Lizzie K. Taylor
(d 18 Aug 1893), and infant Taylor, daughter of Dr. John M. and Mary E.
Taylor (d 1861). Martha Elizabeth Robertson Taylor died at Mauvilla, the
Taylor plantation in Oldham County KY, 25 Feb 1868. Many of the Taylor
family possessions, including china and furniture, are on permanent display
at the Drew County Historical Museum in Monticello, Arkansas. The
historic Rives cabin is also on the grounds of the museum.

≈≈✿≈≈

Watson-Rabb
Submitted by Janie Rabb Fuller

James Richardson Watson and his wife, Lucretia Robinson, came to
Arkansas in the 1850s from Winsboro, SC. They had land holdings in
Drew, Lincoln, and Desha Counties. One of their farms was at Garrett
Bridge in Lincoln County. There are seven great-grandchildren and two
great-great grandchildren living on the Watson property on Rabb Road
north of Monticello. Janie Rabb Fuller, a great-granddaughter, lives on the
site of the original James R. Watson homeplace.
James R. Watson (b 4 Feb 1832, SC; d 3 Oct, 1908, Monticello) was the
son of Harriett (Spann) and Richard Walker Watson. Harriett Spann was
the daughter of Anna (Jennings) and James Spann. Richard Walker Watson
(b Fairfield, SC) was the son of Anne (d 1813) and James Alex Watson.
James R. Watson married Lucretia Robinson 4 Sep 1850. She was born 1
Dec 1834 in SC, the daughter of Mary Ann (Mobley) Woodard and John A.
Robinson. Mary Ann Mobley was b 1799, the daughter of Elizabeth
(Pickett) Whitehead (b 13 Sep 1774; d 12 Sep 1836) and Samuel Mobley (b
1771; d 16 Aug 1854 ?). John A. Robinson (b 1810, Fairfield, SC) was the
son of Lucretia (Mobley) (b 1780; d 27 Apr 1863; bu Lebanon, MS) and
John Robinson (d 1853). Elizabeth Pickett Whitehead is buried in
Woodward, SC. Lucretia Robinson died 9 Jan 1901 and was buried in Oak
Ridge Cemetery in Drew County.
Lucretia Watson, daughter of Lucretia (Robinson) and James R. Watson,
was born 22 Aug 1873 in AR and died 19 Feb 1916 at Monticello. She
married Edward Joel Rabb, who was born 14 May 1857 in SC, the son of
Keziah "Cassandrah" (Robinson) and Thomas Rabb. Keziah Robinson was

a sister to Lucretia Robinson. (See above.) Thomas Rabb was born 6 Jul 1833, the son of Renthea (Glazier) and John Rabb. Renthea Glazier was born 27 Jul 1793, the daughter of Elizabeth (Edwards) (b 5 Sep 1759; d 20 Jan 1840) and Captain John Glazier (d 4 Dec 1831, age 76; Revolutionary War patriot). John Rabb was born 6 May 1781, probably in SC, the son of Hannah (Barnett) and James Rabb. He died 1 Oct 1849 in Fairfield County SC.

Lucretia (Watson) and Edward Joel Rabb were married 19 Nov 1889. Their children were Thomas Watson (b 29 Aug 1891; d 16 Sep 1962; m Jewell Calhoun), Hallie Mae (b 20 Oct 1894; d 7 Apr 1978; m Neil Owens), Ruth (b 19 Oct 1896; d 11 Dec 1908), Walker (b 27 May 1899; d 20 Jul 1905), James Richardson "Doc" (b 10 Aug 1902; d 21 Jul 1990; m Mary Jane Holland), William Stitt "Bill" (b 4 Apr 1905; d 5 Jun 1967; m Ellen McGough), Mittie Lucretia (b 1 Sep 1908; d 2 Aug 1977; nev m), and Edward Joel "E. J." (b 26 Jun 1911; d 16 Jan 1979; m Hazel Ross).

Thomas Watson Rabb married Jewell Calhoun, who was born 25 Dec 1897 in Monticello, the daughter of Eula (Sawyer) and Eddie Lee Calhoun. Children born to Jewell (Calhoun) and Thomas Watson Rabb were Katie Mae (m Lawrence Raines), Colby (d infant), Grover Edward (m Betty Sue Cater), Roth Lee (m 1st Frances Elizabeth Jones; m 2nd Florence Huffman), Tom Jr. (m Imogene Henderson), Lester Mobley (m Ann Lytle), Joe Walker (m Gay Nell Hoover), Camille (m Houston Berryman), James Ibb (m 1st Ann Norris; m 2nd Bernice Murry), and Janie Beth (m Larry Fuller). Larry Fuller was the son of Mabel (Keene) and LaVelle Fuller. (See Fuller family history.)

✺

Edward Wiley
From information submitted by Dan Wiley
Information in brackets supplied by the author

Edward Wiley was born c1790 in PA and died in Chicot County (in present Drew County) 5 Nov 1846. Homestead and cash entry patent records reveal that he claimed at least five tracts of land along the bayou in present Drew County in 1838. These tracts lay in 36-13S-4W and 1-14S-4W, the area north and south of Baxter. He was married to Dovey ? who was born c1803 in NC. Their known children were Martha Ann (b 1829; d before 1860; m Jessie Bowden 10 Sep 1853 in Drew County), Eliza Jane (b 1837; m ? Hart), Dovey Ann (b 1840), and Mary Emily (b 1842). Robert S. Taylor was appointed guardian for these three minor children (under age 14) on 8 Jan 1850. By this time Dovey Wiley had married Thomas S. Newman. Living with them was a child, Nancy Newman, who was born c1846.

Stephen Gaster was later appointed as guardian of Martha Wiley.
[According to an article in the Arkansas Gazette, 8 May 1833, Nancy
Wiley, daughter of Edward Wiley, married Reece Bowden on Bayou
Bartholomew 18 Apr 1833. The article also noted that both Edward Wiley
and Reece Bowden had come from LA. According to research compiled by
Mildred Bowden Oglesby, Edward Wiley may have had other children. She
listed Elizabeth (m ? Hart), Martha Ann (m Jessie Bowden), Elizabeth Jane
(m James M. Austin), Dovie Ann, and Mary Emily (m D. A. White).] There
was another Edward Wiley in Drew County. He was born 16 Apr 1830 in
MO and married Caroline Delane Touchstone in Desha County 30 Oct
1851. Children born to them were George Washington (b 23 Aug 1854
Drew County; d 19 Mar 1942 Woodson, TX; m 26 Dec 1888 Caroline
Cynthia Martin, Dublin, TX), Jane Alathe (b 22 Aug 1856 Drew County; d
8 Aug 1918 Alexander, TX; m Claudius O. Oliver), Cass Somerset (b 30
Oct 1861 AR; d 3 Jan 1882), Dove Ann (b 22 Jul 1864; m Henry Carter),
Theory Adaliza (b 5 May 1866 Drew County; m 21 Aug 1884 Erath County
TX, Cicero Harrison Shaw; d 16 Jun 1945 Eolian, TX), Barbara Sebeler (b 7
Sep 1869, in AR; m John Morrison; d 22 Oct 1940 Woodson, TX), and
Cora Caroline (b 1 Nov 1877; m Fred Carnes).

[Was this Edward Wiley also a son of Dovey and Edward Wiley? Were
they in MO in 1830, move to LA, and then to AR by 1833? Caroline
(Touchstone) and Edward Wiley named one of their children Dove Ann.
That was also the name of Dovey and Edward Wiley's daughter.] Edward
Wiley was living very near the Newman household in Drew County in
1860.

Edward Wiley (b 1830) enlisted 20 Jun 1861 in Capt. Taylor's Company
of the Arkansas Infantry at Selma, which was north of Baxter. He received
a medical discharge 25 Oct 1861 following an attack of typhoid fever with
spinal irritation, which led to paralysis of the lower limbs as well as loss of
power in his right hand, caused by previous abscesses. He eventually
moved his family to Erath County TX where he died 22 Jul 1894.

Caroline Delane Touchstone was born 27 Jan 1832 in MS, the daughter
of Jane/Jenny Randal (b 1802 GA) and James M. Touchstone (b 1798 SC).
Their other children were Jesse A. (b 1824 MS), Allen D. (b 11 Jan 1826
MS), Pembroke S. (b c1830 MS; m 1850-55 Artemisia R ?), James Jackson
(b c1835 MS; m 9 Nov 1853 Susan Margrett Mitchell, Drew County; d Jul
1863 Fort Delaware), George (b c1837 MS), Mary (b c1839 MS), William
P. (b c1843 MS), and T. Adaliza (b c 1845 MS). The father of James M.
Touchstone was Jesse (b 1774 NC). Caroline (Touchstone) Wiley died 26
Dec 1923 in Eolian, TX.

Columbus Wolf
Submitted by Beth Thurman

Christian Columbus "Lum" Wolf was born 6 Jan 1835 in AL, the son of Judy T. (Berryman) (d 1866) and Phillip Samuel Wolf (d 1874). Judy T. Berryman was the daughter of Burrell (or Byril) Berryman, and Phillip S. Wolf was the son of Mary (Stephens) and Jonathan J. Wolf[e] of SC. (Neither Phillip nor Columbus Wolf used the e on their last name, but some in the family retained it. The original spelling was Woolf.) The Phillip Samuel Wolf family moved to Drew County in the 1840s. After serving in the Confederate army, Columbus Wolf returned to his father's farm. In 1887 he moved to Poplar Bluff (Parkdale) in Ashley County and farmed. He married Mary J. Daniel, the daughter of Phereby Penny (Daniel) and Lewis Howell Daniel, in 1856 and they had three sons and three daughters. The Wolf house still stands on the banks of the bayou south of Parkdale.

A daughter, Ella, married Frank Barnes of Parkdale. A son, Dudley Daniel, died 23 Jun 1903, and his wife, Nettie, died 1902. They are buried in a family plot at McGinty. Others buried there are Mary Esther Wolfe (d after 1903) and Oliver Woodman Wolfe (d after 1903). Wolfes buried in the Parkdale Cemetery are Capt. C. C. (b 6 Jan 1835; d 14 Mar 1913), Calvin C. (b 1861; d 1938; husband of M. J.), Charles Eugene (b 13 June 1916; d 24 Oct 1918; son of M. C. and Freddie), Ida C. (b 1875; d 1929), Lawrence Lemuel (b 8 Nov 1898; d 29 Jul 1917; son of C. C. and I. C.), Louis P. (b 1874; d 1957), M. J. (b 14 Mar 18?8; d 10 Sep 1895; wife of Calvin C.), and Murray C. (b 25 Oct 1874; d 1932).

Robert H. Wolfe
From Herndon's Centennial History of Arkansas, Vol 3

Robert H. Wolfe was born 1 May 1867, the son of Elizabeth (Hagood) and James M. Wolfe. Elizabeth Hagood was born in Hopkinsville, KY, and James M. Wolfe was born near Granada, MS. The couple was married in LA c1857, moved to Tyro in Lincoln County about two years later with two young children, and began farming. James M. Wolfe served in the Confederate army and died in 1875. His widow later married J. T. Wilkins.

Robert H. Wolfe attended public school and eventually completed a commercial course at the University of Kentucky. He began working at the age of fifteen as a farm laborer for ten dollars a month plus room and board. In 1886 he went to work for McCain, Atkinson & Houston, a retail grocery in

Pine Bluff. His cousin, E. T. Hagood, purchased a farm near Winchester, and in 1889 Wolfe became his partner. He sold his interest in January 1893 and in September of that year joined partnership with J. T. W. Tillar of Winchester, the mercantile firm being named R. H. Wolfe & Company. The company also contained a large farming operation.

Robert H. Wolfe married Susie A. Bowles of Tyro 2 Feb 1893. Children born to this marriage were Lorena (m V. C. Harrell), Lawrence (m Frances Bear), and Marnette (m Wiley McGehee). Children born to Lorena (Wolfe) and V. C. Harrell were Robert W. and Ann. The only [?] child of Frances (Bear) and Lawrence Wolfe was Jane (m Roy Oldrup). Marnette (Wolfe) and Wiley McGehee had no children but adopted a son, Wiley McGehee Jr. \

Appendix
Signers of the Canal Petition to Congress
by Citizens of Chicot County, 1833

Sam Parker
R. D. Browne
A. H. Davies
John T. White
William Clark
H. Morrell
W. K. Estill
John Mathis
Wm. W. Rose
Jn Ingles
John Smith
James Purvis
James Estill
John W. Mauldin
John W. Allen
S. R. Gilmore
James Patterson
Joseph Marlow
Samuel Jenkins
Brinkley Ward
Walter Jackson
William Russell
Francis Roycraft
Hugh McGary
Warwick W. McGary
Noah Lingard
Jesse Skinner
Frederick Skinner
Daniel Farrell
Stephen H. Farrell
Eligah Barton
Rubin Staten
John Stuart
William Boukeloo
N. C. Allen
Philip Booth
Wm Terhune

Thos Blue
John Lewis
John O. Tunstall
Thos. Tunstall
George Tunstall
John Blue
John F. Harrison
John J. Bowie
Charles S. Reed
William Reed
William Howard
Samuel Patten
Alfred C. Parker
Amos W. Taylor
Edward Wiley
Stephen Gasten [Gaster]
William Jones
John Smith
John Sorels
James McGee
Wm Hunt
Moses Hays
Reese Brewer
Thomas Brady Jr.
Samuel Uselton
Abner Johnson
De La F. Raysdon
Wm B. Duncan
Joshua Croom
J. Van Matre
James Blaine
Theororick M. Dabney
H. Triplett
W. B. Patton
James B. Collinsworth
Isaac Adair
Abram Latting

W. DeVilemont
Stephenson Ellison
Tho. J. Young
John Rhd Offutt
William L. Oliphant
L. L. Davis
E. Ventdes
Gear W. Archer
Reymond P. Mathis
Thomas F. Ferrell
Samuel Estill
Josiah Hoskins
Josiah Ward
Joel Johnson
Wm Pratt
J. D. Parker
Samuel I. Ussery
H. S. Smith
G. G. Lane
Jeremiah Leach
William C. Norton
A. D. Galloway
S. H. Dabney
P. Samuel Wallise
Cyrus Hathaway

John Mills
Jese McCary
John P. Fisher
William C. Gibson
William Ferrell
William Hopkins
Thompson Clark
William L. Brady
Thomas Brady
Thomas Millse
Stuard Millse
Lewis Johnson
Leroy P. Johnson
Esaws Russell
Jacob Obanon
Solomon Hopkins
James Thomson
Andrew Carson
Samul Carson
Reese Bowden
Preston Gague
Robert Dabony
Sam Anderson
B.Williams
James B. Farrell

Selected Bibliography
Books

Advertisements of Lower Mississippi River Steamboats 1812 – 1920. Compiled by Leonard V. Huber. West Barrington, RI: Steamship Historical Society of America, 1959.

Arkansas: A Guide to the State. Compiled by the Workers of the Writer's Program of the Works Projects Administration. New York: Hastings House, 1941.

Arkansas Colonials: A Collection of French and Spanish Records Listing Early Europeans in Arkansas 1686-1804. Edited by Morris S. Arnold and Dorothy Jones Core. Gillette, AR: Grand Prairie Historical Society, 1986.

Arnold, Morris S. *Colonial Arkansas 1686-1804.* Fayetteville: University of Arkansas Press, 1991.

Baker, Russel Pierce. *From Memdag to Norsk: a Historical Directory of Arkansas Post Offices 1832-1971.* Hot Springs: Arkansas Genealogical Society, 1988.

A Baptismal Record of the Parishes Along the Arkansas River, August 5, 1796 – July 16, 1802. Edited by Dave Wallis and Frank Williamson. Pine Bluff: Jefferson County Historical Society, 1982.

Barry, John M. *Rising Tide: The Great Mississippi Flood of 1927 and How It Changed America.* New York: Simon and Schuster, 1997.

Bayou Bartholomew Alliance Technical Group. *Short and Long Term Strategies for Protecting and Enhancing Natural Resources in the Bayou Bartholomew Watershed.* Privately published, 1996.

Ben Lilly's Tales of Bear, Lions and Hounds. Edited by Neil B. Carmony. Silver City, NM: High-Lonesome Books, 1998.

Biographical and Historical Memoirs of Southern Arkansas ofPulaski, Jefferson, Lonoke, Faulkner, Grant, Saline, Perry,Garland and Hot Springs Counties, Arkansas. Chicago: Goodspeed Publishing Company, 1889.

Biographical and Historical Memoirs of Southern Arkansas [Clark, Miller, Sevier, Howard, Pike, Lafayette, Hempstead, Columbia, Little River,

Nevada, Cleveland,Ouachita,Dallas, Bradley, Calhoun, Union, Ashley, Drew, Lincoln, Desha, and Chicot Counties.] Chicago: Goodspeed Publishing Company, 1890.

Birch, Clifton L. *Bayou Bartholomew: A Regional Stream.* Privately published, 1999.

Blassingame, John W. *The Slave Community: Plantation Life in the Antebellum South.* New York: Oxford University Press, 1976.

Bolton, S. Charles. *Arkansas, 1800 – 1860: Remote and Restless.* Fayetteville: University of Arkansas Press, 1998.

Bowie, Walter Worthington. *The Bowies and Their Kindred: A Genealogical and Biographical History.* Cottonport, LA: Polyanthos, 1971.

Boddie, James H. Jr. *A Glimpse of Bastrop's Past.* [Pamphlet.] Bastrop: City of Bastrop, 1978.

Bushnell, David I. Jr. *The Choctaw of Bayou Lacomb St. Tammany Parish Louisiana.* Smithsonian Institution Bureau of American Ethnology Bulletin 48. Washington: Government Printing Office, 1909.

Collection of Recollections: Wilmot, Arkansas. Edited by Barbara Sharik Babb and compiled by Janet Clifton. Privately published, 1993.

Collier, Calvin L. *They'll Do To Tie To! The Story of the Third Regiment, Arkansas Infantry, C.S.A.* Little Rock: Pioneer Press, 1959.

Daniel, Pete. *Deep'n as It Come: The 1927 Mississippi River Flood.* Fayetteville: University of Arkansas Press, 1996.

Davenport, C. C. *Looking Backward: Memoirs of the Early Settlement of Morehouse Parish.* Mer Rouge: Press of *Mer Rouge Democrat*, 1911.

DeArmond, Rebecca. *Old Times Not Forgotten: A History of Drew County.* Little Rock: Rose Publishing Company, 1980.

DeArmond-Huskey, Rebecca. *Beyond Bartholomew: The Portland Area History.* Conway: River Road Press, 1996.

Dictionary of Americanisms On Historical Principles. Vol. 1. Chicago: University of Chicago Press, 1951.

Dobie, J. Frank. *The Ben Lilly Legend.* Curtis Publishing Company, 1950; reprint, Austin: University of Texas Press, 1997.

Eastern Louisiana: A History of the Watershed of the Ouachita River and The Florida Parishes. Vol. 1 and 3. Edited by Frederick Williamson and George T. Goodman. Louisville, KY: The Historical Record Association, 1940.

Edward Palmer's Arkansaw Mounds. Edited by Marvin D. Jeter.Fayetteville: University of Arkansas Press, 1990.

Etheridge, Y. W. *History of Ashley County, Arkansas.* Van Buren: Press Argus, 1959.

Ferguson, John L. and J. H. Atkinson. *Historic Arkansas.* Little Rock: Arkansas History Commission, 1966.

Fortier, A. *Louisiana: Comprising Sketches of Parishes, Towns, Events and Institutions*, Vol. 3. Century Historical Association, 1914.

Foster, William C. *The La Salle Expedition to Texas: The Journal of Henri Joutel 1684-1687.* Translated by Johanna S. Warren. Austin:Texas State Historical Association, 1999.

The Fur Animals of Louisiana. Bulletin 18. Edited by Robert S. Maestri, et al. New Orleans: Department of Conservation, 1931.

Genealogy of Wilkinson and Kindred Families. N.p.

Gibson, Jon L. *Poverty Point: A Terminal Archaic Culture of the Lower Mississippi Valley.* Baton Rouge: Louisiana Archeological Survey and Antiquities Commission, 1996.

Greene, Glen Lee. *Baptists of Oak Ridge.* Nashville: Parthenon Press, 1960.

Hanson, Gerald T. and Carl H. Moneyhon. *Historical Atlas of Arkansas.* Norman: University of Oklahoma Press, 1989.

Havighurst, Walter. *Voices on the River: The Story of Mississippi Waterways*. New York: Macmillan Company, 1964.

Hedges, Vera Lee. *Bartholomew United Methodist Church 1796 – 1996: A Great Cloud of Witnesses*. West Monroe: Scott Sherman, 1996.

Herndon, Dallas T. *Centennial History of Arkansas III*. Little Rock: S. J. Clarke, 1922.

History of Lincoln County Arkansas, 1871-1983. Edited by the Lincoln County Historical Society. Dallas: Taylor Publishing Company, 1983.

Hull, Clifton E. *Shortline Railroads of Arkansas*. Conway: UCA Press, 1988.

Images From the Past: A Pictorial History of Desha County, Arkansas and Southeast Arkansas Delta. Edited by Charlotte T. Schexnayder. Marceline, MO: Heritage House Publishing, n.d.

Jones, Amos. *The Dean of Dermott: The Life Story of Dr. York Wayland Williams Jr.* Nashville: Bethlehem Book Publishers, Inc., 1998.

Kay, George F. *The Shameful Trade*. New York: A. S. Barnes and Company, 1968.

Known Burials in Morehouse Parish Louisiana and South Ashley County. Edited by the Family History Club. Crossett, AR: Nowlin Printing, 1994.

Kouns, Sharon and Peggy Wells. *Folklore and Legends, Burlington, First County Seat, Lawrence County, Ohio*. Privately published, 1996.

Ladd, Kevin. *Gone to Texas: Genealogical Abstracts from the* Telegraph *and* Texas Register *1835-1841*. Bowie, MD: Heritage Books, Inc., 1994.

Leslie, James. *Saracen's Country "Some Southeast Arkansas History."* Little Rock: Rose Publishing Company, 1974.

Louisiana: A Guide to the State. Compiled by the Workers of the Writers' Program of the Work Project Administration in the State of Louisiana. New York: Hastings House, 1945.

Martinez, Raymond J. *The Story of Spanish Moss.* New Orleans: Home Publications, 1959.

Merchant Steam Vessels of the United States 1790 – 1868. Edited by C. Bradford Mitchell. Steamship Historical Society of America, Inc. Fair Lawn, NJ: De Troy Bergen Press, 1975.

Moore, Waddy William. *Territorial Arkansas.* Ann Arbor: University Microfilms, 1977.

Neuman, Robert W. and Nancy W. Hawkins. *Louisiana Prehistory.* 2nd ed. Baton Rouge: Louisiana Archeological Survey and Antiquities Commission, 1993.

1992-1993 Texas Almanac. Edited by Mike Kingston. Dallas: *Dallas Morning News*, 1991.

Pearson, Charles E. and Allen R. Saltus Jr. *Underwater Archaeology On The Ouachita River, Arkansas: The Search for the Chieftain, Haydee, and Homer.* Baton Rouge: Coastal Environments, Inc., 1993.

Reflections of Ashley County. Edited by Mary Imogene Nobel Carpenter and Robert A. Carpenter. Dallas: Curtis Media Corporation, 1987.

Report of the Chief of Engineers. Part 1, Vol. 5. Washington: Government Printing Office, 1904.

Robin, C. C. *Voyage to Louisiana.* Translated by Stuart O. Landry Jr. New Orleans: Pelican Publishing Company, 1966.

Saucier, Roger T. *Geomorphology and Quaternary Geological History of the Lower Mississippi Valley.* Vicksburg: U.S. Army Engineer Waterways Experiment Station, 1994.

Sealander, *A Guide to Arkansas Mammals.* Conway: River Road Press, 1979.

Shinn, Josiah H. *History of Arkansas,* Richmond, VA: B. F. Johnson Publishing Co., 1905.

Sisters, Seeds, and Cedars: Rediscovering the Nineteenth Century Life Through Correspondence From Rural Arkansas and Alabama. Conway: UCA Press, 1995.

U.S. Congress. House. 45th Cong., 3d sess.,Doc. 61.

U.S. Congress. House. 46th Cong., 3d sess.,Doc 38.

U.S. Congress. House. 48th Cong., 2d sess.,Doc. 147.

War of the Rebellion: A Compilation of the Official Records of the Union and Confederate Armies. Vol. 5, 33, 39, 48. Washington: Government Printing Office, 1891.

Way, Frederick Jr. *Way's Packet Directory, 1848 – 1994.* Rev. ed. Sons and Daughters of Pioneer Rivermen. Athens: Ohio University Press, 1994.

Williams, E. Russ. *Encyclopedia of Individuals and Founding Families of the Ouachita Valley of Louisiana from 1785 to 1850.* Monroe: Williams Genealogical and Historical Publications, 1997.

____. *Filhiol and the Founding of the Spanish Poste d' Ouachita: The Ouachita Valley in Colonial Louisiana 1783-1804.* Monroe: Monroe-Ouachita Valley Bicentennial Commission, 1982.

____. *Spanish Poste d' Ouachita: The Ouachita Valley in Colonial Louisiana 1783-1804 and Early America Statehood 1804-1820.* Monroe: Williams Genealogical and Historical Publications, 1995.

Willis, James. *Arkansas Confederates in the Western Theater.* Dayton: Morningside Press, 1998.

Articles

Adams, Horace. "Drew County Pioneers." *Drew County Historical Quarterly* (1987): 76-77.

"Bayou Pigeon and the Atchafalaya Basin." *Images of Iberville: Places Embodied in Art* 1(1998): 5.
<http://www.parish.iberville.la.us/m/dupre5.htm>.

Bearss, Edwin C. "Marmaduke Attacks Pine Bluff." *Arkansas Historical Quarterly* 23 (winter 1964): 296-297.

Bocage, Judge Jos. W. "Old Memories." *Jefferson County Historical Quarterly* 2 (autumn 1969): 8.

Bohinger, Mrs. C. H. "The Noel Family." Arkansas Historical Quarterly 14 (summer 1955), 117-118.

Bower, David R. "A Credo for the Earth." In *Hidden Passage: the journal of Glen Canyon Institute* (winter 1999): 8.

Bry, Hon. H. "The Ouachita Country, III." *DeBow's Review* 3 (May 1847): 408.

Bry, R. M. "Northern Louisiana and Arkansas." *DeBow's Review* 5 January 1848): 69.

Burman, Ben Lucien. "My Touchstone to the Mississippi," *Reader's Digest* (May 1946): 93, 95-97.

"Canal Between Ouachita and Mississippi Rivers, Benjamin L. Miles to Delegate Sevier, November 18, 1833." *Kin Kollecting* 4 (fall 1990): 42-43.

Davis, Caleb W. "St. Bartholomew." *Colliers Encyclopedia* 3 CD-ROM, Infonautics Corporations, 1998.

Davis, Hester. "Preserving the Past for the Future." Arkansas Archeological Survey flyer, n.d.

DeWoody, Mary Sorrells. "Life In The (1860) Sixties." *Jefferson County Historical Quarterly* 7 (summer 1977): 15-18.

DeWoody, Mrs. W. L. "Arkansas Daughters of the American Revolution." Fifth Arkansas State Conference Report, 1913.

Dickinson, Samuel Dorris. "Colonial Arkansas Place Names." *Arkansas Historical Quarterly* 48 (summer 1989): 141.

___. "Don Filhiol at Ecore a Fabri." *Arkansas Historical Quarterly* 46 (summer 1987): 135-136.

___. "An Early View of the Ouachita Region." *Old Time Chronicle: Folk History of Southwest Arkansas* 3 (July 1990): 15-16.

"The Dixon-Farmer Place." *Journal North Louisiana Historical Association* 15 (spring-summer 1984): 130.

"Extent of Steam Navigation in the United States." *DeBow's Review* 25(August 1858): 284.

Faye, Stanley. "The Forked River." *Louisiana Historical Quarterly* 25 (October 1942): 929.

"Hardwick to Trulock." *Jefferson County Historical Quarterly* 4 (spring 1972): 11-12.

Holley, Donald. "Drew County's Carpetbagger: The Life of S. A. Duke, Or How A Yankee Shoemaker Became a Wealthy Southern Merchant." *Drew County Historical Quarterly* 10 (1995): 5-17.

___. "The Man for the Times and Place." *Drew County Historical Quarterly* 4 (1989): 7.

Humble, Sallie Lacy. "The Ouachita Valley Expedition of De Soto." *Louisiana Historical Quarterly* 25 (July 1942): 628.

House, John H. "Archaic Occupation in the Arkansas River Lowland." *Field Notes* 171 (1980): 5.

___. "Resurveying the Bartholomew Bypass Route Near Pine Bluff." *Field Notes* 243 (1991): 3.

House, John H., and Marvin D. Jeter. "Excavations at Boydell Mound A (3AS58), Southeast Arkansas." *Arkansas Archeologist* 33 (1994): 4.

Hudson, Charles. "De Soto in Arkansas: A Brief Synopsis," *Field Notes* 205 (1985): 7-9.

Hudson, Walter C., ed. "Memoirs of James Madison Hudson." *Arkansas Historical Quarterly* 19 (autumn, 1960): 271-277.

Jackson, H. Edwin and Marvin D. Jeter. "Preceramic Earthworks in Arkansas: A Report on the Poverty Point Period Lake Enterprise Mound (3AS 379)." *Southeastern Archeology* 13, no. 2 (1994): 158.

Jennings, Oliver W. "Among the Arkansas Bayous; or, Recollections of a Camp Hunt." *Drew County Historical Quarterly* 6 (1991): 28-32.

Jeter, Marvin D. "Archeology and Indians In and Near Drew County." *Drew County Historical Journal* 5 (1990): 64, 72.

____. "Following a tough act with many more fine things: plans for the 1992 Big Dig at the Taylor Mounds (3DR1)." *Field Notes* 245 (1992): 3.

Kilpatrick, A. R. "Historical and Statistical Collections of Louisiana." *DeBow's Southern and Western Review* 12 (June 1852): 636.

Kouns, Sharon Milich. "Obituaries of Riverboatmen and Women," 1999. <http://home.pacifier.com/~history/Obrivermen.html>.

Leslie, J. W., ed. "Judge Bocage Memoirs: Memories of the Old Second Judicial District." *Jefferson County Historical Quarterly* 5 (summer 1947): 16-17.

"The Levees and Overflows of the Mississippi." *DeBow's Review* 25 (October 1858): 438.

McKelway, Henry. "Preliminary Investigations of 'The Eatman Place.'" *Field Notes* 169 (1980): 9-11.

Mitchell, Jennie O'Kelly and Robert Dabney Calhoun. "The Marquis De Maison Rouge, The Baron De Bastrop, and Colonel Abraham Morhouse: Three Ouachita Valley Soldier of Fortune: The Maison Rouge and Bastrop Spanish Land 'Grants.'" *Louisiana Historical Quarterly* 20 (April 1937): 294-453.

Moore, Clarence B. "Antiquities of the Ouachita Valley." *Journal of the Academy of the Natural Sciences of Philadelphia*, 2d ser., no. 14 (1909-1912): 111.

Norman, N. Phillip. "The Red River of the South." *Louisiana Historical Quarterly* 25 (January – October 1942): 402.

Pritchard, Walter, ed. "A Tourist's Description of Louisiana in 1860." *Louisiana Historical Quarterly* 21 (January 1938): 1199.

Pugh, Robert D. "Portland: A Sense of Place with a Strength of Differences." In *Somewhere Apart "My Favorite Places in Arkansas" Arkansas Residents Past and Present.* Compiled by the staff of Arkansas *Times* and the staff of the University of Arkansas Press. Fayetteville: University of Arkansas Press, 1997.

Rolingson, Martha Ann. "Archeology Along Bayou Bartholomew, Southeast Arkansas." *Arkansas Archeologist* 32 (1993): 1.

___. "The Bartholomew Phase: A Plaquemine Adaptation in the Mississippi Valley." *Cultural Change and Continuity, Essays in Honor of James Bennett Griffin.* New York: Academic Press, Inc., 1976.

Roosevelt, Theodore. "In the Louisiana Canebrakes." *Scribner's Magazine* (January 1908).

Sanders, Joe W., Thurman Allen, and Roger T. Saucier. "Four Archaic? Mound Complexes in Northeast Louisiana." *Southeastern Archaeology* 13 (winter 1994): 134-142.

Saucier, Roger T. "Quaternary Geology of the Lower Mississippi Valley." *Arkansas Archeological Survey.* Research series no. 6 (1974): 15-18.

Shea, William L. "Battle at Ditch Bayou." *Arkansas Historical Quarterly* 39 (fall 1980): 195-205.

Sherwood, Diana. "Clearing the Channel – The Snagboat in Arkansas." *Arkansas Historical Quarterly* 3 (spring 1944): 56-59.

Simpich, Frederick. "The Great Mississippi Flood of 1927." *National Geographic Magazine* 52 (September 1927): 259.

Superior Water-Logged Company. "The Science of Soaked Wood." 1997. <http://www.oldlogs.com/showroom/science.html>.

___. "Timeless Timber." 1997. [Pamphlet.]

Sutton, Keith. "Here Today...A Guide to Arkansas's Endangered and Threatened Animals." *Arkansas Wildlife* 27 (spring 1996): 24.

Treiber, Jacob. "Legal Status of Negroes in Arkansas Before the Civil War." *Arkansas Historical Association* 3 (1911): 175-183.

Watts, J. Carter. "Battle of Pine Bluff." *Jefferson County Historical Quarterly* 10 (spring 1982): 4-11.

___. "The Pursuit of Captain R. A. Kidd, January 15 – May 27, 1865." *Jefferson County Historical Quarterly* 10 (summer, 1982): 25-33.

Woods, Thomas A. "Nature Within History: Using Environmental History to Interpret Historic Sites." *History News* (summer 1997): 5.

Worley, Ted R., ed. "Tenant and Labor Contracts, Calhoun County, 1869-1871." *Arkansas Historical Quarterly* 13 (spring 1954):105.

Young, Pearl E. "Memories of an Ashley County Childhood." *Arkansas Historical Quarterly* 16 (winter 1957): 355-356.

Watkins, Beverly. "Human Adaptation in the Grand Marais Lowland." *Ouachita County Historical Quarterly* (spring 1983): 8

Newspapers

Advance-Monticellonian, 1907, 1971.
Arkansas Daily Gazette, 1871, 1874.
Arkansas Democrat, 1952, 1954.
Arkansas Democrat-Gazette, 1999.
Arkansas Gazette, 1867, 1871, 1875, 1882, 1887, 1889, 1892, 1895, 1896, 1907, 1938, 1941, 1959.
Arkansas Times, 2000.
Ashley County Eagle, 1901, 1917, 1908.
Ashley County Ledger, 1997.
Ashley County Times, 1871.
Bastrop Clarion, 1978, 1979.
Bastrop Daily Enterprise, 1956, 1965, 1979, 1980, 1983, 1987, 1988, 1992, 1993, 1996, 1998.
Chicot Spectator, 1973.
Delta News, 1939, 1940.
Dermott News, 1931, 1964, 1973.
Drew County Advance, 1894, 1896, 1898, 1907.
Irontonian (OH) Register, 1869, 1896.
Little Rock Daily Republican, 1868.
Louisville (KY) Times, 1950.
McGehee Times, 1975.
Morehouse Enterprise, 1939.
Monroe Bulletin, 1881, 1883.

Monroe Morning World, 1954.
Monroe News Star World, 1985.
New York Times, 1922, 1923.
Ouachita Telegraph, 1874.
Pine Bluff Commercial, 1887, 1907, 1976.
Pine Bluff Daily Graphic, 1908, 1924.
Pine Bluff Press-Eagle, 1887.
Shreveport Times, 1956.
Southeast Arkansas News-Press, 1976.
Texas Trans-Miss-Bulletin, 1864.

Unpublished Material

Armstrong, Loyce Arrington. "Story Telling -- Linking Generations." Typed paper in possession of author, n.d.

Balthazar de Villiers to Governor Bernardo de Galvez. Archivo General de Indias, Papeles Procedentes de Cuba, *legajo* 194:44.

Barnett, Alma Daniels. "Genealogy of the John Buford Daniels Family Dating from 1821 to 1963." Typed paper in possession of author, 1963.

Birch, Clifton L. Arkansas Archeological Survey Site Survey Form, State Survey No. 3DR242, 1997.

Burleigh, Martha Crenshaw. "Memories of Dermott and Dermott Public Schools." Typed paper in Leonard Evans Memorial Library, Dermott, Ark., 1961.

Crawley, Ida Jolly. "The Doll." Handwritten short story in possession of the author, n.d.

Crawley, Martha. *My Legacy.* Martha Amanda (Phillips) Tiller Crawley's Journal, 1852-1856. Transcribed by Robert Knight. Copy in possession of author.

Cryer, E. B. Accounts Receivable Ledger, June 1888 – September 1889. (All Cryer books were loaned to the author by Darrell Mobley of Bastrop.)

____. Bills of Lading Ledger, August 1875 – April 1883.

___. Cotton Book, March 1880 – February 1888.

___. Passenger Book, January 1890 – February 1896.

___. Portage Book, January 1880 – January 1896.

___. Receipt Book, August 1888- December 1888.

Curry, Corliss Colby. "A History of the Timber Industry in Ashley, Bradley and Drew Counties, Arkansas," master's thesis, University of Arkansas, 1953.

George B. Gregory, letter to Wiloughby Gregory, July 18, 1845. Copy of original in Gordon Hartrick Papers, Paul Sullins Library, Crossett, Ark.

Hammond, William Richard. "An Abstract of Economic History of Transportation on Ouachita-Black River of Northeast Louisiana." Ph.D. diss., George Peabody College for Teachers, 1945.

Harp, Thomas Young. *"Me" and "Highroads to Education" and "My Kin Folks."* Privately printed, n.d. (ca. 1945.)

John Doe Civil War Diary. Copy of original in possession of   author, 1862 - 1864.

Leavell, Elizabeth Littlejohn and Susan Sturdivant Strong. Typed paper in possession of author, n.d.

Minutes of Monticello Klan Number 108, September 28, 1922 to October 6, 1925. Original in Drew County Historical Museum Archives.

"Morehouse Klan." George Patton, comp. A collection of papers with original minutes in the Snyder Museum, Bastrop, La., 1991.

Morrison, Larry. "Steamboats at the Port of Camden." Typed paper in possession of author, 1975.

"National Register of Historical Places Continuation Sheet,"   Section 8. United States Department of the Interior, National Park Service, 1995.

Oliver, Blanche. "Sterlington, LA." Typed paper in Ouachita   Parish Library, Monroe, n.d.

Patton, George. *Whiskey, Mischief, and the Courthouse Gang: A Story about the Ku Klux Klan in Morehouse Parish in the Early 1920s.* Privately printed, 1999.

"The Pioneer Rivermen 1800-1835." McGehee (Ark.) Library. Unsigned, typed paper, n.d.

Saunders, Mrs. Dillard H. Letter to J. A. Hughes. Drew County Historical Museum Archives, Monticello, Ark. 1963.

Short, Hazel. "A History of Sterlington." Typed paper in Sterlington (La.) Library, 1962.

Simmons, W. J. *The Practice of Klanishness*, Imperial Instructions, Document No. 1, Series AD, 1918, AK, Lii. Atlanta: Ku Klux Press, 1918. Copy of original in possession of author.

Smith, John I. *Reminiscences of Ed T. Smith As Told to His Family.* Privately printed, 1992.

Smylie, Mrs. E. S. Letter to her children. Typed paper in Leonard Evans Memorial Library, Dermott, Ark., 1941.

Spyker, Leonidas Pendleton. Diary. Transcribed by Lillian Herron Williamson. Copy in the Snyder Museum, Bastrop, La. Original in Sandal Library, University of Louisiana, Monroe, 1860.

Taylor, Thomas E. Letter to Louise Godwin. Drew County Historical Museum Archives, Monticello, Ark., 1992.

White, Patsy K. "The Archeological Story." Typed paper in   possession of author, 1995.

Witherington, Hattie. Letter to Bennie Prentice Finch, c1915. Copy in possession of author.

The Oral History Respondents
*African-American
^Known Deceased
+Joint Interview

Name	Date of Birth	Date of Interview
1. Robert Mitchell		10 Jul 1997
2. Lois Baldwin Thomas^	19 Jul 1896	15 Jul 1997
3. Sue Gipson*	3 Jul 1913	16 Jul 1997
4. Ruth Tracy Teal*	17 Feb 1901	17 Jul 1997
5. Clifton "Curly" Birch^	29 Jun 1923	19 Sep 1997
6. Earl Kitchens*	13 Oct 1922	6 May 1998
7. Leroy Haynes^	30 Jan 1896	6 May 1998
8. Garvin Adcock	24 Mar 1912	8 May 1998
9. William deYampert III	28 Aug 1918	12 May 1998
10. Helen Byrd	13 Aug 1919	13 May 1998
11. Herbert "Von" Greenway	10 Nov 1926	13 May 1998
12. Estelle Kimbrell Works+	8 Jun 1926	15 May 1998
13. W. A. "Dub" Kimbrell+	1 Oct 1930	15 May 1998
14. Bessie Fuller Green*	7 Aug 1912	15 May 1998
15. Lloyd Smith	16 Mar 1928	18 May 1998
16. Susie Wright Fuqua^	3 Aug 1904	18 May 1998
17. John Edd Curry	4 Dec 1935	19 May 1998
18. Vernon Scott	28 Mar 1915	19 May 1998
19. John B. Currie Sr.	21 Feb 1921	25 May 1998
20. Amos Sledge^	4 May 1914	28 May 1998
21. Betsy Morris Rodgers	25 Mar 1927	28 May 1998
22. Mark Hawkins	4 Aug 1938	3 Jun 1998
23. Ernestine Nobles Sprinkle	16 Jul 1918	4 Jun 1998
24. Mary Morris Foster	25 Sep 1912	4 Jun 1998
25. Ella Mae McDermott White	8 Aug 1912	6 Jun 1998
26. Siegfried Johnson	17 Sep 1919	1 Jun 1998
27. Gaston Harrison+^	14 Aug 1900	14 Jun 1998
28. Launa Sawyer Harrison+^	16 Jul 1901	14 Jun 1998
29. James Bealer*	29 Aug 1894	16 Jun 1998
30. Dr. Roy Grizzell	14 Mar 1918	16 Jun 1998
31. W. D. "Shorty" Lyle+	13 Sep 1915	9 Jul 1998
32. Nell Fullbright Lyle+	9 Mar 1915	9 Jul 1998
33. Murphy Brockman+	12 Dec 1919	9 Jul 1998
34. Willie Vick Brockman+	18 Apr 1918	9 Jul 1998
35. Andrew Pickens	25 Feb 1941	14 Jul 1998
36. Robert A. Crawley+	1 Dec 1931	17 Jul 1998
37. Ella Crawley Vail+	21 Jan 1924	17 Jul 1998
38. Alvie Lee Pugh*	9 Mar 19122	9 Jul 1998

Name	Date of Birth	Date of Interview
39. Edgar Norris	14 Dec 1923	29 Jul 1998
40. Harvey Chambliss	15 Mar 1930	31 Jul 1998
41. Dr. Ralph Douglas	7 Apr 1906	31 Jul 1998
42. C. C. "Sam" Williamson	1918	6 Aug 1998
43. Virgil Amason	1922	7 Aug 1998
44. Mary Alice Cottrell Nelson	30 Dec 1930	7 Aug 1998
45. Ralph Kinnaird	4 Dec 1934	11 Aug 1998
46. Billy Bobby Abraugh	3 Oct 1933	11 & 13 Aug 1998
47. Katie Bell Parker	22 Jan 1916	18 Aug 1998
48. Bealie Harrison+ ^	12 Nov 1907	18 Aug 1998
49. Mildred Sikes Harrison+	9 Sep 1924	18 Aug 1998
50. Edwin Robertson+ ^	20 Dec 1910	20 Aug 1998
51. Marion Robertson Doles+	23 Oct 1913	20 Aug 1998
52. Oren T. Robertson+	8 Feb 1917	20 Aug 1998
53. Marion Robertson Means+	2 May 1920	20 Aug 1998
54. Mary Ann Dixon Johnston	Aug 1919	24 Aug 1998
55. Cecil Harp^	Aug 1918	24 Aug 1998
56. Duke Shackelford	30 May 1926	27 Aug 1998
57. Thelbert Bunch	1 Oct 1933	10 Sep 1998
58. Benton B. Hunt	12 Dec 1926	20 Sep 1998
59. James "Buster" Ford*	19 Jun 1915	22 Sep 1998
60. Page Webb*^	9 Jul 1913	22 Sep 1998
61. Frank Day+	22 May 1921	24 Sep 1998
62. C. L. "Chuck" Day+	24 Mar 1931	24 Sep 1998
63. Winifred Day+	3 Jun 1921	24 Sep 1998
64. Jack Gibson	30 Mar 1920	27 Sep 1998
65. Mary Dean Naff Pugh+	8 Oct 1922	28 Sep 1998
66. Charles H. Naff+	14 Dec 1940	28 Sep 1998
67. Ed Jones^	8 Jun 1912	6 Oct 1998
68. Dan P. "Buck" Mayo^	3 May 1917	6 Oct 1998
69. Nancy Oberton Tharp*	9 Jun 1894	7 Jan 1999
70. Herman King*	21 Feb 1910	7 Jan 1999
71. Ruth Mayo Boone	19 Feb 1924	21 Jan 1999
72. R. H. "Butch" Dennington+^	5 Sep 1910	26 Jan 1999
73. Clifton Trigg+	17 Aug 1914	26 Jan 1999

NOTES

Chapter 1 – Ancient Springs, Rivers, and Peoples

[1] William Richard Hammond, "An Abstract of Economic History of Transportation on Ouachita-Black River of Northeast Louisiana," unpublished Ph.D. dissertation, George Peabody College for Teachers, August 1945, 172. This report was from the Secretary of War, November 19, 1878 (45th Congress, 3d Session, House Document No. 61, 13).

[2] Map in "Arkansas History Scrapbook," 1943, Pine Bluff Library.

[3] *Biographical and Historical Memoirs of Southern Arkansas of Pulaski, Jefferson, Lonoke, Faulkner, Grant, Saline, Perry, Garland and Hot Spring Counties, Arkansas* (Chicago: Goodspeed Publishing Company, 1889), 131, hereafter cited as Goodspeed, *Memoirs*.

[4] Mary Roane Tomlinson, "Stream of History," *Arkansas Gazette Magazine*, September 11, 1938.

[5] Ibid.

[6] Timothy Flint, as quoted in Hammond, "Abstract," 42, from Timothy Flint, *Journal*, 1835.

[7] Roger T. Saucier, "Quaternary Geology of the Lower Mississippi Valley," *Arkansas Archeological Survey* Research Series No. 6 (1974): 15-18.

[8] John H. House, "Archaic Occupation in the Arkansas River Lowland," *Field Notes* 171 (1980): 5.

[9] Saucier, "Quaternary Geology," 21, 23.

[10] John H. House, e-mail to author, March 28, 2000.

[11] House, "Archaic," 7.

[12] John H. House, e-mail to author, February 12, 2000.

[13] Roger T. Saucier, *Geomorphology and Quaternary Geological History of the Lower Mississippi Valley* (Vicksburg: US Army Engineer Waterways Experiment Station, 1994), 274. Saucier wrote, "In the most recent interpretation (Autin et al., 1991), that channel was estimated to have been active between about 4,000 and 1,800 years B.P. However, it is now known that artifacts dating to the Late Archaic Period are common on the Plum Bayou Meander Belt (House 1980), meaning that the initiation of the meander belt must predate 4,000 B.P. by at least several hundred years. A recently acquired, strategically located radiocarbon date [superscript references a footnote: "Personal communication, 1993, H. Markewich, U. S. Geological Survey, Atlanta, GA] from point bar deposits of the Bayou Bartholomew Meander Belt is even more indicative. The date of 3,890 years B.P. indicates that the meander belt was well developed and several cutoffs had already taken place prior to that time. Direct evidence is not available as to the abandonment of the Stage 2 channel [the bayou], but archeological sites indicate

that the Stage 1 or modern channel of the river was active by about 2,500 years B.P., about 500 years earlier than previously estimated. If the time estimate is correct, it is reasonable to move the terminal date of the Stage 2 channel from 1,800 years B.P. to 2,200 years B.P....."

[14] John H. House, e-mail to author, July 21, 1998; February 12, 1999.

[15] John H. House, e-mail to author, August 19, 1999.

[16] Goodspeed, *Memoirs*, 130.

[17] C. C. Robin, *Voyage to Louisiana 1803-1805*, trans. Stuart O. Landry Jr. (New Orleans: Pelican Publishing Company, 1966), 137.

[18] "The Pioneer Rivermen 1800-1835," unsigned typed paper in McGehee Library, n.d.

[19] Marvin D. Jeter, "Following a tough act with many more fine things: plans for the 1992 Big Dig at the Taylor Mounds (3DR1)," *Field Notes* 245 (1992): 3.

[20] John H. House, e-mail to author, March 3, 1999.

[21] Tomlinson, "Stream of History," 1.

[22] Charles E. Pearson and Allen R. Saltus Jr., *Underwater Archaeology On The Ouachita River, Arkansas: The Search for the Chieftain, Haydee, and Homer* (Baton Rouge: Coastal Environments, Inc., 1993), 5, 7.

[23] David I. Bushnell Jr., *The Choctaw of Bayou Lacomb St. Tammany Parish Louisiana*, Smithsonian Institution Bureau of American Ethnology Bulletin 48 (Washington: Government Printing Office, 1909), 16.

[24] Hon. H. Bry, "The Ouachita Country, III," *DeBow's Review*, (May 1847): 408.

[25] Clarence B. Moore, "Antiquities of the Ouachita Valley," *Journal of the Academy of the Natural Sciences of Philadelphia* 14, Second Series (1912): 111.

[26] Raymond J. Martinez, *The Story of Spanish Moss* (New Orleans: Home Publications, 1959), 1, May 3, 1998, <http://www.terrebonneparish.com/local/culture/spanishmoss/spanishmoss8.htm>.

[27] Map, "Washita River in Louisiana from the Hot Springs to the Confluence of the Red River with the Mississippi. Laid down from the Journal and Survey of Wm. Dunbar Esq. In the Year 1804 by Nicholas King."

[28] Hester Davis, "Preserving the Past for the Future," Arkansas Archeological Survey Flyer, n.d.; Gerald T. Hanson and Carl H. Moneyhon, *Historical Atlas of Arkansas* (Norman: University of Oklahoma Press, 1989), 9; Robert W. Neuman and Nancy W. Hawkins, *Louisiana Prehistory*, Second Ed. (Baton Rouge: Louisiana Archeological Survey and Antiquities Commission, 1993), 1-2.

[29] John H. House, e-mail to author, February 12, 1999.

[30] John H. House and Marvin D. Jeter, "Excavations at Boydell Mound A (3AS58), Southeast Arkansas," *Arkansas Archeologist* 33 (1994): 4.

[31] John H. House, "Resurveying the Bartholomew Bypass Route Near Pine Bluff," *Field Notes* 243 (1991): 3.

[32] John H. House, e-mail to author, September 13, 1999.

[33] Marvin D. Jeter, ed., *Edward Palmer's Arkansaw Mounds*, (Fayetteville: University of Arkansas Press, 1990), 208, 210, 211.

[34] Marvin D. Jeter, "Archeology and Indians In and Near Drew County," *Drew County Historical Journal*, 5 (1990): 64, 72; Marvin D. Jeter, "Following a tough act," 3.

[35] Jeter, "Archeology," 64, 66-67.

[36] Martha A. Rolingson, "Archeology along Bayou Bartholomew, Southeast Arkansas," *Arkansas Archeologist* 32 (1993): 1.

[37] Ibid., 28, 30, 42, 44.

[38] Ibid., 45, 59, 60.

[39] Ibid., 61-63, 82, 83.

[40] Ibid., 85-90, 110-112.

[41] Ibid., 115, 118, 126, 127, 129, 131.

[42] Martha Ann Rolingson, "The Bartholomew Phase: A Plaquemine Adaptation in the Mississippi Valley," in *Cultural Change and Continuity, Essays in Honor of James Bennett Griffin* (New York: Academic Press, Inc., 1976) 119.

[43] Rebecca DeArmond-Huskey, *Beyond Bartholomew: The Portland Area History* (Conway: River Road Press, 1996), 458. An undated, clipped article from the *Ashley County Ledger* states, "After coming to Arkansas [in 1859] Mrs. Waddell [who was widowed] married a Mr. Womack. He did not live long and was buried on an Indian mound on the bank of Bayou Bartholomew."

[44] Patsy White, e-mail to author, September 25, 1999.

[45] House and Jeter, "Excavations," 23,25, 73, 75.

[46] Patsy K. White, "The Archeological Story, " 1995, 4. Unpublished paper in possession of the author.

[47] John H. House, e-mail to author, January 18, 2000.

[48] H. Edwin Jackson and Marvin D. Jeter, "Preceramic Earthworks in Arkansas: A Report on the Poverty Point Period Lake Enterprise Mound (3AS379)," *Southeastern Archeology* (winter, 1994): 158.

[49] David Moyers, "Archeologists Excavate State's Oldest Indian Mound Near Wilmot," *Ashley County Ledger*, November 5, 1997; Jackson and Jeter, "Preceramic Earthworks," 153, 161.

[50] Jon L. Gibson, *Poverty Point: A Terminal Archaic Culture of the Lower Mississippi Valley*, Second Ed. (Baton Rouge: Louisiana Archeological Survey and Antiquities Commission, 1996), 18-19.

[51] White, "Story," 8.

[52] Clifton L. "Curly" Birch, interview by author, tape recording, Tillar, AR, September 19, 1997.

[53] Archeologists use the "Dare" spelling for this site. R. B. Sadler sold 95 acres to Jacob Niemeyer (also spelled Neimeyer) and Thomas J. Darragh. The deed, dated January 20, 1891, was recorded as Niemeyer and Darragh.

[54] Moore, "Antiquities," 111-120. The pipe and pottery periods were identified for the author by Marvin Jeter.

[55] Ibid., 120-130. Period, pottery, and hematite pendant information provided by Jeter.

[56] Ibid., 151-157.

[57] Ibid., 157-161.

[58] Ibid., 161-169.

[59] Ibid., 169-170.

[60] Joe W. Saunders, Thurman Allen, and Roger T. Saucier, "Four Archaic? Mound Complexes in Northeast Louisiana," *Southeastern Archaeology*, (winter 1994):134, 138, 139, 142.

[61] Morris S. Arnold, *Colonial Arkansas 1686-1804* (Fayetteville: The University of Arkansas Press, 1991), 69-73.
[62] White, "Story," 11.

Chapter 2 – The Colonial Wilderness

[1] Charles Hudson, "De Soto in Arkansas: A Brief Synopsis," *Field Notes* 205 (1985): 7-9.
[2] Clair N. Moody, "Bartholomew Among First Arkansas Colonist," *Arkansas Democrat*, March 21, 1954.
[3] William C. Foster, *The La Salle Expedition to Texas: The Journal of Henri Joutel 1684-1687*, trans. Johanna S. Warren (Austin: Texas State Historical Association, 1999), maps 252, 268.
[4] Morris S. Arnold and Dorothy Core Jones, eds., *Arkansas Colonials: A Collection of French and Spanish Records Listing Early Europeans in Arkansas 1686-1804* (Gillette: Grand Prairie Historical Society, 1986), 1; Stanley Faye, "The Forked River," *Louisiana Historical Quarterly* 25 (October 1942): 29 n. 929.
[5] Faye, "Forked River," 29 n. 929, 36 n. 930, 931; Samuel D. Dickinson, letter to author, February 4, 1999; E. Russ Williams, *Spanish Poste d' Ouachita: The Ouachita Valley in Colonial Louisiana 1783-1804 and Early American Statehood 1804-1820* (Monroe: Williams Genealogical Publications, 1995), 111; E. Russ Williams, *Filhiol and the founding of the Spanish Poste d' Ouachita: The Ouachita Valley in Colonial Louisiana 1783-1804* (Monroe: Monroe-Ouachita Valley Bicentennial Commission, 1982), 40.
[6] Jennie O'Kelly Mitchell and Robert Dabney Calhoun, "The Marquis De Maison Rouge, The Baron De Bastrop, and Colonel Abraham Morhouse: Three Ouachita Valley Soldiers of Fortune: The Maison Rouge and Bastrop Spanish Land 'Grants'," *Louisiana Historical Quarterly* 20 (April 1937): 294.
[7] Ibid.; E. Russ Williams, *Encyclopedia of Individuals and Founding Families of the Ouachita Valley of Louisiana from 1785 to 1850* (Monroe: Williams Genealogical and Historical Publications, 1997), 281;Frederick William Williamson and George T. Goodman, eds., *Eastern Louisiana: A History of the Watershed of the Ouachita River and The Florida Parishes* (Louisville, KY: The Historical Record Association, 1940), 27, 67, 68.
[8] Samuel Dorris Dickinson, "Don Filhiol at Ecore a Fabri," *Arkansas Historical Quarterly* 46 (summer 1987): 135-136, 140; Arnold, *Colonial Arkansas*, 20.
[9] Dickinson, "Don Filhiol," 142, 144; Williams, *Filhiol*, 20.
[10] Dickinson, "Don Filhiol," 145-146.
[11] Williams, *Filhiol*, 20.
[12] Mitchell, "Grants," 309-310.
[13] Ibid., 311-312; Hazel S. Short, "A History of Sterlington" (privately printed, 1962), 26, 37, 42, 45, 54-59, 81; Williams, *Spanish Poste*, 162..
[14] Mitchell, "Grants," 321; Sallie Lacy Humble, "The Ouachita Valley Expedition of De Soto," *Louisiana Quarterly* 25 (July 1942): 628.
[15] Samuel Dorris Dickinson, "Colonial Arkansas Place Names," *Arkansas Historical Quarterly* 48 (summer 1989): 141.
[16] Mitchell, "Grants," 376.

[17] Williams, *Spanish Poste*, 160, 173, 185.

[18] Mitchell, "Grants,"377; Williams, *Spanish Poste*, 188; Robin, *Voyage*, 140.

[19] Williams, *Spanish Poste*, 188, 192, 202.

[20] Williamson, *Eastern Louisiana*, 60, 61.

[21] Robin, *Voyage*, 137, 142.

[22] Williams, *Spanish Poste*, 200; Mike Kingston, ed.,*1992-1993 Texas Almanac* (Dallas: *Dallas Morning News*, 1991), 35, 39.

[23] Mitchell, "Grants," 447, 449-453; Williams, *Spanish Poste*, 196-197, 200-201.

[24] Kevin Ladd, *Gone to Texas: Genealogical Abstracts from The Telegraph and Texas Register 1835-1841* (Bowie, MD: Heritage Books, Inc., 1994), 68; Walter Worthington Bowie, *The Bowies and Their Kindred: A Genealogical and Biographical History* (Cottonport, LA: Polyanthos, 1971), 270.

[25] Hanson and Moneyhon, *Historical Atlas*, 25; Walter Brown, "News, Notes, and Comments," *Arkansas Historical Quarterly* 48 (spring 1989): 86. Brown's article states that Lefevre arrived at Arkansas Post in 1770. Research by Morris S. Arnold documents that Lefevre was not in the state until about 1789 and that although his tombstone has a death date of 1770, it is in error. (Morris S. Arnold, letter to author, June 1, 1999.)

[26] Williams, *Spanish Poste*, 42-43, 46 n. 15,16.

[27] Samuel Dorris Dickinson, "An Early View of the Ouachita Region," *Old Time Chronicle: Folk History of Southwest Arkansas* 3 (July 1990):15, 16.

[28] Ibid., 14-15.

[29] Ibid., 16-17.

[30] Ibid., 17; Arnold, *Colonial Arkansas*, 62, 63.

[31] Williams, *Spanish Poste*, 111; Dickinson, "Colonial Arkansas."

[32] Short, *History*, 28-29.

[33] Caleb W. Davis, "St. Bartholomew," *Colliers Encyclopedia* III (CD-ROM, Infonautics Corporation, 1998).

[34] Arnold and Core, *Arkansas Colonials*, 2, 3, 25.

[35] Dorothy Jones Core, ed., *Abstract of Catholic Register of Arkansas 1764-1858* (Dewitt, AR: DeWitt Publishing Co., Inc.), 20-23, 46-47, 59.

[36] Dave Wallis and Frank Williamson, eds., *A Baptismal Record of the Parishes Along the Arkansas River, August 5, 1796 - July 16, 1802* (Pine Bluff. Jefferson County Historical Society, 1982), 4-7, 17-19, 24, 48-50.

[37] Copy of original grant in possession of Morris S. Arnold.

[38] Balthazar de Villiers, letter to Governor Bernardo de Galvez, 12 January 1781, Archivo General de Indias, Papeles Procedentes de Cuba, *legajo* 194:44. Copy of transcription provided by Morris S. Arnold. See actual quote in slavery segment.

Chapter 3 – Early Bayou Settlements in Southeast Arkansas

[1] Goodspeed, *Memoirs, Jefferson County*, 127-129, 134; Dickinson, "Colonial Arkansas," 141; Josiah H. Shinn, *History of Arkansas* (Richmond, VA: B. F. Johnson Publishing Co., 1905), 77.

[2] Goodspeed, *Memoirs, Jefferson County*, 131-134.

[3] Helen Byrd, interview by author, tape recording, Pine Bluff, AR, May 13, 1989.

[4] *Pine Bluff Daily Graphic,* April 19, 1908. This account also published in the *Jefferson County Historical Quarterly* (spring 1983).

[5] "Hardwick to Trulock," *Jefferson County Historical Quarterly* 4 (spring 1972) 11-12; Mrs. C. H. Bohinger, "The Noel Family," *Arkansas Historical Quarterly* 14 (summer 1955), 117-118.

[6] Harvey Chambliss, interview by author, tape recording, Pine Bluff, July 13, 1998.

[7] Lincoln County Historical Society, *History of Lincoln County, Arkansas, 1871-1983* (Dallas: Taylor Publishing Company, 1983), 75.

[8] Lois Baldwin Thomas, interview by author, tape recording, Tarry, AR, July 15, 1997.

[9] Sue Gipson, interview by author, tape recording, Tarry, AR, July 16, 1997; *Goodspeed Biographical and Historical Memoirs of Southern Arkansas* (Easley, SC: Southern Historical Press, 1978; reprint of original published in 1890 by Goodspeed Publishing Co.), 985; Robert Mitchell, interview by author, tape recording, Yorktown, AR, July 10, 1997.

[10] *Lincoln County History,* 31, 48.

[11] Ibid., 31; Bessie Fuller Green, interview by author, tape recording, Yorktown, AR, May 15, 1998; Gipson, interview.

[12] *Lincoln County History,* 31; Green, interview; Gipson, interview.

[13] Russell Pierce Baker, *From Memdag to Norsk: A Historical Directory of Arkansas Post Offices 1832-1971* (Hot Springs: Arkansas Genealogical Society, 1988), 242; *Lincoln County History,* 31; Ruth Teal, interview by author, tape recording, Yorktown, AR, July 17, 1997.

[14] W. D. "Shorty" Lyle, interview by author, tape recording, Star City, AR, July 9, 1998; Murphy Brockman, interview by author, tape recording, Star City, AR, July 9, 1998; John Edd Curry, interview by author, tape recording, Garrett Bridge Community, AR, May 19, 1998.

[15] Mrs. Mary Sorrells DeWoody, "Life In The (1860) Sixties," *Jefferson County Historical Quarterly* 7 (summer 1977), 15, 18; Goodspeed, *Southern Arkansas,* 992.

[16] Lyle, interview; Brockman, interview; Alvie Pugh, interview by author, tape recording, Rose Hill Community, AR, July 9, 1998.

[17] Goodspeed, *Southern Arkansas,* 976-977.

[18] Ibid., 975-78; John I. Smith, *Reminiscences of Ed T. Smith As Told to His Family* (privately printed, 1992), 33-34.

[19] Alvie Pugh, interview; Brockman, interview; *Lincoln County History,* 148, 209.

[20] William and Joseph R. Batchelor, brothers, were living in Smith Township (then in Drew County) in 1850. William, age 33, had two children, Sarah A. (age 6) and Henry (age 4). Joseph R. Batchelor was born in 1814 in Nash County, North Carolina, and married Sarah Elizabeth Collins. Their children were William (born c1839, NC), Martha (born c1840, NC), Sarah (born 1842, MS; died 1860, Desha Co.), Adeline (born c1844, AR), and Stephen Wilson (b 1845, Drew County). Joseph R. Batchelor died before 1914 at "Bayou Bartholomew, Drew County." Jann Woodard, e-mail to author, February 26, 2000; 1850 Drew County census.

[21] Siegfried Johnson, interview by author, tape recording, Pine Bluff, AR, June 11, 1998.

[22] Edgar Norris, interview by author, tape recording, Batchelor Bridge Community, AR, July 29, 1998; Charlotte T. Schexnayder, *Images From The Past: A Pictorial History of Desha County, Arkansas and Southeast Arkansas Delta* (Merceline, MO: Heritage House Publishing Company, Inc., nd), 8; *Lincoln County History*, 209.

[23] *Lincoln County History*, 75 ; Norris interview.

[24] Curry, interview; Smith, interview; Susie Wright Fuqua, interview by author, tape recording, Wilmar, AR, May 18, 1998.

[25] Typed paper, "Tyro, Lincoln County, Arkansas," given to the author by Mrs. Lloyd Smith. The name changed from Tyro to Green Mount in March 1880 and back to Tyro in May the same year.

[26] Fuqua, interview; Smith, interview, Curry, interview; Goodspeed, *Southern Arkansas*, 978, 979, 987, 993; Hazel Hancock Cash in *Reflections*, 277.

[27] *Cemetery Records of Lincoln County* (Lincoln County Extension Homemakers Council: privately published, 1984), 280; *Lincoln County History*, 48.

[28] *Lincoln County History*, 149.

[29] Amos Jones, *The Dean of Dermott: The Life Story of Dr. York Wayland Williams Jr.* (Nashville, TN: Bethlehem Book Publishers, Inc., 1998), 2-4, 21-24.

[30] Carolyn Kelley Porter, "The Holmes Family: First Homesteaders of the Dumas Area," *McGehee Times*, February 26, 1975; Goodspeed, *Southern Arkansas*, 12, 82, 1052, 1019-1020.

[31] Schexnayder, *Images*, 37, 72, 92, 106, 125.

[32] Goodspeed, *Southern Arkansas*, 1001; Schexnayder, *Images*, 8, 23, 39, 51, 96, 124, 126, 128; Marcia Schnedler, "Dumas has a song in its heart, colorful characters in its past," *Arkansas Democrat-Gazette*, May 30, 1999.

[33] Goodspeed, *Southern Arkansas*, 1023-1024; Porter, "The Holmes Family;" Andrew Pickens, interview by author, tape recording, Pickens, AR, July 14, 1998; Schexnayder, *Images*, 5.

[34] Goodspeed states that Mrs. Pickens moved to the county in 1869 and that her husband died in 1883 in Mississippi. Family history indicates that he moved to the county; Pickens, interview.

[35] Smith interview; Curry interview; Norris interview.

[36] Goodspeed, *Southern Arkansas*, 1039.

[37] Pickens interview; Schexnayder, *Images*, 25.

[38] Baker, *Post Offices*, 145. "Leland Lockhart, Oldest Citizen in Point of Residence, Here in '03," *1980 Programs of Desha County Historical Society*, Spring 1981, 8, 10.

[39] Mrs. C. B. Kidd to Marlene Waldrup, Reporter, "Early History of McGehee, Arkansas," nd, typed paper in Desha County Library History Room.

[40] Leoda Evans, "McGehee's Eldest Physician – Dr. Jim Chennault," *Arkansas Democrat Magazine*, September 3, 1950; Kidd, "Early History."

[41] Lockhart, 10.

[42] Mary Roane Tomlinson, "Home of the Early Days," *Arkansas Gazette*, Sunday Magazine Section, August 28, 1938, 3; James Leslie, *Saracen's Country: Some Southeast Arkansas History* (Little Rock: Rose Publishing Company, 1974), 67. Leslie states that an inscription on the back of a 1914 photograph of the Taylor house says the Rives cabin was built in 1819.

[43] Tomlinson, "Home;" Leslie, *Saracen's Country*, 66, 67; "National Register of Historic Places Continuation Sheet," Sec. 8, 8 (United States Department of the Interior, National Park Service, 1995). Dendrochronology performed in 1991 on log samples from first and second story floors revealed the logs were cut from 1844-46.

[44] "National Register," Sec. 7, 2; Leslie, *Saracen's Country*, 67.

[45] Mrs. Dillard H. Saunders, letter to J. A. Hughes, January 31, 1963, copy in Drew County Historical Museum Archives; Tomlinson, "Home;" *Louisville Times*, September 1, 1950. The Kentucky home, Mauvilla, was razed in 1950.

[46] Mrs. Dillard Saunders, letter.

[47] Mrs. Nannie Lee Staudinger, "Winchester: Incorporated 1912, *Advance Monticellonian*, June 17, 1971.

[48] Virginia Flesher, letter to author, February 22, 1999.

[49] Staudinger, "Winchester;" Virginia Flesher, letter.

[50] Gene Hull, "Historic Rails to Monroe" (The Arkansas Railroad Club and Union Pacific Railroad, 1995), 2.

[51] Hutch Landfair, "Early History of Town of Tillar Related," *Dumas Clarion*, March 17, 1971.

[52] Ibid.; Mrs. Bertha T. Tillar, "Selma Timber Industry Gave Birth to Tillar," *Advance Monticellonian*, June 17, 1971; "Tillar, Child of Selma, *Advance Monticellonian*, February 26, 1997; Goodspeed, *Southern Arkansas*, 1007, 1014, 1023. According to Goodspeed, 1014, Chelsey Clayton opened his Tillar store in 1878.

[53] Dallas T. Herndon, *Centennial History*, III, (Little Rock: S. J. Clarke, 1922), 1056, 1059; Vernon Scott, interview by author, tape recording, Tillar, AR, May 19, 1998.

[54] Landfair, "Early History."

[55] Tillar, "Selma;" Landfair, "Early History;" *Drew County Advance*, July 3, 1894.

[56] *Drew County Advance*, July 3, 1894. J. P. Burks and J. D. Welch established this paper in 1892. Capt. W. H. Isom gave the address at the Tillar visit.

[57] Landfair, "Early History."

[58] Jane Ladd, "Frank Tillar Memorial Methodist Episcopal Church," Arkansas Historic Preservation Program, State Review Board, December 4, 1996, 147-48; Tillar, "Selma."

[59] Tillar, "Selma."

[60] Drew County Association for Family and Community Education, *Drew County, Arkansas Cemetery Records*, Second Edition (Crossett: Nowlan Printing, 1994), 413, 421.

[61] Dorothy M. Lowe, "On Selma, A Proud Community," *Advance Monticellonian*, June 17, 1971; DeArmond, *Beyond Bartholomew*, 414; J. T. W. Tillar Obituary, *Arkansas Gazette*, June 5, 1908; Herndon, *Centennial History*, III, 6.

[62] Goodspeed, *Southern Arkansas*, 966, 1014, 1039.

[63] Goodspeed, *Southern Arkansas*, 966, 1014, 1039.

[64] Lowe, "On Selma."

[65] Tillar, "Selma;" Vivian Barrett Peacock, "Selma Tragedy," *1980 Programs of Desha County Historical Society*, Spring 1981, 60.

[66] Tillar Obituary; Herndon, Centennial History, III, 5-6.

[67] Clifton L. Birch, Arkansas Archeological Survey Site Form, State Survey No. 3DR242, May 10, 1997.

[68] Goodspeed, *Memoirs*, 628, 927; Rebecca DeArmond, *Old Times Not Forgotten: A History of Drew County* (Little Rock: Rose Publishing Company, 1980), 15, 223, 225; 1830 Chicot Census.

[69] James W. Leslie, "Monticello History," *Pine Bluff Commercial*, May 6, 1976.

[70] Betsy Morris Rodgers, interview by author, tape recording, Dermott, AR, May 28, 1998; *Dermott News*, December 3, 1931.

[71] Rebecca DeArmond-Huskey, *Beyond Bartholomew: The Portland Area History* (Conway, AR: River Road Press, 1996), 459. Duke's date is given as 1857 in this book; it should be 1867.

[72] *Arkansas Gazette*, June 13, 1832.

[73] Donald Holley, "Drew County's Carpetbagger: The Life of S. A. Duke, Or How A Yankee Shoemaker Became A Wealthy Southern Merchant," *Drew County Historical Quarterly*, 10 (1995), 5, 7-12, 17 n. 26.

[74] "Col. Chas. T. Duke," *Advance Monticellonian*, December 17, 1907; "Baxter, Ark.," *Advance Monticellonian*, June 17, 1971; DeArmond, *Old Times*, 310.

[75] "Baxter, Ark;" DeArmond, *Old Times*, 15.

[76] "Baxter, Ark;" Garvin Adcock, interview by author, tape recording, Monticello, AR, May 8, 1998.

[77] Estelle Kimbrell Works and W. A. Kimbrell, interview by author, tape recording, Pine Bluff, AR, May 15, 1998.

[78] Mrs. L. O. McKeown, "Recollections of Collins," *Dermott News*, 1971.

[79] Amy Sasser Hoffman, "Community History of Collins," *Advance Monticellonian*, nd. Much of this article appears to be a copy of one published in 1933. Map, Topographical Bureau Dist. Ark., April 7, 1865

[80] DeArmond, *Old Times*, 15; Clara McGowan, "Warm Springs Georgia Has Another Local Name," *Times-News* [McGehee], October 4, 1979; Hoffman, "Community History;" Smith, interview (McShan information); Goodspeed, *Southern Arkansas*, 940; *Arkansas Gazette,* June 14, 1893.

[81] "Crumbs from Collins," clipped article, signed T. L. E., July 17, 1883.

[82] Graham Stevens Collins Jr., "Collins, Drew County, Arkansas," *Arkansas Family Historian,* March 1993, 9.

[83] Hoffman, "Community History;" McKeown, "Recollections."

[84] Sledge interview; Anne Robirds, "Jerome: from a small town to a city and back again," *South Arkansas News-Press,* November 10, 1976; Baker, *Post Offices*, 24.

[85] *Delta News*, March 9, 1939.

[86] Mrs. John Carr Willis, letter to author, July 16, 1997.

[87] Dr. John L. Ferguson, statement to author, Arkansas History Commission; Caldwell Brandon, *Arkansas Gazette*, May 31, 1959.

[88] Willis, letter.

[89] Greenway, interview.

[90] Dr. John L. Ferguson, statement to author, Arkansas History Commission; Caldwell Brandon, *Arkansas Gazette*, May 31, 1959.

[91] Robirds, "Jerome."

[92] Charles McDermott, "Charles McDermott Journal," in DeArmond, *Old Times*, 404. The transcription of the journal records a marriage date of 1837, but

genealogy documents December 19, 1833. The journal also states that he took his wife in 1834 to visit her relatives.

[93] Ibid. The transcription of the journal has Edward Riley, but this should be Edward Wiley. Wiley, Gaster and Smith were listed together on the 1830 census. A William Jones signed the 1833 canal petition.

[94] Ibid. He makes no mention of the year Edward returned, but the second Seminole war lasted from 1835-1842.

[95] Some early news articles (Kinney, 1952, and Hammock, 1985) give 1832 as the arrival date. Goodspeed gives 1838. McDermott clearly states in his journal that he arrived in 1844. All his children up to Annabelle were born in Louisiana. Annabelle was born at Dermott in 1848. The child before her, Jane, was born in 1844 in Louisiana.

[96] "McDermott Journal,"405; Emma Shaw Smylie, letter to her children, 1941, typed copy in possession of author.

[97] Abbott F. Kinney, "125 Years of History Woven Into a Short Story," *Arkansas Democrat Magazine*, February 17, 1952, 9. The visitor was a Mrs. Hotchkiss who stopped on her way to Oklahoma in 1858 as a missionary with Rev. Cyrus Kingsbury.

[98] Mrs. Hardy Daniels, letter to author, June 9, 1998.

[99] Goodspeed, *Southern Arkansas*, 1078; Kinney, "125 Years," 9; Abbott F. Kinney, "Arkansas Flying Machine Inventor," *Arkansas Gazette Sunday Magazine*, October 5, 1941, 8.

[100] McDermott, "Journal," 405; Smylie, "Autobiography," 2.

[101] Mrs. C. C. Stark, "Story of Pioneer Family 100 Years Ago," *Dermott News*, February 20, 1964; Kinney, "125 Years."

[102] Kinney, "125 Years."

[103] George P. Kelley, "Bowie Family History Given By Kelley at Historical Meet," *Dermott News*, May 29, 1974, 5.

[104] John Jones Bowie's name is on the 1833 petition for a canal to be built from the Mississippi River to Bayou Bartholomew.

[105] Kelley, "Bowie Family."

[106] Walter Worthington Bowie, *The Bowies and Their Kindred: A Genealogical and Biographical History* (Cottonport, LA: Polyanthos, 1971), 265. Goodspeed, 1062, states that J. W. Bowie was sheriff of Chicot County 1860-62.

[107]. Bowie, *The Bowies*, 267.

[108] Martha Crenshaw Burleigh, Memories of Dermott and the Dermott Public Schools," speech to Chicot County Historical Society, November 1961, 1, copy in possession of author; Alma Daniels Barnett, "Genealogy of the John Buford Daniels Family Dating from 1821 to 1963," 1963, 1, unpublished copy in possession of the author.

[109] McDermott, "Journal," 406; Rev. N. Smylie, "History of Dermott Church," clipped article, n.d., ca 1929; Abbott F. Kinney, "Dermott Has A Birthday," *Arkansas Gazette*, July 6, 1941, 2.

[110] Kinney, "Dermott;" Clifton E. Hull, *Shortline Railroads of Arkansas* (Conway, AR: UCA Press, 1988), 8-13. Hull, 13, gives 1875 as the date the MO&RR became part of the Little Rock, Mississippi River & Texas. Holley, "Drew County's Carpetbagger," 12, gives 1872 as the date the MO&RR reached Baxter

based on the original plat of Baxter. The *Gazette* reported July 18, 1871, "Arrangements are made for enough iron to bring the road [MO&RR] within four or five miles of Monticello." Some early news articles (possibly based on Goodspeed, *Southern Arkansas*, 1067) claim the MO&RR was actually built through Dermott before the Civil War. It was not.

[111] Burleigh, "Memories," 2, 3; "In Retrospect," *Dermott News*, January 17, 1935; "From Dermott," clipped article, April 15, 1883 .

[112] Arkansas Gazetteer, "Advantages Unexcelled by Any Community in That Section," November 18, 1892; Goodspeed, *Southern Arkansas*, 1087.

[113] ."Dermott Dots," clipped, signed January 5, 1888.

[114] Kinney, "Dermott,"7.

[115] "Retrospect;" Goodspeed, *Southern Arkansas*, 1069, 1088; *Arkansas Gazette*, April 5, 1895.

[116] "Retrospect;" Burleigh, "Memories."

[117] *Dermott News*, December 3, 1931; *Southeast Arkansas in Pictures and Prose*, (James Ivie, nd), 42.

[118] *Dermott News*, October 25, 1923; April 11, 1929; *Southeast Arkansas*, 38-40.

[119] DeArmond, *Old Times*, 17; *Dermott News*, July 17, 1913; September 25, 1919; *Southeast Arkansas,* 37, 39, 40, 42; R. H. Dennington and Clifton Trigg, interview by author, tape recording, Dermott, AR, January 26, 1999.

[120] *Dermott News*, June 22, 1910; March 14, 1912, September 26, 1912; December 21, 1912; April 13, 1913; *Southeast Arkansas*, 37, 38; Amy Bishop Flowers to author, 1998; Betsy Rodgers, interview.

[121] *Dermott News*, February 20, 1913; April 13, 1913, November 13, 1913; February 5, 1914; July 30, 1914; September 16, 1915.

[122] Ibid., May 28, 1914; August 6, 1914.

[123] Southeast Arkansas, 38; *Dermott News*, February 5, 1914; February 11, 1915; January 6, 1916; December 28, 1916.

[124] *Arkansas Democrat*, "What Dermott Has," October 16, 1916.

[125] Jim Wagner, statement to author, March 31, 1999.

[126] *Dermott News*, January 24, 1918; March 21, 1918; May 25, 1918; September 12, 1918; December 18, 1919.

[127] *Southeast Arkansas*, 38.

[128] *Dermott News*, January 10, 1924. November 13, 1924. December 25, 1924. January 5, 1925. June 11, 1925.

[129] Ibid., January 6, 1927; February 17, 1927; July 14, 1927; *Southeast Arkansas*, 39-42.

[130] *Dermott News*, February 7, 1929; February 28, 1929; May 2, 1929; July 18, 1929; October 10, 1929; *Southeast Arkansas*, 37, 39, 42; Dennington-Trigg, interview.

[131] Kinney, "125 Years."

[132] Dennington-Trigg, interview.

[133] *Southeast Arkansas*, 37, 39,40.

[134] "What Dermott Has;" *Dermott News*, November 27, 1927; Charles Ernest Bishop, interview by Amy Bishop Flowers, tape recording, McGehee, AR, October 1998, transcript in possession of author.

[135] *Dermott News*, June 19, 1924.

[136] Rev. N. Smylie, "History of Dermott Church," clipped article, nd, c1929.

[137] "Dermott Dots," clipped article, signed December 12, 1883; *Dermott News*, January 22, 1914; March 20, 1924, August 27, 1925.

[138] John C. Hammock, "Bowie Township Alludes to Brother of Jim," *Chicot County Spectator*, June 26, 1985; Rodgers, interview; *Dermott News*, November 11, 1926.

[139] *Dermott News*, July 4, 1912; July 3, 1913; Mrs. Leo Malnar, *The Catholic Church in McGehee*, clipped pages, nd, 48; *State Review Board Meeting*, December 2, 1998 (Little Rock: Arkansas Historic Preservation Program, 1998), 221-225; Kinney, "125 Years."

[140] Kinney, "125 Years;" Stark, "Story;" Kinney, "Dermott;" Burleigh, "Memories."

[141] Kinney, "125 Years;" Kinney, "Dermott;" Burleigh, "Memories."

[142] Burleigh, "Memories;" Kinney, "Dermott;" *Arkansas Gazette*, "Advantages."

[143] *Dermott News*, November 4, 1915; *Arkansas Democrat*, October 16, 1916; *Dermott News*, October 30, 1919.

[144] Kinney, "125 Years;" *Dermott News*, April 20, 1916.

[145] Jones, *Dean of Dermott*, 32.

[146] Ibid., 32, 33, 34, 35, 42, 66-75, 80, 93-99.

[147] Ibid., 32; "Retrospect;" Goodspeed, *Southern Arkansas*, 1078, 1079, 1086; *Dermott News*, February 9, 1911; May 15, 1913; November 13, 1919; January 7, 1926; July 8, 1926.

[148] Burleigh, "Memories;" Kinney, "125 Years;" Hammock, "Bowie Township;" Kinney, "Dermott;" *Dermott News*, January 8, 1920; *Wilmot Weekly*, December 27, 1912.

[149] *Dermott News*, March 16, 1911; February 29, 1912; April 11, 1912; May 28, 1914; August 31, 1916; July 22, 1920; Kinney, "125 Years."

[150] John C. Hammock, "A Thumb-nail Sketch of Dermott History," *Dermott News*, November 14, 1973, quoted from an older unknown paper.

[151] Amos Sledge, interview by author, tape recording, Grace Community, AR, May 28, 1998; Works-Kimbrell, interview; Delta *News*, August 3, September 7, October 5, 1939.

[152] Sledge, interview; Herbert Von Greenway, interview by author, tape recording, White Hall, AR, May 13, 1998.

[153] Baker, *Post Offices*, 158, 204, 152; DeArmond, *Beyond Bartholomew*, 91; Gordon Hartrick, in *Reflections of Ashley County*, Mary Imogene Noble Carpenter and Robert A. Carpenter Sr., eds. (Dallas: Curtis Media Corporation, 1987), 78; Goodspeed, *Southern Arkansas*, 888.

[154] DeArmond, *Beyond Bartholomew*, 91, 93, 458; Jack Gibson, interview by author, tape recording, Ozment Bluff Community, September 27, 1998; *Drew County Advance*, December 12, 1901, gives notice of the marriage of Dr. J. P. Barker, physician of Morrell, to Olive Hart.

[155] DeArmond, *Beyond Bartholomew*, 93.

[156] Hartrick, in *Reflections*, 78.

[157] DeArmond, *Beyond Bartholomew*, 116-118.

[158] Ibid., 71-82.

[159] DeArmond, *Beyond Bartholomew*, 17, 18, 22, 24.

[160] "Dashing Days of Early Portland Recalled by Visit of Old Timer," *Delta News*, August 31, 1939.

[161] Ibid.; Goodspeed, *Southern Arkansas*, 892, 915, 925.

[162] DeArmond, *Beyond Bartholomew*, 460.

[163] "Dashing Days."

[164] DeArmond, *Beyond Bartholomew*, 18, 19.

[165] "Dashing Days;" Goodspeed, *Southern Arkansas*, 884; DeArmond, *Beyond Bartholomew*, 20-21.

[166] DeArmond, *Beyond Bartholomew*, 25-29, 30-31, 34, 35, 38-40, 183, 220-221, 460.

[167] *Delta News*, August 10, 1939.

[168] DeArmond, *Beyond Bartholomew*, 30-32, 38, 41.

[169] *Wilmot Weekly*, December 27, 1912;

[170] *Delta News*, March 23, 1939; DeArmond, *Beyond Bartholomew*, 65.

[171] DeArmond, *Beyond Bartholomew*, 42, 44, 49, 52, 53, 54, 55-56, 59-60, 343-244.

[172] Etheridge, *History*, 23; DeArmond, *Beyond Bartholomew*, 95, 401.

[173] Moore, "Antiquities," 170.

[174] DeArmond, *Beyond Bartholomew*, 95; Etheridge, *History*, 118; Goodspeed, *Southern Arkansas*, 887.

[175] William deYampert, interview by author, tape recording, Wilmot, AR, May 12, 1998; *Delta News*, June 22, 1939.

[176] DeArmond, *Beyond Bartholomew*, 96.

[177] Goodspeed, *Southern Arkansas*, 887, 915.

[178] DeArmond, *Beyond Bartholomew*, 115.

[179] Herman King, interview by author, tape recording, Wilmot, AR, January 7, 1999.

[180] DeArmond, *Beyond Bartholomew*, 116.

[181] Goodspeed, *Southern Arkansas*, 884, 913; Mary Alice Cottrell Nelson, interview, tape recording, Calion, AR, December 7, 1998; Etheridge, History, 153.

[182] Ernestine Nobles Sprinkle, interview by author, tape recording, Parkdale, AR, June 4, 1998; Susanne Files Flowers, in *Reflections*, 336; Store receipt in possession of Ernie N. Sprinkle.

[183] Goodspeed, *Southern Arkansas*, 891, 904.

[184] Sprinkle, interview; Mary Lee Echols, "Parkdale Was founded About 1857," *Delta News*, March 21, 1940; Goodspeed, *Southern Arkansas*, 901-902, 904, 844, 894, 919.

[185] Goodspeed, *Southern Arkansas*, 887, 894, 906-907, 917, 994; Etheridge, History, 35.

[186] Sandra Fuller Fisher to author, June 17, 1999; Goodspeed, *Southern Arkansas*, 924-925; Beth Thurman to author, July 4, 1998; Susanne Files Flowers, in *Reflections*, 249-250.

[187] Baker, *Post Offices*, 124, 180; Mary Lee Echols, "Parkdale Was founded About 1857," *Delta News*, March 21, 1940.

[188] Goodspeed, *Southern Arkansas*, 884, 915; Echols, "Parkdale;" Sprinkle, interview.

[189] Echols, "Parkdale;" Statement by Hazel Hawkins, June 3, 1998.

[190] Goodspeed, *Southern Arkansas*, 884; Una Bethune Barnes, "Parkdale Methodist Church," in *Reflections*, 120; Crefonia Coleman Brame, Mollie Nobles, Howard Nobles, Mrs. Lee Austin, "Parkdale Baptist Church," in *Reflections*, 122; Mary Lee Echols, "The Mississippi Outlet for Poplar Bluff," *Delta News*, March 28, 1940.

[191] Barnes, "Parkdale Methodist;" Echols, "Parkdale.

[192] Mary Morris Foster, interview by author, tape recording, Parkdale, AR, June 4, 1998; Mark Hawkins, interview by author, tape recording, Parkdale, AR, June 3, 1998.

[193] Echols, 'Poplar Bluff;" *Delta News*, March 16, 1939.

[194] Echols, "Parkdale;" *Wilmot Weekly*, December 12, 1912. Etheridge, *History*, 124; Dr. M. C. Hawkins documents, in possession of Mark Hawkins.

[195] Sprinkle, interview; Hawkins, interview; Foster, interview; statements by Hazel Hawkins, June 3, 1998.

[196] *Delta News*, September 14, 1939; Hawkins, interview; Flowers in *Reflections*, 250.

[197] Goodspeed, *Southern Arkansas*, 913; *Ashley County Eagle*, May 5, 1898; Flowers in *Reflections*, 292.

[198] *Delta News*, April 11, 1940; June 27, 1940.

[199] Colton's railroad and township map of Arkansas, 1854; Colton's map of the state of Louisiana and eastern Texas, 1863; Goodspeed, *Southern Arkansas*, 905; Etheridge, *History*, 133; Baker, *Post Offices,* 102; Williams, *Encyclopedia*, 282 (listed as "Harkin's Landing"); Etheridge, *History*, 133.

[200] Etheridge, *History*, 143; Baker, *Post Offices*, 13, 57, 124, 198, 237. Etheridge, History, states that this post office was near Wilmot "on the bayou."

[201] Etheridge, *History*, 23, 100; 1844 map of Township 19; Goodspeed, *Southern Arkansas,* 913, 1893; Barbara Sharik Babb, ed. and Janet Clifton, comp., *Collection of Recollections: Wilmot, Arkansas* (privately published, 1993), 16; DeArmond, *Beyond Bartholomew*, 400.

[202] Sandra Fuller Fisher, e-mail to author, June 5, 1998.

[203] Babb and Clifton, *Collection*, 57, 59, 62.

[204] Etheridge, *History*, 171-172.

[205] Joy Willson to author, June 6, 1999.

[206] Babb and Clifton, *Collection*, 130.

[207] Etheridge, *History,* 172; Babb and Clifton, *Collections*, 18.

[208] Babb and Clifton, *Collections*, 84, 118-121.

[209] Ibid., 82, 83; Currie, interview; deYampert, interview.

[210] Currie interview; deYampert, interview, Etheridge, *History*, 172.

[211] Leroy Haynes, interview by author, tape recording, Wilmot, AR, May 6, 1998; Babb and Clifton, *Collection*, 24, 27.

[212] Babb and Clifton, *Collection*, 22-24; Sandra Fuller Fisher, e-mail to author, June 17, 1999.

[213] *Wilmot Weekly*, December 27, 1912; Gibson, interview; Babb and Clifton, *Collection*, 82, 111.

[214] Etheridge, *History*, 173; Babb and Clifton, *Collection*, 134, 157; *Wilmot Weekly*, December 27, 1912.

[215] Babb and Clifton, *Collection*, 29, 132; The *Daily Graphic*, Pine Bluff, July 27, 1924.

[216] Currie, interview.

[217] Babb and Clifton, *Collection*, 91.

[218] Currie, interview; deYampert, interview.

[219] Etheridge, *History,* 124; Babb and Clifton, *Collection,* 51.

[220] *Daily Graphic, Pine Bluff,* July 27, 1924; *Wilmot Weekly,* May 31, 1912; Babb and Clifton, *Collection,* 19, 46.

[221] Babb and Clifton, *Collection,* 76-79.

[222] Ibid., 57; Etheridge, *History,* 171.

[223] Babb and Clifton, *Collection,* 58-59.

[224] Ibid., 62.

[225] Ibid., 31, 61, 65-66.

[226] *Wilmot Weekly,* December 27, 1912; Babb and Clifton, *Collection,* 46.

[227] *Delta News,* December 12, 1940.

[228] Etheridge, History, 171; Robert Arnell Crawley and Ella Crawley Vail, interview by author, tape recording, Little Rock, AR, July 17, 1998.

[229] Bartle Eatman was executor of Daniel C. Fudge's will in 1862, and Battle Eatman was a ruling elder in the Hamburg Presbyterian Church around 1880. See Carpenter, *Reflections,* 111, 260.

[230] Etheridge, *History,* 155. Briscoe C. Tatum was living in the area, perhaps in Morehouse Parish, in 1880, according to Morehouse Parish courthouse records. B. F. Tatum was captain of the steamboat, *Roberta,* owned by the Monroe Navigation Company, in 1903. Way, *Way's,* 400.

[231] Crawley and Vail, interview; Dr. Roy Grizzell, interview by author, tape recording, Monticello, AR, June 16, 1998; Robert Knight, letter to author, 1998. Dr. Roy Grizzell of Monticello is a great-grandson of J. Fred Crawley Sr.

[232] Haynes, interview; Crawley-Vail, interview.

Chapter 4 - Early Bayou Settlements in Northeast Louisiana

[1] Ruth Mayo Boone interview, January 21, 1999; "Bonita Centennial creates interest for the McDowells," clipped article, April 20, 1990; Family History Club, eds., *Known Burials in Morehouse Parish Louisiana and South Ashley County, Arkansas* (Crossett, AR: Nowlin Printing, 1994], 129, 136. (The cemetery at McGinty is called McGinty Cemetery in *Known Burials* but is registered at the courthouse as Sawyer Cemetery.)

[2] Others buried in the Wolfe plot are Dudley Daniel Wolfe (d 23 Jun 1903), Mary Esther Wolfe (d after 1903), and Oliver Woodman Wolfe (d after 1903). *Known Burials,* 237; Beth Thurman, e-mail to author, July 1999; Morehouse Parish 1900 Census; Billy Bobby Abraugh, interview by author, tape recording, Bonita, La, August 16, 1998.

[3] Marion Robertson Doles to author, 1998; Virginia McCready Nightingale, e-mail to author, June 1999.

[4] Thelbert Bunch, interview by author, tape recording, McGinty Community, LA, August 27, 1998; Ruth Mayo Boone, interview by author, tape recording, Bastrop, LA, January 21, 1999.

[5] Boone, interview; John Calvin Yeldell, letter to author, 1998; Bunch, interview.

[6] Duke Shackelford, interview by author, tape recording, Bonita, LA, August 27, 1998.

[7] Abraugh, interview.

[8] Addye M. Mitcham, "Dr. Thomas Cleveland Richmond Among First Black Doctors to Practice in South," *Bastrop Clarion*, May 20, 1978, 3A; Ralph Kinnaird and Billy Bobby Abraugh, interview by author, tape recording, tour of the bayou in Morehouse Parish, August 11, 1998.

[9] James "Buster" Ford, interview by author, tape recording, Bonita, LA, September 22, 1998; Mitcham, "Richmond."

[10] Mitcham, "Richmond;" Kinnaird-Abraugh, interview.

[11] Ford, interview; Page Webb, interview by author, tape recording, Bonita, LA, September 22, 1998; Kinnaird-Abraugh interview.

[12] Research compiled by Ruth Mayo Boone.

[13] Boone interview; Fay Bowe research; "New Hope Baptist Dedication," *Bastrop Daily Enterprise*, April 8, 1965.

[14] Morehouse Parish census, 1850, 1900; Launa (Sawyer) and Gaston Harrison, interview by author, tape recording, Bastrop, LA, June 14, 1998; Crawley, interview; Ford, interview; Bunch, interview; Kinnaird-Abraugh interview.

[15] Eloise Robertson Means, Marion Robertson Doles, and Edwin Robertson, interview by author, tape recording, Bastrop, LA, August 8, 1998.

[16] John Calvin Yeldell and Dorothy Mack, letters to author, 1998; Kinnaird-Abraugh interview; Property Map Parts of Wards 9 and 10, January 1920.

[17] Mildred (Sikes) and Bealie Harrison, interview by author, tape recording, Berlin Community, AR, August 18, 1998; Kinnaird-Abraugh, interview.

[18] Benton B. Hunt, interview by author, tape recording, Zachary Community, LA, September 20, 1998; Dorothy Mack to author, 1998.

[19] Katie Bell Parker, interview by author, tape recording, Bastrop, LA, August 18, 1998; Loyce Arrington Armstrong, "Story Telling – Linking Generations," nd, typed article in possession of author; Dorothy Mack to author, 1998.

[20] *Known Burials*, 131; Menn, *1860 Large Slave Holders of Louisiana*, clipped article, nd.

[21] Elizabeth Littlejohn Leavell and Susan Sturdivant Strong, typed paper in possession of author, 1982; *Known Burials*, 131; Morehouse Parish court records, "Petition in the matter of the tutorship of the minors Jesse D. and Amelia A. Peterkin," 13 February 1879, and "Affidavit of Heirship, 12 January 1937."

[22] *Known Burials*, 131; Kinnaird-Abraugh interview; 1900 Morehouse Census.

[23] "Letter from a Little Arkansas Boy: Log-Cabin, Ashley Co. Ark., January 1859," clipped article, no date. This article was addressed to Mr. Gillespie and thanked him for his advice to children in the *Advocate*. It was written by Martha Amanda "Mattie" Crawley, who corresponded with the newspaper "From a 'Log Cabin' on Bayou Bartholomew" and signed her articles M. A. C.

[24] Williamson, Eastern *Louisiana I*, 253. Williamson states that the railroad was constructed in 1889. It was not completed, however, until 1890. See Harp, *Highroads*, 5-6. Railroad historian, Gene Hull, states that construction began in 1890, see Hull, "Historic Rails."

[25] Steve Sanders, "Small Morehouse town was settled in 1850s," *News Star World* (Monroe), nd, [c1981; Fay Bowe research (Morehouse Parish post offices); A.

Fortier, *Louisiana: Comprising Sketches of Parishes, Towns, Events and Institutions*, Vol. 3, (Century Historical Association, 1914), 543; Morehouse Parish 1900 Census.

[26] *Eastern Louisiana* III, 1216.

[27] Ibid.; Kinnaird-Abraugh, interview.

[28] Kinnaird-Abraugh, interview; Bunch, interview.

[29] Bobby Abraugh research, Conveyance Book Q, p 192, 196; Book V, p 531, Morehouse Parish County Court records.

[30] Armstrong, "Story Telling;" Kinnaird-Abraugh, interview; Gibson, interview.

[31] Gibson, interview.

[32] Means research, from Burris Ann Mitchell, *Medical Doctors of Morehouse Parish*, 1989; *Known Burials*, 83; Armstrong, "Story Telling."

[33] "Old Landmark Torn Down," clipped article, nd; Shackelford, interview.

[34] Sanders, "Small Morehouse town."

[35] *Louisiana: A Guide to the State*, Compiled by Workers of the Writers' Program of the Work Project Administration in the State of Louisiana (New York: Hastings House, 1945), 598.

[36] Gaston and Launa Harrison, interview; *Known Burials*, 107; Bealie and Mildred Harrison, interview.

[37] C. C. Davenport, *Looking Backward: Memoirs of the Early Settlement of Morehouse Parish* (Mer Rouge: Press of Mer Rouge Democrat, 1911), 39; Vera Lee Hedges, *Bartholomew United Methodist Church 1796-1996: A Great Cloud of Witnesses* (West Monroe: Scott Sherman, 1996), 1.

[38] Eloise Means, "Lind Grove: the bayou's early steamboat destination," *Bastrop Daily Enterprise*, February 26, 1998, 3.

[39] Davenport, *Looking Backward*, 10, 15; Williamson, Eastern *Louisiana*, 74 (Williamson gives Watt's name as H. A. Watt); Eloise Robertson Means, letter to author, September 8, 1998.

[40] Means, letter; Store receipts in possession of Fay Bowe. The January 25, 1880 receipt for W. F. Watt has Watt's name crossed out with Geo. T. Ellis written above it indicating Ellis possibly bought this store. However, the December 15, 1881 receipt was not changed.

[41] Means research. (From *Medical Doctors of Morehouse Parish*.)

[42] Means, letter; Means-Doles-Robertson, interview.

[43] Fay Bowe research; J. D. Lovett Certificate of Death.

[44] Thomas Young Harp, *"Me" and "Highroads to Education" and "My Kin Folks"* (privately printed; nd, c 1945), *Me*, 3, *My Kin Folks*, 36, hereafter cited as Harp, *Me*, *Highroads*, or *My Kin Folks*. Each section begins with page one.

[45] Harp, *Highroads*, 17-19.

[46] Moore, "Antiquities," 169.

[47] "Bonita Centennial;" Means research

[48] M. M. Wilkinson, *Genealogy of Wilkinson and Kindred Families*, 477-481. (The names of various Bunckley family members bear a striking resemblance to the black Hunter and Richmond families. Poca Hunter acquired several hundred acres after the Civil War, and his daughter, Mahala, married Seymour Richmond. It is possible that both families were descended from Richmond-Bunckley slaves and that the family gave the land to Hunter.)

[49] Means research.

[50] Harp, *Highroads,* 2-5.

[51] Ibid., 3.

[52] Ibid., 5-6, 13.

[53] Gene Hull, "Historic Rails."

[54] Wolff & Montgomery store receipt, March 31, 1892, in possession of Fay Bowe. There are some Wolffs buried in the Jewish Cemetery at Bastrop.

[55] Means research; Virginia Harp, "The History of Bonita Morehouse Parish," *La Raconteur: Le Comite des Archives de la Louisine* XV, # 3, 4 (December 1995), 163-164.

[56] Harp, "*Highroads,*" 6.

[57] Ibid., 6-7.

[58] Ibid., 7-9, 23.

[59] Ibid., 11-13; Means research.

[60] Marion Doles, "Seligman's in Bonita: remembering a Morehouse landmark," *Bastrop Daily Enterprise*, February 26, 1998, 6.

[61] Harp, "*My Kin Folks,*" 18; Virginia Harp, "History," 164.

[62] Means research; *Monroe Morning World*, April 11, 1954; Ann DeVillier Riffel, "Lind Grove and Bonita Postmasters," *La Raconteur: Le Comite des Archives de la Louisine* XV, # 3, 4 (December 1995), 165.

[63] Eloise Means research. The Bonita Lumber Company information from Records of Charter, Book 1, p 110, Morehouse County Court Records and *The West Side Delta, Arkansas-Louisiana* (Memphis, TN: Southern Alluvial Land Association, 1920), 61.

[64] Eloise Means research.

[65] Bobby Abraugh, letter to author, February 23, 2000.

[66] Hawkins, interview; Gaston and Launa Harrison, interview; Robertson-Doles-Means, interview; Kinnaird-Abraugh, interview; Abraugh, interview; Parker, interview; Harp, interview; Gibson, interview; Means research.

[67] Means research; Harp, interview; Abraugh, interview.

[68] Ibid.; "Bus, train lines benefited the town of Bonita," clipped article, nd, first appeared in the *Morehouse Enterprise* Industrial Edition in 1929.

[69] *Louisiana: A Guide*, 598.

[70] Marion Doles to author, 1998; Means research.

[71] Robertson-Doles-Means interview; Virginia McCready Nightingale, e-mail to author, May 1999.

[72] "Bus, train lines;" Wally Gallian and DeEtt Carroll, eds., *Morehouse Parish: A Pictorial History* (Bastrop: Bastrop Daily Enterprise, 1995), 31,33, 69; Means research.

[73] Means research. (Some information taken from Barbara Tubbs Vail, *Bonita Methodist Church*.)

[74] Means research (From *Medical Doctors of Morehouse Parish*.); Mitcham, "Richmond." According to *Medical Doctors*, Dr. Nathan Bunckley was practicing in the area in 1838.

[75] Doles, "When Bartholomew."

[76] Armstrong, "Story Telling." Loyce Arrington Armstong and her husband bought Dr. Owens' home and office where they lived for twenty years. When they moved

to Bastrop, they donated the office to the town for a museum. It was moved to property donated by Walter Polk.

[77] Davenport, *Looking Backward*, 43; Gaston and Launa Harrison, interview; Bealie and Mildred Harrison, interview; *Known Burials*, 179.

[78] Hand-drawn map "From 1851 Morehouse Parish Map," in Snyder Museum; Moore, "Antiquities," 161, 166.

[79] Hedges, *Bartholomew Church*, 63-64, 70.

[80] Davenport, *Looking Backward*, 38.

[81] Hedges, *Bartholomew Church*, 1-2, 12, 56-57, 105-106. Hedges' endnote for this information states, "Houston Roberts, D.D., pastor of the church and also a member of the Masonic Lodge located the story of *Bartholomew's founding, History of Bartholomew F & A M Masonic Lodge (and Meeting House of the Methodist Society) Morehouse Parish, Louisiana,* in Masonic archives. Dr. Roberts did not provide the exact location of his source and, unfortunately, in spite of persistent research, no further documentation of this story was found." Cf. v-vi, 91.

[82] Ibid., 2, 57-60, 67.

[83] Ibid., 65; *Known Burials*, 1-6.

[84] Hedges, *Bartholomew Church*, 57; Walter Prichard, ed., "A Tourist's Description of Louisiana in 1860, Louisiana *Historical Quarterly* 21 (January 1938), 1199; Williams, *Encyclopedia*, 282; Fay Bowe, letter to author, May 2000.

[85] Means research. (From *Medical Doctors of Morehouse Parish*. This source lists Dr. Levell in Bastrop in 1926, but Means has documentation that he was in Plantersville in 1917.)

[86] Clipped article from calendar, nd.

[87] Moore, "Antiquities," 161; Robertson-Means-Doles, interview.

[88] Robertson-Means-Doles, interview; Gaston and Launa Harrison, interview (Steve Atkins).

[89] Fay Bowe research (Morehouse Parish post offices); Gaston and Launa Harrison, interview; Bealie and Mildred Harrison, interview.

[90] Gaston and Launa Harrison interview; Map, Morehouse Parish, 1851.

[91] Marjorie Day Huber, letter to author, September 15, 1999; Moore, "Antiquities," 157, 161.

[92] Map, Morehouse Parish, 1851; Huber, letter; Moore, "Antiquities," 151; Davenport, *Looking Backward*, 38.

[93] Marjorie Day Huber, letter to author, January 21, 1999; Moore, "Antiquities," 156; Frank, C. L. "Chuck," and Winifred Day, interview by author, tape recording, Wardville Community, LA, September 24, 1998.

[94] Kinnaird-Abraugh, interview; Hunt, interview; Day, interview.

[95] Day, interview; *Known Burials*, 195; Davenport, *Looking Backward*, 43.

[96] Davenport, *Looking Backward*, 40; James H. Boddie Jr., *A Glimpse of Bastrop's Past*, September 9, 1978, 1; Fay Bowe research (Morehouse Parish post offices).

[97] Davenport, *Looking Backward* 40-42; Hedges "Church," 105; Boddie, Glimpse, 6.

[98] Prichard, "A Tourist's Description," 1198-1199; Boddie, *Glimpse*, 4, 6.

[99] *Pictorial History*, 5; *Louisiana: A Guide*, 598-599.

---

[100] Boddie, *Glimpse*, 5; Morehouse Parish Police Jury, *Morehouse Parish*, (Bastrop: *Morehouse Enterprise*, nd [early 1930s]), pages not numbered.

[101] P. G. Jones, "Seligman's in Bastrop: a living corner of Morehouse history," *Bastrop Daily Enterprise*, February 26, 1998, 10; *Pictorial History*, 20, 34,95; William Pendleton, "Dunn Candy grew from efforts of legendary entrepreneur," *Bastrop Daily Enterprise*, February 26, 1998, 6.

[102] *Pictorial History*, 21, 87.

[103] Glen Lee Greene, Th.D., Baptists *of Oak Ridge* (Nashville: Parthenon Press, 1960), 77-78. No references were found that indicated Shakers ever established a colony there.   The Shakers were an austere religious group that advocated collective property ownership, celibacy, and a simple lifestyle.

[104] Short, *History*, 41, 32.

[105] Greene, *Baptists,* 77-78; *Known Burials*, 109.

[106] Williamson, Eastern *Louisiana*, 27, 67; *Arkansas Territorial Papers*, "Canal Between Ouachita & Mississippi Rivers," Benjamin L. Miles to Delegate Seivier, November 18, 1833. Published in Kin Kollecting 4 (Fall 1990), 42-43.

[107] Williamson, *Eastern Louisiana*, 68; Davenport, *Looking Backward,* 14.

[108] Mary Dean Pugh family history; Huber correspondence. Louise Naff Larsen, great-granddaughter of Naff, discovered Naff's tombstone holding a block of salt in a pasture. She and Freddy Harvey had it moved to Christ Church Cemetery.

[109] Hedges, *Bartholomew Church*, 58; Davenport, *Looking Backward,* 37; Williams, *Encyclopedia*, 281.

[110] Short, *History*, 77.

[111] Susan Holley led the author to this site and to the Spyker home site May 9, 1999. Mrs. Holley found the cornerstone of the old church building and gave it to the present church in 1994.

[112] Davenport, *Looking Backward*, 38; "Autobiography of Wm. M. Guice, MD," <http://www.geocities.com/~cpguice/wmgp2.html>.

[113] Map, Morehouse Parish, 1851.

[114] Gen Francis, "From 'Hard Times' to 'New Hope'," *Shreveport Times*, July 1, 1956.

[115] *The Diary of Leonidas Pendleton Spyker*, transcribed copy, 55, 136, 142, 297, 282.   Page numbers refer to original diary pages.   Original in Sandal Library Archives, University of Louisiana, Monroe.

[116] Hedges, *Church*, 29, 33, 105; Francis, "Hard Times."

[117] Spyker, *Diary,* 50-52, 55, 122, 139, 296, 282, 290, 298, 301.

[118] Ibid., 50, 52, 54, 122, 128, 282, 287, 291, 292, 295, 298. Other people mentioned were: Hannibal Faulk, Col. Ross, Mr. and Mrs. Beachum, Mr. Hunter, Mr. Rooks, Mrs. Todd, Mrs. Brigham, Mr. Willard, Col. Polk, Mr. and Mrs. Bochelle, Mr. Jacobs, Ray Beachum, Penny Ross, James Watson, Wilds Ross, Mr. Bates, Peter McLeish, Mr. Wilson, Mr. Weaks, Miss Mason, Miss Douglas, Puss Ross, Wm. Barham, Mr. Rhodes, Mr. Brown, Mr. Taylor, Mr. Shelton, F. I. Smith, Judge Temple, Mrs. Dunlap, Mr. Schardt, Bob Briscoe, Mrs. Cook, R. R. Todd, Mr. Hinson, Mr. Douglas, Mr. Burns, Miss Bartlett, Mrs. Hamilton, Mrs. Weeks, Mr. Caldwel, Miss Hinson, Mr. McGrurder, Mr. Shelton, Mr. Headen, Charles and Horace Polk, Mr. Williamson, Mrs. Isaac Ross, Mjr. Potts, Mr. and Mrs. Eugene Polk, Mr. and Mrs. H. M. Polk and John and Leon, Mr. Gonder, Mr. Matthews, Mr.

and Mrs. Compton, Mr. Hamlett, Mr. Flerwellen, Mr. Allen, Mrs. Moore, Mrs. Weaks, and Mr. Little. Mr. Dalrymple was the carpenter who built the slave hospital.

[119] Francis, "Hard Times."

[120] Davenport, *Looking Backward, 39.*

[121] Moore, Antiquities, 11 (map), 112, 120.

[122] Kinnaird-Abraugh, interview.

[123] "Miscellaneous," *DeBow's Review*, December 1850, 9: 6, 670.

[124] Short, *History*, 28-30, 42, 45, 59, 81. 28-30.

[125] Ibid., 26, 31-32, 37, 54-58.

[126] Paul Rawson, "Moore Plantation Parish Landmark," *Bastrop Daily Enterprise*, November 1, 1979. Mrs. Short in *History*, 76, spells the name Elden.

[127] Paul Rawson, "Two Frenchmen-the Cavets, at Bartholomew Woods," *Bastrop Daily Enterprise*, November 17, 1983.

[128] Short, *History*, 32, 40, 52-53. On p 32 Mrs. Short wrote that Elizabeth Smiley Miller, daughter of John Miller, married Benjamin Scriber and William F. Collier. On p 52-53 she wrote that Mary Elizabeth Miller, daughter of Guild Miller, married these men and that John G. Miller was her brother.

[129] Ibid., 50-51; Davenport, *Looking Backward*, 7-9.

[130] *Journal North Louisiana Historical Association* 15: 2-3 (Spring-Summer, 1984), clipped article.

[131] Short, *History*, 50-51, 80, 82-84.

[132] Map, Ouachita River Survey, 1895, Sheet No. 19. Vicksburg, Mississippi River Commission Archives.

[133] Short, *History*, 13, 19, 36, 40, 65, 76.

[134] Ibid., 78, 80. Mrs. Short wrote (83) that Elizabeth Sterling sold Arthur L. Smith 787 acres of the Sterling plantation. Elizabeth Sterling died in 1878.

[135] Mary Ann Dixon Johnston, interview by author, tape recording, Sterlington, LA, August 24, 1998; Short, *History*, 18.

[136] Johnson interview; Blanche Oliver, "Sterlington, LA," typewritten paper, 1936, on file at Ouachita Parish Library.

[137] Paul Rawson, "One-Room School Started It All," *Bastrop Daily Enterprise*, December 7, 1979.

[138] Paul Rawson, "Old Bartholomew Cemetery Has Lot of History in It," *Bastrop Daily Enterprise*, May 16, 1979; Short, *History*, 9, 14. The story of finding the Spanish soldier's grave came from an interview with Mrs. Bessie McInnis by Mrs. Short.

[139] Stephen Wilson, "Couch's Sterlington plant tapped 'North Louisiana Field'," (AP&L publication, 1986), 5.

[140] Johnston, interview.

[141] "Sterlington – The Roots of LP&L," 1992, typed paper by the employees and retirees of Sterlington in possession of the author.

[142] Hon. H. Bry, "The Ouachita Country," 408; R. M. Bry, "Northern Louisiana and Arkansas," 69.

[143] Ed Jones, interview by author, tape recording, Ouachita City Community, LA, October 6, 1998; Map, Morehouse Parish, 1851.

[144] Ouachita River Survey; Johnston, interview; Jones, interview.

Chapter 5 – A Steamboat Thoroughfare

[1] Pearson and Saltus, *Underwater*, 12; Rodney Bowers, "Canoe found in river drifted from history: Likely Indian artifact may be 1,000 years old," *Arkansas Democrat-Gazette*, September 5, 1999.

[2] Pearson and Saltus, *Underwater*, 12; Williams, *Spanish Poste*, 20-22.

[3] Davenport, *Looking Backward*, 6.

[4] Pearson and Saltus, *Underwater*, 13-14; Williamson, *Eastern Louisiana*, 194, 197.

[5] Walter Havighurst, *Voices on the River: The Story of the Mississippi Waterways* (New York: Macmillan Company, 1964), 34.

[6] Tomlinson, "Home;" Mrs. Dillard Saunders, letter; "Steamboat Days Back Again?" *Bastrop Daily Enterprise*, March 9, 1956.

[7] Havighurst, *Voices*, 54, 58; Pearson and Saltus, *Underwater*, 15.

[8] Dr. A. R. Kilpatrick, "Historical and Statistical Collections of Louisiana," *DeBow's Southern and Western Review* 12 (June 1852): 636; Williamson, *Eastern Louisiana*, 207-208; Sharon Kouns, e-mail to author, September 29, 1999. Kilpatrick named Nancarrow, and Williamson wrote that Captain Paulfrey was the one who made the first trip to Monroe.

[9] Herndon, *Centennial History*, I, 513.

[10] Larry Morrison, "Steamboats At The Port Of Camden," unpublished manuscript, 1975, 4, copy in possession of author. *Way's Packet Directory* lists the *Jim Barkman* as a 65-ton sternwheeler built in 1859, owned by Capt. James R. Bangs and others, operating on the Ouachita River.

[11] "Canal," 42. (See Appendix for the signatories of the petition.)

[12] Etheridge, *History*, 28.

[13] "The Levees and Overflows of the Mississippi," *DeBow's Review* 25 (October 1858): 438.

[14] "McDermott Journal," 402.

[15] Havighurst, *Voices*, 73; Diana Sherwood, "Clearing the Channel – The Snagboat in Arkansas," *Arkansas Historical Quarterly* 3 (spring 1944): 56-59.

[16] Williamson, *Eastern Louisiana*, 208-209; C. Bradford Mitchell, ed., *Merchant Steam Vessels of the United States 1790-1868*, Steamship Historical Society of America, Inc. (Fair Lawn, NJ: De Troy Bergen Press, 1975), 39; Leonard V. Huber, compiler, *Advertisements of Lower Mississippi River Steamboats 1812-1920* (Steamship Historical Society of America: West Barrington, RI, 1959), 16.

[17] Hammond, "Abstract," 42, 214.

[18] Hedges, *Bartholomew Church*, 58; Davenport, *Looking Backward*, 37; Williams, *Encyclopedia*, 281.

[19] Davenport, *Looking Backward*, 46-47. Judge Temple was born February 29, 1812. See Williams, *Encyclopedia*, 283.

[20] Williamson, *Eastern Louisiana*, 209-212; Huber, *Advertisements*, 6.

[21] Sharon Milich Kouns, "Obituaries of Riverboatmen and Women," September 10, 1999, ◇; Sharon Kouns, e-mail to author, September 25, 1999; N. Philip Norman, "The Red River of the South," *Louisiana Historical Quarterly* 25 (1942): 402.

Norman gives the date as "around 1849" and lists Ben B. Kouns as an owner at that time.

[22] Havighurst, *Voices*, 136.

[23] Hammond, "Abstract," 214-215.

[24] Huber, *Advertisements* 6, 7, 16, 22, 29, 32, 35, 36, 42, 48, 56, 61, 57, 64, 67; "Documents and Articles #7," October 4, 1998 < >; Beverly Watkins, "Human Adaptatin in the Grand Marais Lowland, *Ouachita County Historical Quarterly* 1 (March 1983), 8.

[25] Frederick Way Jr., *Way's Packet Directory, 1848-1994*, rev. ed., Sons and Daughters of Pioneer Rivermen (Athens: Ohio University Press, 1994), 287; Honeycutt. Honeycutt wrote that Harry Williams, a pilot, built the *Addie* at Monroe.

[26] DeArmond, *Beyond Bartholomew*, 11, from Chicot County Court Minutes, Book D, 107, April 5, 1842.

[27] "100 Year Old House Has Seen Many Changes," *Morehouse Enterprise*, April 27, 1939.

[28] Hon. H. Bry, "The Ouachita Country," 408; R. M. Bry, "Northern Louisiana and Arkansas," 69; "Extent of Steam Navigation in the United States," *DeBow's Review* 25 (August 1858): 284, from a Report to Congress by Col. Abert, January 12, 1848.

[29] Spyker, *Diary*, 48, 51, 53, 54, 123-130, 130-133, 136, 138-140, 142-144, 146-150, 155, 157, 211-217, 219, 222-223, 226-227, 229, 232, 239, 245, 250, 282, 287-288, 290-301, 303-304, 306, 308.

[30] Morrison, "Steamboats," 9-10.

[31] Ibid., 14-15.

[32] Correspondent, "An Irontonian Down South," *Irontonian Register*, April 1, 1869.

[33] Huber, *Advertisements*, 27, 66, 68, 77, 79; Advertisement for the *Big Horn* from "Documents and Articles #12, October 4, 1998 < >.

[34] E. B. Cryer, Bills of Lading Ledger, August 1875 – April 1883; C. C. Honeycutt, "Steamboating in the Early Days," *Crossett Observer*, clipped article, 1916; Williamson, *Eastern Louisiana*, 221; Paul Rawson, "Steamboats on the Bartholomew in 1883," *Bastrop Daily Enterprise*, clipped article, 1983.

[35] Huber, *Advertisements*, 37,38; Way, *Way's*, 118; Rawson, "Steamboats 1883." See also Pearson and Saltus, *Underwater*, 35.The *Lotawanna* was advertised as connecting with the *Ora* for Bayou Bartholomew in the *Ouachita Telegraph*, May 1, 1874.

[36] Williamson, *Eastern Louisiana*, 222.

[37] Hammond, "Abstract," 143-144.

[38] Huber, *Advertisements*, 9, 29, 37; Original document in possession of Fay Bowe; Way *Way's*, 38.

[39] Huber, *Advertisements*, 76. John Tillman Hughes, who owned a mercantile store at Poplar Bluff, may have been part owner of the *Ella Hughes* as he had an unmarried daughter named Ella (born 1860; died 1884).

[40] Cryer, Lading.

[41] E. B. Cryer, Cotton Book, March, April 1880.

[42] Hammond, "Abstract," 145-146.

[43] Jim Rider, *Bastrop Daily Enterprise*, February 18, 1993.

[44] Original document in possession of Ernestine Nobles Sprinkle.

[45] Hammond, "Abstract," 88, 172, from U. S. Army, *Chief of Engineers, Annual Report, 1881*, 1421, 1423; *Monroe Bulletin*, May 24, 1882. These Reports hereafter cited as *Annual Report* with year.

[46] Rawson, "Steamboats 1883."

[47] Way, *Way's*, 481.

[48] Rawson, "Steamboats 1883."

[49] DeArmond, *Beyond Bartholomew*, 12, from *Arkansas Gazette*, May 2, 1875.

[50] Donald Holley, "The Man for the Times and Place," *Drew County Historical Journal* 4 (1989), 7.

[51] Hammond, "Abstract," 215-216, from *Annual Report to Louisiana State Legislature, 1848*, 12; 45th Congress, 3d Session, House Document No. 61, 13; U. S. Congress, House, 46th Congress, 3d Session House Document No. 38, 4.

[52] Ibid., 216, from *Monroe Bulletin*, February 23, 1881.

[53] Ibid., 216-218, from *Annual Report, 1896*, 1602; U. S. Congress, House, 48th Congress, 2d Session, House Document No. 147, 2,3; *Annual Report, 1896*, 1602; *Annual Report, 1888*, 1353.

[54] "Navigable Rivers of Arkansas," *Arkansas Gazette*, September 13, 1887, 1. Bartholomew was under the Vicksburg District of the Corps of Engineers as noted by Captain Taber.

[55] Tomlinson, "Stream of History."

[56] Birch, *Bayou Bartholomew*, 114, 115.

[57] Hammond, "Abstract," 174, from *Annual Report, 1888*, 1353, and *Annual Report, 1890*, 1885; E. B. Cryer, Accounts Receivable Ledger, June 1888 – September 1889; Original document (bill of lading) in possession of Fay Bowe; *Arkansas Gazette*, March 13, 1889; Goodspeed, *Southern Arkansas*, 929.

[58] Cryer, Cotton Book, March 1880-February 1888.

[59] Hammond "Abstract," 113, from *Monroe Bulletin*, January 24, 1883, April 9, July 2, 1884.

[60] *Annual Report, 1894*, 1,473-1,475.

[61] Ibid., 1474.

[62] E. B. Cryer, Portage Book, January 10, 1894 – July 1, 1895; Hammond, "Abstract," 175, from *Annual Report, 1895*;

[63] Morrison, "Steamboats," 19; Rawson, "Steamboat Days;" Huber, *Advertisements*, 52, 53.

[64] Martinez, *Spanish Moss*, 4, 7.

[65] Hammond, "Abstract," 176, from *Annual Reports, 1900, 1905*; "Steamboat Days."

[66] Hammond, "Abstract," 218-219, from *Annual Report, 1896*, 1602.

[67] Drew County Historical Society, "Did You Know That?" *Advance-Monticellonian*, July 1976; Huber, *Advertisements*, 57. No other documentation for these boats being on the bayou was found.

[68] Hammond, "Abstract," 219-220; *Annual Report, 1914*, 877, 879; DeArmond, *Beyond Bartholomew*, 12.

[69] *Annual Report, 1904*, 390-301.

[70] Hammond, "Abstract," 220-221, from *Annual Report, 1916,* 1030; *1914,* 877; *1925,* 995.

[71] Ibid., 178, from *Annual Report, 1915.*

[72] Spyker, *Diary,* 229,308,309; Goodspeed, *Southern Arkansas,* 905; "Steamboat Days."

[73] Havighurst, *Voices,* 64, 140, 147.

[74] Honeycutt, "Steamboating."

[75] Morrison, "Steamboats," 6-7.

[76] Williamson, *Eastern Louisiana,* 217-218.

[77] Havighurst, *Voices,* 148.

[78] Mitchell, *Merchant Steam Vessels,* 292.

[79] Way, *Way's,* 456. Her length is given as 1,103, which is in error; it should be 103.

[80] *Official Records,* Series I, Part 1, 48, 70; Way, *Way's,* 247 (dimensions).

[81] Way, *Way's,* 286. The *Lightwood* was later raised and rebuilt; see Norman, "Red River."

[82] Pearson and Saltus, *Underwater,* 41, 43; Mitchell, *Merchant Steam Vessels,* 246, lists this boat as foundered.

[83] Pearson and Saltus, 41; *Way's,* 38, and Williams, *Eastern Louisiana,* 219, list this boat as sunk. William's also gives 1876 as the date. The source in Williams is Captain Elisha Austin's list which was composed from memory in 1881.

[84] Way, *Way's,* 355; Honeycutt, "Steamboating." Honeycutt wrote that the *Ollie B.* and *Ora B.* were named for "two Jew girls of Farmerville, La., who were twins. Their father was a merchant and owned stock in the boats."

[85] Pearson and Saltus, *Underwater,* 42; "Steamboat Days;" Honeycutt, "Steamboating."

[86] Ibid., 294.

[87] Williams, *Eastern Louisiana,* 218.

[88] Ibid., 219; Corps of Engineers Map, 1879, shows location.

[89] Way, *Way's,* 140, 294.

[90] Paul L. Rawson, "Dry Weather Helps Turn up Treasure in River," *Bastrop Daily Enterprise,* October 2, 1980.

[91] Jim Rider, "Low water allows look at bayou bottom," *Bastrop Daily Enterprise,* July 5, 1988.

[92] "Steamboat Days."

[93] The following day, August 15, 1998, the author and Ralph Kinnaird accompanied Louis and Carmen Redden to the site who filmed it for their "Louisiana Backroads" program on KNOE-TV, Monroe. (According to Honeycutt, the *St. Francis Belle* sank near Lind Grove.)

[94] Among those present were Louis and Carmen Redden who filmed the episode for their "Louisiana Backroads" program on KNOE-TV, Monroe. The location is recorded as the Tatum Bend Site #3AS388 with the Arkansas Archeological Survey.

[95] Way, *Way's,* 322-323, states that William Freeman and a Mr. Jenkins took flats of fire clay, bricks, et cetera south in 1877. The flats were towed by the steamer *Mink.*

[96] Tom Harp, letter to unknown person, October 29, 1960; Julia Huff Bryan, statement to author, February 19, 2000.

[97] Mitchell, *Merchant Steam Vessels*, 247; Davenport, *Looking Backward*, 37. In Paul Rawson, "Exploration Sites of Steamboat Sinking Probed," *Bastrop Daily Enterprise*, March 12, 1979, Rawson mistakenly wrote that the *Buckeye* collided with *Old River* on Bayou Bartholomew and that she later collided with the *DeSoto* on the Ouachita.

[98] Williamson, *Eastern Louisiana*, 226; Honeycutt, "Steamboating." (Although Honeycutt stated that the D. Stein burned in 1886, the Cryer ledgers document that she was still running in 1888.)

[99] *Arkansas: A Guide*, 52.

[100] Way, *Way's*, 173.

[101] Havighurst, *Voices*, 140, 147-148.

[102] Kouns, Sharon and Wells, Peggy, *Folklore and Legends, Burlington, First County Seat, Lawrence County, Ohio* (privately published, 1996), 230, from *Ironton Register*, August 13, 1896.

[103] Havighurst, *Voices*, 129-131; Goodspeed, *Southern Arkansas*, 922; Grizzell, interview; Crawley-Vail, interview.

[104] Way, *Way's*, 449, 462; Ben Lucien Burman, "My Touchstone to the Mississippi," *Reader's Digest* (May 1946), 93, 95-97.

[105] Way, *Way's*, 328, 340, 289, 445.

[106] Davenport, *Looking Backward*, 21.

[107] Hammond, "Abstract," 90; Beth Thurman, e-mail to author, May 4, 2000; Cryer, Receipt Book, November 16, 1888.

[108] DeArmond, *Beyond Bartholomew*, 21.

[109] Cryer, Receipt Book, August 7, 1888.

[110] Way, *Way's*, 392

[111] Havighurst, *Voices*, 2-4, 12, 84, 88.

[112] Ibid., 242; Paul A. Rawson, "Special Sound of Steamboat Whistles Is Recalled," *Bastrop Daily Enterprise*, January 14, 1980. Rawson states in this article, as well as in "Davenport Memoirs" that the *Silver Moon* mentioned in the Spyker diary had a calliope and was the last boat up the Mississippi before traffic closed for the Civil War. The first *Silver Moon*, the bayou boat, burned in 1858. The second boat of the same name (1859-1872) is the actual one concerning his reference and was not a bayou boat. See *Way's*, 427.

[113] Way, *Way's*, 206; Pearson and Saltus, *Underwater*, 36; Williamson, *Eastern Louisiana*, 226.

[114] Pearson and Saltus, *Underwater*, 39.

[115] Hammond, "Abstract," 41, from Stoughton Cooley, "Up the Ouachita on a Cotton Boat," *Cosmopolitan* 12 (1892), 548.

[116] Way, *Way's*, 453.

[117] Huber, *Advertisements*, ix.

[118] "An Irontonian Down South."

[119] Havighurst, *Voices*, 95-97.

[120] Cryer, Portage Book, February 22, 1893.

[121] Honeycutt, "Steamboating."

[122] DeArmond, *Old Times*, 155.

[123] Williamson, *Eastern Louisiana*, 219.

[124] Spyker, *Diary*, 50, 157.

[125] Norman, "Red River," 527.

[126] "Steamboat Days."

[127] Spyker, *Diary*, 53, 215, 290; Cryer, Portage Book, May 13, 1893; DeArmond, *Beyond Bartholomew*, 12, 370; Gibson, interview.

[128] Cryer, Passenger Book, January 29, 1890 – [February] 1896.

[129] George M. Patton, e-mail to author, August 17, 1997. Mr. Patton is the grandson of Robert and Fannie (Harris) Moore. The verse was written March 30, 1879. Code Swain married Thomas H. Elfred in her hometown of Saint Joseph, Louisiana.

[130] Honeycutt, "Steamboating." John Gomillon settled in Ashley County. John McClendon married Fannie Barnes "daughter of one of Ashley County's wealthy planters."

[131] "An Irontonian Down South;" Watkins, "Human Adaptation," 8.

[132] Way, *Way's*, 20.

[133] Williamson, *Eastern Louisiana*, 206. J. G. Flugel made his first trip down the Mississippi in 1817 and was later the American consul at Leipzig, Germany.

[134] Davenport, *Looking Backward*, 16-17.

Chapter 6 – A Watery Land

[1] Goodspeed, *Southern Arkansas*, 628.

[2] Hedges, *Church*, 13-19.

[3] "Judge Bocage Memoirs: Memories of the Old Second Judicial District," ed. J. W. Leslie, *Jefferson County Historical Quarterly* 5 (summer 1974): 16-17. First published in the *Pine Bluff Commercial*, September 12, 1887. The second judicial district included present Jefferson, Arkansas, Desha, Lincoln, Chicot, Drew, Bradley, Ashley, Calhoun, Cleveland, Grant, Ouachita, Columbia and Union Counties.

[4] Davenport, *Memoirs*, 21-23.

[5] Horace Adams, "Drew County Pioneers," *Drew County Historical Quarterly* (1987): 76-77.

[6] "History of Mt. Zion Church 1858-1995," *Drew County Advance*, clipped article, 1907.

[7] Bohinger, "Noel Family," 118.

[8] "Dashing Days." An eight-year old son with this family was Marshall Whitesides. Anna Cola Cammack married A. J. Camak.

[9] Clifton L. Birch, *Bayou Bartholomew: A Regional Stream* (privately published, 1999), 40.

[10] *Lincoln County History*, 31.

[11] Topographical Survey [Drew County] District of Arkansas map, 1860, a National Archives map at the Arkansas History Commission; *Drew County Advance*, August 7, 1894; DeArmond, *Beyond Bartholomew*, 16, from a 1913 map in possession of Hunter Hollaway;

[12] Goodspeed, *Southern Arkansas*, 929-930.

[13] James W. Leslie, "Monticello History," *Pine Bluff Commercial*, May 6, 1976; "Drew's First-Built Home Still Stands," *Advance-Monticellonian*, clipped article, n.d.

[14] *Arkansas Gazette*, October 9, 1907.

[15] DeArmond, *Beyond Bartholomew*, 15.

[16] Corps of Engineers Map of Bayou Bartholomew in Ashley County, 1879. Original in possession of Mr. and Mrs. William deYampert.

[17] "Dashing Days."

[18] DeArmond, *Beyond Bartholomew*, 15-16.

[19] Echols, "Parkdale" gives 1910 as the year the bridge was built; Etheridge, *History*, 185, states that the money was appropriated in 1908.

[20] Arkansas Public Land Survey Map of Township 19 South, Range 5 West, April 1844. Copy provided by Janet Clifton.

[21] Etheridge, *History*, 23.

[22] *Ashley County Eagle*, July 19, 1917.

[23] Yeldell-Mack, letter.

[24] Florence Winkler Millard, letter to Dorothy Mack, December 1998.

[25] Crawley-Vail, interview.

[26] Spyker, *Diary*, 151, 222, 244, 282, 292.

[27] Pearl E. Young, "Memories of an Ashley County Childhood," *Arkansas Historical Quarterly* 16 (winter 1957): 355-356.

[28] Dorothy Mack to author, 1998.

[29] *Arkansas Gazette*, June 11, 1867.

[30] *Daily Gazette*, May 15, 1874. A May 10 article said that the flood had lasted two months.

[31] *Arkansas Gazette*, March 18, 1882, May 21, 1892; Pete Daniel, *Deep 'n as It Come: The 1927 Mississippi River Flood* (Fayetteville: University of Arkansas Press, 1996), 3; Ken Hubbell and Janis Kearney Lunon, eds., *The Arkansas Delta: A Historical Outlook at Our Land and People* (Little Rock: Department of Arkansas Heritage, 1990), 11, 12.

[32] Daniel, *Deep 'n as it Come*, 2.

[33] John M. Barry, *Rising Tide: The Great Mississippi Flood of 1927 and How It Changed America* (New York: Simon and Schuster, 1997), 40.

[34] DeArmond, *Beyond Bartholomew*, 176, from a recorded interview by Patricia Taylor, 1982.

[35] Mildred Edwards Tilbury, "Journey in Time – The big flood of 1927 in Bonita and Wilmot area," *Bastrop Daily Enterprise*, October 14, 1999.

[36] Eloise Means, e-mail to author, December 29, 1999.

[37] Addye M. Mitcham, "Flood," *Bastrop Clarion*, May 21, 1997.

[38] Ibid.

[39] Barry, *Rising Tide*, front jacket flap.

Chapter 7 – Bondage, Rebellion, and Aftermath

[1] Balthazar de Villiers, letter.

[2] F. George Kay, *The Shameful Trade* (New York: A. S. Barnes and Company, 1968), 151.

[3] Arnold, *Colonial Arkansas*, 64, 65.

[4] Waddy William Moore, *Territorial Arkansas* (Ann Arbor: University Microfilms, 1977), 370.

[5] Etheridge, *History*, 35, 88.

[6] Spyker, *Diary*, 236-237.

[7] Davenport, *Memoirs*, 6.

[8] Francis, "Hard Times."

[9] DeWoody, "Life," 15-16.

[10] Tomlinson, "Home;" Mrs. Dillard Saunders, letter.

[11] John I. Smith, *Reminiscences of Ed T. Smith As Told to His Family* (privately printed, 1992), 2-3, 23-24.

[12] *Delta News*, June 22, 1939, statement by Riddie deYampert.

[13] "McDermott Journal," 398-399. See Kay, *Shameful Trade*, 48, 183 for reputed cannibalism.

[14] Davenport, *Memoirs*, 31-32, 48.

[15] Smylie, "Autobiography," 2.

[16] Spyker, *Diary*, 51, 53, 149, 239, 296, 302.

[17] Ibid. (Unnumbered pages at back.)

[18] Davenport, *Memoirs*, 48-49.

[19] Spyker, *Diary*, 292, 298.

[20] Mrs. W. L. DeWoody, "Arkansas Daughters of the American Revolution," Fifth State Conference, Helena [AR], February 21 and 22, 1913.

[21] "McDermott Journal," 399, 406.

[22] Davenport, *Memoirs*, 49.

[23] Hedges, *Church*, 26-27.

[24] John W. Blassingame, *The Slave Community: Plantation Life in the Antebellum South* (New York: Oxford University Press, 1976), 82-83.

[25] Kay, *Shameful Trade*, 139.

[26] Harp, *Me*, 4.

[27] Jacob Treiber, "Legal Status of Negroes In Arkansas Before The Civil War," *Arkansas Historical Association* 3 (1911): 175-183.

[28] DeArmond, *Beyond Bartholomew*, 18.

[29] S. Charles Bolton, *Arkansas, 1800-1860: Remote and Restless* (Fayetteville: University of Arkansas Press, 1998), 142.

[30] Williamson, *Eastern Louisiana*, 138-139.

[31] *John Doe Civil War Diary*. Unknown Arkansas Confederate in Monticello Battery. Copy of original in possession of author. (Diary found in ruins of old boarding house in Gladys, Texas, in the 1930s.)

[32] Etheridge, *History*, 100.

[33] Calvin L. Collier, *They'll Do To Tie To! The Story of the Third Regiment, Arkansas Infantry, C.S.A.* (Little Rock: Pioneer Press, 1959), 11; Robert Lane, e-mail to author, November 8, 1998; Thomas E. Taylor, letter to Louise Godwin, June 6, 1992.

[34] Bohinger, "The Noel Family," 118.

[35] Tomlinson, "Home;" Mrs. Dillard Saunders, letter.

[36] Kinney, "125 Years," 9; Smylie, "Autobiography," 2.

[37] J. Carter Watts, "Battle of Pine Bluff, October 25, 1863," *Jefferson County Historical Quarterly* 10 (spring 1982): 1, 4-11; Edwin C. Bearss, "Marmaduke Attacks Pine Bluff," *Arkansas Historical Quarterly* 23 (winter 1964): 296-297.

[38] William L. Shea, "Battle at Ditch Bayou," *Arkansas Historical Quarterly* 39 (fall 1980): 195, 196, 205.

[39] Williamson, *Eastern Louisiana*, 146, 149.

[40] *The War of the Rebellion: A Compilation of the Official Records of the Union and Confederate Armies*, Series I, Part I, Vol. 39 (Washington: Government Printing Office, 1892), 900.

[41] Ibid., 899-900.

[42] *Official Records*, Series I, Part 1,Vol 48, 69-71; In Carl Moneyhon, "1865: A State of Perfect Anarchy," in Mark K. Christ, ed., *Rugged & Sublime: The Civil War in Arkansas*, 149, Moneyhon gives the number of troops as around 4,000. The "Judge Belzer" may have been L. H. Belser who represented Chicot, Drew, and Ashley in the state senate from 1860 to 1862 and in 1864. See Goodspeed, *Southern Arkansas*, 1,063. An 1860 map of Drew County indicates a "Col. Belcher" living on the bayou in southern Drew County.

[43] *Official Records* Series I, Vol. 5, 1064; Vol. 33, 867.

[44] Goodspeed, *Southern Arkansas*, 922.

[45] DeArmond, *Beyond Bartholomew*, 158.

[46] Williamson, *Eastern Louisiana*, 157-158; Francis, "Hard Times."

[47] Eloise Robertson Means, e-mail to author, October 26, 1999.

[48] DeWoody, "Life," 14-19.

[49] Williamson, *Eastern Louisiana*, 143.

[50] Sarah M. Fountain, ed., *Sisters, Seeds, & Cedars: Rediscovering Nineteenth Century Life Through Correspondence From Rural Arkansas and Alabama* (Conway: UCA Press, 1995), 174, 176, 178, 179.

[51] Smith, *Reminiscences*, 7-10.

[52] Ibid., 11.

[53] Janet Gardner, e-mail to author, July 17, 1998, from a history of the Gardner family by Malcolm E. Gardner, 1963.

[54] Fountain, *Sisters*, 179.

[55] Adams, "Drew County Pioneers," 78; *Trans-Miss-Bulletin* (Jefferson, Texas), May 6, 1864; DeWoody, "Life," 15.

[56] Hattie Witherington, letter to Bennie Prentice Finch, c1915. Copy provided by William C. Finch.

[57] Copies of original orders in possession of William C. Finch.

[58] *Official Records*, Series I, Vol. 48, 1404-1405.

[59] Morrison, "Steamboats," 11; Way, *Way's*, 259; W. David Daugherty, e-mail to author, October 12, 1999. Information from the Jefferson (Texas) Museum.

[60] Way, *Way's*, 171, 245, 291, 437; Williamson, *Eastern Louisiana*, 218. The *Official Records* states that the *Mattie* sank in Bayou Bartholomew "55 miles above the mouth of the Red River," but the distance is greater than that.

[61] Havighurst, *Voices*, 173-175; James Willis, *Arkansas Confederates in the Western Theater*, (Dayton: Morningside Press, 1998), 190. Havighurst gave the number dead as 13,000, but this is not confirmed by the *Official Records*.

[62] Way, *Way's*, 455.

[63] *Official Records* 13, 162.

[64] J. Carter Watts, "The Pursuit of Captain R. A. Kidd, January 15 – May 27, 1865," *Jefferson County Historical Quarterly* 10 (summer 1982): 25-33.

[65] *Known Burials*, 89; Steve Sanders, "Knife bears telltale inscription," *Monroe News Star World*, September 9, 1984.

[66] Smith, *Reminiscences*, 24.

[67] Kinney, "125 Years;" Smylie, "Autobiography," 2; Ida Jolly Crawley, "The Doll," an unpublished short story in possession of the author, n.d.

[68] Francis, "Hard Times;" Tomlinson, "Home;" Mrs. Dillard Saunders, letter.

[69] DeArmond, *Old Times*, 310.

[70] Ted R. Worley, ed., "Tenant and Labor Contracts, Calhoun County, 1869-1871," *Arkansas Historical Quarterly* 13 (spring 1954): 105.

[71] "Dashing Days."

[72] DeArmond, *Beyond Bartholomew*, 163.

[73] Walter C. Hudson, ed., "Memoirs of James Madison Hudson," *Arkansas Historical Quarterly* 19 (autumn, 1960): 271-272, 275, 277.

[74] Smith, "Reminiscences," 42-46.

[75] "Dashing Days."

[76] John L. Ferguson and J. H. Atkinson, *Historic Arkansas* (Little Rock: Arkansas History Commission, 1966), 162, 164-168; Holley, "Drew County's Carpetbagger," 12.

[77] Williamson, *Eastern Louisiana*, 163, 165, 168, 169, 172.

[78] Steve Sanders, "Mayor, sheriff murdered in 1876," *Monroe News Star World*, February 10, 1985; Williamson, *Eastern Louisiana*, 173, 179, 180.

[79] Smith, "Reminiscences," 12, 13.

[80] *Arkansas Gazette*, October 4, 1892; October 5, 1892.

[81] Harp, *Me*, 4-5; *Kin Folks*, 113.

[82] Tomlinson, "Home."

Chapter 8 – From Forests to Plantations

[1] "Judge Bocage Memoirs," 18.

[2] Etheridge, *History*, 153; Spyker, *Diary*, 232, 233.

[3] Birch, *Bayou Bartholomew*, 115.

[4] Tomlinson, "Home;" "100 Year Old House Has Seen Many Changes," *Morehouse Enterprise*, April 27, 1939; Hedges, *Bartholomew Church*, 58; Spyker, *Diary*, 138, 219, 226.

[5] Corliss Colby Curry, "A History of the Timber Industry in Ashley, Bradley and Drew Counties, Arkansas," unpublished master's thesis, University of Arkansas, 1953, 33; Goodspeed, *Southern Arkansas*, 940; Clifton Birch, letter to author, September 4, 1997.

[6] Curry, "Timber Industry," 21.

[7] Honeycutt, "Steamboating."

[8] DeArmond, *Beyond Bartholomew*, 195; Marvin Jeter, e-mail to author, August 19, 1998.

[9] *Arkansas Gazette*, February 2, 1892.

[10] *Picturesque America*, 1872, clipped page; DeArmond, *Beyond Bartholomew*, 195.

[11] "The Science of Soaked Wood," Superior Water-Logged Lumber, Inc., June 12, 1998, "Timeless Timber," (Ashland, Wisconsin: Superior Water-Logged Lumber, Inc.), 1997.

[12] Jim Rider, "Mill Operator found uses for sunken logs," *Bastrop Daily Enterprise*, April 15, 1993.

[13] "Timeless Timber."

[14] Gregory Dupre in "Bayou Pigeon and the Atchafalaya Basin," Center for Landscape Interpretation, *Images of Iberville: Places Embodied in Art* 1 (Port Allen, LA: Center for Landscape Interpretation, 1998), 5. .

[15] Quoted in *Hudson Humor*, 1936, in Mitford Mathews, ed., *A Dictionary of Americanisms On Historical Principles* 1 (Chicago: University of Chicago Press, 1951), 318-319; Frederick Simpich, "The Great Mississippi Flood of 1927," *National Geographic Magazine* 52 (September 1927): 259.

[16] The author acknowledges Joe Cope, Sammy Wells, Buck Burton, and Roy Wayne Huskey for their assistance in retrieving the log.

[17] Carol A. Clausen, e-mail to author, January 13, 1999; Jerrold E. Winandy, e-mail to author, December 21, 1998.

[18] W. Ramsay Smith, letter to author, July 29, 1999; Terry L. Amburgey, e-mail to author, August 10, 1999.

[19] Carol A. Clausen, e-mail to author, July 22, 1999; Malcolm K. Cleaveland, e-mail to author, September 21, 1999.

[20] DeWoody, "Life," 16.

[21] A. J. McShan, letter to Feaster McShan, August 1, 1855. Typed transcript provided by Jane Duke McAshan.

[22] "Crumbs from Collins," clipped article, signed T. L. E., July 17, 1883; George W. Sawyer, letter to James H. Sawyer, October 31, 1886 (Jo Sawyer, e-mail to author, July 2, 1999).

[23] *Pine Bluff Daily Graphic*, July 27, 1924. (deYampert acreage.)

[24] George B. Gregory, letter to Wiloughby Gregory, July 18, 1845; Goodspeed, *Southern Arkansas,* 130; Goodspeed, *Southern Arkansas,* 879, 935.

[25] DeArmond, *Beyond Bartholomew*, 206.

[26] Joel Newcome, letter to author, December 15, 1999.

[27] DeArmond, *Beyond Bartholomew*, 165.

[28] *Delta News*, March 7, 1940.

[29] Felix Pugh to Whom It May Concern, December 21 (no year given).

[30] Jim Rider, "Wesley Bunch relates history," *Bastrop Daily Enterprise*, May 4, 1987.

[31] Etheridge, *History*, 57; DeArmond, *Old Times*, 71; Jim Rider, "Tilbury helped plant first rice here half-century ago," *Bastrop Daily Enterprise*, September 18, 1992; Marion Doles research. The 1850 Ashley County census reported 3,850 pounds of rice on hand.

[32] DeArmond, Beyond Bartholomew, 225.

Chapter 9 – Living on the Edge

[1] Judge Jos. W. Bocage, "Old Memories," *Jefferson County Historical Quarterly* 2 (autumn 1969): 8.

[2] "Pioneer Rivermen;" "County Formed October 25, 1823," *Chicot Spectator*, November 15, 1973.

[3] John Edward Miller, *Treasure in Louisiana: A Treasure Hunter's Guide to the Bayou State* (privately published by John Miller, 1996), 128-129.

[4] Bocage, "Old Memories," 8.

[5] "McDermott Journal," 405-406.

[6] Harp, *My Kin Folks*, 84. According to Thomas Swafford, John Murrell died in Pikeville, Tennessee, on November 3, 1844. See ◇.

[7] "Community History of Collins," *Advance-Monticellonian*, clipped article, 1933; Ron Bulloch, e-mail to author, May 10, 1999.

[8] "Dashing Days."

[9] DeArmond, *Beyond Bartholomew*, 318; *Delta News*, May 18, 1939.

[10] "About Jesse James," clipped article n.d., based on an early interview with Mary Haynes Ober.

[11] Julia Huff Bryan, statement to author, February 19, 2000; "About the James Brothers from Mr. Tom Y. Harp," clipped article, n.d. Williamson, *Eastern Louisiana*, 95-96, 103-104, says that the James Gang was in the Carroll Parishes and Richland Parish during the war and that they and the Younger brothers were there afterwards.

[12] "A Partial List of African Americans Lynched in Arkansas." ◇

[13] "Partial List of African Americans Lynched;" Brian Greer, "A Reign of Terror," *Arkansas Times*, August 4, 2000.

[14] DeArmond, *Old Times*, 225. Frances Condren was born the year of the murder and lived with the David Agee family. The other children were Mary Helen, who lived with David Smith, and Silas, who lived with John Stewart.

[15] *Arkansas Gazette,* July 18, 1871; *Drew County Advance*, October 2, 1894.

[16] Ibid., May 19, 1896; *Arkansas Gazette*, September 29, 1896.

[17] *Drew County Advance*, May 19, 1896; *Arkansas Gazette*, May 14, 1896; *Drew County Advance*, June 6, 1896, July 25, 1898.

[18] R. H. Dennington and Clifton Trigg, interview by author, tape recording, Dermott, AR, January 26, 1999.

[19] *Arkansas Gazette*, February 20, 21, 1908.

[20] DeArmond, *Beyond Bartholomew*, 257-262; "Partial List of African Americans Lynched."

[21] Ibid., 259-260.

[22] Earl Bishop, e-mail to author, September 13, 1999.

[23] *Arkansas Gazette*, June 21, 1908; *Ashley County Eagle*, June 18, 1908.

[24] Clipped article, n.d.

[25] Etheridge, *History*, 157.

[26] DeArmond, *Beyond Bartholomew*, 262.

[27] Etheridge, *History*, 157-158.

[28] George Sims, "Cabbages and Kings," *Bastrop Daily Enterprise*, July 8, 1996.

[29] Smith, *Reminiscences*, 66.

[30] Bill Bishop, interview by Amy Bishop Flowers, tape recording, Keithville, LA, November 1998.

[31] DeArmond, *Beyond Bartholomew*, 272 (Spivey story); *Wilmot Weekly*, December 27, 1912.

[32] Ed Sanders, e-mail to author, October 2, 1998.

[33] Ashley County Court Records, 1849-1855, (July 17, 1849, p. 22), from a typewritten transcript (p. 17) by Marilyn Hudgens in Paul Sullins Library, Crossett.

[34] *Drew County Advance*, August 11, 1896.

[35] DeArmond, *Beyond Bartholomew*, 269.

[36] Harp, *Highroads*, 6.

[37] W. J. Simmons, *The Practice of Klanishness*, Imperial Instructions, Document No. 1, Series AD, 1918, AK, Lii (Atlanta: Ku Klux Press, 1918), 1-7, copy of original in possession of author.

[38] Minutes of Monticello Klan Number 108, September 28, 1922 to October 6, 1925, copy of original in possession of author.

[39] George Patton, Introduction to "Morehouse Klan," 1991, a collection of papers in the Snyder Museum.

[40] George Patton, *Whiskey, Mischief, and the Courthouse Gang: A Story about the Ku Klux Klan in Morehouse Parish in the Early 1920s* (privately printed, 1999), 8-9.

[41] Ibid., 19-22.

[42] *New York Times*, December 28, 1922; January 1, 1923; Patton, *Whiskey*, 34-35, 39-55.

Chapter 10 – Hunters and Their Prey

[1] Robert S. Maestri, et al., ed., *The Fur Animals of Louisiana* Bulletin 18 (New Orleans: Department of Conservation, 1931), 168-170; Arnold, *Colonial Arkansas*, 69.

[2] *Arkansas Gazette*, May 7, 1895; Dave Sadler, e-mail to author, July 31, 1997.

[3] J. Frank Dobie, *The Ben Lilly Legend* (Austin: University of Texas Press, 1997), 85-86.

[4] Maestri, *Fur Animals*, 170; Dickinson, "Early View," 16; Dunbar map.

[5] Keith Sutton, "Here Today: A Guide to Arkansas's Endangered and Threatened Animals," *Arkansas Wildlife* 27 No. 1 (1996), 24.

[6] *Delta News*, May 11, May 18, 1939.

[7] Maestri, *Fur Animals*, 88, 90, 111, 117, 126, 129.

[8] Carolyn Haisty, e-mail to author, March 2000.

[9] John A. Sealander, *A Guide to Arkansas Mammals* (Conway: River Road Press, 1979), 16; Goodspeed, *Southern Arkansas*, 629; "McDermott Journal," 404.

[10] "Dashing Days."

[11] *Arkansas Gazette*, August 8, 1871; *Ashley Times*, as quoted in the *Daily Gazette*, May 12, 1871.

[12] Sealander, *Guide*, 204, states that the red wolf was "apparently exterminated" in a large part of the Gulf Coastal Plain during the first two decades of the century, but firsthand accounts attest to a rudiment population lasting into the 1940s.

[13] DeArmond, *Beyond Bartholomew*, 5-6.

[14] Sealander, *Guide*, 204.

[15] *Ashley County Eagle*, November 14, 1901; DeArmond, *Beyond Bartholomew*, 4.

[16] Dobie, *Legend*, 23; *Press-Eagle*, January 25, 1887.

[17] Oliver W. Jennings, "Among the Arkansas Bayous; or, Recollections of a Camp Hunt," *Drew County Historical Journal* 6 (1991): 28-32.

[18] *Delta News*, October 26, November 23, December 14, 1939.

[19] W. F. Skipper, letter to Charles Skipper, June 27, 1892. Original in possession of Betsy Rodgers.

[20] Joe Craig , e-mail to author, January 23, 1999.

[21] Brian Cofer, "Hog hunter roots out wild razorbacks," *Arkansas Democrat-Gazette*, May 16, 1999.

[22] Dobie, *Legend*, 16, 21, 24, 30, 33, 34, 36, 86; Neil B. Carmony, ed. *Ben Lilly's Tales of Bears, Lions and Hounds* (Silver City, NM: High-Lonesome Books, 1998), 2; Jim Rider, "A memorial for Lilly, maybe?" "Farming was not for Ben Lilly," *Bastrop Daily Enterprise*, November 2, November 9, 1992. Rider places Vernon Lilly's home "near Bonita."

[23] Dobie, *Legend*, 89; Theodore Roosevelt, "In the Louisiana Canebrakes," *Scribner's Magazine*, January 1908.

[24] Dobie, *Legend*, 94-98, 118, 127, 116, 217; Carmony, *Tales*, 3-6, 10, 151.

[25] Clyde Venable, e-mail to author, August 2, 1998; Roosevelt, "Canebrakes."

[26] Birch, *Bayou Bartholomew*, 103.

Chapter 11 – Good Times on the Bayou

[1] Bocage, "Old Memories," 7; George B. Gregory; "Dermott Dots," clipped article, July 24, 1883; *Wilmot Weekly*, May 31, 1912.

[2] Francis, "Hard Times;" B. J. Gray, e-mail to author, December 13, 1999. Ms. Gray wrote, "Very early in Ohio the people of color celebrated the 5th of July with speeches, programs, and coming together. Newspaper articles and the *Christian Recorder* have articles about this. They stated in speeches that the 'Negro' was disenfranchised and therefore had no part in the celebration of the 4th."

[3] *Delta News*, July 6, 1939; July 11, 1940.

[4] Joe Craig, e-mail to author, January 25, 1999.

[5] Marion Doles, "When Bartholomew."

[6] *Delta News*, February 1, 1940.

[7] Paolo Canulla, e-mail to author, June 25, 1998.

[8] *Delta News*, July 5, 1940.

[9] Jones, *Dean of Dermott*, 80.

[10] *Lincoln Ledger*, December 9, 1919.

[11] Dorothy Mack, letter to author, 1998.

[12] Martha Crawley, *My Legacy*. (Martha Amanda Phillips Tiller Crawley's Journal, 1852-1856, copy in possession of author.)

[13] M. A. C. [Martha Amanda Crawley], "From a 'Log Cabin' on Bayou Bartholomew, Ashley Co., Ark., March 16, 1858," clipped article.

[14] Crawley, "The Doll." (Jones Chapel was in the area before the Civil War. Frank W. Page, age 25, was living in the area by 1860.)

[15] Fred W. Allsopp, in Tomlinson, "Stream of History."

[16] Jones, *Dean of Dermott*, 5, 6, 23.

[17] Rev. W. T. Tardy, *Trials and Triumphs: An Autobiography* (Marshall, TX: Mrs. W. T. Tardy, 1910), 27. Reverend Tardy was born in Drew County in the early 1870s and became the founder of East Texas Baptist College in Marshall, Texas.

[18] *Delta News*, September 19, 1940

[19] Ibid., April 11, 1940.

[20] Tomlinson, "Stream of History;" Dorothy Mack, letter to author, January 10, 1999.

[21] DeArmond, *Beyond Bartholomew*, 317.

[22] Earl Kitchens, interview by author, tape recording, Wilmot, AR, May 6, 1998. Bailey Sherrer joined the interview during its progress.

[23] DeArmond, *Beyond Bartholomew*, 320.

[24] Eloise Means, e-mail to author, September 8, 1998, from a clipped article by Mrs. Emma Williamson in a Bastrop newspaper. A John A. Williams from Lind Grove was a member of the parish school board in the early 1890s.

[25] *The WPA Life Histories Collection*, Accession No. W 3716, Betty Burke, project worker, July 25, 1997, <> [Keyword, Bayou Bartholomew.]

[26] Ida Margaret Newton, *Delta News*, March 9, 1939.

[27] Tomlinson, "Stream of History."

[28] M. A. C. [Martha Amanda Crawley], "From a 'Log Cabin' on Bayou Bartholomew," clipped article, n.d.

[29] Robert D. Pugh, "Portland: A Sense of Place with a Strength of Differences," in *Somewhere Apart "My Favorite Place in Arkansas" Arkansas Residents Past and Present* (Fayetteville: University of Arkansas Press, 1997), 97-98.

[30] Dennis Tilbury, *Delta News*, March 21, 1940.

[31] Lily Strickland, "Keep On Singin,' Ol' Bayou," (New York: G. Schirmer, Inc., 1938).

[32] DeArmond, *Beyond Bartholomew*, vii.

Afterword - Sing on Bayou, Sing On!

[1] Thomas A. Woods, "Nature Within History: Using Environmental History to Interpret Historic Sites," *History News* (summer 1997): 5.

[2] Bayou Bartholomew Alliance Technical Support Group, *Short and Long Term Strategies for Protecting and Enhancing Natural Resources in the Bayou Bartholomew Watershed*, (Pine Bluff: Bayou Bartholomew Alliance, 1996), 4.

[3] Tomlinson, "Home" and "Stream."

[4] *Delta News*, May 11, 1939.

[5] *Annual Report, 1904*, 1473-1474.

[6] Charter members of the board were Curtis Merrell, Sonia Byrd , Janis Gill Ward, Dr. Bill Layher, Cynthia and Howard Kimbrell Jr., Robert Mitchell, John Scott McClendon, John Frank Gibson, and Jack Edwards. George Pugh became a board member in 1998. The majority of the members are landowners in the bayou's watershed.

[7] *Strategies*, 2-4, Table 1, 1-2.

[8] Curtis Merrell, letter to author, February 20, 2000.

[9] David R. Bower, "A Credo for the Earth," in *Hidden Passage: the journal of Glen Canyon Institute* (winter 1999): 8.

Family Histories

[1] Oscar McCarty (born in 1907), the son of John Thomas McCarty (born in 1876) and grandson of Esther (Rawls) and William McCarty of Drew County, said that William's brothers were Larkin, Matthew, and Henry.[1] This William McCarty was much older than William Phillip McCarty, who was born in 1894, and Larkin, Matthew and Henry could not have been his brothers. Oscar McCarty's grandfather, William, disappeared two years after the birth of his son, John Thomas, and was never heard from again. See Rebecca DeArmond, *Old Times Not Forgotten: A History of Drew County*, 170-71.

[2] The author acknowledges Marjorie Day Huber for sharing her extensive research on the Day and Naff families.

[3] *Greene County Democrat* (AL), clipped article, nd.

[4] *Delta News*, June 22, 1939.

[5] *Greene County Democrat*.

[6] Triplett family history, clipped page, 2, January 20, 1972.

 # Index

BAKER, 259 Dan 259 Dr 64 E F 433
Elwood 450 81 86 Evelyn 78 Hester 450
India Olive 394 Lula A 433 Mr 77 R L 64
R M L 63 W K 68 81 Walta Aline 506
BALDWIN, Charles William 446 Lois 36
390 446-447 Mary Elizabeth 446
BALDY, Martha J 470 Thomas 85 Thomas
H 85 William H 470
BALES, Della 418 Sid 418
BALL, Catherine 417 Louise 417 Margaret
Sara 417 Sampson 417 William 417
William Robert 417
BALLARD, J H 56 R H 56
BANCROFT, Cora Charlotte 48
BANGS, James R 159
BANISTER, Tom 119
BANKS, A B 107 57 75 Dr 81
BANKSTON, 48 Eulavee 445 Odel 445
BANNISTER, Tom 431
BARBER, Clara 146
BARFOOT, Dolly Bell 376 Hamp 376
BARHAM, Connie 448 Dora 448 Era Aline
384 Gray 123 Thomas N 141
BARINGER, Georgiana 89
BARKER, J P 86 Nancy Lewis 397 U E 88
U E Mrs 88
BARKMAN, Jacob 159
BARKSDALE, 35 Hazel Jean 411 W B 64
BARLOW, Brian E 82 E E 81-82 John 138
Lavern 419 Martha Amanda 147 Sarah
452
BARNARD, Elizabeth 126 Ellen 126
BARNES, 294-295 99 443 Bernice 382
Bessie May 444 Big Boy 212 Charles 443
Daniel 444 Daniel T 443-444 Daniel W L
444 Edward 444 Edwin 444 Eliza 443
Elizabeth Hettie 466 Ella 100 513 Evan
443 F A Mrs 101 Fannie Julia 443 Fannie
Sue 398 Frances Jennet 443 Francis 443
Frank 100 104 294-295 513 Frank Allen
294 443 Gabriel 443-444 Gran 444
Granville 444 Harry O 443 Hawkins 294
Henry 444 Honey 398 J C 466 J K 103 J S
101 J S Mrs 101 James Nobles 443 Jeffie
443 Jim 398 John 398 507 John K 443
John Sims 294 443-444 99 John Sumner
295 398 Johnnie 398 Leonard 443 Lucy
443-444 Lucy Ann 444 Mag 443 Martha
Ann 443 Mary Jane 398 444 Mataline 398
Michael Crute 466 Mr 295 330 Robert
443 Sally Jeff 398 Sophronia 507 Susan
507 Susan Rebecca 443 99 Susanna 443
Susannah 444 Swepson 443 Thomas 443
Tot 398 W E 102 Wash 444 William 443

BARNES (continued)
William Evan 443 William Evans 443
Willie 443 Willie Kathryn 443
BARNETT, 45 Alice 468 Alma 468 80
Alma Daniels 467 Amanda 468 Ander
367 Ander P 367 Charle Conditt 468
Dolly 367 E L 428 Ellis Foster 468 Elsie
Mae 367 Florence 468 Frances 468
Frances Foster 468 Frances Victor 468
George F 107 Hannah 511 Iva 393 J W 56
Joseph W 44 Mary Bentley 468 Mary Lee
468 Nancy Catherine 367 Robert Emmit
468 Robert Julius 468 Sam 367 Sarah 428
U C 80 U C Mrs 80 Uzal Conditt 468
William D 44 Willie 481
BARNHART, L C 111
BARNS, Alonzo Theodore 417 Elizabeth
417 George Alonzo 417 Gladys 410
Isabella Louisa 417 Julia Elizabeth 416
Julia Jane 417 Susan Laura 506 Theodore
417
BARR, Owen 377 R L 81 Velma 377
BARRACK, Claudette 489
BARRETT, Adelaid Etta 480 Dorothy
Louise 481 Fannie Lula 480-481 Franklin
Pierce 480 Helen Lucile 481 Ida Mae 480
Inez 477 John David 480 John Robert
480-481 Labonne Willene 480 Marie
Lucile 480-481 Mary Idelle 481 Nancy
427-428
BARRINGER, John Albert 89
BARROW, 254 98 Charles 253 J C 254 Mr
98
BARRY, John M 216
BARTELEMI, Margarita 32 Teresa 32
Therese 32
BARTELEMIAS, 31
BARTELEMY, Angelica 32
BARTELL, Elizabeth 158
BARTELMEY, Genovesa 32 Maria 32
BARTHELEMI, Felicete Duchassin 31
Francois 31 Helene 31 Joseph 31 Louis 31
Margarita 31 Marianna 31 Martin 31
Pierre 31 Therese 31
BARTHELEMY, Jacques Michel 31 Joseph
31 Louis 32 Martin 32 Renaul 31
BARTHOL, Clara Lee 370 Renear Laurie
370
BARTHOLOME, Louis 33
BARTHOLOMEW, 22 31 Ambrose 33
Joseph 32
BARTLETT, Caroline 476 Churchwell 475-
476 Cinthie E 476 Dionitia 476 Elizabeth
476 Henry 148 Henry C 147

GREESON (continued)
Philip Hartwell 501 Ruth Mae 501
GREGG, 149 Bruce Frizell 414 Durwood 83
Harvey Lee 149 414 Jerry Baird 414
Lorraine 186 Marjorie May 149 414
GREGGS, T C 111
GREGORY, A B 134 A J 94 Claude M 394
E D 103 Edwin 101 Edwin Mrs 97
George B 276 329 Hattie Elizabeth 394
Hugo H 94 Ida 410 Lola B 91 Martha 99
Mary 508 Mr 277 Roy 244
GRENWAY, Von 340
GRICE, 138 Ada Ruth 370 Christual
Lemuel Washington 369 Christual Pouis
369 David 369 Edith 370 Eira Elva 369
Ella Mae 370 Elma Jean 370 Elva Jewel
370 Etta 370 Henrietta 371 Henry 369 J D
192 Martha Ann 369 Wash 369 William
Benjamin 370
GRIFFIN, 112 Dorothy Marie 478 Francis
M 432 Ida Mae 152 Margaret E 432
Margaret Pickens 432 Rebecca 113
Rebecca Genevia 112 Rebecca J Genevia
379 402
GRIGG, Sara 118
GRIMES, Billy 322
GRISHAM, 55 Arthur 55 Carolyn 447 Ed
54 Frelan 55 Lamar 48 Rasco 55
GRISWOOD, J B 448
GRIZZEL, Roy 182
GRIZZELL, Charles 402 Ida 401-403 Julia
401 403 Linda 403 Rena 401 Roy 379
401-403 Virginia 403
GROCE, Ina Mae 476-477 Karen 505
GROGAN, Gladys Hartland 385 Richard
385
GROH, Dorothy 464
GROSS, 67 Parson 67 Sterely 67
GROVER, Mrs 118
GRUBB, Bruce Cody 437 Ellen 437 73 78
Maude 437 Maude Mae 437 Samuel
Curtis 437
GRUBBS, Lois 419 Sherman 419
GRUMBLES, Andrew Thomas 447 Fred 38
John 37 Judith Lynn 447 Lois Evelyn 447
Lois Thomas 390 Rebecca 482 Rebecca
Thweatt 447 Rita Rebecca 447 Robin Till
447 Thomas Harold 447 Winfred 385
GUAGLIARDO, Carolyn Clark 500 Paul V
500
GUESS, Ben Franklin 499 Helen Virginia
499
GUICE, 103 142 144 Bertha Lee 471 Enoch
Simmons 471 J D 103 Mary Alice 471

GUICE (continued)
Mary Louisa 471 Moses 143 Moses S 144
William W 471
GUINN, W M 37
GUISE, William 88
GULLEDGE, Lillie 495
GULLEY, Catherin Octavia 495
GUMPERT, Barney 497 Lucille 497
Rosemary 497
GUNNS, 284
GUNTER, Hardy 385 Helen Patricia 385
Mary Jones 408
GUPTON, Dana 381
GURLEY, Keziah 503 Mary Almeda 496
498
GUTHERIC, L T 101
GUTHRIE, Grayson Mrs 149
GUY, Abba 236 Abby 236
HADDICK, 136 198 Scott 178 184 186 197
HADLEY, 121 E L 121 Eliza L 121 Ellie
Belle 121 H H 121 Hanna Holmes 121
Hannah 410 Harriet Eliza 396 410 James
121 410 Jesse D 121 Liza 121 Mabel A
121 Ocatavia 121 Robert J 121 W H 121
William 121-122 William H 122 William
Holmes 121
HAGGERTY, Jack 135
HAGLER, Foeba 446
HAGOOD, 45 47 E T 514 Eddie T 44
Elizabeth 513 Thomas 44
HAILE, Robert 140
HAISTY, 474 476 Alma 479 Anna Lora 477
Annie Lou 478 Barbara Ann 477 Bertha
479 Betty Jane 477 Betty Lou 477 Brett
Stanton 477 Brooks Barrett 477 Caldonie
478 Carolyn 315 474-475 493-494
Carolyn Mae 477 480 499 Carroll Wesley
479 Carroll Wood 480 Chirsta Renata 477
Conrad Leopold 479 Delancy 474 476
Dona 478 Dorothy Nell 480 Ecil Christina
479 Edna Bernice 480 Emma Lou 479
Esther 477 Evelyn 479 Everett 479
Frances E 480 Fronnie 478 Grace Barton
477 Gwendolyn 477 Harriet 475 Harriet
Elizabeth 476 478 Henry Erastus 479 Inez
477 James 474-478 James Oneill 475
Jesse Brooks 477 Jesse New Year 479
Jessie Ida 475-477 480 John 474-476 58
John Byron 479 John Dale 477 John
Patrick 475 John Quintin 479 John
Sherwood 477 John Stanley 477 480 499
John Wesley 475 478-479 Kimberly
Susan 478 Kittie 479 Labonne Willene
480 Lela 479 Lettie Lee 478

MAYO (continued)
Rose Marie 370 Ruby Nell 370 Ruth 371
Sandra 368 Sandra Elaine 372 Sarah
Eveline 368 370 Sherrie Ann 372 Shirley
June 423 Steve 423 Tammy Lee 372
Tanya Lynn 423 Teresa 372 Terri 372
Tommy Mack 423 Vala Mae 368 Verlene
423 Versal Harold 370 Versel Joe 372
Virginia Dare 422-423 William Norris
422-423 William Philip 368 370 William
Phillip 422 Zelma Lee 370
MAYOR, Dorman Edgar 372
MAYS, Callie 398 Charlie 291 Sally 118
395 Sam 398 Virgia 446
MAZANTI, Emma 95
MCADAMS, Annie B 124
MCAFEE, Layton H 506 Opal G 506
MCALISTER, Sherry Dale 500 William
Henry 500
MCARTHUR, Shelby 14
MCASHAN, Jane Duke 492
MCBETH, E E 45
MCBRAUGH, 119
MCBRIDE, 37 Jack 89 John 143 146 Nancy
89 R J 91 Richard J 91
MCBROOM, Audrey 371 Wayne 371
MCCAIN, 119 212 Alexander Hamilton 488
Alice 488 Annie Bellita 489 Audrey Mae
489 Bell 119 335 Bernice 423 Bernice
Poke 422 Callie 488 Catie Deen 488
Claude Vernon 489 Claudette 489
Darthula Katie 488 Davie L 489 Dollie
488 Dorothy 489 Dorothy Mack 214
Elmer 489 George Oscar 488 Grandma
214 Irma 489 James Aubrey 489 Jeff 389
Jesse 212 Jim 489 John 489 John
Anderson Iii 488 John Anderson Jr 488
John Anderson Sr 488 Juanita 489 Katie
Dean 488 Lawrence Edward 489 Lillie
335 Lincoln 488 Louisa L L 488 Ludie
Bell 488-489 Marion Monroe 488 Martha
Jane 488 Mary Jane 488 Mary Lillie 116
488-489 Mary Mollie 488 Mildred 489
Naomi 488 Ralph 489 Sabina 489
Theodore Edward 489 Velma Lee 489
Verna 489 William Jesse 488 William
Penn 119 212 214 488-489 Willie 488
Zora 488
MCCALEB, Carol 431
MCCALL, Albert 469 Bahannon 469 Jane
469 Josephine 469 Margaret 469 Margaret
Ferguson 469 Rohannon 469
MCCAN, Mary Parizade Parry 488

MCCARTY, A E Mrs 118 Anna Eliza
Mcclellan 368-369 Annie 118 Audrey 369
Bill 369 Buddy 369 Claude L 369 David
389 Della 369 Ella M 369 Ella Myra 370
Elmira Jane 368 422 Erma 369 Ethel 369
Ethel Leona 369 H 369 Henry Jackson
116 267 368-369 Henry? 220 Jesse J 369
Lavelle 369 Lucille 369 Luke 369 M R
368-369 Mala M 369 Mala Mabel 369
Margaret 369 Margarette 369 Martha Ann
369 Mary E 368 Matthew Y 368-369
Mattie Merle 369 Maude M 369 Maye
422 Mildred 369 Missouri 368 Missouri
Mayo 369 Myrtle Eva Leona 369 N T 368
Ora 369 Ora Belle 369 Othel 369 Precilla
369 Robert Leslie 369 Rosie Evans 369
Sarah 368 Theodocia 368 Viola Ruth 369
Wilbur Douglas 369 William Henry 369
William Jackson 116 William Jackson
Mrs 118 William James 369 William P
368-369 William Phillip 369
MCCARVER, Emma D 54 Will Mrs 56
William 54
MCCARY, Jese 516
MCCATE?, Martha J 469
MCCCAIN, Annie Bellita 489
MCCLANAHAN, Emily 408 Samuel 408
MCCLEARY, 131 Agnes 131 Arthur Rood
409 Marie Theresa 409 Pat 131
MCCLELLAN, Mary Alice 451
MCCLENDON, John 200
MCCLERKIN, Eleanor 416 James 416
MCCLINTOCK, Rev 95
MCCLOUD, Betty 408 Harvey 319-320
Tebb 319-320 Tebe 408 Vennie 408
MCCLOY, 42 Elizabeth 62 Mrs V B 466 W
R Mrs 62 Will 62
MCCLURE, Nancy Lou 499 Robert Jerome
499
MCCOLLUM, Nettie Winters 398
MCCOMBS, 276 87 Addie 164 Ashton 179
87 Fannie 86 Laura 86 W F 86 91
MCCONE, H Wayne 498 James Gill 496
498 James Thomas 498 500 James
Thomas Jr 500 Jane 498 500 Jane English
500 Julia 500 Majen 500 Peyton Gill 500
Virginia Gertrude 496 498
MCCONKEY, 145 Dr 145
MCCONNICO, Ann Kennard 424
MCCORD, Irma 129
MCCORVEY, Maude 436
MCCOY, Lizzie 492
MCCREADY, 492 Bert 391 Billy Wayne
491 David Earl Willis Bertrand 491

Bartholomew's Song

Subject
Index